VESPASIAN

VESPASIAN

Barbara Levick

ROUTLEDGE
ROUTLEDGE
Taylor & Francis Group

London and New York

First published 1999
by Routledge
11 New Fetter Lane, London EC4P 4EE

Simultaneously published in the USA and Canada
by Routledge
29 West 35th Street, New York, NY 10001

Routledge is an imprint of the Taylor & Francis Group

Typeset in Garamond by RefineCatch Limited, Bungay, Suffolk
Printed and bound in Great Britain by
Biddles Ltd, Guildford and King's Lynn

British Library Cataloguing in Publication Data
A catalogue record for this book is available from the British Library

Library of Congress Cataloging-in-Publication Data
Levick, Barbara.
Vespasian / Barbara Levick.
Includes bibliographical references and index.
1. Vespasian, Emperor of Rome, 9–79.   2. Emperors – Rome –
Biography.   3. Rome – History – Vespasian, 69–79.   I. Title.
DG289.L48   1999
937′.06′092 – dc21   98–52448
[b]   CIP

ISBN 0–415–16618–7

To Marion Taylor
and my other friends at St Hilda's College

CONTENTS

PLATES

MAPS

ACKNOWLEDGEMENTS

First must come thanks to the publisher of *Claudius* (1990), Mr Peter Kemmis Betty, Managing Director of B.T. Batsford, Ltd, who entertained the idea of a *Vespasian* from me and encouraged the work from the beginning; more recently I have owed much to the forbearance of Dr Richard Stoneman, Senior Editor at Routledge.

To colleagues and friends I owe as great a debt of gratitude as ever, for their generosity and patience in answering enquiries and reading draft text, and for gifts of their works. It is a pleasure to name, in alphabetical order, Dr R. Ash, Professor A. Barrett, Dr E. Bispham, Dr A. Cheung, Professor K.M. Coleman, Mr G.E.M. De Ste Croix, Ms B. Crutch and the Oxford University Computing Centre (much help with disks), Dr R.H. Darwall-Smith (who gave me permission to use *Emperors and Architecture* before publication), Dr J. Davidson, Professor W. Eck (who allowed me to read an illuminating paper on Vespasian's exploitation of Judaean balsam before it was published), Dr C.F. Eilers, Dr A.T. Fear (who allowed me access to *Rome and Baetica* before publication), the late Professor W.G. Forrest, Dr K.A. Forsyth, Professor J.F. Gardner, Dr I. Gradel, Dr M.T. Griffin (who has allowed me to cite her chapters for the second edition of the *Cambridge Ancient History* 11), Dr R. Laurence, Mr J. Legg (admission to Nuffield College Library), Dr P.C.B. MacKinnon, Professor F.G.B. Millar, Mrs B. Mitchell (who read the entire text and notes), Mr R.B. Moberly, Mlle V. Naas, Professor J. Nicols (for help with the Four Emperors), Mrs G. Piddock (admission to Lincoln College Library), Dr J. Pigoń (who read the section on Vespasian's relations with the senate and gave me A. Kunisz's work on Clodius Macer), Dr T. Rajak, Dr J. Rea, Mrs T. Ross (St Hilda's College Computing Manager), Dr J. Rowlandson, Professor D. Saddington, Professor O. Salomies, Dr H. Sidebottom (who allowed me to read his paper on Dio of Prusa before publication), Dr M.G. Simpson, Dr P.R. Taylor (who allowed me to read her work on Valerius Flaccus before publication), and Professor T. Wiedemann.

For many illustrations I am once again deeply indebted to the skill and discrimination of Dr C.J. Howgego of the Heberden Coin Room in the Ashmolean Museum, Oxford, and to his good offices in securing prints kindly supplied by the Museum and published by permission of the Visitors; Dr Andrew Burnett has done me the same kindness in selecting coins from the British Museum, and the prints are published by permission of the Trustees. The Administrators of the Staatliche Museen zu Berlin – Preussischer Kulturbesitz Münzkabinett were particularly prompt and generous in sending photographs, and I am also much indebted to the Landschaftsverband Rheinland (for the photograph by L. Lilienthal); to the Ny Carlsberg Glyptotek; to The Centre Camille Jullian, Université de Provence – C.N.R.S., for permission to publish the photographs by Ph. Foliot of the Vespasianic inscription in the Musée Municipal d'Orange which they supplied through the good offices of the Conservateur, Mme Marise Woehl; to the Deutsches Archäologisches Institut, Rome; and to the Direzione Generale of the Monimenti, Musei, e Gallerie Ponteficie, Città del Vaticano, who have generously allowed me to publish the photographs that they have sent me. The cover illustration, The Emperor Vespasian by Peter Paul Rubens (1577–1640) Noortman (London) Ltd, UK/Bridgeman Art Library, London/ New York, was obtained with the kind help of Ms Zoe Stollery of The Phaidon Press and Ms Charlotte Kelley of the Bridgeman Art Library.

B.M. Levick
St Hilda's College
Oxford

ABBREVIATIONS

See also Bibliography. Dates are of the Christian era except where indicated.

b.	bar, ben (son of)
cos. (*ord.*)	consul (*ordinarius*, holding office first in the year and giving his name to it)
HS	*sestertius*, sesterce (money unit; purchasing power: B. Levick, *The Government of the Roman Empire* (London and Sydney, 1985) xvif.)
m.p.	(*mille passuum*) one Roman mile (1479 m; 1618 yds)
SC, SCC	*Senatus consultum, -a*, decree(s) of the senate
suff.	suffect consul (substitute holding office for the later months of the year)
V.	(in notes) Vespasian
AP	*Anthologia Palatina*
DC	Dio Cassius, *History of Rome*
DP	Dio of Prusa (Dio Chrysostom), *Discourses*
GI	Gaius, *Institutes*
JA; *B*; *CA*; *V*	Josephus, *Antiquitates Judaeorum*; *Bellum Judaicum*; *Contra Apionem*; *Vita*
PEp.	Pliny the Younger, *Epistulae*
Ph*VA*	Philostratus, *Life of Apollonius of Tyana*
Ph*VS*	Philostratus, *Lives of the Sophists*
Pl*G*; Pl*O*	Plutarch, *Lives of Galba*; *Otho*
PNH	Pliny the Elder, *Natural Histories*
P*Pan*	Pliny the Younger, *Panegyric on Trajan*
Q*IO*	Quintilian, *Institutio Oratoria*
RGDA	*Res Gestae Divi Augusti* (*Achievements of the Deified Augustus,* EJ[2] 1)
SHA	*Scriptores Historiae Augustae*
S*D*; *G*; *N*; *O*; *T*; *V*	Suetonius, *Domitianus*; *Galba*; *Nero*; *Otho*; *Divus Vespasianus* (other biographies with fuller title)

TA; *Agr.*; *D*; *H*	Tacitus, *Annals*; *Agricola*; *Dialogus*; *Histories* (ed. H. Heubner, (Leipzig, 1978))
AA	*Deutsches Archäologisches Institut, Archäologischer Anzeiger*
ABSA	*Annual of the British School at Athens*
AC	*L'Antiquité classique*
AE	*L'Année épigraphique* (twentieth-century dates not prefixed by '19')
AH	*Acta Archaeologica Academiae Hungaricae*
AJ	F.F. Abbott and A.C. Johnson, *Municipal Administration in the Roman Empire* (Princeton, 1926)
AJA	*American Journal of Archaeology*
AJAH	*American Journal of Ancient History*
AJP	*American Journal of Philology*
Album	A.E. and J.S. Gordon, eds, *Album of Dated Latin Inscriptions* (4 vols, Berkeley, 1958–65)
ANRW	*Aufstieg und Niedergang der römischen Welt,* ed. H. Temporini (Berlin, 1972–)
Ath.	*Athenaeum*
Ath. Mitt.	*Mitteilungen des deutsches archäologischen Instituts (in Athen)*
Atti	*Atti: Congresso internazionale di studi flaviani, Rieti Settembre 1979* (2 vols, Rieti 1981); *Settembre 1981* (2 vols, Rieti, 1983)
BAB	*Bull. de la Classe de Lettres de l'Acad. Royale de Belgique*
BAR	*British Archaeological Reports*
BCH	*Bulletin de correspondence hellénique*
BEFAR	*Bibliothèque des Ecoles françaises d'Athènes et de Rome*
BGU	*Ägyptische Urkunden aus den Staatlichen Museen zu Berlin, Griechische Urkunden*
BICS	*Bulletin of the Institute of Classical Studies*
BJ	*Bonner Jahrbücher*
BMC	*British Museum Catalogue*
BRGK	*Bericht der Röm.-Germanischen Kommission des Deutsches Arch. Instituts*
Brit.	*Britannia*
Bruns	K. Bruns, *Fontes iuris romani anteiustiniani*[7], ed. O. Gradenwitz (Tübingen, 1909)
Brunt, *RIT*	P.A. Brunt, *Roman Imperial Themes* (Oxford, 1990)
Bull. com.	*Bulletino della commissione archeologica del comune di Roma*
CAH	*Cambridge Ancient History*
CEFR	*Collection de l'Ecole française de Rome*
Chilver	G.E.F. Chilver, *A Historical Commentary on Tacitus' Histories I and II* (Oxford, 1979)

Chilver/Townend	G.E.F. Chilver, completed and rev. by G.B. Townend, *A Historical Commentary on Tacitus' Histories IV and V* (Oxford, 1985)
CIG	*Corpus Inscriptionum Graecarum*, ed. A. Boeckh (4 vols, Berlin, 1828–77)
CIL	*Corpus Inscriptionum Latinarum*, ed. F. Ritschel *et al.* (Berlin, 1862–)
CP	*Classical Philology*
CPJ	V. Tcherikover, A. Fuks, and M. Stern, *Corpus Papyrorum judaicarum* (3 vols, Cambridge, Mass., 1957–64)
CQ	*Classical Quarterly*
CR	*Classical Review*
CRAI	*Comptes rendus de l'Académie des Inscriptions*
CREBM	H. Mattingly *et al.*, *Coins of the Roman Empire in the British Museum* 1 (London, 1923; 2^2, 1978)
CW	*Classical Weekly/World*
Docs G–N	E.M. Smallwood, *Documents illustrating the Principates of Gaius, Claudius, and Nero* (Cambridge, 1967; repr. Bristol, 1984)
Docs N–H	E.M. Smallwood, *Documents illustrating the Principates of Nerva Trajan and Hadrian* (Cambridge, 1966)
EE	*Ephemeris epigraphica*
EJ^2	V. Ehrenberg and A.H.M. Jones, *Documents illustrating the Reigns of Augustus and Tiberius*[2], ed. D.L. Stockton (Oxford, 1976)
ESAR	T. Frank, ed., *Economic Survey of Ancient Rome* (5 vols, Baltimore, 1937–40; repr. Paterson, NJ, 1959)
FGH	F. Jacoby, *Die Fragmente der griechischen Historiker* (14 vols, Berlin, Leiden, 1923–58)
FIRA	S. Riccobono *et al.*, eds, *Fontes Iuris Romani anteiustiniani* (3 vols, Florence, 1940–43)
G&R	*Greece and Rome*
GRBS	*Greek, Roman and Byzantine Studies*
Hist.	*Historia*
HN	B.V. Head, *Historia Numorum. a manual of Greek numismatics*[2] (Oxford, 1911)
HSCP	*Harvard Studies in Classical Philology*
IG	*Inscriptiones Graecae* (Berlin, 1873–)
IGB	G. Mihailov, ed., *Inscriptiones Graecae in Bulgaria repertae. Acad. Litt. Bulg. Inst. Arch, Ser, epigr.* 2, 5–7, 9f. (4 vols, Sofia, 1956–66; 1^2, 1970)
IGLS	L. Jalabert and R. Mouterde, eds, *Inscriptions grecques et latines de la Syrie* (10 vols, Paris, 1929–86)

IGR	R. Cagnat, ed., *Inscriptiones Graecae ad res Romanas pertinentes* (1, 3, 4, Paris, 1901–17)
ILA	S. Gsell and H.-G. Pflaum, eds, *Inscriptions latines de l'Algérie* (3 vols, Paris, 1922–76)
ILS	H. Dessau, ed., *Inscriptiones Latinae Selectae* (3 vols, Berlin, 1892–1916, repr. 1954–5)
IMS	*Inscriptions de la Mésie supérieure. Centre d'Et. épigr. et num. de la Fac. de Phil. de l'Univ. de Beograd* 1- (Belgrade, 1976–)
IRT	J.M. Reynolds and J.B. Ward-Perkins, eds, *The Inscriptions of Roman Tripolitania* (Brit. Sch. Rome, 1952)
IvE	*Inschriften griechischer Städte aus Kleinasien* (Bonn, 1972–), Ephesus volumes
JHS	*Journal of Hellenic Studies*
JNG	*Jahreshefte für Numismatik und Geldgeschichte*
JRS	*Journal of Roman Studies*
JS	*Journal des Savants*
Lat.	*Latomus*
LCM	*Liverpool Classical Monthly*
LF	*Listy Filologické*
MAAR	*Memoirs of the American Academy in Rome*
MAMA	*Monumenta Asiae Minoris Antiqua*
MEFR	*Mélanges de l'Ecole française de Rome (Antiquité)*
MH	*Museum Helveticum*
Millar, *ERW*	F.G.B. Millar, *The Emperor in the Roman World* (London, 1977; repr. with afterword, 1991)
Mommsen, *St.*	Th. Mommsen, *Römische Staatsrecht* (3 vols, Berlin, 1³, 1887; 2³, 1886; 3³, 1887; repr. Basel, 1952)
MW	M. McCrum and A.G. Woodhead, *Select Documents of the Principates of the Flavian Emperors including the year of revolution AD* 68–96 (Cambridge, 1961) (see Concordance, p. 273)
NAC	*Quaderni ticinesi: Numismatica e antichità classiche*
NC	*Numismatic Chronicle*
OCD	S. Hornblower and A. Spawforth, eds, *Oxford Classical Dictionary*³ (Oxford, 1996)
OGIS	W. Dittenberger, ed., *Orientis graecae inscriptiones selectae,* (2 vols, Leipzig, 1903–5)
PBA	*Proceedings of the British Academy*
PBSR	*Papers of the British School at Rome*
PCPS	*Proceedings of the Cambridge Philological Society*
PE	R. Stillwell, ed., *The Princeton Encyclopedia of Classical Sites* (Princeton, 1976)

PEQ	*Palestine Exploration Quarterly*
Pflaum, *Carrières*	H.-G. Pflaum, *Les Carrières procuratoriennes équestres sous le Haut-Empire romain. Inst. fr. d'Arch. de Beyrouth, Bibl. arch. et hist.* 57 (3 vols, Paris, 1960–1)
PFuad	D.S. Crawford, ed., *Fuad I Univ. Papyri* (Alexandria, 1949)
Phil.	*Philologus*
PIR	H. Klebs *et al.*, eds, *Prosopographia Imperii Romani* (3 vols, Berlin, 1897–8); *PIR²*, E. Groag *et al.*, eds (2nd edn, Berlin, 1933–)
PLond.	F.G. Kenyon and H.I. Bell, eds, *Papyri in the British Museum* (London, 1893–1917)
POxy.	B.P. Grenfell and A.S. Hunt *et al.* , eds, *Oxyrhynchus Papyri* (London, 1898–)
PP	*La Parola del Passato*
PStras.	F. Preisigke, *Griech. Pap. d. kais. Universitäts- u. Landsbibliotek zu Strassburg* (2 vols, Strasbourg, Leipzig, 1906, 1920)
RE	K. Wissowa *et al.* , eds, *Paulys Real-Enzyclopädie der classischen Altertumswissenschaft* (Berlin, 1894–1980)
REA	*Revue des Etudes anciennes*
REJ	*Revue des Etudes juives*
REL	*Revue des Etudes latines*
RFIC	*Rivista di filologia e d'istruzione classica*
RHDFE	*Revue historique du Droit français et étranger*
RIB	R.G. Collingwood and R.P. Wright, eds, *Roman Inscriptions of Britain* 1 (Oxford, 1965)
RIC	H. Mattingly and E.A. Sydenham, eds, *The Roman Imperial Coinage* 2. *Vespasian to Hadrian* (London, 1926)
RIN	*Rivista Italiana di Numismatica e di scienze affini*
RM	*Rheinisches Museum für Philologie*
Röm. Mitt.	*Mitteilungen des deutschen archäologischen Instituts, Römische Abteilung*
SEG	J. Hondius *et al.*, eds, *Supplementum Epigraphicum Graecum* (Leiden, 1926–)
SEHRE	M. Rostovtzeff, *Social and Economic History of the Roman Empire²*, ed. P.M. Fraser (Oxford, 1957)
SNR	*Schweizerische Numismatische Rundschau/Revue suisse de Numismatique*
Syme, *DP*	R. Syme, *Danubian Papers* (Bucharest, 1971)
Syme, *RP*	R. Syme, *Roman Papers* (7 vols, Oxford, 1979–91)
TAM	E. Kalinka *et al.*, eds, *Tituli Asiae Minoris antiqua,* 1 (Vienna, 1901–)

ABBREVIATIONS

TAPA	*Transactions and Proceedings of the American Philological Association*
WS	*Wiener Studien*
YCS	*Yale Classical Studies*
ZPE	*Zeitschrift für Papyrologie und Epigrafik*
ZSS	*Zeitschrift der Savigny-Stiftung (Rom. Abteilung)*

KEY DATES

66–7	Nero's tour of Greece, Vespasian in attendance
66	Enforced suicide of Corbulo. Revolt in Judaea. Vespasian put in charge of operations
67	Reduction of Galilee
68	Vespasian reduces Judaea, Idumaea, and Peraea. Revolt of Vindex and Galba. Fall of Nero (8–9 June)
69	'Year of Four Emperors':
	Otho overthrows Galba (15 January)
	Vitellius' forces defeat Otho at Bedriacum (14 April); Otho's suicide (16th)
	Vitellius recognized by the senate (19th)
	Vespasian proclaimed Emperor in Egypt (1 July) and Judaea (3rd)
	Flavian forces defeat Vitellianists at Cremona ('second battle of Bedriacum', 24–5 Oct.)
	Execution of Flavius Sabinus (19 Dec.)
	Vespasian's troops take Rome (20 Dec.). Full powers conferred on him (21st)
70	Wrangling in Senate (January–?March)
	Ceremony for restoration of Capitol (21 June). Jerusalem: Temple burned; Titus captures City (August–September)
	Vespasian returns to Rome. He becomes supreme pontiff and 'Father of his Country' (autumn)
	End of revolt on the Rhine and in Gaul (autumn)
71	Triumph of Vespasian and Titus (June)
	Titus given Tribunician Power and proconsular power (1 July)
73	Masada taken. Vespasian and Titus censors (April 73 – October 74)
73–4	Establishment of Roman power in *Agri Decumates*, S.W. Germany
74?	Killing of Helvidius Priscus
75	Dedication of Temple of Peace
75–9	Josephus publishes *Jewish War*. Eprius Marcellus and Alienus Caecina die as conspirators against Vespasian
77	Publication of Pliny's *Natural History*. Agricola goes to Britain (late summer)
78	Successful campaign against Bructeri
79	Death of Vespasian (24 June); accession of Titus. Vespasian deified Eruption of Vesuvius and Destruction of Pompeii (24 August)
80	Fire of Rome
81	Death of Titus (13 September); accession of Domitian (14th)

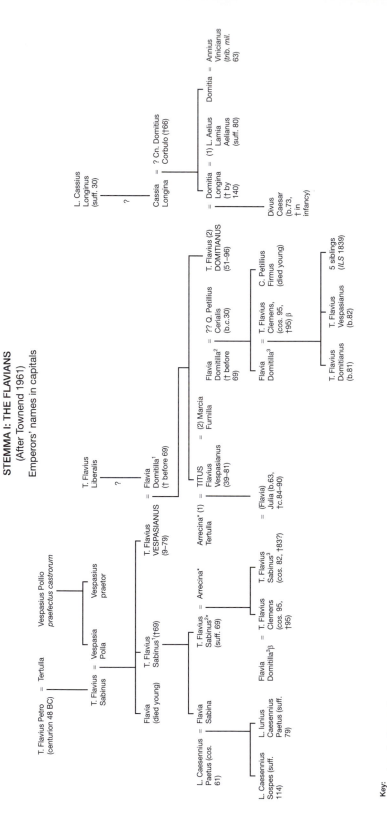

STEMMA I: THE FLAVIANS
(After Townend 1961)
Emperors' names in capitals

Key: * see also Stemma II
        β see elsewhere in this stemma

STEMMA II: THE ARRECINI AND JULII
(After Townend 1961)

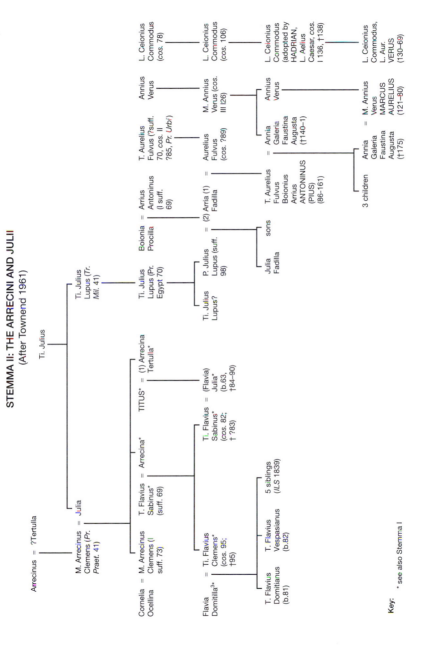

Key: * see also Stemma I

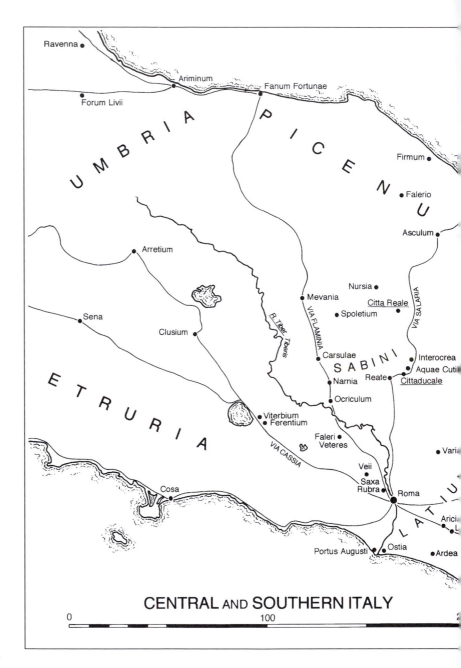

Map 1 Central and Southern Italy

N

ABRUZZI   Histonium ●

● Terventum

S A M N I U M

● Bovianum
● Saepinum

● Arpinum

LATINA

Aquinum ●

Aeclanum
Beneventum ●   ●

Mt Tifata
Capua ●   C A M P A N I A

Formiae ●   Sinuessa ●   Nola ●

Herculaneum   Salernum ●
Tarracina ●   Neapolis ●   ● Pompeii
Puteoli ●
Cumae ●   Paestum
● Misenum

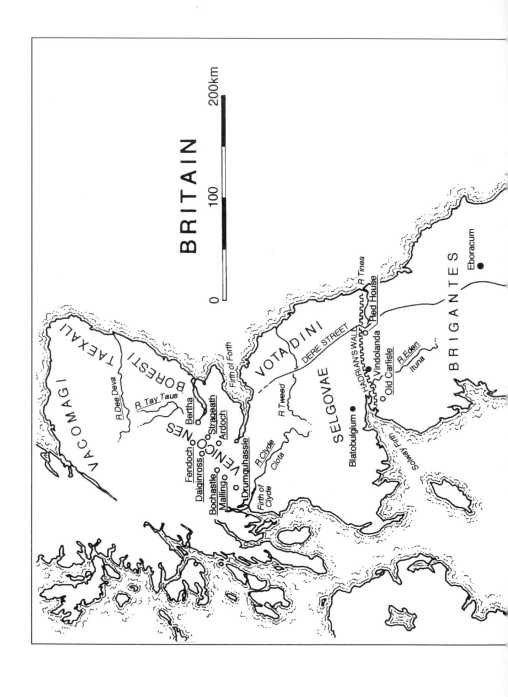

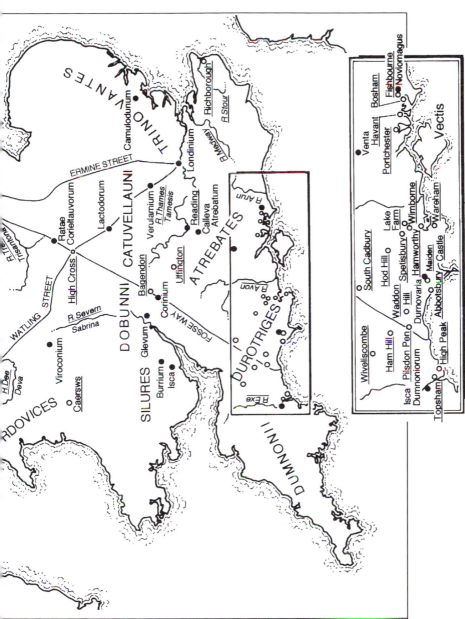

Map 2 Britain

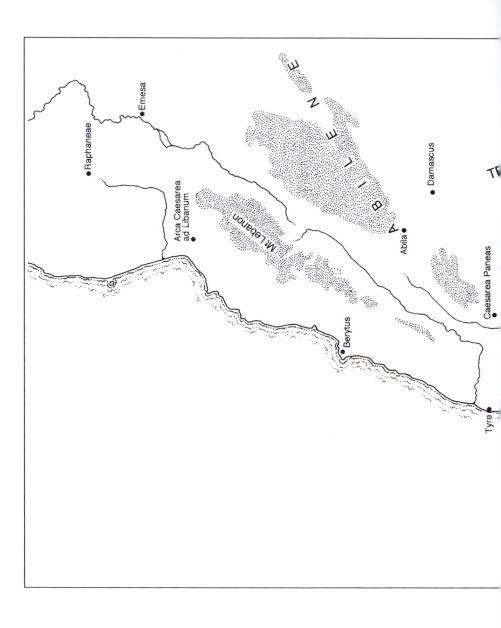

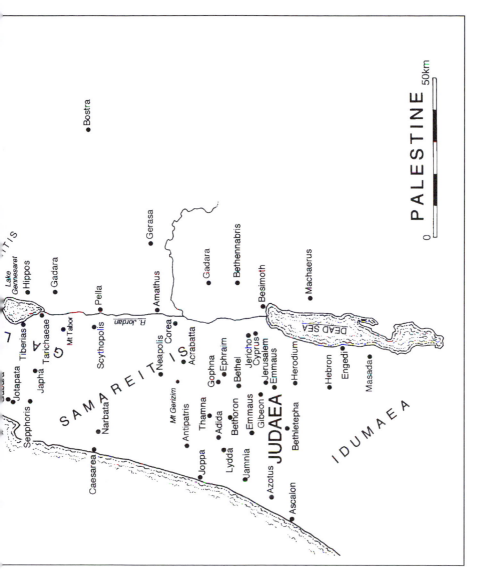

Map 3 Palestine

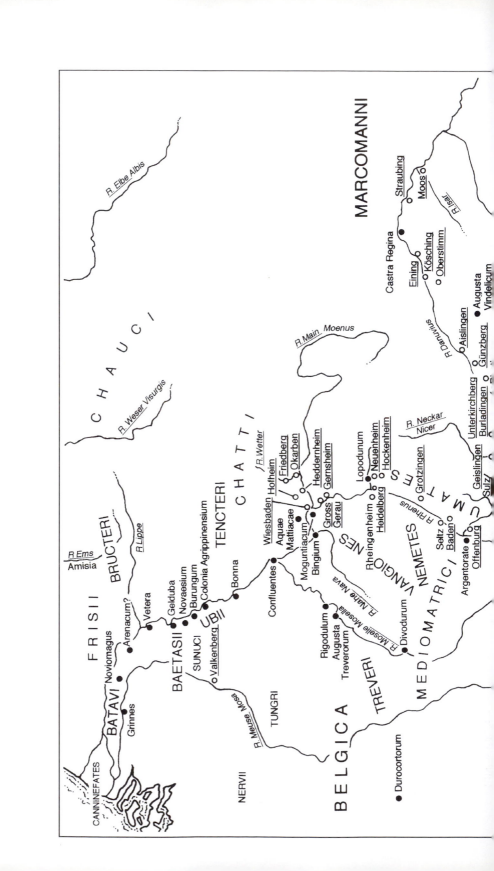

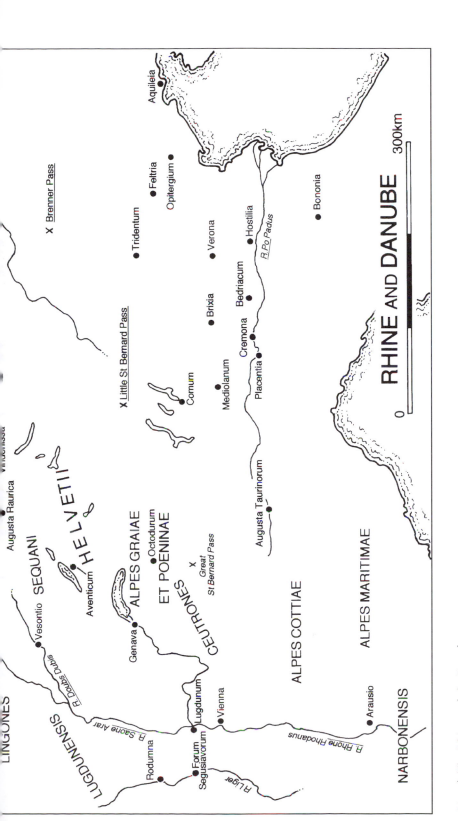

Map 4 The Rhine and the Danube

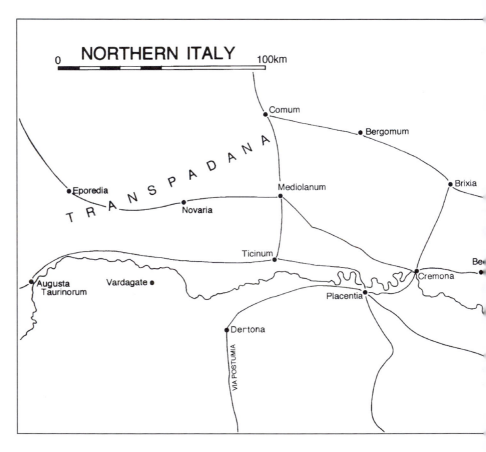

Map 5 Northern Italy

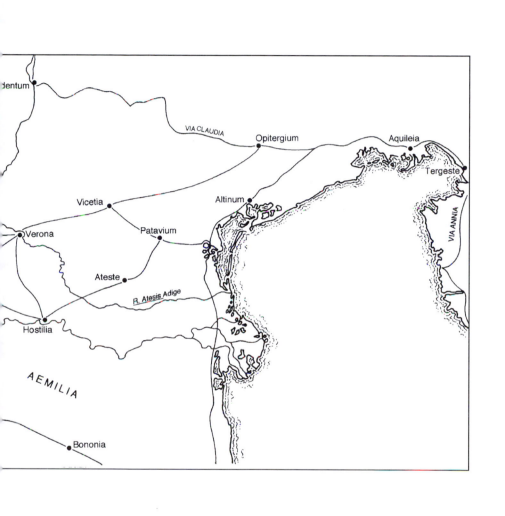

dentum

VIA CLAUDIA

Opitergium

Aquileia

Tergeste

Vicetia

Altinum

Verona

Patavium

VIA ANNIA

Ateste

R. Atesis Adige

Hostilia

AEMILIA

Bononia

Map 6 Spain

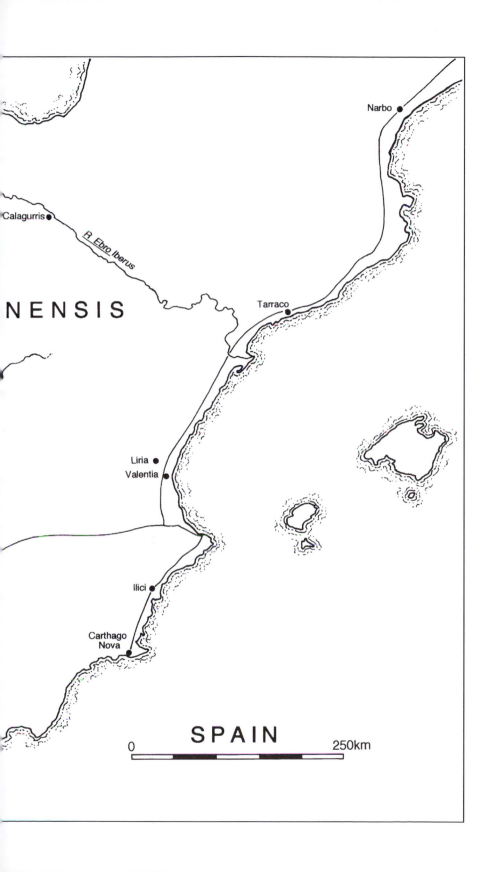

Narbo

Calagurris

R. Ebro Iberus

NENSIS

Tarraco

Liria
Valentia

Ilici

Carthago
Nova

SPAIN

0   250km

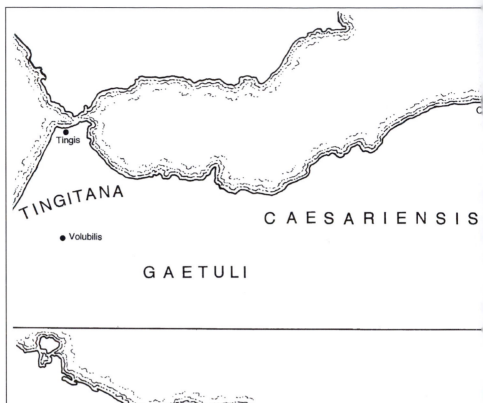

Map 7 North Africa

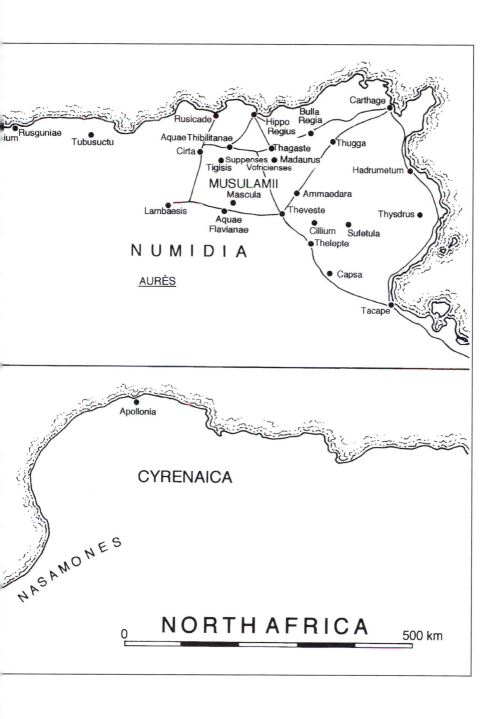

Rusguniae
ium Rusguniae
Tubusuctu
Rusicade
Carthage
Bulla
Regia
Hippo
Regius
Aquae Thibilitanae
Thugga
Cirta
Thagaste
Suppenses
Madaurus
Tigisis
Vofricienses
Hadrumetum
MUSULAMII
Mascula
Ammaedara
Lambaesis
Theveste
Thysdrus
Aquae
Flavianae
Cillium
Sufetula
Thelepte
NUMIDIA
Capsa
AURÈS
Tacape

Apollonia

CYRENAICA

NASAMONES

NORTH AFRICA

0   500 km

Map 8 Asia Minor

Map 9 The Danube

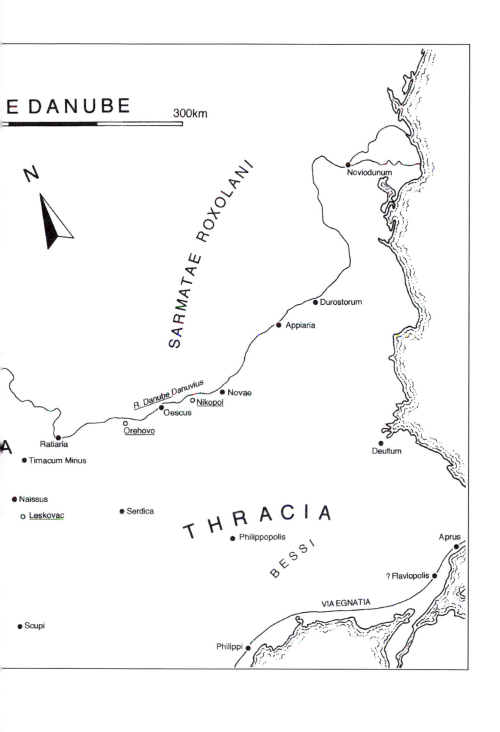

E DANUBE

300km

N

SARMATAE ROXOLANI

Noviodunum

Durostorum

Appiaria

R. Danube Danuvius

Novae

Nikopol

Oescus

Orehovo

Ratiaria

Deultum

Timacum Minus

Naissus

Leskovac

Serdica

THRACIA

Philippopolis

BESSI

Aprus

? Flaviopolis

VIA EGNATIA

Scupi

Philippi

INTRODUCTION

This is a success story, as medieval traditions about 'the noble Emperor' make clear. In one French, Spanish, and Portuguese romance, printed in Lisbon in 1483, Vespasian, a sufferer from leprosy, is cured by the handkerchief of St Veronica, and proceeds to take Jerusalem, avenging Christ and punishing Jews and Pilate; he converts his entire Empire to Christianity.[1]

The individual's success, set against the downfall of a dynasty, is the straightforward subject of the first four chapters of this book. The unglamorous new senator Vespasian pursued his career under the Julio-Claudian emperors, Tiberius, Gaius, Claudius, and Nero (14–68), and his accumulating experience made him useful to the declining dynasty without making him dangerous. He survived politics as well as the rigours of campaigning in Britain (Ch. 1–2) to emerge in 67 as the military man chosen by Nero to bring Judaea back into the Empire (3). So he came to be in charge of three fighting legions and in alliance with the governors of Syria and Egypt, who controlled five more, precisely when the emperors of 68–9 were fighting for survival (4.1). The success of the bid itself depended on his being able to rally legions and individuals in key positions military and civilian through calculation or principle, fear or ambition, usually a complex amalgam (4.2).

When Nero fell in June 68, it was a portentous blow to stability. The dynasty founded by Augustus had kept Rome and the Empire free from civil war for a century. One man's supremacy, based on superior powers and control of the army and politely known as the Principate, passed normally to an heir at law and had been accepted as a necessary condition of peace. Now the laurel bushes planted by Livia, Augustus' wife and Tiberius' mother, wilted and died, like her breed of white chickens, whose progenitor had brought her the original laurel berry. At first Nero's death seemed easily remediable. The claimant in the wings, Galba, was an aristocrat with military merit, wealthy, experienced, and free from natural heirs to turn out like Nero. Yet he had prestigious connections with the previous régime, since his career had been promoted by Livia, giving him a kind of legitimacy.

Galba spoilt men's hopes by coming to power. He fell to Otho in January 69, Otho in April to Vitellius, in December Vitellius to Vespasian. Why

1

should the sequence end? Tacitus describes the year as 'nearly Rome's last'. The second part of this book (5–13) shows the parvenu surviving where Galba and the others had been swept away. It is the second part of his success story: the rôle of Princeps made higher demands, Tiberius justifiably thought, than that of a magistrate, and Tacitus judged that Vespasian's reputation rose to it.[2]

In 70 the Empire was disordered, demoralized, and ill-disciplined. Judaea was still in revolt, and the Rhine and the provinces of Gaul about to be threatened by dissident movements (8). Vespasian had also to cope with an acute shortage of reserves and revenue (7). But there were good reasons to hope for recovery. There was no radically new constitution to be devised: the Augustan and Julio-Claudian principate, adapted, would do. Vespasian could concentrate on making it work and presenting himself as a worthy ruler along accepted lines (5 and 12). He came to power after only a year and a half of disorder, unlike Augustus, who emerged supreme after thirteen years of civil war or uneasy peace and decades of political and social turbulence before that.

Vespasian's principate and those of his sons Titus and Domitian (79–81; 81–96) equalled only the years of the later Julio-Claudians. But they are seen as initiating a new age. Nerva, Trajan, and Hadrian (96–138), and the Antonine Emperors (138–93) assumed power comparatively smoothly and the reigns of all but the last, Commodus, could be presented as the Golden Age of the Empire. The Flavian period seems to mark a settlement: there was a clearer idea of what an emperor's functions were, and what rôle the senate still had to play (6 and 11); of what could and could not be achieved against peoples currently beyond Roman writ (10); provinces attained new privileges and increasing wealth in relation to Italy (7 and 9), and a new élite, Italian and provincial, gave society a different tone (11).[3]

Historians face three problems, all acutely posed by the medieval romance. First, how much could the actions of an individual contribute to momentous changes? Or were they brought about, perhaps not intentionally, by the small actions of millions? Regions and classes had their own social and economic rationale. There is no blanket answer, but the Emperor did wield real power; he controlled the army, which potentially could wield force. Power in turn made him influential in habits of thought and manners. But he could also grasp, share, and sometimes forward, the wishes of subjects.[4]

Second, how far did Vespasian seek to change rather than restore? How much of what he did was remedial, *ad hoc*, and learned from predecessors, and how much had new long-term objectives? Like Septimius Severus (193–211), he would have engaged in discussions on what was advantageous to the Empire. They had to be based on principles derived from shared experience and knowledge of history.[5]

The biographer Suetonius asserts that Vespasian had two prime aims: to restore stability to a tottering State, then to enhance its lustre. Equally favourable, the fourth century writer Aurelius Victor claims that Vespasian 'restored' the State 'within a short time': the first aim was achieved by Vespasian's censorship in 73–4, if not by his triumph of 71. How did Vespasian hope to achieve his other purpose of 'enhancing' ('*ornare*') the State? Enhancement was material, but had moral, social, and military dimensions. Suetonius follows his observation with sections on measures against indiscipline among the troops; the ending of cities' 'freedom'; reconstruction of Rome; attention to the upper class; restoration of looted property; regulation of legal procedure; and measures against luxury. None of this was novel; changes of policy ascribed to Vespasian need scrutinizing (9, 10, 13).[6]

Last, the problem of disentangling the 'story' from the stories. We may put theoretical scruples aside and claim that we manage even our daily lives under the same dependence on others' 'representations', though they do not involve the cultural gulfs created by the lapse of two thousand years, to be bridged only by strenuous efforts of the imagination; but there is a particularly thick overlay of propaganda that obscures the truth about the Jewish War, the Year of the Four Emperors, and the entire reign. Contemporary information concerning the War and the Flavian coup comes from Josephus, a disingenuous source close to the Emperor, while the loss of most of Tacitus' *Histories* has left literary material meagre and conformist. Official productions, coinage, inscriptions, and architectural monuments are relatively plentiful. The student is edged towards favourable views. Yet the ideology itself is something to exploit. As a response to the demands made on an emperor, it made Vespasian, like other emperors, a prisoner. He had to some plausible extent to stand by his own declarations and public persona. The success or failure of political measures can be gauged from their effects and from the reactions of politicians and writers judged independent; and military achievement is often measurable from evidence on the ground (10 and 13).[7]

1

A NEW MAN IN POLITICS

Vespasian's career was a product of the social revolution that accompanied the change from Republic to Augustan Principate. Not only Marxist class but rank kept Roman society stable. Lines between Roman and non-Roman, slave and free, between plebs and the equestrian and senatorial orders, and between these orders, were reinforced under the Principate. But deserving men could cross them and look forward to seeing sons and grandsons crossing others. Permeability strengthened the system.

A parvenu underwent severe scrutiny. His beginnings could be presented by detractors as degrading. A poverty-stricken boyhood, involving manual work on his parents' farm and preventing him from acquiring an education, was ascribed to Gaius Marius, the great general from near Arpinum. Origin outside Rome (Arpinum had not received Roman citizenship until 188 BC) made a man liable to attacks that were hard to disprove when he had grown up in obscurity. Titus Flavius Vespasianus, born in the evening of 17 November AD 9 at a hamlet in the Sabine country, was, with his elder brother T. Sabinus, the first of those Flavii to rise to senatorial rank; both reached the consulship, Sabinus rose to the Prefecture of the City, and Vespasian unthinkably high for a man of his origins, whatever his gifts and industry.[1]

Suetonius did research. On his father's side Vespasian was descended from T. Flavius Petro of Reate, who had fought as centurion or *evocatus* for the Republicans at Pharsalus in 48 BC, escaping home from the battlefield. The sixty centurions of a legion could come from the stratum of society just below that of the knights, or rise slowly from the ranks. *Evocati* were men recalled after retirement, with prospects of promotion, and Petro may have been a veteran of Pompey's Eastern campaigns (67–63 BC). He secured a pardon and honourable discharge from Caesar and, back in civilian life, took up the profession of debt collector.

Petro married a woman from Etruria, Tertulla, and his son, Vespasian's father, is the first known T. Flavius Sabinus of the family, which is the earliest attested in which brothers had the same forename, and in successive generations. The ethnic surname may be taken from a forebear, or be intended to distinguish this from another branch elsewhere. On Sabinus' career, some said that he reached the post of leading centurion in a legion, as one might have expected from a man of his background, others that he reached only an ordinary centurionate when he had to retire for health reasons. Suetonius, however, states roundly that he did no military service before undertaking collection of the 2.5 per cent due on goods entering or leaving the province of Asia, where statues were erected in tribute to his fairness. Sabinus went on to become what Suetonius describes as a money-lender or, more politely, banker ('*faenus exercuit*') amongst the Helvetii, where he died. It was a shrewd enterprise, with the advance of Roman control to the Danube: their homeland between the Rhine, Jura, and the Lake of Geneva was developing and there would be demand for capital from ambitious pro-vincials keen to better themselves. But it was probably official functions that originally took Sabinus north: service in the company responsible for collect-ing the 2.5 per cent tax in Helvetian territory; as a centurion he might already have been involved in tax-collecting. There he died, survived by his wife and two sons; his eldest child, a girl, had not lived to her first birthday. The conventional view has Sabinus' service in Gaul in the principates of Augustus and Tiberius, but a seductive hypothesis of D. Van Berchem puts his sojourn later: when Claudius opened up the Great St Bernard pass in 46 the devel-opment of Helvetian territory gave scope for the banker's activities; hence it may have been Vespasian himself who recommended Aventicum to his father, when he was already legionary legate at Argentorate – and after the expenses of his praetorship caused him financial difficulties. A nurse of 'our Augustus' is commemorated on a funerary monument of Aventicum, not Vespasian's nurse, as is usually supposed, surviving until her charge was at least 60, but that of Titus, his son, who was left with his grandfather while Vespasian took part in the invasion of Britain. In support Van Berchem cites the opposition put up by the Helvetii to the Vitellians in 69, the elevation of Aventicum to a colony, and the favour shown it after that by Titus. All this attests connections with Aventicum, not when they were forged; and Helvetian territory did not develop so suddenly under Claudius as to preclude Sabinus from operating there two decades previously.[2]

The careers of father and son, in the versions of Sabinus' early life rejected by Suetonius, are suspiciously parallel, military service at just below eques-trian level, then financial enterprises; Pliny the Elder's *History* is probably the source for one of them. The point of both versions, illness causing premature retirement, would be the same: he would have become a leading centurion. Both are apologetic. What Suetonius accepts is also interesting. The later financial activities of the son, Sabinus, required capital, which he presumably augmented as a tax-collector in Asia and among the Helvetii. Even though he did not serve in the army he seems likely, as a man playing a responsible if minor part in the collection of taxes in Gaul, to have reached just below equestrian rank or to have been close enough to pass as an *eques*. Suetonius' confidence suggests that he thought that he was using a good source, though evidently not Vespasian's own memoirs, which dealt with the Jewish War.[3]

A different purpose lay behind a story about Petro that Suetonius rejects. He claims not to have been able to find any evidence for it – which brings out the obscurity of the family. In this version, Petro's father came from Transpadane Gaul as a contractor of the farmhands from Umbria who were hired annually in the Sabine territory. In other words, he was a newcomer to Reate, without landed property, and his claim to consideration there was based on his wife being a native; worse, he was a Gaul. This tale was uncovered or developed – the name Petro is certainly Gallic – by a source hostile to Vespasian. It could be oral or written, in the form of a political pamphlet, and belong either to the months between Vespasian's bid for power on 1 July 69, and the fall of Rome nearly six months later or to scurrility circulating after Vespasian's accession.[4]

Sabinus married up, something once frowned upon in English society but not worth comment at Rome, as Gaius Marius' uncontroversial marriage (*c*.111 BC) to a Julia of the Caesars shows. Vespasia Polla came from a family eminent at Nursia, an Umbrian town abutting on Sabine territory, and her father Pollio, as well as holding the post of Camp Prefect, served three terms as military tribune, a post for intending senators as well as *equites*. Suetonius notes a place 6 miles from Nursia on the road to Spoletium known as 'Vespasiae' which showed many sepulchral monuments of her family and proved its distinction. Her brother had entered the senate as one of the propertied men from all over Italy encouraged by Augustus, and reached the praetorship. Not surprisingly, the second son took his *cognomen* (surname) from his mother.[5]

The financial activities of Petro and Sabinus are stressed in the opening pages of Suetonius' biography, but respectable landed property recurs in stories of Vespasian's forebears and early life. He was brought up on the considerable estates of his paternal grandmother Tertulla at Cosa in Etruria, perhaps while his parents remained in Asia or the Alps. 'Vespasiae' may have been the site of another property, and it is possible that Vespasian's mother also owned a house in Spoletium. These properties belonged, significantly enough, to the families into which the Flavii married. Their own base may have been in the hamlet where Vespasian was born, at Falacrina. A.W. Braithwaite located it 32 km along the Via Salaria (Salt Road) on the other side of Reate from Rome: S. Silvestre in Falacrino i Collicelli near Città Reale preserves the name. Here we may put the home of Sabinus. Another story from Suetonius' biography seems to provide the family with a residence just outside Rome as well. An ancient oak in the grounds, sacred to Mars, put out shoots on each occasion when Vespasia gave birth. The third, when Vespasian was born, was like a young tree. But the word for his estate, '*suburbanus*', need not refer to places outside Rome. We are not prevented from seeing the Flavians as small entrepreneurs, marrying into the landed gentry of the Sabine territory, and may even suspect truth in the story of Petro's father's origins as a labour contractor.[6]

The land from which Vespasian sprang and which gave him his countrified accent was well described by L. Homo. Five thousand square km of upland north-east of Rome, surrounded by Etruria in the west, Umbria in the north, Picenum in the east and the central Italian tribes of the Abruzzi in the south. Only a third was cultivable. Mountainous and forested towards the north (it was known for its acorns), it had more amenable plains surrounding Amiternum and Reate to the south. Cultivation of olive, vine, and herbs, and stock-raising, were the staple occupations. Tough conditions and an early entry into Roman history, illustrated by the tales of the Roman rape of the Sabine women and of Romulus' sharing of power with the Sabine king Titus Tatius, gave these people a reputation for courage and high morals, as well as entitlement to participate in Roman life at the highest level, as the Claudii had done for centuries. They succumbed to Roman power in 290 BC and received full Roman citizenship twenty-two years later.[7]

Vespasian would spend summers in this country, on at least one occasion lingering until his birthday in November, or returning to celebrate it. His favourite spot, where he was to die, was Aquae Cutiliae near Cittaducale, close to his birthplace, only 12 km east of Reate towards Interocrea. But he also loved the time he spent on his grandmother's estate; he kept it as it had been, and would celebrate her memory by using for special occasions, perhaps her birthday, a silver cup she had owned.[8]

If Vespasian cared so much for his home country and for his family it would not be surprising if he assumed the manners of his hard-working countrymen and made no secret of what he learnt from his parents and grandparents, as Homo observed. He could not or would not rid himself of his accent, and probably told the truth, or enough of it, about his origins, avoiding pretentious claims such as those of the family of his rival Vitellius (that they were descended from Faunus, king of the Aborigines, and his divine consort Vitellia), which merely provoked the outspoken Cassius Severus into attributing them a very different origin – from a freedman. His own career and principate, combining military achievement with administration that was notably canny over money, recalls the preoccupations of his father and grandfather; his unabashed sense he may have learned from his grandmother Tertulla. One story projects it back on her. When she was informed by his father that the omen of the oak branch, which he had confirmed by inspecting the entrails of a sacrificial animal, showed that her grandchild was born to be a Caesar, she laughed at being still in her right mind when her son had gone senile.[9]

Vespasian's mother was ambitious: her sons should reach the status of her brother the ex-praetor, and the combined fortunes of the families provided the census of two senators, 2m *HS*. Vespasian's upbringing is unknown, and although in his reign he encouraged education, nothing is said of a taste for literature or philosophy, or of oratorical gifts. Vespasian knew Greek, but it may have been acquired in Achaea or in Judaea, relatively late in his career. All the same, his education must have been adequate, even if his literary attainments were only mediocre.[10]

The elder Flavius applied for the permission to wear the *latus clavus* (the broad stripe on the tunic), prerogative of members of the senatorial order, in token of his ambitions. No doubt he was supported by his uncle the senator. Vespasian, who must have taken the toga of manhood in 25–6, at the age of 16, declined to apply – for a long time, according to Suetonius, and until his mother provoked him into agreement by calling him his brother's *ante-ambulo*, 'footman' or 'dependent'. Perhaps the senator's sister was particularly ambitious, as Homo suggested, for the son who derived his *cognomen* from her own name. How long Vespasian's intransigence really lasted is uncertain: it could have been years, months, or only weeks. The story is of a familiar type: how close a great man was to losing his chance of greatness, but for his mother's intervention. It could have become known, and from Vespasian's own mouth, at any time, on his first successes in Britain, at the time of his consulship, at his mother's death, or when he became Emperor. In the year of his refusal, lack of adequate funds, or the desire to follow in his father's footsteps need not have been the only deterrents: it was the decade in which, since the death of the Tiberius' son Drusus Caesar in 23, the struggle for the succession became more intense and more dangerous for anyone in politics, with the ascendancy of Tiberius' minister L. Aelius Sejanus (24–31).[11]

Aspirants to the quaestorship, the first magistracy that gave membership of the senate, should have two periods of service to their credit: one as tribune of the soldiers, the other in one of the minor magistracies known collectively as the Vigintivirate, the Board of Twenty. As the sons of a non-senator, Sabinus and Vespasian are likely to have held the military post first. Vespasian served in Thrace, a troublesome dependency where disturbances broke out probably in 25 and continued until 26 or even 27; 26 was the year in which the governor of Moesia, C. Poppaeus Sabinus, won triumphal decorations for suppressing them. Vespasian would have been in one of the Moesian legions that were sent to put them down, IV Scythica rather than V Macedonica, since no reference is made to a previous term with V when Vespasian took it for the Jewish War. But he is likely to have arrived in 27, after the main fighting was over, and so to have spent his time on garrison duty. Legionary detachments remained in Thrace after the disturbances ended, and J. Nicols believes that Vespasian spent three or four years in post; a three-year stint would bring him home in 30.[12]

Vespasian's post in the Vigintivirate is unknown, but, given his origins, it is not likely to have been one of the more prestigious of the four posts, those of the three-man board of masters of the mint or of the ten men with judicial functions (*IIIvir monetalis*; *Xvir stlitibus iudicandis*): even under Augustus most moneyers came from families bearing senatorial names or at least had forebears who had held the same post. He was probably either one of four men in charge of street cleaning in the City or, worst, one of the three who supervised executions and book-burnings (*IVvir viarum curandarum*; *IIIvir capitalis*). The street-cleaning post gives no clue when it might have been held; but if Vespasian served as *capitalis* in 31, he would have shared responsibility for carrying out the most notorious executions of the early Principate: those of Tiberius' fallen minister Sejanus on 19 October, and of his children, strangled in November or December and exposed on the Gemonian Stairs. Those deaths were remembered with horror, as Tacitus' account of them shows. If Vespasian had a part in this or in the subsequent witch-hunt, which culminated in 33 with what Tacitus called 'a massacre of enormous proportions' – the execution of twenty of Sejanus' associates – it would have been exploited in the propaganda war of 69 or by dissident circles during Vespasian's principate. We hear nothing. Either Vespasian served before Sejanus' fall, in 30, or he held the innocuous IVvirate, which would have been a natural step towards his later aedileship.[13]

Once over the Vigintivirate, Vespasian was entitled to stand for senatorial office proper, the quaestorship, on which he could have entered on 5 December 33 at the age of just 24, but he may have waited, held office in 34–5, one year after his brother, or 35–6. As quaestor it was only to be expected that he should receive one of the (less prestigious) provincial posts, whose holders acted as financial assistants to the governors of public provinces, the proconsuls. Theirs were the least sought-after of the twenty postings available. It was Crete with Cyrene that fell to Vespasian, 'by the lot', but the high-grade positions that kept young men at Rome as assistants to the consul or to the Emperor himself must have been given before the provincial posts were drawn; Vespasian's province was not even one of the two in which the quaestors served under proconsuls who had actually held a consulship, Asia and Africa: Crete with Cyrene, like Bithynia and Narbonensian Gaul, was governed by an ex-praetor, who might never reach the consulship and so be able to help on a young subordinate. The functions of the provincial office, although it formally began in December, necessarily ran from June to May, because that was when the governor himself (if he set out as early as Tiberius demanded) was in his province. Reaching an overseas province when the seas were closed from October to March could cause problems. Overseas quaestorships could occupy eighteen months of a young man's life, twelve of them committed to routine that might be mind-numbingly boring. If he entered office on 5 December 34, Vespasian would not be free until May 36, perhaps not until July if we allow some weeks for his homeward journey.[14]

The next formally obligatory post in the senatorial career was the crucial praetorship, which carried with it independent *imperium*, the power to command, and opened the way to governorships. It could be held at the age of 30, and during Tiberius' principate there were between twelve and sixteen annual vacancies. Very well-born young men were able to pass straight from quaestorship to praetorship, within the age-limits prescribed and provided that they observed the rule that two years had to elapse before a magistrate entered his next position. Patricians in particular achieved this, for of the sixteen optional intervening posts, the ten tribunates of the plebs devoted to the defence of the people's rights and the six aedileships that were concerned with the proper conduct of Rome's markets, all but two, the 'curule' aedileships, were restricted to plebeians. Augustus had sometimes found these posts hard to fill and had offered the tribunate to knights as a means of entry to the senate; Claudius found the same problem. In the senate, where elections had effectively been held since 15, it would be a merit (especially in the eyes of men who themselves had held them!) to have taken on one or both posts at this level. That is, having held them gave a man, especially if he were 'new', a greater chance of winning the praetorship. Lucky men escaped with one such post; others chalked up two.[15]

Returning to Rome from his province, Vespasian tried for the aedileship. This would have been in the late summer of 36, and, for all the difficulties that Augustus had experienced in filling this post, he failed; shortage of time for the canvass is the easiest explanation, as J. Nicols suggests; but, as he also observes, Vespasian did not do much better at the second attempt. The first candidature was badly timed in another way: it came very close to the end of Tiberius' principate, six months before the Emperor's death on 16 March 37. The Roman world was looking forward to a new young emperor, the son of the dead hero Germanicus, and at court men were keeping an eye on the health of the old one, who began to avoid contact with his doctor. Not only the protégés of the expected heir Gaius and his friends would be marked out for advancement but the most pedestrian politicians could hope for freedom and opportunity. That may have intensified competition for posts in the middle range at this time; a new man would be behind in the queue if ex-quaestors of long standing were emerging from semi-retirement.[16]

For a worse setback we have to go to C. Marius, although at a time when the aedileship was more sought-after and rejection not uncommon, even for aristocrats. Marius, tribune of the plebs in 119 BC, stood for the curule aedileship the following year and suffered defeat; he immediately transferred his candidature to the plebeian aedileship, to be defeated for a second time. Vespasian stood for the second time in 37, was elected to the last place, and held office in 38.[17]

Gaius changed electoral practice in 38, the year after he came to power. He abolished the senate's pre-election of candidates, which had been making a mockery of popular assemblies since 14, theoretically restoring free choice to the people. It did not work: senators had become used to making electoral pacts, bartering mutual support and avoiding the possibility of public rejection. In 39 or more probably 40 Gaius admitted defeat and allowed a formal electoral procedure to be held in the senate once again. Vespasian's election to the praetorship brought him to office either in 39, the earliest year that his age permitted and without an interval between the two offices, or more probably in 40, as J. Nicols has argued: the brief gap of three years (including one of electoral failure) between quaestorship and praetorship would have been anomalous for a man not specially favoured. Gaius' tinkering with the electoral arrangements is unlikely to have been the reason for Vespasian's relative success in his candidature for the praetorship, when he came in among the leading candidates. He does not seem to have done anything to win popular favour, and his record as aedile does not suggest either that he enjoyed or had yet won the special favour of Gaius: the Emperor noticed thick mud in an alley and ordered it to be thrown on Vespasian's toga, since he was the official responsible for supervising street cleaning.[18]

Another explanation for Vespasian's setbacks and his unexpected success suggests itself. At some point he had entered into a long-standing relationship, suspended during his marriage, with Antonia Caenis, the freedwoman and confidential secretary of the Emperor's grandmother Antonia. Marriage with a freedwoman was illegal, and when Vespasian took up with her again after his wife's death affection would have been reinforced by the wish to avoid complicating succession to property. Antonia may have freed Caenis in her will; if emancipated earlier, at the requisite age (30), Caenis must have been born in 7 at latest, two years before Vespasian. The liaison gave Vespasian access to the circle of courtiers and servants round the Emperor (Caenis was associated with the group who had succeeded in removing Sejanus in 31), although Antonia did not stay on good terms with Gaius and in any case she died in May 37, weeks after his accession; no good offices on her part were available that summer. On the other hand it was not long before Gaius began to antagonize the senate. By autumn 39 Gaius could claim to have discovered plots involving his brother-in-law M. Lepidus and Cn. Gaetulicus, commander of the Upper Rhine army, which he put down with dispatch, dashing north to take over Gaetulicus' legions and assert himself as the worthy son of their hero Germanicus. Throughout his term of office as praetor (it is not known which of the posts he held) Vespasian was at pains to keep on the right side of the Emperor, and it may be that the unpretentious new man was supported by Gaius for the praetorship, as hostility developed during the summer of 39. Another upstart loyalist, C. Velleius Paterculus, had been supported along with his brother for the same magistracy in the crucial year of 14, at the moment of Augustus' death, coming in among the first four. When Gaius' sister Agrippina was on her way home with the ashes of the executed Lepidus, Vespasian as praetor designate took part in a debate on the punishment of the conspirators and proposed aggravating the penalties: the remains should be denied burial. In honour of the success that Gaius claimed against the Canninefates in Germany during the spring of 40 Vespasian selflessly demanded that special games should be held. The cost would be met from public funds, but a praetor would have to enhance their magnificence out of his own pocket. When eventually Gaius returned to the neighbourhood of

Rome in May 40, or when he entered the city to hold his ovation (a lesser triumph) on his birthday, 31 August, Vespasian was duly invited to dine and took the opportunity of expressing thanks in the senate. We need not assume that the entire speech was devoted to the subject, only that an unfriendly reporter, turning over Vespasian's record, found this servile reference to the tyrant.[19]

Expenses incurred during the period when elections were again in the hands of the people may be why Vespasian seems to have been short of funds at this stage of his career: his eldest child Titus was born at Rome on 30 December 39, in what Suetonius calls a dingy house near the Septizonium. Contributing to the victory games would have aggravated his difficulties.[20]

Unlike his father, Vespasian did not marry above him. His wife was Flavia Domitilla, and it was easy for detractors to find material from her antecedents. Domitilla had been another man's mistress, not a senator's either, but a knight's, and a knight from Sabratha in Africa at that. Moreover, her title to full Roman citizenship had been called into question (a provocative issue when the succession to Vespasian came under discussion). She had been of Latin status, but eventually brought suit and, Suetonius says, was declared freeborn and a Roman citizen. This suggests that she either was or had been deemed an ex-slave. She bore the name of her father Flavius Liberalis, who presented her claim, and it is likely that her mother was his freedwoman and concubine, freed without good cause shown, contrary to the Lex Aelia Sentia, so acquiring only Latin status. However, the supposition that Domitilla was the illegitimate child of a woman who had already acquired Latin status on emancipation from slavery is virtually ruled out by Suetonius' specification that she was declared freeborn. Alternatively Flavius Liberalis had freed his daughter as a Latin and for the purposes of the marriage to Vespasian there was a (collusive) law-suit claiming *ingenuitas e libertinitate* (vindication of the free birth of a person currently of freed status). The suit was probably occasioned by the marriage because Augustus' legislation forbade senators and their sons to marry freedwomen, and the marriage would not have been possible without the vindication of Domitilla's free birth. Flavius Liberalis himself was respectable enough: he came from the flourishing Etruscan municipality of Ferentium 88 km north-west of Rome, home of a senatorial family that was to produce a short-lived emperor in 69, that of the Salvii Othones, and he rose to the position of quaestor's clerk, an official post that itself was not closed to freedmen, although often held by knights.[21]

As to why Vespasian wanted the marriage, nomenclature offers an answer: he was marrying a kinswoman (who must have been the only eligible one he had): Ferentium, half-way between Reate and Cosa, was within the stamping ground of the dynasty. Later marriages between cousins in the family helped to keep power within the dynasty (they were used by the Julio-Claudians also). In a private family such marriages conserved family property. If Vespasian married for money there were no immediately favourable effects on his finances, to judge by Suetonius' account of Titus' birthplace; but Vespasian had high expenses, and his father-in-law may have kept tight control of the purse-strings, although Domitilla's marriage represented a considerable social advance. The dowry may have been smaller than the sum to be expected when Flavius Liberalis died, probably leaving his daughter sole heir. And marriage and the possession of children should have given Vespasian an advantage in his career through the operation of Augustus' legislation. It was some time, however, before Domitilla gave birth to a second child that survived: the later Emperor Domitian was born on 24 October 51, almost twelve years after Titus, and his sister Flavia Domitilla either after Vespasian's return from Britain or, if we keep to Suetonius' order for the children, not long after Domitian. The gap is not surprising: in 41 his career took Vespasian abroad for a number of years; even if his wife went with him to his Rhine posting she cannot have crossed into Britain. Domitian too is said to have had a poverty-stricken adolescence, without a single silver vessel to his name – unless this is his critics' interpretation of his own claim of frugality; but he was born in a better district than Titus was, the sixth, on the Quirinal, and in a house that he was later to convert into a temple to his family. Vespasian was about to become consul.[22]

2

VESPASIAN AND THE ARISTOCRACY

The command in Britain

A new man needed friends of distinction, as well as a mistress at court, and it was surely with the encouragement of friends that Vespasian took his first political steps, fluctuations in his success to some extent following theirs. So Marius was a protégé of the noble Caecilii Metelli. The first name that might be associated with Vespasian's advancement is that of Pomponius Labeo, the praetorian legate who brought a legion into Thrace in 26 during the revolt; he was a subordinate of the governor of Moesia, C. Poppaeus Sabinus. If Vespasian had been too young to see active service under him as military tribune, Labeo may still have recommended his appointment to Sabinus and supervised his first months in the army.[1]

The Pomponii were of senatorial stock from the Republic, and produced consuls in AD 16 and (suff.) 17. They belonged to an interlinked group of families that seem to have owed their rise in the mid-first century AD to Tiberius and members of his family. Some associations may go back to Tiberius' brother Nero Drusus, to be taken over by Tiberius when Drusus died in 9 BC; and they could have been continued by Drusus' son Germanicus, who was adopted by Tiberius in 4 and seemed likely to reach supreme power. The other families involved were the Plautii, Petronii, and Vitellii.[2]

It was these, whose first representatives, four brothers Vitellii, entered the senate in the last decade of Augustus' principate, who were to climb highest, with Aulus Vitellius, from the next generation, becoming Emperor in 69. One brother, Publius, served Germanicus both on the Rhine and in Syria, and two others reached the consulship: A. and L. Vitellius were suffects in 32 and 34. The less spectacular Plautii of Trebula Suffenas among the tribe of the Aequi reached the consulships of 2 and 1 BC (suff.), AD 29 (suff., a man who had already been close to the Emperor Tiberius when he served him as quaestor in 20) and 36; they were particularly to distinguish themselves in the field. The Petronii, coming probably from Umbria, produced an eminent equestrian, Prefect of Egypt, early in the Principate, suffect consuls in 19 and 25, and the *ordinarius* of 37. Flavian ties with these families surely go back beyond Vespasian and his elder brother. The praetor of 51 BC, A. Plautius, probably great-grandfather of the suffect of 29, may have been an early senatorial associate of the Flavii: like Petro, he fought at Pharsalus under Pompey.[3]

The group persisted: links forged by intermarriage between Plautii and Vitellii under Augustus were renewed in the next generation when Plautia, daughter of the consul of 1 BC, married P. Petronius (suff. 19) and Aulus (suff. 29) married Pomponia Graecina, daughter of the consul of 16; in the third generation Petronius' daughter married Vitellius the future Emperor. At the same time political ups and downs were disruptive. The death of heirs in the imperial house, allowing others to rise, imposed difficult decisions. The death of Germanicus in 19 frayed the edges of the group; some may have transferred their allegiance to Tiberius' son Drusus Caesar, while others, Vitellii and Petronii, seem for a while to have attached hopes to Germanicus' younger brother Claudius. The death of Drusus in 23 posed another dilemma and a problem of loyalty: how closely should they be associated with Tiberius' minister L. Aelius Sejanus, who could be seen as a supporter of the interests of Drusus Caesar's surviving son Tiberius Gemellus against those of Germanicus' three boys Nero, Drusus, and Gaius? When Tiberius, 63 when he lost his son, finally died, which of them would come to power?[4]

The rise of Gaius, from 31 onwards, and his accession in 37, brought fresh lustre to members of families who had remained loyal to the children of Germanicus and survived. One of the most eminent members of the nexus, L. Vitellius, who had gone on from his consulship of 34 to distinguish himself as governor of Syria by intimidating the Parthians, claimed to be a son to Antonia. Vespasian's connection, with Antonia's freedwoman, was humbler. When Gaius was assassinated in 41 and his uncle Claudius seized power, there was no interruption in the success of members of these families. Q. Pomponius Secundus took over Gaius' consulship, and his brother Publius received the post as suffect in 44. In particular, Claudius enhanced the brilliance of the Plautii and Vitellii. A. Plautius, the suffect of 29, commanded the expedition to Britain in 43 and in acknowledgement received the unique honour (for a man in a private station) of an ovation, a minor form of triumph; his nephew Ti. Plautius Silvanus Aelianus was suffect consul in 45. L. Vitellius became consul for the second time in 43 and again in 47, both times *ordinarius* as Claudius' colleague, and in 47–8 he shared Claudius' censorship; his sons both held consulships in 48.[5]

The heyday of these families benefited their protégé Vespasian, who in 69 was contemptuously claimed as a 'client' by the Emperor Vitellius. He enjoyed help from another quarter. As an ex-praetor, Vespasian might eventually find himself in charge of a province of his own, but it was likely to be no higher ranking than Crete and Cyrene, and in the public service there were preliminary posts to fill as assistants to governors. Help from friends, experience in the army, and, reported by Suetonius, a word from Narcissus, then Claudius' most powerful freedman, took him out of the ballot by securing him the command of a legion, II Augusta, stationed at Argentorate.

Perhaps Narcissus was tipped or listened to Caenis; he was giving his recommendation to a member of a group familiar with the new Emperor. Claudius himself had been humiliated by Gaius, and should not have held subservience against Vespasian. He was on his way as a useful soldier.[6]

Legions on the Rhine saw action very early in Claudius' reign, repercussions from Gaius' campaigns of 39 and 40. Northern tribes, the Chauci (between the mouths of Ems and Elbe) and Canninefates, and the more southerly Chatti (east of the Moselle–Rhine confluence), began or went on raiding. Gaetulicus' successor Ser. Galba and his colleague on the lower Rhine, P. Gabinius Secundus, were coping with them in 41, perhaps winning Claudius a salutation as *imperator*. Gabinius, who recovered what may have been the third of the eagles lost with the legions in 9, was allowed to assume the name Chaucius, the last time such a name was acquired by a man in a private station. These were significant operations. No doubt Vespasian's legion was affected: something should lie behind Josephus' claim that he had 'restored peace to the West when the Germans were disturbing it'. Silius Italicus recorded his restraining of the Rhine by means of banks; either Vespasian, arriving in 42, too late for the campaigning, had to deal with the Rhine in flood, or he strengthened fortifications that kept down rebellious Rhine tribes.[7]

Early in the same year A. Plautius, governor of Pannonia, played a part in bringing to a smart end the attempt of his neighbour in Dalmatia, Camillus Scribonianus, to put down Claudius' new 'tyranny'. He could be trusted with an enterprise that would establish Claudius as the legionaries' as well as the praetorians' Emperor: the invasion of Britain. The plan, mooted by Gaius, was firm by the end of 42 at the latest. Plautius was assigned four legions, equivalent auxiliaries, detachments of the praetorian guard, and massive resources. From his own province he took IX Hispana, from the Rhine XX, XIV Gemina, and II Augusta, still under Vespasian. Intense preparation and training must have begun. Vespasian was making ready for four years' frontline service in Britain under a commander with whom he was already connected; he was to win a distinction that was the foundation of his later career. Even though he did not, as Josephus goes on to claim, 'win Britain for Claudius', nor yet conquer Thule or even lead an army against the Caledonian forests, as Flavian poets claimed, Tacitus was right to stress the importance of his achievements: 'Fate pointed to Vespasian.'[8]

Other legionary commanders selected for Britain included the experienced Cn. Hosidius Geta, who had recently been fighting in Mauretania, and Vespasian's older brother Sabinus, though which legion he was assigned is unknown. As this was a show-case display of Roman military might in which nothing must go wrong, the confidence of A. Plautius and the commander-in-chief in the ability and loyalty of the legates must have been strong.[9]

A walk-over was not expected. The Roman force was divided into three and the main landing-place was either at Richborough (the most commonly held view) or some other spot on the Kentish coast, or much farther to the west, in Hampshire or Sussex not far from the later palace at Fishbourne, just west of Noviomagus, where there were several other harbours to choose from: Porchester, Havant, and Bosham. It is possible that bridgeheads were established in both east and west, but two major landings widely apart would have given the Britons the chance to take divided Roman forces one after the other. In any case, the advance from the landing-place to London and Camulodunum was not easy. The Britons had to be brought to battle. A preliminary success was followed by the establishment of a fort at the crossing of a river traditionally identified with the Stour. Some native troops, on the conventional view the Gloucestershire Dobunni, who had been conscripted against Rome, declared for the invaders but there was fierce resistance on the way to London, at a river which on the conventional account was the Medway in Kent, but which J.G.F. Hind identifies with the Sussex Arun. It was dealt with by a feint crossing by auxiliaries. The main crossing was accomplished by legionaries and both Vespasian and his brother distinguished themselves. Once over the river the Romans still had difficulty in maintaining their bridgehead, and Hosidius Geta's attack ended a two-day struggle. The way was clear to cross the Thames near London; this operation was helped by the capture of a bridge upstream (at Staines, in Hind's view), but over the river the marshy ground proved as much a hazard as the enemy. Plautius, claiming to be in difficulties, summoned the Emperor to his aid, and they marched into Camulodunum. Claudius' stay of sixteen days was marked not only by this capture of the Trinovantian centre, now a focus of Catuvellaunian power. but also by his reception of chieftains from all over Britain who wished to surrender or claim Roman help against nearer enemies. Attractive though the proposal for a main landing near the Isle of Wight is, its dangers (due to the presence of the enemy on the island behind the Roman landings) seem to rule it out. It was at Richborough that Agricola set up the great monument 'marking the conquest of all Britain'. Claudius' visit also raises doubts about discounting Richborough as one of the original landing spots: the Emperor would have to pass through areas which there had not yet been time to subdue. A push from Richborough to Colchester may have been followed by a descent from Essex into Berkshire, Hampshire, and Sussex by II Augusta under Vespasian.[10]

The slow business of conquering southern Britain went on under Plautius, then from 47 to 53 under another well-connected general, P. Ostorius Scapula. Vespasian, transferring to the left flank after Claudius' departure at latest, had a vital task: it was the defection of southern Britain, confronting the coast of Gaul with a power centring on Verulamium in Hertfordshire and Camulodunum in Essex and expanding into Kent and Sussex under the defiant sons of Cunobelin, that was the strategic justification for the invasion. Vespasian may have begun operations by consolidating the Roman hold on west Kent and Sussex, but his main operations, using Fishbourne as a supply base, were towards Hampshire, Dorset, and Devon. If the dependent monarch Ti. Claudius Cogidubnus (or Togidubnus) was installed in his kingdom in southern Britain at the same time as the invasion he and Vespasian must have become well acquainted. Collaborating in a war need not cement good relations, but Cogidubnus survived as ruler at least into Vespasian's reign, as 'Great King' (*Rex magnus*). He could have been useful in 69, if he thought Vespasian would win.[11]

It was a combined land and sea operation, with the troops being supplied by the fleet at such bases as Hamworthy in Poole Harbour and Topsham on the Exe (this part of the Channel is particularly well suited to coastal navigation), and with the hinterland being penetrated up river valleys such as that of the Hampshire Avon. Suetonius enumerates a spectacular series of successes, culminating – although this must have come very early in the sequence of events – in the taking of the Isle of Wight (Valerius Flaccus has Vespasian sailing the Caledonian Ocean!). There were thirty battles, some of them no doubt accounted for by the conflicts of the first campaigning season, the subjugation of two tribes, and capture of twenty 'townships' (*oppida*) – hill fortresses that is, for which Vespasian on this prestigious campaign would have had fifty-five state-of-the-art siege engines at his disposal, a third of those he was to have at Jotapata in 67. One tribe he subdued was the Durotriges of Dorset, the masters of Ham Hill, Hod Hill, Pilsdon Pen, Maiden Castle, South Cadbury, and more than forty other strongholds, and another western Belgic tribe, either part of the Dobunni of Gloucestershire or the Dumnonii to the north of the Durotriges in Devon and Cornwall or a branch of one of the other tribes involved, the Atrebates or Durotriges themselves. The conquests (by assault through the wooden gates, preceded by a devastating artillery bombardment rather than by siege, since no traces of circumvallation have come to light), included, besides Maiden Castle, Hod Hill, where attempts to extend the defences could not be carried out in time, and Waddon Hill; the massacres at South Cadbury, Spetisbury Rings, and Ham Hill seem to be later. The Romans left these dominating sites well defended. Forts were constructed inside Hod Hill, with accommodation for a cohort (480) of legionaries and half an *ala* (256) of auxiliary cavalrymen and artillery at the gates, and perhaps at Ham Hill. The fort for Maiden Castle lies under Dorchester. Lake Farm near Wimborne Minster and Wivelscombe west of Taunton were occupied, and Hamworthy, for the fleet. Coastal stations were also established at Abbotsbury and at High Peak west of Sidmouth. Even if he did not lead II Augusta beyond it and occupy the territory of the Dumnonii in Devon and Cornwall, Vespasian brought the site of Exeter under occupation before he left, probably in 47 with A. Plautius, after four full seasons of independent campaigning.[12]

How far north Vespasian's operations extended is not clear. If Hind is right a vexillation had been despatched north to Corinium in the land of the Dobunni at the outset of the invasion, rather dissipating, it must be said, the forces available to the Romans. In any case, the activities of the three other legions in Britain left II Augusta plenty of scope. XIV advanced into the Midlands along the line of Watling Street to Towcester and High Cross. One of the forts Vespasian captured was probably that on White Horse Hill near Uffington in Berkshire, on the borders of the Atrebates and Dobunni; he may have sent a division south-westward along the Ridgeway from the Thames near Reading, perhaps on his return from the capture of Colchester, or north from Dorset after his successes there. The ground covered by A. Plautius and his subordinates in the five years of campaigning is remarkable. The line of the Fosse Way hingeing on Exeter in the south had been secured and although the legionary fortress at Lincoln is mid-Neronian the headquarters of IX Hispana were already in fortresses nearby. The sensational achievement proved not to be solid, as might be expected, but it was immensely valuable to Claudius, who was able to claim further credit.[13]

Aulus returned to his ovation. Claudius wanted to show particular appreciation of Plautius' successes from 43 to 47, perhaps tacitly to recognize his support in 42. This compromise gave Plautius a real military parade without eclipsing Claudius' own full triumph, and his subordinates must have basked in his glory, though the distinction of triumphal ornaments (*ornamenta trumphalia*) had probably been announced with the culmination of the first year's campaign and conferred, where necessary on absentees, when Claudius celebrated his triumph in 44. Vespasian received not only the *ornamenta*, which were normally beyond what a man of his rank might expect, but also a pair of priesthoods, which with their social cachet would be particularly significant for a new man. One may have been of great distinction, for example membership of a board of seven men charged with the management of sacred banquets (Septemviri Epulonum), but only members of the imperial family held more than one of the four preeminent priesthoods. The other must have been an unexciting sodality, perhaps as one of the Augustales created in 14 to honour the late Emperor.[14]

Vespasian was back in Rome by the end of 47 at latest, then, but he did not receive his consulship until the last and least prestigious two months of 51. He was nearly 42 when he took office, and that age was normal for a new man, perhaps statutory for all who were not entitled to remissions by patrician birth or number of offspring. Yet Vespasian had distinguished himself in bringing Claudius' cherished and indeed most important scheme to successful fruition. Something better might have been expected. Perhaps Vespasian's return to Rome was ill-timed. 47 saw the beginning of the chain of events that was to lead to the downfall of the Emperor's wife Messalina. Eliminating a powerful politician in that year, the Narbonese senator Valerius Asiaticus, concentrated opposition and forced her to seek new allies in senatorial and equestrian circles, notably the consul designate C. Silius. Claudius' freedmen were threatened by this move: they would not survive a swing towards senate and *equites*. Nor would Claudius' power, since he had become emperor in the first place against the wishes of the senate. There was a purge of Messalina and her allies in autumn 48 but the imperial house was so badly shaken that Narcissus' coup damaged his own position: he could be held responsible for the convulsions. The confidence apparently implied by ceremonies held in these years – tenure of the censorship; celebration of the Secular Games; taking of the Augury of Security (*Augurium Salutis*) – should not deceive us, as they were intended to reassure contemporaries about Claudius' political plight. The success in Britain had worn off; a political crisis at home posed a severe threat to his régime and he had to look for further support. At the beginning of 49 the Emperor married his niece Agrippina, the daughter of the beloved lost leader Germanicus and great-grandchild of Augustus himself, and began to advance her son L. Domitius Ahenobarbus, engaging him to his daughter Octavia and adopting him so that he became heir on equal terms with the Emperor's own son Britannicus; better terms, since Nero was three years the elder.[15]

Agrippina was the woman who had brought Lepidus' ashes to Rome in 39–40, when Vespasian had publicly advocated sharpening the penalties of the conspirators; Narcissus allegedly had secured him his first significant post. Vespasian's friend at court was becoming a man of the past, an enemy in all likelihood of the woman of the future. Yet not all the men associated with Claudius in the early years of his régime fell from power as Agrippina rose. Vitellius astutely held aloof from the struggle between Messalina and the freedmen and it was he who smoothed the way for Claudius' new marriage. Vitellius, consul for the third time in 47, died in 51, but he may have survived long enough to promote the consulship of Vespasian.[16]

After that consulship, according to Suetonius, came a period of retirement and inactivity. Vespasian could not legally stand for the governorship of one of the public provinces open to ex-consuls for five years after his consulship, and the system of suffect consulships created a queue of men waiting for these posts, so that the actual interval was by now one of about ten years. There were imperial provinces and commands available, but nothing came Vespasian's way. Agrippina has taken the blame. He had good reason later to exaggerate his distance from her, but at the very least she and her clique, led by the returned exile Seneca and the Prefect of the Praetorian Guard, Afranius Burrus, whose appointment she secured in 51, had supporters who had to come first.[17]

Titus later claimed that he had been educated alongside Claudius' son Britannicus, his junior by fourteen months. It was the Flavians' policy to associate themselves with Claudius' régime, but the claim may be true, since it was verifiable. After her marriage to the Emperor, Britannicus' education was now controlled by Agrippina's men, who kept the boy out of the way. Claudius died, worn out with the struggle to maintain his position after the fall of Messalina or actually by poison, in October 54; Narcissus, away in Campania, was forced to suicide almost at once.[18]

Britannicus was now 13, and not a serious contender when Nero was smoothly put into power. He became a threat, however, when Nero's mother began to lose control over the new Emperor in the first months of his principate. Her style of government was authoritarian; Nero's other advisers, Burrus and Seneca, considered that it was better long-term policy to turn the Emperor's back on Claudius' 'tyranny' and secure the support of the alienated senatorial and equestrian orders. Seneca made it clear through Nero's accession speech that there was no room for petticoat government in a régime that boasted of giving the senate a say in decision-making; women and freedmen had had their day. Agrippina's response was to threaten Nero with Claudius' legitimate heir. If Britannicus came to power all the men who had flourished in the earlier part of Claudius' principate could hope for a return of prosperity. Shortly before his fourteenth birthday, in February 55, after which he might reasonably have assumed the toga of manhood, Britannicus was taken ill at a banquet in the Palace, died in the night, and was hastily cremated. Nero was now the only scion of Augustus' family who was also the son (although by adoption) of the previous Emperor; he was hardly to be challenged. The Flavians claimed that Titus had been sitting next to Britannicus at the fatal banquet and had even been affected by the poison used to kill him. Embroidery, but if Titus was still being educated with Britannicus in 55 it suggests that his father's career was unlikely to prosper for the moment. As a protégé of Claudius, Vespasian could not hope for much from the reforming régime of Burrus and Seneca, and he was already alienated from Agrippina. It was only when both these influences were removed from governing circles that Vespasian's prospects began to brighten.[19]

The years from 48 onwards involved politicians in choices as hazardous as those of 19–31, until in 59 Nero began the process of freeing himself both from Burrus and Seneca and from Agrippina by the neat expedient of having his mother murdered. Under such extreme pressure the old alliance of Vitellii, Plautii, and Petronii seems to have broken up: between Petronia and A. Vitellius there was a bitter divorce at the end of Claudius' principate. The sons of L. Vitellius did not suffer, and R. Syme detected a resurgence of a Vitellian faction in about 60. The evidence is slender: the consulships in 61 of P. Petronius Turpilianus, elderly son of P. Petronius (suff. 19) and of L. Caesennius Paetus, Vespasian's kinsman; his brother T. Flavius Sabinus' City Prefecture, beginning in 61; and Vespasian's advancement to Africa. The Plautii, however, were subjected to a series of attacks, probably due to their loyalty to Claudius. They began in 57, when Pomponia Graecina, wife of the late Emperor's commander in Britain, was accused of embracing foreign superstition; another A. Plautius was killed some time after 59; Plautius' nephew Q. Lateranus died in Piso's conspiracy against Nero in 65, and Ti. Plautius Silvanus Aelianus received no acknowledgement of his successes when he left his governorship of Moesia in 67. J. Nicols sees this patrician as a close friend of the brothers: he was a member of the Vitellian–Plautian group, in Britain at the same time as as the Flavii, and held positions of trust under Vespasian. Yet capital was to be made out of generosity to surviving members of the nexus, especially in contrast with Nero's meanness; younger generals could expect due reward for their deserts; and the able Aelianus was to hold posts under Vespasian, notably the City Prefecture, that conferred distinction rather than power.[20]

Vespasian's brother had presumably benefited from the help of the Plautii and their associates, but his praetorship, if he entered the senate at the end of 33 as quaestor for 34, may belong to comparatively uncontroversial years, 37 or 38; he evidently did not share his brother's misfortune of having to speak out on matters that made an enemy of Agrippina. Sabinus' consulship belongs to the first half of Claudius' principate. He is known to have been the colleague of another of the former legates, Cn. Hosidius Geta, on 1 August in 44, 45, or more probably 47. The changing political climate of Claudius' last years did not prevent him securing appointment to the most important of the Danubian provinces, Moesia, which he held, far from the political upheavals that were taking place in Rome, probably from 53 to 60, before he became Prefect of the City. It would be allowing the brothers too much calculation – and freedom – to suppose that they decided towards the end of Claudius' reign to split their support between contending parties to safeguard the wealth and standing of their family, and that it was Vespasian's choice to stand with Narcissus. When politicians were confronted by such decisions, they would often be too deeply committed to make a convincing retreat; past actions or favours limited their freedom.[21]

3

FROM NERO'S COURT TO THE WALLS OF JERUSALEM

The Flavii developed their own alliances, among younger men or men of lower status. Some of them seem to go back far into Flavian history. One of Vespasian's kinswomen, probably not his daughter, became the wife of the Umbrian Q. Petillius Cerialis Caesius Rufus, legionary legate in Britain during the revolt of Boudicca. L. Caesennius Paetus, sent in 62 to annex Armenia Major, who was married to Sabinus' daughter, had a son old enough to be military tribune in 63; that marriage, if he sprang from it, belongs to the mid-40s. Then there was M. Arrecinus Clemens, Prefect of the Guard at the time of Gaius' assassination. His daughter married Titus, not before 60. It is possible that there was an existing connection between these families: both Titus' wife and the wife of T. Flavius Petro three generations previously bore the name Tertulla. Ti. Julius Lupus is expressly said to have been a friend of Vespasian's in private life: he was a cousin of Arrecina, and from the same equestrian rank, or a little below: his father of the same name, brother-in-law of the Prefect Arrecinus Clemens, had been a tribune in the Guard, summarily executed by Claudius for his part in the assassination. That cannot have hindered the career of his son: the execution was designed to encourage loyalty in the officer corps. Given his connection with Clemens it seems likely that he too was on good terms with the Flavii well before the recall of Sabinus from Moesia. Naturally the building of connections continued; Titus was probably quaestor at Rome in 63 or 64 and had married his second wife, Marcia Furnilla, the highborn daughter of Q. Marcius Barea Sura, as he became a senator.[1]

In about 62 Vespasian came to draw lots for his proconsulship. It was Africa that fell to him and his tenure, if energetic, was unpopular, even notorious: at one point he was pelted with turnips at the port of Hadrumetum. That may have had to do with food, or a shortage of it: Claudius had been pelted with stale crusts during a grain shortage at Rome in 51. Africa could have known a shortage if ships destined for Rome had priority, and in 62 300 grain ships were lost and fears at Rome were allayed by Nero's intervention, perhaps at the expense of Africans the following winter. Turnips may have been what they were having to eat. Political opponents, informed of the riot, would have used it against him: the contrast drawn by Tacitus and Suetonius between Vespasian's ill repute from Africa and Vitellius' popularity was a product of the civil war of 69.[2]

Vespasian did not enrich himself from his province; rather the reverse: he had to mortgage his estate to his brother, who was evidently unwilling to make a free loan. His poverty went back at least to 39, but it is possible that keeping up supplies to Rome had involved Vespasian in personal expenditure. To recoup, Vespasian allegedly went into a business plausible at Reate, which was famous for its mules. Men nicknamed him 'the muleteer', but mule-driving or dealing on a large scale becomes 'transport operations'. According to one story (which Suetonius does not guarantee), Vespasian also took a fee of 200,000 *HS* from a young man, perhaps while he was still in Africa, in return for securing him permission to stand for senatorial office. Impoverishment through holding office was not dishonourable, and Vespasian may have boasted of it, but the rest of the fabric looks like a further attempt to belittle the incoming Princeps, made in 69 and perhaps with a reference to the fact that if the worst came to the worst he could return to an hereditary occupation, but there may be something in the allegation. Epigraphic evidence gives a different glimpse of Vespasian in society, presumably some time after his consulship. He was called in to arbitrate in a property dispute between two sons of the consul of 27, M. Crassus Frugi: L. Piso Frugi Licinianus, soon to fall as Galba's heir, and Crassus Scribonianus, who died in 70. Vespasian, if agreed by them rather than imposed by the senate, was respected in circles close enough to the Emperors as to be in repeated danger from them.[3]

In the last three years of Nero's reign the Flavii were to enjoy power and prestige: Vespasian was in charge of three legions in Judaea, his brother was Prefect of the City, and Titus as his father's legate was on his way to a praetorship; the younger Arrecinus Clemens also reached the office. Only Caesennius Paetus had met with a reverse: his command in the East had ended with a humiliating capitulation to the Parthians at Rhandeia. But Nero had taken it lightly, and a kinsman, A. Caesennius Gallus, was commanding XII Fulminata in Syria when the Jewish War broke out.[4]

These were destructive years to the aristocracy: first in 65 came the conspiracy of C. Piso, involving officers of the Praetorian Guard. That resulted in the death of Seneca, who was suspected to be the man intended, at least by some conspirators, to take over after Nero's murder. In the same year other attacks destroyed Seneca's relatives Annaeus Mela and Lucan. The writer Petronius was a friend of another man involved in the 'Pisonian' conspiracy, and so, genuinely or otherwise, could also be implicated. In 66 another conspiracy, attributed to Annius Vinicianus, was discovered at Beneventum, and led to the enforced suicide of Barea Soranus and his daughter Servilia. Annius Vinicianus was son-in-law of the general Cn. Domitius Corbulo, and his brother Pollio, husband of Servilia, had already been exiled in connection with the plot of the previous year; so was the son of Corbulo's half-brother, P. Glitius Gallus. In 66 Ser. Salvidienus Orfitus (*cos.* 51), another nephew, fell victim. Nero left for Greece happily freed from a dangerous combination of members of a family that had already been promoting a change of dynasty at the beginning of Claudius' reign. In October the arrogant and dangerously well-connected Corbulo (Gaius Caesar's brother-in-law) was summoned to Greece and ordered to kill himself. Vespasian's rise to a position of eminence was due to the death of a man whose diplomacy and generalship, deployed against the Parthians for most of the reign, had secured an honourable peace; and if M.T. Griffin is right to see the future governor of Syria, C. Licinius Mucianus, as an adherent of Corbulo, it helps to explain the original hostility between the two men and shows how Vespasian's appointment might have been seen.[5]

Discussing speculation rife in mid-69, Tacitus says that Vespasian's reputation was equivocal. Not surprisingly, given his success in the last years of Nero, and the men with whom he shared it. Vespasian's friendship with victims of Nero was made use of in a debate at the opening of his reign. But Titus had renounced the connection with Soranus when it became dangerous, and from the debate of 70 emerged a hint that Vespasian had been as guilty as other members of the House in the destruction of their peers. Men who were successful in Vespasian's reign had benefited from the catastrophes that followed the Pisonian conspiracy: M. Cocceius Nerva, the future emperor, won his triumphal ornaments not with the army but by informing in 65; Cn. Arulenus Caelius Sabinus, who took over the place of leading jurisconsult from the deported C. Cassius Longinus; T. Clodius Eprius Marcellus; Q. Vibius Crispus, both suff. II in 74. To a greater or lesser degree each was ready to seek advancement under an unacceptable Emperor or to profit from the misfortunes of others. Vespasian claimed not to be in high favour when the call came to repress the revolt in Judaea: he had fallen asleep at one of Nero's performances and the next day was refused admission when he came to pay his respects; taking this hint, he had retired to a small village and was expecting a different order when the messenger came. So it was said, in a nice variant on the theme of greatness almost missed.[6]

What led to the war in Judaea, whose diminutive size had been a reason in 6 for loose attachment to Syria under a mere equestrian Prefect, and the aims of the rebels, will always be a lively topic, given the disparity of belief and class amongst them, their regionalism and personal rivalries, and the various springs of their discontent: economic, political, religious; a peremptory formulation will put the Roman reaction into context. Rule by an alien gentile power was against the will of God, except as punishment; but better-off sections of society, especially in the cities, managed to accommodate themselves to it: they were in authority, some even members of the equestrian order. It was when the alien Emperor demanded cult, as Gaius Caligula did, or governors made claims on his behalf, as Pontius Pilate had for

Tiberius, that there was potential conflict. But in the country economic prob-lems, debt, shortage of land, aggravated discontent, class hatred, and animos-ity to town dwellers; authority for rebellious action came from Scripture, which anyone could interpret: the Messiah would end foreign and upper-class oppression alike. The local ruling class did not command respect and was seen to be in league with governors mostly inept or corrupt. The last two in the half dozen years before the revolt broke out in 66 were reportedly among the worst: their actions and those of the Greek-speaking troops under their command offered the final provocation, along with continuing disorder over civic rights in Caesarea and outrages, allegedly condoned, against Jews there and in cities of the neighbouring provinces, notably Syrian Antioch. Class war between Jews who were doing well out of the Roman régime and those who were suffering hardship from their countrymen's command of economic resources has been established as a central factor both in the original struggle for Jerusalem that marked the outbreak of the war and continuing as the struggle developed. Josephus' account of the factions and his naming of them are tendentious.[7]

On S. Applebaum's view the original but not the only Zealots were those who followed Judas the Galilean against the Roman takeover of Judaea as a province in 6. He had called for resistance to tribute and to mortal masters. In 66 they were led by Judas' descendant Menahem and on his assassination, disappointed in their messianic hopes, retired to Masada, leaving Jerusalem to the radical priests under Eleazar b. Ananias, son of a former High Priest, and his successor Eleazar b. Simon; to the adherents of John b. Levi of Gischala in northern Galilee and of the Leveller Simon b. Gioras. *Sicarii* ('knifemen' or 'assassins') was a word applied by the Roman government to armed insurgents as a whole. E.M. Smallwood and C. Hayward distinguish religious-minded Zealots and *sicarii,* led by Menahem, although they may have been related doctrinally: the Zealots were a close-knit and well-defined sect centring on Jerusalem, splitting into two factions when John of Gischala arrived to lead the more extreme. For Josephus and the Romans, personalities structured the rebels; these leaders, some ideologues, others opportunists, and broad terms like 'extremist' and 'moderate', will have to differentiate the groups. For all religion was of prime importance and God the trump card: with the support of a supreme God each group was ready to dare or bear beyond measure. The only valid counter-argument, or rather assertion, in favour of quietism or surrender, was that God intended Rome to prevail, for the time.[8]

Open unrest began in the month of Artemisius at Caesarea, over a building-site that impinged on a synagogue, and continued in Jerusalem when the governor Florus made a withdrawal of seventeen talents (408,000 *HS*) from the sacred Temple treasure, perhaps to make up tax-arrears. Florus is accused of encouraging the disorder with brutal reprisals and Berenice, daughter of Claudius' friend King Agrippa I of Judaea, who was in Jerusalem at the time, was unable to placate him (16 Artemisius). But insurgents cut Florus off from the Antonia fortress and he had to evacuate the city, leaving only one cohort to support the chief priests and the Sanhedrin.[9]

The elderly governor of Syria, C. Cestius Gallus, sent a military tribune to investigate and he was joined by Berenice's brother, M. Julius Agrippa II, who currently ruled territories north and east of the Sea of Galilee, parts of Galilee itself, the tetrarchy of Lysanias round Abila, and territory on Mount Lebanon. Agrippa's aim was to come by grace of the Emperor into his father's entire realm and that made him loyal, but he had failed to secure order among his people. He refused to support the demand for an embassy to press for Florus's recall, which had little chance of success – and would reveal his own inadequacies. His plea for quiet in the face of Rome's God-given power, for the payment of arrears and the reconstruction of the porticoes linking the Antonia fortress with the Temple, which insurgents had demolished to prevent an attack on the Temple from the fortress, has been reworked by Josephus. The original plea succeeded only for a moment, if that, and Agrippa was stoned out of Jerusalem. Elsewhere the definitive struggle began with the occupation of Masada. There the Roman guards were massacred; equally definitively, sacrifice made in the Temple on behalf of Rome and the Emperor was ended by the High Priest Ananias' son Eleazar, and a struggle for Jerusalem broke out between the revolutionary and moderate factions (the moderates held the Temple and the upper city). The guilty Florus refused to send troops to end the fighting; Agrippa despatched 2,000 cavalry. The struggle ended when Josephus' *sicarii* penetrated the Temple. The upper city fell and the record office, where creditors' bonds were kept, went up in flames, like the palaces of Agrippa and Berenice and that of Agrippa's appointee, the High Priest. The Antonia fortress was captured and its garrison butchered after a two-day siege beginning on 15 Lous and the royalist and Roman troops were then shut up in Herod's palace. A siege conducted with weapons brought from Masada by Menahem of Galilee lasted into September, outliving its organizer: Eleazar's men made away with him and it was to Eleazar that the Roman garrison, by now confined to the three great towers on the north side of the palace, surrendered on terms, perhaps on 26 September, only to be butchered in their turn; their commander accepted conversion to Judaism, being circumcised. The dénouement in Jerusalem coincided with a massacre of Jews in Caesarea and atrocious reprisals and counter-reprisals throughout the country; in Syria the great cities remained quiet, but the violence set off the powder keg in Alexandria; the new Prefect Ti. Julius Alexander, nephew of the philosopher Philo but a renegade Jew, unleashed his troops on the Ghetto.[10]

There was no road back. The Romans lost two other Herodian fortresses, Cyprus over Jericho and Machaerus, the first with its garrison massacred; from the second the Romans left under truce. Cestius had to strike from Syria at the focus, taking XII Fulminata and detachments of 2,000 from his other legions, III Gallica, VI Ferrata, and X Fretensis (about 11,120 men in all), with ten auxiliary units, of which four were cavalry (about 4,928 men, if they were regular units), and contributions of nearly 14,000 (about 5,300 of them horse, and with many invaluable bowmen) from Agrippa and the other dependent rulers Antiochus IV of Commagene, and Sohaemus of Emesa, that should have given him more than 30,000 (including about 7,300 cavalry), a number swollen by irregulars recruited from the towns to a total estimated by M. Gichon at 35,000–40,000. Against a city of about 60,000–90,000 inhabitants, many non-combatant, and swollen by pilgrims to the Feast of Tabernacles, defended by a force of irregulars, some bent on slaughtering their rivals, he failed. Cestius neither succeeded in an assault nor persisted in a siege, probably because of supply problems, especially for the cavalry; and on retreat he suffered a defeat at Bethoron that lost him 5,780 men and his siege engines. XII Fulminata was a discredited legion, and Cestius died soon afterwards; he had to be replaced promptly by a competent and reliable general, experienced in independent command (as Cestius perhaps was not), one who could learn from Cestius' mistakes and whose confidence and decisiveness would restore morale.[11]

The size of the province did not lead Nero and his advisers to underestimate the potential seriousness of the rebellion, which had to be prevented from spreading. If it did not threaten the survival of Roman power in the East, as Josephus claims, it might have involved Jews beyond the Euphrates in supporting the insurgents and so embroiled Rome with Parthia, which had an obvious interest in destabilizing the eastern provinces. Jewish communities within the Empire were a focus of unrest and likely to become targets for violence if war broke out in Judaea.[12]

This was the end of the year of Corbulo's death; two other governors of high birth, the brothers Scribonius on the Rhine, had also been liquidated and replaced, in Upper Germany with the new man L. Verginius Rufus of Mediolanum, in Lower Germany with Fonteius Capito. Moesia was to pass from Ti. Plautius Silvanus Aelianus to Pomponius Pius. Every factor weighed in favour of appointing Vespasian to the task of putting down the Jewish rebellion: he was in Greece and and it would take only a few weeks for him to be on the scene of action, even travelling overland through the Anatolian winter. Years in Britain had demonstrated his competence as a soldier, and his origins made him safe. With the exception of Titus, Vespasian's legates also came, as J. Nicols points out, from non-consular families.[13]

There may have been existing connections between Vespasian and prominent easterners involved in Judaea. That smoothed his path when he was in post and may even have been a factor in his appointment. Agrippa I had been a friend of Claudius, his mother Berenice of Antonia. Ti. Julius Alexander, a former Prefect of Judaea (46–8) and since the spring of 66 Prefect of Egypt, belongs to this circle: his father had been Alabarch (chief customs officer) of Alexandria and likewise friendly with Claudius. The Alabarch had been one of the men from whom Agrippa I was able to borrow money, and he had married his son Marcus to Agrippa's daughter Berenice.[14]

The scope of Vespasian's command remains a matter of discussion, like that of Corbulo during his term in the East from 55–66. Their tasks were to regain control of a people, and a territory that had slipped from Rome's grasp, and it has been suggested that their titles reflected that precise task: Vespasian would be Propraetorian Legate of the Army of Judaea (*Legatus Augusti pro praetore exercitus Iudaici*). None the less the best account of Corbulo's positions has him governor of one province or another during each segment of his time in office, and Vespasian too may have been (notionally at first) Propraetorian Legate of the province of Judaea, with the task of restoring order specifically added ('*ad componendum statum*'). Perhaps he enjoyed a period as governor of Syria as well, if the death of Cestius occurred after he arrived. As J. Nicols points out, that would help to explain the later devotion to him of the Syrian III Gallica. Mucianus arrived to take over Gallus' post in 67, perhaps during the siege of Gamala, by 23 October. Early relations were bad.[15]

Vespasian came down into Syria from the Hellespont and through the Cilician Gates and took over at Antioch by 1 March. There he met two of the legions that were to play a key role under him in Judaea, X Fretensis and V Macedonica, which had both seen service under Corbulo, and was assured of their loyal support by local dignitaries, Agrippa II, Antiochus IV of Commagene, Sohaemus of Emesa, and Malchus II of Nabataean Arabia. XV Apollinaris had been placed under his 27-year-old son and legate Titus, who had travelled to Alexandria by ship, probably the great Alexandria rather than the Syrian Alexandria ad Issum, if the legion was there in preparation for Nero's eastern expedition. He brought it and perhaps some auxiliary troops to Ptolemais, a forward base occupied as a necessary precaution after the defeat of Cestius. Before the rendezvous Vespasian had been restoring the morale and bearing of troops still in the north.[16]

Given the city's importance to Jews, capturing Jerusalem was always a prime objective in Vespasian's strategy, as it had been Cestius' aim. But it could not safely be attacked without securing control of territories between it and the Romans. Hence Vespasian directed his first efforts at the conquest of Galilee. Besides that, there was obvious value in controlling the coastal strip (as there had been in controlling the south coast of Britain in 43–7) as launching-pad. In these preliminaries Vespasian was following Cestius' plan, but in a deliberate way and without at the same time committing himself to an attack on the capital.[17]

Vespasian was confronted by a tougher military nut than A. Plautius had cracked in 43, although there was no seaborne landing; the conquest of Britain presented obstacles to communication and movement only when the Pennines, Wales, and southern Scotland had to be mastered. Mountain masses running north–south made movement west–east difficult and provided shelter for rebels. Apart from guerrilla strongholds, there were regular settlements which would have to be subdued one by one in a series of sieges, of the kind that Cestius had shirked. It would be hard to over-estimate the significance of Vespasian's experience in reducing hill-top forts, though the terrain of Britain was far less cruel. The Romans knew the problem and Vespasian deployed massive equipment against Jotapata and Jerusalem. There were human differences too: the Britons had seen Gaul brought under the Romans, and observed some advantage in it; they were not sustained by a value system that made little of material considerations in comparison with obedience to an almighty God; and their society was not so fissured by want and injustice as to foster desperate fanaticism at the bottom of the heap.

What they had achieved prompted the insurgents into redeploying their defence and their political structure. The High Priests and their associates had either worsted Menahem and his extremists and taken control, or were collaborating with them, with the Sanhedrin (*synedrion*) as council and a popular assembly meeting in the Temple court. A mint was established, and Joseph b. Gorion and Ananus b. Ananus, a former High Priest, moderate men, were given command in Jerusalem, although control was eventually wrested from them by Eleazar b. Simon, who with Eleazar b. Ananias had been passed over as 'despotic'. There were six subordinate commands for the country districts: Josephus b. Matthias, the future historian, was assigned to Upper and Lower Galilee, which would take the brunt of the first attack, and the city of Gamala. Their administration he in turn, confronted with the task of unifying the disparate interests of town and country, and of the brigands outside settled society, entrusted to a council of seventy and to seven magistrates in each of the cities. Fortification of the towns and strong points of an area that he found under the influence of the revolutionary John of Gischala, and far from ready to accept his own say-so, came next, and the recruitment of 100,000 defenders (Josephus' figures for troops, casualties, and prisoners are probably all too high, no matter the source). Of these he trained 60,000 infantry and three hundred cavalry on Roman lines; 4,500 mercenaries and a bodyguard of 600 completed his troops. The effectiveness of Josephus' fortifications is in evidence throughout, and the spirit of the defenders is shown by the way a premature attack on Jotapata in Galilee was repulsed: they came out of the town and ambushed the Romans. At the same time, the political complexion of the first government in Jerusalem, and the appointment of a Pharisee (if Josephus already was one) to Galilee, does not suggest a determination to fight to the death. If they resisted and then surrendered on terms they might win concessions, especially with Agrippa as an intermediary. That had to be achieved before they were overthrown by men who did not want an ameliorated *status quo*. Undeclared readiness to compromise made Josephus a 'traitor' and his writing apologetic.[18]

As soon as the command structure and discipline of his troops organized during his two-week stay satisfied Vespasian, he marched south, reaching Ptolemais in about mid-April 67, and incorporated Titus' XV. When completely assembled, which took some time, the forces also contained twenty-three auxiliary infantry cohorts (including the garrison of Judaea, five units from Caesarea), of which ten are said to have been *milliariae* (notionally twice the regular size), and six regiments of auxiliary cavalry. The contribution of the monarchs was still considerable: 2,000 archers and 1,000 horse each; and the Nabataean Malchus offered a further 1,000 cavalry and 5,000 foot archers. Vespasian must have had nearly 50,000 men under his command, the core of a concentration of might vital at the end of the decade. His highly competent legates, besides Titus, were M. Ulpius Traianus in charge of X Fretensis, who in ten years would be governing Syria, and Sex. Vettulenus Cerialis, later legate of Moesia. Vespasian's first task was to address himself to Lower Galilee and to rally the people of Sepphoris, who were still loyal, and a detachment of 7,000 men was sent under the military tribune Placidus.[19]

The extraordinary elaboration of the order of march, officers in close attendance on the commander, illustrates the complex organization of the Roman army – and Vespasian's ostentatious deployment of its might: he would not be taken *en route* like Cestius. Tacitus offers a succinct but impressive portrait: a keen soldier, marching at the head of the column, choosing the camp site, using his tactical skill to press day and night on the enemy and if necessary taking his part in the fighting; he ate his food when he could and differed little from the common soldiery in dress and demeanour. In short, a worthy successor of the commanders of old, Hannibal and most notably Marius, and their later emulators, Caesar, Tiberius, and the Elder Drusus – but for his stinginess. It was Flavian propaganda and a *topos,* as Mrs B. Mitchell points out, but for Tacitus' undermining last phrase, and showed the dynasty's aspirations. The first resistance was to be expected at Garis, 4 km from the beleaguered Sepphoris. But Josephus could not control his troops: they fled and he had to return to Tiberias, which spread despondency there. Headquarters in Jerusalem were informed that Galilee could not hold out. Vespasian proceeded to Gabara, making the neighbourhood an example of what the entire country might expect for the repulse of Cestius.[20]

The Romans advanced on the precipitous stronghold of Jotapata, nearly 10 km south of Gabara, arriving according to Josephus on 17 Artemisius. It was a different proposition and had already repulsed Placidus' attack. Josephus now re-entered the fortress and Vespasian surrounded it without delay. A first assault, using earthworks and then the full force of artillery, failed; only after a five-day struggle was the stronghold fully invested. The siege lasted more than forty days, with Roman siegecraft and technology tested to their limits by the ingenuity of the defenders, who, even though tormented by thirst, persisted in raising the height of their fortifications and even found ways of deadening the blows of the formidable 'ram', finally crippling it by breaking off the iron head. Vespasian himself did not escape unscathed: he was wounded in the instep or knee, but the infuriated Romans continued their assault into the night, their *ballistae* creating carnage, and followed it up next day with the escalade. Even this was successfully countered: Josephus' story is that the Jews poured boiling oil on their assailants and boiled fenugreek on to the gangplanks to make them slippery. Vespasian had to call his men off and resort to more earthworks and a trio of 50-foot fire-proofed towers, which eventually overtopped the Jewish fortifications. A dawn assault was launched on the north side of the depleted garrison under the leadership of Titus and the tribune Domitius Sabinus. Jotapata fell on 1 Panemus, with a massacre that brought the Jewish dead to a total alleged to be 40,000 (only 1,200 women and children were enslaved), and was destroyed.[21]

From the bowels of the city emerged the historian, a man of property and realism. He had already proposed to leave the siege, but the defenders inexplicably could not recognize that he was more use to the cause outside Jotapata than in. Josephus responded to the promises of Vespasian's emissary, the tribune Nicanor, who had probably served under Agrippa II, and surrendered after two score of his companions killed each other in a suicide pact, he happening to be the man drawn last to die. Titus and Vespasian also spared their highly placed prisoner: Josephus had topographical knowledge, inside information, and encouragement to offer the Romans, besides influence to bring on other insurgents. The loss of Jotapata was taken hard in Jerusalem; it did nothing to break resolution.[22]

Vespasian's flexible use of legionary detachments in this war was probably another device that he had learned in Britain. During the siege of Jotapata the legate of X, M. Ulpius Traianus, had been sent to deal with Japha, some 17 km to the south, with a force of 2,000 foot and 1,000 cavalry, and succeeded in trapping some of its inhabitants outside the walls, with the idea of defeating the Romans before they could settle down to their forte, siege warfare. With surrender imminent Traianus discreetly asked Vespasian to send Titus with reinforcements; so it was Titus who here too had led the final bloody assault on 25 Daesius. Samaria to the south, whose population in any case was unfriendly to the Jews, was under garrison, but the Romans thought that there was the threat of a rising in a gathering on Mt Gerizim, and Sex. Vettulenus Cerialis, legate of V, had dealt with that by 27 Daesius by blockading it during a heat-wave with a force of 3,000 infantry and 600 cavalry. The eleven thousand and six hundred who refused to give themselves up were simply surrounded and massacred. No Roman casualties are reported.[23]

After the capture of Jotapata Vespasian returned to Ptolemais without delay, breaking camp on 4 Panemus, and then turned south to Caesarea, where winter quarters for Legions V and X were established. XV was to be quartered due east at Scythopolis, the largest city of the Decapolis and overlooking the valley of the Jordan, 10 km distant. Vespasian continued southward in line with Cestius' strategy of controlling the coastal route and encountered opposition only at Joppa, which Cestius had sacked and where the insurrection, renewed as piracy, had been damaging communications and trade between Egypt, Judaea, and the north. By the end of July the pirate ships had been shattered in a northerly gale and the city had been captured and razed, and 4,200 bodies thrown on to the sea-shore. Vespasian installed a garrison and laid waste the hinterland.[24]

Vespasian now took a break from campaigning to visit Agrippa II in his kingdom north-east of Galilee. There were twenty days of celebration in Agrippa's capital, but the visit had a serious purpose. Agrippa was not safe from the insurgents: there was a threat of unrest in Tiberias; at Tarichaeae, another town on the Sea of Galilee, 10 km south, the threat had materialized. Titus was despatched to fetch the legions at Caesarea for a rendezvous at Scythopolis, only 32 km south of Tiberias. All three legions were deployed and there was little difficulty: Tiberias opened its gates after a skirmish with the decurion Valerianus, who had been sent with a token force of cavalry to negotiate a surrender and prudently withdrew before a trap sprung by the extremist Jesus b. Saphat (Saphias). The city's cause was pleaded by Agrippa and its leading inhabitants, and it was spared. By securing Agrippa's kingdom Vespasian was consolidating the Roman hold on northern Palestine.[25]

Jesus and his insurgents fled to the well-fortified Tarichaeae with the Romans in cautious pursuit. Vespasian made camp at Amathus and, attacked from the lake, sent Titus at the head of 600 élite cavalry against the insurgents left on the plain outside the town. Heavily outnumbered, he sent for reinforcements, Traianus arriving with 400 more horse, and Antonius Silo with 2,000 archers. The importance of the engagement in Roman eyes, and perhaps its importance for Titus' glory, may be indicated by the number of ships in the joint triumphal procession of 71, and allusions to it on the coinage; Josephus puts a stirring and miraculously effective address into the mouth of the young commander faced, before reinforcements arrived, with immense odds and the dismay of his troops. Now there was no holding them, and the enemy were swept back into the unwelcoming town. Titus, after a second harangue, took the city in a daring assault from across the lake, on the side where it was still unfortified. Fugitives from the town took to the water and were annihilated on 8 Gorpiaeus by a rapidly constructed fleet of rafts. Their total casualties appear as 6,000.[26]

Within Tarichaeae the Romans sensibly discriminated (after the massacre had gone on some time) between insurgents and passive inhabitants of the town. That raised Agrippa's stock and avoided returning his realm in a ruined state. So too after the final battle on the lake: Vespasian, seated in state on his tribunal, divided natives of Tarichaeae from the newcomers from Gaulanitis, Trachonitis, Hippos, and Gadara, who had instigated the revolt. He intimated an amnesty for these too. At Tiberias they were herded into the stadium; 1,200, old and unfit, were slaughtered; 6,000, the fittest young men, were selected to work on Nero's Corinth canal; of the remaining 39,000, Agrippa had his subjects returned to him and Vespasian sold the rest, 30,400. According to Josephus it was Vespasian's military and civilian advisers who persuaded him that there was nothing wrong in breaking a promise made to Jews. But Roman history is rich in treachery practised by men well thought of and leading to the convenient deaths of opponents: Julius Caesar and Trajan are convicted; Tiberius quoted and followed a different tradition when he ostentatiously refused to allow a German opponent to be poisoned.[27]

The capture of Tarichaeae deserved its special attention in the Triumph. It was followed by the surrender of remaining rebel strongholds except Gischala and Mt Tabor, west of the lake, while in Gaulanitis Agrippa II now had to deal only with Gamala, built on a ridge with a hump that sprang from the mountainside and gave the town its name of 'Camel'. The other rebel towns in Gaulanitis, Sogane and Seleuceia, had long since come to terms. It was its inaccessibility on the precipitous mountain, its water supply within the walls, and Josephus' fortifications, stronger even than those of Jotapata, that gave Gamala's inhabitants, stiffened by the refugee insurgents who had now swollen their numbers, the courage to continue its seven months' rebellion against Agrippa. Vespasian, accompanied by the king, broke camp at Amathus and brought up his three legions. Total investment was out of the question: earthworks were constructed by the legions where the ridge abutted the mountain, sentries posted all round, and the ground above occupied. When the earthworks were complete, an artillery bombardment kept the defenders off the walls while three battering rams were applied. But when the Romans broke in, their weight brought down the houses on the slopes catastrophically about them; Vespasian himself was hard put to escape from the highest quarter of the town and had his shield spiked with spears. After regrouping and encouraging his men Vespasian had to revert to siege tactics and look for the gradual attrition of the garrison; finally a watchtower was demolished and on 23 Hyperberetaeus Titus entered the town, followed in full force by Vespasian; all there but two women were slaughtered or committed suicide.[28]

As a diversion during the siege (comparable with the attacks on Japha and Mt Gerizim) Vespasian undertook the reduction of Mt Tabor, which had also been fortified by Josephus. Placidus lured the defenders into the plain for negotiations; they are said to have attacked the Romans first but Placidus was ready enough: he cut most of them down with his 600 horse and kept the rest away from the fortress, so that they had to make their way to Jerusalem. Lack of water forced the remaining garrison to surrender.[29]

The last major conquest of this campaign, that of Gischala, which had been taken over by extremist insurgents under John b. Levi, was again the work of Titus and his thousand cavalrymen; Vespasian meanwhile (Josephus says with Jerusalem on his mind) sent X to its base at Scythopolis and led the other legions back to Caesarea. Titus offered terms, and the following day saw the surrender of the town, which Titus garrisoned, tearing down part of its fortifications. He sent cavalry after John, who had seen what was coming and used the sabbath to escape to Jerusalem, but was able only to kill 6,000 of his followers and take 3,000 women and children prisoner. When Titus returned to Caesarea, Vespasian moved south again and received the surrender of Jamnia, Azotus, and Lydda, with numerous prisoners of war.[30]

The loss of Galilee and the fortresses in Agrippa's realm provoked intense dissension in Jerusalem and throughout the rest of the country. The moderates had failed. Entering Jerusalem early in November 67, John of Gischala and his followers first imprisoned, then massacred the secular moderates; they then proceeded to bring the religious hierarchy under control by using the lot to secure the appointment of a nonentity, a man of the people, as High Priest. Strong resistance was put up by Ananus, the senior High Priest, by his colleague in the high command, Jesus b. Gamaliel, and by Rabbi Simon b. Gamaliel; their followers forced John's allies to convert the Temple into their fortress. When open violence broke out, Ananus's party succeeded in taking the outer court but decided not to attempt the more sacred inner court, and took to a blockade. John now put in another bid by denouncing their 'treachery' to the Idumaeans, who sent him reinforcements; a sally was made from the Temple and the gates opened to them. Ananus' blockading guards were taken in the rear and slaughtered. Ananus and his supporter and immediate subordinate in the hierarchy Jesus were soon found and suffered the same fate, which Josephus regarded as the beginning of the end: Ananus would have been able to negotiate peace with the Romans. A reign of terror against the upper class and moderates, partly organized as show trials, ensued. Some of the Idumaeans left the city, Josephus says in disgust at what had happened, but they had only the arrival of the Romans to look forward to. The extremists were in unchallenged control, which they reinforced by making away with men who had distinguished themselves against the Romans, such as Niger the Peraean who was known from the encounter with Cestius and two attacks on the Roman garrison at Ascalon.[31]

Vespasian was urged by his war council to attack the divided Jerusalem at once, but preferred to leave the Jews to fight among themselves, while the Romans recruited their strength. He was right: the insurgents were weakened by daily desertions, to the advantage of Roman intelligence, and exacted a savage price from anyone they caught making off (which to some extent inhibited the exodus). A rift now developed in the extremist leadership itself: John lost control after falling out with Eleazar b. Simon, who had played a leading part in the defeat of Cestius. But disorder in the countryside also seems to have increased, and it is at this point that Josephus mentions the stronghold of Masada, which had been occupied by the *sicarii*. Now that the Roman army was inactive and the Jerusalem authorities paralysed by dissension, its occupiers were emboldened to carry out raids, including one on Engedi.[32]

In Josephus' account Vespasian was moved by the plight of Jerusalem to take action to relieve it, but the only sign that his plans were speeded up is the early start of activities in 68. In any case he still intended to isolate the capital by dealing with intervening strongholds, such as Gadara, capital of the Peraea N.E. of the Dead Sea, which he attacked first. He entered it on 4 Dystrus 68, with the connivance of the propertied citizens, who tore down its walls and accepted a garrison. The defenders had put the chief traitor to death and fled, with the tribune Placidus and 500 horse and 3,000 foot in hot pursuit, to a village called Bethennabris in Peraea, nearly 20 km to the south. Again, and presumably for the same reason as before, to avoid being shut up in a siege, the defenders allowed themselves to be lured out on to level ground and were cut to pieces. The inhabitants of the town shared their fate. Of those who survived to make for Jericho 15,000 allegedly were massacred at the Jordan and others uncounted threw themselves into the river, which carried their corpses down into the Dead Sea. Placidus followed up by subduing a cluster of neighbouring settlements, using boats to round up stragglers on the Dead Sea. The settlements he left in the hands of newly loyalist Jews. Traianus and his subordinates had restored to Roman rule the whole of Peraea as far as the Dead Sea. Only Machaerus held out.[33]

Here Josephus introduces news of the revolt of Julius Vindex, governor in Gaul, probably of the Province of Lugdunensis, against Nero, as a factor in Vespasian's conduct of the war, stimulating him to greater efforts, so that the pacification of the East should allay the anxieties of Italy. The open declaration of hostilities against Nero, in which Vindex was supported by Ser. Sulpicius Galba, governor of Nearer Spain, who had a legion at his disposal, VI Victrix, was able to raise another locally, VII Galbiana, and carried with him the governor of neighbouring Lusitania, M. Salvius Otho, came only on 14 March or a little earlier and would have been known to Vespasian by mid-April, too late for him to have reacted to it by intensifying his efforts to settle the districts he had recovered 'while the winter lasted' or with a campaign that Josephus puts 'just at the beginning of spring'. J. Nicols holds that Vespasian had already heard of Vindex's intentions on 9 March, from one of the letters that Vindex sent to his fellow-governors. Whether a governor so distant would have been worth informing is a question, and Josephus writes as if the open revolt of Vindex and the Gallic chieftains were already under way. He has pushed the news far back into the winter so that Vespasian's activities in garrisoning and policing the communities that he had already pacified, as well as in extensive rebuilding, and his zeal for the next phase of the reconquest, can be given credit.[34]

Vindex's revolt was soon, perhaps within five weeks, put down by the legions of the Upper Rhine under L. Verginius Rufus. In Spain Galba was near suicide. But the discontent that produced it was Empire-wide and it was known that an explosion was imminent: Nero had been urgently called back to Rome from Greece at the end of 67 by his man in charge, Helius. The causes were complex and overwhelming, most important the ever-increasing shortage of cash that was forcing Nero to squeeze every penny he could from the provinces. It arose primarily from the cost of warfare that had lasted in the East from 54 to 63 and from which no gain could be expected; when it ceased at the eastern end of Asia Minor it was resumed three years later in Judaea; in a gap in eastern operations, 60–61, had come the revolt in Britain, which meant, like the Jewish revolt, the loss of revenue from the area, enhanced army costs, and a heavy price in reconstruction. The army was behind in its pay, but that was nothing new, and the overwhelmingly greater part remained loyal. At the beginning of the last phase of the reign, in 64, the fire of Rome imposed further burdens on State and Imperial treasuries, not much lessened by a donation of 4 million *HS* from the colony of Lugdunum, which was only returning the amount it had received after its own fire of a few years earlier.[35]

Nero compounded the unpopularity by self-seeking extravagance: costly leisure pursuits, the tour in Greece, theatrical performances, racing, and palace-building in the ruined city, the Golden House, all fiddling on the grand scale. Even in the East he damaged his popularity by ransacking the provinces for works of art destined for the new Rome. Once the provincials too had begun to feel the financial pinch they naturally shared political and moral grievances which were brought out by the men and women who took part in the Pisonian conspiracy of 65: the murder of his mother in 59 and the ensuing political upheavals: the divorce and killing of his wife Octavia, Claudius' daughter, the retirement of Seneca and the suspect death of Burrus. In the aftermath of this conspiracy, and of the Vinician plot, fear shook the ruling class, especially army commanders. It was a plausible excuse that the blue-blooded military man Galba offered when he claimed to have intercepted orders for his own death. All this might have been borne if Nero had had an heir to avenge him. The trail that Vindex lit in mid-March 68 led in less than three months to the Emperor's suicide and to the proclamation of Galba by Praetorian Guard, senate, and people.[36]

Vespasian meanwhile, during Traianus and Placidus' Peraea campaign, marched south from Caesarea to Antipatris north-east of Joppa, which he restored to order in two days, the toparchy of Thamna, Lydda, and Jamnia to the south-west, where deserters from the rebels were now quartered, and to the toparchy of Emmaus north-west of Jerusalem, where he left V Macedonica in camp. The next approach to Jerusalem that he tackled with the rest of the army was south-west of the capital, in the toparchy of Bethletepha, which he fired, and over the border of Judaea into the more troublesome Idumaea, where in the two central villages 10,000 were massacred and 1,000 made prisoner. Substantial forces were left behind as a garrison, while Vespasian crossed the hills by way of Emmaus and Samaria, making camp at Corea on 2 Daesius. The following day saw him at Jericho; Traianus joined him from Peraea with news of his own success.[37]

At Jericho Vespasian established a camp to guard the north-eastern approaches of Jerusalem. A similar guard was placed at Adida near Lydda, about 32 km north-west of Jerusalem, and the encirclement was complete. An expeditionary force under L. Annius was sent to Gerasa (not Jerash but on the frontier of Peraea), and captured it with the loss to the Jews of 1,000 dead, the remainder captured. Gerasa was destroyed and the surrounding countryside ravaged. Only Herodium in eastern Judaea and Masada, besides Machaerus, still held out. From Masada a new and formidable force now entered the scene, and eventually took a leading rôle in Jerusalem itself: Simon b. Gioras, who was treated with suspicion by the *sicarii* on the rock. When he heard of the death of Ananus, Simon had left Masada, gathered a force of insurgents in preparation for a takeover of the capital, and succeeded in terrorizing Idumaea and capturing the ancient little town of Hebron, about 28 km from the capital, from which he carried off a quantity of booty.[38]

It was when Vespasian returned to Caesarea from his operations in the neighbourhood of Jerusalem that he learnt of Nero's death, which had taken place on 9 June, and of the recognition of Galba. The news brought Vespasian's projected campaign against Jerusalem to a halt; he needed confirmation in his appointment (it could be claimed) and in the autumn he sent Titus, along with Agrippa II, to greet Galba and receive instructions. Operations were not resumed until 69, when Vespasian already knew of the opening events in the momentous Year of the Four Emperors: the refusal of the Rhine legions at the beginning of January to take the oath to Galba and M. Salvius Otho's successful coup with the Praetorian Guard against Galba a fortnight later. Meanwhile the city was being torn by regional, class, and sectarian war: John of Gischala, who had lost his Idumaean allies, stood at the head of one section, and already had Eleazar b. Simon against him; in Xanthicus (March–April) 69 Simon b. Gioras was brought into Jerusalem to counter him. In the stalemate Simon became its master, except for part of the lower city, but could make no headway against John's captured Roman artillery, which was trained on his men from the outer court of the Temple, while 400 men under Eleazar held the inner court. It was catastrophic for all that the city's grain stocks were burnt in the struggle.[39]

The last campaign that Vespasian conducted seems to be assigned by Josephus to about the time that he should have heard of Otho's defeat by the Vitellian forces on 14 April 69: having sworn allegiance to Vitellius in the first half of May he set out from Caesarea on 5 Daesius to deal with the parts of Judaea and Idumaea that Simon had covered, and took control of the road into Jerusalem by way of the mountains north of the city. In succession he took Gophna and Acrabatta, Bethel and Ephraim, which he garrisoned, and now for the first time swept up to Jerusalem itself, taking a number of prisoners in the raid. Meanwhile Cerialis, legate of V, tackled Upper Idu-maea: he burnt one little fortress, received the surrender of another, and forced Hebron, burning it down and massacring the inhabitants. It was on return to Caesarea that Josephus has Vespasian learning of Vitellius' victory. A final consultation with Mucianus, not recorded by Josephus, led to his acclamation at the beginning of July.[40]

Josephus' narrative is problematical, not just because (despite professing to avoid interrupting the narrative of events in the war) he is intent on filling in Vespasian's inaction from mid-68 to mid-69, and to some extent covering it up, with two sections on the civil war and an account of Simon b. Gioras' activities in Jerusalem. First, Vespasian ought to have heard of Vitellius' victory before his final campaign, not after it. Second, it is hard to find room for the campaign between 5 June and 1 July, especially if preparations for the declaration were to be put in hand only after his return. B. Niese's solution was to put the entire campaign back into 68, but the narrative, though loosely joined to the events of the civil wars at its outset, is even there set in the midst of events of January–April 69, and it seems firmly enough attached to the victory of Vitellius at its latter end for the transfer to be unacceptable. W. Weber connected Josephus' opening date, 5 Daesius, which he took to be the Tyrian equivalent of 23 June, with the end of the campaign, while J. Nicols believes that either Dystrus (March) should be read for Daesius, or Josephus deliberately falsified the timing to make Vespasian's elevation seem more spontaneous. The first of Nicols' alternatives is simple and attractive, the second, even as a lie going back to the general's own memoir, is unlikely: there were too many survivors. Probably Daesius should be retained: Vespasian suspended all operations when he heard, perhaps in early February, of the rising of Vitellius and, in the middle of the month, of the death of Galba. Preparations for the campaign – admittedly a very com-pressed one – delayed from the spring were resumed as a blind as soon as Vespasian knew of Vitellius' accession; at the same time Titus and Mucianus were secretly preparing for 1 July. All Josephus has done is to postdate Vespasian's knowledge in a half-hearted way, by refraining from mentioning it at the beginning of the campaign and stressing it at the end in phraseology guilefully vague, encompassing Vitellius' elevation to power, which took place in mid-April, and disturbances 'in Rome' caused by his arrival – as late as mid-July, after Vespasian's declaration.[41]

From 1 July until Titus resumed operations after the Flavian victory there is nothing to record from Judaea but road-building and reorganization (Judaea proper was divided into two toparchies centring on Bethel and Ephraim). The agony of Jerusalem dragged on.[42]

Appendix: Josephus' dates for the Jewish War

See esp. Niese 1893; Nicols 46f.; Schürer 1973, 587–601; E. Bickerman, *Chronology of the Ancient World* (rev. edn, London, 1980) 22–8; 47–51. Preferred dates italicized.

Jos. ref.	Jos. date	Equiv. if Maced. name used in Tyrian system	Equiv. if Maced. name imposed on Roman months	Equiv. if Maced. name imposed on luni-solar calendar	Event
A.D. 66					
2,284	Artemisius	*19 May–18 June*	May	Aiaru/Iyyer: 15 May–12 June	Outbreak
315	16 Art.	*3 June*	16 May	31 May	Unrest in Jerusalem
430	15 Lous	*3 Sept.*	15 Aug.	Abu/Ab: 27 Aug.	Antonia attacked
440	6 Gorpaeus	*24 Sept.*	6 Sept.	Ululu/Elul: 15 Sept.	Palace besieged
528	30 Hyperberetaeus	*16 Nov.*	30 Oct.	Arasamnu/Marheshvan: 9 Nov.	Cestius attacks
555	8 Dius	*25 Nov.*	8 Nov.	15 Nov.	Defeated
A.D. 67					
3,142	17 Art.	4 June	*17 May*	21 May	Romans at Jotapata
142	21 Art. (?)	8 June	*21 May*	24 May	Jos. enters Jotapata
282	20 Daesius	6 July	*20 June*	Simanu/Sivan: 21 June	Attack repulsed
306	25 Daes.	13 July	*25 June*	26 June	Japha taken
315	27 Daes.	15 July	*27 June*	28 June	Garizim taken
316	1 Panemus	20 July	*1 July*	Duzu/Tammuz: 2 July	Jotapata taken (on 47th day!)
409	4 Pan.	23 July	*4 July*	5 July	V. at Ptolemais
542	8 Gorp.	26 Sept.	*8 Sept.*	6 Sept.	Tarichaeae falls
4.69; 83	23 Hyp.	9 Nov.	*23 Oct.*	21 Oct.	Gamala falls
A.D. 68					
413	4 Dystrus	21 Mar.	*4 Mar.*	Addaru/Adar: 26 Feb.	Gadara falls
449	2 Daes.	20 June	*2 June*	24 May	V. at Corea
450	3 Daes.	21 June	*3 June*	25 May	At Jericho

Jos. ref.	Jos. date	Equiv. if Maced. name used in Tyrian system	Equiv. if Maced. name imposed on Roman months	Equiv. if Maced. name imposed on luni-solar calendar	Event
A.D. 69					
550	5 Daes.	23 June	5 June	13 June	V. invades Judaea from Caesarea
577	Xanthicus	18 Apr.– 18 May	April	Nisanu/Nisan: 12 Apr.– 10 May	Simon in Jerus.
654	3 Apellaeus	20 Dec.	3 Dec.!	Kislimu/ Kislev: 8 Dec.!	Death of Vitellius
A.D. 70					
5.99	14 Xant. Passover	1 May	14 April	14 April	John enters Temple
133; 567	14 Xant.	1 May	14 April	14 April	Titus encamps against Psephinus
302	7 Art.	25 May	7 May	7 May	1st wall taken
466	12 Art.	30 May	12 May	12 May	Siegeworks building
466	29 Art.	15 June	29 May	29 May	Works finished
6.22	1 Pan.	20 July	1 July	28 June	Jewish sally
67	3 Pan.	22 July	3 July	30 June	Antonia attacked
68	5 Pan.	24 July	5 July	2 July	Antonia falls
94	17 Pan.	5 Aug.	17 July	14 July	Sacrifice ceases
166	24 Pan.	12 Aug.	24 July	21 July	Romans fire Portico
177	27 Pan.	15 Aug.	27 July	24 July	W. portico burns
220	8 Lous	27 Aug.	8 Aug.	4 Aug.	Earthworks complete
236	(9 Lous)	28 Aug.	9 Aug.	5 Aug.	Titus' council
244	(8 or 9 Lous)	27 or 28 Aug.	8 or 9 Aug.	4 or 5 Aug.	Sally; retreat into inner court
250	10 Lous	29 Aug.	10 Aug.	6 Aug.	Temple burns
374	20 Lous	8 Sept.	20 Aug.	16 Aug.	Siege of upper city

41

Jos. ref.	Jos. date	Equiv. if Maced. name used in Tyrian system	Equiv. if Maced. name imposed on Roman months	Equiv. if Maced. name imposed on luni-solar calendar	Event
392	7 Gorp.	25 Sept.	7 *Sept.*	1 Sept.	Upper city attacked
407; 435	8 Gorp.	26 Sept.	8 *Sept.*	2 Sept.	Jerus. falls
A.D. ?73					
7,401	15 Xant.	2 May	15 April	10 April	Fall of Masada

4

THE BID FOR EMPIRE

1 The year 69

For all the claims of our earliest source, Josephus, the proclamation of
Vespasian was made first in Egypt on 1 July, in Judaea two days later,
although Alexandria and Caesarea are 535 km apart by sea. It was planned
months before, took place on the day agreed, and, like the declaration for
Vitellius, outside the candidate's own province. Tacitus, like Josephus,
stresses the zeal of the soldiers at Caesarea. They did not wait to be har-
angued by their officers (essential work would have been done beforehand),
but saluted Vespasian as he emerged from his bedroom. The state of Italy and
the Empire, the will of the gods, and above all the demands of officers and
men, acting as an electoral assembly, forced Vespasian to accept. Reluctance
was expected.[1]

Ironically, another story of Josephus goes back to 67 for the origin of
Vespasian's plans: his claims to have predicted Vespasian's elevation have
made scholars suppose that Vespasian was contemplating an attempt on the
Principate as early as that summer. That is not credible. However shaky
Nero's position, Josephus' final prophecy was likely to lead to his own
execution as a precaution on the part of a nervous general. No doubt he
predicted brilliant military success to rival Corbulo's, and offered help – a
disgrace for a Jewish commander – but Josephus knew that Vespasian was
unstoppable in Judaea, and he needed some toehold in the Roman camp.[2]

Galba, though recognized throughout the Roman world, does not seem to
have issued instructions to his commander in Judaea, and news from Rome
in the second half of 68 was disquieting: not only was he in the hands of
undesirable advisers such as T. Vinius and his freedman Icelus, who was
given equestrian status; he was vengeful, slaughtering the marines who had
been Nero's prop in Italy, summarily executing Nero's general Petronius
Turpilianus, member of a family with which Vespasian had been associated
and a consul designate. Old-fashioned severity he would have called it, but it
was not backed by public opinion or adequate force. He had L. Clodius
Macer, the insubordinate legate of III Augusta in Africa, assassinated by the

local procurator, and lacked nerve to investigate the murder of C. Fonteius Capito, commander on the Lower Rhine. More particularly, Vespasian's brother Sabinus was removed from the Prefecture of the City and his son lost a promised consulship; J. Nicols suggests that it was in connection with this that Vespasian sent Titus to Rome with Agrippa II towards the end of 68. The ostensible reason was to obtain a mandate for future campaigning, and support for Titus' candidature for the praetorship (his 29th birthday fell on 30 December). Titus is said by Tacitus and Suetonius to have been regarded *en route* as an aspirant to another position: that of Galba's heir. That is a later invention, flattering to the dynasty; Titus can have hoped for no more than accord between Galba and his father at this stage.[3]

The first sign of Flavian independence came when Titus heard at Corinth, early in February 69, of the death of Galba in the coup staged by M. Salvius Otho at Rome on 15 January and of the rising of Vitellius on the Rhine. He conferred with his suite and did not go on to greet a new, probably ephemeral Emperor. Sabinus' position was promptly resolved by reinstatement. Titus' change of plan was still discourteous. But if he continued to Rome he would become hostage to one of the two new contenders for the behaviour of his father; so Nero is said by Josephus (inaccurately) to have regarded both Flavian boys.[4]

Titus would have realized that Otho's chances against the Rhine legions were slender, unless he could bring up the Danubian armies (XI Claudia in Dalmatia, X and XIII Geminae in Pannonia, III Gallica, VII Claudia, and VIII Augusta in Moesia) – whose officers were less keen on Galba's successor than the men were. There were two legions at Vetera, V Alaudae and XV Primigenia, one each at Novaesium and Bonna, XVI and I, while the upper reaches were held by IV Macedonica and XXII Primigenia at Moguntiacum and XXI Rapax at Vindonissa. It was the Moguntiacum legions, at the former headquarters of Verginius Rufus, whose troops six months previously, after massacring the army of Galba's ally Vindex, had tried to make him emperor, that took the long-envisaged initiative on 1 January by refusing Galba their oath. Within a few days the Lower Rhine army had declared for their recently arrived commander A. Vitellius, and the Upper dropped lip-service to Senate and People. Vitellius soon had behind him not only the neighbouring tribes, the Usipetes, Treveri, and Lingones, victims of punishment inflicted by Galba, but the governors of Britain (with II Augusta, IX Hispana, and XX Valeria), of the Belgic and Lugdunensian Gauls and Raetia, as well as his kinsman by marriage, L. Tampius Flavianus, governor of Pannonia. A. Caecina Alienus, a legionary legate in Upper Germany, probably of IV Macedonica, had played a leading part, like Fabius Valens, as legate of I. They were bringing with them more than a third of the Rhine legionary forces in a two-pronged advance, Caecina taking those of the Upper German army over the Great St Bernard Pass, Valens those of the Lower by way of Lugdunum and Mt Genèvre. It was when Titus returned to the East, according to Tacitus, that the Flavians began their build-up to war.[5]

On the journey back he called at Rhodes and may have diverted to Ephesus to meet the governor of Asia, C. Fonteius Agrippa, whom Vespasian was soon to put in charge of Moesia. He certainly visited the oracle of Paphian Aphrodite on Cyprus and received a comforting reply to an enquiry as to the success of his hopes and plans (Josephus kept silent about it). At Caesarea Titus found that the army had already sworn allegiance to Otho, a recognition that would have helped to legitimize Vespasian's rebellion against Vitellius – if he had not also acknowledged Vitellius' supremacy when he heard of it at Caesarea in mid-May. That, however, was the moment when Vespasian and his associates, aware both of the danger they were in from the new Emperor (Vespasian's brother had been Otho's man), and of the disaffection among Otho's defeated Praetorians, and those who had not been defeated, the Balkan legions, and of resentment among their own that they had played no part in making an Emperor, could begin to draw up plans and timetables. Vitellius for his part laid claim on his coinage to Vespasian's successes: 'Victoria Augusti' has the goddess fixing a shield to a palm-tree.[6]

Titus' ruthless grasp on power in the next ten years suggests that his diplomatic activity was not due to disinterested concern for the ambitions of his 60-year-old father. His own ambitions and powers of persuasion played a role, perhaps decisive, in bringing Vespasian to act. We cannot know how hard he had to work: to remove either Otho or Vitellius would be legitimate but dangerous. There could be no move without massive forces, and if Otho, supported by the Danubian legions, had been victorious, nothing could have been done, as E. Flaig indicates. Real hesitation on Vespasian's part, in the face of Vitellius' legionary strength, and the fear of assassination on the order of Galba or Vitellius, was natural, and it is found, most impressively, in Tacitus who contrasts the deliberation of Vespasian and his main ally, the governor of Syria, with the determination of their officers.[7]

Syria with its remaining legions would play a vital part, though governors of the grandest province in the East had a history of wrangling with generals on special missions, who abstracted troops, pulled rank, and stole thunder. Cn. Piso's fatal dispute with Germanicus Caesar in 19 was special, but since then there had been C. Ummidius Quadratus quarrelling with Cn. Domitius Corbulo in 55, and Mucianus at odds with Vespasian himself. But in the dangerous time after 66, when Nero could destroy either man separately, but only with the collaboration of the other, they had made up. Titus journeyed to Mucianus during the siege of Gamala, in October 67. One subject of this mission may have been the implications of Nero's own projected campaign in the East: his forces would have been assembling. Again, J. Nicols notes Titus' apparent absence from the early campaigns of 68. When Vindex's revolt broke out the need for a common front was greater still, as it was when Galba was accepted as Emperor. Now early in 69 on the initiative of the returning Titus a more active collaboration was planned. Tacitus presents Mucianus as openly exhorting Vespasian to make his move and so demonstrating their solidarity. Second only to Mucianus was Ti. Julius Alexander in Egypt, with two legions and control of grain shipments. Rome had felt the threat since the abortive rising of Clodius Macer in Africa, as reassuring coin legends of Galba, Otho, and Vitellius betray.[8]

In Rome prudence, as well as Otho's policy of returning to arrangements in force before Nero's death, had dictated the restoration of Sabinus. His son the consul designate was accordingly committed to the Othonian cause and the campaign in the north. Four legions were summoned from Pannonia and Dalmatia, sending an advance guard of 8,000. Ap. Annius Gallus and T. Vestricius Spurinna were to secure the line of the Po (Caecina was through the Alps) while the Emperor, setting out on the Ides (15th) of March, a bad day for Caesars, brought up the rest of his troops: I Adiutrix, up to nine Praetorian cohorts, and a scratch force of 2,000 gladiators. But Otho's men were over-confident and insubordinate and his staff, which he mistrusted and eventually put under his brother Titianus, top-heavy and divided. It is also possible, as A. Powell has suggested, that troops who had less to hope for from victory than the Praetorians would have been ready for a peaceful compromise. Whether he had the main body of any legions from the Balkans other than XIII Gemina from Poetovio available by the time of the final battle is disputed; XIV Gemina was absent, but in spite of Tacitus' silence VII 'Galbiana', perhaps from Carnuntum, and XI Claudia from Burnum may have arrived. The distinguished commander Suetonius Paullinus, who wanted to delay challenging until reinforcements arrived, was overruled. After the battle of Bedriacum on 14 April and the death of Otho, Fabius Valens wrote to the consuls at Rome on behalf of the victors.[9]

Sabinus had no option but to take the oath to Vitellius, administering it to Cohorts and Watch on 18 April. During his march to Rome in June and early July Vitellius heard the good news that the East had also sworn (the procedure, including provincials as well as military, would have been completed by the end of the third week of May). The new Emperor's early decisiveness and moderation, not loyalty to his former 'patron', would give Vespasian pause. None the less, the mint at Antioch, which had struck coins for Galba and Otho, did nothing for Vitellius. At the same time a decline of discipline in the Vitellian forces came to be known, something to raise Vespasian's hopes: legionaries were at loggerheads with auxiliary troops; Vitellius' tour of the stinking field of Bedriacum, echoing Caesar's of Pharsalus, did not do him any good. Flavian preparations, delicate negotiations with eastern officials and potentates, the gathering of information about feeling in the West, ensuring that there were funds sufficient to pay for the troops, who also had to be sounded, took time. Two and a half months after the death of Otho Vespasian took the irrevocable step. It was preceded by a meeting with Mucianus, by Vespasian's consultation of the oracle of Ba'al Carmelus at the beginning of June, and by a final mission of Titus to Syria on about the 25th.[10]

So on 1 July Ti. Julius Alexander addressed III Cyrenaica and XXII Deiotariana in camp at Nicopolis; at the Hippodrome in Alexandria crowds of civilians enthusiastically endorsed the proclamation. Two days later the 'spontaneous movement' at headquarters in Caesarea produced a definitive salutation. The duty guard addressed his general as 'Imperator', the traditional greeting offered a new Emperor. At Antioch, 426 km north, Mucianus at the end of the first week in July swore in IV Scythica, VI Ferrata, and XII Fulminata and rallied civilians, assembling them in the theatre and addressing them in elegant Greek.[11]

After the first phase, securing the armies, was assured, the leaders met in Berytus in the latter half of July. There Vespasian was greeted by the dependent rulers Sohaemus of Emesa and (richest of all) Antiochus of Commagene, and by Agrippa II and Berenice. Agrippa, knowing of the coming coup, had slipped away from Rome before Vitellian agents could stop him. Embassies came from Syria, led by Mucianus himself, who had secured all the Syrian cities by 15 July, and the provinces of Asia Minor, and from the theoretically free Achaea; latecomers were still arriving when Vespasian was in Alexandria. According to Josephus all the cities were holding festivals in Vespasian's honour and offering sacrifices on his behalf; some sent crowns and congratulatory decrees. But the agenda at Berytus was serious: the next moves.[12]

The campaign in Judaea, where the legions were weakened by the departure of vexillations assigned to Mucianus, was suspended, to be resumed by Titus, with Alexander as chief of staff, when Vespasian was securely in power. Vespasian, unwilling to risk reputation in the struggle, adopted Tiberius' principle of being the last resort. He was to stay in the realm he had already won over, leave IV Scythica in Syria, and consolidate his hold on Egypt and its grain. He might also lead the Egyptian legions west along the coast to join C. Calpetanus Valerius Festus in Africa and complete the blockade. This remained an option even after he knew of the Flavian victory at Cremona. But cutting Rome's supplies of grain would not bring Vitellius down, only set the populace rioting. A task force from the legions of the Orient (VI Ferrata and 13,000 other legionaries and auxiliaries) were to pass through Anatolia and along the Via Egnatia through Thrace and Macedonia and to command the Adriatic from Dyrrachium, a threat to Brundisium and Tarentum, and to the entire heel and instep of Italy, splitting the Vitellian forces. Vespasian was strong in cavalry and he had the fleets of the eastern Mediterranean and Black Sea, even if the commanders of the Ravenna and Misenum fleets did not come over. Letters went to legates and armies making a point of promising to restore ex-Praetorian Guardsmen to their posts. The crucial work of leading the force was assigned to Mucianus, and an acting governorship of Syria was allocated to Cn. Pompeius Collega, previously legate of IV Scythica. By the time Mucianus' columns moved out in mid-August on their measured way the leaders knew that the Moesian legions had recognized Vespasian; he could expect detachments from all six Balkan legions (about 12,000 men) to occupy the north-eastern approaches of Italy. He instructed them to wait at Aquileia for Mucianus, who was now to take this more northerly route.[13]

To finance operations Vespasian must have raided the Judaean war-chest. He certainly practised economy. The donative mentioned at the parade of 3 July was moderate according to Tacitus, and paid later. Booty amassed from Judaean campaigns was available, but significantly perhaps not such voluntary offerings as Vitellius' troops made him in January; Mucianus demanded enormous sums from other provinces. Vespasian's friends were expected to contribute, with advancement in rank as a reward, and Mucianus set the example. This was where the wealth of the client kings came in.[14]

Another problem was the attitude of the Parthian King Vologaeses I, who might see a chance to encroach on Syria or Asia Minor, given that there was unrest in Armenia, Cappadocia, and Pontus. Levies were held and veterans recalled; arms factories were to be set up in fortified towns; and Vespasian sent a mission to obtain a promise of non-intervention. The Parthian promised nothing, but had no intention of bringing a victorious Vespasian, still based in the Orient, down on him. After the conference Vespasian moved up to Antioch to supervise the final preparations, showing exemplary energy.[15]

By mid-July Vitellius, now in Rome was unable to pay donatives even to the 60,000 he had (unnecessarily) brought with him; the jealousies of legions and auxiliaries were intractable; rivalry between Caecina and Valens mirrored hostility between the Upper and the Lower Rhine armies. Caecina was already in contact with Flavius Sabinus and Rubrius Gallus and contemplating a change of allegiance in July and August.[16]

As soon as they knew in mid-July of the proclamation III Gallica in Moesia declared for Vespasian, and their defection was reported to Vitellius by the governor M. Aponius Saturninus. When VIII Augusta and VII Claudia of Novae and Viminacium committed themselves, Aponius too changed his allegiance, but his authority was lost. The Moesians jointly sent to demand the allegiance of Pannonia and Dalmatia. When Vespasian's own appeal arrived VII 'Galbiana' and XIII Gemina were together, perhaps on manoeuvres, as K. Wellesley suggests, and while other officers were in favour of temporizing, M. Antonius Primus, legate of VII, carried the day, catching the mood of the troops. Only XI Claudia hesitated, perhaps over the immediate invasion of Italy. From the Balkans letters went to other possible supporters: Nero's crack legion XIV Gemina in Britain and I Adiutrix in Spain, both ex-Othonian, and to the Gallic tribes who, with the Raetians, were being approached by messengers from Vespasian himself.[17]

With Asia Minor secured, Mucianus had an unhindered passage by way of Byzantium. There he assembled the Pontic fleet. Once in Thrace he found a

Dacian attack on the denuded fortresses of Oescus and Novae to deal with, and sent VI Ferrata against them. By then Mucianus, whose arrival was rumoured in the course of the battle, already knew of the outcome of the battle of Cremona (24–5 October) between Vitellian forces and the Flavian troops from the Balkans. He would lose no time in resuming the march; C. Fonteius Agrippa was summoned from Asia to take charge of the defence of Moesia.[18]

The rivalry and self-interest of officers and men had transformed the course of the Flavian advance. At a conference held towards the end of August at the winter quarters of XIII Gemina at Poetovio the ambitious activist Primus successfully advocated invading Italy immediately instead of waiting for Mucianus and the main army. The Danubian legions need not content themselves with blockading north-eastern Italy at the Pannonian Alps. That could be evaded by Vitellian reinforcements coming from the Rhine through Raetia, whose governor was loyal, and from Britain, as well as allowing Vitellius to retrain the five legions already in Italy. Unauthorized, and with the leading centurion Arrius Varus, who had served as a commander of auxiliary infantry under Corbulo in Armenia, Primus marched off his mainly auxiliary striking-force at once, telling Aponius Saturninus to bring up his three legions, despatching a force to keep watch on the Inn, and leaving defence to the dependent Suebian rulers Sido and Italicus. This was against Vespasian's instructions: allegedly he supposed that Vitellius' army could be reduced by a shortage of pay and supplies from Egypt; certainly he ordered the Balkan armies to await Mucianus at Aquileia. Primus' gamble ran the risk of piecemeal defeat, but it left no time either for Vitellius' reinforcements to arrive. It paid off, but Primus' usurpation issued in political rivalry before the war was over. In addition Primus wrote to the Batavian auxiliary commander Julius Civilis to do all he could to prevent the mobilization of Vitellius' remaining forces; on the spot Civilis was encouraged by Hordeonius Flaccus, commander of the Lower Rhine army.[19]

The striking force occupied Aquileia, Opitergium, and Altinum, then Patavium and Ateste, winning the war's first engagement in the neighbourhood; VII 'Galbiana' and XIII followed it to Patavium. They then moved westward to Vicetia – Caecina's home town – and Verona, a base that protected the debouchement of the Adige from the Alps and the route from the Brenner Pass, and awaited the arrival of the Moesian reinforcements. The legions were still discontented with their nominal commanders, and Primus had to rescue Tampius Flavianus and Aponius Saturninus from their violence – thus providentially being rid of two superfluous ranking officers.[20]

It was now the line of the Po, not the Alps, that the Vitellians had to defend, with Hostilia, where the Via Postumia crossed, the vital point. Vitellius had heard of the defection of the Balkan legions after his birthday celebrations on 7 September and summoned aid from Britain, Spain, and Germany. First he, then Valens fell ill, leaving defence to the treacherous

Caecina. The troops set out for the north on or about 17 September, and Valens' men went along with Caecina's, making nearly 60,000, although some 15,000 experienced men had been transferred to the Praetorian Guard: detachments of I, IV Macedonica, XV Primigenia, and XVI; V Alaudae and XXII Primigenia; XXI Rapax and I Italica; and the detachments from the British II Augusta, IX Hispana, and XX Valeria, with cavalry and auxiliaries. Once in the north they were split between Hostilia and Cremona – and the Moesian legions had time to arrive.[21]

The fleet nearest operations, at Ravenna, after their commander Sex. Lucilius Bassus' discussions with Caecina, now went over to Vespasian. This immediately preceded Caecina's final abandonment of Vitellius, datable to 18 October from the eclipse with which Dio makes it coincide. Caecina used the fleet as a bargaining counter, and it was a valuable asset, driving Vitellian forces towards Cremona away from the sea and from Hostilia, which could now be cut off by a fleet on the Po. Having failed to carry the legions, he went with them to Cremona in chains. Primus moved his troops from Verona to Bedriacum, where he arrived on 23 October, to deal with the Vitellians on his right flank before the loyalists could arrive under Valens.[22]

He had set out on 25 September and (Tacitus claims) could have prevented Caecina's treachery or at least led his side at Cremona but lingered, waiting for inadequate reinforcements at Falerii, 400 km distant. The crushing defeat of numerically superior Vitellian forces, ironically on a field not far from the site of the first battle in which they had seen off Otho, was followed by an atrocity: the sack of Vitellian Cremona. The engagement itself was bloody: Vitellius lost 30,200 men, Primus 4,500; civilian casualties in Cremona where, civil war or no, a fair had been going on, were massive. The Alpine passes were manned to block the Flavian rear and the defeated legions dispersed in the Balkans. News of the victory, which soon put Vespasian in control of Italy east of the Apennines, was despatched throughout the West.[23]

Valens heard of the defeat on 30 October in Etruria and took the only possible decision: to raise Gaul and seek reinforcements from Germany. This also failed; the Flavians ordered the provincial procurators to seal the routes. Valens reached Narbonensis but was intercepted by the Procurator, Valerius Paullinus, a personal friend of Vespasian. He was sent back to Italy and executed by Primus. News of Valens' capture had a decisive effect. In Spain a legion hostile to Vitellius, I Adiutrix, gave the lead, in Britain Vespasian's old legion II Augusta; now too XI Claudia took the decisive step.[24]

For Vitellius the news of the defection of Bassus and the fleet, along with that of Caecina which he received at Aricia, 20 km south of Rome down the Appian Way, had been bad enough. He returned to Rome on the 28th, addressed People and Senate on successive days, speeches forgotten when the news of Cremona was taken in. Tacitus censures the apathy, indecision, and panicky largesse of Vitellius' last weeks; Z. Yavetz rightly sees him as putting on a show before the populace, but does not banish suspicion that

Vitellius lacked nerve to launch a full-scale attack over the Apennines or even to defend them until the enemy were nearly at Fanum Fortunae.[25]

After Cremona the Flavian forces returned to their Verona headquarters. The way was clear for an advance south while Cornelius Fuscus with the Ravenna fleet put the eastern coast of Italy in their control, securing the food supply, and they reached Fanum. But Vitellius' new Praetorian Guard, fourteen cohorts, the legion of marines, II Adiutrix, all men with everything to lose, and cavalry support, under the new Prefect, Alfenus Varus, were on their way, and were thought to have blocked the passes of the Apennines: the main force had to be summoned from Verona to win them.[26]

Vitellius' men took up position at Mevania, and were joined by their commander-in-chief. The leading Flavian force arrived on about 3 December. The defection of the other Italian fleet, based at Misenum, meant the opening up of a second front south of Rome. Vitellius divided his forces, mistakenly, and sent his brother with six cohorts to deal with the rebels at Tarracina (18 December), making these men unavailable for the last battle before the capture of Rome. He retired to Rome and his remaining force fell back on Narnia. The arrival of the Verona troops on the 13th made the Flavians, now at Carsulae only 18 km to the north, more formidable, as did the sight of Valens' head on a pole paraded in front of the fortifications. This was the man who had inspired the Vitellian movement and who at that moment should have been drumming up reinforcements from Germany. The garrison surrendered and Vitellius was beginning to lose more by desertion: one of the city cohorts went over to the Misenum fleet.[27]

It was two days at most before Vitellius heard the news of Narnia. Primus, Mucianus, Varus, and Flavius Sabinus in the City offered the option of abdication, which not surprisingly he seemed ready to accept, unrealistic though it was. The principals met on 17 December in the Temple of Apollo, with the consulars Cluvius Rufus and Ti. Catius Asconius Silius Italicus (the historian and the poet) as witnesses. Vitellius' safety was guaranteed, and he was to be pensioned off with 100m *HS*. The formalities approved for the following day were novel, and not to be got through smoothly. Early on the 18th Vitellius summoned an assembly, but it would not listen. On the contrary, such feeling was roused that Sabinus had to retreat to the Capitol, with the suffect consul C. Quinctius Atticus and a noblewoman, Verulana Gratilla, presumably to hold out until Vitellius succeeded in abdicating. There they were joined by Domitian and the grandchildren of Sabinus. The Flavian advance guard of 1,000 cavalry under Q. Petillius Cerialis failed in an attack and the desperate followers of Vitellius stormed the Capitol as the Temple of Jupiter Optimus Maximus blazed to destruction, the most shameful event in Roman history in Tacitus' view; Cerialis, appointed in part because of his kinship with Vespasian, comes in for his share of criticism for incompetence and ill-discipline. The Flavians used the fire as a ground for refusing to negotiate when they entered the city. Now it gave Sabinus to the Vitellianists, and they had him executed, depriving the Emperor of any hope of abdication. Domitian slipped out in disguise and took refuge in a house nearby. Sabinus' leading supporters – senators, *equites*, junior officers – had advised him to stage a coup, but he went on to the end with his conciliatory approach, correct as long as Vitellius had a chance of winning, and even after Cremona when Flavian legions were not yet within striking distance of Rome. The forces he had at his disposal – 9,000 Othonian praetorians, disbanded but not disarmed, 2,000 in the City cohorts (if Vitellius had doubled the size of each), 7,000 in the Night Watch – may have amounted to about the same in numbers as Vitellius had on the spot (18,000 according to J. Nicols), though they were not of the same quality or experience. But Sabinus' claim just before his end that he had done nothing against Vitellius shows only obstinate loyalty to Vespasian's proclaimed purpose of a bloodless victory.[28]

It is extraordinary that Primus had halted at Ocriculum, to begin celebrating the military holiday of the Saturnalia (17–21 December), and did nothing but send forward Cerialis to try the defences. Recriminations flew later: Primus was treacherous, Mucianus held him up. But Primus may have been convinced that Rome would fall into his hands without another blow being struck, which from the political point of view the High Command preferred and was desirable for a man who had already exceeded instructions; he was certainly under pressure from Mucianus (now about 250 km behind) to make a joint entry and take over power from an Emperor already abdicated.[29]

The Flavians left the party on the 19th when they understood that Rome was not to be taken without a struggle and that their supporters were in danger. When they reached Saxa Rubra they could see the glow of the Capitol. Two embassies from the Vitellian leaders were received, and their terms refused. The praetor and Stoic philosopher, Q. Iunius Arulenus Rusticus, was wounded in the approach to Cerialis; another distinguished Stoic, the knight C. Musonius Rufus, barely escaped untouched in that to Primus, who would not grant a day's respite to a delegation of Vestals. In the morning of 20 December the troops entered Rome under Primus, who remained in charge until the arrival of Mucianus perhaps a week later. Scenes of carnage were played out against the background of Rome's normal activities, cafés, bathing establishments, and prostitutes still plying their trade. Vitellius' Praetorians fought to the last in the barracks; he was dragged out of the Palace by soldiers who had once been Otho's, forced past the spot where Galba had been murdered, and butchered on the Gemonian Stairs where the body of Sabinus had lain. Domitian came out of hiding, to be saluted Caesar and conducted to Vespasian's house on the Quirinal. South of Rome mopping up led to the capture and execution of L. Vitellius, while Sex. Lucilius Bassus, back in his original rôle of cavalry officer, restored order in Campania.[30]

In October Vespasian completed work at headquarters, and left for Egypt, accompanied by Titus. On the march he heard of the battle of Cremona and in Alexandria of Vitellius' death. In Suetonius' version, he had reached Alexandria when he heard of both, separated though they were by nearly two months, which is eloquent for the importance of Cremona in the minds of writers (with the capture of Rome and Vitellius' death an epilogue). Vespasian had chosen the best place, emulating not only Tiberius but Claudius. The exorbitant financial demands of the Flavians had been put down to Mucianus. Certainly Vespasian could not be held responsible for the sack of Cremona. His hands were clean, although ultimate power rested with him. His strategy, to win Italy with the minimum of bloodshed, had been abandoned by Primus; post-war cruelties were Mucianus'. The fate of cashiered officers and the standing of Mucianus and Primus were reserved for Vespasian.[31]

2 Vespasian's success

What brought officers and men, highly placed individuals, and cities to the new man's side? Such questions make Vespasian himself a prime factor in men's thinking. For courtiers and others in the imperial service they were; in provincial and municipal circles, the man at the centre was a means to success in local ends.

Vespasian's power grew out of the possession of three victorious legions with associated auxiliaries, and from being a proven fighter. Tacitus stresses the vital core: of Vespasian's own legions one was commanded in 69 by his son, one by his fellow-Sabine – and protégé? – Sex. Vettulenus Cerialis. Junior officers of these legions, auxiliary prefects, and common soldiers could connect duty to the man appointed their commanding officer with their united power, and see how to benefit.[32]

The calculations that Tacitus ascribes to Vespasian were also made in neighbouring and more distant provinces. Renouncing any claim of his own and preferring to be kingmaker like the Earl of Warwick, Mucianus took the same risk if the attempt went wrong, with a secondary position to gain. L. Homo points to lack of ambition, but Mucianus' determination to control events at Rome in 70 does not suggest that. Scholars have overestimated Mucianus' birth, and so his claims, but Tacitus makes him bracket himself with Vespasian: he was a native of Spain, at best of Apennine Italy, like Vespasian himself. His active military experience was as a subordinate – he had probably been in Armenia under Corbulo – while Vespasian, who may have begun in the East as commander of the entire Syrian force, went on to his own war. There were blots on Mucianus' career (he had been suffect consul in the 60s, after years at praetorian rank) and, a notorious homosexual with a theatrical manner, he had no sons, a disadvantage as he is made by Tacitus to acknowledge. He made the realistic choice between backing the marginally preferable Vespasian, with the chance of substantial gains, and of being swept away.[33]

Politics, strategy, and his family connection with Judaea made the accession of Ti. Alexander, Prefect of Egypt, inevitable and early. He had already shown suppleness in securing his own position on the death of Nero, who had appointed him in 66. An edict of 6 July 68 blamed the late régime for abuses in Alexandria and Egypt. He could offer Galba the loyalty of his province (which entailed the security of the grain supply from Egypt), at the price of reforms which would make Alexander a popular Prefect – and so able to guarantee the deal. His connections with Judaea and so with Vespasian made him unlikely to continue under Vitellius. He could not have resisted the Flavian conglomerate, but he could contribute two legions and deprive Vitellian Rome of grain; the adoption of 1 July as Vespasian's *dies imperii* (accession date) was acknowledgment of his contribution.[34]

The total of Vespasian's troops, without princes' contributions, was nearly a third of the imperial establishment. In the past the prestige of eastern legions had not been equal to those in the West, but Vespasian's in 69 were of high quality and had had more combat experience than the Rhine legions: three, V Macedonica, X Fretensis, and XV Apollinaris, had been on active service with him since 67; V and X, along with VI Ferrata, had campaigned under Corbulo in Armenia (III Gallica was removed to Moesia in 68). Even the two Egyptian legions, II Cyrenaica and XXII Deiotariana, had sent detachments. Only IV Scythica, humiliated by the Parthians at Rhandeia, and XII Fulminata, defeated in Cestius' retreat, were below par.

The same considerations that affected Alexander drew in dependent princes who for the sake of their thrones had already contributed to the war effort in Judaea, most intimately Agrippa II, who slipped away from Rome when Vespasian declared, and Berenice. Even without existing ties these princes had to adhere to their powerful neighbour: their kingdoms depended on it. Financial and military support might win titles at worst, at best territorial extensions; failure to help, instant deposition. If the cause did not succeed, adherence was at least excusable, and amends might be made by a last-minute change. Octavian had left most of Mark Antony's partisans in place after his victory in 30 BC.[35]

As the strength of the movement grew, its gravity increased, and the closer any individual or group was to it, the stronger its attractive power. At a distance cooler calculations would be made. Vespasian might have hoped for help from Ti. Claudius Cogidubnus, whose kingdom had been the base for his own conquests of 43–7, if Cogidubnus had not been vulnerable to the Vitellian legions and by himself could do no more than sabotage Vitellian reinforcements and encourage pro-Flavian subversion. Much closer at hand, in autumn 69 Anicetus, a usurper in Pontus, declared for Vitellius: he hoped he was far enough from Vespasian's forces to break free of Rome.[36]

Not only possession of military capability, but skill and resolution in deploying it, contrasted with the much publicized irresolution of the man he was supplanting, enhanced Vespasian's drawing power. The talents of a good general, Tacitus was to make Domitian reflect, should be the monopoly of the Emperor. Josephus presents Vespasian as the elected choice of his victorious army, outclassing the inferior candidate of the Rhine legions, which had been in eclipse during Nero's last years. In what had become with the elevation of Vitellius a soldiers' revolution, Vespasian was, in J. Nicols' words, a soldier's soldier, the virtual conqueror of Judaea. His physical prowess, paraded as one of his merits, showed that, though elderly, he was healthy, a candidate who could do more than jog.[37]

Other factors, minor by comparison, were birth and record. If Nero was ousted, Galba, with his lineage and connection with the Julio-Claudians, was the obvious candidate, though he had done nothing to enhance his reputation since Claudius' reign. His own choice of successor was the blameless aristocrat Piso Licinianus, with his family history of independence of the Caesars, while the challenge came from two men who owed their rank to successive members of the former dynasty. As 69 went on, lack of ancestry became insignificant. Attempts were made to nominate L. Verginius Rufus, the new man from Mediolanum, first when he had defeated Vindex or more probably when the Upper Rhine army learnt of Nero's death, then when the Othonians lost at Bedriacum. An Italian from the Sabine country was an obvious possibility. Vespasian's birth simply provided material to committed opponents, or for later ambiguous anecdotes.[38]

Other men still had a better title than Vespasian. Ti. Plautius Silvanus Aelianus, Nero's aristocratic and distinguished general, now out of office, springs to mind. He sprang to Vespasian's mind too, and early in the new régime was given the prestigious but influential rather than potent Prefecture of the City. He carried with him triumphal ornaments earned years before which Vespasian pointed out should not have been left for himself to confer; the gesture fixed Silvanus in his place. Then there was C. Suetonius Paullinus, conqueror of Boudicca and one of Otho's generals, his loyalty suspect. Even Vespasian's own elder brother might have seemed a more obvious choice. Tacitus reports rumours of rivalry, but does not confirm them. Senior in the consulship, he had been richer and more influential; and he was popular with the troops. No scandal attached to him; Tacitus has little but praise. In 69, however, he was in charge only of the City Prefect's cohorts.[39]

Personal merits other than military credibility were marginal. The pretenders were recognized as adventurers. Vespasian's servility to Gaius and careerism under Claudius and Nero, not even consistently successful, made his reputation almost as equivocal as his predecessors', but he kept his head and turned out better than people feared. Suitable qualities of character could be played up after the event: Vespasian's patriotism and righteous cause became articles of faith as soon as he looked the winner. Vitellius turned out worse, or had no time to bring subordinates under control; and much could be made of gross and costly appetites suggested by his portraits.[40]

Vespasian had assumed in the East a position once held by other powerful commoners: L. Vitellius in the mid-30s and Corbulo from 54 to 66. Did the memory of Corbulo, and the sense of loss engendered by his enforced suicide, work for Vespasian with the legionaries or with an officer corps who found prospects of advancement blighted? Corbulo was a martinet who in Germany in 47 had a man executed for discarding side arms when engaged in construction and whose retraining of the eastern legions had culminated in a winter under canvas on the Anatolian plateau. Officers were another matter: a tie was supposed to exist through shared service. Although one of Corbulo's junior officers, Arrius Varus, prefect of a cohort, was said to have obtained the leading centurionate of III Gallica by informing on him, others might be suspect to Nero. His leading officers included L. Verulanus Severus, whose kinswoman Verulana Gratilla was with Sabinus on the Capitol in December 69, M. Vettius Bolanus, Vitellius' governor of Britain, T. Aurelius Fulvus, probably Mucianus, perhaps M. Ulpius Traianus. In fact, they did not suffer. Verulanus had his consulship towards the end of Nero's reign, and Mucianus was safe enough to be given Syria; Fulvus remained in charge of III; Traianus retained a legateship. The equestrian Ti. Julius Alexander was transferred to Egypt, one of the most responsible posts open to him. Their success in Armenia was rewarded. Networks formed during the fighting under Corbulo were available in 68–9, but not every officer would take to the man who had the command in Judaea that might have been Corbulo's – who had benefited from Corbulo's enforced suicide. Early in Vespasian's principate Domitian was married to Corbulo's daughter Domitia Longina, perhaps to attract his prestige to the new dynasty.[41]

Partisans of Otho who believed that they had nothing to hope for from Vitellius or saw Vespasian as the winner were more likely to support him. A prime example is Rubrius Gallus, chosen by Nero to campaign against Vindex; a loyalist, then. In 69 he was a trusted adviser of Otho, helped bring Caecina over to Vespasian and passed straight to the command of Moesia. Vedius Aquila, legate of XIII Gemina, roughly handled by his men after the Othonian defeat at Cremona, saw his best chance with Vespasian and took them to Patavium. At a lower level the same was done by L. Antonius Naso, who had risen from the position of leading centurion in a legion to that of tribune in the Praetorians. In that post he had been decorated by Nero, and perhaps because of that was cashiered by Galba. Next he is found in charge of XIV Gemina, entrusted by Otho with the task of bringing it from Illyricum to the Po valley. Under Vespasian Naso rose high in the procuratorial service: in 77–8 he held a position of importance in Bithynia, where the senatorial governor was often a lightweight. Aemilius Pacensis, cashiered from the Urban Cohorts at the same time as Naso, was restored by Otho and received joint command of the forces sent to the Maritime Alps and Narbonensian Gaul. He died on the Capitol for Sabinus. It was a centurion cashiered by Galba, Claudius Faventinus, who tried first to win the Misenum fleet for

Vespasian. Even the son of Antiochus IV of Commagene had been wounded fighting on the Othonian side at Bedriacum. But there was more than one way to the Flavian lines. Cornelius Fuscus, who had brought over his native colony (perhaps Vienna) to Galba and had been rewarded with the procuratorship of Illyricum, also joined the Flavians and became Prefect of the Ravenna fleet. For any opponents of Vitellius Vespasian's chances of success were a determining factor.[42]

Fear and self-interest governed most behaviour; where does loyalty come in? It had been conspicuous in the Jewish War. All were united against a fanatical enemy in defence of Rome's interests, the Emperor's, and their own; spectacular feats were performed by all ranks. Historians of 69 have to single out instances of loyalty to established authority, mainly exhibited by professional soldiers: a centurion of the Guard cut down in the Forum defending Galba's litter single-handed; men killing themselves at Otho's funeral pyre, an example followed by officers and men at Bedriacum, Placentia, in the camp of VII Gemina, and at Cremona; the refusal of the defeated Vitellians to surrender at Rome. Civil war exposed the complexities of 'loyalty', and the true priorities of groups and individuals. A promising known leader commanded interested fidelity, and that came to stand for a principle. What had the men of Otho to look forward to from Vitellius after Bedriacum? And Vitellius' troops knew in December 69 that by surrendering to Antonius Primus they would save their lives at best. The unit, which looked after its own, commanded most loyalty in 69.[43]

Tacitus remarks that Vitellius' execution of leading centurions on the Othonian side was what most roused the Balkan legions against him. Such brutality was one of his worst mistakes. But these men were already set against him and his king-making Rhine legions. Long-standing regional, besides professional rivalries, as between legionaries and Praetorian Guard on the one hand or auxiliaries on the other, had a violent issue, or went on festering: rankers, unlike their commanders, changed unit only infrequently. Hostility between Nero's favoured XIV Gemina and the Batavians went back to their defection from Nero. The troops had an eye to their own prospects and compared them with those of others. This had led to agitation on behalf of Verginius Rufus and then Vitellius in the Rhine armies; it was equally powerful in the East in the spring of 69. How much effect the promises of Vespasian's agents had is problematical. His likely success was a prior requirement, but some targets were easier to hit than others.[44]

The superior pay and conditions of service enjoyed by the Praetorian Guard made them objects of envy. Men favoured with transfer to Guard units fought for Otho and their privileges to the end; they were offered honourable discharge and replaced in a Praetorian Guard of sixteen cohorts and four Urban Cohorts each of a thousand men by 20,000 of the 60,000 legionaries of Vitellius who were at Rome. Vitellius' Praetorians in turn were his last defenders; the turnover in the Urban Cohorts was less speedy and many were to rally to Sabinus at the end. Vespasian's letter, circulated to the governors of the West, promised reinstatement to men removed from the Guard.[45]

Sailors came below legionaries in pay and status. Not only the placing of the Ravenna fleet but its Othonian background and the recruitment of its sailors from Danubian provinces made defection to Vespasian likely. The carrot was promotion: the higher status and pay of legionaries in the new II Adiutrix. It took more effort to win the fleet at Misenum. The appeal allegedly from Vespasian that the sailors were shown by the cashiered Claudius Faventinus was not enough; only a praetorian senator who happened most fortunately to be in the neighbourhood had sufficient authority to guarantee their future and their support.[46]

Unit-loyalty led to rivalry between units on the same side, dissension and the degradation of officers. Valens heard at Ticinum of the setback that Caecina had suffered at the temple of Castor and Pollux near Bedriacum on about 5 April. His troops were keen to rescue their defeated comrades, and so to display their own superiority. And it may have been resentment and jealousy of Vitellius' troops throwing their weight about in Rome that kept the Watch faithful to Sabinus. When the Flavian forces invaded Italy and assembled at Verona the troops made it threateningly plain that they wanted the dynamic Antonius Primus not to be superseded by the senior but half-hearted Tampius Flavianus and Aponius Saturninus.[47]

Changes of allegiance seemed to betray shallowness of support, contrasting with the solidity of the backing that Vespasian received. They should not be taken for mere fickleness on the part of the common soldiery. Their behaviour was rational, given self-interest – the hope of donatives and pro-motions, with plunder in the immediate outcome – and fear – the prospect of removal from a familiar base, dishonour. Vespasian knew how to play on this: Mucianus told the populace of Antioch and no doubt his troops too that 'their' legions were to be transferred to the inhospitable Rhine: IV Scythica had been in Syria since about 56, XII Fulminata since Augustus, and VI Ferrata since 30 BC. There was nobody to contradict.[48]

The particular history of some units made them easier to win. The Upper Rhine legions under L. Verginius Rufus had remained loyal to Nero and slaughtered 20,000 Gauls who claimed to be allies of the rebel Galba. When Nero fell they declared for Verginius, only to be refused, giving Galba a second grudge. In 69 all the Rhine legions had been in Germany for twenty-eight years at least, XV Primigenia at Vetera for fifty-nine. Some could expect to be removed from their homes. They tried again with Vitellius in January and found a candidate willing to accept the sword of Julius Caesar that was thrust into his hand. The defeated troops of Otho approached Verginius Rufus after the battle of Bedriacum; the original choice might still prove acceptable to Vitellius' forces. Verginius slipped away and saved his life, while the misgivings of the defeated Othonians proved well justified.

Vitellius' supporters, having placed their bet, had to leave their chips down. When Vitellius left for Italy the remaining troops were as obstinately loyal to the Emperor they had made as those who went with him: he depended on them and would look to their interests. In the struggle for Italy, his men gave in only after the battle of Cremona, or when confronted by the alternatives of total defeat or acceptance by the Flavians at Narnia. At Rome they fought to the end: surrender left them with bare life at best. The legionaries under Caecina who had taken the lead against Galba on 1 January, especially those of V Alaudae, took his switch to Vespasian extremely ill. Minor grievances such as failure to distribute booty adequately only inflamed existing mistrust between legate and rankers.[49]

Vespasian had no hope of the Rhine armies; but the men of the Balkans played a decisive rôle. Their commanders could be won over or swept aside by men spurred on by Vitellius' resentment at their abortive attempt to save Otho. The humiliating fate of XIII Gemina, set to work building amphitheatres at Cremona and Bononia, showed the Vitellian temper. Other legions that had fought for Otho were dispersed: XI Claudia was returned to Dalmatia, VII Gemina (formerly Galbiana!) went to Carnuntum in Pannonia, and I Adiutrix to Spain, where X Gemina had already been sent from its quarters in Pannonia. There are three scenarios. According to Suetonius, 6,000 Moesians on vexillation to support Otho had already shown their resentment at Aquileia at the end of April by mooting alternatives to Vitellius and, on the urging of men from III Gallica, by inscribing Vespasian's name on their standards. The movement was gradually repressed, but the publicity it received led to Ti. Alexander's declaration. Then, basing their views on Suetonius' account, K. Wellesley holds that the Moesian legions declared for Vespasian in May, E. Flaig that the vexillations from eastern Moesia, arriving back at the bases at Oescus and Novae, in late June, carried their legions with them into revolt, with the Pannonian legions joining at the beginning of August. The orthodox view based on Tacitus is that III Gallica, reassembled at Oescus, once the home of V Macedonica, became a solid core of support for Vespasian. Still under the man who had commanded it in Armenia, T. Aurelius Fulvus, it carried with it pride in the achievement of the eastern legions, probably envy, and potentially sympathy with their cause; as E. Flaig notes, three of the six eastern legions had come from the Danube, V Macedonica, IV Scythica, and XV Apollinaris. Vespasian became a real alternative to Vitellius and to L. Verginius Rufus in the Balkans as soon as Otho was dead, but at a time when Vitellius seemed increasingly entrenched it was unlikely for their original resentment to lead to a second and decisive outbreak. Legionaries of individual units acted first, involving leading centurions, tribunes such as Vipstanus Messalla of VII Claudia, and finally commanding officers such M. Aponius Saturninus. We may well accept from the story that the detachments named Vespasian, but as an apparent flash in the pan, offering hope but no certainty of support.[50]

Even in western provinces far from the action, the same factors – the likely winner, the past history of a unit and the probable future effect of that – were operative, and there was additional frustration and indiscipline amongst troops unable to decide events. The Balkan legions on going over addressed themselves to the Othonian XIV Gemina from Britain and Otho's creation I Adiutrix in Spain. Vitellius had no ardent partisan in charge of Tarraconensis and the province changed allegiance immediately after the battle of Cremona. In Britain L. Antistius Rusticus, tribune or acting commander of Vespasian's II Augusta, had particularly good material to work on. His success was rewarded with medals and advancement. But Vitellius had done his best with promotions, and they had an effect on IX Hispana and XX Valeria under Roscius Caelius, soon to be replaced with Cn. Agricola; it refused the oath. XIV Gemina was vulnerable because of its obstinate loyalty to Nero and then to Otho. Hence when Vitellius called up reinforcements there was alacrity only in his old province of Africa, only a few days from the capital.[51]

As J. Nicols observes, Tacitus attributes the revolutionary events of 68–9 to sedition among the troops and destructive greed on the part of the leaders. Without troops who thought their interests threatened none of the pretenders could have moved, and events on the Rhine in 70 supported a later perspective in which 'soldiers in the grip of irrational forces' loomed conveniently large. When Vitellius arrived in Germany in December 68 to replace Verginius, there was an outbreak of what Nicols calls the 'revolutionary spirit of the soldiers': the split between men and officers – except for the most astute opportunists – that resulted from the battle of Vesontio continued after the elevation of Vitellius, and on the Danube: the interests of individual officers and men in their units no longer coincided. Officers from the centurionate upward had fears and ambitions comparable with those of the men, but more volatile loyalties. They had quicker and more reliable access to information, were better equipped to assess it, and at the rank of tribune and above did not spend enough time with one unit to develop the *esprit de corps* unfailing in rank and file.[52]

Among the supple and unscrupulous officers thrown up in 68–9, Antonius Primus of Tolosa is one of those especially noteworthy for their later importance. He entered the scene as a Neronian exile in his own province, for offences criminal rather than political, but Galba appointed him commander of his new legion VII. At Carnuntum he swore allegiance to Otho but was too late at Bedriacum to take part in the battle. Vespasian gave Balkan officers a fresh chance of service, and he was quickest to take it. His immediate invasion of Italy, the way opened up by auxiliaries, was much to the taste of the troops, who could expect booty and credit with Vespasian for success.[53]

A. Caecina Alienus is the most flagrant example of successful betrayal. Quaestor in Baetica, he had been sent at the end of 68 to Germany, where there had been unrest ever since Galba's recognition, to take over IV Macedonica, when Galba (allegedly having discovered embezzlement in

Spain) recalled him. So he became instrumental in rousing Vitellius to make his bid. (Did the troops of IV Macedonica who rushed the tribunal in January do so without any prompting?) Caecina had everything to expect from Vitellius – if Vitellius survived and continued to favour him; with his rival Fabius Valens, another man fatally disappointed by Galba, he was awarded the consulship of 1 September–31 October 69. It was fear of Valens' influence combined with an estimate of the strength of the eastern task force that induced Caecina to sound out Sex. Lucilius Bassus, commander of the Ravenna and Misenum fleets, so we are told. When he knew that the fleet had been won for Vespasian he too entered into negotiations with Primus. Bassus had his own grievance: he had been disappointed of the Prefecture of the Guard. Historians of the Flavian period spoke of 'concern for peace' and 'patriotism'. Tacitus scorns that: it was wickedness. The traitors were naturally irresponsible, had already betrayed one emperor, Galba, and were jealous of rivals for Vitellius' favour. Yet Tacitus' insistence on Valens' power is not altogether convincing: Caecina could not have supposed that he would supplant Mucianus or even Antonius with Vespasian; his estimate of the outcome, stressed by Josephus, is likely to have weighed more heavily.[54]

Ties of marriage, however strong in normal times, took second place to expediency in this year. Both C. Calpetanus Festus, legate of III Augusta in Africa, and Tampius Flavianus, governor of Pannonia, were connections of Vitellius. Flavianus' hesitation in face of unrest among his troops, and his attempt to resign his post, were to his credit. But the Flavian activist Cornelius Fuscus persuaded him to return from Italy and resume his command. Festus' action, the murder of the aristocratic governor L. Piso, eliminating a man whose very name made him a source of fear, perhaps a real threat, was calculated to find favour whoever won, and his recognition of Vitellius was balanced by clandestine correspondence with the likely winner.[55]

Not all commanders were as decisive in their movements as Caecina and Valens. Sometimes contending motives led to paralysis, as with M. Pompeius Silvanus, governor of Dalmatia, who had been manoeuvred into action by the legate of XI Claudia, L. Annius Bassus. Aponius Saturninus of Moesia was committed to Vitellius – as long as he seemed secure. In token of his loyalty he ordered the assassination of the legate of VII Claudia at Viminacium, Tettius Julianus. They were already at loggerheads and Julianus' anti-Vitellian troops had got out of hand at Aquileia. But Tettius did not wait. After five months in hiding he made his way to Alexandria. Saturninus soon transferred his own allegiance, and had a narrow escape from his soldiers.[56]

Quietist officers were subject to pressure from above and below. Before Cremona they were approached and promised that Vitellius' appointments to centurionates and tribunates would be honoured. In Britain assurances would have been needed that those promoted by Vitellius would retain their rank. Such promises were of immediate value to the victor, but the Flavians could be sure of these men only if their victory was complete and decisive.[57]

Circumstances brought other useful men of rank over to Vespasian's side. Property in the East was one factor. With the praetorian senator M. Plancius Varus the heat of political events at Rome, where he had, possibly unwillingly, become involved in prosecuting Cn. Dolabella, as well as the site of his home city, Perge in Pamphylia, and his estates in Asia Minor brought him into the Flavian camp. Back in the East, Varus may have been found useful work as acting governor of Asia. K. Wellesley chooses the story of the dim Arval Brother P. Valerius Marinus, whose retention on the list of consuls designated for 69 suggests that he was a favourite of Otho. He seems to have attended Otho on his journey north, fleeing Bononia for Rome after the battle of Bedriacum. Vitellius' régime had nothing for him; he took ship for Alexandria. There were men of more promise: Cn. Julius Agricola immediately (according to Tacitus) joined the cause when he heard of it, *en route* for his family estate in Gaul, where his mother had been murdered by Othonian raiders before Bedriacum; perhaps then before 1 July and at latest when the letters despatched by the Flavians reached Gaul and his home town of Forum Iulii was occupied in about October by Vespasian's supporter Valerius Paulinus, another native of the place; Agricola in all likelihood had already come to know Petillius Cerialis when they were serving in Britain during the revolt of Boudicca. Another able young *eques*, M. Hirrius Fronto Neratius Pansa, also rallied to Vespasian as soon as practicable, perhaps even before Flavian forces reached Italy.[58]

Civilian populations in Italy and the West were moved less by sympathy than by fearful regard for the attitude of the nearest force. Feeling would have been strongest in Gaul: parts had supported Vindex, the Aedui, Sequani, Arverni, Vienna, capital of the Allobroges, while other tribes, Treveri and Lingones, were with the Rhine legions. The Spanish peninsula had a similar but weaker allegiance to Galba, then to Otho, never tested by a hostile army. Vespasian's agents in the West made little headway against the threatening presence of the Rhine legions, encountered when Valens marched south. Valens' troops had not been sufficiently propitiated by the women and children of the Mediomatrici to prevent a massacre at their centre. The Narbonese learnt the lesson: Vienna, suspect from its associations with Vindex, grovelled to the Vitellian column. A 'fine' was imposed and it lost its right to levy militia.[59]

In Corsica a conflict of interest between the governor, D. Pacarius, and his subjects led to his assassination without positive advantage to the Corsicans. Pacarius had sought credit by bringing the island over to the advancing Vitellians and reinforcing them with local recruits, whose enthusiasm was extinguished when they realized what supporting Vitellius meant. They were safely distant from the scene of action and thought to curry favour with Otho; but the sideshow attracted no attention from either side.[60]

In the East and the Balkans cities and other administrative units had responded to unopposed Flavian power. Men brought over their native cities, like Valerius Paulinus. Catilius Longus, an equestrian officer later adlected into the senate at praetorian rank, may have brought over the city of which he was patron, Apamea in Bithynia. With the cities came wealthy civilians and their contributions. In Italy the news that Vitellian forces had occupied Mevania and the prospect of an armed struggle for the peninsula caused consternation. Concern for property would make landowners look only for the end of hostilities. Communities had their own concerns. When the Misenum fleet went over, it carried Puteoli with it, but fear for gains from the ships that should be sailing into it every year was also at work. And if Capua stayed obstinately faithful to Vitellius it was because local rivalries remained vital, as they had in the rising of Vindex, at Lugdunum and Vienna. But as the Flavian bandwaggon rolled its size and power, and the skill of the drivers, made it a juggernaut. The fate of Vitellian Cremona issued an awful warning. J. Nicols attributes the welcome the Flavians received at Opitergium and Altinum to the fact that those cities, on the main route to the Danubian provinces, were familiar with their soldiers; but terror may have played a part. Central Italy went over to Vespasian when the Praetorians proved unable to hold out at Mevania. The army of Primus was helped on its way – out of local territory.[61]

In the City Vespasian's cause roused no enthusiasm. For the propertied classes the Flavians were another set of plunderers, while the *plebs* was pro-Vitellian. Z. Yavetz holds that Vitellius' politically directed generosity – his *liberalitas* – and his commemoration of Nero, which chiming in with popular feeling, kept them, even to the point of joining up, until his indecisiveness alienated them. This view has been challenged. Vitellius could hardly afford to pay donatives, and the spring of 69 had been a wretched harbinger of famine. For J. Nicols, the Cremona atrocities, and Vespasian's intention of cutting off grain supplies, were more important. Necessarily the people cheered in turn for Nero, Galba, Otho, and Vitellius, and they all feared famine and violence. But something must be allowed for conflicting affections. Nero had been a favourite for his ancestry and his youth; his tastes and courting of the populace laid down lasting affection. Otho benefited as Nero's friend. Others (the better off, or dependants of the wealthy, who could afford principles) were ready when they heard in the theatre of Otho's death to take busts of Galba, garland them with laurel, process to the Lacus Curtius where he had been killed and heap up the garlands at the scene. The Flavians had nothing to offer that the affable Vitellius did not promise. He was execrated after his death for deserting his supporters. There was nothing to be said for welcoming another set of greedy and brutal soldiers. At best the Flavii themselves were not unknowns: Sabinus, with his long tenure of the City Prefecture, could have been an asset.[62]

Key adherents joining at crucial moments had foresight rewarded. The preliminary negotiations and the conference of Berytus provided for promotions, immediate or future, and the promises were kept. Adherents in the

East and big men who had brought over armies or fleets, regions or cities in the West before the victory could look forward to the new régime with confidence. As E. Flaig has pointed out, Vespasian was looking for competence, even if it had not served him; but merit combined with loyalty was a known formula for success. Tacitus mentions appointments to prefectures and procuratorships as well as to the senate. Those who served or contributed money founded careers on what they did. Vespasian did not let his rankers down either. The legions received a donative before he left the East in 70, and there were promotions to look forward to. The heroes who had marched on Rome received 100 *HS*, or more probably 300 *HS*, on entry.[63]

So the trained legions under the hard soldier and irresistibly attracting all the resources of the East won the day. These forces were split, but so were those of Vitellius. And Vitellius' constituency, essentially the Rhine legions and neighbouring Gauls, was inherently narrow: resentful survivors of his predecessors' supporters and armies could confidently turn to Vespasian.

5

IDEOLOGY IN ACTION

Vespasian wrote memoirs, and contemporaries were loyal: so he had the old Roman military merits and in public life nurtured the State, was watchful, just, energetic, and unpretentious, in private life simple. Pliny the Elder openly admits bias. He had coincided with Titus during the latter's military tribunate on the Lower Rhine (57–8) and dedicated his *Natural Histories* to him. He survived Vespasian by two months but the thirty-one books of his lost *Histories* may prudently have concluded on a high point, the triumph. Josephus completed the *Jewish War* late in the reign at earliest. He used the imperial memoirs, and had his work authenticated by Titus – whose gallantry and forbearance it in turn certifies. But Josephus had a greater problem: to reconcile the historian and prophet of Israel, a new Jeremiah, with the celebrant of emperors who had brought her down and destroyed the Temple; worse, to make sense of his transition from fighting like the Maccabees to playing Joseph at the court of a latter-day Pharaoh.[1]

The difficulties of these historians have created difficulties for their successors. But the ideology acceptable to a war-weary Empire imposed itself on its holders. Against the luridly painted failings of Vitellius, Vespasian's was a persona that he put on, grew into, and had to live with and, when practicable, up to. He did follow earlier popular politicians, and set the tone of his reign, by living with ostentatious modesty. Less time was spent on the Julio-Claudian Palatine than in the Gardens of Sallust, where he received senators and humbler persons. He was accessible in the street and his doors were open all day, without a guard. To assure friends speedy admission Claudius had distributed rings bearing his own image. Vespasian abolished a practice that had led to abuse – false pretences, subsequent informing. The custom of searching visitors, another Claudian innovation, he also abolished, without much danger. Vespasian had grown sons to avenge him, not so Claudius.[2]

The ideology found expression in every medium, notably in buildings restored or freshly constructed at Rome. Coinage was banal. Types were borrowed from past reigns, allusions reassuringly predictable. Some to be expected are absent (no new building figures); and it seems not to matter that some – Concord, for example – had undesirable antecedents, having been used by Nero or the arch-villain Vitellius. But novelties are instructive. *AETERNITAS* outbids *ROMA RESVRGENS* or (already under Galba) *RENASCENS*. The idea of the Eternal City went back to Augustan poetry, to a time when destructive civil war, which Livy saw as the one threat to everlasting prosperity, seemed over. Velleius Paterculus in about 30 hoped for the *aeternitas* of the Empire, which depended on the Emperor; Tiberius himself took it for granted that the State, unlike politicians, was *aeternus*. Concern for the *aeternitas* of Italy was ascribed to Claudius. Now the claim to everlasting life was simply asserted, sometimes without qualification, some-times as a property of the Roman People. The steady good health of the state was a benefit conferred, it seems, by the Emperor, formerly by Galba, now by Vespasian, since it was *SALVS AVGVSTI*; but the idea went back to Tiberius' obverse *SALVS AVGVSTA*.[3]

The salutation of the legions signalled Vespasian's dependence on mili-tary power. He emphasized that and his prowess by becoming 'Imperator T. Flavius Vespasianus Caesar'. 'Commander' had been Augustus' forename alone until Nero assumed it in 66; the regular way of marking military glory was to tot up salutations. Galba, once recognized by the senate, added the names of Caesar and Augustus to his own, which had already been followed by 'Imperator' in token of his salutation and of his claims to military merit. Then Otho, as the choice of the Praetorian Guard, or following Nero, placed Imperator first. Vespasian's troops also addressed him by the name of Caesar, which belonged to the imperial Julii, and through having been assumed by Claudius on accession had become a title, prerogative of an Emperor, his sons and heirs; so Nero and evidently Galba's shortlived heir Piso. 'Augustus' had been conferred on the first Princeps in 27 BC, and it passed to his son in AD 14; Tiberius never expressly acceded but subscribed 'Augustus' in official documents. Other Julio-Claudian emperors did not hesitate. In 68–9 Vitel-lius held back until the people insisted on his arrival in Rome, refusing even 'Caesar' until November: his coinage shows 'A. Vitellius Germanicus Imp.'. In an attempt to find something fresh, civil, and appealing, Vitellius, taking a hint from his own soldiers, assumed the resonant name conferred on Nero Drusus and inherited by his son, near-conquerors of Germany. 'Germanicus' would draw both the people of Rome and the legions. 'Augustus' is omitted from Vespasian's titulature on Alexandrian coins and is adopted in August: he then allowed the use of the supreme title unauthorized. Vitellius played up his father, the military man three times consul and colleague of Claudius in the censorship, but Vespasian needed all conventional props.[4]

A milestone of the second half of 69 displays Vespasian with full nomen-clature, without mention of tribunician power, consulship, and chief pontifi-cate, and B. Isaac remarks that the milestone would bear out Suetonius' remark (in a faulty text) that Vespasian was 'slow' to take tribunician power, but he is not known to have taken it later than the rest (21 December 69). In any case, theoretically for use within the City and overshadowed even there by *imperium*, tribunician power did not matter, except as a means of indicating a successor. More significantly, Vespasian was to count his years of tenure as if they had begun on 1 July and celebrated his 'imperial day' (*dies imperii*) on that same date, as Suetonius himself reveals: what the senate had said about Vitellius had been overridden by the army's 'vote' for Vespasian.[5]

The fact that Suetonius fails to mention the senate's formal grant of powers to Vespasian, while telling how he was acclaimed by the army and acquired *maiestas* and *auctoritas* (majesty, prestige, and influence) with the help of oriental gods, is not to be overplayed as showing a new form of leadership or focus of Empire. Emperors were being made outside Rome, and every aspirant to exceptional positions at Rome needed divine patronage: exceptional favour or gifts validated claims and guaranteed the leader's essential good luck (*felicitas*).[6]

Strenuous efforts were made to present Vespasian as the reluctant Emperor, chosen by heaven to take the Roman Empire under his charge. Low origin (and rapid success) enhanced the rôle of Destiny in Flavian ideology. It is stressed by Josephus and attested by the reappearance of Fortune on the coinage and her introduction into military cult. Suetonius offers eleven supernatural items supporting Vespasian's claims to power, meant to be in chronological order; a complete list may have been drawn up in Pliny's *Histories*, based on material provided in the Emperor's own memoir, and used by Tacitus, selectively for his literary purpose, and Dio. Anecdotes of the early career were *post eventum* fabrications or reinterpretations: the mud that Gaius spattered on Vespasian's toga, the dog that brought him a human hand at lunch, the ox breaking into his dining room and doing obeisance. Two items from the period before Vespasian's declaration are more pointful: when Galba was elected to his second consulship, or during Otho's reign at Rome, a statue of Julius Caesar on the Tiber island turned from west to east. That may already have been the work of partisans intent on fulfilling the 'prediction'. The story of eagles fighting at Bedriacum and the victor defeated by one coming from the east is certainly late enough for a rumour purposefully set going. After 1 July all the resources of Eastern lore were at the disposal of Vespasian and his friends. When he arrived in Egypt Vespasian was offered the fertile flood of the Nile by a priest of Amun Re at Montou (Medamud); perhaps in appreciative response, he dedicated the quartz statue of the river with its sixteen children – sixteen cubits (8.5 m) of optimum flood height – in his Temple of Peace.[7]

There was a prophecy that the future ruler of the world would arise in the East (Tacitus' version makes the rulers plural, accommodating Titus). The prisoner Josephus asked for an interview and told Vespasian that he would become Emperor. His prophecy belongs after Nero's death. At the siege of Jerusalem in the summer of 70 Titus was also equipped with a wonder: God's anger caused the city's water supplies to dry up; for Titus they flowed plentifully. T. Rajak notes that the prophecy is used more to exculpate Josephus for giving up the cause of the rebels than to extol the Roman Messiah. (The same goes for the other Jewish prophecy made to Vespasian, that of Rabbi Johanan b. Zakkai.) In 69 more stress on the future Emperor's rôle was likely. The immediate gain to both sides was clear: Vespasian secured the support of heaven in the eyes of some Jews, and the prophet, if proved right, could expect rewards. The same rationale goes for Titus' visit to the shrine of Aphrodite at Paphos at the beginning of 69, and Vespasian's own, whenever it was, to that of the deity of Mt Carmel, where a priest told him, in the presence of his entourage, that 'his plan, whether to build a house, extend his property, or increase the number of his slaves [a nice touch from a provincial!], would succeed: he would be the master of a mighty seat, vast properties, and an abundance of men'.[8]

Few events of Vespasian's life have attracted more attention than his dealings with Alexandrian deities. The sources differ on timing and details. Vespasian, unaccompanied, entered the temple of the venerated oracular god Serapis to enquire about his future and 'saw' a man called Basilides ('Son of the monarch') whom he knew to be elsewhere; Basilides presented him with palm branches, garlands, and cakes. On another occasion Vespasian was approached by a blind man and one with a crippled hand or foot, and asked for a cure: wiping the eyes with his spittle and treading the limb with his own foot. His courtiers encouraged Vespasian, but it was only when qualified men assured him that cures were medically possible that he agreed.[9]

Besides differing as to whether miracles or vision came first, Tacitus and Suetonius diverge on their place in the history of the coup. Suetonius has the visit to Serapis heralding the coming of messengers with news of the second battle of Cremona and of Vitellius' death (events separated by almost two months); and the miracles perhaps when Vespasian had been recognized at Rome: they enhanced the prestige and majesty of a man new to his position. Tacitus puts both events (miracles first, the reason for consulting Serapis) after the Flavians were known to have occupied Rome: Vespasian is waiting for winds favourable to his return. The two datings lead to different perceptions of what happened. On Suetonius' view, the apparition is aimed in part at reassuring Vespasian; on Tacitus', both events are directed more at the local population. There is force in the view that Vespasian consulted a local deity to achieve sacral legitimation soon after his arrival. Backed by Jewish royalty and a Prefect of Jewish descent, Vespasian, although known as the general who had put down the Jewish revolt, needed the Alexandrian Greeks. It is plausible to put both events close together in the winter of 69–70, before the capture of Rome was known.[10]

To the world at large the miracles were a metaphor of the new régime's healing powers, reluctant though the physician was. But in Alexandria the Emperor was a thaumaturge such as Apollonius of Tyana or Jesus of Nazareth, with powers to put predecessors in the shade. The descendants of Mark Antony (Germanicus and Claudius; Gaius and Nero) had enjoyed particular devotion from the Alexandrians; neither Antony nor Germanicus – the only other member of this family to visit – had ever done anything like this.[11]

The implications of the episodes turn out the same: Vespasian was the legitimate King of Egypt, and one favoured by and intimately associated with Serapis. At some time during his stay, possibly immediately after his arrival, or perhaps after he had attended a performance in the Hippodrome and after the miracles, Vespasian was saluted by his Prefect in terms that included not only 'Caesar the god', but 'son of Ammon', that is, of Re, a title of Pharaohs and Ptolemies in their capacity as kings. In the temple, he was King, and received the garlands due to one, and the boughs of a victor. The disabled men he cured were directed to him by Serapis in a dream, and the miracles were fit for Serapis himself, whose mediator he was, one involving precisely the part of Vespasian's body that was venerated for its powers in the deity.[12]

All classes in a difficult city alien to Vespasian were being won over. The vision legitimated him as the protégé of a deity once of particular importance to upper-class Greeks, while the miracles had an instant effect on a mixed crowd like the audience assembled for Ti. Julius Alexander's speech. Those who delivered the loyalty of the Alexandrians also benefited. The priests of Serapis, who vouched for the fact that Vespasian was alone in the temple, earned at least as much gratitude as those of Paphos and Carmel, while Serapis and the Fortune of Alexandria rose in status as protectors of the Emperor. Indeed, Alexandrian priests might well have been concerned to rival the hold that Mt Carmel had gained. What Suetonius presents as conferring charisma on the Emperor enhanced the status of the city where it was conferred. Puny communities joined in. The people of Tegea in the Peloponnese convinced themselves of Vespasian's divine right when the Emperor's features were discerned on antique vases that they unearthed. It was worth claiming credit from him for the minutest share in the elevation – especially if Tegea was engaged in local rivalries.[13]

Such political factors do not turn Vespasian into a cynical manipulator of religion and superstition: he seems at worst a willing dupe of stage-managers, notably Alexander, who had already won over the city in the summer of 68 by concessions that exalted Galba and strengthened his own position. Josephus ignores these events: the manipulation of gentile cults in a city notorious for virulent hatred of Jews was repugnant – and put his own work in the shade. But Alexander's efforts did not make up for Vespasian's money hunger. In 71 Titus returned from Judaea and took part, with studied affability, in the consecration rites of the Apis bull at Memphis. Suetonius does not reveal where he got the idea that because Titus wore a diadem at the ceremony, he was thinking of rebellion; perhaps it went back to Alexandrian wishful thinking, and was taken up by disaffected Romans.[14]

Tacitus argues for the influence of omens on the Emperor, and points out that Vespasian kept a personal astrologer, a colourless claim by comparison with the lurid anecdotes that surround Tiberius' relationship with Thrasyllus. Any emperor needed to be seen to know his stars. A court astrologer was insurance against reckless assassination attempts. Vespasian's man was the royally named Seleucus, presumably recruited in Syria. There must have been others, for Dio says that although he banished astrologers from Rome (an edict apparently issued while he was still in Egypt) he habitually consulted the best; Dio names the famous Ti. Claudius Barbillus of Ephesus, son of Thrasyllus and linked with the royal house of Commagene. Late in the reign, in about 77, an extraordinary episode shows Vespasian's way with a hostile seer, the captured German prophetess Veleda. The delighted Vespasian apparently consulted an oracle: what should he do with the 'tall maiden whom the Rhine-drinkers revere'? He was told (it seems) not to keep her in idleness but to make her work, polishing temple furnishings, probably at Ardea where the response was found.[15]

Vespasian's recognition of 1 July as his accession day was a minute step towards the open 'military monarchy' of the third century, but the overriding justification for stressing military power was that victory brought peace – the pretext that Tacitus makes Caecina use when he betrayed Vitellius. The victor had a strong ideological card to play – and a claim to keep up. *VIRTVS AVGVSTA* ('the courage of the Emperor') occurs on early coin issues. It led to *VICTORIA* and *PACIS EVENTVS* ('the coming of peace') for Rome and the *ORBIS TERRARUM* ('the Roman world'); *HONOS* and *VIRTVS*, *FORTVNA REDVX*, and Janus on coins of 71 have convincingly been brought into connection with the Augustan altars of Fortuna Redux and Pax, voted for 19 and 13 BC. Alert tribal corporations of the city of Rome recognized the nexus with their dedications to Fortuna Redux of the Augustan House, the Victory of the Emperor, and the everlasting peace of the Imperial House. By mid-reign numismatic elaborations had given place to plain *PAX*, or the Emperor's: *PAX AVGVSTA/I*. Vespasian is made to leave Alexandria in 70 enjoining Titus to raise up the State by achievements in the field; his own concern was with peace and domestic matters. But Titus' activities meant that he too could be styled 'preserver of the Augustan peace'. The new régime ended a period of frenzy, when troops were out of hand.[16]

Pax was also what Rome imposed on her subjects. Both conceptions have their place in the ideology of the Temple of Peace. The elder Pliny takes a longer, grander view, though he gave Vespasian his place in the scheme: he celebrates, and prays for the eternity of

> the immeasurable majesty of the Roman peace, a gift of the gods, who, it seems, have made the Romans a second sun in human affairs. And all the wonders of the world have been matched in Rome itself over its eight hundred years' history: the buildings it has accumulated are enough to make another world, and of these the culmination is the Temple of Peace itself.[17]

Vespasian and Titus, granted one each, celebrated a joint triumph. One of Vespasian's arches, voted according to Dio the year before, certainly commemorates his military success. The army that had invaded Italy had to have its part in the procession. That was a delicate matter, not to be mishandled as it was when Vitellius' coinage celebrated victory over the Othonians; Vespasian had no real foreign enemy to shelter behind as Octavian had for his victory at Actium. Probably the suppression of Jewish revolt was the main theme, for Suetonius, Dio, and the coins refer to Vespasian's triumph as being 'over the Jews' (*DE IVDAEIS*) and some of the Temple spoils won by Titus are represented on his most famous arch; another bears the claim that he had been the first to succeed in capturing a previously inviolable Jerusalem. They refused the title *'Judaicus'*: they had reconquered a small rebellious province, and the name would have laid them open to the mocking charge of being proselytes; perhaps the offer was made tongue in cheek.[18]

The triumph presupposed a salutation as Imperator. The first for Vespasian had come in the form of his proclamation, but before he died ten years later he had received nineteen more, and Titus fourteen, the first in 70, for Jerusalem: a high rate of striking. Augustus had twenty-one salutations when he died after four and a half decades of supremacy; Claudius, who reigned for less than fourteen years and was saluted Imperator twenty-seven times, has an even higher rate. Given the intense activity of his generals in Britain and Germany, Vespasian's probably seemed better justified.[19]

Victory and peace were an opportunity for display. Nero had closed the Temple of Janus, following Augustus' example, when peace with Parthia was achieved in 63. Vespasian and Titus did the same after their triumph. (It was re-opened in 72.) In the first half of 75 they extended the Pomerium, which carried aggressive connotations, symbolizing an extension of Roman power (*fines*). When Claudius carried out the ceremony in 49 he had been criticized: extending the bounds of the Empire outside Italy was a novel basis; Claudius, who had conquests beyond Ocean itself, was justified. Vespasian and Titus, who used Claudian wording on the inscriptions that marked out the new boundary, must have been able to claim that they had not done less than he had. It may be on the basis of Q. Petillius Cerialis' campaigns in Britain that the Pomerium was extended. Claudius' demonstration of 49 put success in Britain back before the People. Vespasian is the last emperor known to have signalized territorial advancement in this way; the boundary stones set up by Hadrian were restorations. It tells something of his and Claudius' concern for public opinion at Rome and of Romans' perception of the Empire as still on the march.[20]

It was an important ingredient of Vespasian's propaganda to denigrate some of his predecessors, contrasting despotism and incompetence with his own steadiness and care for the free functioning of the State. Nero had destroyed himself, but Vitellius, like his troops (after the Flavian sack of Cremona), needed demolition. Cruel military tyranny drove Josephus' liberator and his troops to almost uncontrollable wrath. Self-indulgence, displayed on the march to Rome and slowing it down, was a failing made plausible by the Emperor's portraits and harped on after his death by Licinius Mucianus: a single serving dish requiring a special outdoor kiln had cost a million *HS*. Lastly, childlessness, a blatant useful lie. Vitellius' offspring had been celebrated on his coinage along with his father the censor; the basis for the assertion must be the age of Vitellius' son: 6 or 7 years old, he was a nonentity, unlike Vespasian's boys. It was ironical that the earliest Roman coinage of Vespasian, struck in his absence, had to adapt a Vitellian portrait. The coinage caught the unassuming tone (*civilitas*) of Vespasian's despatch, read to the senate at the end of 69: *LIBERTAS*, it read (a principal theme of Galba and his allies, though used by Vitellius too) and type of a garland; from 70 until the spring of 71 the claim was even more explicit. Coins struck at Rome and *cistophori* styled Vespasian 'Vindicator of the Freedom of the Roman People' and are dedicated to its 'Champion'. The first legend recalls the pretensions of Galba's ally Vindex, the second, as A. Watson has shown, was more explicit: '*adsertor libertatis*' was a legal term for any Roman citizen who 'vindicated the freedom' of another out of slavery.[21]

It was impossible to be consistent in handling the intermediate Emperors, Galba and Otho. Vitellius' victim Otho demanded consideration that would win over troops loyal to him and still in service. Otho's name, unlike that of Vitellius and his brother, stood in the Acts of the Arval Priesthood. But Otho had also rebelled against Galba, whom the Roman world had recognized as the man to take over from the Julio-Claudians – though he tried to rally followers of the dead Galba against their common enemy Vitellius. The logic was impossible, and there were powerful survivors to placate or neutralize. The connection between Otho and Vespasian was factitious: Otho's letter asking Vespasian to avenge him and come to the aid of the State was communicated to the troops in the summer of 69. It had the same purpose as the rumour of legionary transfers to the north-west. Once the war was won Vespasian could forget an emperor whose image was unacceptably like Nero's.[22]

On one view, Vespasian was Galba's successor; Antonius Primus in northern Italy ordered busts of Galba out of store when he had none of Vespasian. There was little mileage with the armies in an emperor who had proved vacillating, vengeful, and mean, more at Rome, among the better off: demonstrations in favour of the late emperor broke out when news of Otho's death arrived. On Domitian's first entry into the senate he proposed that tribute should be paid by restoring Galba's measures to the statute book; his are the only ordinances besides those of Augustus, Tiberius, Claudius, and the Flavians which have to be observed by magistrates in the Flavian Municipal Law of Irni; offices conferred by him were also validated. The senator Curtius Montanus proposed that Piso should also receive honour. The logic was good, but the hint of regret, and the encouragement to surviving

Pisones, unwelcome. Officials responsible for carrying out the decree did nothing. The senate also voted Galba a statue surmounting a column decorated with ships' beaks, to be placed at the spot in the Forum where he died. Suetonius claims that Vespasian disallowed the statue too. Restoring the measures had a practical value and was adequate recognition; the column with its reminiscence of Augustus' victory in the civil wars would overshadow Flavian public life (probably the purpose of its promoters), and Vespasian annexed the Augustan column for his own coinage. The excuse for refusing was factitious: Galba in Spain had sent undercover assassins against him (as Nero had against Galba himself). In the range of possibilities between '*damnatio memoriae*' (itself allowing selection from a menu) and deification the content of honours determined whether they were acceptable to current rulers or not. Under Titus coin types of Galba were revived; it may have been then that the story of Titus' hopes of being declared his heir began circulating.[23]

New emperors routinely made reference to the Founder, as incoming Soviet Communist Party secretaries would promise a return to Marxism-Leninism. Gaius and especially Claudius, after Gaius had destroyed faith in novelties, promised a return; the innocent Nero was to be an improvement. For Vespasian, instant founder of a ready-made dynasty which in statue groups at Brixia and Olympia supplemented or replaced that of Augustus, the analogy was closer than it had been for any Julio-Claudian. The centenary of Actium fell in 70: like Octavian Vespasian had the 'duty' of wresting power from unworthy hands. For the elder Pliny he slipped easily into the rôle of the new proponent of moral and physical regeneration.[24]

Invoking Augustus implied claims about the free working of organs of State, especially the senate. We shall see how the senate fared in practice; A. Stylow notices *libertas* disappearing from the coins after 71. Vespasian had statements to make more closely related to the needs of the post-war age. His greatest building, the Colosseum, had originally been planned by Augustus, he discovered. There were parallels between Vespasian's useful programme, temples, roads, and bridges, and that of Augustus, and he restored the Augustan Theatre of Marcellus. Suetonius and others mention Vespasian's modesty in ensuring that the names of the original builders were inscribed on his reconstructions; that recalls Augustus' own claim to have given credit to his predecessors – so multiplying his own.[25]

There was a closer model: Claudius, though he had made brutal inroads on the ranks of the aristocracy, had, like Vespasian, restored stability and could be presented as going wrong in his last five years when Nero was forced on him as heir. Vespasian restored the cult of the Deified Claudius – although that title was not obligatory – and completed the temple begun by Agrippina; he held the censorship that Claudius had revived, improved Claudian legislation, and adopted a style of government attentive to the people's needs, including attempts to reclaim public land for the State.

Vespasian resumed the conquest of Britain where his own career had taken off, and Philostratus makes him claim in Alexandria that he bore with Nero for the sake of Claudius, who had made him consul and adviser. So he also showed *pietas* (due devotion), a quality of Augustus, towards Caesar and other great Romans. The only snag was that Claudius' being Vespasian's model gave point to the sneer that Titus was a coming Nero (so would replacing Nero's head with that of Titus on a statue group at Olympia, if it had been well known).[26]

If we took his death-bed words seriously ('Oh dear! I think I'm turning into a god') Vespasian would seem to have held his own 'cult' in slight regard. In fact they show critics mocking it. His position and the dynasty's had been enhanced through cult, and the immortality of the dynasty as a whole was implied in the '*Aeternitas*' of the coinage. Deceased members might be exploited when official cult of the living was out of the question, as in Rome, but it remains uncertain when Vespasian's daughter Domitilla (or his wife of the same name) was posthumously granted the title Augusta and joined the thin ranks of deified women: the elevation of either is more convincingly to be assigned to Titus or Domitian. In the proemion of Valerius Flaccus' *Argonautica*, the Emperor's apotheosis as a constellation offering guidance to navigators is 'predicted'. That suggests early concern with Vespasian's future as a deified emperor (*divus*), but on balance the passage still looks most like a work of hindsight, composed under Domitian rather than Titus.[27]

There were developments in the imperial cult. In intellectual circles, represented by the elder Pliny, a tired convention was rejuvenated by attaching it to Vespasian's benevolent deeds and enterprises:

> For mortal to help mortal, that is God, and this is the way to everlasting glory. This is the road that Roman leaders have taken, and it is this road that the greatest ruler of all time is treading, at a pace favoured by heaven, along with his offspring, as he brings relief to an exhausted world.

Cult was no longer adulation demanded as a right, but 'the very ancient custom of showing gratitude to benefactors by enrolling such men in the ranks of the divine'.[28]

Individual tributes have to be distinguished from those of communities and province-wide establishments, and arrangements set up on the initiative of the worshippers from those imposed from above. In Italy it had become accepted in Augustus' time for individuals to take oath by the Genius of the Emperor; under Vespasian a wax tablet from Herculaneum shows his 'offspring's' tutelary deities invoked. Some cities offered worship: Vespasian at Pompeii had the annual Flamen of the living Emperor, functioning presumably in the 'Temple of Vespasian'.[29]

In the provinces the reign was a 'climax'. More provinces are found participating, and practice developed, as in Tarraconensis and in the East, into cult of the Julio-Claudian (and then Flavian) *Divi* and the incumbent ruler, with Roma as adjunct. But when new cults were instituted, and by whom, is uncertain. Vespasian is credited with introducing it within his first three years into Baetica, Narbonensis, and Africa; into the *conventus* of north-west Spain, perhaps into Upper Germany and elsewhere, his purpose to secure loyalty. More probably initiatives came from the provinces rivalling each other for attention: Baetica had already been refused permission for a cult of Tiberius in 25. The first three areas had long been loyal to Rome, and Baetica and Narbonensis were showing more signs of 'Romanization', however defined, than Tarraconensis and Lusitania, where the cult had existed since Augustus' death. In Africa Otho adumbrated new rights ('*iura*'), which may have included the provincial council that was soon to maintain and staff the cult. For Baetica there is a more cautious view, that the provincial cult was organized only after Vespasian's death. But provincials were less restrained than Romans in the capital. In 77 the province of Lusitania dedicated 5 pounds of gold, probably in the form of a bust, to Titus. Another advance: Augustus and Livia alone were the objects of cult under Claudius, the son of the Emperor here. But enthusiasm for Vespasian was only to be expected in the peninsula, after his grant of Latin rights, and attention to an old emperor's heir equally natural. Of individual cities, Ipsca Contributa in Baetica celebrated higher status by putting up a temple to the benefactor.[30]

In the East temples had always been allowed to emperors during their lifetime, and this continued, while cities and individuals went on seeking attention with various offerings. Early dedications to the Emperor are recorded, as might be expected, from Pamphylia, Rhodes, Lesbos, and Bithynia. At Cestrus in Cilicia a dedication to Vespasian by the People was erected in the Emperor's temple in the second half of 76. It was mild language when the proconsul of Bithynia in 77–8 'consecrated' the new gymnasium at Prusias ad Hypium that a local benefactor had constructed in honour of 'the House of the Augustan Imperatores'. Even in Egypt the Emperor did not always figure as a deity but sometimes in conservative style as the person for whom dedications were made, as at Karanis in the Fayyum, following Neronian precedent, to the crocodile gods Pnepheros and Petesouchus, on behalf of Vespasian and his whole house.[31]

The dynasty notoriously lacked *auctoritas* (prestige), but acquired ready-made *maiestas* (majesty) from the *Lex Iulia* that provided a capital penalty for diminishing the majesty of the Roman People and its magistrates. What constituted 'diminishing majesty' was elastic: certainly violence or material damage but, by extension, insult written and oral, direct or in a history or drama. By AD 14, too, the majesty of the dynasty had taken on a quasi-religious aspect: to attack it was an act of irreligion (*impietas*). Vespasian's reign, unlike Domitian's, never became notorious for these trials. None the less 'impiety toward the house of the Augusti' remained a real bogey.[32]

The resurgence that Vespasian's success was to bring about was intellectual and moral as well as physical, but he was far from establishing the control of intellectual activity that has been credited to him. The Emperor's education was evidently unremarkable, and he posed as a plain man, bringing Cato the Censor and his imitator C. Marius to mind, though like Cato he was an author and agile with words. The Homer and Menander that he quoted is brought out by Suetonius in the context of witticisms, some earthy; R. Herzog's picture of his intercourse with savants of the Alexandrian Museum has something of Hadrian about it. Vespasian had his sons well educated, especially Titus, if he shared a school-room with Britannicus. Both were known as poets – in 76 Titus had boldly written on that ill-omened phenomenon, a comet – with a taste for literature and architecture. Wise Minerva, Domitian's patron deity, already had a temple in Vespasian's Rome. For wider benefit he founded chairs of Greek and Latin rhetoric at Athens and Rome, with salaries of 100,000 *HS* paid from the imperial treasury; one of the earliest holders was Quintilian. Philosophy was passed over, not surprisingly given the trouble that Vespasian experienced with Stoics and Cynics; the theory was that they did not work for pay. At the end of 75 he accorded teachers of grammar and rhetoric, doctors, and physiotherapists (again not philosophers, who waited until Trajan's reign) privileges in the cities in which they resided, on pain of a 40,000 *HS* fine for infringement; violence against them was answerable to the Roman people as impiety towards the dynasty. Eighteen years later Domitian found abuses: teachers and medical practitioners took on slave pupils for money; they lost their immunity. Both decisions evidently pleased the cities, since both were published on the same stone at Pergamum. For the long-established guild of Travelling Athletes Dedicated to Heracles, whose members' performances gave pleasure to hundreds of thousands, Vespasian confirmed existing privileges, as Claudius had before him.[33]

Vespasian is presented as a supporter of individual men of letters and artists, although Pliny laments that his enthusiasm did not produce the success it deserved in the sciences. A poet named, probably, Saleius Bassus, who sold out his recitals but allegedly remained hard-up, received half a million *HS*, a tragedian probably called Apellaris 400,000, which would qualify him, if he met the other requirements, to be a knight, and the cithara-players Terpnus and Diodorus, who had probably appeared at the old-fashioned performances of music and declamation that inaugurated the restored Theatre of Marcellus, 200,000 each; lesser artists received tips of ten or forty thousand. The man who altered the head of the Neronian colossus to that of Helius, and perhaps the restorer of Praxiteles' Coan Venus, if this was the statue Vespasian dedicated in his Temple of Peace, earned personal fees.[34]

Social and political factors play their part in forming the aesthetic of an age, along with literary and stylistic drives. The elegance and allusive brevity of late Julio-Claudian art and literature was vulnerable to social changes that brought to the fore new and 'provincial' men; and in Petronius' novel the vulgar extravagance of the freedman Trimalchio was held up to mockery. A return to plainness was safe, and undercut *nouveaux riches*. Under Vespasian there was an evasive reaction to the fear of annihilation that Nero's régime and the Year of the Four Emperors engendered: the *outré* was dangerous, hierarchy defined by usefulness rather than display. Tacitus ascribed the new style and manners to imitation of the Emperor himself, but a public figure and the public interact. Consensus in politics and acceptance of the Princi-pate as a framework for political activity were further advanced in reaction to Domitian's 'terror' of 93–6: Pliny's *Panegyric* is their monument, Tacitus' *Annals* a sceptical commentary.[35]

In Latin there emerges a staider, more classical style, with the prose of Cicero as an antecedent admired by Quintilian, who died in his mid-sixties at the end of the Flavian era; his pupils included the younger Pliny. Tacitus of the *Dialogus* (set in 74–5, written perhaps a generation later) is Ciceronian. Both writers knew that oratory was in decline, but only Tacitus exposed the political cause; Quintilian had expressed approval of Flavian practitioners and hopes of the future. In verse Martial (*c*.40–104) published his celebration of the Colosseum shows (*De Spectaculis*) in 80, but his epigrams and the late *Silvae* of P. Papinius Statius (*c*.45–96), modelled on Lucan's, were not in the genre that was most in vogue: epic, with Virgil as a model. The most famous exponents are C. Valerius Flaccus Setinus Balbus, son of a Naples school-master, who died in the early 90s, leaving his *Argonautica* unfinished, and Statius. Ti. Catius Silius Italicus (*c*.25–101 and *cos*. 68), was author of an epic on a theme handled by his fellow-townsman Livy, the Second Punic War; a careful writer in Pliny's eyes, whose choice of subject shows him in tune with his times, as did his restoration of Virgil's tomb at Naples. Statius' *Thebaid*, begun in about 79, treated dangerous topics: power, the rivalry of brothers. 'Court' poets, absent from the decade of Vespasian, reappear under Domitian. As their reputations have been reassessed, views of their tributes to the dyn-asty, once thought servile, have also changed: 'fury' is ascribed to Statius' praise of Domitian. But the picture is complex; darkness is present, as the background to felicity, at its deepest under Nero and in 68–9. This is the weapon of the literary man: boldness in portraying tyrants is a challenge to the ruler of the day, who dare not recognize himself in them and is forced to learn the lessons of the past; the poet is interpreter and guide.[36]

In architecture too there was a return to older classical styles, in sculpture to Atticism, in portraiture to realism, 'illusionistic art', skilfully rendered and technically effective. The epoch has a flavour of its own, but there is a danger of over-schematization. In painting it was naturally a merit for Attius Priscus, an artist involved in a programme of restoration, to be close to the ancient style. And the 'Fourth', intricate, style at Pompeii, exemplified in the House of the Vettii, with painted architectural features apparently enlarging the room and plain panels alternating with *aediculae* in which the larger pictures seem to be hung on screens, is no longer thought of as a final, 'classical', phase in accord with literary tastes; it is one of several styles available contemporaneously, and goes back to the time of Claudius.[37]

In religion the intellectual climate of Flavian Rome (and the Empire) began to change, for all Silius Italicus' emphasis on traditional Roman religion. Established State religion did not suffer, but a renaissance of Egyptian gods outside Egypt was noticed by A. Henrichs, perhaps due in part to the origin of Vespasian's principate in Alexandria, but in the main a product of the increasing unity of the Empire, economic, cultural, and political, after a century of peace. The decisive change, pin-pointable to this decade, was the precipitation of Christianity into an Empire-wide religion, from being a sect of Judaism, although as yet it did not attract unfavourable attention from the authorities. The process begun by Paul in Claudius' time needed the upheavals of the Jewish War, in particular the destruction of the Temple of Jerusalem, for success. No longer would converts to Christianity look to Jerusalem as the centre of the church. It began a life independent of Judaism and the Jews, often one of pernicious hostility to them. For Judaism itself the loss of the Temple and the reinforcement of the Diaspora with refugees from Judaea achieved its effect more slowly: the development of individuals' consciousness of what it meant to be a Jew.[38]

6

A NEW EMPEROR AND HIS OPPONENTS

With Rome under Flavian occupation the senate met on 21 December, the day after Vitellius died, to legalize Vespasian's position. Their conferment, on the motion of the consul designate Valerius Asiaticus, of tribunician power, *maius imperium*, and customary prerogatives such as membership of the four leading priesthoods would then be ratified by the people. There also had to be consulships for Vespasian and Titus, and a praetorship with *imperium* equal to a consul's for Domitian. The young men were each honoured with the designation 'Caesar' and 'Leaders of the Youth' (*Principes Iuventutis*), a title devised for Augustus' adopted sons and picked up for Nero as first in the younger generation of the imperial family. Then a delegation had to be appointed to present the senate's respects to Vespasian, as they had done to Galba in 68.[1]

Augustus had taken decades to perfect the cocktail. His first attempt was in 27 BC, but an upheaval followed in 24–3, and there was a major adjustment in 19, when *imperium* within the city lost when Augustus had given up the consulship in 23 was added to his tribunician power; he did not become Pontifex Maximus until 12 BC, nor receive the honorific title of Father of his Country (*Pater Patriae*) until 2 BC. Tiberius too came into his powers gradually, and with a lacuna in the period between his first grant of tribunician power in 6 BC, combined with *imperium* in the East, and AD 13, when his *imperium* was made equal to that of Augustus; it was only in March 15, the year after Augustus' death, that he became Pontifex Maximus, and he steadfastly refused nomination as Father of his Country. At the moment of his 'accession' there was embarrassingly little more to offer him than the name Augustus itself (that was Augustus' plan). It was quite different with the youthful Gaius Caligula in 37, who received the powers in a bunch on accession. Claudius too was a private individual at the time of Caligula's assassination in 41, and took them *en bloc*; Nero on the other hand had been invested at least with proconsular power outside the city three years before his accession. There were no such preparations in 68. Each claimant of that and the following year, took his essential powers, except the supreme Pontificate, all at once.[2]

79

The speed that Tacitus unfairly stressed in the case of Vitellius, contrasting it with the slow build-up of earlier emperors, was the inevitable aftermath of violence for Vespasian too. Josephus innocently stresses the speed of events: the people had a single festival celebrating Vespasian's accession and Vitellius' downfall. The votes were taken with greater alacrity because of the promising letter from Vespasian, necessarily composed weeks before the final victory, at latest in November after he heard of the victory at Cremona, but designed for this occasion.[3]

Mucianus had also written a letter to the senate, which preceded his own arrival by a matter of days. It was anomalous, coming from a mere legate, and it was heard with distaste, probably at the first meeting. But Mucianus was the possessor of a ring given him by Vespasian, as the hated M. Agrippa had been in 23 BC of one entrusted him by Augustus when he supposed himself on his deathbed. Mucianus' and Primus' supremacy was recognized at once by the grant of triumphal and consular insignia respectively, those of Mucianus nominally for success against the Dacians. The lesser men Cornelius Fuscus and Arrius Varus, who became Prefect of the Praetorian Guard on the suicide of the Vitellian incumbent Julius Priscus, obtained those of a praetor. All that T. Flavius Sabinus could receive was a censor's funeral. The agenda was completed by a decision to restore the Capitol; as a religious matter it should have come at the top.[4]

Votes of thanks to commanders, armies, and dependent rulers, like the conferment of lesser offices, followed on 1 January. Tettius Julianus was deprived of his praetorship for failing to follow his legion over to Vespasian's side and D. Plotius Grypus received it instead. Governors, prefects, procurators, new consuls were designated, and Vespasian's freedman Hormus was allowed the status of a Roman knight.[5]

Mucianus had entered Rome and taken command as an emperor might. There was work on two fronts (besides getting army and provinces under control): he must confirm the political foundations of the new régime, and secure his own position in it. When he parted from Vespasian he had been called the Emperor's 'colleague', a resonant word first applied to M. Agrippa. The first task committed him to distasteful acts: the execution (outside the city) of Calpurnius Galerianus, son of the man who had conspired against Nero in 65 and, equally importantly, son-in-law of the suspect governor of Africa, his cousin L. Piso; Vitellius' young son was also killed, and probably Crassus Scribonianus, elder brother of Galba's chosen heir. When Vespasian arrived he could balance Mucianus' ruthlessness by an easy act of generosity, conferring a dowry on Vitellius' daughter. Truly Vespasian improved on Claudius' performance in keeping his hands clean; physical absence on State business gave him an alibi far superior to absent-mindedness or weakness of character. But for the moment public opinion did not matter to a victorious commander who was now legate of a legitimate Emperor and from 1 January able to work on a guilty and frightened senate through the incoming praetor

Domitian. A senior consular, Mucianus would speak early in debate and could afford to coat his speeches with civility.[6]

Mucianus' rival Antonius Primus was soon brought low. For a few days he was man of the moment, although even then his reward was one that had gone to equestrian Prefects of the Praetorian Guard. But beside him stood Domitian, who had been in the city the whole time, would think of himself as having participated in the same struggle, and had been saluted 'Caesar' by Primus' troops. It was a high priority for Mucianus to shatter this constellation. If it came to a fight Primus and his ally Arrius Varus, now Prefect of the Guard, could not win, although they could count on the Praetorians and the troops victorious at Cremona, especially VII Gemina and Varus' III Gallica. Mucianus temporized, rewarding his opponents' subordinates and promising Primus the governorship of Tarraconensian Spain, which in the event went to a senior figure, Ti. Plautius Aelianus (suff. 45), who was to enjoy a glorious culmination to his career. Three of the Danubian legions (VIII Augusta, XI Claudia, and XIII Gemina) were despatched to Germany to deal with the Batavian revolt; VII Gemina and III Gallica went into their permanent quarters (Pannonia and Syria respectively) along with VII Claudia. The disarming continued with the reduction of Varus from the Guard Prefect to administration of the grain supply (*Praefectura Annonae*), and Primus was withdrawn from Domitian's advisory board. While the rebellion on the Rhine and in Gaul raged, Primus was invited by Domitian to accompany him to Gaul. Mucianus flatly refused to allow it, and when Primus left it was for the court of last resort, Vespasian in Alexandria, and under shadow of the dangerous accusation that he had incited Crassus Scribonianus to aim for the Principate. The Emperor was unwilling to do anything for him, whatever he thought of the charge: Mucianus was in control, and in any case Primus, using force to bring Vitellius down, had failed to save Vespasian's own brother from it. Primus was lucky to be allowed retirement in his native Tolosa, where he would have scanned the memoirs and histories as they came out and found himself charged with insubordination, arrogance, and responsibility for the sack of Cremona.[7]

With the end of civil war, senatorial politics began again, a familiar game played for high stakes (personal advancement and the functions and status of the House as a whole) by known rules. But now there were important matters to settle, and the senate divided, perhaps recalling the shortlived liberty that it had enjoyed when Nero was dead and Galba absent. Some began looking to punish the miscreants who had flourished under the last Julio-Claudian emperors by sycophancy, informing, or prosecution. They acted for personal vengeance or as a matter of principle or to deter further villainy or for all three reasons. Some, looking forward, had a far-reaching concern for the form that Vespasian's principate should take and the part that the senate itself was to play in government. The long run, too, directed attention to the way in which the new but elderly Emperor's successor was to be chosen, and who he was to be. All this was also of interest to miscreants, to whom the 'constitution' of the Principate meant very little but who depended for their success on proven reliability and loyalty to a current régime. These two groups are known from the names of their most prominent representatives, C. Helvidius Priscus of the first, Eprius Marcellus of the second. They were separated by a mass of senators ranging from energetic careerists such as Cn. Julius Agricola and M. Ulpius Traianus, whose rise did not involve threats to the life and property of their peers, to undistinguished quietists who hardly rose at all, or only by birth. Few men brought in by Claudius and Nero can have stood for senatorial rights. Others may have shifted ground after the dangers of the last years. Vespasian won over Thrasea Paetus' associate Q. Paconius Agrippinus, who by 71 was his legate in Cyrenaica.[8]

Amid such divisions the cause of the senate stood no chance. Events followed one another swiftly, revealing the issues at stake, the composition of the groups and the currents of politics at the very first meeting of the new régime. Most consulars had nodded approval of or applauded Asiaticus' proposals for Vespasian's honours, and those for his subordinates, and of the motion to restore the Capitol; a minority demonstrated loyalty with orotund verbal support. After consulars came praetors designate, and Helvidius Priscus, who had been elected under Galba (more probably than under Vitellius, with whom he had conducted a verbal duel in the House during the summer), expressed himself in language designed to pay due respect to an emperor who merited it; there was nothing insincere in what he said. We have no details, but this speech made Helvidius' stance clear and, Tacitus tells us, was well received.[9]

Immediately after the honours on the agenda of 21 December must have come the question of choosing members of the embassy sent to hail the new Emperor. It raised two issues: who was to be offered to Vespasian as the senate's representative, more fundamentally whether the senate was to take up a position on this point at all by expressing its judgment (*iudicium*) on the method of their choice, and so on any point of political significance. The position of the consul designate, Valerius Asiaticus, was delicate, mainly because of his adherence to Vitellius, who had offered him his daughter, partly because of the influence in his native Gaul that had proved fatal to his father under Claudius. Following inoffensive precedent he proposed that the members should be selected by drawing lots, Eprius Marcellus offering heartfelt support, as well he might, given his history as a Neronian accuser. Helvidius Priscus suggested a delegation hand-picked by magistrates under oath, which was evidently to be followed by a vote of the senate on the men proposed. Helvidius made a neat point: the composition of the embassy touched upon the honour of the Emperor, who had been a friend of three of Nero's victims of 66, including Thrasea Paetus (Helvidius' father-in-law) and Q. Barea Soranus, with whom Titus had been connected by marriage.

The senate should give the Emperor a clear idea of whom it approved as men fit to be his advisers.[10]

This was a well-chosen battleground. The issue of imperial friends went back to Julius Caesar. He and all the emperors, even Augustus, had been indiscreet in their choice of friends: Maecenas and Sallustius Crispus, whom Augustus bequeathed to Tiberius, and the latter's Sejanus, above all the freedmen Narcissus and Pallas under Claudius, and their Neronian successors, had usurped the consiliar rôle, using it against the interests of the senate as a whole and against individual senators, earning hatred as well as envy. A new Principate was time to start afresh. An emperor could not do without advisers; Vespasian had held councils of war throughout his attempt on the Principate, and his advisory board would now have to be amplified; the men chosen for the embassy should figure in it. Just for that, Marcellus had to stand his ground. He cited precedent and, more sinister, the anxiety of a 'new' Princeps, looking round to see who his true friends were (it was clear who took the place of eyes). Worse, Marcellus, showing prophetic insight as well, reminded the senate that it was they who had condemned the victims, expressing *iudicium senatus* with a vengeance; they were all incriminated. He won: traditional procedures attracted the moderates; prominent personalities were afraid of jealousy if they were picked.[11]

So Vespasian's *consilium*, chosen by him, as Trajan's was to be, showed continuity with that of an earlier epoch, and there was no radical change under his successors: Vibius Crispus, the elder Acilius Aviola who had served under Claudius, the general Rubrius Gallus, A. Didius Gallus Fabricius Veiento (*cos.* II 80), a former friend of Nero, and the notorious blind prosecutor L. Valerius Catullus Messallinus (*cos.* I with Domitian in 73), all figure in Juvenal's skit on the Domitianic council, summoned to consider a monstrous fish. That some of Vespasian's counsellors were disliked is suggested by a point offered by Suetonius in favour of Titus: he brought in new faces, which his successors kept.[12]

The problem persisted, becoming acute when Domitian in 96 left behind a hated memory and a problem for Nerva, who was in no position to alienate his predecessor's power brokers. The younger Pliny in 100 declared in his panegyric on Trajan that that Princeps chose his friends from among the best men, those who had been particularly hated by the late tyrant; in the fourth-century *Scriptores Historiae Augustae* survived a critic's comment on the great men who were powerful in both reigns and beyond: Domitian had chosen good friends. The two accounts may be reconciled, if we allow Pliny to treat Trajan's tolerance of a now helpless group of 'good men' as 'friendship' and Trajan's critic to express a high regard for potentates who might have been his emperor's rivals.[13]

Another aspect of the senate's rôle arose from the agenda of 21 December: the restoration of the Capitol. Financing it was the problem. From public funds, Helvidius proposed, with the help of Vespasian, a suggestion which – with its pointed implication that the financial resources of the supreme council of State were having to be supplemented from those of an individual – his peers passed over. The problem over the Capitol was indeed only part of the whole plight of the State Treasury. It was presumably the expenditure proposed for this that gave rise to the complaints of the officials in charge of it and so to the idea of setting up an economy commission, which Helvidius warmly espoused; as praetor designate, perhaps a future Prefect of the Treasury, he had a legitimate interest in its health. This met with a tribunician veto. As to the Capitol, it had been a bone of contention between leading senators, Catulus and Pompey, on an earlier occasion, 62 BC; that must not happen again. A distinguished knight, L. Vestinus, was commissioned to oversee the work. The site was rededicated on 21 June – with Helvidius in official attendance. When the work was begun, later in the year, Vespasian carried off the first hod of rubble, showing who was in charge.[14]

Third, a theme implicit in the debate on the embassy, the future of the men who had betrayed the House and their peers for their own interest, began to sound out brassy and discordant. At the first session of the senate Musonius Rufus, after the dispute over the State Treasury, succeeded in getting P. Egnatius Celer arraigned for his part in the prosecution of Barea Soranus. J.K. Evans has shown the rationale behind this: under Galba Helvidius had failed in his attempt to bring Eprius Marcellus to book, so those intent on vengeance adopted an oblique approach by tackling a man who had given evidence against Soranus, Vespasian's friend and former connection by marriage. The trial was set for the next session, but was delayed until 1 January, with a second hearing on the 9th or the 15th, which suggests that negotiations were going on behind the scenes. None the less, when the trial came on, Celer was convicted and returned to the exile from which he had emerged, with loss of property. It was a small beginning: Celer was a provincial, probably from Berytus, and no senator, but the arraignment promised greater things.[15]

This success encouraged Junius Mauricus to demand access to the imperial archives, so that all informers might be unmasked. This was unthinkable to the new régime, not just because it would mean the senate being torn apart by the revelations, but because the men who would go under were just those who might be most useful. They would be loyal, if protected, and some were of a rank that made them key members of the senate and potential governors of important provinces. Domitian declined, without the Emperor's sanction, to release papers for inspection.[16]

An alternative, less satisfactory, method of exposing the guilty men was now proposed: each member of the senate should take oath by the gods that he had not profited from ruining any of his peers. Swearing such an oath before the full House was an ordeal, opening the way to murmurs, direct challenge, even a threat of violence: failing to take it amounted to confessing.

In the event only three men, including an ex-consul, C. Paccius Africanus, who had helped bring about the death of the Scribonii, were hounded out of the House, though not out of membership; but Africanus managed to implicate a bigger man, who had been harrying him with questions. Polished and indispensable, Q. Vibius Crispus was linked with Vitellius' gluttonous orgies in an ambiguous anecdote: they would have killed him if he had not been ill. Crispus was to be immortalized by Juvenal for his ability to swim with the tide. The young Vipstanus Messalla leapt to the defence of his hated brother the ex-quaestor M. Aquillius Regulus, but was met by a blistering reply from another champion of liberty, Curtius Montanus: there was nothing to fear from a man of Vespasian's age and self-control – but he was not going to be the last Roman Emperor, and later generations of miscreants would learn how they might behave if criminals were let off.[17]

Helvidius guessed from the senate's reception of Montanus' speech that he might even bring down Eprius Marcellus. He began by lauding the harmless orator Cluvius Rufus, using him as a foil for Marcellus. This too was heard with passionate approval. But Marcellus knew that he was in no danger and contemptuously quit the House, followed by Vibius Crispus, leaving it, as he said, to Helvidius to rule over – if he thought he could, with the Emperor's son present. The sitting ended in chaos. At the next session, after a lecture from Domitian on reconciliation, implying that the offenders had had no option, Mucianus spoke up at length for them, and reminded Helvidius of a legal point: resuming an abandoned prosecution would infringe the SC *Turpilianum* of 61.[18]

The pleas for reconciliation were self-interested, made for men who deserved punishment. At the same time, there would have been wisdom in keeping the revolution a velvet one. A compromise might have been achieved, if the senate had had the courage to keep incriminated men off the embassy; but avengers could have taken that in itself as a signal for attack. In the confusion of the days after Vitellius' death, insisted on by Tacitus, nobody had the weight to lay out ground rules, put deals in hand, and guarantee them; even Mucianus' authority was provisional.[19]

Helvidius' failure bred resentment, though the senators were not left to brood in idleness. Two small token fish were dealt with: Octavius Sagitta, guilty of murdering his mistress in 58, and Antistius Sosianus, who in 66 had been brought from his island to aid the prosecution of P. Anteius Rufus and M. Ostorius Scapula and had slipped into Italy again in 69 under cover of the Othonian amnesty. Both went back into exile. Two new cases, from areas always considered within the senate's sphere of interest, also came to its attention. From Sena in Italy came complaints of violence offered to a member of the House, and from the public province Crete and Cyrene a case of extortion by its governor. Together these cases showed the senate what remedy it might adopt.[20]

The paramount issue was still the rôle of the senate as a whole, in spite of its recent setbacks. Once Vespasian's men in Rome had noted the mood of certain senators and seen that they could be defeated piecemeal, it was tempting to find a permanent means of minimizing obstructiveness. This is what seems to have been achieved by the '*Lex de imperio Vespasiani*', which embodied prerogatives available to Vespasian's predecessors rather through the position they held than rights formally granted them, and, in C.E. Stevens' words, 'made him a member of the Julio-Claudian club'. This emerges from the sixth clause preserved, which legalized any action that Vespasian 'deems' (*censebit*) to be of advantage to the State. No senatorial preference could stand before that. And the final clause, legitimating actions taken before the passing of the bill, virtually denied, as Vespasian's choice of date for the celebration of his accession explicitly did, the validity of the senate's recognition of Vitellius from 1 July 69 onward. The sixth clause established a principle; the first liberated the Emperor from the trammels of consultation with the senate in his dealings with Rome's allies and adversaries; and the second and third enabled him to manage the senate to produce legitimate enactments at his discretion; and the fourth strengthened his control over elections to magistracies and so over members who hoped for further advancement by making it easier for 'his' candidates, some of whom might not be widely acceptable, to secure election: the House was faced with a stark choice with Vespasian's candidates: they had to be voted in or out, not be allowed discreetly to come in too low on the poll to win a place; no attempt is made to suggest a precedent for this procedure. It is appropriate, and ironical, that the Tribune Cola di Rienzo, expounding the *Lex* in 1347, suggested that the *Lex* advertised itself as being passed in accord with the expressed wish of the senate.[21]

Such an enactment would not have been introduced without the Emperor's consent, although the clauses may have been drawn up from precedents hastily compiled by friendly legal experts. By the middle of February, the narrative of Tacitus suggests, the senate was already learning its lesson. There may have been further incidents from 70, lost with the rest of Book 5, wrangling at the elections, for example; but they are unlikely to have occurred in April or May, when the senate was in recess. The choppy water that Mucianus, Marcellus, and the others went through in January and February could have been enough to generate the idea of supplementing Vespasian's formal powers. Once drafted, the enactment could have been in Vespasian's hands by the middle of March and passed by the beginning of the recess.[22]

The encounters of January and February 70 were for some only the beginning of a campaign. Helvidius' respectful tone on 21 December was belied by the content of his proposal on the Capitol, and a different tone is alluded to by Suetonius. Vespasian arrived back in Italy at about the end of September to an ecstatic welcome, the mood well caught by the coinage of the year. Crowds poured out to meet him and celebrate his arrival with sacrifices and festivities; those of higher rank could afford to travel furthest, and did. (Vespasian could not receive less than Vitellius.) Helvidius had already been ignoring Vespasian in his praetorian edicts, legitimately, unless they concerned the Emperor directly. Now he greeted him merely by his given name.[23]

The silence of the edicts showed a Roman magistrate managing his office as his own man; but depriving Vespasian of titles confirmed by the senate, though not conferred on their own initiative, was untoward, given his original deference. However, it did not necessarily amount to a denial of Vespasian's position. 'Imperator' within the city was inappropriate, as Tiberius had made clear to the obsequious; the omission of 'Caesar Augustus', now part of Vespasian's name, is more serious, but was probably given greater significance in retrospect, and could be taken less tragically as an attempt to detach the new Princeps from the Julio-Claudian dynasty and all that that meant.[24]

None the less, there was a hardening of Helvidius' attitude after the first failures, and the subsequent passing of the 'Lex de imperio' gave additional reason. When Vespasian arrived in Rome they were brought face to face in the senate. In one episode, Helvidius went so far that the tribunes of the *plebs* (pliable as in December 69) handed him over to lictors and Vespasian left the House. Dio seems to date this scene to Helvidius' praetorship, that is to October–December 70, but it may belong to the following year. Altercations between praetors and tribunes were a paradigm Republican scenario, familiar even under the Empire. But this quarrel was not with tribunes. Insolence was the test for what Helvidius, like Thrasea, cared for: senatorial freedom of speech; it had been a commonplace in Republican public life and emperors keen to show concern for it, like Tiberius and Vitellius, made a point of treating such altercations with subjects (Vitellius' was with Helvidius!) as if they were between equal members of the senate.[25]

Dio, following a pro-Flavian source, attributes Helvidius' demeanour to 'hatred' of Vespasian: he could not leave him alone in private or public; he was courting death with his behaviour and was bound to pay in the end. Doubts are reported, perhaps shared, by Tacitus. Hence A.W. Braithwaite's claim that Helvidius was anxious to find traces of the autocrat in what Vespasian did and was disappointed when there were none to find, and that it was 'opposition for the sake of opposition', a self-seeking attempt to outdo Thrasea Paetus, the model of true glory. It does Helvidius no justice; nor does M.P. Charlesworth's assertion that Helvidius was opposed to any form of Principate, hereditary or elective. Yet there was more to it than a mere desire to 'enhance the prestige of the senate', which is as far as Ch. Wirszubski would go. There was a specific and fundamental disagreement about the rôle of the senate and senators in politics and decision-making. Should the Princeps genuinely consult the senate on matters of importance, as Suetonius claims that Tiberius did in his early years, or get what he 'deemed' advantageously rubber-stamped?[26]

The way that Helvidius made this point, and the fact that he was not content with making it, alienated men who might have sympathized. The philosopher Epictetus, for whom Helvidius was a model of virtue, has Vespasian begging him not to attend the senate, and Helvidius insisting on fulfilling his rôle as a senator – a contrast with Thrasea, who in his day had been criticized for pulling punches, and who for some time had boycotted the House. Helvidius too had been criticized, for lack of persistence in prosecuting Marcellus under Galba, and that was a spur.[27]

One subject roused particular contention, something not touched in 70, although the capture of Jerusalem made Vespasian's clear intentions easier to fulfil: the selection of the next Princeps. Consultation on that was vital, if it were to be guaranteed in the long term. Tiberius wrote and 'asked' the senate to vote tribunician power to his son Drusus. Tacitus mocks a ritual that did not present the House with a ready-made bill. Helvidius is unlikely to have fought for that mere form: a point of substance was at stake: was Vespasian to impose his offspring on the senate, and Titus at that? (Dio has one son to succeed, Suetonius a plural, perhaps using hindsight, or an author writing under Domitian; *liberi* could be either.) The proposal for tribunician power for Titus, to date from 1 July 71, did not go through on the nod. In 71 mints produced the poignant reverse 'Senatorial Accord' (*CONCORDIA SENATVI*), 'Foresight' (*PROVIDENTIA*) made its first appearance, and 'Liberty' fades from the coinage, giving place to themes appropriate to the Triumph: the reduction of Judaea, Peace, Titus and Domitian. Significantly, it was from 71 also that Titus' unprecedented command of the Praetorian Guard dated.[28]

The alternative was genuine selection by the senate itself. This method was appealing after Julio-Claudian heredity and the imposition of a series of emperors by their troops in 69. The senate had been applying it after Gaius Caligula's assassination when Claudius, backed by the Praetorian Guard, concluded the debate. The procedure to be followed once the senate had made the selection was another matter. Possibly Galba had shown a way, although he had promoted Piso Licinianus in a crisis and without consulting the House, the formalities openly assuming the heir. Galba ostentatiously avoided the conventional form of familial adoption employed for Tiberius, Germanicus, and Nero, and the procedure was public rather than a quasi-private matter; it could have been developed into imperial acknowledgment of senatorial choice. Much has been made of his action and its possible relation to the 'adoption' of Trajan by Nerva in 97, which Trajan's panegyrists exploited, and altogether too much of adoption as a method of securing the succession; it conferred distinction on the heir however chosen. Both Galba and Nerva acted in an emergency, men who had no obvious heir. Vespasian – and his son – were having nothing of it. Their immediate predecessor Vitellius had resumed the dynastic approach, having titles conferred on his mother and son. The proposal of mid-71 that Titus should have tribunician power conferred on him, as it had been conferred on Drusus Caesar in April

22, probably led to the relegation of Helvidius Priscus, whether Vespasian walked out of the debate exclaiming apocalyptically that his offspring would succeed him or nobody would, or simply spoke with the confidence of a man with astrological backing. Already in 71 Titus had the military clout and prestige to impose his will.[29]

It is to this period, 70–72, that the exile of Helvidius Priscus and the street philosophers is assigned in the mutilated account of Dio. On the issue of powers for Titus Vespasian could not yield, and Helvidius was relegated. The reason publicly given for the relegation may have been more general: obstructiveness, conduct unbecoming to a senator, giving aid and comfort to seditious aliens. The political attacks, allegedly slanderous, that Helvidius made on Vespasian's 'friends', chief among them Eprius Marcellus, providentially absent since the spring of 70 on his three-year term in Asia, should not have figured prominently: raking over the accusations would only do Helvidius' work for him. The mild form of Helvidius' exile shows Vespasian taking the minimum steps to silence him, but agitation continued and was taken to be seditious, giving a pretext for his execution in about 74 or 75. Friction is in evidence in Tacitus' *Dialogus*, set in the sixth year of the reign: the poet Curiatius Maternus has ruffled the feathers of courtiers by reading his *Cato*, but is not to be intimidated. The piece has intimations that his death is near, as A. Cameron has shown, but the claim that the dialogue preceded condemnation – not natural death – is not convincing; as a victim he has left no other trace. Lesser and younger associates noticeably failed to make their mark during the reign, some to be conceded consulships by a conciliatory Domitian: the younger Helvidius, consul perhaps within the first half-dozen years of Domitian's reign; Q. Junius Arulenus Rusticus, plebeian tribune in 66, praetor in 69 – and suffect only in 92; T. Avidius Quietus, suffect 93; the first two were killed in Domitian's last years.[30]

Outside the senate there was vociferous opposition from Stoic and Cynic philosophers, who should not be lumped together. While Stoics had nothing against monarchy as such, provided that it did not degenerate into tyranny, Cynics left nothing unquestioned. Then there was social status: a well-groomed beard was acceptable in a Roman upper-class household, but street-corner orators are implausible guests: it is the difference between St Paul and St John the Baptist. Cynics who were genuine anarchists must have been independent. Dio implausibly links the exile of Helvidius with the activities of these street-corner philosophers by calling him a rabble-rouser. That may be part of the case against him, showing at best that there was an ideological continuum between respectable practitioners and ranters. It is also a question how far the politics of Helvidius, his family and associates – the 'Stoic Opposition' – were determined by theoretical principles. It is good to recall Ch. Wirszubski's dictum on Thrasea: 'a courageous and upright senator who held Stoic views, not . . . a Stoic philosopher who happened to be a senator'. 'Professional' philosophers had long been associated with great Roman houses. Blossius of Cumae, an associate of Tiberius Gracchus, paid a high price for the connection in 133 BC. The greatest house of all, that of the Caesars, was itself a focus for philosophers. But Roman tradition was strong enough to make it unlikely that the views of senators were determined, rather than merely being bolstered, by doctrine. Vespasian himself had had connections with Barea Soranus and Thrasea, but the story of his being lectured by Apollonius of Tyana in Alexandria is a fiction and there is little to be said for intimacy with Dio of Prusa.[31]

Street-corner opposition was a surprising novelty. It may have been fed precisely from Alexandria and mainland Greece: Alexandria had speedily shed its illusions about the new régime; Achaea had lost its freedom again. The malcontents, Cynics by the sound of them, though Dio calls them Stoics and remarks that Demetrius the Cynic was actuated by Stoic principles, were repeatedly denounced by Mucianus for eccentricity and arrogance and for their doctrines. As M.T. Griffin has pointed out, Mucianus had no reason to reveal the philosophical allegiances of opponents of the régime. So in 71 or 72 (Mucianus was consul May–December 72), all except the equestrian Musonius, who had enjoyed licence at the beginning of the reign to prosecute Celer, were exiled from Italy. With them went the astrologers, a long-standing bugbear whose predictions unsettled high and low alike. The expulsion included men from the highest circles, Demetrius and the Stoic amateur C. Tutilius Julius Hostilianus of Cortona, who were confined to islands. It was a clean sweep of the articulate opposition to 'monarchy', perhaps too to the treatment of Greece. Musonius went later, to be recalled in Titus' reign.[32]

Vespasian's friends, for all their ill repute in the senate, continued to reap the rewards of collaboration. However, in spite of his third consulship, the influence that Mucianus enjoyed when he allegedly instigated Vespasian to exile the philosophers seems to have declined before his death, which preceded the publication of Pliny's *Natural History* (77). He is not found in further office and apparently came to talk of Vespasian with scant respect, picking at his claim to power and asserting his own achievements in 69, in the field and as an orator when the declaration was made. Vespasian bore it with good humour. As to the Principate, he implied when he complained about the carping to a common friend, bound to report the remark back, Mucianus' homosexuality – and childlessness – made him a no-hoper: 'All the same, *I'm a man.*' Vespasian may have been paraphrasing a remark about the countrified Marius: 'A boor, but a real man.'[33]

Marcellus with Mucianus' help was advanced to a governorship of Asia, twice prorogued (mid-70 to mid-73) and to a second consulship, and Crispus likewise to the governorship of Africa and to a second consulship (both suffect 74); this in spite of having made no known contribution to the Emperor's elevation. They were too pliable in politics, and useful in the House with their oratory, to discard. On the contrary, the high favour they were shown, the wealth their eloquence brought them, and their occupation of posts that were keenly sought by ex-consuls, illustrate Vespasian's ostentatious determination not to be intimidated by intransigents. Crispus and Marcellus are presented in high favour, even venerated by the old Emperor, in the *Dialogus*; R. Syme suggested that the agreeable manners of Crispus – his sagacity and good humour – made Vespasian reluctant to allow him too long abroad. Crispus survived into the reign of Domitian and reached a third consulship (suffect) before 83; friendship with him became a thing for decent men like the younger Pliny to conceal after the dynasty fell. It was otherwise with Eprius Marcellus and Caecina: they died towards the end of the reign, detected by Titus in unlikely conspiracy. What L. Valerius Catullus Messalinus had done to earn the regular consulship of 73, as colleague of Domitian, is not clear, but he was well born and may already have shown readiness to speak up loyally; he was to acquire a poisonous reputation in his colleague's Principate. Two years earlier M. Cocceius Nerva had shared the *fasces* with Vespasian; he was noble too, a known time-server, and perhaps had made his legal background useful in 70. The only other consuls *ordinarii* of the reign came late, in 78: a pair of loyal and serviceable Italians, soon to command in Germany and Syria.[34]

The new Emperor had his own preferences to satisfy: it was safest to confer office on members of his own family. Relatives by marriage took high provincial office, although their careers were not unspotted: the strong word 'tainted' has been applied to them. L. Caesennius Paetus, who married Sabinus' daughter, had led Roman forces across the Euphrates in 62 to their humiliating surrender at Rhandeia. He now went East again to the prime diplomatic post of Syria. Q. Petillius Cerialis, perceived as rash, had met a reverse in Britain under Nero. It was to Britain that he returned under Vespasian, but those appointments were not due solely to merit or relevant experience. Some men of merit are conspicuous by their absence from the record, L. Verginius Rufus the most obvious.[35]

Vespasian had arrived in Rome probably at the end of September 70. He had maintained his court at Alexandria for eight months; like Octavian in 30 BC, Galba and Vitellius, and Trajan after him, he showed no haste to enter his capital but let domestic politics shake down while he stood aside. It had emerged through the summer that there would be no early end to the siege of Jerusalem, and he left while it was still in progress. He put off his Triumph until 71, to share it with Titus, though that was a solecism. None the less, his entry, celebrated at the moment of his meeting with Domitian on the Cancelleria sculptures, was triumphant, and brought relief to the tensions that he had allowed to mount in his absence, just as they had in 19 BC when Augustus returned to a strife-riven city, both occasions justifying the senate's faith in Good Fortune the Restorer (*Fortuna Redux*), who now first appeared on coinage in person. This was probably when senate and people conferred the title 'Father of his Country' (*Pater Patriae*) that Augustus had taken after twenty-eight years in sole power and which Tiberius had firmly refused. For later Emperors it was conventional to wait and Vespasian is credited by Suetonius with waiting remarkably long. No new success is required to account for Vespasian's grant, even though the fall of Jerusalem made a stir: his mere return was enough. The ceremony and addresses that went with conferment enhanced its value. The same was true of the supreme pontificate, which Vespasian seems also to have taken on his return. There was no point in holding the post in absence (there were no competitors to keep out); election and inauguration glossed the Emperor's splendour.[36]

Vespasian's presence meant the renewal of contact with peers whom he had known as a private individual; they were known to Mucianus too, but Vespasian may have viewed the political scene differently and even have changed some of his governors: the appointment of Ti. Plautius Aelianus to Spain was soon reversed. However, Vespasian's sanction would have been obtained for everything done after the first few days.[37]

Vespasian soon felt at home in his rôle, as is witnessed by his familiar reference to 'his dear little people', which belongs to the period of the restoration of the Capitol. Humour as well as firmness marks his response to attempts to put him down politically, socially, or culturally, whether by opposition in the senate, criticism of his accent delivered to his face, or anonymous pamphlets; the same near-imperturbability met flatterers who tried to claim that his family had been responsible for the foundation of Reate and traced their descent to a companion of Hercules whose statue was to be found on the Via Salaria; he knew that they were always ready to make statements so outrageous as to seem ambivalent. This was a confident man, and one with a good conscience. After emerging victorious from the contest of 69 over men who on the face of it had better title to power, Vespasian had little to fear from civilian rivals. Even Mettius Pompusianus, a man denounced for being in possession of an imperial horoscope, who would have been courting death in earlier principates and was to die in Domitian's, was a subject of mirth: he was allowed the consulship – on the understanding that he would return the favour some time.[38]

All the same, Vespasian built up the prestige that he had so lacked. He did it in the traditional way, through holding the consulship, which Augustus had also accumulated from 31 to 23 BC. That had proved unacceptable, and Augustus was to hold the office only twice more, when he introduced his grandsons into public life. Vespasian was prepared to run the risk of offending in his own and his sons' interest; in any case there were now suffect consulships open in generous numbers to private individuals, and it is said that Vitellius meant to go further by becoming *consul perpetuus*, presumably relinquishing office each year after months or days. K. Waters points out that three-quarters of the *ordinarius* posts were held by members of the family: Vespasian and Titus occupied it seven times; but a hundred men are known to have achieved the consulship between 70 and 95. The promotion of kinsmen, and intermarriage between branches of the family, were part of the same effort. Flavian inbreeding would have reached a level previously attained only by Claudius' marriage to his niece Agrippina if Domitian could have been induced to wed Titus' daughter Julia, and Waters has described it as a 'blind spot'. He attributes Flavian success to a 'natural' tendency to regard monarchical power as hereditary.[39]

Having made it clear to the senate who was master, in particular with Titus in possession of tribunician power, Helvidius and the Cynics in exile, and with relatives and trustworthy friends in prime commands or lucrative governorships of public provinces, while over-ambitious supporters were allowed to languish on the back benches or at their country residences, upheaval seemed unlikely. In 73–4 Vespasian and Titus jointly conducted a census that subjected every member of the two upper orders, senators and knights, to scrutiny and made it possible for the two men to admit promising supporters. They entered office in April and concluded the final ceremonies in the autumn of the following year, the same period of time that Claudius and republican predecessors had occupied. When they were designated is uncertain, but late 72 is a possibility. It is unlikely that the move was prompted by any external event: the advantages of holding the office, both functional and as conferring prestige, were too obvious, and Vespasian had had the example of Claudius before him ever since he came to power.[40]

The poverty of our sources makes it unclear how far political unrest was dampened after the crisis of 71 and the aftershocks. Pliny seems to have ended his history with the Triumph of June 71, a reasonable date – that exempted him from tackling the controversies that broke out days later. Even then he withheld it for his own lifetime. Pliny's caution has impoverished our knowledge of the aftermath. There are notable items, though date and context are uncertain. First, the trouble that led to the execution of Helvidius. It made Helvidius a martyr, the Roman Socrates; but that would have been worth it if Helvidius were disposed of as the scapegoat for lesser figures' 'plotting' (which might mean no more than meeting to grumble). Then the unlikely 'conspiracy' of Caecina towards the end of the reign is a sign of insecurity felt by some members of the régime, probably over the quiet transmission of power to Titus. When the time came, and the new Emperor made his first dispositions, he was at pains to discourage 'informers' (*delatores*) by exiling existing practitioners. These offenders are usually associated with the notorious charge of diminishing the majesty of the Roman People (*maiestas minuta*), and Titus also specifically said on his accession that he would not allow such prosecutions if they were concerned with slanders of himself or his predecessors. The same had been done by Gaius Caligula in 37, after the bitter in-fighting that had darkened the last years of Tiberius' reign, and he was followed by Claudius and Nero, also after periods of oppression. It may be a conventional gesture or it could signal continued unease in the later years of Vespasian's reign. But there is no other sign of such cases in this decade, and delation was a method of prosecuting all manner of offences – those against Augustus' marriage legislation, for example, giving sure evidence only of indigent, ambitious, and unscrupulous pleaders. For all the impoverishment of the sources it is hard not to believe that the second half of Vespasian's reign was more settled than the first. Tacitus wrote at the beginning of his *Histories* that the conferring of supreme power on a single man was in the interest of peace, referring to the advent of Augustus, but it was even more true of Vespasian, with the autocracy a confirmed fact. After 71 the opposition was left criticism in a lighter vein: mockery, irony. There was no unravelling the purpose behind an extravagant proposal of honours, and the proposer was safe. Political commentary now conducted with all but financial impunity in *Private Eye* had to be kept at home, creeping out only when an emperor was safely dead, or a régime defunct. It was to Vespasian's credit that there was no gratuitous violence, only what was seen to be required for the dynasty's security.[41]

7

FINANCIAL SURVIVAL

Here is an area in which the management of individuals makes a perceptible difference, by maximizing and managing revenue, but also by affecting confidence. Vespasian asserted (perhaps in announcing tax rises) that 4,000m *HS* were needed to put the state on its feet. Suetonius' MS reads 40,000m, 'the largest sum mentioned in antiquity'. If we accept the emendation, which provides a figure within Roman ken, and the estimate of K. Hopkins that annual revenue from taxation was about 800m. *HS*, Vespasian would be claiming that the Empire needed five years' revenue to restore it, a period that was sometimes allowed for tax remission after earthquake damage. The interpretation that while Nero restored one city (Lugdunum after the fire) he was restoring a thousand is not warranted. Vespasian's immediate straits are suggested by the small sum – 100 *HS* each – distributed to troops on the fall of Rome. Even with the tip he added on arrival from Egypt the total came nowhere near the gross sum promised legionaries by Nymphidius Sabinus on behalf of Galba eighteen months previously: 1,250 *HS* each, with six times that for the Praetorian Guard. Already in July 69 Vitellius, hard put to find anything for his victorious legions, had devised a special tax on the freedmen of leading Romans. Vespasian's financial needs were a prime factor in his principate, and that is reflected in the sources: for they provided a prime grievance to the disaffected, however generously he spent on the proper commitments of a Princeps. Monuments set up to two distinguished generals in the reign mentioned that they had brought in more revenue.[1]

On Vespasian's solution to these problems depended the maintenance of adequate government, immediate security, and in the long run, confidence in Roman power. Much of the huge sum was needed to pay the troops that were left on Vespasian's hands and to pay some off; to say nothing of restoring war-damaged installations and looted equipment. Direct taxation had always and explicitly been devoted to the upkeep of the army. The overthrow of Nero and the Year of the Four Emperors had repeatedly broken the thread that ran from the acknowledged emperor to the armies responsible for order within the Empire. It had to be seen to be restored, and for that money was vital.[2]

The problems were on three different levels of immediacy which were inversely related to their seriousness. First, confiscation of property, physical damage, and consequent loss of confidence (and so a diminution of money available for property purchase and improvement and for trading ventures). Major cities such as Vesontio, Cremona, and Rome itself had suffered looting and fire damage. Swathes of devastation came from the repeated passage of armies over main highways, especially through Gaul, the Alps, and Italy, the scenes of fierce struggles, and to a lesser extent in the Balkans, Asia Minor, and Africa. Yet it is easy to overestimate the physical damage that ancient warfare could cause; the temporary end of all but vital and local trade and credit in affected areas was probably more serious. When it was realized that the wars were over, confidence, trade, and customs dues would rise again. In Rome sites abandoned by their owners were given over to anyone who would develop them, although physical restoration there besides reparation for looted property had to be led and often paid for by Vespasian.[3]

Second, losses to the state caused by Nero's high level of expenditure over his reign, some of it on the upkeep of Roman power abroad (the advance in Britain and the Boudiccan revolt, 57–61; the conflict with Parthia, 54–63), some on keeping up Nero's own position (2,200m *HS* are said to have been expended on gifts). The last five years, when he had undertaken the rebuilding of Rome on a magnificent scale and was fighting the war in Judaea, were particularly costly. Increasing signs of bullion shortage at Rome have been detected, with the number of branches of the mint (*officinae*) striking gold and silver there falling from six to three in his last four years, and the purity of the silver coinage in decline. It must have been in Nero's own reign that a statue of Alexander by Lysippus, which the Emperor had ordered to be gilded, was stripped again, to its improvement, according to the elder Pliny. Galba then was short and, like Vespasian after him, acquired a reputation for parsimony: 'he did not go for other people's money, but looked after his own, and was a miser with public funds'. But political considerations still came first, and they were not well judged. Galba tried to recover Nero's gifts up to 90 per cent through a thirty-man equestrian commission, while Cn. Julius Agricola was appointed to investigate misappropriations of temple treasures. The gifts had passed beyond recovery. Finally Galba made a gross blunder, posturing over saving on additional praetorian donatives: 'I'm in the habit of selecting my troops, not of buying them.' Otho and Vitellius faced the same problems, but no stringency is reported: on the contrary. Otho is recorded as having set aside 50m *HS* to complete Nero's Golden House; in his last days Vitellius had desperately awarded exemptions from tribute, adding to his successor's problems. The personal extravagance of Vitellius too ('serving dishes the size of lagoons') was a Flavian theme; it occurred in one of Mucianus' speeches during his consulship of 70 (probably one dealing with post-war problems), and is prominent in Tacitus' *Histories*.[4]

It was probably such extraordinary problems that Vespasian had in mind when he estimated needs. But there was a third, of long standing, that of funding the Empire at a time when profitable war had virtually come to an end but the standing army still had to be maintained: Domitian publicly complained that the provinces could hardly meet necessary demands. Further, under the Empire much revenue was spent in the provinces where it was collected, on armies stationed there or on development. There was less to go to Italy, either to the Treasury or for immediate expenditure on games and buildings, perquisites of the victorious Roman people. Taxation revenue rose as the prosperity of the provinces increased under the Roman peace and as a result of incorporating more peoples into the Empire, but there was an undesirable side-effect: the comparative failure of Italy to keep pace.[5]

It did not matter in which part of the State financial system public resources were placed, as long as they were available for use all over the Empire. Overall imperial control ensured that they were: Augustus left a financial account of the entire Empire, available to the senate from procurators and freedmen. Under Claudius and Nero the freedman in charge of imperial finances public and private ('a rationibus') Pallas emerged as the man in overall charge of public finance. There was no going back from this costly arrangement (when he took early retirement in 55, Pallas demanded that his accounts with the State should be considered balanced). It is attested under Domitian. The finances of the entire Empire precisely were Vespasian's concern. We do not know when or where he expressed it, in a letter or orally to the senate on his return from Alexandria. If so, his remarks came after an effort had been made in the senate itself immediately after the fall of Vitellius to deal with the problems of one section of the financial system, the Aerarium Saturni. Theoretically this was the main State Treasury, and the organization that handled funds belonging to it but made available to Emperors for their official purposes (the imperial Fiscus) was a section of it.[6]

During a debate concerned primarily with restoration of the Capitol, the low state of the Aerarium was deplored by the praetors in charge, who asked for a limit on 'public' expenditure, that is, from that Treasury. This would entail either immediate senatorial action or the setting up of a commission of enquiry, similar to those established previously on the motion of emperors. The consul designate was alarmed at the idea of the senate's taking action when 'commitments were so heavy and the problem so intractable'; Helvidius Priscus, himself praetor designate, demurred and pressed for positive steps. The consul invited other opinions, and the tribune Vulcacius Tertullinus vetoed any action taken in the absence of the Emperor. Eventually a commission was allowed; its members were chosen by lot, a recipe for the participation of nonentities and a futile end. Nothing more is heard of it.[7]

This problem had a political dimension. Perhaps the commission's advocates designed it to adjust relations between Aerarium and Fiscus. The Aerarium and its officials had long been rendered virtually impotent by concentration of funds in the hands of the Emperor both as an individual owning private property (*res privata*) and what he inherited from his predecessors (*patrimonium*), and as an official controlling the Fiscus. If its position were to be improved, that would entail restrictions not only on Treasury expenditure but on that of the Emperor himself; to reach any conclusions a commission would have to know all about such expenditure, an arcane matter since Gaius at latest had ended the publication of accounts. It could have incalculable implications about the legions in each province and imperial use of funds beyond the cost of the army; it might even lead the reckless to call for accountability and the return of revenues derived from the property of those who died intestate or who were convicted on criminal charges (*bona caduca; bona damnatorum*), which were habitually diverted either to the Emperor's official funds, reasonably given the heavy burdens on them, or, illegitimately, into the private funds of an emperor. (Vespasian kept his own old property separate, for he made a will.)[8]

Economy commissions were either attempts on the part of the Emperor to get the Aerarium to make ends meet (so with Nero in 62: he attacked his predecessors' practice of anticipating its revenues) or as sops to senatorial fears. Such was the five-man commission set up in 97. It was a political gesture, perhaps resuming the enquiry of 70 after the assassination of the autocrat, and included the 83-year-old L. Verginius Rufus (cos. III 97), brought out of shameful retirement to demonstrate the right-mindedness of Nerva's new régime. The commission's achievements were minimal, but Nerva restored profits from public water supplies from the Fiscus to the Aerarium. The problem of relations between Aerarium and Fiscus fades in the second century along with that of relations between Emperor and senate. Discussions based on the appearance of new officials and focusing on what revenues went into which treasury neglect the main point, effective control: emperors ran finances in their own provinces and had additional funds made available because their expenses were so high; indirectly, by subvention, recommendation, and preventing redistribution of revenue, they controlled the Aerarium too.[9]

If the occasion for Vespasian's remark about the Empire's needs was a resumption in the senate of the problem of Aerarium solvency, then Vespasian would naturally pass to a more pressing topic: solvency of the State; he may have been announcing fresh taxes. In 22 Tiberius had exploited senatorial breast-beating about personal extravagance to lecture the House on Italy's problems. Or Vespasian's remark could have been an immediate reaction to the commission's report. But in this area as elsewhere he made characteristically firm long-term responses to attempts by the senate or by individuals to assert themselves. Under Vespasian appeared two new provincial treasuries, the *Fiscus Alexandrinus* and the *Fiscus Asiaticus*. The former presumably contained monetary taxes from Alexandria, perhaps from residents liable to the poll tax, and receipts from the sale of Egyptian grain taken in tax and not required for Rome, or, in T. Frank's view, supported by the apparently depleted quantity of imperial property held in the province, cash raised from the sale of crown lands. The latter may also have received specifically the poll tax, but the generalizing title suggests that other revenues may have left their route into the Aerarium and been diverted into a separate chest. This would be a blow to the Aerarium, since Asia was one of the few profitable provinces, a drain only in crises such as destructive earthquakes. It was probably for the peculiar problems of the Aerarium that the senate sought another remedy: to borrow 60m *HS* from patriotic individuals. The scheme was charged to the ex-praetor Pompeius Silvanus. It was modest, and ineffective: individuals needed all they had.[10]

We do not know the date of the appointment of Vespasian's financial agent, Ti. Julius, an imperial freedman born in Smyrna who had been a procurator under Claudius and who may have proved his ability during the civil war or as treasurer to Titus: he participated in the Jewish triumph. His service in the post that Pallas had held under Claudius and Nero was satisfactory: he held office for more than ten years and reached equestrian status.[11]

To deal with financial problems long-term and short-term, Vespasian began reclaiming and exploiting public property; he increased the rate of old taxes (Suetonius writes of the tribute being doubled) and devised new ones. No time was lost in Egypt, or in Gaul: when Domitian arrived there in 70 it was 'to conduct the census'. Special enquiry commissions often provided the information, but there were also the traditional census of Roman citizens (73–4), and provincial censuses such as those conducted in Spain under Q. Vibius Crispus and in Africa by C. Rutilius Gallicus, or in Egypt. Josephus benefited from census information when he was able to set the resources of the rest of the world against those of the Jews. So Gallicus is credited by Statius with having raised the level of tribute. The shortfall did not vanish overnight; Vespasian is said to have become even more rapacious as time went on.[12]

In Italy Vespasian restored to communities lands that had illegitimately passed into private possession. That did not directly benefit his exchequer: but cities with adequate revenues were less likely to call for imperial aid. There was immediate profit from his recovery of public property to the Roman State. Vespasian squeezed sums out of colonial territory that had not been distributed to the settlers (*subseciva*), on the grounds that (Frontinus was conceivably using the Emperor's very words) 'land allocated to no-one could not belong to anyone except the person entitled to allocate it', and distributing it for the benefit of the Fiscus. In Italy these sales provoked such protests from those who had been enjoying free use of the land that Vespasian had to give up his plan. Titus' attempt to renew it was shortlived; in the interests of political unity Domitian brought it to an end early in his reign.[13]

At the colony of Arausio in southern Gaul, the survey carried out in 77 on Vespasian's orders with the purpose of restoring public property that

Augustus had given the soldiers of II Gallica and which had passed some years previously into private hands also led to the publication of a map recording the annual rent payable on each of the unofficial centuries (allotments of 200 *iugera* or 50ha.) within the *subseciva*. In Cyrenaica, Vespasian took back former royal lands that belonged to the Roman people, now also in private possession, a 'garden' in Ptolemais and an estate of the Ptolemies in Cyrene. Claudius began this work, unsuccessfully it seems. His agent, the legate L. Acilius Strabo, charged with extortion under Nero by influential Cyrenaican landowners, reached a suffect consulship in 71. To further Claudius' work, Vespasian in 71–4 employed the legate Q. Paconius Agrippinus, whose boundary stones have been found in the coastal area east of Apollonia, to restore the land to 'the Roman People'. South of Apollonia the Emperor seems to have sold public land to the city, as J. Reynolds and R.G. Goodchild suggest, and to have intervened, through the proconsul, in its leasing. In Corsica his procurator sold land to the Vanacini (72). Raising money by disposing of unwanted property went back to the days of Vespasian's coup, when a Ptolemaic palace in Alexandria went.[14]

When provincial boundaries were adjusted, as they were in Africa and between Baetica and Tarraconensis by Vespasian and Domitian, fiscal exactness may have been a motive: the public province of Baetica lost the cinnabar mines at Sisapo and Mirobriga Turdulorum to Lusitania, a province under an imperial legate. There was no question of the mines becoming the Emperor's private property, but they fell under his control. But in the view of T. Frank most mines were already under imperial control by Vespasian's day. In Africa Rutilius Gallicus and Sex. Sentius Caecilianus (suff. 75 or 76) in 73–4 revived the boundary line between Carthaginian and Numidian territory established by Carthage and Masinissa and confirmed by Aemilianus, conqueror of Carthage – the 'Royal Ditch'. This division into two dioceses, coinciding with the census of Roman citizens, had a practical purpose, as G. Di Vita Evrard has insisted: easing tax collection and maximizing revenue from fertile land. To the south-east the Nasamones were to revolt against Domitian's tax-collectors.[15]

Vespasian's interest in the mines of Spain is not proved by these boundary changes, but in Domitian's time Ti. Julius was controlling 'whatever Iberia spews out from her gold-rich trenches'. Concern is attested by Pliny's statement that mines that had been thought to be exhausted were reopened and operated more intensively than before. R. McElderry brought this into connection with the rules drawn up for the management of mines ('*Lex metallis dicta*'), the workings at Vipasca in Lusitania ('*Lex metalli Vipascensis*'), and iron workings ('*Lex ferrariarum*'), though the Vipasca documents date from the reign of Hadrian. We should be equally cautious in associating Vespasian with a measure or practice concerned with the surface cultivation of Africa – the *Lex Manciana*, probably of Neronian or Flavian date. Mancian tenure is succinctly defined by J. Percival: 'a form of tenure arising from the clearing and cultivation of waste land, available primarily ... to *coloni* on estates already existing', and found on the edge of centuriated land, so that extended operations would add to the revenues of the imperial treasury or to the Emperor's own income. But the career of the man most plausibly associated with the 'law' culminated in a consulship early in the reign of Nero; and if it is rather a practice introduced on his property by him or a member of his family, Vespasian's interest cannot be demonstrated.[16]

Besides raising existing taxes, Vespasian reintroduced some abolished by Galba, perhaps for the benefit of his Gallic allies, and devised new. A third new Fiscus was placed under a freedman procurator. The *Fiscus Judaicus* received the 8 *HS* that free male Jews between the ages of 20 and 50 had previously contributed annually to the upkeep of the Temple. News of its destruction came to Rome three months after the first ceremony on the Capitol had taken place on 21 June, but the decision to claim the revenue for Jupiter did not have to wait for that: how to pay for the Capitol had been an early controversy. Now women up to 62 and children of 3 or more had to pay or be paid for. Gentiles also contributed: he took fines levied on offenders against doctors under their right granted on 27 December 75. When the Capitol was complete, perhaps in 76, there would have been enormous sums available for other purposes, since the persons liable to the Temple levy had been multiplied perhaps fourfold; the fund could have been drawn upon again for restoration after the fire of 80. The revenue was separated from other taxes in Egypt; in other provinces accounting could have served the same purpose. The size of the Jewish population of the Empire at this time has been estimated at five to six million, and if that were accepted the new tax would have produced 40–48m *HS* a year, 5–6 per cent of Hopkins' suggested annual revenue. In Egypt alone, according to one estimate, the tax produced a regular 8m – a figure based on inflated ancient ideas of the Jewish population there: one million. The tax was known to be harsh; the burden on fathers of families was particularly severe, and under Titus it is found being paid in instalments and in arrears. Suetonius was shocked as a young man by the brutal disregard for dignity with which enquiries about liability were carried out, and Nerva mitigated the way the tax was collected.[17]

Jewish contributors in Egypt may have been consoled for the outrage by one against Alexandria, whose citizens now had to pay poll tax that hitherto had fallen only on unprivileged Egyptians. Shrines, perhaps the priesthood too, likewise lost immunity. In the African and Asian provinces Vespasian may have tightened management by setting up new financial administrative areas. In Rome itself there was the tax that gave French the obsolescent '*vespasienne*': one imposed on the laundries that collected the products of public urinals. In raising a new tax in Rome Vespasian in his need was following the dangerous example of Gaius. It was less controversial to set up additional customs posts to collect revenue where goods passed into and out of the Empire.[18]

Revenue played its part in Vespasian's decision to take back the freedom of the larger regions that Nero had released from direct Roman control, and so from tax, as it will have as he decided to annex Commagene; the centurion who brought refugee princes from the Parthian court to Rome was noted as having brought in a goodly company of taxpayers too. The motive of gain is expressly stated in connection with Achaea by Pausanias and is probably true of the other areas, which suffered promptly, if it is true that freedoms were lost on Vespasian's homeward journey in 70 rather than in 73–4. The revenues of Achaea would have been modest for its size and development, especially as its two greatest cities, Athens and Sparta, remained free, but the Emperor may have enhanced the value of Greece and Macedonia by adding a poll tax (*tributum capitis*) to the existing land tax. On the other hand, it is hard to believe with L. Homo that taking Sardinia into the 'imperial' sector had the same motive. Sardinia, if profitable, was also troublesome and needed the security of a military presence. In Corsica the imperial property now had a procurator of its own under the equestrian governor.[19]

Financial considerations must have played their part too in Vespasian's attitude towards the granting of citizenship. Roman citizens, free from poll tax, did not escape the tax imposed on provincial territory, unless they were members of those Roman colonies whose territory was treated as if it were part of Italy, which was exempt (*ius Italicum*). Vespasian's colony at Caesarea did not escape tribute. There was another consideration: when the Emperor Augustus was hard put to fund his discharge grants to legionaries, a hated tax had been devised which fell only on Roman citizens: the 5 per cent inheritance tax (*vicesima hereditatium*). When Caracalla in 212 granted citizenship to freeborn inhabitants of the Empire, Dio Cassius could accuse him of doing it for money. There were exemptions for property inherited from close kin – not extended to new citizens, we do not know on what grounds, or if that was an innovation. When Pliny delivered his panegyric on Trajan in 100, he claimed, no doubt exaggerating, that the burden had made men unwilling to accept the boon of citizenship – only Trajan had relieved them of it.[20]

Vespasian went further, generating a crop of scurrilities and accusations, one of them remembered from his days as a private citizen in the 60s. Irregular levies in crises are normal; but those imposed by Mucianus in 69 continued in peace, and malicious prosecutions that enriched the treasury became a subject of complaint. Allegedly Vespasian sold the citizenship (with the aid of Caenis), magistracies and other posts without regard for merit, and acquittals without regard for justice, and (a nice twist!) to have promoted his procurators, especially those of a rapacious bent, until they were bloated with wealth – to condemn them with greater benefit to the exchequer. Illegal as well as ill-gotten gains, where they are not merely malicious fictions or the interpretation of a single case, passed directly into Vespasian's own pocket, although in all probability they went for public purposes. It was only to be expected that Domitian, keen to secure his financial hold over the army, should, like Tiberius and Gaius, have begun confiscating from provincials as well as the Italian aristocracy. Vespasian could be shamed out of such actions by clever counsel: Hipparchus of Athens was acquitted when Salvius Liberalis asked what it was to Caesar if Hipparchus possessed 100m *HS* and Vespasian applauded; neither Hipparchus nor Liberalis survived Domitian's reign.[21]

Outlandish devices won Vespasian his reputation for 'avarice'. In Alexandria his demand for new taxes and peremptory sale of the palace and its old glory made him a sham king with no future, like the interloper Cybiosactes in the last years of the Ptolemies. The story goes that a complaint from the Alexandrians about a tax error – the tax was six obols per person in excess – was remedied by the addition of six obols to the tax. The numerous anecdotes on avarice that have made their contribution to Vespasian's 'character', masquerading as factual, show how hard pressed the Empire was to pay its way. We are to believe that Titus protested about the revenue from urine and that Vespasian replied by putting a copper under his nose and asking him if it smelt (after all, the money had been laundered); and that Vespasian summoned a man whose brother was being tipped for advancing him to a post and, taking on the rôle of power-broker in which he had figured as a consular in the 60s, pocketed the tip; and that on being offered a statue valued at a million *HS* he put out his hand to the donors and told them that the base was all ready. The insistent underlying truth is that Vespasian maximized revenues and was felt to be unscrupulous about their source.[22]

Vespasian is not simply to be put in the category of 'parsimonious Princeps' like Tiberius and Galba (whose reign was too short for judgment). Misguided efforts on the part of Tiberius to set an example of how to behave as *primus inter pares* obscured the needs of the Empire and hindered the development of a flexible attitude towards finance. Tiberius behaved like a private individual instead of a statesman, hoarding money like everyone else. Recognition that the Principate was indeed a monarchy was an advance. Vespasian understood the value of disbursement, which his pronouncement implied that he needed for immediate use. He built splendidly in Rome, providing employment and cash for contractors, suppliers, and their workmen. In keeping account of expenditure, even if it was a gift (400,000 *HS* – the knight's census) to a woman for sex, which Vespasian allegedly instructed his cashier to put down to 'a passion for Vespasian', he was no stricter than Nero had been, for Nero's gifts could be totted up and pursued.[23]

Tiberius' housewifely attitude, imitated by patriots who locked up precious metal in dedications, contributed to the inadequate monetization of the Roman Empire. Motives for minting are still under discussion. But the incident of 33, when upper-class men short of liquid assets had to be bailed out and their creditors satisfied, shows Tiberius disbursing coin from the Treasury as a last resort: he had not understood what should be done. Disbursement seems to remain an act of *liberalitas* until the mid-fourth century; but senators who recognized that they were living under a *de facto* monarchy could claim that the monarch should pay for everything, a view that Dio Cassius, writing in the early third century, makes M. Agrippa put into their mouths. Like Galba, who in A. Wallace-Hadrill's words 'came to power on a wave of protest against the extravagances of an emperor best known for the Domus Aurea', but who did not restore currency to the old standard, Vespasian recognized imperial responsibility for the weight and fineness of the coins issued by his mints: that is how the reverse legend *AEQVITAS* has been explained, while *FIDES PVBLICA* reflects wider concern. None the less, Vespasian, like Nero, had to debase the silver: the *denarius* fell from *c.*3.00 g of silver to *c.*2.85.[24]

Whatever came into provincial treasuries could be reissued or converted into fresh currency for the support of government throughout the Empire. Vespasian responded to the gap between need and supplies by stepping up the minting of bullion. Mints for gold and silver were put to work in the earliest years of his principate at Rome, Tarraco, and Lugdunum; and in the East at Byzantium, Ephesus, and Antioch. They met the need until normal levels of expenditure were restored, surviving at Tarraco and at Byzantium and Ephesus from 69 perhaps until 71 and at Lugdunum until 73, while the Antioch mint functioned, naturally enough, in 69, and then again in 72–3, a year of political and military activity in the East. There was a factor working against these mints: the Emperor's need for central control.[25]

Lucan writes that it was in 49 BC that 'Caesar' – Julius in the first instance, and compendiously all his successors to Nero – became richer than the State. Caesar broke into the Aerarium, and some of the contents passed by will into the hands of his heir Augustus. Much booty and private property went the same way. He had the lion's share of the spoils of Egypt, and many friends bequeathed him legacies. I. Shatzman estimates his property at 1,000m *HS*, although the contents of his will proved modest, and Augustus apologized for it. As the imperial family diminished in size, so that Nero could claim that he was the sole heir of the dynasty, the survivors' property increased: Nero's patrimony was dented by his expenditures but estates were not being alienated. The possession of these huge properties and the revenues they brought in were important enough to embolden procuratorial administrators to defy or bypass senatorial governors in the reign of Tiberius, and to win them powers of jurisdiction under Claudius. The private property of the Emperor was acquiring official status because it belonged to the Emperor.[26]

This property should have passed, with the death of Nero, intestate or with a will that was suppressed, to Galba and the shortlived emperors of 69, and so to Vespasian, to become, minus a subsidy to Otho's nephew and a dowry for Vitellius' daughter, 'crown' property, the imperial *patrimonium* proper, that an emperor inherited in virtue of his position – and which he was expected to use to maintain it. So the brickworks of the central and northern Adriatic, whose products, labelled once with the name of A. Hirtius

Pansa, *cos.* 43 BC, then with Tiberius', came in their final phase of production to bear the name of Vespasian. The accession of a new dynasty meant recognizing the status of the inheritance, and that entailed administrative changes, even without taking account of the enormous size of the private property that Vespasian 'inherited'. State property controlled by the Emperor as administrator, and the *patrimonium* passed on by his predecessors, and his own private property, all was put to imperial use and for practical purposes was a unified resource. But accounting kept it distinct, for Vespasian made a will that must have bequeathed the overwhelmingly larger part of his property, tacitly or explicitly including the *patrimonium*, to his political heir but will have provided also for his second son and other relatives and dependants, as well as people and troops. Whatever the status of the royal balsam gardens round Jericho and Engedi in Judaea, Pliny envisages them paying tribute like the Jews and relishes the prices the product fetched. Emperors had long needed to exploit the revenues of any property that they could claim; Vespasian's need was pressing, and any reform of organization that he conducted will have been maintained by his successors. Yet it is only from the later Flavian period that sales from imperial marble quarries increase significantly, becoming part of a market economy, rather than the original command economy, and the driving force should have been demand from prospering customers rather than pressure from above.[27]

The view that the Flavians consolidated and reorganized the imperial domains both in Egypt and elsewhere has been held since M.I. Rostovtzeff advocated it. It is inherently plausible, his view of a positive drive against big landowners and absentee landlordism less so. In Egypt the Estate Account (*ousiakos logos*) emerged, a special treasury to receive these revenues, and permanent departments for their administration. As founder of a new dynasty Vespasian certainly needed to establish the category of 'crown' as opposed to personally owned imperial property. Traces of the latter ownership, in the form of properties called 'Vespasian's', remained in the third century. Now imperial land (*ge ousiake*) took on its definitive form, absorbing earlier emperors' estates. In Africa, where reorganization was necessary because of Nero's confiscations, Vespasian has been credited with dividing the province up into regions with headquarters later attested at Hippo Regius, Hadrumetum, and Theveste; and in Asia Rostovtzeff also found 'regions' (*eparchies*) each in the charge of a procurator, subject to the procurator of the entire province based in Ephesus. An inscription of 79 set up by an imperial freedman at Appia in Phrygia shows him working like his father and grandfather in the local marble quarries; and he acted as 'Guardian of the Peace' (*Irenophylax*) for a 'region'. On a contemporary inscription from Ephesus we find T. Flavius Pergamus, sub-procurator of the '*regio Syriatica*'; some of these positions may go back unattested beyond Vespasian, others may be later creations.[28]

Other significant and far-reaching reforms in financial administration are credited to Vespasian: he substituted individual farmers for the traditional societies in the collection of indirect taxes, a reform which (like the reorganization of imperial domains in Africa) was completed only under Hadrian. Then he attached imperial servants, slaves or freedmen, to the operatives, strengthening state control over them. Finally, working out an Augustan initiative, there was the creation of the three new Fisci – if indeed there were no more. Accordingly Vespasian is also vulnerable to the accusation of initiating the 'Statism' to which the Empire succumbed four centuries later. Acts, intentions, results, all must be treated with scepticism. Most telling is the failure to complete the reforms until Hadrian's time – if they were 'reforms', rather than a series of *ad hoc* decisions suggested by conditions of the day. And the final, undesirable 'result' had causes far beyond these.[29]

The grasping parsimony of the anecdotes is humorously portrayed, and wry satisfaction may be detected. Later generations, exemplified by the fourth-century author of the *Historia Augusta* admired Vespasian's financial management. More: financial security meant political security. Vespasian's measures kept his dynasty in power, but they also showed the Empire that firm control was being exercised from the centre: it was seen to be a going concern. At the same time, money was spent on worthwhile projects, reconstruction, road-building, which redistributed revenues, while Vespasian's measures for economizing and enhancing revenue seem by the end of his reign to have had a contributory effect. Titus was known for generosity, and it is not certain that, even after his disbursements on shows and on relief and restoration after the eruption of Vesuvius and the fire of 80, Domitian was seriously short of money; if he was his grant to the legions of a one-third rise in pay was a prime cause.[30]

PLATES

Plate 1 Obv. Nero, laureate; Rev. Roma in military dress, with Victory and parazonium (Aes, Lugdunum, *c.* 65). *The Ashmolean Museum, by permission of the Visitors*

Plate 2 Obv. Galba, laureate; SER. SVLPI. GALBA IMP. CAESAR AVG. TR.P. Rev. Galba, bare-headed in military dress on platform and backed by officer, haranguing troops with shield, standard, and spear; ADLOCVTIO S.C.: 'Address to the troops'. (Aes, Rome, *c.* December 68). *The Ashmolean Museum, by permission of the Visitors*

I

Plate 3 Obv. Otho, bare-headed; M.OTHO CAESAR AVG. TR.P. Rev. Securitas standing, holding wreath and sceptre; SECVRITAS P(opuli) R(omani) (Gold, Rome, mid-January–mid-April 69). *The Ashmolean Museum, by permission of the Visitors*

Plate 4 Obv. Vitellius, laureate; A.VITELLIVS GERM. IMP. AVG. TR.P. Rev. L. Vitellius in toga, seated on curule chair, r. hand extended, l. holding eagle-tipped sceptre; L.VITELLIVS COS. III CENSOR (Gold, Rome, late April–20 December 69). *The Ashmolean Museum, by permission of the Visitors*

Plate 5 Head of Vespasian. *By permission of the Ny Carlsberg Glyptotek, Copenhagen*

Plate 6 Portrait of Titus. *By permission of the Vatican Museum*

Plate 7 Portrait of Domitian. *By permission of the Vatican Museum*

Plate 8 Obv. Nero laureate; Neron Seb. Caisar: 'Nero Augustus Caesar'. Rev. Within wreath 'Epi Ouespasianou Caisare. L ID ': 'In Vespasian's term of office; Year 14. Coin of the people of Caesarea' (Aes, Caesarea Maritima, 68). *The British Museum, by permission of the Trustees*

Plate 9 Obv. Vespasian laureate. Rev. Jewish woman seated at foot of palm tree, mourning; behind palm, Vespasian standing, holding spear and parazonium; IVDAEA CAPTA S.C. (Aes, Rome, etc., 71). *The Ashmolean Museum, by permission of the Visitors*

Plate 10 Obv. Vespasian radiate. Rev. Victory standing on prow, holding wreath and palm; VICTORIA NAVALIS S.C. (Aes, Rome, 71). *The Ashmolean Museum, by permission of the Visitors*

Plate 11 Obv. Vespasian laureate. Cais. Flavi. Ouespasianus. Rev. Titus laureate; AUTO. TIT L A: 'Imperator Titus. Year 1'. (Aes, Alexandria, before 29 August, 69, with anomalous titulature). *The British Museum, by permission of the Trustees*

Plate 12 Bronze text of the *'Lex de imperio Vespasiani'* (Rome). *By permission of the Deutsches Archäologisches Institut, Rome*

Plate 13 Vespasian's return, 70, greeted by Domitian (Cancelleria Relief B). *By permission of the Vatican Museum*

Plate 14 Obv. Titus laureate; Autocra. Titus Caisar Sebas. Hyius: 'Imperator Titus Caesar, son of Augustus'. Rev. Palm tree between trophy, shield, and spears; Epi Maiciou Roufou Anthypatou: 'In the Proconsulship of (M.) Maecius Rufus'. (Aes, minted by the Provincial Council of Bithynia, 71/2). *The British Museum, by permission of the Trustees*

Plate 15 Coin of Sardes restruck on coin of Apollonos Hieron; traces of previous types. Obv. Bust of Athena or Roma, with aegis; Epi T . . .: 'In the magistracy of T . . .'; from previous type: Apollo standing; Ere iton: 'Coin of the people of Apollonos Hieron'. Rev. Temple front of four columns; in field To B: 'For the second time'; Epi Marcellou Sardianon: 'In the Proconsulship of (T. Clodius Eprius) Marcellus. Coin of the people of Sardes'; from previous type: Nero; Neron Cais. (Aes, Sardes, Lydia, 70/1–72/3; the Marcellus is Vespasian's friend). *The British Museum, by permission of the Trustees*

Plate 16 Obv. Vespasian laureate. Rev. Vespasian extending hand to raise kneeling Roma; behind, Minerva; ROMA RESVRGE(N)S S.C.: 'Rome rising again'. (Aes, Rome, 70). *The Ashmolean Museum, by permission of the Visitors*

Plate 17 Obv. Vespasian laureate. Rev. Hexastyle temple of Jupiter Capitolinus, with statues on ground-work and in pediment; S.C. (Aes, Rome, 77–8). *The Ashmolean Museum, by permission of the Visitors*

Plate 18 Obv. Titus laureate; T. CAES. VESPASIAN. IMP. PON. TR. POT. COS II. Rev. Pax standing, holding branch and cornucopia; PAX AVGVSTI S.C. (Aes, Rome, 1 January–30 June, 72). *The Ashmolean Museum, by permission of the Visitors*

Plate 19 Obv. Vespasian laureate. Rev. Triumphal procession; Vespasian in quadriga, trumpeter, captive, etc. TRIVMP. AVG. (Gold, Lugdunum, ?70–1). *The Ashmolean Museum, by permission of the Visitors*

Plate 20 Obv. Tyche or city goddess wearing calathus, holding ears of barley and cornucopia; Et. DI Ba(sileos) Agrippa: 'Year 14 of King Agrippa'. Rev. Vespasian laureate; Autocra(tori) Ouespasi(ano) Caisari S(e)basto: '(Dedicated) to Imp. Vespasian Caesar Augustus'. (Aes, 74/5). *The British Museum, by permission of the Trustees*

Plate 21 Obv. Vespasian laureate. Rev. Victory standing, crowning Vespasian who sacrifices at an altar in front of an arch bearing statues of *?Genius Populi Romani* and *?Genius Senatus*; VICTORIA AVG. S.C. (Aes, Rome, etc., 71). *By permission of the Administrators of the Staatliche Museen zu Berlin – Preussischer Kulturbesitz Münzkabinett*

Plate 22 Obv. Vespasian laureate, 'Ouespesianos [*sic*] Caisar'. Rev. Head of Senate, hair rolled and bound with diadem; E. Aegaianou Thean Syncleton Lebedi.: 'During the magistracy of Aegaianus, (the people honour) the Divine Senate; coin of Lebedus'. (Aes, Lebedus, Ionia). *The British Museum, by permission of the Trustees*

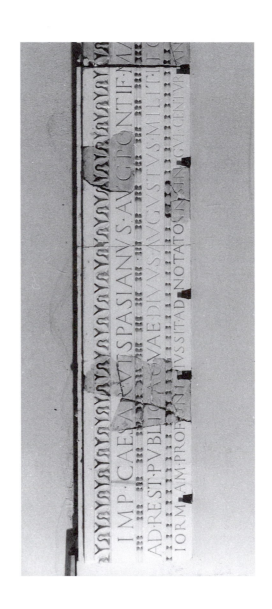

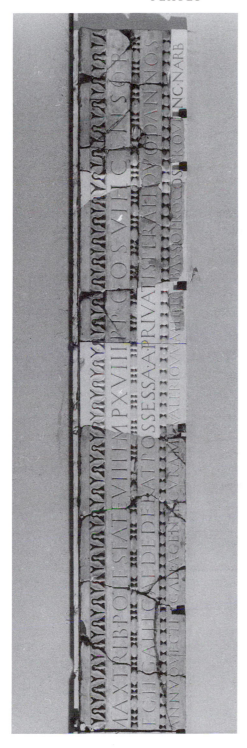

Plate 23 Vespasian on reclamation of public land, Arausio: Imp. Caesar Vespasianus Augustus, Pontifex Maximus, in the eighth year of Tribunician Power, eighteen times hailed Imperator, Father of his Country, eight times Consul, Censor: for the purpose of restoring the public lands that the Deified Augustus had granted to soldiers of the Second Legion Gallica and which have been occupied by private individuals for a number of years, has ordered a plan to be set up, with a note attached to each century of land [*c.*50.4 ha.] of the annual tax due from it, under the supervision of ?Valerius Ummidius Bassus, Proconsul of the Province of Narbonensis (1 January–30 June, 77; lighter sections of the inscription are restorations). *By permission of the Musée municipal d'Orange; Photo Université de Provence, C.N.R.S., Centre Camille Jullian, Ph. Foliot*

Plate 24 Obv. Domitian laureate; CAESAR AVG. F. DOMITIANVS. COS. V. Rev. Annona seated holding bundle of corn-ears in both hands; ANNONA AVGVST. S.C.: 'The Augustan grain supply'. (Aes, Rome, 77–8). *The Ashmolean Museum, by permission of the Visitors*

Plate 25 With [Imperator Caesar Vespasian Augustus, Pontifex Maximus, holder of Tribunician Power for the fourth year, hailed Imperator for the tenth time, four times Consul and designated for the fifth, Censor designate, Father of his Country, and Titus], son of Imperator Vespasian Augustus, holder of Tribunician Power, hailed Imperator for the fourth time, twice Consul and designated for the third time, Censor designate, and with Aulus Marius Celsus as Propraetorian Legate of Augustus and Sextus Caelius Tuscus as Legate of Augustus, the Sixth Legion Victrix (erected this monument) (April–30 June, 73; commemorative inscription by Legio VI Victrix from Xanten-Vynen, Lower Rhine, on the site of the battle of 69; VI Victrix remained on the Rhine until the reign of Hadrian). *Photo by L. Lilienthal, published by permission of the Kommission Rheinland*

Plate 26 Obv. Vespasian laureate wearing aegis. Rev. Titus and Domitian galloping r.; T. ET DOMITIAN. CAESARES PRIN. IVVEN. S.C.; 'Titus and Domitian Caesars Leaders of the Youth'. (Aes, Lugdunum, 69–70). *The Ashmolean Museum, by permission of the Visitors*

Plate 27 Obv. Titus laureate as 'Autocrator': 'Imperator'; and Domitian bareheaded as 'Caesar', confronted. Rev. River god Hermus, himation over lower limbs, holding in r. two ears of corn and in l. cornucopia, and leaning on vase from which stream flows; Epi Hypaticou (Ti. Catiou . . . Siliou) Italicou; Strat. Agronos: 'Under the Proconsul Italicus, during the magistracy of Agron'. (Aes, Smyrna, 77/8; the Proconsul is the poet Silius). *The British Museum, by permission of the Trustees*

Plate 28 Obv. Domitian, laureate; CAES. AVG. F. DOMIT. COS. III. Rev. Spes (Hope) advancing, holding flower; PRINCEPS IVVENTVT. (Silver, Rome, 74–5). *The Ashmolean Museum, by permission of the Visitors*

Plate 29 Interior of the Colosseum

Plate 30 Obv. Titus seated, holding branch; around him weapons. Rev. Colosseum, with Meta Sudans r. and portion of a building l. (Aes, Rome, 80–1). *The British Museum, by permission of the Trustees*

Plate 31 Obv. IMP. T. CAES. DIVI VESP. F. AVG P.M. TR. P. P.P. COS. VIII round S.C.: 'Imperator Titus Caesar, son of the Deified Vespasian, Augustus, Pontifex Maximus, holder of the Tribunician Power, Father of his Country, eight times Consul, By Decree of the Senate'. Rev. Ceremonial carriage drawn by two mules; DOMITILLAE IMP. CAES. VESP. AVG. S.P.Q.R.: 'Dedication of the Senate and Roman People to Domitilla wife of Imperator Caesar Vespasian Augustus'. (Aes, Rome, 80–1). *The British Museum, by permission of the Trustees*

Plate 32 Obv. Titus laureate; IMP. TITVS CAES. VESPASIAN. AVG. P.M. Rev. Vespasian seated, radiate, holding Victory and sceptre; DIVVS VESPASIAN. (Gold, Rome, 79–80). *The British Museum, by permission of the Trustees*

Plate 33 Obv. Domitian laureate, wearing aegis; IMP. CAES. DOMIT. AVG. GER. COS XVII. CENS. PER. P.P.. P.M. TR.P. XVI. Rev. Temple or chapel showing two columns, in which figure is seated on throne; in front, Victory on each side. (Gold, Rome, 95–6; Jupiter Feretrius or the Flavian Gens have been canvassed as dedicatees, but the authenticity of the coin is in question). *The British Museum, by permission of the Trustees*

Plate 34 Obv. IMP. CAES. DOMIT. AVG. GERM. COS. XV. CENS. PER. P.P. round S.C.: 'Imperator Caesar Domitian Augustus Germanicus, fifteen times Consul, Censor for an unlimited period, Father of his Country. By Decree of the Senate'. Rev. Ceremonial carriage drawn by two mules; DIVAE IVLIAE AVG. DIVI TITI F. S.P.Q.R.: 'Dedication by the Senate and Roman People to Julia Augusta, daughter of the Deified Titus'. (Aes, Rome, 90–1). *The British Museum, by permission of the Trustees*

8

STABILIZATION

The winning of peace

'The death of Vitellius ended the war; it did not bring peace', says Tacitus, of the City; in Germany, the Balkans, Africa, Judaea, and Britain there were new outbreaks, or old wars continued, to distract the centre from its work. It was a chance for animosities to emerge, distinct or in combination: anti-Roman feeling; class war; nationalism, already exhibited in Judaea and now showing in the West as tribalism. At a low level it manifested itself in opportunistic communal violence in Campania, Gaul, and Africa. By the end of the reign the only operations attested were in Britain, aggressive and imperialist. Such was the régime's military success, founded on Vespasian's success in Judaea and against Vitellius; and each step in reducing dissidence gave confidence to producers, traders, and politicians: their world would survive.[1]

In Britain the army's loyalties had been divided, and Rome lost control of the complex and powerful dependency of the Brigantes ('Hillmen', 'High Ones'), whose territory stretched coast to coast from the Don to near the line of Hadrian's Wall, and who had been kept faithful under Cartimandua, probably since the invasion. She needed Rome's support, and Rome hers. In 69 her husband Venutius, whom she had rejected in favour of his 'armour-bearer' – a vassal chieftain - took advantage of Rome's weakness to seize power. He was supported by the mass of the people and reinforcements from other tribes, and all Roman auxiliary forces could do in response to calls for help was rescue her. Vitellius' governor M. Vettius Bolanus and his two predecessors all had trouble with their troops. British disturbances were good news for Gallic rebels, and the problem of the now hostile presence in the north was left for the new Emperor, although Bolanus won some success against the rebels, and had a breastplate for trophy.[2]

More serious was the situation on the Rhine. Before he could think of further advance into Germany even as a possibility (one decisively rejected by Claudius), Vespasian had to stabilize the existing military situation. The story is controversial: the Flavians had reason to adjust their account of their dealings with the Batavian Julius Civilis and represent the revolt as a nationalistic uprising; participants on all sides had hidden agenda, concealed from fellow-combatants; fortunately Tacitus was not committed to a Flavian account. Scholars have argued accordingly that the movement was not separatist, that Civilis was drawn into war through the 'Gallic Empire', and that this was why, unlike the Treveran Julius Valentinus and Julius Sabinus the Lingonian, he and his troops are not known to have suffered punishment, and Batavians continued to serve in the army. The revised view is not convincing. Many Rhine legionaries had favoured their candidate Vitellius too intensely to accept Vespasian even after Vitellius' death; fearing Vespasian, they preferred to join Gallic neighbours in the search for an alternative. Batavian auxiliaries defected from Vitellius in the main because of the demands of recruiting officers, threatening long service abroad. In August 69, Vespasian was the obvious alternative, but intrinsically no better. The tribe had long been under economic and social pressure caused by recruitment and consequent lack of manpower at home: theirs had to be a separatist movement, and it was led by a general (providentially one-eyed like Hannibal) who allowed his beard to grow and dyed it red. After the Flavians captured Rome the rebellion flowered into an attempt to create a confederation of German and Gallic tribes, 'strongest' and 'richest'. Some Gallic tribes too, already alienated from Galba because of their connection with the Rhine legions who had put down Vindex's revolt, had helped promote Vitellius, and feared Vespasian. Now apparent instability at the heart of the Empire and the nearness of strong dissident forces put their leaders in mind of superior positions to be held in a breakaway Gaul. It was a formidable combination. Yet it meant different things to different participants; even without the Roman comeback, it would have fissured within months: besides rivalry between individual tribes and within them, there was Gallic fear of German dominance, sectional interests within the movement, and the material losses that Gaul would have sustained through seceding.[3]

The Batavians and their ability to swim rivers in full kit while controlling their horses had proved useful in the invasion of Britain, and they knew Vespasian and his brother. They had also earned Vitellius' gratitude at the first battle of Cremona: eight cohorts, once associated with XIV Gemina, were present when Valens' army assembled at Andematunnum, the Lingonian capital. The cohort commander Civilis, a man of royal descent, had been sent to Rome in May or June 68 by Nero's legate on the Lower Rhine for involvement in the revolt of Vindex, and his brother Paulus executed. Galba acquitted him, but in 69, Galba gone, he was rearrested by the army of the Rhine. Vitellius, keeping his valuable auxiliaries sweet, released him once again. When Vitellius took his forces to Rome he left four depleted legions, reinforced only by local levies: on the Lower Rhine XVI Gallica remained at Novaesium, XV Primigenia at Vetera, with the relic of V Alaudae, I at Bonna: on the Upper, IV Macedonica and the remains of XXI Rapax and XXII Primigenia. Hordeonius Flaccus, successor to Verginius Rufus on the Upper Rhine, was in overall command after Vitellius left, old, lame, vacillating, and without leadership, according to Tacitus. But he had the self-interest of the troops against him too.[4]

The Batavians declared for Vespasian in response to Antonius Primus' appeal. After serving in northern Italy the cohorts had been sent back to the Rhine in May. They found willing allies: the Canninefates and their kinsmen the Frisians were already in revolt against Vitellius' recruiting officers. The legions were now further weakened: Tungrian auxiliaries and Batavian rowers went over, ostensibly still to Vespasian, and the Romans lost control of the Batavian homeland, the Island between the Rhine and Waal. Hordeonius was for Vespasian, and it was in the Flavian interest for him to connive at what was going on to prevent the arrival of more Vitellian troops in Italy. Attempting to recover the Island, the Romans removed detachments of V Alaudae and XV Primigenia from Vetera, and added them to the normally dependable Ubian infantry, Treveran cavalry and (still!) a cohort of Batavians. Their failure was fatal to morale. Vitellius called the eight cohorts south again to his defence, but the order met a sluggish response; Hordeonius refused the Batavians the pay they demanded and they moved instead down the Rhine virtually unopposed. In September Vetera itself, with its depleted garrison, became their target, but they could not take it by storm. Hordeonius sent Dillius Vocula with IV Macedonica and Vocula's own XXII Primigenia to relieve the garrison, but the Romans were still short of supplies. Three attempts were made to bring in convoys, ending in a mutiny when the troops refused to return. Meanwhile Civilis was being reinforced from across the Rhine, and he was able to plunder and demoralize Rome's friends on the river and further west.[5]

Early in November news of Cremona arrived. Hordeonius administered the oath of loyalty, but misjudged his troops' fidelity. While the struggle for Vetera went on, a donative offered in Vespasian's name merely provoked the troops at Novaesium, augmented by men of V Alaudae and XV Primigenia, to a mutiny in which Hordeonius fell. The dead Vitellius' portraits were restored. But Vocula succeeded in obtaining the allegiance of I, IV Macedonica, and XXII. News of Vitellius' death brought the legionaries the choice of acquiescence in Flavian rule (after the murder of Hordeonius!), or joining Gauls and Germans: hatred of Vespasian consumed the legions' loyalty to Rome, and the Twilight of the Romans, signalled by the fiery destruction of the Capitol, was a potent symbol to people who practised self-immolation in defeat. Civilis went on attacking 'Vitellian' Romans even after he had been told that the civil war was virtually won. The question was whether calling off his men from lucrative fighting would lose him face with them without securing a worthwhile pay-off from Vespasian. Delay might raise his price. Civilis began negotiations with the Treveran prince Julius Classicus, who had unsuccessfully commanded a cavalry squadron in Vitellius' expeditionary force, and Julius Tutor, Vitellius' Prefect of the Rhine bank (an exceptional post, appropriate to a Treveran), with Sabinus the

Lingonian, and a few Ubians and Tungri. The Treverans, long associated with the Rhine legions, backed them against Vindex, supported Vitellius and once more had nothing to look for from the victor. The officers' service under Vitellius made disloyalty to Rome look better; Tutor's prestigious command enhanced his value to the rebels, so making it more worthwhile for him to take part. The Gauls showed their hand just as Vocula was marching to the relief of Vetera; his Vitellian soldiers deserted him, and his assassin, a deserter from I, was promoted centurion. Gauls, German tribes, Rhine legions, were Civilis' for the asking. Classicus appeared in Roman officer's uniform, the greatest distinction now known in the area, and interpretable by those whose identity was bound up with Rome, the Ubii, who had given way to pressure from the Tencteri, and the remnants of Vocula's army, as that of a Roman *imperator*. But the *imperium* belonged to an independent Gaul. Civilis held his Batavians aloof, an élite distinct from Gauls and Germans; Tutor then proceeded south to Moguntiacum, where recalcitrant officers of IV and XXII were killed, while Classicus completed the siege of Vetera: the garrison was forced to swear to the Gallic Empire – and was massacred. Rome's presence on the Rhine was over, her fortresses destroyed; Vindonissa and apparently Moguntiacum, where collaboration by other ranks assuaged the insurgents, survived.[6]

The intimidation of the Ubii strengthened Civilis' hand still more and brought over Sunuci, Baetasii, and Nervii, but the monster they had helped to conjure up frightened the Gauls. The faithful Sequani in April defeated a mass of Lingonians under Sabinus, who was now styling himself 'Caesar'. That checked the movement, like news of Roman preparations.[7]

Mucianus himself was needed at Rome. Safe men were sent, and safe troops, in revealingly crushing numbers. In Italy Mucianus requisitioned three Flavian supporters, VIII Augusta, XI Claudia, and XIII Gemina, along with II Adiutrix (from men of the Ravenna fleet) and the Vitellian XXI Rapax, which was already on its way back to base at Vindonissa; two, eventually three, were summoned from Spain, I Adiutrix and VI Victrix, X Gemina, and one British, XIV Gemina, old enemies of the Batavians, and the Channel fleet. The Italian contingent went mostly by the Great St Bernard and Mt Genèvre passes, some by the Little St Bernard. Annius Gallus, the Othonian general, with I, VIII, and XI, took on the Rhine and supervision of the Lingones to the west in the nascent province of Upper Germany. These activities Tacitus described in the missing part of the *Histories*; the campaign against the ringleaders of the Lower Rhine was more urgent. Operations under Q. Petillius Cerialis deployed II, VI, XIII, XIV, and XXI, as well as legionaries on the spot returning to loyalty, X Gemina, and massive auxiliary forces, six squadrons of cavalry and up to nineteen infantry cohorts (probably with the brothers Cn. Domitius Tullus and Lucanus, who had served in V Alaudae at Vetera, in charge).[8]

At Durocortorum, capital of the Remi, a conference was held in April or

May. Valentinus spoke eloquently for the struggle, but Julius Auspex of the host delegation stressed Roman power and the advantages of peace. Gaul was flooding the world with her goods, and even if the *Imperium* survived it would be cut off from Britain and the Rhine army market; the Remi needed both. Only the Treveri themselves, with Tungri, Nervii, and Lingones, persisted, and the main danger was over. Success itself split the protagonists: Civilis was pursuing a rival Batavian leader, and Tacitus accuses Classicus of resting on his laurels, while Tutor failed to garrison the Upper Rhine and close the Alpine passes. Some Roman forces were already near: XXI Rapax had passed its old camp, the procurator of Noricum was *en route* from Raetia with auxiliary cohorts, and an élite squadron (*singulares*) who had defected from Vitellius were being led against Civilis by his nephew Julius Briganticus. Fresh levies from left-bank tribes south of Moguntiacum, along with deserters from the legions, reinforced Tutor's Treveri. But both abandoned Tutor, who fell back on the left bank of the Nahe at Bingium; the procurator turned the position and there was a massive Treveran surrender. The disgraced XVI and I, who had been transferred to Treveran territory from Novaesium and Bonna, now took the oath to Vespasian and withdrew into camp amongst the Mediomatrici. But Valentinus and Tutor, by killing their legates, forced the rebels back.[9]

Cerialis, a Roman inclined to put subjects in their place verbally as well as in battle, arrived at Moguntiacum in May. The Gauls were duly impressed, and Civilis and Classicus sent messages to Valentinus, telling him to temporize. Cerialis' first objective was the Treveri. I and XVI marched down the Moselle while Cerialis, with the expeditionary force and the remains of IV and XXII, moved up from the Rhine confluence, arriving at Rigodulum, nearly 13 km downstream from Augusta Treverorum, where he defeated and captured Valentinus. Cerialis mercifully let the Gauls off with a stock lecture offering protection from predatory Germans, peace, and a share of Empire; he treated the men of I and XVI with similar forbearance (June). It was good policy: Cerialis' camp outside the city was an obvious target.[10]

Classicus and Tutor fled to the Batavians, the military core of the resistance. In a desperate preliminary ruse, they wrote to Cerialis that Vespasian was dead, offering him the Gallic Empire if they might keep their Batavian and Treveran principalities, but Cerialis prudently passed the note to Domitian with the captured Valentinus, who was duly executed. The surviving rebels' next move, the attack on the Roman camp, took Cerialis by surprise (he was in bed in the city with an Ubian, one Claudia Sacrata, it was duly noted, when the assault came), but within the day his men were destroying the enemy camp.[11]

Now in July Colonia Agrippinensium massacred the Germans billeted there, including Civilis' keenest unit, and surrendered his womenfolk. XIV Gemina went on to the reduction of Tungri and Nervii, whose leaders fled north into the heartland of rebel territory; but that campaign kept the legion from co-operating with the fleet and descending on Batavian territory, and the Canninefates were able to take the fleet in isolation and cripple it. Civilis gathered his forces at a strong point with encouraging memories: Vetera.[12]

Cerialis, coming into possession of II, VI, and XIV, with auxiliaries, made for the enemy's own territory (July–August). The battle wavered two days over ground that Civilis had flooded, and he was able to escape because the Romans lacked the fleet to trap him. Civilis burnt Batavodurum and retreated to the Island with Classicus, Tutor, and 113 leading Treverans. They broke down Nero Drusus' dyke, allowing the river in full force down the Waal on the Roman side of the Island and lowering the Rhine. Cerialis had despatched XIV Gemina to Annius Gallus, who had to deal with tribes upstream such as the Chatti, who threatened Moguntiacum; he now had X Gemina at Arenacium, and II Adiutrix at Batavodurum, building a bridge to the Island; the auxiliaries were further west at Grinnes and Vada. In August the rebels attacked the several camps simultaneously. The assaults failed, though Briganticus and a number of Roman senior centurions were killed. Cerialis drove the the enemy back into the river with his élite cavalry, but was unable to wipe them out: his rowers were not ready – so he must have complained. Discipline was not at its peak, and Cerialis was not the man to restore it, as another episode showed. On returning from an inspection he was ambushed and only escaped because (once again) he was not in his quarters, a flagship that the enemy towed off to present to the seer Veleda.[13]

The flotilla, ready at last, had a brief encounter with Civilis' blockade at the mouth of the Maas and the Waal. It was Civilis' last defence. In September he retired beyond the Rhine, leaving the Island to Cerialis. The Romans avoided damaging the chief's property, and when negotiations opened, Cerialis tried to use them to detach Civilis' allies, notably Veleda and her formidable Bructeri between Ems and Lippe. The Batavians themselves were losing heart. At a meeting on the stumps of a severed bridge over the Ijssel or Vecht, Civilis was probably allowed refuge on the east bank of the Rhine, with Classicus, Tutor, and the councillors. Cerialis had achieved his main purpose, re-establishing Roman, specifically Flavian, authority, on the Rhine. The Romans were in difficulties from rain and flooding, coming winter prohibited eastern operations, and Civilis was a failed leader. But Trier was probably punished by confiscation of rebel leaders' land. Sabinus and his wife held out in hiding for years. When they were betrayed they were taken to Rome and executed, though their infant sons were spared. Without practical purpose (the chance of deploying a man later to advantage) Vespasian would not demonstrate compassion as Claudius had to Caratacus, and Sabinus had called himself Caesar.[14]

Now rebuilding could begin from the North Sea to the Upper Danube. and legions be deployed in long-term positions. There was destruction or damage to Vetera, Novaesium, and Bonna along with the auxiliary forts at Valkenburg (10 km east of Maastricht) and Ad Confluentes, and in the southern sector Moguntiacum, Rheingönheim, perhaps Seltz, and Argentorate; Hofheim too, in the Taunus north-east of Moguntiacum. Rebuilding was in stone, if that change was not already a Julio-Claudian initiative, as at Vindonissa.[15]

XXI Rapax and XXII Primigenia, the survivors from the pre-war Rhine army, went respectively to Bonna and Vetera II (rebuilt as a single fortress 1.5 km east of the original site); the other Lower German fortress, Novaesium, was taken over by VI Victrix, and Noviomagus constructed between two settlements destroyed in 70 for X Gemina (II Adiutrix continuing with Cerialis to Britain). On the Upper Rhine Moguntiacum remained a double fortress, for I Adiutrix and XIV Gemina, while VIII Augusta took over Vespasian's old base of Argentorate and XI Claudia Vindonissa, replacing XXI Rapax. Gaul was not neglected: a long-standing military presence was continued and strengthened.[16]

As to auxiliaries, in spite of the trouble they had caused, there was a strong presence, filling gaps between existing forts. They had played an important part, especially in the south after the withdrawal of II Augusta in 43. A few pre-Flavian forts are attested. Now stone housing was constructed or rebuilt, as at Ad Confluentes, along the left bank. Attention to such routes is implied by the bridges constructed there (70) and at Moguntiacum (probably 74). Immediate problems were dealt with by disbandment or transfer: three cavalry units disappeared and more than a score of infantry. Units went to the Balkans and notably to Britain, where D. Knight finds a cavalry unit and twenty-three cohorts, including four Batavian, two Tungrian, three Lingonian, and four Nervian, transferred under Vespasian, with perhaps three each of cavalry and infantry units crossing with Cerialis in 71; Ala I Hispanorum came west with Mucianus, passed to Germany with ten other auxiliary units for the revolt and then went to Britain. Moesian units were stationed on the Rhine, and others moved from Upper to Lower Rhine, where only two units were left from before the revolt. It received twin cohorts I and II Civium Romanorum (perhaps from ex-legionaries), VI Ingenuorum, and II and VI Brittonum, and new auxiliary forts were built, making 27 in all; units were deployed according to the strength of the enemy they faced, sparingly in the south, densely and in the form of cavalry in the centre opposite the Tencteri, with infantry cohorts in the northern sector.[17]

On the Danube, especially on the lower reaches, the problem was different. Tacitus blames Roman preoccupation with civil war for reverses there, but they resulted from opportunistic attacks on the part of tribes already troublesome. East of the Quadi and Marcomanni, who could be dealt with by diplomacy, the Romans faced the Sarmatian Iazyges on the Hungarian plain between Danube and Tisza, less truculent than the Roxolani, and the Dacians of Transylvania, a people sufficiently developed in the first century BC to have threatened the province of Macedonia. During the civil war some Romans showed sensitivity in dealing with neighbouring tribes. Tampius Flavianus and Cornelius Fuscus had to send forces to Italy, and they dealt differently with their potential allies, as A. Mócsy observed. Sido and Italicus, loyal to Rome in their rule over the Marcomanni and Quadi, but not popular at home, took their troops to fight at Cremona, leaving no forces to unseat them; the chiefs of the Iazyges were kept as hostages and their troops sent home leaderless.[18]

Moesia was less well handled. There had been increasing activity in the Julio-Claudian period. The original province, with two legions, IV Scythica at Viminacium and V Macedonica, at Oescus by 42 at latest, had been augmented by Tiberius with Macedonia and Achaea (15–44). Then Claudius annexed Thrace and sent VIII Augusta from Pannonia to Novae. Nero's Parthian war was demanding, but Moesia could not be left for long with only two legions: in the mid-50s IV Scythica was replaced by VII Claudia from Dalmatia, and when in the early 60s V Macedonica was also transferred east it was only a few years before III Gallica took its place.[19]

The extension of Roman control to the mouth of the Danube and shores of the Black Sea had put that lake, with the transport of grain supplies from Russia, under the protection of the governor of Moesia. A fleet forty-strong based on Sinope ensured Roman power on the eastern coast, which was particularly subject to piracy; backed up by 3,000 legionaries, it controlled the tribes round the Black Sea and the Sea of Azov. In Rome's Crimean dependency, the Bosporan kingdom, a presence was also maintained, and a share of the monarch's revenues taken. Under Claudius the governor had replaced one Roman nominee with another, Cotys I; Vespasian confirmed his son Rhescuporis II.[20]

Ti. Plautius Silvanus, governor of Moesia under Nero 60–7, achieved successes celebrated only under Vespasian. He had brought over more than a hundred thousand tribesmen to pay tribute on the southern side of the Danube. He had smashed an incipient Sarmatian movement (precursor of the invasion of 69); brought over rulers to pay homage; restored their relatives to friendly monarchs; and received hostages. He had kept his province peaceful, relieved the Chersonese of a siege by the king of the Scyths – in which Cotys may have been killed, since he ceased to coin in the 60s and Rhescuporis II was in office by 68 – and provided the people of Rome with grain. The movements that made Silvanus' action necessary came from eastern tribes nudging those further south and west against areas under direct Roman control. It was not only Nero who neglected Silvanus' achievements: Tacitus has nothing of them, perhaps because no decree of triumphal ornaments attracted his attention. They were open to criticism if the vacancy left by tribesmen brought over the Danube gave scope to those behind; but that would not have weighed with Tacitus. Movements further west, perhaps repercussions, also led to the transfer of tribes across the Danube by Tampius Flavianus, before the death of Nero, given his early Claudian consulship; but his achievement too was probably recognized by Vespasian.[21]

In the winter of 67–8, the Roxolani, now in Wallachia, had cut up two auxiliary cohorts, helpless against their horse. In February 69, when a thaw made roads slippery and the countryside was under deep soft snow, an expedition of up to 9,000 was ambushed and destroyed by III Gallica and auxiliary troops. Otho rewarded M. Aponius Saturninus, the governor of Moesia, with a triumphal statue and all his legates, not merely T. Aurelius Fulvus of III, with consular ornaments. His own glory demanded it, but the interests of politicians and Empire did not continue harmoniously. Tacitean criticism applies particularly to the Flavian leadership, notably Antonius Primus and Saturninus, who withdrew troops from the Danube; Vitellius had been more responsible. In late September 69 the Dacians moved in on both Roman banks below Ratiaria against Oescus and Novae; Sarmatians too may have been involved, as in the following years. Mucianus' taskforce, *en route* for Italy, turned north by way of Philippopolis. VI Ferrata went from there or from Serdica or Naissus to confront the Dacians; their repulse was to justify Mucianus' triumphal ornaments. In the late autumn, C. Fonteius Agrippa was brought up from Asia with additional forces, including Vitellian survivors, such as those of V Alaudae, to coordinate defence. Fonteius was killed early in 70 and the province ravaged. Rubrius Gallus, sent in his place, succeeded, with I Italica and VII Claudia, in beating off the Sarmatians and restoring the defences of Moesia.[22]

These events and setbacks foreshadowed future problems; greater attention would have to be paid to this area, as it would be by Domitian and Trajan: another reason for the retrospective recognition accorded to Silvanus. Vespasian's permanent legionary dispositions, as well as the advance on the Upper Danube, showed that he was aware of that. The Balkans had always had pull, stronger as time went on; now, although the establishment of the Rhine army was restored to eight, those on the Danube were raised to a new level, from four to six.[23]

On the southern shore of the Black Sea there was only minor, isolated trouble, coming in the autumn of 69, when Vespasian already controlled the region. It was instigated by Anicetus, ex-commander of the royal Pontic fleet, who had found service directly to Rome benefiting him less than service to the former dependency had until five years previously. Anicetus used the name of Vitellius to call rebels to arms. He cut a Pontic cohort to pieces at Trapezus and clinched his victory by forming an improvised fleet, but was soon annihilated by a legionary detachment. News of the success arrived before Vespasian reached Alexandria, at the same time as he heard of the victory of Cremona. Recognition of the new Emperor is attested in Pontus: a basis dedicated to him by the people of Heraclea, while across the water Phanagoria in the Crimean Bosporus left no doubt of its allegiance in mid-71.[24]

The major problem area within Vespasian's power base was Judaea, where in 68 he had already been planning the offensive against Jerusalem. Plans for the post-war era were in hand in 69, when M. Ulpius Traianus, legate of X Fretensis, constructed a road from the capital, Caesarea, to Scythopolis. Since the declaration the insurgents had regrouped, but the supporters of John of Gischala had split; some of the dissidents were holding the Temple, while Simon b. Gioras controlled the Upper City and most of the Lower. In the factional struggles grain had been burned, when the city was full of refugees from the countryside (600,000 bodies of lower-class dead were eventually and implausibly reported to have been thrown out of the city).[25]

In Alexandria Vespasian had planned the final reduction of Judaea with Titus, who had been assigned the war at the conference of Berytus. Titus set out in spring 70, taking with him Ti. Julius Alexander, governor of Judaea in the 40s, and Josephus (Egypt was assigned to L. Peducaeus Colonus), and detachments totalling 2,000 men from III Cyrenaica and XXII Deiotariana under Aeternius Fronto, making up for the men in Mucianus' taskforce. Titus now brought an additional legion into play: beside V Macedonica, still with Sex. Vettulenus Cerialis, X Fretensis under Traianus' successor A. Larcius Lepidus Sulpicianus, and XV Apollinaris under Tittius Frugi, XII Fulminata came into action for the first time since Cestius' defeat. Then there were twenty auxiliary infantry cohorts and eight squadrons of cavalry and Syrian and royal allied contingents, larger than they had been under Vespasian and led in person by Sohaemus and Agrippa, almost the last appearance in the field of dependent forces. Josephus includes 3,000 'guards' from the Euphrates – half a legion from Zeugma, as F. Millar notes. A total of 50,000–60,000 men assembled at Caesarea.[26]

Titus' campaign began shakily. V and X were despatched by Emmaus and Jericho, while Titus himself led XII and XV, with the Syrian auxiliaries and allied contingents, through Samaria and Gophna to Gabath Saul, 5.5 km. from Jerusalem. After a reconnoitre in which he was almost cut off at the Psephinus Tower, Titus advanced two legions, XII and XV, to Scopus; V was stationed 500m. behind it, and X on the Mount of Olives, 1 km from the city on the east and beyond the Brook Kedron. The besieged checked their quarrels and cut up X, which Titus had to rescue.[27]

This success was a signal for renewed struggles for the leadership. At the Feast of the Unleavened Bread, 14 Xanthicus, John of Gischala gained entry to the Temple gates and Eleazar b. Simon was killed. The two surviving claimants, John, with 6,000 soldiers and 2,400 irregulars, and Simon b. Gioras and his 15,000 men, 5,000 of them Idumaeans, stayed at loggerheads until the Roman battering rams swung into action. It was on the day of John's entry, Josephus implies, that Titus, despairing of a surrender, decided to move up to the walls. After another ambuscade a more cautious approach allowed Titus to encamp at about 370m from the ramparts, opposite the Psephinus Tower, an octagonal structure nearly 30m high; another group dug in at the same distance opposite the even taller (34m) Hippicus Tower, while X remained on the Mount of Olives. Titus had chosen the most vulnerable spots in the ramparts (the outermost of the three walls, that of Agrippa I, had never been completed) and those that gave easier access to the Upper City, the Antonia fortress, and the Temple; the suburbs were scoured for material to make siege platforms.[28]

For his attack Titus chose a point north-west of the Jaffa Gate, under fire from weapons captured from Cestius; the 38 kilo missiles that the more skilled X Fretensis sent back had a range of more than 370 m. When the works were complete, battering rams, the biggest christened 'Nikon' ('Victor') by the defenders, were brought up at three points. To gain height, Titus had constructed three mobile wooden towers, each 21 m high, which proved their worth as support to the rams.[29]

On 7 Artemisius the defenders were forced to give up Agrippa's wall. Titus went straight on to the second wall, concentrating on the central tower of the north side. In spite of the concerted efforts of the defenders a breach was made after only four days. Titus' men were hard pressed in the narrow streets, and extricated themselves with heavy losses; four more days were necessary to end resistance. There was now a pause, in which the Jews were subjected to the awe-inspiring sight of four legions on parade, receiving pay in full dress; the respite did nothing to break their resolution.[30]

The next phase lasted until 5 Panemus. Two legions, V and XII, collaborated against the Antonia, with the Temple the ultimate objective, and the others in the north opposite the Hyrcanus tomb, Titus' original target. Hunger tormented the besieged, and the two leaders had to guard the gates against desertions – the atrocities alleged against allied troops and legionaries looking for coins swallowed by the deserters should have been deterrent enough. Despite their sufferings, the defenders made increasingly skilful use of the 340 captured artillery pieces. It was seventeen days before the massive terraces from which the assault was to be mounted, begun on 12 Artemisius, were complete, and then the Antonia approach was undermined by John of Gischala's men and destroyed by fire. Rams were operating from the northern works when a sally under Simon b. Gioras set them on fire too and even threatened the Roman camp. Titus decided on total investment to cut the city off, starve it out, and protect his men from further sallies. When the besieged still held out, Titus ordered more massive approach works, but only opposite the Antonia fortress; fetching timbers meant a round journey of 16 km. The new terraces, the last attempt at an assault, were built in three weeks, defended from the Jews' now enfeebled sallies, and gave the rams their chance to shatter the wall – only for a second, improvised wall to be revealed behind it. This was stealthily scaled in the small hours by a party of twenty-four, a trumpet sounded at the top to summon the main force, and the Antonia fell.[31]

Temple and Upper City remained. Titus cleared the ground by razing the fortress, on 17 Panemus, the day the Jews had to stop the daily sacrifice in the Temple for want of victims. With an eye to fighting in confined spaces,

Titus redeployed his troops into élite groups of a thousand, under the legate of V, Sex. Vettulenus Cerialis, and ordered a night attack. The engagement ended indecisively, but the rest of the army were preparing to destroy the Temple defences by building four ramps, two each on the north and west sides. The defenders made daring sallies and finally made another assault on the troops encamped on the Mount of Olives. On 22 Panemus, to hinder the advance into the Temple, they fired and hacked down the portico that joined it to the Antonia – destruction continued by the Romans – and five days later lured legionaries on to the roof of the western portico, which they fired, causing heavy casualties. The destruction of the porticoes took away the defenders' vantage-points. On 8 Lous the Romans had rams poised against the west wall, but they had already been withstanding assault for six days and the gate in the northern wall was equally resistant to undermining. Scaling parties against the outer Temple court also failed, and Titus ordered the gates to be fired.[32]

Josephus shields Titus from responsibility for destroying the Temple: on 9 Lous, the day after the Romans penetrated the court, Titus ordered a ramp for easier access, and summoned his six-man council to decide the fate of the Temple. His clemency was frustrated by the fury of the Jews and his soldiers' indiscipline. On the 10th the Jews twice sallied from the inner courts, the wall separating the outer and inner courts was razed, and a soldier torched the priests' rooms on the north side of the sanctuary. Along with the Temple burned the Treasury and other public buildings and 6,000 refugees in one of the porticoes, which were deliberately fired by the Romans to complete the job. But before the Temple burnt Titus and his staff entered the Holy of Holies and carried out the Table of the Shewbread and the seven-branched candlestick which were displayed in Titus' triumph for the Temple of Peace. The booty – or its estimated worth – brought down the price of gold in Syria by 50 per cent. At the end of the day the standards were brought into the outer court and sacrifice offered, while Titus was saluted Imperator. Israel began a new unhappy era.[33]

Josephus' testimony is contradicted by two late sources, Sulpicius Severus and Orosius, who claim that Titus ordered destruction, in Sulpicius' view with the anachronistic idea of cutting out two alien branches of the same stock, Judaism and Christianity. Scholars offer varying scenarios for Josephus' council – and if present might still have done so. H. Montefiore suggests that Titus gave orders that he knew could not be carried out; E.M. Smallwood credits him with intending to save the Temple, but the renewed Jewish attack forced his hand. A less favourable view is to be preferred. The Romans did not intend cult to continue. Sacrifice had ended, they executed the priests after the capture, and the tax payable to Jupiter Capitolinus imposed in 70 was a grinding reminder to Jewry of his superiority to the God of the Temple. Even a discussion on whether the Temple, if it survived the actual attack, should be razed was unlikely at this point.[34]

Only the Upper City remained in Jewish hands. The leaders asked for a parley, but their request for safe conduct was refused. The captured Lower City was burned, and surviving insurgents took to passages beneath it. In the Upper City slaughter continued too, 8,400 dying in Herod's palace at the hands of Simon and John's men, so Josephus claims. This, with the three towers, was their last fortress. For the final assault new approach works at the north-eastern and north-western corners of the Upper City had to be put in hand on 20 Lous, inducing the Idumaeans to begin negotiations. They were killed by the fanatics, but other desertions followed. On 7 Gorpiaeus the Romans mounted their rams on the terraces; part of the wall was breached and the defenders fled, abandoning the Hippicus, Phasael, and Mariamme Towers, which Titus left to commemorate his success. They fled to the ravine of Siloam, then underground, into a trap. The prisoners included John of Gischala, who was deported to Italy and perpetual detention. The last 'free' parts of the city were destroyed with indiscriminate slaughter, and all the remaining fortifications except on the west, where the garrison was to be quartered, razed. Towards evening they stopped the killing, but in the night the fire took hold and dawn on the 8th broke over Jerusalem in flames.[35]

Simon b. Gioras in the Upper City had also gone underground, but emerged on the Temple site to surrender. He was reserved for execution during Titus' triumph. Other prisoners confined in the Temple court were examined over a period of days. Allegedly 11,000 starved to death during the process, but the surviving activists (and the old and feeble, allegedly without instructions) were killed, 700 impressive-looking captives were reserved for the triumph, persons over the age of 17 were sent to hard labour in Egypt or to provincial arenas, and children sold. Those who died in the siege are calculated by Josephus at 1,100,000, but Tacitus' 600,000 for the total besieged is more persuasive; Josephus' figure for those taken prisoner in the war is only 97,000.[36]

Titus celebrated with a three-day feast. Victory had been hard won: the siege had lasted 140 days, forcing Vespasian to leave for Italy without him, and his tactics had needed repeated revision. For Romans and their eastern friends it was time for rewards. Agrippa II had his kingdom extended. Flavius Josephus received charge of the sacred writings, freedom for his brother, and landed property. Behind Jerusalem's surviving walls, X Fretensis remained with its auxiliaries under the acting governor, Sex. Vettulenus Cerialis; the bulk of the army returned to Caesarea, still the administrative centre, and Titus celebrated again there and at Caesarea Philippi with gladiatorial programmes featuring the prisoners. Domitian's and Vespasian's birthdays were marked in the same way, Domitian's on 24 October at Caesarea Maritima, Vespasian's on 17 November at Berytus. At Zeugma Titus received another tribute: a golden crown from the Parthian king.[37]

This was the end of the war for Titus. He marched south again to Alexandria and organized the despatch to Pannonia of the 'European' legions,

V and XV, and to Rome of selected captives. He himself embarked in the spring of 71 and returned to Italy with speed, leaving subordinates, first Sex. Lucilius Bassus, who arrived in 71 from his prefecture of both Italian fleets to take over from Vettulenus as governor, with the task of finishing the work round the Dead Sea. There remained Herodium, Machaerus, the strongest fortress in Judaea after Jerusalem, and Masada. Herodium surrendered to Bassus, probably in 71, but Machaerus would have had to be dealt with by siegecraft, if Bassus had not negotiated its surrender, bartering a captured Jewish soldier for it. The garrison escaped, the inhabitants of the town below were massacred or enslaved, and Bassus proceeded to mop up defenders who had passed his lines. Machaerus may have been put under an auxiliary garrison. On Bassus' death in 72 or early 73 he was succeeded by L. Flavius Silva, who conducted a siege better known than that of Jerusalem itself.[38]

Masada was manned by 967 *sicarii* under Eleazer b. Jair, grandson of the Zealots' founder. They were pillaging for their living, but the fortress contained weapons for ten times as many, and provisions for years. It had two entrances, a carriage road on the west and, facing the Dead Sea, a path aptly called 'the Snake', and never used by the assailants, though boulders were found above it ready to use. Silva, short of supplies for one legion, four cohorts (one part-mounted, one milliary), totalling more than seven times the besieged, saw that he could not starve Masada and would have to conduct a regular siege. He set up headquarters to the north-west and another large fort to the south-east, each accommodating part of the legion. The circumvallation, aimed against forays or escapes, was more than 3.54 km in length, 3 m high and 1.8 m thick. On the east it linked a string of eleven stone towers constructed at intervals of between 80 and 100 m., on the other sides twenty-nine towers, and the wall was patrolled. On a massive natural promontory, Leuce ('White (spur)') on the west, which rose to 128 m below the edge of the plateau, an 85 m high terrace was constructed. It was crowned by a 21 m platform, bringing the Romans into striking distance of the rampart. This was the base for siege weapons which included a 25 m iron-clad tower housing artillery and a ram. The ram brought down the outer wall, but a resilient timber wall constructed behind that proved vulnerable only to fire. The Romans prepared a final assault but according to Josephus found all but seven of the besieged dead in a suicide pact. Whatever the numbers who perished in this way, were massacred, or hid and starved to death, Masada fell on 15 Xanthus 73, after a siege of four months. For a short while troops remained in the south-western corner of the headquarters camp; then Masada was reoccupied by a Roman garrison. Silva achieved high honours, but not triumphal decorations: as W. Eck suggests, the war had ended officially with the fall of Jerusalem and the joint Triumph. Romans would see the siege as designed to demonstrate Roman inexorability. In world history the grandeur of the site and the heroism of the defenders have created a different image.[39]

120

Not all insurgents were rounded up. *Sicarii* escaped to Egypt from Herodium and Machaerus. Egypt and Alexandria had problems without being invaded from outside. Some were due to anger between Jews and Greeks that had hardly gone off the boil since the reign of Gaius and was reheated by the war in Judaea and disorder elsewhere in the Levant. When Titus arrived in Alexandria in 71 he had been presented with a petition of the same type as he had seen at Antioch, and evidently gave the same reply, preserving the *status quo* for Jews.[40]

The refugee *sicarii* set on wealthy members of the Jewish community, and tried to provoke an uprising. They had been preceded by the prisoners of war destined for the mines and by demands for the new didrachm Temple tax. If collection of the tax began only in 71–2, and arrears for the two previous years of Vespasian's reign (by the Egyptian calendar) were added, discontent with Roman rule may have been at a high level. But the Jewish establishment, leaders of the Alexandrian Elders (*Gerousia*), denounced them in assembly. Six hundred were seized, and the rest fled up-country to Thebes. The Prefect, Ti. Julius Lupus, reported the incident to Vespasian, who ordered the demolition of the Jewish temple at Leontopolis in the Delta, in spite of its long and blameless history. Lupus' successor Paulinus, in office by the end of August 73, made the Jews surrender the sacred ornaments and locked the precinct. Onias' temple had been an obscure local rival to Jerusalem, the only other place where sacrifice was offered. Vespasian must have believed that the *sicarii* would reach it and turn it into a resistance centre. In Egypt Judaism was certainly resurgent: amongst the names already commonly in use by Jews Biblical names like Abraham and Rebecca became prominent. But pagan cult suffered too: Vespasian closed the temple at Heliopolis.[41]

There were analogous disturbances in Cyrenaica, where Greek cities clung to the coast of a massive tract of inhospitable land dominated by Berbers. The province was more rent than most by class tensions, race-hate (as the savagery of the Jewish revolt of 115 was to show), and factional rivalry. The Jewish community had prospered, but Jonathan, a refugee tailor, led some two thousand of the less well-off into the desert, to the alarm of the propertied. The governor, Catullus, sent cavalry and infantry and massacred the secessionists. Jonathan, taken alive, claimed that the wealthy who had informed on him were actually involved. Catullus accepted this information, according to Josephus to satisfy his own greed, get rid of political opponents, and win his own Jewish war. Perhaps too he intended to curry favour with the Greek community and with Vespasian by supporting the exchequer. Three thousand died and there were extensive confiscations. Further accusations were made against leaders of the Jewish communities of Rome and Alexandria, as well as against Josephus, preempting efforts aimed at discrediting the story. But when Catullus returned to Rome with his prisoners and his list, Vespasian's investigation, whether or not Titus intervened, as Josephus claims, at least discredited accusations against Jews outside Cyrenaica. Jonathan paid for secession by being burned alive; Catullus received only a reprimand from Vespasian; Josephus attributes a frightful death – 'eaten of worms' – to the vengeance of God. Deadly feuds, rooted in poverty, were reinforced in 72, and, as J.M. Reynolds suggests, the governor may have undermined the loyalty as well as the numbers of the class he attacked.[42]

At the western end of the coast the provinces of Africa and the Mauretanias were troublesome too. The latter faced Spain and had interacted with it as the civil wars progressed, and Africa, Rome's main supplier of grain at three days' sail from Rome, had been of prime potential importance throughout, a target for Vespasian himself. Its resident legion stayed in place, but the cohorts of L. Clodius Macer, reconstituted for Vitellius, were disbanded. Before Africa could be definitively considered stable the death of the governor L. Piso, brother-in-law of Galba's heir, had to be brought about by the legionary commander, Valerius Festus: rebellion had been imminent. Once in control Festus put down a struggle over crops and herds between the inhabitants of Oea and Lepcis, which was becoming more serious because the outnumbered Oeans were bringing in Berber Garamantes from the Fezzan and forcing Lepcis to fortify itself. But Festus was able to quieten Garamantian brigandage, as the Romans saw it: he found a shorter route into their territory, making Roman troops less dependent on the goodwill of its inhabitants for water (the Garamantians filled the wells with sand). By taking the route 'by the Head of the Rock' he cut four days off the journey and brought the Garamantians to terms.[43]

Mauretania, troublesome when the Romans had annexed it, had accordingly been divided between two equestrian procuratorships with auxiliaries and detachments of legionaries at their disposal, based on the cities of Tingis and Iol-Caesarea; independent nomads on the borders aggravated underlying unrest. In 68–70 the hopes of malcontents soared, and would be hard to extinguish. Five years later, in 75, the two regions are found, as they had been during the original conquest, under a single senatorial legate, Sex. Sentius Caecilianus, who had had recent experience in nearby Africa as commander of III Augusta. Caecilianus' job was to 'regulate' the provinces and to put down tribal unrest. Incursions into southern Spain were a threat, felt under Nero and again, in organized form, in spring 69. For the moment Caecilianus was successful: he passed to a consulship in the same year or the next, and relief felt in the Roman cities may have found expression in a dedication to the Emperor by the colony of Tubusuctu in eastern Mauretania. But the area was a recurrent source of trouble: eight episodes are catalogued between 84 and 182.[44]

Vespasian and his associates dealt pragmatically and piecemeal with cracks in the fabric of the Empire, and applied practicable remedies. One, apparently obvious, was for Rome to disarm her subjects. Plentiful evidence emerged in 68–70 from Raetia, the Maritime Alps, and Mauretania, that no such rule had been pronounced. Vespasian did not pronounce it either. It is the region of most obstinate resistance, Judaea, that P.A. Brunt has used to refute the theory that emperors entertained the idea: the seriousness of later Jewish rebellions bears him out. General acquiescence in Roman rule was more of a deterrent to piecemeal disturbance than unenforceable irritants.[45]

9

ENHANCEMENT

The physical and moral
restoration of the Roman World

1 Rome and Italy

Parts of Italy, where the end of all the emperors who died in 68–9 had come and over which two campaigns had been fought, suffered most from the wars, after the military zone on the Rhine. The resurgence of Rome, which escaped damage until struck in its heart by the fire on the Capitol, was vital to Vespasian's own position: coins proclaim it, conjoining '*ROMA RESVR-GENS*' with the type of Vespasian extending his hand to raise Roma from her knees and presenting a high proportion of types showing public buildings. Returning to visible normality helped other kinds of wounds heal: members of one family had met in conflict.[1]

There were interlinked aims, involving overlapping groups: immediate relief, long-term supplies, amenities, entertainment, a sense of well-being. 'Rome' embraced not just an undifferentiated population but, in particular, citizens who were officially members of the *plebs urbana*, beneficiaries of grain distributions as the *plebs frumentaria* (about 200,000 males). The people had been as compliant as the senate in face of new emperors during 68–9; as a political force they had only nuisance value, but they still had symbolic political importance and a surviving tribal organization, and they had to be shown to be satisfied, especially after the success of Nero and Vitellius. Beyond Rome was citizen Italy, where men of property domiciled in the City had their estates and in many cases (like the Emperor) their roots, and which came second to Rome in the attentions it received. The régime seems to have claimed to have achieved the first stage of restoration for the year of the triumph, 71, at latest with the closing of the censors' term in 74.[2]

Most immediately, Rome had ten days' grain supplies left. As coinage shows, Galba, Otho, and Vitellius had all acknowledged grain as a prime concern. Both Galba and Vitellius had been under threat from Africa, Vitellius from Egypt too. Immediately Rome came into the control of Vespasian's troops, it was his responsibility. From Alexandria he sent a fleet as soon as the seas were open at the end of March; African grain might have been expected before then. The most conscientious emperors, such as Tiberius and

Claudius, were hard put to secure supplies, but we have no evidence of more trouble under Vespasian. This may be for lack of evidence, but he may have been helped by Claudius' measures rewarding carriers and by Nero's improvements to the harbour at Ostia, and he had the Horrea Galbae, granaries behind the Porticus Aemilia that had been given to the State by Galba or more probably his private property taken over by his successors, for storage.[3]

Besides regular distributions of grain there were occasional *congiaria* (monetary tips, theoretically an oil ration of about 3.4 litres) to men on the list. Claudius was not as generous as the conventional picture of Suetonius makes out: only two occasions are known; one more, at the stormy opening of the reign, has been surmised. Vespasian himself gave cash to the people when he returned in 70; it took the place of the tip to be expected from an emperor on accession as a legacy from his predecessor. Vespasian's generosity measured up to the norm, 300 *HS*. In 72 a *sestertius* displayed Titus distributing tips 'for the first time', no doubt in connection with the triumph of 71. A third distribution for Titus would be attested by a coin of 80 in the British Museum, if it is authentic, making Vespasian's first distribution a gift made in Titus' name. Certainly, like Octavian in 29 BC and Claudius in AD 44, Vespasian made his triumph the occasion for a distribution; but like Augustus in 5 and 2 BC, Tiberius in AD 20 and 23, and Claudius in 51, he aimed at popularity for his heir, neglecting his own gifts on the coinage.[4]

Another priority was the water supply, as Agrippa had shown, and Claudius, who had spent enormous sums on it. Vespasian lost no time in restoring at his own cost the Claudian aqueduct, out of use for nine years; he recorded the fact in the first half of 71 on the Porta Maggiore below Claudius' own inscription of 52 commemorating the construction of Claudia and Anio Novus.[5]

After supplies, amenity. Claudius had concerned himself with flooding, which caused damage and loss of life into the twentieth century. In 73–4, perhaps after another inundation, Vespasian was having the channel regulated again by the Curators of its Banks and Bed. M.T. Griffin notes how the form of the authorization to act changed with time: once from the senate ('*ex SC*'), now it came directly from the Emperor, to his greater credit. In December 69 Rome had not recovered from the more widespread fire of 64: in Suetonius' words, Vespasian took over a city still ugly with fire damage and, in line with a sentiment expressed in a senatorial decree of Nero's time, began to set it to rights (there had been a flood that spring as well). Vespasian's endeavours made him one of Rome's great builders and, according to a priesthood that owed its own importance to the restoring work of Augustus, the Sodales Titii, Vespasian in 78 was the 'preserver of public ceremonies and restorer of sacred buildings'. Temple building, and the revival of the ceremonies that belonged to the state religion, were outward signs of the inward regeneration essential to individuals and Commonwealth.[6]

Prime among long-term measures and among the first to be considered by the senate was the rebuilding of the Capitol. It had symbolic value for the resurgence of Rome, and for the renewal of the relationship between the Roman People and the triad of gods who had overseen their rise. The ruins loomed over Rome's inhabitants as a sharp reminder of the events of 69; its rebuilding was a signal to all that Rome's power was undiminished and that the Empire would survive. The ceremonial to inaugurate restoration, probably the return to its original position of a '*Lapis Terminus*', was held on 21 June 70, before Vespasian's arrival, but he carried off the first hod of rubble, physically taking the lead, as in the war in Judaea and when he prepared for the campaign against Vitellius.[7]

The Capitol was built on the foundations of the old temple. Coins show the traditional Corinthian columns of the triple-chambered building, which like other temples soon became an art museum, but they are not reliable as indicators of its appearance. The public record office nearby, the Tabularium, was rebuilt and stocked with copies of 3,000 documents under the supervision of a senatorial commission selected by lot early in 70, a useful work that symbolized Rome's continuing life. As a pendant to his work on the Capitol Vespasian appropriately undertook the restoration of C. Marius' temples of Honos and Virtus as well as of the stage buildings of the Theatre of Marcellus (of which he was a patron), but inscribed them with the name of the original builders (gaining double merit).[8]

Another enterprise was the unfinished Temple of Claudius on a huge platform on the Caelian. The structure had been pulled down after 64 to make way for Nero's Golden House; resuming the building served an additional symbolic purpose: the Golden House, a villa within the walls, had deprived the people of housing to gratify Nero's selfishness, its parks and gardens open to them as an act of grace. Now Vespasian, successor of the last reputable, and with the people deservedly popular, Julio-Claudian ruler, had the temple completed, probably hexastyle and within a garden, and cult instituted.[9]

After the triumph, and using Jewish booty, he began a new temple, dedicated to *Pax* and situated between the Basilica Aemilia and the Argiletum, an area that had suffered in the fires of 64 and had not been reclaimed for its previous use, a meat market. The structure, lauded by Pliny as one of the most beautiful in Rome, and recalling and outdoing the Altar that Augustus had dedicated in 9 BC, constituted a declaration of normality restored after the civil wars. It was completed in 75, but plans to develop the Argiletum into a Forum were left for Domitian to carry through; it is named after Nerva, who dedicated it in 97, or called the Forum Transitorium, since it led from the Temple of Peace (which only later attracted the title 'Forum') to the Forum of Augustus. The 135 by 110 m precinct had an internal colonnade and was chequered with flower-beds (or shrubbery or pools). The pedimented shrine, not raised on a podium, stood on the south-east side; to this were consigned the spoils of Jerusalem. Of the four halls that flanked it, two were libraries, one in all probability containing a marble plan of Rome, forerunner of the Severan plan. It would have been based on the results of his census, housed in another hall. To the north-west rose the Temple of Minerva, with its tall Flavian columns.[10]

Works of art, possibly including Myron's heifer and a bronze ox, perhaps by Lysippus, many looted by Nero and now assigned to the Roman public, adorned the Temple, as did a great statue of Nile with his sixteen children (the 16 cubits of optimum flood). R. Darwall-Smith sees the Temple as an ostentatiously public art gallery, related to the Porticoes of Livia (which enshrined the Temple of Honos and Virtus) and Octavia. The collections are doubly significant: the orderly arrangement in captivity of works of art had long been making Rome into an image of her Empire, reminding the conquerors of their position; objects carried in triumphs, such as the balsam plant from Judaea in Vespasian's, now noted as a source of revenue, had a similar significance. In the Republic governors such as C. Verres had gorged their appetite for plunder; now emperors good and bad had their pick. Tiberius, an emperor of ill-repute, sneaked a single statue away from Agrippa's Baths, and had to return it; Nero looted Greece wholesale. Vespasian departed emphatically from Nero's bent for luxury combined with self-glorification, setting bounds to imperial behaviour. Republican politicians had known how much the people, disliking private luxury, valued public splendour, and the popular-minded M. Agrippa had advocated recalling private collections from exile in wealthy villas. Significantly, his speech is reported by the elder Pliny, who contrasts Vespasian's consecration in the Temple of Peace and elsewhere of works of art 'plundered' by Nero for his new 'sitting rooms' – unless the word he uses means 'privies'. The new collections encouraged popular self-regard as well as providing an amenity. Claudius and Vespasian's practical gifts brought them particularly close to ordinary people.[11]

The greatest and most enduring monument of Vespasian's attention was to occupy the focus of Nero's self-regarding Golden House. Vespasian opened up the upper end of the Via Sacra and used the site of the Pool at the centre of the complex as the basis of a building in which a sample 45,000–50,000 of the Roman population were to meet, representing not just the plebs, but, as M.T. Griffin has stressed, the entire people, in serried fashion, and as an awe-inspiring embodiment of its identity – to enjoy itself. (Students of philosophy had been accused by Seneca of attending to their subject only in the intermissions of shows.) As a place of assembly the Colosseum had a more general significance than that of offering to the public what had been the property of one man: Nero's Golden House, it was claimed, would actually have driven out the people as far as Veii, like the Gallic attack of 390 BC. Vespasian financed the building from Jewish spoils, so an architrave inscription in bronze letters attested (it was replaced when the building was restored in 443–4). He completed and no doubt inaugurated the arena and the three lower storeys of the Amphitheatrum Flavium, 'Hunting theatre' (so Dio), or 'Colosseum' (first in Bede), probably planning the highest storey but leaving it unfinished. Titus, who devoted another part of the Golden House site to public baths, inaugurated the extended building in 80 with games lasting a hundred days and involving the killing of 9,000 animals; accordingly his name was inserted into the inscription, eliminating Vespasian; so important was it to claim the building to which the booty from Jerusalem certainly contributed major funding. Finally Domitian probably added the hypogeum. The shows of all kinds that Vespasian gave were correspondingly fine – for example, those that marked his restoration of the Theatre of Marcellus. The building came to stand for Rome and served as a model: Puteoli, Urbs Salvia, Arelate, Nemausus, perhaps Carthage. A destructive lightning strike in 217 was taken to herald the death of an emperor. This was the city's first stone amphitheatre, of travertine for the supporting structure, and tufa blocks in the intermediate walls (brickwork in the upper storeys), with plaster facing, marble seats, and *opus spicatum* pavements (wood in the arena to allow scenery to be brought up). With axes of 188 m and 156 m and an arena covering 3,357 m^2, the four stories reached 52 m (the original three passing like Augustus' Theatre of Marcellus from Tuscan through Ionic to Corinthian) and were crowned with battlements. Annexes housed gladiatorial schools, the main Ludus in the valley between the Esquiline and Caelian Hills, the Matutinus on the Caelian.[12]

On the Via Sacra already rose the colossal statue, 29.5 m high on the least estimate, 35.5 on the largest, that probably gave the building its familiar name. It had been intended as a portrait of Nero, for a huge atrium at the entrance of his Golden House on a site later used for Hadrian's Temple of Venus and Rome. In 75 Vespasian spent a vast sum on a new head, that of Helius, the original of the Colossus of Rhodes, who brings light daily from the East.[13]

The Triumph was also kept in mind by arches bearing trophies, so Dio says; identifying them is difficult. One may be shown in the scene depicting the spoils of Jerusalem on Titus' arch in the Forum. It was surmounted by two four-horse chariots, those in which Vespasian and Titus rode, with the equestrian Domitian and probably Minerva between. Because of its military decorations (prisoners bound to palm trees), F.S. Kleiner connects another triple arch with the triumph: that on the early second-century tomb of the Haterii on the Appian Way inscribed 'by the Temple of Isis' (*'ad Isis'*). He places it on the Via Labicana near the Colosseum. This is uncertain; the three crowns displayed on the arch, two smaller to the left, the larger to the right, may allude, not to the achievements of Titus and Domitian (he had no part in the Jewish victory) and of Vespasian, but to those of Vespasian and Titus and of Domitian himself; only the destruction of Domitianic monuments tells against the later date; R. Darwall-Smith prefers the traditional view: the arch is that in the Campus Martius near the Temple of Isia and Serapis.[14]

Another arch acutely brought to light by Kleiner was different in design. It appears only on coins of 71, where Vespasian is shown sacrificing in front of it, while being crowned by Victory. Four-sided, it bears in the attic two figures, identified by Kleiner with Genius Senatus and Genius Populi Romani. Vespasian's attention to these personalities, whose iconography was becoming codified in the Flavian period, may have won favour with the People as well as with the senate, with its celebration of each being's inherent divinity; in fact, the abstraction distances him from both.[15]

The reconstruction of Rome, like that going on at Pompeii since the earthquake of 62, provided work, as well as funds for contractors. In connection with the Capitol, in particular with the problem of transporting the huge columns of the Temple of Jupiter, an engineer offered Vespasian a labour-saving device. He refused: it would prevent him feeding his 'little plebs'. The story has given rise to scepticism, trenchantly expressed by G.E.M. De Ste Croix. Vespasian, no fool, could have had no motive for refusing an invention that could have been employed elsewhere, especially for military fortifications. We never hear of any attempt to recruit a labour force from the poorer citizens as a means of sustaining them: labour for the reconstruction was probably organized through contractors using slave-gangs and sub-contracting to independent artisans and transport workers. And if the lower classes depended to any large degree on employment in public works, they could not have survived periods of little or no building. The story is to be dismissed; humble free men did have a part in public works, but hired labourers played a far smaller rôle than skilled and semi-skilled men performing specific tasks. It is certainly rash to accept Vespasianic anecdotes at face value. The source of this story might be a jibe against the Emperor's populism, or, if the words are his, uttered after the event to display it. Similar alternative interpretations are available for the claim that the frequent and elaborate banquets Vespasian held were intended to benefit the meat market. Yet the exact nature of the machine is unknown; it may have been a crane too specialized for building fortifications; in any case military labour already paid for was available. And if the lowest classes went through times when there was hardly any public building going on (not that private building need have stopped as sharply), it does not mean that they did not seek desperately for means of support. Emperors knew that and could sympathize, though organizing wholesale 'employment' for a free and self-respecting population was not in their remit.[16]

Vespasian also urged private contractors towards restoring the city. Unoccupied sites were allowed to anyone who would build, a measure at one with care long-standing for city centres and intermittent for the housing of the city population. A Claudian measure was reiterated which forbade demolition of private buildings for gain, the SC Hosidianum: materials such as marble might be removed from one structure to another, but not if the result was unsightly. Strabo tells of building mania at Rome in the age of

Augustus, possible because of abundant supplies of timber and stone, brought in by water; perhaps there was less money available after the Augustan boom. Streets also needed speedy attention, not so much because of war damage as from the 'neglect of earlier times'. Vespasian acted, using his own money, in the second half of 71. Tiberius' neglect and Gaius' destructiveness had been attacked by Claudius; Vespasian is more oblique, but Nero is a target. Even now the former aedile who had failed to keep Gaius' streets clean was not wholly successful: Juvenal still uttered familiar complaints about crowds and filth. It is natural to ask too how Vespasian came to be using and mispronouncing the word 'waggon' (*plaustra*); perhaps in connection with Rome's traffic problems: waggons were banned for most of the day except for religious purposes.[17]

In pursuit of stability not only the wealthy were constrained. The demagogue Caesar showed himself as Dictator tough and unyielding in the face of popular feeling: all except licensed clubs were abolished, because they could be used against authority. Augustus followed suit. Another constraint imposed by Emperors including Claudius and Nero concerned cookshops: Vespasian now banned them from selling hot food except pulses, perhaps merely a measure against luxury, unless it was designed to prevent customers sitting down and talking. Chickpeas were no incentive to linger.[18]

The census that Vespasian and Titus carried out in 73–4, the first for twenty-six years and last of its kind, had symbolic as well as practical purposes. The Emperor needed to know what resources he had, and the People, in whose name those resources were deployed, had comfort from having survived. The *lustrum* was closed, and the numbers of citizens declared, with their particulars. Pliny the Elder interested himself in cases of longevity that the census threw up: the real survivors.[19]

Concern over the total, so of those capable of fighting for Rome, went back into the Republic; since the second century the population of Italy had been perceived as declining, the place of free men being taken by slaves. Emperors were better placed to complain than to remedy the problem. Private benefactors had already begun the alimentary schemes which on a small scale subsidized the upbringing of respectable children in Italian towns and which were later taken up by Nerva or Trajan. Vespasian made no such attempt, tying up funds on permanent loan. In any case, Roman arms were still being carried forward. Successes, probably those that continued Claudius' work in Britain, were visibly commemorated by the advancement of the Pomerium, in the Collis Hortulorum in the north and on the plain of the Tiber in the south. This came in 75, the year after the census was completed, as it had in 49 under Claudius.[20]

Ordinary people had to know in their justified envy that public property and revenue were being exploited for public benefit, not for that of a few powerful men. This point had been made by the Gracchi. Vespasian tackled resumption and reorganization, in Italy and the provinces. He took back the

Public Vineyards south of the Aventine Hill in 75, and in 77–8 regulated the property of Diana Tifatina near Capua and Formiae, which had been dedicated by Sulla the Dictator, on the lines laid down by Augustus; it had fallen into the hands of private persons, Capuans or Romans. In 76 the community of Cannae, or possibly Canusium, which it served as an emporium, likewise had its boundaries restored. The regulation of boundaries in Campania emerges in the *Liber Coloniarum* as the result of a law or ordinance (*lex, constitutio*) of Vespasian, evidence of importance in people's minds.[21]

In Campania at the beginning of the reign, necessary measures for law and order and for billeting were combined with disciplinary measures. Capua had to pay for recalcitrance and enmity to Tarracina, which does not seem to have been rewarded, by having III Gallica quartered on it; Puteoli became Colonia Flavia Augusta Puteolana; but the view that it was now that it gained the southern strip of the Ager Campanus, taken from Capua, has had to be given up: that change belongs to Augustus' reorganization. Enhanced status with repopulation provided increased income and more men to share the burdens of office. Reate received veterans, as Antium had under its native Nero, and Emerita in Lusitania under Otho, a former governor. Nola, Sinuessa (Colonia Flavia), Paestum, and Bovianum Undecimanorum in Samnium also received new settlers, the last from XI Claudia. More inhabitants without additional territory should mean less land for each, but only common land (*subseciva*) may have been taken. The north, indifferent though it was, had been violently affected by the war, with Cremona suffering worst. Other acts of destruction could be blamed on local enmities, as when the Placentia amphitheatre was burnt. Physical and moral order had to be put on display: Vespasian himself reconstructed the Capitolium of Brixia. At Patavium, one magistrate took the opportunity to stress that his office was held 'in accordance with the Julian municipal law'.[22]

The state of the main roads in Italy was obvious to commanders and troops who had been conveyed or trudged along them, although Vespasian himself saw nothing of them between 66 and 70. He passed into history as a restorer of roads on a grand scale: he repaired the Appian Way to Brundisium, the Viae Latina and Cassia to Capua and Luca respectively, and the Flaminia to Ariminum, and created the Flavia from Tergeste to Pola; this route, like the Flaminia, required impressive cuttings. Along with road restoration went repair of bridges, as at Viterbium on the Cassia in Etruria, probably restoring Claudian work.[23]

Sacred buildings in Italy, such as the Brixia Capitolium, were important as they were at Rome. It may have been an act of personal gratitude to reconstruct the ruinous temple of Victory, Sabine Vacuna, who was also identified with Bellona and Minerva, at Varia Latina, and, in the spring of 76 after an earthquake identified by H. Newton with that of the early 60s, the temple of the Mother of the Gods at Herculaneum. Both this and Vespasian's tenure by proxy of the leading magistracy in an Italian city such as Firmum in Picenum are significant, demonstrating his concern for the survival of Italy for all time ('*aeternitas*' in the *SC Hosidianum*), and for morale as well as material welfare.[24]

Rome was the Empire's centre of justice: there sat the supreme judicial authority, with the dispensing of justice one of his main functions; the senate, the jury courts. Litigation brought strangers to Rome, and some had a long wait. Delay was an old complaint, which Galba had refused to solve by creating a sixth panel of jurymen, instead demanding additional winter and New Year service from existing members (one of the complaints against him). Queues were especially long after civil war, through inanition and fresh wrongs. Vespasian exerted himself to clear the backlog, with the help of jurist friends, Cn. Arulenus Caelius Sabinus and Pegasus. A commission chosen by lot tackled the contentious job of restoring looted property and clearing the backlog of the Centumviral Court, which dealt with inheritance. Vespasian knew the effect of Claudius' erratic judgments on litigants and audience. He was assiduous in jurisdiction, and won a reputation for fairness and for patience with advocates. He would sit in the morning and probably left the rest of the day's business to his advisers, who were also kept busy: the Emperor got up before dawn and expected associates at his *levée*; a judicial session might follow.[25]

Under Vespasian the bar was lively, within limits: it accepted the régime and collaborated. Besides Eprius Marcellus and Vibius Crispus and the less notorious M. Flavius Aper, there was P. Galerius Trachalus, the unusually free-spoken C. Salvius Liberalis (subtle and successful with it, he was adlected into praetorian rank). Of the jurists, little more than names survived: Pegasus, perhaps the brother of the more durable jurist Plautius, and his successor under Domitian Juventius Celsus the Elder, leaders of the Proculian school; C. Cassius Longinus, exiled by Nero, Cn. Arulenus Caelius Sabinus, of the Sabinian, to which Arulenus gave his name. They were not unproductive, but Pegasus and Celsus were tainted by association with Domitian and their works made little impact; Longinus composed a treatise on the civil law which was abridged by L. Javolenus Priscus, Sabinus a commentary on the aedilician edict. But the consulars Javolenus, who composed fourteen books of '*Consultations*', Neratius Priscus, son of one of Vespasian's generals, and the younger Celsus are judged more distinguished; Vespasian's reign was only the cradle of the great epoch of private law. His stable rule showed the Principate as a fixture, not a ramshackle superstructure on the Republican constitution; Domitian's wilful autocracy was a temporary interruption of a trend towards security and the rule of law.[26]

Vespasian's 'modest and wise' legislation has won the approval of modern scholars, who have seen it as a continuation of that of Augustus and Claudius. It was almost bound to be that: Tiberius was sparing in the use of enactments, especially of laws passed by the people, in which he expressed little faith; Nero's work tails off. Vespasian's was one of fine-tuning. He modified the *SC Claudianum* of 52, which provided that the children of a slave by a free woman were to be slaves, the property of the slave's master, like the free woman who formed such a liaison without his consent. Some time in the history of this legislation, not merely the ignorance of the owner but his formal refusal of permission for the liaison came to be required for the woman's enslavement, and this humane modification may belong to Vespasian's reign. In another enactment, apparently not the *SC Claudianum* (Gaius refers to it as a *lex*), there was an anomalous provision that if a free man (not specifically a Roman citizen) unwittingly cohabited with a slave woman, children were to follow the status of the parent of their own sex. Vespasian's legislation brought back the normal rule, that children of an irregular union were to follow the status of their mother: in this case as slaves of the woman's owner. Another Claudian enactment was strengthened, probably through the *SC Macedonianum*, allegedly named after the parricide who inspired it. (That perhaps was a jibe against its senatorial author.) The *SC* aimed at preventing sons from borrowing on the strength of their prospects as heirs: it may have introduced the provision that no action for recovery would lie even after the son became independent. The *SC Pegasianum* (c.70–1), improving the *SC Trebellianum* of 56, dealt with inheritances and *fideicommissa* (requests made to an heir in a will to make certain gifts). It extended rules governing inheritance by celibates to *fideicommissa*, ordained that they should not stand between Greeks and Romans, and allowed the heir to keep one quarter of what he received, so giving him an incentive to discharge them. An *SC* of Pegasus and his fellow-consul granted the same right of obtaining citizenship to slaves who were emancipated over the age of 30 and so became Junian Latins (a class of freedmen created by a law of the early Principate), as was already possessed by younger men who had year-old sons.[27]

Care for Rome and Italy may seem to be undermined by novelties still to come: the preponderance of provincials in the legions, the admission of senators from the provinces, massive extension of Latin rights. Vespasian has been seen departing from Augustus' careful distinction of Italy from the provinces and credited with special boldness in continuing Claudius' policies and, like Caesar and Claudius, with a tendency to assimilate the two, even 'admitting the Romanized provinces of the West as full partners in the government of the Empire'. In the sense that Italy eventually became a 'province' and that taxation was imposed, as the Bithynian consular and historian Dio had urged, putting the case in the mouth of Maecenas, assimilation did take place; Rome and Italy faded politically and economically before disparate problems: emperors' need to win support for themselves outside Italy; the relative impoverishment of Italy in comparison with provinces such as Spain, the Gauls, and Asia, so that materially they caught up with and surpassed her; the distance of Rome from the centre of military operations along the Rhine, Danube, and Euphrates. Change was signalled by the failure of

short-lived third-century emperors to visit Rome at all, by the development
from 325 onwards of a new Rome in Constantinople, and by the advance to
preeminence of Mediolanum in northern Italy. But the Sabine Vespasian did
not abolish distinctions. Many new senators came from Italy, and he may also
be seen as bringing Augustus' integration of Italy to completion. It was in
Vespasian's reign and in a work dedicated to his son that Pliny the Elder,
from northern Comum, penned eulogies of Italy, its people and resources, as
highlights of his *Natural History* – revealing as much by his enthusiasm and
his choice of criteria as had the misgivings of Tiberius. Already in 19
Germanicus lauded Tiberius as benefactor of the whole human race, and
when Titus died, it was the loss of their darling, not just that of Rome, Italy,
or Roman citizens, that was mourned. But when Domitian's edict sought to
redress the balance between the production of grapes and grain it favoured
Italy (no more vines to be planted), against the provinces (half the existing
ones to be uprooted). The disbursements of Vespasian likewise suggest that
for practical as well as ideological purposes Italy came first; in Pliny's recon-
ciling phrase it was to become the native country (*patria*) of all races
throughout the world.[28]

2 Provinces west and east: gifts, status, Romanization, titles

By the time Pliny opened *Natural History* 27, in which he dealt with drugs,
he could thank, for remedies from the Sea of Azov, the Atlas, and Britain, the
'immeasurable majesty of the Roman peace . . . May it last for ever!' The
Triumph marked the end of war and rebellion and 'the establishment of the
Empire on the firmest foundation'; the basis for future happiness was charted
in the census. The provinces had suffered less than northern Italy in 68–70,
with the exception of eastern Gaul and the Rhineland. But improvements
and repairs were always due to this Forth Bridge of an Empire. For all his
reputed avarice, Vespasian's service is lauded by Suetonius and later writers
(following a contemporary historian or a commemorative speech): restoration
of cities, construction of mighty roads. Modern writers elaborate, praising
'centralization and prosperity under the Flavians' in Asia Minor, decisive
blows for Romanization in Africa, egregious servants, generosity with the
citizenship, the encouragement of trade. Certainly, the advance in the 'epigraphic habit' or 'epigraphic culture' means something. A rise in the number
of inscriptions when a new régime begins may mean enhanced prosperity,
increased confidence, keenness to display loyalty, or a combination of these
and other factors. Scholars have overestimated the contribution of the stable
new régime, whose greatest achievement may have been precisely its promise
of stability; denigrating predecessors or justifying Roman imperialism plays
the Flavian game. Cooler scrutiny is needed, first of crisp questions of
'administration' then of the wider issues, development, privilege, and cul-

tural change. Is the material reliable? Were the results intended? If so, for what purposes?[29]

Injustices and anomalies had to be put right, some long-standing, others the product of recent struggles. First, the unspectacular work of reassessing community boundaries, known from a rich crop of markers. They belong to different contexts, censuses, advancements in status, appeals to the Emperor, the flare-up, during the civil wars, of old feuds. The routine was liable to be put off: Claudius attacked Tiberius for neglect. The quantity of material suggests that Vespasian was keen; there were implications for accurate tax assessment. The boundaries of Asseria and Alveria in Dalmatia may have been regulated before the outcome of the civil war was known; Vespasian had those of Lepcis in Tripolitania marked in 73–4 by C. Rutilius Gallicus, and in Spain between March and December 73 the line between the Lac(in)imurgenses and the people of Ucubi, citizens of the colony Claritas Julia, was adjusted. Corsica saw a new boundary dispute: in about 77 Vespasian instructed the governor to measure lands bought by the Vanacini from a previous procurator, and sent a surveyor for the purpose; they were in dispute with the people of Colonia Mariana in the north-east. In Dalmatia, C. Petillius Firmus, tribune of IV Flavia Firma, was appointed on the authority of Vespasian to mark the boundary between two Liburnian communities. Firmus was connected with the dynasty, and his rank, in a centurion's job, gave his decision additional authority. A third colony involved in a dispute (old land-confiscations may have rankled) was Vienna, which had suffered in the Vitellian advance. The line between Vienna and the Latin Ceutrones of the Graian Alps was redrawn in 74 by the neutral and authoritative legate of Upper Germany. In Thasos the procurator attempted to resolve a boundary question, perhaps involving responsibility for the imperial post (*vehiculatio*), by sending a soldier. Certainly two ancient enemies, Sparta and Messene, had their boundaries regulated by the Emperor's freedman surveyor in 78. It was probably in about 73–4 that the boundaries between Mopsuhestia and Aegeae on the coast in Cilicia Pedias were adjusted – not the end of disputes in that province.[30]

Personal attention is a sign of importance in the ruler's eyes, but visits were often incidental to a military purpose. After the age of 55, Augustus, like Tiberius after him, depended on imperial princes. The journeys of Claudius and Nero to Britain and Greece were self-seeking, although gifts made *en route* enhanced their glory. The example of Hadrian, traveller and inspector, was not followed by Antoninus Pius, an omission that had to be defended by the provincial orator Aelius Aristides. Vespasian and Titus, laureate before accession, also remained at home: relatives and adherents carried out missions abroad.[31]

Vespasian's appointments are highly praised. One governor is on record as charged with extortion, and one subordinate official. The case against Antonius Flamma had probably been prepared by the people of Cyrenaica before the end of 69; it seems to have been politically motivated and a product of local feuds: Cyrenaica was the proconsul's home province. In the other case C. Iulius Bassus, former quaestor in Bithynia, was acquitted. The innocence of neither is assured, and other victims may have been afraid to prosecute the Emperor's men. We do not know that Vespasian kept a tight rein on governors; he lacks the commendation that Suetonius gives Domitian. As to prorogations, Eprius Marcellus, who was twice prorogued in Asia, was in ill repute politically and well away from Rome, but not necessarily a bad governor. The need for post-war stability in Asia may have been important; the proconsul of Crete and Cyrene, C. Arinius Modestus, was also continued (73–5?), in the wake of the disturbances that Catullus had put down. Normally proconsulships went to ex-consuls and ex-praetors annually, by seniority and the lot. Domitian's governors of Asia Minor, in particular the men started by Vespasian, were highly praised by D. Magie, but although men promoted after 69 are also commended by Tacitus, it is in unspecific terms.[32]

Some governors have been accounted 'specialists', as Agricola might be in Britain; there were eastern 'specialists', such as M. Hirrius Fronto Neratius Pansa. Other things being equal – tested loyalty, support enjoyed by other contenders – experience in an area, especially if it were as troubled as Britain in 70, would be a factor in appointments. But Agricola as ex-praetor governed Aquitania, and expected to hold the proconsulship of Asia. Specialists are often persons of narrow range, and Agricola's disappointment has been put down to lack of eastern experience. Yet sortition determined whether an ex-consul governed Asia or Africa and Pliny the Younger's most recent experience of the East before being sent there in 109 to set Bithynia-Pontus to rights was gained in the Roman courts.[33]

Vespasian is credited with a particular novelty, that of attaching assistant law officers, *legati iuridici*, to governors, notably in Spain, where the advocate Larcius Licinus is found early in the reign, and in Britain, beginning in Agricola's governorship: C. Salvius Liberalis, a more distinguished advocate, Javolenus Priscus, *iuridicus* under Titus, the leading jurisconsult. Vespasian developed the practice, certainly. The enormous Galatia-Cappadocia concatenation with its military functions demanded a subordinate, and C. Rutilius Gallicus had served there under Nero. When it was reconstituted, Greek-speakers were employed, Ti. Julius Celsus Polemaeanus the earliest known (78–80). In Britain governors were occupied with the offensive, though the original function of the legate here may have been, as A. Birley suggested, to incorporate Cogidubnus' realm. Law officers would be concerned not only with settling disputes peacefully, but (Spain in its entirety having been granted the 'Latin right', *Latium*) with the changing relationship between local and Roman legal institutions.[34]

It is not surprising, either, that Vespasian did not hesitate, as J. Reynolds and R. Goodchild pointed out, to give instructions to the proconsuls of public provinces; their dignity had long yielded to imperial needs, even to the perceived welfare of provincials. Augustus informed governors of their duty in the Cyrene edicts; a Claudian proconsul of Asia set out with instructions. Changes in the relation of procurators to governors were also to be expected in straitened circumstances; after Nero, whose procurators drove Vindex to revolt, a governor would be aware of the danger of flouting men who were so important to the Treasury.[35]

To pass to the material developments that impressed ancient writers, Vespasian continued Claudius' interest in colonization. He had the spur of troops to discharge, and had to pay: the title of Madaurus in Africa, Flavia Augusta Veteranorum Madaurensium, shows old soldiers involved. Scarcely a province failed to receive such settlements in areas where Roman control was insecure, as in Africa, or where, as in Italy, existing foundations needed reinforcement. The welfare of provincials did not necessarily come first, as it did at Aventicum, administrative centre of the Helvetii since mid-Augustan times. Now, probably in 73–4, and recognizing and advertising damage inflicted by the advancing Vitellianists, Vespasian created Pia Flavia Constans Emerita Helvetiorum, veterans again revealed in the title. Colonies performed police functions. On the Loire, Forum Segusiavorum, Colonia Flavia, lay on important routes from Lugdunum. In northern Lusitania, off the beaten track but important for controlling Augustus' conquests of Asturia and Callaecia, where there had been unrest under Nero, Flaviobriga on the Cantabrian coast also became a colony. The gold-rich region was worth securing.[36]

The Balkans attracted particular attention. Dalmatia received veteran colonies; amenity rather than any threat must have been a factor in their siting. In Pannonia Flavia Sirmium and Siscia had been bases in subjugating lands west of the Danube. They were to become stages on the route that linked East and West for emperors fighting to keep them together and under control. Moesia, fronting the tribes beyond the Danube, was dominated by the military, but not a cultural unity. It was becoming urbanized, and although the colony of Scupi (Flavia Felix Dardanorum) served peace it was too far from the front line to be much more than a convenient retirement place for veterans. The colonists came from the Moesian VII Claudia and VIII Augusta. E. Birley has shown that an effort was made to enrich the foundation by including men from XIV Gemina and III Augusta; Tacitus notes lack of cohesion in latter-day colonies, and under Hadrian more settlers were sent, as Scupi's title Aelia suggests; it may not have thrived as Vespasian planned, although some colonists knew city life: they came from northern Italy and Narbonensis, including the colony of Forum Julii.[37]

Claudius' arrangements for Thrace, annexed in 46 and put under an equestrian governor, were kept, and Vespasian followed up the probably Claudian colony of Aprus. He reduced the number of the 'satrapies' (*strategiae*) of the hellenistic domain, and their territories began to be attributed to cities.

Flaviopolis was probably on the neck of the Chersonese and the colony Flavia Pacis Deultum, near the Black Sea coast, was a provincial police post. Even so, Trajan had to replace equestrian governors with ex-praetors.[38]

In Palestine, Caesarea, Vespasian's base, became Colonia Prima Flavia Augusta. It might have to serve again against Judaea, like Ptolemais, Claudius' foundation to the north, but its existence made that less likely. Something similar took place in Africa when Ammaedara passed from being the home of III Augusta to colonial status as Flavia Augusta Emerita. These colonies recall what Claudius did less successfully in Britain: XX Valeria moved out in 49 and Camulodunum became a colony, a bulwark against rebels. Such colonies, based on an existing military presence, may owe much to local initiative.[39]

Like colonies, roads and dykes cost money; here slaves or impressed local labour could be used, and local resources maintain the imperial post. Road-building had a military purpose, and belongs later. It was a necessity, not directed at the welfare of provincials. At the same time, visible decay in a peaceful province did a governor no credit. As Roman control advanced westwards in Africa, eastwards in Asia Minor, roads nearer the coast had to be kept up. The route from Hippo Regius to Carthage and Theveste was restored in 76, and the proconsul of Asia was active the year before on the routes between major cities. Vespasian and Titus, after Cilician road-building in 75, were credited in 78 with reconstruction 'from public funds' of the bridge over the Gök Su at Seleucia.[40]

In Spain the road system was overhauled, having last received serious attention late in the reign of Tiberius. Its backbone, the Via Augusta that led down the east coast and turned west in Baetica to reach the Atlantic at Gades, was restored with its bridges by Vespasian, and C. Calpetanus Festus was active in Citerior in the first half of 80 on the vital Asturica-Bracara route that contributed, like Flaviobriga, to the control of the north-west. A key site on the road was at Chaves (Trás os Montes), where it crosses the Tâmega, and where an inscription of 78/9 records the contribution of the ten peoples of the area to a work that was probably the predecessor of Trajan's bridge.[41]

Sardinia was also restive. In 19 Tiberius deported 4,000 freedmen there to mop up outlaws. Once considered too small for a senatorial legate, it had passed into the hands of proconsuls in 44, an exchange for Achaea. Vespasian, restoring Achaea to direct Roman rule as a public province, took back Sardinia and assigned it once more to a knight, attested in 74. Control was tightened by the proconsul in the first half of 70 by continuing Neronian road improvements on the road from Caralis to Sulcis; in 73–4 the route to Turris was being repaired.[42]

Under the Flavians a number of cities without new settlers or military functions reached the rank of *municipium* with *Latium* or Roman citizenship, Roman-style constitution, and sometimes the imperial name incorporated in their title. In Spain it followed Vespasian's grant of *Latium*, conferring citizenship on magistrates at the end of their term. The process illuminates Flavian thinking on extension of the citizenship and lesser privileges. There were precedents for blanket awards: Transpadane Gaul had received the same privilege in 89 BC, the Maritime Alps in AD 63; Claudius may have made extensive concessions. The older view was that the grant formed part of the censorship of 73–4. More probably it belongs, as A.B. Bosworth argues, to the beginning of Vespasian's principate and aimed at conciliating the inhabitants of the peninsula, which had supported the lost Galba and Otho, and kept quiet afterwards. Concessions made by Vitellius at the end could have spurred Vespasian into action; rewarding Spain split it from Gaul at a time when two legions of its garrison were needed, as A. Fear notes, for the campaign against Civilis. In his respectful mention of the grant, Pliny the Elder describes *Latium* as 'tossed about in storms of State', a phrase probably drawn from the preamble to the edict. In the epigraphic record both Vespasian and Titus are given credit, which favours the later date, but any reference, especially after 79 and after changes to the original grant, might courteously mention the Emperor's partner. Vespasian's edict was modified as abuses and obscurities came to light. The final form was regulated by the highly Roman Domitianic Municipal Law that survives in versions inscribed on bronzes datable to the early 80s or 90s from communities that became *municipia*, Irni and elsewhere. But some towns were in possession of their rights by 75.[43]

The whole peninsula benefited. But there are various interpretations. It has been assumed that all the citizens of towns with *Latium* were 'Latins' and enjoyed privileges intermediate between those of non-citizens and full Roman citizens, and the detailed provisions of the *Tabula Irnitana* support that assumption. So the grant both enhanced the position of a community and expected that the mass of its citizens should accept the rules of Roman civil law: in section 22–3, those who acquire citizenship are already subject to Roman rules on *manus*, *mancipium*, *tutoris optio*, and *patronatus*. It has also been argued, however, on the one hand that *Latium* affected only personal rights, making no change in the position of cities themselves, and on the other that under the Empire it was confined to communities; the individual 'Latin' ceased to exist in this context. It seems likely that, as Pliny's mention of Spain rather than Spaniards suggests, grants were made to communities, but that for inhabitants who were not in the curial class immediately affected there was leeway between the rules that Rome prescribed and the way they were actually interpreted; advance of a community to the status of a chartered *municipium* was a stage, particularly frequent in the south and east, reached on application after it made changes in its own organization as it determined.[44]

The grant encouraged rural communities, notably in Lusitania, to develop into townships or regular cities, and some dependent communities into independent organizations, as at Ipsca Contributa in Baetica. When a town became a chartered 'Flavian municipality' (*municipium Flavium*) the constitution took account of local conditions, prescribing the number of councillors that a town could be expected to support, and regulating the pecuniary level of cases that the magistrates were competent to take. Preserving councils at the same size as their predecessors, and allowing only men already members of the council to hold the magistracies that brought citizenship helped to ensure the stability of the societies that were advanced.[45]

Physical changes ensued. In July 77 magistrates and council of a hill-top community, the Saborenses, sent envoys to the Emperor complaining of problems, presumably logistic and financial, that they were presently unable to solve and asking to rebuild their town centre on the plain. To make the proposal more acceptable they asked to name the new centre after him ('*Flavium*') and to secure their future requested him to confirm revenues, perhaps customs dues granted under Augustus. This Vespasian allowed, but reserved for the governor their request to levy additional taxes. As ever, the claims of the Treasury, clarified in Tarraconensis in a census conducted by the Emperor's friend Vibius Crispus, came first. Enthusiasm sometimes outran resources: Munigua was rebuked for extravagance by Titus.[46]

Its new urban centre will have made Sabora look like a Roman town. Changes were taking place elsewhere too. At Munigua the baths are Flavian, and Flavia Conimbriga constructed a larger forum. N. Mackie noted that in Spain most datable evidence for public works and their administration comes from Vespasian's reign onwards. The same is true elsewhere. At Lepcis Magna, where boundary revision followed the disturbances of 70 and was followed in turn by elevation to the status of *municipium* with Latin rights, there succeeded 'incredible' building activity. But Vespasian regulated and acquiesced without putting anything in the local kitty, the tacit object, as N. Mackie suggested, of the Saborenses. At Cartima, it was a local benefactor who was responsible for much building, and this town also got itself into debt; nor would Vespasian have paid for his own temple at Ipsca.[47]

In Spain the number of inscriptions dated by the Emperor's regnal year rose significantly under Vespasian. R. Duncan-Jones convincingly takes this for a response to the concession, achieving the main aim of the grant. Taking the name of the Emperor demonstrates the same loyalty, due perhaps when particular favours, material or constitutional, were conferred, as at Sabora; several 'Flavian' towns are to be found in the north-western region of Spain, where Rome (apart from her army) had had least impact.[48]

Constitutional advances elsewhere were sporadic and probably on petition rather than as part of a policy of urbanization. Significant communities were allowed civic privileges and the rewards of citizenship for their leaders. Scardona, on the borders of Liburnia and Dalmatia, and Doclea in south-east Dalmatia, were to retain their importance until the fourth century at least. In Noricum Solva may have been added to the four Claudian municipalities. In

Pannonia Scarbantia, on the Danube–Adriatic route, also became a *municipium*, along with Neviodunum and Andautonia up the Save from Siscium. Scarbantia's commerce and its rôle in the military operations of the fourth century justified the choice. In Africa veteran colonies were rare; if Claudius' award to Volubilis is a guide, other grants of status, many of controversial date, and other benefactions were made in response to requests. *Municipes*, such as those of Hadrian's later colony of Bulla Regia, and other beneficiaries might show gratitude, and others join in out of emulation. In the governorship of Vibius Crispus, Thysdrus was provided with a water supply by the imperial benefactors. One of the two leading families of Cillium, whose mausoleum survives as its chief monument, bore the Flavian name. At Bulla a huge statue of Vespasian was set up in the forum; at Thugga an arch and statues of Vespasian and Titus – one of Domitian was added later; and at Oea's western neighbour Sabratha an arch to Vespasian and Titus, dedicated in 77–8. H. Bengtson counted honorific inscriptions from eleven North African cities; competition promoted their production and magnified insignificant benefactions.[49]

The development of cities hastened changes in the life of tribal people, whether sedentary, following their flocks to high ground in the summer, nomadic, or something between. Now we find them assigned territory, not merely being harassed or driven into the interior. Lands belonging to Cirta were allocated by the legate to two tribes near Tigisis. D. Mattingly and R.G. Hitchner note a dramatic and sustained increase in sedentary settlement from the Flavian period onwards in the pre-desert Sofeggin and Zem-Zem region of indigenous *wadi* farmers cultivating the olive. The authors surmise that a dynamic form of share tenancy, probably based on Mancian tenure, was facilitating agricultural development and tenurial arrangements of private estates. The greatest development did not necessarily go with the most intense 'Romanization', but rises in production would benefit marketing cities, underpinning material development.[50]

Some settlements developed under military influence. Arae Flaviae in south-west Germany, like Aquae Flavianae in Africa, near the station of Mascula, were on or close to roads tramped by the army. Civilian settlements outside installations (*canabae*) throve on the symbiosis; Professor Saddington notes idiosyncratically named villagers of Vindonissa setting up an arch under Titus (79) to the unusual triad Mars, Apollo, and Minerva; three Hadrianic municipalities on the Danube, Carnuntum, Aquincum, and Viminacium, began as *canabae*.[51]

The colony of Corinth, like Paphos on Cyprus, became 'Flavia', perhaps on restoration by Vespasian after the earthquake of 77. But the grant of the title, enhancing distinction on both sides, did not always mean imperial expenditure. Of the Greek words of gratitude, Saviour, Founder, and Benefactor, the second implies material help and the last was still available for eminent subjects. In the East colonies are rare, *municipia* still rarer. Being a city state

141

(*polis*), especially one with a treaty or freedom and immunity from taxation, or an assize centre (*conventus*), or with titular primacy in a province, counted most. In Asia Minor E. Dąbrowa finds only one 'city' newly founded, probably a substantial entity beforehand, differently organized: Flaviopolis among the people of Characene in northern Cilicia (73/74), completing the formal urbanization of that district. At latest when the territory was annexed in 72 Neronias in Lacanitis was renamed as the city of peace, Irenopolis. Now the whole of northern Pedias was divided between the territories of these cities and Augusta in Bryclice. The Flavian name spread in the Asian province too. The list of assize centres found at Ephesus shows an unidentified people of Sardes district becoming 'Flaviocaesares', like those of the city of Daldis. They and the Loreni are 'Flaviopoleitae', the first on coins presenting Vespasian as benefactor. Here is local emulation, the Emperor awarding status and titles to applicants, rather than intervening in the affairs of minute communities. City status and awareness, through issuing coins, was eventually asserted by more than half the 500 cities claimed for the province. To the east cities remained sparse. In Flavian Asia forty-nine cities struck coins, in Galatia-Cappadocia seven, and epigraphic material is similarly weighted: Asia showed more than twice the number of attested Flavian monuments as Galatia-Cappadocia, Bithynia-Pontus, and Cilicia combined.[52]

Along with advancement in status and building construction went cultural changes, but causal connections are not tight or one-way, and it is unclear how far they were promoted from above. Tacitus' model governor Agricola spends attention, and evidently imperial money, on helping British communities to acquire polish and amenities; specifically he encourages them to build shrines, market-places, and houses (*domi*), and the young aristocrats to study, to acquire what they called civilization (*humanitas*), so ensuring their subjection. Agricola could have justified his expenditure; it had a practical, ultimately a fiscal aim. When Agricola acted Pliny had already written his panegyric on Italy's destiny: to give *humanitas* to Man, a *post eventum* justification for imperialism.[53]

Humanitas was originally a Greek possession, but the process has been called 'Romanization', an ill-defined, misused term half superseded by 'acculturation'. Either can operate from above or (usually) below; it can be voluntary, encouraged, or imposed: subjects alter habits, adapt ways of thought; Romans ban practices like Druidism or remodel constitutions. 'Romanization', used approvingly by scholars in sympathy at least with ancient imperialism, binds together a bunch of disparate strands, only individually measurable. ('Americanization' is equally uninformative, but usually not used with approval.) The strands mark changes motivated by snobbery, eagernesss to conform, ambition, or desire for amenity: adopting a grid plan for towns, building *gymnasia*, drinking wine not beer (all as much Greek as Roman), putting on or attending gladiatorial shows, endowing a local deity with a Roman name and Olympian characteristics, speaking Latin in public, calling the magistrate 'duovir' or 'prefect' instead of the Gaulish 'vergobret' or Punic 'suffet'; adopting the tripartite Roman name. And fashions apparently Roman may carry references from older culture; the motif of the four seasons in North African mosaics was part of the imagery of *stelae* to Tanit and Baal-Hammon.[54]

In Flavian Africa the spread of Roman nomenclature and the development of the cult of Baal-Hammon-Saturn are two such strands, the impulse coming from the provincials. How many strands justify a claim that until Caesar North Africa was Punico-Roman, between Caesar and Vespasian Romano-Punic, and only in the Flavian era Roman, when the same material evokes a different summary from another scholar? The judgment that Roman North African society was a 'new world', its cities 'hybrids' is just. The subjective sense of 'Romanization', awareness of being Roman, in one part of one's being at least, is detectable in literature and inscriptions, strongest in Roman colonies and amongst the cosmopolitan propertied class. When the Empire came under military threat second-century Greek writers began calling the Roman army 'ours', by contrast with Parthian forces or the hordes beyond the Danube; that does not mean that on other occasions they forgot differences within the Empire.[55]

The homes (*domi*) that Agricola promoted would be town houses to go with the market-places (*fora*) such as he dedicated at Verulamium (79 or 81) in the name of the Emperor. Loans taken out by Britons in the two decades after the invasion had been a factor in the outbreak of revolt in 60. Since then governors had concentrated on the peaceful development attested by archaeological changes; the Verulamium Forum itself on the earlier dating was started under Sex. Julius Frontinus (73/4–77). Britons were achieving the production level necessary to meet the demands of the tax-collectors who supplied the army of occupation, as the opening up of new farmlands and the extraction of minerals suggest. Agricola found upper-class Britons sharper pupils than Gauls, keen on the toga; and on porticoes, baths, and dinner parties. The Greek language teacher from Tarsus, Demetrius, who may have operated a school at the governor's headquarters in Eboracum, would have been welcome at British tables too. Again, Tacitus represents the foundation of the colony at Camulodunum as a means of accustoming natives to Roman law; the introduction of *iuridici* points in the same direction. The end of Cogidubnus' kingdom made room for self-government in southern Britain, it can be argued: the development of *civitas* (canton) capitals at Calleva Atrebatum, Venta, and Noviomagus and of the public structures, forum and basilica, that went with them. Similar developments occurred in Londinium. Further afield, at Isca Dumnoniorum and Ratae Corieltauvorum, the evacuation of troops also left space for urban development.[56]

Agricola's perception of his subjects attracts attention away from Gaul. Wealth and status had come under the Principate, interrupted by the disturbances of 21 as Roman taxes bit and individual aristocrats lost place to each other or to newcomers; the upheavals of 68–70 hastened such changes, but it is over-schematic to represent them as the bringing the doom of a class of 'Julii' whose ancestors were enfranchised by Caesar and Augustus. After the revolt Gaul had to recover poise and Rhine army markets. As well as baths and *fora*, theatres and amphitheatres appear, though the chronology is inexact. Little had been permanently lost, and it was especially northern Gaul that developed in the Flavio-Trajanic period, in part because of the conquest of the greater part of Britain; stone replaced wood in construction, sculpture and inscriptions became commoner. No longer at the end of the line, the Gauls themselves could supply British wants by routes already in use in Strabo's time, the Seine and Rhine. Change was also due in part to veterans of the Rhine legions settled in the region, bringing their language and habits.[57]

Scholars agree that there was an advance in the production of North African oil, wine, and ceramics during the reigns of Vespasian and his sons. Other forms of progress attributed to the era, such as the construction of the theatre at Cillium, were made easier by improvements to the African road system. Though not intended as such, they were a prime factor in economic, social, and cultural change, the adoption of Roman nomenclature and the transformation of religious dedications. Occasional direct gifts such as the Thysdrus aqueduct had a major impact: Thysdrus became an oil capital in the early stages of the African boom of the late first and second centuries.[58]

The 'feel-good' factor in Proconsularis, like the grant of *Latium* to Spain, resulted in an increase in the number of dedications made to Africa's rulers. Such grants made a strong impression. Josephus' approving but exaggerated claim in the late Domitianic *Against Apion* that Iberians (as well as Etruscans and Sabines) were known as 'Romans' may be compared with Seneca's acid attack on the deceased Claudius for wanting to see Gauls, Greeks, Britons, and Spaniards in togas. Winning provincials to the Emperor's cause was hymned by a writer favourable to the régime, and acceptable within Italy as a contribution to stability.[59]

Tacitus' *Histories* contrast eastern and western affairs in 69, to the advantage of the former. After the help Vespasian received from his backers, much of it extorted cash, only key players benefited; dependent monarchs were not even secure. Special problems of the East – the survival of the city-state as a focus of loyalty, volatile politics, lower-class discontent – were aggravated. In the late summer of 70, when Vespasian visited Greek cities *en route* for Rome, hopes of favour were high and he was fêted, although the actions of only a few cities are recorded: Perge, Rhodes, Ionia, and Mysian Apollonia.[60]

Concessions to needs and sensibilities were peripheral, granted on petition, and cheap. Apart from the grants of title to individual communities Vespasian encouraged education and guaranteed the privileges of aristocratic associations. The 'Travelling Athletes Devoted to Heracles' were assured that he intended to secure those that Claudius had granted at their request.

Another measure, dated to 27 December 75, protected physicians, instructors, and physiotherapists, who were freed from the duty of billeting Roman soldiers and from extraordinary levies; if they were mistreated the perpetrators were liable to a fine. They were permitted to hold their gatherings in sacred precincts; violators incurred a charge of 'impiety towards the House of the Augusti'.[61]

In the East the upheavals of 68–9 handed Rome's rivals, the Parthians, a weapon of lasting value: the pretender, previously exploited by Rome. Verbal attacks on Vespasian began while he was still in Alexandria, from common people and Cynic philosophers. Vespasian, who developed his conception of the Empire as a hard-headed Italian under Tiberius, and had an Italian constituency to please, proved a disappointment after the philhellene Nero (the first such emperor, he claimed), who had freed Achaea from Roman rule. The first of three 'false Neros' had appeared in 69, and attracted many supporters, though he 'terrified' Asian property-owners. The second came late in the reign, a third under Domitian. Malcontents hankering for days when Greeks were free, outlaws and down-and-outs swarmed from their hiding places. The fourth '*Sibylline Oracle*', composed by a Jew just after Vespasian's death, encapsulates the grievances of Jews and Greeks, interpreting the eruption of Vesuvius as requital for the fate of Jerusalem, prophesying natural destruction and the return of Nero leading a Parthian army to liberate oppressed or pillaged lands, including Asia, which was to recover its property, and Cyprus, recently shaken by earthquake. *The Book of Revelation*, cataloguing loot from the East, confirms the impression. There was no danger that the massacres of Romans carried out in 88 BC would be repeated, but unrest might be expected.[62]

The wooing of Alexandria, the under-privileged Ptolemaic capital, had ended predictably in a squabble over taxation. The Alexandrians nicknamed Vespasian Cybiosactes ('Fishfingermonger'), originally a shortlived husband of Queen Berenice IV (54 BC): the boorish interloper Vespasian was likewise destined for early death; but the Alexandrians told Titus that they forgave Vespasian, as he had no idea how to play Caesar. (They had seen a real Caesar in Germanicus, fifty years before.) Vespasian's withdrawal of freedom from Achaea (except for a few privileged cities such as Athens and Sparta), Rhodes, Byzantium, Samos, perhaps Lycia and Cos, gave general offence: Philostratus' fiction has Vespasian reproved by the sage Apollonius of Tyana. Disturbances in Greece before these changes gave a pretext: Greeks could not govern themselves. The fact that Vespasian seems also to have withdrawn Corinth's right to coin suggests a punitive aim. Need for revenue played a part in the decision, while taxation perceived as heavy aggravated discontent.[63]

Byzantium and Samos were free in 77; either they were reduced with Achaea but soon recovered their freedom or they forfeited it only later. When Vespasian deprived Achaea remains unclear: according to Philostratus it was when he arrived there in late summer 70; Rhodes and Lycia were also on his route. Vespasian may well have been sufficiently secure to act then, but 73/4 cannot be excluded: there Eusebius-Jerome's *Chronicle* places the change and it fits the date for Sardinia's return to equestrian rule, a proconsular post having been made available in Achaea.[64]

The case of Lycia is particularly unclear, partly because of Vespasian's strategic reorganization of Asia Minor, in which it might have been involved. On the strength of Suetonius' statement Lycia too has been thought to have been freed by Nero, or perhaps by Galba: his governor L. Nonius Calpurnius Asprenas took over 'Galatia and Pamphylia' early in 69. When it lost its freedom and joined Pamphylia remains a matter of controversy. The seductive scenario of W. Eck has been widely accepted: Lycia was never freed, but run as a unit by one governor, Sex. Marcius Priscus, from the last years of Nero until the beginning of Vespasian's reign: reunification took place in 73/4, like the reduction of Achaea to direct Roman rule. But as R. Syme remarked, arguing in favour of liberation by Galba, Suetonius is unlikely to have made such a mistake about Lycia; and the inscription recording Marcius' tenure remains hard to interpret.[65]

Vespasian's arrangement, perhaps embodied in a constitution for the province (*lex provinciae*), proved definitive in Lycia-Pamphylia, as for Achaea. The Lycians made the best of it. Courtesies were offered and reciprocated, with benefactions tangible or otherwise. The Lycian League established games in Vespasian's honour, 'Grand, Pentaeteric, and of Olympic status' and at local level there were dedications at Myra and Xanthus, where he was Saviour and Benefactor of the World; for him and his sons the people of Balbura set up their 'Augustan' aqueduct. At Patara and Cadyanda Vespasian created the baths, or gave his name to them, since they were funded from local resources that had been 'kept close' or 'recovered'. It was Vespasian – or at Patara Nero, whose name is erased from the stone – who was responsible for saving these funds. From what were they saved? It is hard language to use of the imperial revenue, and uncharacteristic of either emperor to impoverish his resources; perhaps the money was saved from being squandered (or embezzled) by local authorities. As S. Mitchell has demonstrated, an emperor's name on a building does not mean that he paid for it. At Ephesus the wall of the Augusteum was restored from sacred revenues, under proconsular supervision; the ruler heads the stone: the city and any real donor benefited from the prestigious association. There is no doubt of the change that began in Lycia from Vespasian's time onwards. J.R. Patterson attributes it to Vespasian's pump-priming, but notes J.J. Coulton's point that the new stability under Roman rule made external water supplies safe. Lycian cities became paid-up members of the Empire, vying with neighbours for attention. In Pamphylia the two rival leaders, Side and Perge, like the Council of Elders at Attaleia, honoured Vespasian with monuments, and Perge, warden of a shrine of the imperial cult, ran games called the Artemisia Vespasianeia.[66]

Asia Minor, besides helping finance the war effort, had borne the passage of the task force. Eprius Marcellus' years in Asia ensured continuity while changes went on in the rest of the peninsula. They were strategic in purpose, but beneficial. Otho already had plans for Cappadocia, even if it was only permission for a provincial council. Vespasian's creation of the great province of Galatia-Cappadocia, and the stationing of a legion at Satala, entailed upgrading the road system, and incidentally enlarged outlets for products from the West, food, clothing, and military equipment. When troops moved, they ravaged; stationary, they were an economic advantage, creating permanent demand. The development of the north and east of the Anatolian peninsula did not suggest to Vespasian that the status of the governors of Bithynia-Pontus needed up-grading. Rapid economic and social change there, connected with the enhanced importance of the Danubian and Euphrates system, remained for Trajan and Pliny to cope with. The only manifest change was the emergence of another Flaviopolis, at Crateia.[67]

Cities on the frontier or its approaches, such as Samosata, Melitene, and Caesarea Mazaca, were pivotal to the new system; the Augustan colony of Antioch-towards-Pisidia, now far from any action, remained the leading city in the south of Galatia-Cappadocia, as Ancyra was in the north. It maintained its conspicuous loyalty, which the Emperor knew from the service of a leading citizen, C. Caristanius Fronto, Prefect of Ala Bosporanorum in Egypt: a new priest emerges, *sacerdos* of Vespasian.[68]

The more cities grew, the more urgent demands for food became. Shortage was well known throughout the Roman world; there had been a long-lasting and widespread visitation under Claudius. In the early 90s Domitian was to tackle the problem using the drastic and unenforceable remedy of ordering the cutting down of half the vines outside Italy. The same years saw an acute shortage in Asia Minor, due to a hard winter. It led to profiteering and unrest. In the reign of Vespasian Dio of Prusa, on his estate, found a hungry mob advancing up the drive. His defence was that he was practically all in stockraising and viticulture. At Cibyra in southern Phrygia the veteran benefactor Q. Veranius Philagrus in 73 provided that funds not expended in any year from his gift of a million *HS* (the sum normally went on the gymnasiarchy, but individuals might remit the allowance) should go exclusively towards the purchase of arable land; account was to be rendered to emperor and senate. The salutary aim was long-term gain, but neither emperors nor generous subjects could ensure adequate supplies.[69]

Syria, the power-house for Vespasian's takeover, still occupied a prime place in the eastern Empire, even after the creation of Galatia-Cappadocia and the transfer of a second legion there, as the base from which control was extended eastwards under the Flavians and Trajan, and attention was given to its roads. The leading city, Antioch, was a hotbed of trouble second to Alexandria in Egypt, though it had been quiet in 66 when disorders broke out elsewhere. Just after Vespasian's arrival in Syria, in 67, Jews were accused of planning arson, and he had not won his cause when an inhabitant of the city, a renegade Jew himself significantly called Antiochus, repeated the accusation. In the autumn of 70 public buildings, including the agora, council building, record office, and basilicas, were indeed destroyed by a fire, for which Josephus holds debtors responsible. A fresh pogrom followed, which the legate of IV Scythica succeeded in ending in the absence of C. Caesennius Paetus, the governor designate. When Titus reached Antioch from Berytus the Greek inhabitants demanded the expulsion of Jews. Nothing came of this petition or one to cancel their political rights, made in the theatre when he returned from meeting the Parthians at Zeugma.[70]

The Antiochenes naturally associated themselves with the reduction of Judaea, and like other communities were encouraged to do so, as F. Millar has remarked. They were awarded spoils, set up at the Epi Daphne gate, insultingly near a Jewish quarter, and gave the district the name of 'The Cherubim'. In Epi Daphne itself a theatre, also said to be constructed from the spoils, contained a statue of Vespasian and perhaps of other imperial figures. Under the supervision of Traianus fullers, and the city generally, were provided with a canal, stretching almost 2.6 km from the Nahr el-Asi river to a pass of the Amanus (commemorated autumn 73–4). Civilian labour was used, but civil works may have prompted the military project of 75. Vespasian's debt to the cities of Syria was acknowledged by other small favours. At Berytus, where his first council of war met, he held the duovirate, acting through a prefect. In the east, where Roman control was to be strengthened with Trajan's province of Arabia, Bostra, future capital of that province but still under King Rabbel II (71–106), Gerasa and Palmyra were entering the upward curve of prosperity that was to give them the buildings that keep them famous.[71]

Augustus had had friends from the eastern intelligentsia, and we have seen Josephus at the side of Vespasian and Titus. But Flavian intercourse with the legendary sage Apollonius of Tyana is fantasy and relations with Dio of Prusa less intimate than supposed. He was beginning his switchback career, which led to exile under Domitian and back to his native city and a precarious preeminence under Nerva and Trajan. Demetrius had fallen irrevocably from grace and the new generation, Euphrates of Tyre and Epictetus of Hierapolis, freedman of Musonius Rufus, made no detectable impression on Flavian government. Under Vespasian easterners of quality, municipal aristocrats and men of royal descent, were emerging in the Roman context of the senate, to join well established representatives of Baetica and Narbonensis; the last two Severans, Elagabalus and Alexander (218–35), were themselves part Syrian. The future of cultured Greeks in the Antonine Empire was as assimilated Romans within the administration rather than as envoys and gurus.[72]

From AD 70 Judaea, probably left the same size as it had been before the war, enjoyed enough respect to be assigned to the governorship of an ex-praetor. The legate's legionary garrison knew the ground and could be reinforced from a settlement of 800 placed in 71 at Emmaus (Qolonia, 'Colony'). Eusebius alleges that Vespasian, after the capture of Jerusalem, rounded up members of the House of David, in case one rivalled the secular Messiah – himself. But casualties and enslavement, the Diaspora swollen by refugees, made controlling Judaea a lighter task. Any new imperial estates were separately administered.[73]

Jewish government was crippled: the Sanhedrin was disbanded, and there could be no High Priest. If Judaism, in the words of M. Rostovtzeff, had an iron ring of hellenism thrown round it, that does not seem to have taken the form of Graeco-Roman cities. There is much to be said for the view that the eleven toparchies into which Judaea was divided were controlled by the Jewish propertied class. Vespasian according to Josephus decided not to found cities, although he had been reconstructing communities in Galilee and Peraea as he went. At his administrative centre, Caesarea Maritima, already largely a Greek, or rather Syrian, city, and now a colony, Vespasian held honorary office. It may have received Samaritan land, and it was presented with an Odeion on the site of the disputed synagogue. Vespasian also restored Joppa and conferred on it too the title 'Flavia'. It may have been after the war that the toparchy capital Emmaus, between Jerusalem and Joppa, received the title Nicopolis; in 72–3 Samaritan Ma'abartha near Shechem acquired a Greek constitution (perhaps with new settlers) and name that has survived: (Flavia) Neapolis. There was no reason to spend money rehabilitating a province responsible for its own downfall and that had cost Rome effort, men, and money to reduce.[74]

The down-graded procurator still managed the province's economic resources, impoverished though they were. The claim that Vespasian held the province as his private possession is not to be taken literally, but restoration and reorganization must have been one of the charges of the procurator M. Antonius Julianus under Titus in 70: supplies were needed for the military. Vespasian may have raised the level of taxation, besides taking the extended Temple tax for Capitolinus and developing the balsam plantations. On B. Isaac's interpretation of Josephus he 'disposed' of properties confiscated from rebels, rather than 'leasing it'. The status of most of the inhabitants was not changed. Only ex-combatants were *dediticii*, enemies who had thrown themselves on the mercy of the victors and had no rights; they, and the dead and captured, would also have lost their property or become tenants on what had been theirs. S. Applebaum indicates west Judaea, between Lydda and the Dead Sea, as the land disposed of, confiscations affecting districts involved in the struggle: Upper Galilee, Narbatene, Antipatris, Lydda, Jerusalem, and parts of Peraea; Vespasian had settled collaborators at Jamnia and Lydda and in Peraea, and E. Smallwood points to Emmaus and its settlers as a place where owners were dispossessed. Military and other, absentee landowners in full legal possession are listed in the *Midrach de-Bei Rav*: consuls and hegemons, cleruchs, non-commissioned officers, centurions, senators, and well-born women. They are all 'harassers', but there was no radical reorganization of Judaea and Jews were free to buy the confiscated land.[75]

Events in Judaea were among the most important of Vespasian's reign. The end of the Temple cult, revived abortively under the pagan Julian (360–1), threw responsibility for maintaining Judaism on to individual communities; a new centre of rabbinic learning grew up in Jamnia under Rabbi Johanan b. Zakkai, a former rebel; its leaders, the Nasi, were heirs of the Pharisees, their appointment had to be ratified by the Romans, and they became the heads of a religion centred on the Law (*Torah*) and its teaching (the *Mishnah*), preoccupied with theory and private morality. At the same time the fall of Jerusalem gradually brought the Jewish branch of the Christian church to an end, encouraging the sect to develop into a Gentile phenomenon, although it would be a generation before the end of circumcision in the Church exempted its adherents from the tax. Already in the winter of 68–9, during the terror in Jerusalem, the Christian community had fled 'as a result of divine guidance' to a Gentile city, Pella in Peraea.[76]

The edict that the governor Ti. Julius Alexander issued in mid-68 exposed as comprehensively as the propaganda purposes of its author could manage the inefficiency, injustices, and abuses of the Roman administration in Egypt. Cure was another matter, and hopes were probably not fulfilled. There were no additional privileges, and one that Alexandrians had enjoyed, exemption from the poll tax, had been removed. This may itself have been a punitive response to early signs of discontent. Another measure designed to prevent loss of financial blood was connected with the *fideicommissa* that were also the subject of metropolitan legislation: where the beneficiaries were non-citizens the provision was to be null and void, and the sum confiscated. The sedition reported under 73 is plausible, though it may be misdated. In the countryside – which had been allowed to go on believing that it was subject to Vitellius until at earliest 23 July – the overriding purpose of the administration, exploitation, stayed the same, made more effective if land categories had now been clarified. The status of the governorship declined slightly, when the Prefecture of the Guard became a post to be held by the Emperor's son; after the Julio-Claudian period, too, previous experience in the province ceased to be a recommendation. A century of Roman rule had made it routine.[77]

Routine indeed, and the entrenched interest of innumerable individuals, were in part the saving and then the remaking of the Empire. Vespasian's achievement in stabilizing the Empire was virtually total, but enhancement by him has been overdrawn, and much in the conventional picture has to be given up; so some of the changes in financial administration credited to him may have begun before his reign, and developments in the imperial cult come from below. Initiatives such as founding colonies, road-building and restoration, care for the public post (*vehiculatio*), and other public works had a military or political aim; privileges were designed to secure loyalty to the dynasty; titles were given, not much money spent. There is little to be said for the view that Vespasian encouraged trade; economic advance was due primarily to confidence in the peaceful background and secure future that it provided, and it was patchy geographically and in content: not surprisingly the Batavians do not seem to have been better off after 70 than before. Activity was heightened by the very need for reconstruction on the restoration of peace: money flowed, into the gaping imperial coffers and out again for necessary expenditure on rebuilding, new construction, and the army. Enhancement was a natural consequence of stabilization.[78]

10

IMPERIALISM

Vespasian's army and the extension of the Empire

The military disorder of 68–70 embodied an old nightmare. But the new events, in which a strong factor was the fear and humiliation of the army that had defeated Vindex, give no reason for seeing in them the beginning of the demoralization and wilfulness of third-century armies. Vespasian, victorious and in control of the centre, had a sharp problem: to restore discipline, among Flavian and Vitellian troops in Italy, eventually in the remnants of the Rhine legions, by showing himself master and by assuaging fear.[1]

Combatants in Italy were dealt with by Primus and Mucianus. Some returned to duty in the provinces. Not only was there an upsurge in the numbers of individuals discharged at the end of civil hostilities, especially from the Italian fleets, which had served their turn well; four legions disappeared from the army list when the German revolt ended: I, IV Macedonica, XV Primigenia, and XVI Gallica had sworn allegiance to the Gallic Empire; the real offence of XV, though it also had a vexillation with the Vitellians at Cremona, was to have surrendered at Vetera. The historic V Alaudae probably survived, although financial stringency was against it: a mere remnant of the legion absent with its eagle with the Vitellians had been massacred at Vetera. Men from IV and V who had been on vexillation with Vitellius are found in the colony at Scupi. Others from IV and XVI made a fresh start in IV and XVI Flavia (Felix and Firma respectively!), the former in Dalmatia, the latter ultimately in Cappadocia. With Alaudae retained and XV Primigenia cashiered the total was 29, one more than it had been before the emergency recruitments of 69. Vitellius' Praetorians had to argue for their place against Otho's men and Antonius Primus' legionaries. They refused to be dismissed quietly, maintained their position, and were dealt with as individuals; some were retained and even after retirement were re-admitted as legionaries. Technical skill seems to have been a recommendation.[2]

Vespasian's own troops had nowhere else to look for reward – which he is said to have been slow to pay. He would not have been likely either to discharge them prematurely: each cash discharge cost 12,000 *HS*; veterans and the casualties of 68–70 would have to be replaced with tiros; at Cremona VII Gemina alone lost six senior centurions. Overall here was no reason for

Vespasian to be confronted by a long-term disciplinary problem, and he was a firm commander in the mould of Caesar, Augustus, and Tiberius and, unlike Galba, consistent.[3]

Vespasian has also been faced in modern scholarship with deteriorating recruits, indeed, with the gradual 'proletarianization' of the army. The myth, propagated by M. Rostovtzeff, was to explain, in particular, the sack of Cremona; the proletarian legionaries loathed the city bourgeoisie. Vespasian dealt with the problem by forbidding the legions to Italians south of the Po, favouring provincials, urbanized and of decent standing. A variant draws attention to provincial recruits' ignorance of and lack of interest in politics.[4]

In the sack of Cremona brutality needs no explanation. After a desperate battle, the victors lucky to escape and emerging on a high, destruction, theft, and rapine proved them alive. As to the claim that Vespasian forbade Italians to serve, that political impossibility has evidence against it: Italians continued in the legions, forming just over one-fifth of the men whose origin is known between the reigns of Vespasian and Trajan; the younger Pliny welcomed Trajan's schemes for government grants (which operated in Italy) towards the cost of rearing children as potential soldiers. Tacitus, surveying the Empire's military strength for the year 23, indicates that Italians – from Etruria and Umbria, Latium and ancient colonies, the Republican recruiting grounds – were serving in the privileged Praetorian Guard. The decline in the proportion of Italian legionaries was gradual, reluctantly accepted, and due to unwillingness to soldier long years abroad if better-paid service at Rome were available, perhaps also to the relative impoverishment of the peninsula. Under Claudius and Nero nearly half of the legionaries recorded came from Italy; Hadrian and the Antonines saw that fall to less than 1 per cent. If Tiberius found Italian 'beggars with nowhere to live' unacceptable in comparison with what was available in the provinces, it shows precisely that Rome was not allowing the army to become 'proletarianized'. The proportion of Spanish recruits of those known rose from less than 2.5 to nearly 5 per cent under Vespasian, of Gallic from 10 to almost 16 per cent, of men from Africa from 2 to nearly 7 per cent, from the Balkan and Danubian provinces from 4 (all Macedonians) to 14 per cent (under 2 per cent from Macedonia); from the eastern provinces the percentage rose from 19 per cent to more than 25 per cent; significant figures, which indicate in particular the increasingly important rôle of the East in running the Empire and the rise of the Danubian provinces, which in the third century were to provide emperors. The army was becoming 'regionalized', stationary units fed locally in part developing ties with the people among whom they lived. The increase in Danubian and eastern recruits was also related to the strength of the legions in those areas. Difficulties caused when local people and a garrison shared interests and grievances did not occur after Vespasian had dealt with Civilis and the Gauls; but he made no attempt to alter the long-standing trend towards provincial recruitment. The Rhine legions were recruited until 69 largely from Italy, Narbonensis, and Spain, afterwards increasingly from north of the Alps, including the Rhineland itself; and it was there that the veterans were settling.[5]

Professor Saddington warns against the temptation to assume an increase in cheaper auxiliary strength. A pair of cavalry Alae, I and II Flaviae Geminae Milliariae (theoretically doubled-sized), an infantry unit with cavalry, I Flavia Hispana Equitata, went to the Rhine, and a new squadron of cavalry, I Vespasiana Dardanorum, to Moesia, but 'Twins' may have been mergers of units that had lost heavily in the war. Units were levied from Africa (Gaetuli, Numidae, and Musulamii), Spain, Britain, Thrace, Syria, Cilicia, and newly annexed Commagene; only the Thracian Bessi and Dardanians cannot be shown to have supplied named units before.[6]

Vespasian has also been credited with changes in recruitment and handling. Claiming double-sized units, epigraphically attested in the 80s, as a novelty means discarding Josephus' evidence that they were available in the Jewish War. Then allegedly Vespasian raised auxiliaries' social level by bringing in Roman citizens. But as yet there were few in the *auxilia*, and the more citizenship spread the less it entailed a rise in the social status of recruits. Most important, Vespasian allegedly broke ethnic unity, integrating tribal bands and replacing native commanders with Romans; and sent recruits to distant lands. Certainly, Vespasian did not allow auxiliaries to hold the Empire to ransom, and dealt with the immediate problem on the Rhine. Other Flavian developments should not be over-dramatized; they continued and intensified earlier practice; as D. Saddington points out, institutionalization of units was under way in Nero's time, and men from newly conquered areas had long been sent where they could not support rebellious compatriots. Once established, units were recruited from districts in which they were stationed, except those with specialized weaponry, slings and bows; that weakened earlier loyalties. Although *numeri* disappear from Lower Germany there is little evidence for an abrupt end to employing 'native' commanders, who, like the most famous rebel of all, Arminius, would have been Roman citizens. Tacitus suggests that the change had come about for the Batavians by his own day, but at the beginning of the second century a 'native' was Prefect of Cohort IX at Vindolanda: the significantly named Flavius Cerialis had a Sulpicia Lepidina for wife, suggesting that his father-in-law had been enfranchised by Galba.[7]

At Rome Vespasian had to confront the problem of the Praetorians, essentially the headquarters troops of an imperator, brought under Tiberius into a single barracks, and the immediate prop or threat to a régime. They had taken the lead in recognizing Gaius, and had been decisive in bringing Claudius to power, in toppling Nero, and in replacing Galba by Otho. There had been twelve cohorts under Nero; Vespasian has been credited with lowering the number from Vitellius' sixteen, each a thousand strong, to the nine mentioned in a discharge certificate of December 2 76; a daunting task – if he took it on, and the 'missing' cohorts were not stationed elsewhere than at Rome; ten appear in a later diploma. He dealt neatly with political activities: for all their *esprit de corps* and their politically conscious officers the Praetorians were a threat mainly for their ambitious Prefects. Vespasian's kinsman the senator Arrecinus Clemens took over in 70, then Titus.[8]

No threat came from the night watch or the four urban cohorts under the City Prefect, a leading senator; they had proved helpless against Praetorians in 41. Urban cohorts XV and XVI at Ostia and Puteoli were disbanded and replaced at Ostia with night watchmen; XIII may have been sent to Carthage by Vespasian, for III Augusta was engaged in the south-west, and Africa, with its vital grain, remained suspect in 70. Yet it is attested there only under Domitian. Another potential trouble-spot was Lugdunum, financial centre of the Gauls. It had held out against Vindex in 68, but loyalty to Nero was no recommendation now. Cohors I Flavia was created for service there.[9]

Vespasian, having fought like Augustus all over the Roman world and knowing three continents, had no need at 60, well beyond the age at which Tiberius had taken the field, to involve himself in campaigning; it was for the inexperienced Domitian to show what he could do. But Vespasian's nineteen imperatorial salutations show him exploiting glory that his troops won for himself and Titus, and he chose commanders prudently. Key positions (Rhine, Danube, Syria, Egypt) were identified and filled, like the Guard Prefecture, with family or loyalists. Vespasian was parsimonious too with triumphal honours. He and his brother had experienced Claudius' generosity with the *ornamenta*; thirteen other award-holders from that reign are attested. The years 70 to 79 offer a meagre list: Mucianus could not be awarded less; Ti. Plautius Silvanus Aelianus in a political gesture had achievements of Nero's reign recognized, and L. Tampius Flavianus a success in Pannonia achieved before he was swept away in the Flavian revolution; Cn. Pinarius Cornelius Clemens won them in Germany, M. Ulpius Traianus in the East. Lesser senators active in the field could expect sets of decorations that were now standardized, as they were for centurions (and excluded for non-citizens), not necessarily by imperial fiat but perhaps from increasing unwillingness to depart from an increasingly narrow range of norms. Another, harmless, form of recognition came into use for military men: adlection into Rome's highest aristocracy, the patriciate.[10]

On E. Luttwak's formulation, that Roman power lay in the perception of it in the minds of men, Roman power was diminished by the events of 68–70. They showed the Empire vulnerable inside and out. The Gauls joined the revolt on the Rhine on hearing of the Dacian and Sarmatian invasions and were told that Britain was defecting; and in tribes moving westwards from the steppes a permanent threat was making itself felt in the Balkans. Tacitus was to write sombrely of 'fates' pressing on the Empire. Vespasian had to consider defence as well as prestigious imperialism. One view of Josephus' Aramaic version of the Jewish War is that it was a tract designed to let people beyond the eastern frontier – Parthians in particular – know how much the power of Rome was to be feared. It is only the genuine problems that Vespasian had to face that lends that conception any plausibility. T. Rajak refuted it; but Josephus' reference to his hopes of deflecting others from revolt suggests nervousness. Decades of comparative peace meant that when Galba made his bid for the Principate Spain had only one legion of the three stationed there under Tiberius; a perception of external threat, less plausibly a distaste for posting legions close to Italy, encouraged a centrifugal tendency, exemplified in miniature by Rubrius Gallus' posting in 70 of more garrisons on the lower Danube after the Sarmatian incursions.[11]

That did not imply a more defensive stance. Legions could move outwards as well as sustain attack. Examination of military activity in the provinces under Vespasian will show that E. Luttwak's view exaggerates the contrast with the period before 68. The idea that Vespasian renounced imperial ambitions or followed any deathbed injunction of Augustus is unfounded.[12]

After the civil wars the Flavians developed what the Julio-Claudians left, for pragmatic strategic and internal political reasons; and the policies, Empire-wide, remained mutually interactive. In Africa the slow extension of Roman control was continued, in the East, a demonstration of strength, with the possibility of deployment in force, made up for shortcomings in Nero's settlement with Parthia. The calling in of dependent kingdoms here and in Britain followed from their success, as it had with the reduction of Galatia to provincial status in 25 BC, of Cappadocia in 17 BC and the Cottian Alps in 64. Even in Germany, where Julio-Claudians had been cautious, there was an advance, which might have been more vigorous if so much had not been committed to the full-scale conquest of Britain that Nero had demitted after the revolt of Boudicca to concentrate on annexing Armenia.

The mapping and delimitation of Africa, begun with the plan for the colony at Carthage in 123 BC and continued with road-building under Augustus and Tiberius, continued on a substantial scale. III Augusta had been taken from the proconsul's command by Gaius Caligula. In the reign of Septimius Severus the work of Vespasian's governor and legate issued in a new province, Numidia, containing the legion and territory acquired to the south-west; surprisingly, when Cn. Domitius Tullus commanded the legion in 70–2 he had still not held the praetorship.[13]

The disturbances that opened the new reign were nothing new as natives lost land, freedom, and transhumance rights: military distinctions had been won in Africa since the beginning of the Principate, most notably during the rebellion of tribesmen under the Musulamian Tacfarinas, 17–24; Galba had been prorogued as governor (45–7) and exceptionally he had commanded III Augusta, against Musulamii. Now Festus' quelling of the Garamantes in 70 created a relationship on which the Romans were able to capitalize. Perhaps it was as early as Vespasian's reign that a Roman officer, Julius Maternus, made a four-month reconnaissance from Lepcis Magna to Agisymba,

'Rhinocerus place', in company with the Garamantian chief; but Pliny ignores it, which suggests a date later than 77.[14]

The defeat of the Garamantians in the south-east eased progress into the western interior towards the Aurès and the Musulamii, making a seemingly decisive phase in the pacification of Africa; terrain and sources make it hard to chart. Probably in the middle of the reign III Augusta moved 35 km south-west from Ammaedara among the Gaetulians to Theveste. Ammaedara accordingly became a colony with centuriated territory, and Cillium, at a key point on the route from Capsa to Carthage, was also founded as a military settlement. The inscriptions of Sufetula, which belonged to Vespasian's Quirina tribe, begin under him; it too may have had a military function. Milestones of Vespasian are found on the roads from Hippo Regius to Cirta by way of Aquae Thibilitanae and to Theveste, through Musulamian territory west of the Flavian veteran colony of Madaurus, and from Theveste to Carthage, establishing the centrality of the base. In the next phase, by the beginning of the second century, the legion advanced further west to permanent quarters at Lambaesis; the existence of Aquae Flavianae between Theveste and Lambaesis, which was occupied under Titus, shows that momentum was not lost. Such military posts have suggested that the Flavians planned the North African boundary system (*limes*, a delimiting path), but its origins are not agreed, and the limits of Roman control had not yet been reached. Vespasian introduced new troops, the Chalcideni from Syria, archers for desert warfare, but no evidence for his strategy. Towns promoted by Vespasian are far from the *Fossatum Africae*, even as the colonies are outside the original province, and their creation must be seen in this context of advancing and deepening control (Madaurus' territory probably occupied Musulamian land).[15]

In Britain expansion begun as a show-case operation under Claudius was decisively resumed as a source of glory and imperatorial salutations on a Claudian scale. 'Britain' was a province, in the sense of a 'job', but in 70 Wales was not subject and northwards direct rule ended at the Brigantes; part of southern England, Hampshire, Berkshire, and Sussex, had been entrusted to the dependent monarch, Ti. Claudius Cogidubnus. Since 60 the advance had been halted for consolidation. Nero withdrew XIV Gemina from Viroconium in the mid-60s to serve in the East, and while the Principate itself was at issue in 68–9 no governor could launch a major offensive. Modest achievements are written up by modern writers suspicious of Tacitus.[16]

With the Continent quieted, Rome was ready for action in Wales, broken off in 60, when Suetonius Paullinus was summoned from his attack on the corn-rich Druidical stronghold on Anglesey, and in the North. XX Valeria had left Burrium to take the place of XIV at Viroconium, and II Augusta moved up from Isca Dumnoniorum to Glevum, both leaving detachments in their old fortresses. When Wales was securely under control in the mid-70s,

Burrium was abandoned altogether and II moved to its permanent home at Isca (Caerleon).[17]

The generals faced a double task, and if Cogidubnus died in this reign, administrative duties in southern Britain became more onerous. The distinguished men appointed revealed the importance that Vespasian attached to the island that he had helped to invade: it was to be the stage for spectacular advance. Q. Petillius Cerialis, governor 71–3/4, had dash, as well as experience of Britain at its worst as legate of IX in 60–1. His subordinate as legate of XX, Cn. Julius Agricola, had also been in Britain then, as tribune. Cerialis brought over II Adiutrix and punished the Brigantes, claiming them for the province and extending direct control to the line of the future Wall, including Carlisle. The Romans consolidated their hold by constructing forts, and the headquarters of IX Hispana were moved from Lindum to Eboracum.[18]

Sex. Julius Frontinus (73/4–77) is conceded even by Tacitus to be a great man for the times. He had probably begun as an equestrian officer, reaching senatorial rank under Galba. Effective service, and knowing his place, helped him rise and stay at the top: he served against the Lingones, and reached the consulship in 72 or 73. Frontinus was another of those governors of Britain (Q. Veranius, Suetonius Paullinus, Vettius Bolanus) experienced in mountain country and particularly well qualified for the advance north and west: like Bolanus he was probably with Corbulo in Armenia. Frontinus conquered Wales, advancing up the valleys and subjugating the Silures, who had given trouble almost since the invasion, and established a network of auxiliary forts, earthen, with wooden ramparts, at such places as Brecon and Caersws so that risings could be checked before reaching serious proportions. For the legion there was the fortress at Isca. Only in north Wales did the Ordovices of Powys, who annihilated an auxiliary *ala*, remain for Agricola to deal with, a 'policing exercise'. There was also another campaign against the Brigantes. Frontinus' success, and perhaps the favour he found in Domitian's eyes by surrendering his post of urban praetorship to him in 70, won him the task of dealing with the formidable German Chatti, as Domitian's subordinate in 83.[19]

Frontinus' successor (77–83), however over-praised by his son-in-law Tacitus, was carefully chosen, loyal and experienced in Britain. Command of the dissident XX in 70 was a successful test. His next charge was a province linked to Britain by culture and trade, Aquitania. Suffect consul in 77 or even 76, he arrived in the late summer of 77 for what turned out to be a seven-year stint. The Ordovices were his first target, and then, seizing the moment, Anglesey. Agricola's despatches that reported his success bore no laurels, from prudence, modesty, or (in cool modern estimates) a sense of proportion. The second summer saw him sweeping through his territory, perhaps against the northern Brigantes and beyond the Tyne–Solway Isthmus beyond the line of the Wall, constructing forts, and exacting hostages; Tacitus is vague, but the season, like the following winter, may have gone on the consolidation that contributed so much to Roman control: expansion put strains on the south, which had to contribute supplies and had its garrisons thinned.[20]

In 79, his third season, Agricola continued the advance from his base at Red House, Corbridge, opening up the Dere Street route into Scotland, laying waste territory as far as the Tay and consolidating gains by constructing forts in the region; he is specifically credited with encountering new tribes, the presumably friendly Votadini and the Selgovae on the Borders east and west of the Street, which supports the view of Agricola's modern detractors that Tacitus' narrative masks the achievement of earlier commanders in the North. The huge extent of Brigantian territory – perhaps from the Trent to Birrens in Dumfries – is the problem: even marked territorial advance would not quickly bring Agricola to 'new' tribes.[21]

This summer Titus alone took credit for Agricola's success, becoming 'Imperator' for the fifteenth time, and decided to call a definitive halt on the Clyde–Forth line. The strangulated language that Tacitus uses to describe this decision shows how ambivalently he felt: it was taken by an admirable emperor, the line was approved by Agricola and sited in detail by him – and the order to resume the advance came from Domitian. For 80 Tacitus has little to report but further consolidation, confirmed by the line of forts that marked the new frontier; but in 81 Agricola crossed the Clyde to take the field against 'hitherto unknown' tribes in the west Lowlands, previously bypassed, and to cast an eye on the island that he supposed lay conveniently between Britain and Spain and was inhabited by kinsmen of the Britons. The frontier did not last another year: Domitian needed glory, even won by others. The pretext for further conquests was a massive rising intended by the enemy. The season saw a combined military and naval operation, against the Venicones in Fife, the Vacomagi or Boresti between the Tay and the Dee, and perhaps the Taexali beyond. Agricola avoided being surrounded by splitting his forces into three, but at the cost of an almost fatal weakening of IX Hispana: it had to be rescued in a dashing night action (it could be reported) which intimidated the enemy.[22]

Agricola's campaigns ended in late 83, when he brought the enemy to battle probably by depriving them of their economic base; the site of his textbook victory at Mons Graupius has not been identified. In the same year Domitian achieved his first personal victory against the Chatti. That meant the end of Agricola's usefulness; and he had had more than twice the normal term. In the aftermath of the victory, auxiliary forts were established at the southern mouths of Highland glens, at Fendoch, Dalginross, Bochastle, Malling, and Drumquhassle, for defensive, offensive, or policing purposes, or for all. But the demands of Germany and above all the Danube, where defeats at the hands of the Dacians began in 85, rightly took precedence, and the unfinished legionary fortress at Inchtuthil and the other forts were abandoned by mid-88, XX Valeria removing to Deva when II Adiutrix returned to the Continent. Agricola had already lost legionary vexillations required for Domitian's campaign of 83. South and east between Bertha and Strageath and then down to Ardoch a second fortified line probably marking a Roman protectorate of the Venicones in Fife was given up by 90, and even the Clyde–Forth line. In the first decade of the new century, whether because of demands elsewhere in the Empire or because of unrest in the province, the line of the Tweed was also abandoned; the scene was set for the construction of Hadrian's Wall.[23]

In the reign of Claudius Germany was a command in which an ambitious general might lament his luck, as Corbulo did. By AD 9 Augustus seemed to have achieved the subjugation of peoples between Rhine and Elbe. After the loss of three legions his successors eschewed immediate conquest, though they kept both banks of the Rhine in Roman hands, using diplomacy to aid pro-Roman leaders and to set one people against another. Now Vespasian settled for something less than the scheme of Augustus' middle years.[24]

Solid foundations were laid, as we have seen, when the havoc of 69–70 ended. In the northern sector, later Lower Germany, the establishment of Noviomagus enabled II Adiutrix, then X Gemina, to oversee the Batavians, part of whose territory was annexed. The Romans turned their attention to the Bructeri, who had taken part in the revolt, were still unchastened, and sheltered the baleful prophetess Veleda. The legate of the Lower German army 76–9, C. Rutilius Gallicus, was sent against them with his legions and she was captured in 77–8, to become a temple-cleaner at Ardea, helping the Roman efforts psychologically if not militarily; she seems to have had a more friendly successor, Ganna, who visited Rome in the early 90s. The Romans were lucky: 60,000 Bructeri (a Roman exaggeration) were later destroyed by German enemies and, perhaps in the first five years of Domitian's reign, perhaps the year after his death, T. Vestricius Spurinna forced them to take back a puppet king they had expelled. It seems that the policy was to weaken resistance among them and make sure that they were under friendly rulers.[25]

It was in the southern sector below the lower Main and the upper Danube and where the Neckar runs through the Black Forest, across a re-entrant angle that called for uneconomical deployment of Roman forces on the upper reaches of both the main rivers, that Vespasian made a modest advance: into what Tacitus calls '*Decumates agri* ', probably lands of a group of ten cantons. He achieved measurable and permanent results, not precluding further gains, building on the hold that the Romans already had on Raetia (Bavaria south of the Danube), which Augustus had annexed. Vespasian's move had the secondary advantage of giving additional cover to the Belfort Gap, where the Doubs leads to the Saône valley. This route had been used by L. Verginius Rufus in 68, when he moved to repress Vindex's rising. Further south, in the later province of Upper Germany, in the Wetterau north and north-east of Moguntiacum the reconstruction of the forts at Aquae Mattiacae and

Hofheim and earthworks at Heddernheim (Frankfurt) on the line of advance along the Wetter which were to be followed up with a stone fort for Ala I Flavia Gemina under Domitian, along with discoveries at Okarben and Friedberg, suggest that the route was already coming under control in Vespasian's time. The claim that there were pre-Flavian forts on the right bank of the Rhine south of the Main has been controverted; the Romans had controlled it since the early Principate, but perhaps through friendly tribes. Now there was a definitive occupation. Between the confluences of the Main and the Neckar a road was constructed either in the immediate aftermath of the revolt or a few years later along the line Gross Gerau, Gernsheim, and Heddernheim; and the garrison of Rheingönheim was moved over to Lopodunum north of the Neckar and Neuenheim (near Heidelberg) on the right bank. Forts south of the Neckar continued the line down to Argentorate: Hockenheim, Grotzingen east of Karlsruhe, and Baden Baden.[26]

The activity was associated with the strengthening of Aventicum, Augusta Raurica, and Vindonissa, and extended Raurican and Helvetian as well as Roman territory among the Suebians; detachments of I Adiutrix and VII Gemina (on its way back to Spain from Pannonia) were stationed at Augusta Raurica; the colony owed its first amphitheatre to the reign of Vespasian. No doubt definitive occupation of this area had repercussions still further west. The Romans moved from Argentorate up the Kinzig into the *Agri Decumates*, and established forts at Offenburg, where a milestone names the governor Cn. Pinarius Clemens, with Argentorate as *caput viae* (the destination, Raetia or the Danube bank, Laiz or Tuttlingen, obliterated), Waldmössingen, Sulz, and between Neckar and Danube probably at Geislingen and at Lautlingen and Burladingen on the route to Laiz. From Vindonissa a second road was driven to Hüfingen and Arae Flaviae at the heart of the region, soon evidently a centre of the imperial cult like Lugdunum and Colonia Agrippinensium.[27]

The area was tackled from the south as well. In Raetia, Vespasian reinvigorated the south bank of the Danube from Hüfingen to Oberstimm, restoring auxiliary forts that had suffered in the struggles of 69, such as Risstissen, Unterkirchberg and Burghöfe, and filled in gaps in the Claudian line, between Oberstimm and Linz; at Günzburg an inscription indicates building in 77–8 (a replacement for Aislingen?). Given the activity in the *Decumates* it is not surprising that Vespasian and Titus, rather than using the awkward terrain of the south bank, built a road on the northern side of the Danube eastwards from near Neuburg. It passed through the new cavalry fort of Kösching and recrossed the river at Eining, a fort under construction in the reign of Titus. Sites at Castra Regina itself, and eastwards towards the confluence with the Inn, at Straubing, and near Moos east of the Isar are thought to have been occupied under Vespasian, though not the other forts on this stretch down to Passau.[28]

The achievement in Germany gave Rome more ground, up to the Weser and the Ems in the north, and right-bank territory in the south, also re-establishing Roman initiative. Mastery of the *Decumates* prepared for further advances by Domitian: he pushed north and east in the Wetterau and established a dense new forward line of forts from there north–south down the Main and middle Neckar, controlling any attempt by tribes coming from the north, notably the Chatti, to approach the Rhine in that area.[29]

In the south the relation between Vespasian's achievements and those of Domitian is unclear. Did Domitian continue a plan drawn up by his father or improve on a more modest one? The question may be misconceived. The establishment of the Mainz–Gross-Gerau–Heidelberg route and of the Wetter forts suggests that the final achievement or more was something that Vespasian might have envisaged. As in the Augustan attack on Germany and in Claudius' invasion of Britain an immediate plan may be distinguished from options tacit or only mooted.[30]

North of the middle Danube Vespasian had faithful allies, the Suebian kings Sido and significantly named Italicus, who had fought at Cremona, in control of Moravia and south-west Slovakia and creating a 'third zone' under Roman influence, political, cultural, and, as L. Pitts has stressed, economic. The Marcomanni had moved eastward out of Bohemia, but the Flavians faced intransigent and aggressive Sarmatian Roxolani and Dacians. There was no permanent advance until Trajan finally annexed Dacia in 106, acquiring its resources for Rome, splitting the Sarmatians, and creating a bulwark against them. Until then the Romans were vulnerable to both tribes, and suffered notable defeats from the Dacians in 84–5 and 86. Mailed horsemen had proved their worth in incursions of the Julio-Claudian period and in 69–70, and could be dealt with, as J. Wilkes has pointed out, only when they dispersed for plunder, while the vast plains swallowed up legions deployed there. Vespasian followed up the success of Rubrius Gallus and the Danubian provinces gained, eventually at the expense of the military zone on the Rhine: after the revolt of Saturninus in 89 Domitian removed XIV Gemina and XXI Rapax from Moguntiacum to Pannonia.[31]

Earlier movements suggest measured redeployment towards the lower Danube rather than a massive upheaval. Pannonia was left with its Julio-Claudian two legions: XIII Gemina was stationed at Poetovio, and at Carnuntum the base of XV Apollinaris was strengthened and enlarged under C. Calpetanus Rantius Quirinalis in 73. But D. Knight notes two each of cavalry and infantry units redeployed from Germany to the Balkans. At Burnum in Dalmatia was buried a Batavian cavalryman from Ala I (Hispanorum?), Imerix, son of Servofredus, who died at the age of 28 after eight years' service; he may have been recruited under Vitellius. Titus moved the squadron again, to Pannonia. There too a new auxiliary fort was constructed at Vindobona, upstream from Carnuntum: Ala I Britannica appears there before the end of the century, and Cohors I Britannica at Brigetio in about 80; each eventually Milliaria, if not originally so. When in 73 the Ala Frontoniana (later I Tungrorum) moved from the Lower German army it went to Italy and then to Pannonia, to be stationed at a strengthened Aquincum. The same site has produced a dedication to Vespasian and his sons by an *ala* whose name is not preserved. Pannonia gained seven units, making a strength in 80 of at least seventeen, and Noricum two, the additions coming from Dalmatia as well as from eastern provinces. Such developments illustrate the downgrading of the establishment in the Dalmatian hinterland for the benefit of front-line provinces. The one legion left at Burnum during the reign of Vespasian, IV Flavia, was to leave in 86 for Domitian's Dacian war.[32]

But Pannonia in turn was soon to lose place to its eastern neighbour Moesia. In response to the problems that had arisen under Nero and during the civil wars, Vespasian built up the establishment on the Lower Danube, moving it definitively up from the Drave and increasing the garrison of Moesia to four legions: VII Claudia at Viminacium (it seems to have taken part in road-building), V Macedonica at Oescus, I Italica at Novae, V Alaudae, if it survived, at an uncertain site, perhaps Durostorum. Besides that, Flavian Moesia had twenty-one auxiliary units. In the Derdap A. Mócsy noted one auxiliary fort coming into existence at Taliata; four others have been added: Hurlec, Leskovac, Nikopol, and Orehovo. But when Trajan annexed Dacia in 106, the new province was to suck in no fewer than twenty-five units, mostly from Upper Moesia.[33]

Another development on the Danube was increased reliance on infantry rather than cavalry: thirteen of the Pannonian strength in 80 were infantry, only four cavalry. On the Danube itself two fleets, both styled Flavia, were allocated one each to Pannonia and Moesia, with bases at Taurunum and Noviodunum respectively. There was no defence in depth, though that would have served Domitian well. But movement from one sector to another was facilitated by the road system and veteran colonies such as Scupi and Deultum (men of VII Claudia also went to Philippopolis) backed the military on active service. Under Vespasian the Danubian garrison was beginning to take on its second-century aspect. In the short run, the success of Rubrius Gallus, and Vespasian's sound dispositions and road-building, kept the area peaceful for a decade and a half and created the basis for Trajan's takeover of Dacia.[34]

In the East Vespasian found himself with an immediate problem – in late 69 eastern forces were denuded and Romans had turned their backs on the Parthian Empire – and with unfinished business. In 66 Nero abandoned Rome's claim to appoint the dependent monarch of Armenia Major. It had been maintained since 20 BC, when Tiberius crowned the Roman nominee replacing Artaxes II. Rome's candidates often faced rivals backed by Parthia, or were found unsuitable for Armenia and its people; if a king stayed the course it needed military back-up to establish a successor. In the last years of his principate Claudius had allowed Armenia to pass from Roman control and the Parthian monarch Vologaeses I (51/2–79/80) was able to settle his brother there. Nero had begun in 54 by taking measures for the restoration of the status quo; he appointed Cn. Domitius Corbulo governor of Galatia and Cappadocia combined, with special responsibility for removing the Parthians from Armenia and replacing Tiridates with a Roman nominee. Tigranes was not a success, and by 62, partly for the sake of his position at Rome, Nero felt that something more prestigious was necessary, and he sent L. Caesennius Paetus to annex Armenia as a province. The humiliation of Paetus, who surrendered to the Parthians at Rhandeia, was wiped out for the Romans when in 63 Tiridates gave up his tiara to Corbulo on the same spot. In 66 he was crowned by Nero in a ceremony that disguised the fact that Rome was recognizing the Parthian choice. With the Armenian issue solved, there need be no trouble between the two empires, except what territorial greed and opportunism provoked. On the Parthian side was the lure of Syria's wealth, on the Roman the fertile land of Mesopotamia and a desire to reassert authority in Armenia.[35]

Nero left much of the far end of Asia Minor under dependent monarchs such as Antiochus IV of Commagene; the easternmost province, Cappadocia, had been in the hands of a praesidial procurator, a governor like Judaea's, since its annexation in AD 17, but whether it reverted to a procurator after Corbulo's death in 66 is not clear. In Parthia a reaction against hellenic influence began in the reign of Vologaeses, perhaps concomitant with a more bellicose attitude; but his success in securing Armenia may have been enough to satisfy his subjects; according to Tacitus towards the end of Nero's reign he was determined to avoid war. One of Vespasian's precautions in 69 was to open negotiations with Parthia and Armenia; when Vespasian seemed sure of victory Vologaeses, who may have begun by addressing Vespasian without the courtesy of his title, offered unwanted reinforcements (Vespasian diplomatically referred him to the senate and assured him of peace), and on the fall of Jerusalem he presented Titus with a golden crown. Relations were to deteriorate.[36]

Months spent in the East after the senate recognized him enabled Vespasian to make sure that unrest caused by the Jewish War, and by alert changes of loyalty among the dependent monarchs, would not be aggravated by his departure or by Parthian opportunism. Vespasian's governors of Syria were experienced and trustworthy. L. Caesennius Paetus his kinsman was given a second chance in the East when Mucianus left, continuing until 73; as stand-in until his arrival he had the safe legionary legate Cn. Pompeius Collega. Next came A. Marius Celsus, perhaps author of a work on tactics, who had served Corbulo as legate of XV Apollinaris. Faithful to Galba, he had – better still – become an adherent and commander of Otho against the Vitellians. It was he who had taken over the Lower Rhine from Petillius Cerialis in summer 71. Celsus' tenure was short and he was succeeded by M. Ulpius Traianus, who held office until 77/8. Traianus may have come from Galatia-Cappadocia, where Collega is soon found (?73/4–76/7). A limited circle of men was in play, none plausible candidates for the Principate. B. Jones has argued that Titus' lingering in the East after the capture of Jerusalem was intended to ensure that the Parthians knew that the new régime, while not intending territorial gains east of the Euphrates, would be firm in the face of Parthian adventures. The prime reason may have been internal security (especially in Egypt) and above all the guarantee it provided of Vespasian's safety in his first months at Rome.[37]

Vespasian made radical long-term rearrangements in Asia Minor. He annexed dependencies adjacent to the Euphrates and recreated Nero's province of Galatia-Cappadocia, under a consular legate controlling two legions, at Melitene, and Satala. What remains controversial is the speed of the change: a smart sequence completed in 72 or something more gradual, ending only in 76–7. A grander controversy envelops the overall intent of the changes. Was it to continue the precautionary measures of 69–70? Or did Vespasian and his *aides* envisage, even plan offensive movements against Parthia, such as Trajan undertook in 113? Accordingly the concept of the Euphrates as a political frontier, except south of Zeugma-Seleucia, has come under criticism. The view taken here is that Vespasian aimed at making Parthian intervention impossible while putting Rome in a position to march eastward in force at will. Vespasian proceeded slowly; after about 75, a new factor played a part in Roman calculations: the presence of the Alans north of the Caucasus, an incentive for posting XVI Flavia to Satala.[38]

For the early 70s reliable information from Josephus shows that Vespasian deprived both Aristobulus of Lesser Armenia and Antiochus IV of Commagene of their kingdoms, the first in 71 or 72, the second in 72/3. Lesser Armenia carried a route between Trapezus and the Upper Euphrates, vital during Corbulo's operations. Its ruler Aristobulus withdrew, compensated perhaps with the principality of Chalcis, and the area was assigned to Galatia. Commagene went under less quietly. The pretext was the accusation made by Caesennius Paetus that Antiochus and his son Epiphanes were intriguing with Vologaeses. An implausible charge before Vespasian's plans were known: Antiochus was one of his first supporters and, accompanied by Epiphanes, brought assistance at the siege of Jerusalem; Josephus, writing after Vespasian's death, and sceptical of the Parthian threat, regards the charge as false. The Emperor was simply determined on new dispositions. Caesennius invaded with VI Ferrata, auxiliary troops, and the luckier dependants Aristobulus of Chalcis and Sohaemus of Emesa. Probably he installed III Gallica at Antiochus' capital Samosata: in 73 a detachment was constructing a hydraulic installation at Ayni near Rumkale ('Roman Castle'). The desire to station a legion at this Euphrates crossing is one plausible motive for annexing the kingdom, apart from revenues and manpower (auxiliaries were recruited soon after the takeover). Antiochus' sons fled to Vologaeses, and the leading centurion of XII Fulminata was sent to summon them to Rome and comfortable exile; Antiochus himself was placed in Sparta. Commagene was united with Syria, as it had been under Gaius.[39]

At about the same time Syria lost Cilicia Pedias, which, with most of Antiochus' territory in Cilicia Tracheia, became a separate province under a praetorian legate. But it was increased by the acquisition of Emesa: Sohaemus disappears after 72. This southern zone of the military area was not neglected, as Traianus' activities at Palmyra, Gerasa, and Bostra, and attendant urban developments attest: this was the period when Palmyra's agora was begun. B. Isaac suggests that there was also a temporary military presence at Beroea and at Apamea.[40]

IV Scythica remained at Zeugma. But Vespasian had already stationed a legion further north in Cappadocia, at Melitene near the Euphrates crossing to Tomisa: XII Fulminata went there in 70 or 71 after the fall of Jerusalem, leaving its former base at Raphaneae in Syria. This militarization of Cappadocia implied its transfer from an equestrian procurator to a senatorial legate, not necessarily consular.[41]

The question then is whether that change took place at about this time, the work of Traianus as first governor of Galatia-Cappadocia, c.70/71–72/73, or later. Other changes in Asia Minor at about this time favour an early date: the accession to Galatia of Lesser Armenia and Galatia's loss of Pamphylia to the separate province of Lycia-Pamphylia. But it looks as if it was some time later, in about 75 or 76, that Vespasian's XVI Flavia, for which men had been recruited in Syria, went to Satala: a stone from the first half of 75 shows detachments of the Syrian legions, along with XVI, constructing a canal near Syrian Antioch.[42]

Strategy was the prime consideration, but domestic concerns, already suggested by the list of governors of Syria, may have played a part. Vespasian had sprung from his eastern command, the last of a series of usurpers. Syria became a source of anxiety again in 97 when the succession to Nerva was in question; at least it was a canard used in promoting Trajan's cause. Vespasian's own attempt had depended on the support of the governor of Syria. At first sight, to create a major command in eastern Anatolia was dangerous. Not so if the two commanders either were both wholly trustworthy or were hostile to each other. Galatia-Cappadocia was the natural counterweight to Syria after Judaea had been entrusted to a praetorian legate. The collaboration of Mucianus and Vespasian had been an exception.[43]

When the changes were completed the Roman military establishment was set for nearly four decades, until Trajan's annexation of Armenia Major in 114 made reorganization necessary. The fortresses were on the north–south route that led from Trapezus at points where it was crossed by east–west routes; the bridge over the Cendere between Samosata and Melitene may go back to Vespasian. In the north, Armenia Minor and Cappadocia, the auxiliary forces that backed up the legions totalled up to 11,500 men in four cavalry and fifteen or sixteen infantry units, three of the latter at double strength, so equalling the number of the legionaries, in a ratio of just under five to one in favour of infantry. These covered the gaps between the legionary fortresses and the Black Sea area north-east of Satala up to Apsarus near Batum, about a day's march between each. In Syria, besides the three legions, there were about 13,500 auxiliaries, nineteen cohorts and eight cavalry units, the higher proportion of cavalry here (between three and four to one in favour of infantry) suiting the terrain. There were detachments from the Cappadocian legions at Trapezus itself, which had fallen to the rebel Anicetus in 69.[44]

Vespasian secured communications too. The absence of milestones does not prove the want of good roads, only of those brought up to Roman specifications: as S. Mitchell has pointed out, the first known on the Caesareia–Melitene highway are Severan. Nor do Vespasian's milestones allow the claim that he created a country-wide road network that needed only maintenance after the Flavian period. It suggests, apart from concern for the internal security of Cilicia Tracheia, a particular preoccupation with communications in the north of the peninsula. Vespasian's work was continued by his sons and by Trajan in Galatia, Lycaonia, and Asia. Vespasian conceived the military scheme, drew the logistical conclusions, and put construction in hand, a notable contribution.[45]

Attention was paid to communications in Syria too. The existing paved road from Antioch to the Claudian colony of Ptolemais was restored in the second half of 72 and the road from Apamea to Raphaneae. Rome's tightening grasp of eastern Syria is shown by a milestone of 75, when a road was constructed which if completed would link Palmyra with the Euphrates at the confluence with the Balikh (near Sura or at Nicephorum-Callinicum), or the Chabur (at Circesium). That would be a continuation of other roads connecting Palmyra with Damascus and the coast and not necessarily the only link with the Euphrates. Traianus was also responsible in 75–6 for work attested by a miletone that could belong to the route Apamea–Palmyra or Chalcis–Emesa and for the 4.35 km stretch of the 'stream of the double river', canalizing the Nahr el-Asi and Kara Su above Antioch. It looks as if the governor given credit for the idea took it from the canal built by the city itself in his time. The canal shortened the journey to Zeugma and could have been connected with the project of a 1.3 km cutting designed to keep viable the port at Seleucia Pieria, 10 km up the coast from the river mouth, perhaps for a Syrian Fleet.[46]

The new installations might be defensive measures, with the Euphrates accepted as the demarcation line between the two Empires, a *limes* being constructed on the west bank. For Suetonius, Vespasian's measures were taken in response to the repeated incursions of 'barbarians', while even Josephus allows the vulnerability of Samosata to Parthian assault. Nor did Vespasian or his sons launch any attack beyond the Euphrates designed to create fresh Roman territory. But it went beyond defence. The Euphrates did not function as a cultural border and the Romans had long-established interests beyond it, notably the protectorate of Sophene. It was not a formidable military obstacle and the legions in Cappadocia and Commagene were well-placed, not only for defence, but for striking into Parthian territory; they were so used by Trajan when he marched by way of Satala to annex Armenia. A more aggressive purpose is discerned by B. Isaac: entrenchment in the Caucasus aimed at Parthian Armenia and Media. Nero's large-scale Caucasus expedition, planned at the end of his reign, came to nothing, like his scheme to probe south of Egypt, but the Flavians pursued them on a more modest scale. Certainly, as Isaac suggests, comparing the advance with that in Upper Germany, secure possession of Trapezus, Cappadocia, and Commagene made military operations in Armenia more practicable: communication lines were shorter and provisioning the troops correspondingly easier; even in peacetime, legions poised on or near the Euphrates would clarify Parthian thought in diplomatic exchanges. Freedom of action for the Roman government would be the aim, with the option of a forward movement if it fitted the military and political situation, and 'political' might include anything from promoting the career of a rising member of the dynasty to curbing unrest within areas already under Roman control.[47]

Yet attention paid to the extreme north of the military zone suggests that another factor besides Armenia and Parthia may have been at work, as in Nero's plans and in Trajan's conquests in Armenia and Mesopotamia in 113–17: the possibility of tribes from the north penetrating the Caucasus and threatening Roman control of lands round the Black Sea, even Asia Minor west of the Euphrates. Stress has been laid on this factor by H. Halfmann, who has based his chronology of Vespasian's arrangements in Asia Minor on it. In 72/3 (according to Josephus) the Alani did move south, into Media and Armenia Major against the Parthians, apparently at the invitation of rebellious Hyrcanians. King Pacorus of Media Atropatene had to flee and later to ransom his family, while Tiridates of Armenia resisted but was unable to prevent his country being plundered, and Vologaeses, who made an expedition of his own across the steppes, had to ask for help of his Roman 'ally' (in 75 according to Dio). It was only in a climate of peaceful co-existence between Romans and Parthians that such a request could have been made. Vespasian refused. He was concerned only if the threat was directly to Roman territory. Ancient accounts of the nadir of Roman–Parthian relations in this decade are brief and unclear. One fourth-century writer, Aurelius Victor, claims that the Parthian king was 'forcibly pacified', while the 'Epitomator of Aurelius Victor', independent of him but using the same source, says that the king was pacified by intimidation. Tacitus, cataloguing the dangers and disasters that threatened Rome between 68 and 96, can bring on only a near-war over a false Nero: the claimant of Titus' reign, or the third, of about 88, rather than the adventurer of 69. It is not plausible to claim that Vespasian's refusal made Vologaeses afraid that the Romans would try to displace Tiridates, and that Vologaeses' response was a movement against Roman territory in the following year; on this view Traianus repelled Vologaeses with the help of an expedition from Cappadocia under M. Hirrius Fronto Neratius Pansa, merely intimidating the enemy but winning triumphal ornaments; after that support for a fresh 'false Nero' was the only shot that Parthia had in 79. The Parthian response is incredibly disproportionate. The increased strains were due to Vespasian's strengthening in 72–3 of Cappadocia and Commagene; and they in turn led to the refusal of help and, with the Alan threat, to the creation of the fortress at Satala, on a route to Elegia and the sources of the Aras in the heart of Armenia.[48]

Under the Flavians forts were established at Apsarus and Dioscurias on the Black Sea. The Roman protectorate over the Iberi was re-established and in the second half of 75 at the strategic site of Harmozica on the Koura River near Tbilisi, at the end of the Grusinian army route through the Caucasian Gates (Sarmatian or Krestovyy Pass), the Roman garrison helped to restore a fort for their friend the Iberian King Mithridates. In the reign of Domitian a centurion of XII Fulminata is found on a mountain near the coast 70 km south-west of Baku. There should be caution on topographical grounds in connecting this with the incursions of Alani: they cannot have been a direct factor: Roman activity focused on supporting the Iberi. The Romans were asserting their strength in eastern Anatolia, Armenia, and the Caucasus. By entrusting Cappadocia to a consular and strengthening the Iberi, they made their presence dominant in the area and kept the initiative for action against either main opponent.[49]

The tone of Vespasian's dealings with Parthia was set by his cool reply in kind to the communication in which he was greeted as plain 'Flavius Vespasianus'; the policy was measured and alert, and aggression unlikely as long as advance in Britain continued, and the redeployment in Germany. The controversies that flourish over Flavian policy in the East represent varying estimates of a balance struck throughout the Empire by an astute and economical strategist, the equal of Augustus and Tiberius, intent on a compromise that would enable him and his successors to select offensive or defensive measures according to their strength and opportunities.

11

ELITES

Vespasian's origin, the contentions of 70 and 71, and Flavian occupation of the regular consulship, will have alienated the senate. L. Homo rightly called it a fundamental organ of state, a prime piece on the board. It remained the source of leading administrators and generals, and as its political functions diminished this aspect became more important. So too the symbolic. Josephus makes Agrippa II warn Claudius against massacring the House in the struggle for power in 41: Claudius will have no one to rule. Vespasian needed no warning. His treatment of the order has won high praise – and tributes for his transformation of it.[1]

Vespasian found the senatorial and equestrian orders depleted and demoralized. Aristocratic houses had gradually been diminished under the Julio-Claudian dynasty. Some attracted adverse imperial attention through kinship with the ruling family, conspicuous consumption, or large client-ships. Some were impoverished and had failed to reproduce. Many lost men and property in the civil war. Augustus had found similar problems, though the senate he had to deal with was over- rather than under-stocked. Augustus redefined and stabilized both the upper orders with a series of painful weedings of the senate, the re-establishment of annual scrutiny of the knights, and legislation regulating upper-class social behaviour, preventing marriages of senators and their descendants with ex-slaves and infamous persons, imposing criminal penalties for adultery, and forbidding them to take part in theatrical and gladiatorial shows, especially for money. The measures were to stabilize the orders and to diminish envy among the less well-off. By Claudius' time a discrepancy between rank and the wealth and standing of the men who held it had developed: the senate had not been systematically weeded by Tiberius and Gaius, though Gaius had remedied Tiberius' neglect of the equestrian order by resuming their annual inspection. Claudius' solution was to use the dormant office of censor.[2]

Vespasian used both *ad hoc* and systematic methods; it is convenient to treat his operations as a whole. He did not hesitate to confer senatorial rank on valuable partisans in 69, before confirmation in power; Ti. Julius Celsus Polemaeanus of Sardes, military tribune of III Cyrenaica, and D. Plotius

Grypus, who passed to the praetorship from command of II Augusta, are known by name. Other individuals who had served, such as Sex. Lucilius Bassus, Vitellius' defecting Prefect of the Fleets, legate in Judaea before 70 was out, were admitted afterwards. L. Antistius Rusticus, tribune of Vespasian's old legion in Britain during the civil war, and C. Caristanius Fronto probably had to wait for praetorian rank until Vespasian took the censorship with Titus as colleague in April 73, twenty-five years since Claudius had laid down the office. They held it for the statutory eighteen months. The census itself was the culmination of, and legitimized, a marked change in the composition of the senate which was only to be expected after the upheavals of Nero's reign and the years 68–9. Domitian took the censorship again in 84, and never laid it down; no later emperor held the office, but its powers were tacitly employed; continuity avoided intermittent upheavals.[3]

In Suetonius' succinct account Vespasian purged and supplemented the two orders, removing members deemed 'least worthy' (adherents of Vitellius might well be found wanting) and bringing in 'all the most respectable Italians and provincials', words that Vespasian and Titus might have used themselves. Merit was supposed to be the criterion, with a political as well as a moral dimension, the standards that Claudius, in his speech of 48 on giving men from northern Gaul the right to stand, had ascribed to Augustus and Tiberius. Wealth was another qualification specified by Claudius. Vespasian too could claim that the new men should contribute their wealth to the Italian store, an argument that Tacitus makes Claudius use publicly in favour of his Gauls. Under Trajan provincial candidates for senatorial office had to invest a third of their cash in Italian land.[4]

One person, a Palfurius, is named as having being removed: delator and (according to the Scholiast) performer in Neronian arenas turned Stoic pleader and poet after his expulsion; he was son of a suffect consul of 56 and of Spanish origin: Some impoverished men deemed worthy to remain received a subsidy, half a million *HS* a year in the case of ex-consuls. That was half the senatorial census requirement, and equivalent to capital of 8.33m *HS*, far higher than the sum (usually a million) that Augustus and Tiberius authorized; but carried a built-in limitation: it could be withdrawn.[5]

Tacitus gave qualified approval to the partisans in the East promoted in 69 (their sons were Tacitus' neighbours in the House as he wrote the *Histories*): excellent men and destined to rise to the top; some had more money than merit. From elsewhere two individuals of little merit are known: Baebius Massa, a notorious Domitianic prosecutor, may have earned his place in a similar way, as procurator in Africa in 70, where he is noted as betraying the proconsul L. Piso to his executioners. The date of his admission is uncertain: he had been only praetorian governor in Baetica when a charge of extortion brought him down in 93. Sex. Lucilius Bassus also appears an ignoble creature in Tacitus' *Histories*, comparable with A. Caecina.[6]

The change that took place was significant, but not revolutionary. First, comparatively large numbers of new men were admitted in two short bursts, irregularly in 69–70, following Galba's precedent, then in the censorship. Some thirty men are known to have been 'adlected' in this way, and the censorship made an impression: the fourth-century figure is of 1,000 families supplementing the surviving 200, making Vespasian refound the senate. Other new men may have entered this way or by election to quaestorships, making for a senate whose standard size for the early Principate is accepted as being about 600. The body had a perceptible proportion of new men and apparently was accessible to a wider range of communities; help from friends admitted under the Julio-Claudians favoured hopefuls from communities already represented. There may also have been an access from a few senatorial families in retirement under Nero. That passed unnoticed. Suetonius stresses the elevation of Italians and provincials alike. Claudius, speaking up for the Gauls, claimed that Italians had had preference, but his stand, and the admission of individual provincials before and after, made Vespasian's task easier.[7]

First the Italians. The reign of Vespasian saw the rise of the Neratii Prisci of Saepinum, the first adlected at the rank of ex-praetor in the censorship, to reach the suffect consulship of 87 and provide the State with the great jurist his son, suffect 97, both useful too as governors of Pannonia. From Berga-mum in Cisalpine Gaul came a bronze inscription dedicated to M. Sempron-ius Fuscus, a local knight who was adlected as ex-praetor in 73–4. Another leading member of the equestrian order from northern Italy, Marius Maturus Arrianus of Altinum, who had brought the Maritime Alps over to Vespasian, refused elevation, like Minicius Macrinus of Brixia, offered praetorian rank; they preferred a peaceful, respected life to high position and struggles.[8]

Men from Baetica and from Narbonensis had already reached the consul-ship – the names of the philosopher Seneca and of Valerius Asiaticus spring to mind. Under Vespasian Spain kept up an earlier lead – six to two known new admissions. One notable career began with the adlection most likely at praetorian rank of M. Cornelius Nigrinus Curiatius Maternus, a connection of the leading speaker in Tacitus' *Dialogus*. He is mentioned in inscriptions of Liria, and went on to hold probably the first consulship of his family and to win decorations on two campaigns as governor of Moesia. His career ended with the legateship of Syria, but in what circumstances? He may have emerged as a potential rival of Trajan in 97, only a generation after Vespasian himself had come to power from Judaea.[9]

Two entrants from Africa, the brothers Q. Aurelius Pactumeius Fronto (adlected at praetorian rank by Vespasian and Titus, the first consul from Africa) and Clemens were harbingers of a flock that would produce Septimius Severus, 'the African Emperor', in 193. They came from Cirta, descendants of a Campanian immigrant.[10]

It was the officers in legions and auxiliaries of the East, equestrian officials, individuals from opulent communities, who as a group underwent Tacitus' particular scrutiny. Their advancement, significant for the State, was not a break in the history of the aristocracy, for the Julio-Claudians had already admitted men from Greek-speaking provinces (at least eight) that were hardly surpassed by Vespasian (twelve, including two from Syria). Services or money had been put at Vespasian's disposal as they committed themselves to the 'Eastern' candidate. Perge in Pamphylia offered a dedication, the Roman citizens resident in the city taking prime position on the monument. There had already been senators from Pamphylia, and there was practical value in drawing attention to loyalty. C. Julius Cornutus Tertullus was admitted to the urban quaestorship and, as ex-aedile, advanced to praetorian status, the beginning of a long wait for the consulship. Men from the East represented the great cities of western Asia Minor, Pergamum and Sardes (respectively C. Antius A. Julius Quadratus and Ti. Julius Celsus Polemaeanus, adlected at aedilician rank), or less opulent but exemplary towns like the Roman colonies of Antioch-towards-Pisidia and Apamea in Bithynia: C. Caristanius Fronto, military tribune of XII Fulminata, who came in at the rank of plebeian tribune, and Catilius Longus. One man from Syria seems to have come from the colony of Berytus; L. Julius Marinus was related to Ti. Julius Candidus, probably from Nemausus, and his son apparently married a daughter of Cornutus Tertullus. These men were available for useful, unprestigious jobs such as subordinate legateships in the provinces (Marinus attained a proconsulship, Bithynia-Pontus, but not until 89). Yet the family of Quadratus embraced one of Trajan's generals, C. Claudius Severus, and a free-spending and distinguished successor of the special legate Pliny in Bithynia, C. Julius Severus. J. Devreker places the decisive moment for the easterners under Domitian: their overall representation in the senate was 15 per cent under Vespasian, 26 per cent under Domitian, with a 22 per cent and 37 per cent share of the new intakes respectively. Percentages are not worth much when small numbers are in question, the information so defective. But Vespasian's reign certainly saw only a small step on the road that was to lead to a strong representation of the Greek-speaking provinces in the senate of the second century; it was left behind by that of Domitian, still further by those of Trajan and Hadrian. And it was not yet time for the admission of redundant royalty. Antiochus IV was removed from Commagene in 72; neither of his recalcitrant sons was admitted: it was his grandson C. Julius Antiochus Epiphanes Philopappus who was adlected by Trajan and reached the suffect consulship; he had an impeccable maternal grandfather: Ti. Claudius Balbillus, governor of Egypt, courtier, and intellectual.[11]

The men admitted were not treated like the northern Gauls who had petitioned Claudius twenty-five years before. They had received permission to wear the tunic with the broad stripe (*latus clavus*) that announced their intention of becoming senators, and perhaps that was all they wanted. Claudius adlected men from elsewhere, but some of Vespasian's entered at a rank higher than Claudius had ventured for his – praetorian rather than aedilician or tribunician. This is long before the first known adlection to consular rank: a former prefect of the Guard under Commodus. Officers who benefited at the beginning of Vespasian's reign entered at the high level of ex-praetor, as became their military experience – which could be drawn on instantly. Senators brought in under the census were less urgently needed, could be given lower rank, and often climbed the ladder more slowly.[12]

Striking as the influx of men from the provinces was, it did not overwhelm the predominantly Italian character of the House. Italians represent a quarter of the 'new' names known, even if regional accents were loud. Rather, the policy that Claudius attributed to Augustus and Tiberius, of bringing in the best men from all over Italy, was finally consummated. Again, to see a sharp distinction between the 'progressive' policies of Caesar, Claudius, and Vespasian on the one hand and the 'caution' of Augustus and Tiberius on the other does not do justice to the complexity of the processes of change. It neglects the unfolding of families and the deployment of influence in individual communities, so that certain cities, such as Corduba or Ephesus, become especially prominent on the roll. Again, it was grants of citizenship made in the provinces by dynasts from Pompey to Claudius that provided the stock from which knights and eventually senators could come. Not only policy was involved, but the way it was presented and perceived: the caution of Augustus looked more cautious because Caesar had unhesitatingly made a few shocking admissions of men (mostly of Roman descent) born in provincial Gaul and Spain. And although Caesar and Augustus (even Claudius, in a sense) came to power after a civil war, Augustus was sententious on cheapening privilege and had tried to establish himself as the champion of Italy before war broke out in 31 BC; Caesar and Vespasian took Italy from a provincial base.[13]

Transpadane senators in particular now enjoyed an acme of influence lasting the half century from about 60, and they made themselves heard. The change of tone towards economy and decorum that Tacitus connects with the arrival of men from the country towns of Italy and the provinces must have originated largely from Italians and Gauls. For a contemporary senatorial poet from Cisalpine Gaul, Silius Italicus, the ideal senate of the second century BC, as L. Homo pointed out, consisted of men who combined impeccable poverty with military virtue. There was no shortage of money now, but not for frivolous use. The impression that Tacitus gives, of the staid 'Victorian' values that were held to prevail in the country districts of Italy, and in such northern towns as Brixia and Patavium, chimes in with appeals for frugality put out by the Comum-born elder Pliny and contemporary portrayals of Vespasian himself as a standard-bearer for the simple life. There was also an intimation of the serious style of the second century. The age emerged from the shock of the near loss of the only known solution to Republican chaos and stretched tranquilly to 192, encompassing Flavians,

Trajan, Hadrian, and Antonines; it saw the senatorial order accepting its social transformation from a Roman aristocracy to one of the nobility and bourgeoisie of Italy and the Empire – 'the glory of all the provinces', as Tacitus makes Otho put it, prematurely – the high tide of imperial confidence, and the coming of the Greek renaissance: a high moral tone combined with intellectual sophistication. The change made itself felt in the private sphere too, in a greater stability in married life. Men were to be conscientious, ambitious for what they could legitimately attain, openly preoccupied with private concerns such as health, which the Emperor's interest, in theirs (as Trajan's correspondence with Pliny shows) and his own, made legitimate. Marcus Aurelius would have been disdained by Tiberius, who kept his illnesses to himself.[14]

The apparent change in mores is not a mere stereotype adopted from Tacitus' remark in the *Annals*, his biography of Agricola, and the self-presentation of the younger Pliny, Cornelius Fronto, and Marcus Aurelius; that would itself demand explanation. Its causes lay, not only in the rise of countrified gentry to fashion and power, but in a sober appreciation of where Italy stood economically in the Empire, and senators in the hierarchy of power, under the stable Flavio-Trajanic Principate, continuing into that of the Antonines. Orderly transmission of power was interrupted by one jolt, in 96–7; speedy action by Trajan and Hadrian to secure their place and Hadrian's ruthless dealing with malcontents at either end of his reign prevented others. From 70 until 180 the Empire possessed masters assured and professional and, equally importantly, knew it. Office was firmly in their gift, as the '*Lex de imperio Vespasiani*' demonstrated. Unseemly electoral scrambles occurred in the aftermath of Nerva's chaotic reign; nothing is heard of them later. A senate composed largely of new men accepted what was offered with gratitude.[15]

It was part of the importance of the upheaval of 68–70 that it produced the successful new élite from which the new imperial dynasts emerged, as J. Nicols has pointed out. Vespasian fostered the careers of M. Ulpius Traianus from Italica in Spain, who was adlected into the patriciate; of M. Annius Verus of Arelate in Narbonensis, made patrician at 16 (his father must have earned him that before a premature death), father-in-law of Antoninus Pius and grandfather of Marcus Aurelius; of the brothers Cn. Domitii Curvii Tullus and Lucanus, great-grandfathers of Marcus through the Domitiae Lucillae; and of L. Ceionius Commodus the noble Etruscan, who was great-grandfather of Lucius Verus and transmitted his name to the last emperor of the Antonine dynasty. These are not evidence for prescience on Vespasian's part, but of the stability of the age and the stamina of the families.[16]

The patriciate, to which Augustus had elevated members of the plebeian nobility and which Claudius had used to distinguish Italian senators, both like Vespasian bequeathing the names of about a score of men favoured, was now for the first time offered to provincials, by an emperor who had not enjoyed the rank himself. Momentarily and paradoxically, for existing patricians had not held high command, it became an honour associated with military success. Distinction in the field, recognized as the second criterion for advancement after birth, had under the Republic provided a route to the consulship and so to hereditary nobility. Now a supplement to the devalued consulship was required. Traianus and Agricola are the prime examples, though Sex. Julius Frontinus, Agricola's predecessor in Britain, is conspicuously absent. Almost as distinguished were the Domitii Curvii, whose military decorations came from service in Germany in 70; they were raised to the patriciate in the censorship. Sex. Vettulenus Cerialis is another case. Highly praised by Josephus for service in Judaea as legate of V Macedonica, he governed the province and was honoured by Titus just before his triumph with multiple military decorations. L. Flavius Silva Nonius Bassus was adlected to patrician and praetorian rank in 73 and passed straight into his command in Judaea; 81 saw him as regular consul, an unusual honour for a man of equestrian origin. The patriciate carried accelerated advancement (no aedileship or tribunate of the *plebs* would be held), and promise of an early consulship, but the sons of the men elevated by Vespasian could still be appointed to consular legateships – if they prepared by holding provincial posts after the praetorship. In the crystallizing senatorial career the ex-quaestor could no longer look for a legionary legateship: all the posts had to be filled by ex-praetors, older rather than more experienced in the field (but adlection and promotion provided a wider choice than the Julio-Claudians had had). At once a stereotyped view of the rise and justification of Rome's aristocracy – merit elevated and continued in suceeding generations – was revamped, and the Augustan élite, some impoverished or effete, others perceived as a threat, were supplemented and eventually replaced.[17]

Besides the patriciate and the extension of desirable proconsulships, such as Eprius Marcellus held in Asia, the Princeps could still make refined differentiations within the aristocracy by manipulating the consulship. Some held it as colleague of a member of the imperial house, others at the opening of the year; above all the device of the repeated consulship reached full working order under the Flavians and Trajan.[18]

Vespasian's own tenures recalled the early years of Augustus, when the founder actually needed the office as a means of invading the state and also sought like Vespasian to acquire prestige. It ran Augustus into trouble, because it kept other men out: there were only two posts available every year. In 5 BC, when he held the office again, Augustus introduced suffect consulships, dividing the year between two pairs, the opening, eponymous positions more prestigious; later other pairs were fitted in. Augustus' successors used the consulship to advance their heirs, and Claudius and Nero, who lacked seniority, occupied it frequently; Vitellius may have contemplated taking it every year, or holding it perpetually, alongside the regular pairs. Now it kept few out of office, holding it had a favourable aspect, the Emperor functioning like an ordinary senator at the height of his career, and honouring lesser men with whom he held it, as Claudius honoured Vespasian in 51. The first imperial consulate of Vespasian lasted a full six months, the others never more than four (72); that of 71 two; after the censorship two are known to have been laid down on 13 January (74, 79); the rest may have been held until February (75–7).[19]

The Emperor's colleagues were predictable. Titus came first (70, 72, 74–7, 79), and when Vespasian gave up office on 13 January, it was to allow Ti. Plautius Silvanus and Domitian to share with Titus. More surprisingly, in 71 M. Cocceius Nerva was found worthy, the future emperor, known as a poet who had won triumphal decorations for his part in exposing the Pisonian conspiracy six years before. The less signal honour of becoming the colleague of Domitian in 73 went to L. Valerius Catullus Messalinus; well-born and perhaps already an associate of Domitian: he won a second term in 85 and became notorious for his savage verdicts in Domitianic trials. Reserving places for his sons as well as himself did not allow Vespasian to offer many eponymous consulships, and there was only one run-of-the-mill tenure without the honour of an imperial colleague, that of D. Junius Novius Priscus, perhaps the son of a friend of Seneca's exiled in 65, and L. Ceionius Commodus, who went on respectively to the Lower Rhine army and the province of Syria. As to the length of time that men were allowed to hold office, there seems to have been a change: Neronian practice had been for the first pair to hold office for six months. By the last decade of Domitian's principate four months were allotted to both types. The importance and prestige of eponymous consuls were in decline.[20]

Under the Julio-Claudians only five private persons achieved second consulships and one, Claudius' friend L. Vitellius, a third. Iteration became a little commoner under the Flavians, in spite of the needs of Vespasian and his sons. The roll is confined to members of the ruling circle: Licinius Mucianus, suff. II 70, with Vespasian's kinsman Q. Petillius Cerialis, and suff. III 72, with T. Flavius Sabinus suff. II; Ti. Plautius Silvanus Aelianus, suff. II 74, with Titus III; Petillius Cerialis suff. II the same year, with Eprius Marcellus suff. II, after another distinguished civilian, Vibius Crispus suff. II; and the two wealthy retired generals L. Tampius Flavianus, who had supervised the Rome aqueducts in 73–4, and M. Pompeius Silvanus suff. II seemed to have served in the same year (?76). Iterated consulships cluster early in the reign, except for imperial tenures, serving the men of 68–9 who were still in favour and loyal civilians.[21]

Preeminent commands were carried off by men connected with the imperial family by marriage, such as Q. Petillius Cerialis and L. Caesennius Paetus, and probably Sex. Vettulenus Cerialis. Vettulenus was a useful man, but as a native of Reate, where the family was united in marriage with the Pituanii, and he may have been connected with Vespasian's mother. Vettulenus' younger brother C. Civica Cerialis followed him in the consulship (suff. *c*.76) and to the Balkans (81/2 to 83/4) but was killed by Domitian for revolutionary designs during his proconsulship of Asia (87/8). The son of a man who held high command could expect special advancement, even though he was unconnected with the dynasty by blood. Petillius Cerialis' son Firmus, not by a Flavia but from a previous marriage, took part in Rubrius Gallus' campaign against the Sarmatians. By mid-71 he was back in Rome to receive his military decorations from Vespasian and Titus, to be elected quaestor as a candidate supported by the Emperor – and to be offered the insignia of a praetor on the motion of the two Imperatores. If he did not reach the consulship it can only have been because he died young. Consular Fasti and the pattern of commands suggest a penumbra of powerful men near the centre of power, just outside the dynasty itself. Sex. Julius Frontinus was one of those whose success and standing were uninterrupted by changes of emperor. They were above the ideological and careerist squabbles of the main body of the senate, intent on keeping their high position but aiming no higher, and hazardous to attack, even for an emperor's favourite; there was enough action in the Flavian Empire for men of ability and loyalty outside this inner circle.[22]

It was in connection with Domitian and Trajan that the conception of 'military men' ('*viri militares*') gained currency; the senatorial career of the Principate achieved stability and fullness, with offices new under the Empire such as the curatorship of roads major and minor filling the idle years inherent in the Republican model and indicating how a man's career was shaping; and the habit had developed of commemorating careers in greater detail than had been the case under Augustus. R. Syme's military men enjoyed a particularly rapid advancement after their praetorships (two offices only), so coming to the consulship early, with the way open to high command. The conception has taken severe criticism, but in a broader sense there were 'military men', favoured and sometimes given work in areas they knew. Keen soldiers like Marius and Vespasian had always stood a good chance of advancement, like the paradigm upstart of Augustus' principate, P. Sulpicius Quirinius, the Cyrenius of St Luke's Gospel, whose loyalty and energetic service as a soldier secured him the consulship of 12 BC. Tacitus counted it a merit of Tiberius that he paid attention to military talent.[23]

During the civil wars the senate showed ready compliance, and as a body did not put up resistance to Vespasian after the passages of 70–1. Julio-Claudian taskmasters and the events of 68–9 hastened loss of self-respect and Vespasian's firmness in the face of Helvidius' resistance delineated clear limits for their activity, though he did nothing to precipitate their development into the rubber-stamp that they seem to have become by the end of Domitian's reign. Vespasian normally showed the House respect by constant attendance and by transacting business through it which emerged as decrees (*Senatus Consulta*, *SCC*), so that in form at least, although what it discussed might have been trivial, and weighty matters were decided elsewhere, it preserved its ancient function as the supreme council of state (*summum consilium*) and seemed to enjoy its inherited authority (*auctoritas*). Urgent business or old age kept him away, but his sons stood in. In 71 coins were struck showing the Emperor sacrificing before an arch bearing images of the Genius Populi Romani and the Genius Senatus – a quaint and sanitized concept.[24]

Involving the senate in the production of enactments was beneficial in two ways known to Vespasian's precedessors. When a controversial act was in question, it could commit them to something they disliked. This was a technique at which, according to Tacitus, Domitian, who had learned it from Nero and ultimately from Augustus, was to prove particularly adept. But in the main complicity enhanced members' sense of their own worth in relation both to the Emperor and to the *plebs*.[25]

Leaving aside votes of powers to the Emperor and his sons, and judicial sentences, the reign of Vespasian offers four known *senatus consulta*. The paternalistic régime of Claudius had a particularly high rate of striking, at least one decree every nine months; none is known for the reign of Titus, and only two at most for Domitian. But information is too meagre for figures to be significant. Holding the consulship so frequently, the Emperor was in a good position to put decrees through, but none bears his name, and he seems to have left steering them through the House to others, as Claudius did with the *SC Hosidianum*, in which he is credited with the foresight that gave rise to the decree. Three items, the two *SCC* of Pegasus and Pusio, and *Macedonianum*, show the senate performing a traditional function, that of modifying existing laws or *SCC*; the *Macedonianum* against loans to persons under paternal authority, like the first *Pegasianum*, tackled a matter of concern to the propertied classes: the safe transfer of wealth from one generation to another. But the measure also fitted Vespasian's concern for the higher education that would nurture potential participants in public life. The fourth *SC*, following a speech of Vespasian in which he advocated the overdue award of triumphal ornaments to Silvanus Aelianus, presents the senate in another traditional rôle, that of regulating the status and honours of its members; there were many such measures and it is only because the special honour found a place on Aelianus' extant *elogium* that this one has come to notice.[26]

Vespasian showed his former peers particular civility in keeping the Palatium and his favourite spot in the Gardens of Sallust open to them and exempting them from humiliating searches before they were admitted to the presence – something he could afford with two adult heirs. This was in marked contrast to Claudius, who in his terror of assassination had instituted these searches that Vespasian himself must have undergone. He abolished another Claudian innovation, grades of admission to the imperial presence: favoured men wore a gold ring bearing a portrait of the Emperor; certainly Vespasian had suffered from one major-domo. He did not repeat Tiberius' mistake of abandoning the capital, but took civility further by exchanging dinner invitations with senators, treating them at least as social equals.[27]

Knights also received attention, particularly at the census. Theirs was the order from which senators were recruited, the source for Vespasian's new men, and it supplied its own grades of administrators. Individuals are not much on show. Noisy wrangling of the orders over the right to staff the juries of major courts had come to an end in the late Republic, or subsided into ill-natured jokes or personal feuds; no conflict of interest involving a principle, or even the orders as a whole, finds its way into imperial history; we hear of demarcation disputes in provinces and quarrels over the rights of provincials against tax gatherers or military enforcers. Augustus and Tiberius had protected distinctions between one order and another, making it clear that both upper-class ranks were to be kept distinct from those below, so securing their position and their gratitude. Vespasian dealt lightly with minor incidents, remarking, when a senator tried to pull rank in a quarrel, that nobody had any business to abuse senators, but it was right and proper for a citizen to answer back: the two orders differed in rank (*dignitas*), not in their right to free speech (*libertas*). The view that Vespasian's reign saw *de facto* parity between them is not illuminating.[28]

Some setbacks the order had, at least until Titus became Emperor. It had lost the prestigious command of the Praetorian Guard, although Pliny loyally describes Titus' tenure as a service both to Vespasian and to the order; Judaea, Cappadocia, and Mauretania were now under senatorial legates. There was still the Prefecture of Egypt and other governorships, notably of Thrace and at first Sardinia; and command of the fleets became a prerogative of knights. In the equestrian service titulature was still evolving. The practice introduced by Claudius of styling the equestrian governor of a province 'procurator' (stressing his relationship to his master) was established, but the title 'prefect' might still be combined with it, distinguishing the governor from the mere financial officer also called 'procurator', and they came also to be marked in their titulature as having the right of life and death in their province ('*ius gladii*', 'the right of the sword'). In spite of increasing formality the Emperor could still refer to his equestrian governors as 'friends'.[29]

In the equestrian as well as the senatorial order men were especially distinguished who had served in 69 or in the Jewish War, like the much decorated C. Velius Rufus, who rose under Domitian to be governor of Raetia. Most notable was Cornelius Fuscus, who had come out in Galba's support, entering the public life he had once eschewed when he stopped wearing the broad stripe of senatorial rank on his tunic. Services to Galba brought him to the Balkan procuratorship from which, behind the legates, he could manoeuvre enormous forces on Vespasian's behalf. Fuscus ended as Domitian's Prefect of the Guard, dying in action against the Dacians in 86 or 87; it was the first time outside Egypt that a knight had borne such responsibility in the field. At a lower level knights could obtain positions of honour, as senators could, through their connections. That was probably how C. Nonius

Flaccus came to act as Vespasian's deputy (*praefectus*) when he held the leading magistracy of Asculum: he looks like a relative of a senatorial Nonius, C. Salvius Liberalis or L. Flavius Silva.[30]

From the point of view of the emperor's later reputation, as the case of Claudius showed, it was almost as important to guard the integrity and prestige of the equestrian as of the senatorial order. Some of the advisory functions of knights had been lost under the Julio-Claudians, Galba, and Vitellius, to freedmen dependent on imperial favour. They had made themselves felt and built up their own fortunes by securing favours and advancement for men who had won them over, or paid for their recommendations. Upstarts had received public honours, galling to the aristocracy, to grace huge fortunes. The trappings (*ornamenta*) of the magistracies that were the prerogative of their betters marked the equivalence in service and power of men who could never be social equals: Narcissus and Pallas, Claudius' freedmen, had received quaestorian and praetorian ornaments respectively, the difference in rank distinguishing the levels of success. (Consular ornaments were reserved for knights; it was a poor Prefect of the Praetorian Guard who did not rise to that level.) Grants of *ornamenta* became less frequent under the Flavians. There was an alternative: Vitellius privately gave his freedman Asiaticus equestrian rank, having publicly refused to do so at the request of his troops – he knew it was wrong. During the campaign for Italy the Flavian freedman Hormus held his place among the Flavian leaders. Early in 70, Mucianus did not shrink from allowing him the rank of knight: such were his responsibilities. The act had a later parallel. The father of Statius' addressee Claudius Etruscus, holder of the same supreme financial post as Pallas held under Nero (*a rationibus*), married into a senatorial family, the Tettii, and both his sons and then he himself (like Asiaticus and Hormus), probably in 73–4, were granted equestrian status. Other men of freedman stock advancing less spectacularly would have escaped notice. The case of Larcius Macedo is known from his sensational death: murdered by his slaves early in the second century, this ex-praetor is unequivocally called the son of a slave – the adopted son of a household favourite, A.N. Sherwin-White suggested. With a son suffect consul perhaps in 123, he is likely to have been born in the mid-50s, embarking on the senatorial career at the end of Vespasian's reign or under Titus.[31]

Philostratus makes the sage Apollonius of Tyana warn Vespasian against the pride and luxury of freedmen and slaves; he would not have needed the advice. His own experience of how much offence had been caused by the power of women and freedmen made it likely that the experienced commander Vespasian, who had a family and friends to advise him and dispense favours, would at least insist that patronage was exercised with discretion. There was no bringing it to an end: advancement had always depended on patronage and imperial freedmen were close to the centre. When Tacitus wrote the *Germania* in 98 it was still worth rubbing in the shameful contrast between Roman and German treatment of this class. Under Vespasian there was no patent resentment in either order at usurpation by freedmen of their right to counsel the Princeps, as there had been under Claudius, Nero, and allegedly Vitellius; it was safe in the new reign to allude to Claudius' failings in that matter as a thing of the past. But perhaps it is significant that the story that it was not Antonius Primus but Hormus who was responsible for the sack of Cremona came from the memoirs of the aristocrat Vipstanus Messalla. And stories inevitably circulated about Vespasian's mistress Caenis: she received enormous sums from a number of sources for the sale of governorships, procuratorships, military commands, priesthoods, and even imperial decisions. Vespasian himself, who had allegedly obtained his first command through the influence of Narcissus, was perceived as willing to profit by these sales, even as outsmarting the vendors and taking the price himself on occasion. These hostile stories show Vespasian 'improving' on Claudius – by taking the bribes himself. Money was at the root of another problem concerned with freedmen, those of private individuals. As a token of civility, Vitellius had allowed destitute exiles returned under Galba to resume their rights over their freedmen, which would have given the former masters access to their freedmen's property on their decease. The catch was that the freedmen hid their fortunes or even transferred to the imperial household, becoming more powerful than their former masters. We are not told that they were repudiated by the new régime.[32]

Vitellius placed army officers in administrative positions formerly held by freedmen, and even G.E.F. Chilver, who plausibly attributed the move to the lack of suitable freedmen in Germany, saw the employment of knights as a feature of Flavian government: Claudius Etruscus, for all his origin, was a case in point. It would be a mistake to read a change of policy into this. The posts were held originally as menial positions in a great household. Closeness to the Emperor had given the freedmen servants what was seen as limitless influence, resented by men of quality. At the same time it diminished the disgrace of service, making the higher posts more acceptable to men who had always been willing to act as the Emperor's land-agents (procurators). The change, such as it was, was gradual and no part of a policy of placating the equestrian order. It was not until the reign of Hadrian that all the high posts once held by freedmen were in the hands of knights.[33]

The development of the Principate was welding together an aristocracy of power and service, the rule of one man levelling the rest, as Seneca implied, and bringing down the aristocracy of birth. The senate, necessarily replenished with useful men, was kept on a tight reign by the victors. The marriage of senatorial Tettia to Claudius Etruscus' father was significant. Senators of slave descent were familiar in political abuse: the Vitellii had suffered, like the Gabinii of the Republic. Nobody heard of these slaves in their time, but a second-century consul, M. Antonius Pallas (suff. 167), bore the name of Claudius' most distinguished freedman.[34] Vespasian's achievement as these inevitable social changes took place was to maintain the senate's formal prerogatives and play down the influence of freedmen, softening the pains of status dissonance.

12

VESPASIAN AND HIS SONS

Transmitting power smoothly to a chosen successor had plagued emperors from Augustus to Galba. Augustus devised the mechanism: such powers were conferred on the chosen man that he was a Princeps before his predecessor died and the two formed virtually a collegiate Principate; in the next generation two boys might be trained for future supremacy. All three were magnified and glamorized before the Empire. A natural son was the obvious choice, but only Claudius possessed one, Britannicus, and he was not of a suitable age at the time of his father's death. Adopting a relative by blood or marriage as a son was a provident substitute legally as effective, but it led to rivalry and instability when other candidates, cognates, were available, as happened when Augustus adopted Tiberius in 4. Before Galba became emperor he was recommended to adopt a relative (*propinquus*) to improve his chances. In the event, and too late, he made a virtue of going outside his family: none of the emperors who had come to power through adoption within the family, Tiberius, Gaius Caligula (whose father Germanicus was Tiberius' adopted son), and Nero, had turned out well. But Galba's selection of the innocuous aristocrat L. Piso Licinianus and his failure to package the deal acceptably for the Guard only hastened his fall. Adult sons were a novelty deployed as an advantage. In January 70 Titus and Domitian were in their thirty-first and twentieth years, and likely to produce sons of their own. The elder, as Tacitus makes C. Licinius Mucianus point out to Vespasian when he urged him act, was already qualified to rule. That solved the problem, at least for quietists and those who accepted this way of transmitting power as legitimate.[1]

For all the grimness of old Galba, Vespasian's age and maturity were an advantage to him after Gaius and Nero, both dead at 30. But a man who took over at 60, for all his excellent health, and equally healthy lack of concern for it, could not be expected to reign for long, and men looked to the future right from the beginning, as they had during the principate of Tiberius, who had come to power four years younger; primarily then to Titus. When Vespasian assumed the style 'Caesar Augustus' by the end of August 69, Titus became 'Caesar'. This surname of the Julian clan had been assumed by Claudius, inherited by his adopted son Nero and conferred by Galba on Piso. It became, potentially at least, another means of indicating the heir; but the Flavians too treated it as a family name, for Domitian was greeted by it as well at the end of the year by troops and senate, and retained it. Not only Augustan precedent but the possibility that much of the initiative for Vespasian's bid came precisely from Titus, made it likely that he would be rapidly advanced to a position of near-equality with his father, as a colleague in fact. Already in 70 Tacitus has Vespasian allocating duties between Titus and himself in a way that encapsulates the rôles of Augustus (after 8 BC) and Tiberius and their heirs: Titus was to raise the Empire with his achievements in the field while he himself took care of peace and domestic matters. Josephus, writing of the same year, makes Titus in a speech to the defenders of Jerusalem refer to himself as well as Vespasian as an 'emperor' whom formerly they had known only as a 'general'; he had already claimed that the soldiers had been undecided between Vespasian and his son.[2]

From two sources there were difficulties to overcome. It was clear to some members of the senate from the disastrous history of the Julio-Claudian emperors, culminating in the reign of the golden boy, Nero, that hereditary succession, by adoption when necessary, did not work. Senators who were not quietists knew that there could be other ways of filling what had by now come to be a recognized office, even Galba's way, if he had not made the choice himself instead of leaving it to his peers. Titus' personality provided ready material for dissidents. He was probably better educated than his father, accomplished and attractive, an effective speaker (though not assiduous as an apprentice barrister) and a gallant and successful soldier, but he was vilified as a ruthlessly ambitious believer in his own star, and as a second Nero (both Vespasian's sons allegedly 'realized' their high state through debauchery). Titus' association with the Jewish princess Berenice, which she would have intended to culminate in a marriage that would transform her brother's position in Judaea, offered ammunition to critics: she could be presented as a new Cleopatra. The 'love and darling of the human race' who turned out better as Emperor than his reputation promised, may have seemed to the aristocracy of Rome more cosmopolitan than a future Princeps should be: Neronian in this too. Elsewhere, and especially in Alexandria, close relations with Jews were resented, as both Claudius and Trajan found. The liaison may have contributed to the spiteful, or over-hopeful, canard that Titus was thinking of setting up an independent Empire in the East.[3]

Vespasian delayed his triumph so that Titus could share it after his arrival in mid-June 71; that made a special renewal of auspices necessary, since he had crossed the city boundary as soon as he had arrived. Now he had the proposal put to the House that Titus should be invested with tribunician power and with proconsular imperium, either outside Rome, if the parallel of Agrippa in 13 BC or Nero in AD 51 was followed, or on the same basis as Tiberius in 13, a joint administration of the Empire; Titus like Tiberius took no salutation as 'Imperator' on accession. Tribunician power was exclusively the prerogative of the Princeps and his partner; only Tiberius in 6 BC, also after a triumph, and AD 4, and Drusus Caesar in 22, after an ovation, had reached that position in the lifetime of the emperor. Held precisely from 1 July 71, Titus' count, like that of his consulships, was two behind that of his father, who began from the salutation of the Egyptian legions; the Arval Brethren are found taking vows for the safety of both father and son (75, 77–8).[4]

Constitutional advancement did not come out of the blue, although prophecies of Flavian success couched in the plural and including Titus, if not Domitian, are propaganda put out when the accession was assured. Titus had already done the things that really counted in a successor, and which Augustus' and Tiberius' sons had been sent abroad to achieve: he had distinguished himself in the field and won the soldiers, not only as his father's legate before July 69, fighting in the front line, but as commander-in-chief, whether (as seems most probable) as senior legate, or holder, either during his first consulship in the first half of 70, or after it, or when Vespasian left for Italy in September, of proconsular *imperium* in Syria, Judaea, and Egypt. On the capture of Jerusalem his soldiers saluted Titus *Imperator*, the first time it had been possible so to salute the son of a reigning emperor since the days of Tiberius and the Caesars Germanicus and Drusus. The senate was expected to recognize such salutations, which constituted a *prima facie* claim to the triumph. There was no ground for refusal: triumphs had been awarded before when war still subsisted: Germanicus' over the Germans is an obvious case. According to Philostratus, it was when Titus had been proclaimed *Imperator* in Rome and had been honoured for his capture of Jerusalem (he heard of the confirmation of the salutation at Tarsus by the following February), that he 'went off to share the power on an equal basis with his father'. He did not use the title as a forename; it belonged to his father, and eastern mints that ascribed it to him while Vespasian was alive did so unofficially out of ignorance or adulation; but they could be referred to jointly as '*Imperatores*'. Titus did not win any more salutations in the field, unlike Tiberius after AD 4, who advanced his adoptive father from his sixteenth to his twenty-first, but took them, along with Vespasian, for other men's achievements, indicating his own removal to the higher sphere. The second was received in 71 after 1 July and shared with Vespasian's eighth; his third to fourteenth corresponded with Vespasian's ninth to twentieth.[5]

In the same passage of Philostratus question arises as to Vespasian's authority over Titus, who is shown acquiescing in it. The record on his triumphal arch likewise makes clear what his achievements in Judaea owed to his father's instruction, advice, and auspices. 'Neighbouring provinces' had recognized his success at Jerusalem by offering him a crown, which he refused; Josephus has him accepting one from Vologaeses, so there were probably at least two offers; Titus spared Rome's subjects the cost, but not the Parthian king. The only thing that can be said for the canard published by Suetonius is that he accepted a diadem from the Alexandrians. There is nothing more to it than malice, or a distorted perception of what Titus' rôle must be even during Vespasian's lifetime. A man of Titus' intense ambition would ask why he should usurp an eastern Empire when by waiting for the death of a man of 60 he could ensure the entirety. Even if Vespasian had remarried instead of taking up again with the unmarriageable Caenis, Titus would have had little to fear from any offspring of such a late union. Loyally he celebrated his father's birthday at Berytus on 17 November 70, then travelled by way of Zeugma, Antioch, Jerusalem, and Memphis to Alexandria, entering it on 25 April 71; 1,700 *m.p.* in eight months, fêted everywhere.[6]

Everything was done to enhance Titus' prestige. He took up his first consulship of 70 in absence (so important was it that he and his father should garner credit), and held six more during the reign (72, 74–6, 77 or 78, and 79), all with his father, none lasting the six months of the first. At the triumph he as well as Vespasian bestowed the people's money on them and his chariot along with Vespasian's surmounted the commemorative arch. His own later arch in the Forum played on that success; another was inscribed with a claim that he was the first man to capture Jerusalem. He too held the censorship of 73–4, echoing the partnership of Augustus and Tiberius in 13–14, although that pair used consular powers for the functions.[7]

Titus' authority was augmented in 71 in an unparalleled way. The dangerous and extensive forces commanded by the Prefect of the Guard were handed over to him. Until another member of the family, the consular Arrecinus Clemens, took it over the previous year the post had been held by knights. Junior members of the imperial family had been associated with the equestrian order as its leading representatives, informally like Claudius, formally as *Principes Iuventutis*; now the association was given substance by conferring the supreme equestrian post, which was normally recognized with the grant of consular decorations, on Titus. What lay behind Titus' appointment was Titus' reading of the situation when he arrived in Rome. Certainly he did not treat it as a sinecure: Suetonius notes precautions against all those most under suspicion, including the use of agents in theatre and barracks to denounce suspects, who were hauled off to immediate execution. Titus' accumulated honours were gross and historically inconsistent; apart from his tenure of the Prefecture, it was only in the narrowest sense in line with Augustan precedent for a man to be made simultaneously consul and *Princeps Iuventutis*; when Gaius and Lucius Caesar, and Nero, had been given the title, it was with the promise of the consulship a few years hence. His preeminence is clearly reflected, not only in Philostratus, but in the work of Josephus (naturally) and Suetonius, who calls him 'part-holder of the Empire, even its supervisor'. From July 71 he was co-regent as Agrippa and Tiberius had been – though he lacked independent administrative apparatus – and enjoyed the homage that went with the position, in the provinces as well as in Italy.[8]

Along with Tribunician Power and effective office went membership of all four of the most prestigious priestly colleges that all emperors enjoyed, and which had been conferred with his other honours on young Nero in 51, as well as of the lesser but appropriate Sodality of Augustus. The new dispensation was understood, though when Titus was honoured alongside his father in the monuments, he was sometimes credited with a status even higher than he had, through venial slips of composer or lapicide. Domitian was also often included, perhaps sometimes only in completion of the Flavian House, but mistakes over him were more blatant: the subtleties of the political position were not always appreciated by provincial dedicators. Monuments even allow Domitian his father and brother's position of censor.[9]

The second difficulty in managing the succession was indeed Domitian, who seems not to have accepted third position with grace. The debate of June 71 had nothing to offer him. It was as Titus' possible future heir, not as his colleague, that Domitian would be seen, so Titus ensured even after Vespasian's death. With the formal justification of the marked disparity in age between the brothers, Vespasian was following the model that Augustus provided in 6 BC and AD 4 when he advanced Tiberius to near collegiality, and younger members of the family to future hopes, not that of 5 BC–AD 2, when Gaius and Lucius Caesar were brought on together as his heirs. Domitian was urban praetor in 70, by special concession and through the abdication of Sex. Julius Frontinus, a praetorship necessarily enhanced with consular power. He reached the consulship itself (suffect) probably on 1 April 71. Only his second tenure was of the eponymous post, that of 73, when Vespasian and Titus were occupied with the censorship. He continued with suffect consulships (75, 76, perhaps 77, and 79), and it was to yet another suffect post (80) that he was designated at the time of Vespasian's death; that transformed the office into the eponymous one. Again, Titus had his portrait on obverses of his father's reign as holder of tribunician power in 71; Domitian had to wait until his second consulship, 73. And while Titus shed his title *Princeps Iuventutis* within two years, Domitian kept it, accompanied by images of *Spes* (Hope), with its unmistakable reference to a future position, even after the death of his father. A similar trick had been played by Gaius on his cousin Tiberius Gemellus, left joint heir in Tiberius' will. He was too young for Empire, Caligula declared, conferring on him the damning title that young Gaius and Lucius Caesar had enjoyed as a pair. Domitian was offered Titus' daughter Flavia Julia in marriage, a link permissible since Claudius married his niece Agrippina. The intention was clear: Domitian, like Tiberius in 11 BC, when he married Augustus' daughter, had prospects – but in the next generation, not as Augustus' partner. Domitian refused, and married elsewhere. Only in his brother's principate did the Arvals take vows for Domitian's safety – and that of Julia.[10]

The most weighty evidence for determination on the part of Vespasian and Titus not to allow Domitian serious advancement is their blatantly continuing to keep him out of contact with the military. Licinius Mucianus had his own eye on Domitian in 70. The Guard Prefect Arrius Varus was a friend of Domitian's, and so was his replacement Clemens. But Clemens had lost favour with Vespasian and was useless as a way of securing prime position with his father, while Mucianus baulked Domitian's efforts to win distinction against Civilis. Domitian accompanied him north, but so pressing did Mucianus' domestic duties turn out to be that they had not reached the Alps before the news arrived of the defeat of the Treviri at the hands of Q. Petillius Cerialis. Domitian was left the choice of returning home or basing himself at Lugdunum to watch mopping-up operations; he received no salutation for his unauthorized intervention, although it was played up during his principate. On the attic of the triumphal arch shown on the 'Jerusalem spoils' relief of the arch of Titus, Domitian is represented as a horseman between the two chariots of Vespasian and Titus, and that scene of 71 was his closest to military glory in their reigns, apart from the laurel he wore on coins; young sons of triumphing generals had always been allowed to take part in the processions, as M. Marcellus and Tiberius had in Octavian's triumph of 29 BC. In the middle of the reign, in 75, fresh hopes may have been dashed. Vologaeses I of Parthia asked for Roman help against Alan invaders, the expedition to be led by one of Vespasian's sons (perhaps Vologaeses was hoping to make trouble). The Emperor declined, and it would be perverse to regard *aurei* struck in Domitian's name in 77–8 and celebrating success against the Parthians as offering him consolation of any kind.[11]

Accounts of his discontent probably began as tittle-tattle during Vespasian's reign; after Domitian's assassination they were coloured by hatred of the late tyrant. With the partial exception of the trip to Lugdunum (Suetonius' report of his attempt to reach the armies is circumstantial), facts are in short supply. After he was baulked in 70, Domitian was believed to have made approaches to Petillius Cerialis, his kinsman by marriage. If he did, and if they were treasonous, they were overlooked: punishing Domitian was not worth the publicity. The question is how they came to be known – if they were not invented. It is the favourable comment that tells, not for truth but for the Domitianic view, by playing up Domitian's rôle in 69–70. Already in Vespasian's reign Domitian demolished the caretaker's lodge that had sheltered him and put up a chapel to Jupiter the Preserver and a marble altar depicting what had happened. How important those terrifying, exhilarating days of siege on the Capitol, escape, adulation, and power were is also suggested by the attention that Domitian paid to the Egyptian deities Isis and Serapis: it was in a group of Isis worshippers that he had escaped from the Capitol, and in the hieroglyphic text on Domitian's obelisk in the Piazza Navona he is called 'beloved of Isis'. After Flavian forces captured Rome, Domitian was hearing in the senate a form of address that had commonly been used there to the emperors themselves: 'Caesar'. Statius, perhaps echoing the theme of Domitian's own poem on the subject, claims that it was he who put an end to Jupiter's war (the battle for the Capitol), as well as to the struggles on the Rhine, crushing an impious civil war and the obstinate resistance of German mountain people; Martial tells how, when Domitian alone held the reins that had once been in the hands of the Julian family, he 'handed them over' to be third in the world that belonged to him. Domitian himself used the same language, claiming when he came to power that he had 'given' the Empire to Vespasian – and the senate had 'duly assigned' it to him. Suetonius is credible here: he is reporting a transaction in the senate. Titus was correspondingly played down: it was correct under Domitian to describe the Emperor as having inherited supreme power from his father Vespasian – by way of Titus. Domitian on at least one occasion seems to have varied this line. After Vespasian's death his will was read out, a significant document for imperial purposes in that it indicated who needed the bulk of his fortune. That of Tiberius had been read out and invalidated because it left his main fortune equally to Gaius and Tiberius Gemellus; Claudius' had simply been suppressed; evidently it mentioned Britannicus. Domitian claimed at some point that he had been left joint heir 'to the Empire' and that Titus had forged the will, removing that item (or rather, presumably, altering Domitian's share in the property and tampering with any separate political testament that Vespasian left). It was a credible charge, given the precedents, but it has no support in anything that Vespasian did. On the south side of the Navona obelisk Domitian 'received the royalty of his father from the hand of his brother'; the names of Domitian's infant heirs, Domitianus and Vespasianus, are also significant. But the strongest presentation of Vespasian with Domitian, Titus obliterated, is that of one of the reliefs of the Cancelleria, on which Domitian is shown being greeted by his father in 70; the other relief may show his 'return' to the Principate eleven years later.[12]

A sinister slant could be given to the Cancelleria episode. Dio has Domitian greeting his father at only Beneventum, not at Brundisium like other notables, because of his sense of guilt, which sometimes made him pretend to be stupid (Claudius' trick). If anything, the act shows him asserting himself. Tacitus alleges that Titus in 70 warned Vespasian against allowing reports of Domitian's activities to turn him against him, which suggests that Titus kept his own informants. But only malicious sensationalism claimed that it was worry about Domitian that caused Vespasian to return to Rome without waiting for Titus to capture Jerusalem; his journey was hardly a hurried one.[13]

Domitian's attempt to secure an eastern command in 75 is the last political effort ascribed to him in his father's reign. His confinement to civil life allowed hostile writers to present him as taking refuge in literature (military epic, as it happened) and debauchery. Domitian gave up literature when he came to power in 81. If he was a 'bald Nero', it was only in his philhellenism;

for him the Principate conferred power for use. Stories of the young Domitian may tell as much about contemporaries' perceptions as they do about his ambitions, but they are borne out by Domitian's later conduct and public words.[14]

Domitian's resentment was allowed to fester, even though Vespasian knew that once he had gone Titus too would have to begin tackling the problem of the succession for the generation beyond. Titus had no sons, only a daughter, Julia, probably the child of Arrecina Tertulla – and had not remarried after divorcing Furnilla as a political liability. He had been on active service since 67 and in any case the volatile politics of the late 60s made a long-term commitment hazardous; when the Flavians began to see themselves as the coming dynasty it was good for aristocratic families with disposable females to be kept in suspense. Hence Domitian might come into play, although Titus at 40 when he took sole power was still young enough to marry and raise a male heir far enough for him to be able to make a claim that would stand up to Domitian's (Nero had taken over at 16 as a possessor of *imperium*).[15]

Some men judged that Domitian would eventually come to power, although another candidate, the cousin Flavius Sabinus who married Julia, was also in the wings. Josephus' account of the expedition to Gaul is such a masterpiece of ambiguity that it has been considered part of a Domitianic completion of the *War*. Even written under Vespasian it could safely be read by either of the brothers: it stresses Domitian's willingness to undertake responsibility, the barbarians yielding to him without a struggle, his definitive settling of Gaul, the sensation and admiration caused at Rome by achievements beyond his years but worthy of his father. Precocious or bumptious; it can be read either way. We do not know much about Domitian's friends during his father's reign, but they may have included C. Rutilius Gallicus, suffect consul probably in September–October 70 and consul for the second time in 85 after a two-year spell as governor of Asia. M. Arrecinus Clemens, Titus' predecessor as Prefect of the Guard and his former brother-in-law, was among them, on the testimony of Tacitus and Suetonius; he was to owe Domitian much of his brilliant success – suffect consul in 73, *cos.* II 85, and governor of Tarraconensian Spain – until his fatal fall from grace, perhaps in the 'conspiracy' of 87. One set of politicians viewed Domitian's future with particular interest: the relations of his wife Domitia Longina, whom he had taken in 70 from the high-born kinsman of Ti. Plautius Silvanus, L. Aelius Lamia Plautius Aelianus, another victim of Domitian's reign. She was the daughter of Cn. Domitius Corbulo and a magnificent prize for that reason, attracting some of the loyalty of Corbulo's personal friends and surviving relatives, who had suffered in the last years of Nero. Longina's son, later deified, was born in 73, giving rise to stronger but short-lived hopes. In the provinces, a few officials, out of ignorance, sympathy, or prudence, gave Domitian the status that we have seen him being accorded by private individuals.[16]

Titus' blatant ruthlessness during his father's reign declares his determination to secure his own future, fear of the opposition and even of his brother's rivalry. In 71 he returned to Rome in some haste to assume his new position, taking a merchantman from Rhegium to Puteoli and so forgoing a triumphal progress from Brundisium to Rome. Circumstantial evidence connects the exile of Helvidius Priscus the elder in 71 with Titus. That, evidently, was not enough. Execution was ordered (probably in 74); then Vespasian sent an order rescinding it, and failed to save Helvidius only because he was wrongly told that he was already dead. This tale exculpates Vespasian, as far as may be done, from the extreme guilt of executing a Stoic paragon. His name is not even mentioned in connection with the issuing of the order. The suggestion that it was forged, emanating from the Prefect of the Praetorian Guard – Titus – who is said to have boasted that he would have made a top-class forger, was made long ago by C.E. Stevens, partly on the basis of Domitian's allegation about Vespasian's will and another suspect document. There was no need for forgery, whether of the original order or (as A. Birley suspects) of the false report. Suetonius describes Titus as dictating letters and composing edicts in the name of his father (the ultimate authority). His order, represented as coming in oral form ultimately from the Emperor, would have been enough. In any case, there is something wrong with the story of the second, saving, message failing because of the false report, which looks like an amalgam of two distinct versions: Vespasian rescinded the order, but did so too late; he would have rescinded it, if he had not been told that it had already been carried out. The successful removal of Helvidius made Titus even more formidable, and gave him confidence for a later, more sudden and blatant weed-out of undesirable politicians. It has caused comment that Domitian, who is held responsible at the end of his reign for an atrocious assault on the son, other kinsmen, and associates of Helvidius Priscus, should previously have shown them so much encouragement by advancing them to high office: the younger Helvidius in about 87, Q. Iunius Arulenus Rusticus as late as 92. If Titus had been involved in the exile and death of Helvidius, that was to be expected. In the early years of Vespasian's principate Domitian and the constitutionalists had at least negative aims in common. So the excluded younger brother kept his hands pure while the irresistible Titus cleared his own path.[17]

Later, just before the Emperor's death, but without specifying a date beyond associating it with the execution of the rebel Sabinus in 79, Dio's epitomator Xiphilinus inserts his story of the destruction of Eprius Marcellus and Aulus Caecina. They were plotting to murder Vespasian but were detected. Josephus, publishing his *War* in the years 75–9, caught the right tone by incorporating the 'disgraceful' story of Caecina's well-rewarded 'treachery' to Vitellius in that work. There is no build-up to their fall – Vespasian considered them among his best friends, Dio remarks – and Josephus would hardly have written as he did before it; but the 'conspiracy' might belong to an earlier year than 79. Caecina died as he rose to leave a banquet in the Palace itself. Titus gave the order, to forestall any attempt by Caecina to use the soldiers he had already won over to his side, for what has deliciously been called 'an autographed copy' of a speech intended for the Guard had been discovered. That done, Marcellus was brought to trial before the senate and he cut his throat. Dio believed in the plot, and has followers, but it is hard to see what Caecina and Marcellus hoped to achieve; nothing suggests that they regarded themselves as suitable candidates for power, even if they had been able to achieve the assassination of Titus and Domitian as well as of the failing Emperor himself.[18]

The authors of the charges, Titus and his accomplices, were confident enough to demand acceptance of a farrago, to which one dissident or jokey version added the decorative detail, either a straight blunder or more probably developed from the fact that Berenice left Rome after the 'conspiracy' was discovered, that Caecina was killed for having sexual relations with her. It is probable that Titus regarded these old advisers as a potential nuisance to a new Emperor and decided to free himself of them beforehand. Suetonius adds convincing detail of Titus' unacceptable use of his power as Prefect of the Guard. Suspects were denounced in the theatre or the Praetorian barracks by men primed for the job and summarily executed as if by public demand. The incriminating item he provides, Caecina's script, once again brings Titus' gift for imitating handwriting forcibly to mind. (It was something noticeable when a Roman lawyer wrote a speech out beforehand; if Caecina had ever read out a speech to the Guard he is likely to have had a frigid reception), and his hailing of Marcellus before the senate and his denunciation recalls Titus' youthful practice at the bar, desultory though that was. The scenario had a model, Nymphidius Sabinus' treacherous attempt while himself Prefect of the Guard in 69 to seize the Empire from Galba. He was cut down as he approached them clutching the text of a speech written for him by Cingonius Varro (although, we are told, he had already learnt it by heart). The despatch of Caecina and Marcellus is for Suetonius a means of providing for Titus' future peace of mind. He may even have thought that ridding public life of men with their reputation would count in his favour – a miscalculation, because of the manner of their going. For the present it made the prospect of his succession additionally unwelcome, a subject of foreboding. It cast a shadow over the beginning of the reign that J. Crook compares with the effect of Hadrian's execution of the four consulars in 118, which secured his future.[19]

Crook plausibly suggested that the bone of contention was indeed Berenice, or rather the group of easterners that her relations with Titus, begun in 67, when these men gathered round the governor of Judaea, made powerful: her brother Agrippa II, Ti. Julius Alexander, once her brother-in-law; their protégé Josephus. They saw without difficulty where future power lay, and so did Mucianus, whose accommodation with Titus had laid the ground for the

Flavian coup and who might have expected to enjoy an ascendancy over the coming man. When Agrippa and his sister arrived in Rome is uncertain (75 is usually given), but Agrippa received the insignia of a senator of praetorian rank. Even if Berenice did not seriously entertain the ambition of becoming 'Queen' – that is Augusta – as emperors' wives could be since Claudius elevated Agrippina, and as Titus is said to have promised her, she is reported to have behaved like one, and her power behind the scenes was considerable. Quintilian relates how he pleaded Berenice's case with Berenice among the judges, presumably then in the imperial advisory Council, as imperial ladies had been in the days of Gaius and Claudius. When Titus returned to Rome in 71 Berenice had been left behind. She was not able to join him until a time when Mucianus was falling from favour (after his third consulship he took to history writing) or already dead. For Vespasian's own return to Rome in 70, wrongly supposed to have been hastened by Domitian's behaviour, Crook has another suggestion: Titus was already warning Vespasian against his friends, perhaps against Mucianus himself.[20]

This puts much emphasis on the princess who may have been more of a useful grievance than a serious objection to Titus and, like Cleopatra, a convenient weapon for the wounding of his reputation. It may be that Marcellus was opposed to her presence in Rome, and that his death ironically secured her dismissal on security grounds – for the present. Berenice returned to Rome once again after Vespasian's death, but Titus, like Henry V, saw that a monarch could not have the same friends as a prince, and her power was gone. As P. Rogers has pointed out, nothing suggests a link between Mucianus and Titus' victims Caecina and Marcellus; indeed, Titus is presented as being on good terms with him. In 69 at least they had been allies. However, Mucianus was not an easy subject, even though he had not aspired to be emperor, and his death, perhaps already by 74, certainly by 77, may have been a relief to both Vespasian and Titus.[21]

It is safer to leave Berenice out of the story of the frame-up. Mucianus may have played a part, if only because, when he died, the passing of a man who had shared centre-stage with the dynasty in its first years left a power vacuum. Lesser politicians cultivated such men, and if they failed or died, had to transfer their loyalties. That happened more than once in this principate. At the end of 69, Antonius Primus was supreme. As the year 70 opened, Mucianus pushed him out, kept him out of Domitian's suite, and made Rome impossible for him. Antonius in turn denigrated Mucianus to Vespasian in Alexandria, but without success. Mucianus and Domitian and, though he was absent for nearly eighteen months, Titus himself were the men to attend to. After Antonius retired from public life his adherents could hardly transfer themselves to a contemptuous Mucianus; Titus himself or Domitian would be the gainers. Then the subordination of Domitian cost him part of his following; they may have had recourse to Mucianus. But Mucianus himself died before the 'conspiracy', releasing another group of secondary politicians to look for dinner invitations elsewhere. The fate of Marcellus and Caecina may have been due to their own commitment to the Flavian house as a whole, to Domitian as well as to Titus; as the surviving old guard, they attracted everything that was not focused on Titus. And for him that would not have been acceptable.[22]

13

CONCLUSION: IDEOLOGY IN THE AFTERMATH

Vespasian, noted for strenuousness in organizing and taking a personal lead in the Jewish War and for vigour in launching his coup, continued his habitual way of life, responding assiduously to the needs of the Empire, as only Augustus and Claudius had, until almost the end; Dio tells of occasions when old age kept him from the senate, but the Theatre of Marcellus saw him as an old man. As the sage Apollonius of Tyana was made to advise, and as leaders do who enjoy their position, he got up early and stayed up late, and he read his daily correspondence before admitting friends, talking with them as he put on his shoes and dressed. Vespasian was visited then by another early bird, the Elder Pliny. When he had dealt with his day's business he would relax with one of the 'numerous' women he kept after Caenis' death; the bathing and eating that followed made him noticeably more inclined to grant requests. The improving nature of this portrait is obvious; but it was accepted by Tacitus, and Vespasian himself may have been its willing prisoner.[1]

In the tenth year of his reign, at the age of 69, Vespasian developed a fever, attributable at first to the spring weather or to the climate of Campania. He returned to Rome and then went on to his native Reate, which he preferred to the watering places on the Bay of Naples, and at Aquae Cutiliae, between Cittaducale and Antrodoco, he took the cure. The stomach was affected, whether the trouble was organic or due to an infection, and the waters, specified for digestive problems and believed to help those who sat in them, did no good. Vespasian went on working, receiving deputations even on his death-bed. Like Tiberius, who knew that illness weakened political effectiveness and refused to be examined, Vespasian disguised his condition. Rumour made headway, and allegedly he had to dismiss ill omens: the doors of Augustus' Mausoleum opened of their own accord, as they were said to have done before the death of Nero. This was kindly reported to the Emperor, who noted its appositeness: Junia Calvina, like Nero a great-grandchild of Augustus, had just passed away (it was a year of pestilence). Another omen, the appearance of a comet – 'hairy star' – he deflected as marking the death of one with more hair than himself, the King of Parthia. Both stories put the dying Emperor within the ambit of the dynasty that preceded him, *pareil* of Nero and his opponent Vologaeses; he was now its true successor.[2]

A final attack of diarrhoea brought the end, probably in the early hours of 24 June. At the last Vespasian tried to rise: 'An emperor ought to die on his feet.' Tiberius again, another emperor who at least began with a strong sense of duty, had felt the same. The position he held validated Vespasian's life and this account of his end presents him as a man ever aware of obligation to the Empire. It would be good to think that he knew that he had fulfilled it and that his achievement would be recognized. But the dying words, 'Oh! I think I'm becoming a god' are a hostile joke of the time; as M. Schmidt shows, they parody the last words cruelly attributed to Vespasian's patron and political model, the hated Claudius: 'Oh! I think I've messed myself.'[3]

The symptoms were not unlike those of Claudius, and Titus was suspected of poisoning, notably by the Emperor Hadrian, a measure of his perceived ambition. But Titus is likely to have been guilty only of having the Mausoleum doors opened early: he knew he would not have to wait long. On Vespasian's death all or almost all the ceremonies devised for the funeral of Augustus and repeated for those of Tiberius and Claudius were observed. There were divergences in what followed. Gaius and his successors including Vespasian had been saluted 'Imperator' when they came to power, but Titus remained 'Imp. XIV' until a victory in Britain increased his tally. The precedent is Tiberius, showing how well the succession had been prepared: like Tiberius, Titus needed no salutation to warrant a substantial accession of new powers. He had those he needed, and only honorific posts and titles remained: 'Augustus', the supreme pontificate, assumed within the week, and the title 'Father of his country', by 7 September. Vespasian and Titus had scored a remarkable success – but one that only accidents of birth and death could continue to the next generation.[4]

More surprising is doubt, due to the silence of the coinage, about Vespasian's deification, which is thought to have been delayed until some six months after his death. Only the inscription over the Marcian aqueduct unequivocally records Titus as the son of a deified emperor in 79 (after 8 September), and may have been edited when it was set up on completion of the repairs. Yet Titus' needs alone should have guaranteed the deification, even if Vespasian had not earned it (in his *Panegyric*, Pliny credits Trajan with genuine devotion to Nerva; earlier emperors had deified their predecessors for the style '*Divi filius*'); but even Domitian's coins have him 'son of Augustus' until 80–1. It is possible that for a while Titus believed that, as a man sharing power since 71, he could dispense with the additional charisma of being the son of a god so uncharismatically bourgeois – and when Domitian would benefit equally. Only Claudius had achieved divine status since the great founder Augustus, and that immediately became a court joke. Vespasian may have run the same risk, as the last words attributed to him show; hence hesitation about exploiting the ceremony. Doubts about consecration come to the surface in a saying of the new Emperor that probably belongs to the earliest weeks of his reign, when he abolished treason as a weapon against those who slandered their rulers:

> I cannot be insulted or abused in any way. For I do nothing that deserves censure, and I am not interested in lying slanders. As for the emperors who are dead and gone, they will avenge themselves if anyone does them a wrong, if they are truly demigods and have any power.

Ambiguity lurks here. Dio connects Titus' saying with his never putting a senator to death, and it is likely that he originated the customary oath which the senate would ratify (it was refused by Domitian) that he would never execute a peer. This was something that Vespasian had done, and Titus was undertaking an improvement; but we have seen not only the expendable Caecina and Marcellus but Helvidius Priscus as probable victims of Titus. The speech and the oath were Titus' tacit promise of reform, with Vespasian left to shoulder guilt; parading condemned 'informers' across the arena before exile also looks like repudiation. Titus may have felt too that his rumoured connection with Galba, as a prospective adoptee, would enable him to short-circuit Vespasian altogether. If so, he shared the ambivalence of Domitian towards his parents: Domitian disposed of both at one stroke when he indulged the fantasy of being the son of the virgin Minerva. At the same time, it is hard to accept the view that Titus' fear of ridicule or a belief that he could do without a deified parent went as far as neglecting to achieve the consecration; Titus certainly acknowledged his father's *PROVIDENTIA* over the succession. What is observable may be no more than tactful failure to commemorate it. That failure in itself was enough to give rise to hostile gossip against an initially unpopular ruler, forcing him to reconsider. T.V. Buttrey draws attention to the 'restored coinage' of 80–1 in which *DIVVS AVGVSTVS PATER* was accompanied by *DIVVS AVGVSTVS VESPA-SIANVS*, both presented as the founders of a dynasty. Meanwhile Domitian legitimately indulged his taste for nomenclature that included 'Augustus'. In general Titus was not averse from promoting the family: on 3 January 81 the Arval Brothers were offering vows for the safety of Domitian, Julia, and their offspring, as well as for Titus.[5]

The temple that went with the cult and its sodality of fifteen Flaviales (Titiales were added in honour of Titus) was completed by Domitian, who added another, to the entire Flavian clan personified, the *Templum Flaviae Gentis* on the Quirinal where Vespasian had had a house in which Domitian had been born. This was for the remains of deceased members of the family, breaking with Julio-Claudian practice, and when it was complete those of Vespasian were removed to it, as were those of his granddaughter Julia. To this Domitian added a portico for the Deified Emperors, *Porticus Divorum*, including two temples at the site on the Campus Martius where the triumphal procession of 71 had set out. These constructions strengthened Domitian's own position (as did the references to Vespasian on the Pamfili obelisk, and the reliefs of the Cancelleria) as much as they honoured his predecessors. If homage continued outside Rome it must have been known to be acceptable to the late Emperor's heir.[6]

From the period immediately after Vespasian's death evidence for Flamens of his cult proliferates; more are known for him than for any other emperor bar Augustus; only Caesar and Trajan come near. But it is evidence for the cult of the living Vespasian, not of the dead, as I. Gradel has warned, unless the monument can be shown to have been cut more than a generation later. Men recorded their year's tenure, perhaps long past, on stones commemorating their municipal careers; only rarely, in the cases of Augustus and Claudius, can the municipal cult of the emperor be shown to have survived his death. For Vespasian this was so at Ostia and further afield at Ephesus, when Domitian, for whom the cult of the Sebastoi had been devised at the end of the 80s, was damned and Titus' cult failed.[7]

By erecting the *Templum Flaviae Gentis* Domitian showed his concern to elevate his family, although the personal achievements of Vespasian and Titus and their deification in quick succession strengthened its position as the accepted reigning dynasty. Female members also benefited. Titus' daughter Flavia Julia received the title 'Augusta' during her father's reign. She was the wife of T. Flavius Sabinus the consul of 82, and became Domitian's mistress when her husband died for plotting against the Emperor, probably in 83. Julia was certainly deified after her death, which occurred some time before 3 January 91; coins show that she had achieved divine status at least by the end of that year. There is a more problematical case, that of 'Diva Domitilla'. There were three Domitillae in the dynasty: Vespasian's wife, his daughter, and his granddaughter by the second Domitilla's marriage. She married T. Flavius Clemens and produced a brood of seven, two of them Domitian's chosen heirs at the end of his reign. The undistinguished origins of Vespasian's wife have prevented her being taken seriously as a candidate for deified status, while the third Domitilla was disgraced in 95 and sent into exile on Pandateria when in that year Domitian eliminated her husband, his last potential rival in the family. Vespasian's daughter has always seemed the strongest candidate, although, like her mother, she died before Vespasian came to power. Received opinion has been challenged by D. Kienast. He has pointed out that Vespasian's wife was not a 'non-person' when the dynasty was in power: she has the title 'Augusta' attested on an inscription of Rome and her memory ('*MEMORIAE*') is alluded to on coins of Titus' first year. At that stage Vespasian's wife would have been awarded the stately carriage (*carpentum*) to take part in processions in her honour as a preliminary to the full consecration that Domitian accorded her. But his sister too could have been honoured in the same way, on the strength of her grandsons' prospects when they were adopted by Domitian, perhaps as late as 95.[8]

Titus as sole ruler learned from his father's example, and there is no reason to look for some 'cause' for his improvement, such as illness: he was now secure and as emperor had little time to make fatal misjudgments. His two-year reign gave the lie to public foreboding and, in spite of events not in his control, the eruption of Vesuvius on 24 August 79, a fire at Rome the following year, and a pestilence, it was looked back on as an idyll. He worked skilfully and specifically to rebut charges of cruelty, extravagance, self-indulgence, and greed, and he is credited with an improvement in public life. The state of the sources obscures detail, but Titus' commonplace opening move, renunciation of treason trials as a remedy for slander, was reinforced by punishments. Vespasian's reign had been fairly free from natural disaster, with the exception of an earthquake on Cyprus and a plague that struck at the end of his reign, but it had opened with a bloody civil war and recrimination and resentment that lingered for years. Titus succeeded in extricating himself from his involvement in all of it.[9]

Domitian, despite being reminded by Titus, disingenuously if the anecdote is true, that he was his partner and heir, was insecure in power from his accession on 13 September 81, when at last he received his first acclamation as *Imperator* and, like his father and brother, assumed the title as a *praenomen*. Until his cousin Flavius Sabinus' death in 83 and his own indispensable personal military success – delayed since 70 – over the Chatti in that year, he behaved with necessary moderation and civility. From 83 on he refused to be content with the possession of power and restraint in its use; control had to be exercised, above all demonstrated in gratuitous insult, or aggravated punishments, especially to subjects nominally his peers. Dio claims that Domitian's particular target was the friends of his father and brother; many may indeed have acquiesced in or actively encouraged his previous relegation to a subordinate rôle. Domitian would want to make a return with interest for that. Not all suffered: Q. Petillius Cerialis seems to have returned to another consulship, in 83 with the Emperor; but as he grew more confident Domitian found himself increasingly able to put out of the way powerful men who had crossed him, or whom he had feared, beginning with Flavius Sabinus, and dealing *en route* with the resentment that such actions roused: Domitian became censor in 84 and was continued for an indefinite term in the following year; he put down a conspiracy in 87 and a revolt on the Rhine in 89, which was followed by a purge of military men; it was his closest courtiers, his wife, freedmen, and commanders of the Praetorian Guard, who removed the tyrant in 96, so that they would not fall with him: his heirs, Clemens' sons, were infants.[10]

Revisionists have done their best, but not everyone will accept the view that Domitian's 'real crime was to be the last Flavian'; Domitian's real crime was to fall disastrously from standards of civility set by Vespasian and Titus, and to luxuriate in heavy-handed use of his powers. His mistake was to take seriously and to its conclusion the image that his father had enjoyed, to such benefit to the Empire: a successful man in control. Hence, for all its grim end, which meant the return of 'liberty' and the rebirth of Rome, at least on the coinage, Roman writers of his and the next generation were willing to give the first two members of the dynasty their due: 'Three Emperors had usurped power and been slaughtered', says Suetonius, opening his account, 'the Empire had long been in a precarious state and had lost its sense of direction when the Flavian dynasty eventually took it in hand and gave it renewed strength. They had no ancestry and nobody had heard of them before, but although everyone agrees that Domitian's greed and cruelty brought to him the end he deserved, the state has certainly no reason to wish they had never come to power.' After the fall of Domitian, and a taste of uncertainty under Nerva, the stock of Vespasian, who compared favourably with both, rose to new heights. At the shrine of the Emperors in Ephesus all but one of thirteen dedications to Domitian had Domitian's distinctive name and title 'Germanicus' ingeniously but not quite undetectably replaced after his death by the name of Vespasian and his style as a god. A slightly more hostile note sounds through, however, appropriate to the early post-Flavian period: the dream in which Vespasian is reported as seeing Claudius and Nero weighed against himself and his sons, with Augustus, contrary to Flavian ideology, playing no part in the facile calculation. Sabinus, son of the executed Lingonian rebel, had good reason to gloat on the extinction of the dynasty as reparation for the death of his parents; his verdict is transmitted without comment by Plutarch, who had good reason, as a Greek patriot, to resent loss of Greek freedom.[11]

One reason for the preservation of Vespasian's good name, or a justification for it, was the view that Domitian was at odds with the friends of his father and brother, besides having made away with the relative that they favoured, Flavius Sabinus. As well as the next generation of the senatorial opposition, his victims were rivals within the dynasty, Sabinus and later Clemens, and men who had made their careers under the Flavians, such as L. Antonius Saturninus, suffect perhaps in 82, the rebel governor of Lower Germany in 89, and above all Sex. Vettulenus Civica Cerialis (suff. 72 or 73). Agricola, withdrawn from Britain in 83 and never to serve abroad again, escaped attention by lying low in retirement, according to Tacitus, and died just before the last phase of the reign began in 93.[12]

Vespasian has had a good press from ancient and modern writers, even up to a point from Tacitus, for moderation and willingness to face the truth. They present him as a man for whom realism, about himself and others, and what follows from it, a sense of proportion and humour, were keys to success as general and Emperor. The extraordinary number of anecdotes about Vespasian that have entered the literary tradition are many of them variants on this theme: the man is put down (occasionally by his own self-deprecating remarks), but bobs up again, like Hašek's good soldier Švejk: Caligula muddying his toga, Nero's freedman humiliating him and being told to go to the devil when he later came grovelling, Mestrius Florus correcting Vespasian's Sabine vowels, and having his own pronunciation turned against him; Titus remonstrating over the tax on urinals and rebuked with a vulgar cliché. Even Vespasian's own realization that he was about to die – and become a god – may be also interpreted as a comment on this trait. Ambiguous jokes intruded on the very funeral: the actor impersonating Vespasian asked the managers how much the cortège cost, and told them that they could give him the 100,000 *HS* and throw his body into the Tiber. This report from a public event may be true: the parsimony that Vespasian displayed at the last was a merit as well as a failing. In the nineteenth century, when social mobility and the career open to the talents were things to notice, the anecdotes became endearing. In first-century Rome they are more ambiguous, and may indeed have served, as rumours do, to bring together two strands of thinking about an upstart emperor in a society that knew he was their only hope of peace and stability. The muddied toga story, and its interpretation as a sign of high destiny, which may belong to 69, mediates between Vespasian's servility to his Emperor as a young *novus homo* and his future rôle as Princeps: an opponent might bring up the episode, a supporter turn it to a new purpose. Vespasian's real failings, social and official, are justly rebuked: he was not up to standard. Yet they prove not to be fatal, to himself or to his critics. The Emperor's response is measured and reassuring: not imperial wrath, but a joke, the small man's answer to unanswerable accusations. All parties have a viable future, and honour is satisfied. Vespasian was ruthless in ridding himself of innocent potential rivals, even chidren, never gratuitously cruel, it was felt. There is a corroborative detail – he did not care for gladiatorial shows. Knowing the reality of slaughter in battle, Vespasian, like Tiberius, another soldier, probably had no time for civilian fantasies. But there was no stigma in enjoying them, Vespasian built the Colosseum precisely for such shows, and it was out of place for the Emperor to show distaste. But the bloodthirsty Claudius liked them too much.[13]

Flavian writers such as Pliny the Elder and Josephus claimed that Vespasian's rise was the work of Fortune or the Fates, taking charge as soon as Vespasian came to Britain. Hardly deniable when the series of events leading to his success had been so unlikely, that also exempted writers from enquiring into surprising details. And whether writing official – semi-commissioned – history, for the instruction of readers, or for their own pleasure, they were under constraint. Revision began as men fell from power or died – Antonius Primus, Licinius Mucianus, A. Caecina and Eprius Marcellus. The case of Primus is illuminating. Losing his struggle for power within the government, he was awarded responsibility for the sack of Cremona. If he had won, an uncontrollable outbreak among the soldiery might have been blamed, as it was for a time under Galba when L. Verginius Rufus' massacre of the Emperor's supporters at Vesontio had to be explained

CONCLUSION

away. Josephus held back a little (Primus merely allowed the soldiers their head); Vipstanus Messalla refused the version altogether.[14]

T. Rajak argues that apart from the history of Pliny the Elder, which covered earlier wars of Vespasian and was a prime example of the adulatory tracts that he stigmatizes, the first history of the Flavians was that of Tacitus. For the downfall of the Julio-Claudians Tacitus had the work of Cluvius Rufus, a man of consular rank. If it concluded with the death of Nero or the end of 68, strictly speaking it did not overlap with the *Histories* but must have influenced its great sequel. Cluvius' reputation fluctuates: a taste for the anecdote and scandal that a courtier was well placed to collect has been thought to deprive his work of seriousness. But Cluvius himself, in pointed conversation with Verginius Rufus, made much of the integrity that history demands, and his claims were taken seriously by the serious-minded younger Pliny. Court history *was* scandalous and lent itself to ancedotal treatment. Another candidate is available for Tacitus' main source for 69, used by Plutarch also: the eloquent stylist Fabius Rusticus, who survived at least until 108. In the *Annals* Tacitus is cautious of a writer biased by attachment to Seneca; Rusticus was clear of that charge for the post-Neronian age.[15]

But Tacitus was old enough, born 56 or 57, to have developed his own ideas on the dynasty, and he had valuable oral sources: old Verginius, whose funeral oration he delivered, had his own view of events of 68–9 and, excluded from politics under the Flavians, probably of their régimes, although he had had to compromise the truth in public versions. Tacitus' cautious handling of his rôle shows that he knew how to evaluate them. T. Vestricius Spurinna had been with the Othonian forces in northern Italy and reached his first consulship perhaps in the middle years of Vespasian. So did Tacitus' father-in-law. Agricola had been in Britain during Boudicca's revolt of 60–1 and may have come to know his contemporary Titus at this time; he went on to serve in Asia as quaestor to L. Otho Titianus, brother of the future emperor. He was at Rome during 68 and was appointed by Galba to investigate temple treasuries. He was an early and active convert to the Flavian cause, though his career then took him away from Rome, except for the years of his praetorship and consulship, 73 and 76 or 77.[16]

For Tacitus, though in private life he credits Vespasian with setting the example of an old-fashioned life-style that helped to change the habits of the aristocracy and in politics singles him out as one emperor who outstripped expectation – he might have proved worse, if he had lived up to the earlier, time-serving, course that had blemished his repute – the meanness was persistent and incontrovertible, and the ideal Princeps would have combined the merits of Vespasian and Mucianus. Tacitus writes of the subject of the *Histories*, which was the Flavian dynasty, their rise from the opening of 69 to their end in 96, as 'sinister even in peace'. It is not clear that he is referring only to the reign of Domitian. What Tacitus thought about Vespasian's closest supporters is revealed by a passage in which he classifies them with the men round Otho and Vitellius, lumping Mucianus and Eprius Marcellus with T. Vinius, Fabius Valens, the freedmen Icelus and Asiaticus. A. Caecina and Lucilius Bassus are among those whom Tacitus can deal a measured judgment, and by contrast he could cast doubt on the responsibility for atrocities laid at the door of the disgraced Primus, by preserving the alternative version and refusing to decide between them. The burning of the Capitol is another case: Pliny, Josephus, Suetonius, and Dio present the followers of Vitellius as guilty; Tacitus reserves judgment, but reports that the commoner story was that the followers of Vespasian were responsible. It was unlikely to have been current under the Flavians, especially Domitian, who was on the Capitol in 69. In written form it can have surfaced only after 96.[17]

Suetonius was born in 70 or later, too late to know much of the reign firsthand. Some of his sources were also products of the Flavian era. For the period after Pliny the Elder's work ended (71), another, unknown panegyrist has been postulated, whose biographical work helped Suetonius to make a unity of the disparate sources that he used for the second half of his sketchy biography. A slight example, acutely observed by H. Graf, illustrates how information could be turned to the advantage of the ruling house: the commission appointed in 70 to restore looted property is accepted by Suetonius as one of Vespasian's achievements in the field of justice; Tacitus, rejecting the 'Flavian' interpretation, treats it neutrally. Yet adulatory sources would not have deterred a man writing a quarter of a century after the extinction of the dynasty from reporting all he could of scandal or cruelty. Suetonius is silent on those topics. The worst that opponents and critics found to fling at Vespasian, orally or in clandestine pamphlets, was stinginess and lack of style in his public life, and unexciting fidelity and lack of ambition in his sexual attachments – the conventionality that was part of the change of tone that Tacitus commented on in the *Annals*.[18]

Dio Cassius by contrast looks as if he is following a source published before the end of the Flavian epoch. Pliny the Elder, who paid attention to Licinius Mucianus (also an author of oratorical works and letters) would be a good candidate if his historical work had not ended in 71. Dio's favourable picture of Vespasian is thrown into an even rosier light by his condemnation of Helvidius Priscus, who comes over as an intolerable gadfly, unable to leave Vespasian alone, bent on martyrdom and unworthy of the father-in-law, Thrasea Paetus, he claimed to follow.[19]

The influential Suetonius' favourable image became definitive and was reproduced by fourth- and fifth-century compilers, Aurelius Victor, and the 'Epitomator' who like him derived from an anonymous writer of imperial history. Other authorities were equally ready to accept the judgment. The orator and poet Ausonius, in his work on Suetonius *Twelve Caesars* (*c.*379), selected the word 'just' to describe Vespasian and Titus – though their gifts were transitory compared with the evil that Domitian did; Vespasian was 'a most agreeable emperor' in Augustine's *City of God* (413–26).[20]

The deification of Vespasian, well-earned as it seemed at the time, and useful to his sons, did not survive the dynasty: for Trajan it did not have the pristine glamour of those of the founders Julius and Augustus. *Sodales Titiales Flaviales* are attested only as late as Septimius Severus. The origin of the Temple of Vespasian was forgotten and it became known as the 'Temple of Janus'.[21]

Other buildings of Vespasian survived, some perpetuating his name. The Colosseum came also to be called 'the Palace of Vespasian'. It underwent restoration in the reign of Alexander Severus (about 230), and saw the celebration – with wild beast shows – of Rome's millennium in 248 and of the victories of Probus a quarter of a century later. In 357, along with the Forum and Temple of Peace, it was one of the monuments particularly admired by Constantius. In 443 or 444 reconstruction led to the name of Vespasian (and of Titus) being replaced by those of Theodosius II, Valentinian III, and their City Prefect Lampadius. The building was still in use in Theoderic's time at the beginning of the sixth century, although the gladiatorial shows had come to an end under Honorius in 404. In 523 it was the scene of a festival held in honour of the consulship of a member of a leading family, Flavius Anicius Maximus, but that was the end of beast shows there. Anglo-Saxon pilgrims (quoted by Bede) said that 'while the Colosseum stands, Rome shall stand; when the Colosseum falls, Rome shall fall; when Rome falls, the world shall fall.' Happily about one-third of the building has survived earthquake and quarrying. It was the Colosseum's rôle as a sanctified place of martyrdom that saved it: in the mid-eighteenth century it was dedicated by Benedict XIV to the Passion of Jesus. A large rectangular hall of Vespasian's Forum survived by being even more decisively Christianized: it was adapted by Felix IV in 527 as the church of Sts Cosmas and Damian.[22]

The most famous achievement of the first two Flavian emperors, apart from their building programme at Rome, and their most important after the restoration of peace Empire-wide, was the reconquest of Judaea and the destruction of Jerusalem, while their Colosseum remained unstained by Christian blood. Hence their high medieval reputation as scourges of the Jews, which emerges in Dante. At lower literary levels also Vespasian and Titus survived, and in distinguished company, showing their high station in popular world history: V. Canotta cites a poem in heroic twelve-syllable verse, preserved in Turin. The characters include David, King of Greece, and his wife Helen of Troy, daughter of Vespasian; Charlemagne; Joseph of Arimathea; Asillius, son of Herod Nicodemus; Mohammed; Vespasian and Titus; and Pontius Pilate; the setting is Greece, Troy, Jerusalem, Lucca, and Rome. In prose and drama 'The noble Emperor' was celebrated in the Romance fable that opens the Introduction to this book. Vespasian's alleged zeal to convert the heathen was taken further by the fable itself: the Portuguese printed version of 1496 was included in a consignment destined in 1515 for 'Prester John', the ruler of Ethiopia, nearly four hundred years before it was finally translated into Nahuatl, a Mexican Indian language, and published in 1909.[23]

Renaissance writers and some more modern, prompted by old cues, have been favourable too and hardly less intent than missionaries on exploiting Vespasian. Leonardo da Vinci, quoted by G. Bersanetti, summed up Vespasian's as a '*vita bene usata*', a life put to good use, a just synopsis of the classical tradition, at least for Vespasian's last ten years. The shadow of Mussolini falls perceptibly over Bersanetti's own study, published in 1941. Entertainingly, and illuminatingly for his own view of civilization, how it spreads, and how it survived in Britain, he claimed on the basis of Tacitus' *Agricola* that Vespasian's governors made a decisive contribution to the dissemination of Roman civilization, the basis of the island's modern history; Britain thus owes him the thanks due to a benefactor. Otherwise Bersanetti accepts the plausible and sympathetic stereotype: a countryman with a sharp sense of reality, a supreme capacity for hard work and a gift for organization. L. Homo, writing in the aftermath of the Second World War, blatantly heroized the Emperor, even romanticized him, as far as that could be done. As H. Bengtson noted, he chose as his motto the favourable judgment of Napoleon I on Vespasian as one of the greatest men that the Empire produced. We are meeting, not just the man who restored order to the Roman Empire in the early 70s, but one to be welcomed into the Fourth Republic, the Charles de Gaulle of his day. When the existence of a state is threatened safety can come only with total reform of a political nature. This dominated the whole of Vespasian's programme, in which he displayed his striving for order and hierarchy, a sense of moral values, and the idea of continuity. They could be achieved only by monarchical government, but not in the oriental form it had taken under Nero. The work of Augustus had to be harmonized with a new atmosphere and changed conditions.[24]

Historians could do without the patina of these modern portraits: we already have contemporary adulation to discount – although it is relevant as a factor affecting the Emperor's behaviour – and the distortions of immediate hindsight. It was right to stress the importance of Vespasian's immediate successes. The Principate itself had come about as the only way of achieving stability when the competitiveness innate in Roman politics got out of hand and led to violence in the City and between legions. One man, Augustus, had made the prize his own and his family's. When after a century they proved inadequate the very solution to Rome's original problem was terrifyingly called into question. The trauma of the loss in the East is shown by the refusal in some circles there to admit that Nero was dead. There were candidates elsewhere than at Rome for what Gaius and Claudius had made a received position. Chaos seemed close. Vespasian's achievement, though he had the exhaustion of the Empire on his side, and the possession of sons to guarantee his security, something that Nero had lacked, was, first, to survive; then to demonstrate that the end of a dynasty did not mean the end of an ordered system or of peaceful transfers of power: the system had outgrown the dynasty. As civil war raged, ordinary inhabitants of the Empire were going about their business, farming, travelling to trade fairs to sell their wares as they always did. Vespasian's victory ensured that this real life and the interests vested in it would continue, and that the peace relied on for a century was a permanency. It had never been seriously tested before: Claudius achieved power in 41 before anyone more than 50 miles from Rome knew that he was being challenged. Now it had been proved.[25]

Steadiness was the Emperor's particular merit: Vespasian's success suggests that he thought actions well out beforehand. He did not allow resentment, however justified, to push him like Tiberius into corners or onto islands of no return. Nor did he often have to revise decisions, unlike Gaius whose attitude towards the senate changed radically in a four-year reign and who even in small matters such as restoring elections to the people had to back-track. Nor was he easily frightened into sudden and violent action, like Claudius, or given to impulsive acts of generosity, like Nero. It was a benefit to Vespasian's court and to his subjects in Rome, Italy, and the provinces, that they knew where they were. It was in providing a framework in which men could return to self-interested normality, not in any reordering of the kind that twentieth-century autocrats have managed, which was beyond the apparatus, knowledge, ideology, and ambition of any Roman emperor, that we should see his achievement. Beyond that were military decisions that might have gone another way but for him: to continue the Claudian conquest of Britain; to take over the *Agri Decumates*, to front up to Parthia.

Vespasian's success in restoring confidence or at least hope for the future may be measured by the number of monuments in stone and bronze that his reign produced: the 'epigraphic habit', the practice of inscribing permanent memorials of achievement, became more prevalent than ever before. At the end of the second century it was to peak again after another revolution, that ended by the successful accession of Septimius Severus and his dynasty (193–217); but at the beginning of the third century confidence proved less well justified. Vespasian's adjustments, though made for the moment, had beneficial long-term consequences: the development of a new Italo-provincial ruling class, a change of political and social style that was to be the making of the age of Trajan and the Antonine Emperors. It was the achievement of a personality, not that of any theory or plan. A product of the Italian aristocracies that had only come into their own with the beginning of the Principate was the right man to restore the Roman political system and the Roman Empire: a new man rose through them and believed in them. Within the city of Rome, and dealing in particular with the senate, he normally combined firmness with restraint and even with humour, a combination that had failed his predecessors; he dispelled panic, inspired calm and the same confidence as he felt himself. Like Augustus, alone of his predecessors, and like Trajan who followed him – but Trajan had an easy ride after the 'tyranny' of Domitian, as the grateful Pliny shows in his *Panegyric* of 100 – Vespasian understood that the possession of real power, derived from the army, did not have to be demonstrated by humiliating contemporaries; he was confident enough to be unassuming even as he accumulated his consulships and imperatorial salutations. The impression he made is a measure of the impact of an individual personality on the course of history. Some scholars see in the Year of the Four Emperors, the reign of Vespasian, and those of his sons, an abrupt shift towards the 'military monarchy' revealed in all its nakedness in the mid-third century, when emperors willy-nilly were the creations of their armies. Less dramatically, it is equated with the first decisive change of direction in the Empire, towards a consciously 'functional' Principate. There was less of a change: the events of 69 and Vespasian's firm tenure of power merely began to unveil as a system the autocracy that had become entrenched a hundred years before; previously it had revealed itself only spasmodically in the quirks of individual emperors, and the functional emperor was not a novelty: Tiberius liked to hold forth about his duty, Claudius loved performing his.[26]

Unprepossessing as his origins and accent were, Vespasian was lucky, in a society that stressed physique, deportment, performance, and style, to have only one physical characteristic to raise a laugh. The Flavians are depicted with an intent and what might be intended as a commanding gaze. Suetonius describes Vespasian as looking as if he were 'straining', a look that has been detected in the portraits. In life it gave an opportunity to a wit whom Vespasian invited to pass a comment on himself: 'I will as soon as you've unloaded your gut'. Other jokes about his interest in money from any source (his father's and grandfather's business too) provoke the suspicion that hostile contemporaries savoured the belief that they were dealing with a personality that would now be summed up as 'anal'.[27]

Artists of the reign were presenting a man in his sixties. Scholars have divided the portrait sculptures into two groups, but they have used different criteria: the apparent age of the subject, and style, especially distinguishing 'idealizing' and 'realistic' portraits. The task is made more difficult because heads of Nero were recut. M. Bergmann and P. Zanker have discredited the first criterion: the reign lasted only ten years and the characteristics of the 'older' Vespasian may be seen on coins of his first year. They distinguish two types, main and subsidiary, with numismatic parallels. To the main type belong the Uffizi and Ny Carlsberg Glyptothek busts; to the subsidiary those in London and the Vatican, as well as the Cancelleria head. Conceding that this type does bear fewer signs of age, they regard it as going back to a pre-imperial representation or as a reaction against the prevailing official portrait, so shockingly removed from Nero's; the relative frequency of reworked material in this series makes them incline to the first view. So it was not Vespasian who aged but the Emperor's image; idealized versions close to those of the Julio-Claudian dynasty, some reworked from those, yielded to the realistic style exemplified in the Ny Carlsberg Glyptothek portrait: a bald and toothless President Lyndon Johnson.[28]

Portraits of Vespasian and his sons show how they wished to think of themselves and be presented and how their image was interpreted by artists. In turn the portraits like written sources and anecdotes contributed to make up ancient literary portraits, which aimed at making the outer man fit the inner. Suetonius, probably using written and oral descriptions as well as portraiture, recalls Vespasian's person, like his personality, affectionately. He notes the Emperor as stocky, with well-built, sturdy limbs. He had always enjoyed excellent health, except for chronic gout (mentioned by Dio); well able, then, to stand up to campaigning in Britain and Judaea. It was probably the active, even restless life Vespasian led that made it unnecessary to maintain his health with faddy practices. Baldness may have come early, as it did for Domitian (though not in Domitian's portraits, nor all of Vespasian's).[29]

Scholars' 'readings' of portraits with such literary backgrounds are suspect. A. Hekler's comments are blatant: Vespasian is the 'veritable peasant, with his narrow, irritable look', while Domitian's smooth cheeks even reveal the 'feminine pallor' of the texts. Hekler neglects Titus, but Suetonius' eulogy of the living Emperor's looks – physical and mental gifts reaching full glory in the adult, well-proportioned person, dignified as well as attractive, and remarkably robust (like his father), contrasting with Domitian's loss of early comeliness – makes it easy to guess what it might have been like. Suetonius had to concede that Titus was not very tall, and a bit paunchy, like his brother, we are informed, and probably his father; only Domitian is described as 'tall'. All three are depicted with the same well-formed lower jaw, slightly cleft chin, and prominent, overhanging nose, noticeable in Vespasian's case over the receding, untoothed upper lip of the Ny Carlsberg portrait; not just the hypocrite Domitian seems ready to smile. It is unsafe to go further. What a modern observer sees in a portrait will be owed, first, to features worked in by a sculptor who had a model to follow but may also have known Vespasian at least by reputation; but it will be in part a creation of the observer. In miniature it will reflect thinking about the reign itself: what Vespasian achieved was largely the achievement of the way his subjects saw him.[30]

NOTES

INTRODUCTION

1 Hook and Newman, Intr., with bibl. Ch. 13 n. 23.
2 Rôle: TA 3, 53, 4; V.'s improvement: TH 1, 50.
3 26 years: SV 25, 2f. Golden Age: DC 72, 36, 4; E. Gibbon, *Decline and Fall of the Rom. Empire* (ed. J.B. Bury, London, 1900) 1; scepticism: C. Wells, *The Rom. Empire* (London, 1984) 278.
4 Luttwak 3. Personality: M.T. Griffin, *CR* 43 (1993) 115.
5 Septimius Severus: DC 77, 17, 1. See Levick 1990, 81.
6 SV 8, 1, with Graf 128 n. 351 (vocabulary). Stability: Aur. Vict., *Caes.* 9, 1 ('*brevi*'; so [Epit. Aur. Vict.] 9, 5); cf. 9. V.'s measures: SV 8–11.
7 V. as source: Weber 186f. Titus, claiming '*indulgentia*' to Munigua, had to display it (*AE* 62, 288).

1 A NEW MAN IN POLITICS

Graf 7–16; Homo 7–22; Townend, 'Connections'; Nicols 1–8; 12; Kienast 1990; Jones, *Tit.* 1–7; Van Berchem 1978; Buttrey 1972; Chastagnol 1976; Ritter; Barrett.

1 A. Stein, *Der röm. Ritterstand. Münch. Beitr. z. Papyrusforsch. d. ant. Rechtsgesch* 10 (Munich, 1927) 301f., regards the rise as 'typical'.
2 Tertulla: SV 2, 1; 5, 2. Jones, *Tit.* 1, makes Sabinus *promagister* in Asia; S.J. De Laet, *Portorium: Et. sur. l'organisation douanière chez les Romains*, etc. (Bruges, 1949) 377 n. 4, the same among the Helvetii; an official position is not attested. Centurions tax-collecting: I owe this point to Mrs B. Mitchell. Gratitude: De Laet 371 n. 2; Brunt, *RIT* 388, cites *Docs N–H* 481 as the only epigraphic parallel for the honour; pro-magisterial functions: 366. Nurse: Van Berchem 268 improves *CIL* 13, 5138 (note that young Caligula was in Germany 14–17). Colony: Ch. 9.2. Titus' favour: Fredegar, *Chron.*, in *Mon. Germ. Hist., Meroving.* 2, ch. 36 p. 60, 24; p. 61, l. 10f., *s.a.* 73, with P. Frei, *MH* 26 (1969) 101–12, esp. 103. Helvetian territory under Claudius: R. Frei-Stolba, *ANRW* 2, 5, 1 (1976) 377–91, is fundamental. Connections with natives, pointed out by Van Berchem (*CIL* 13, 5106, 11480, cf. *AE* 72, 352, with H. Herzig, *Jahr. Bern. Hist. Mus.* 53 (1973) 39f.; *CIL* 13, 5063) may have been inherited from before Claudius' reign. Repeated *praenomen*: O. Salomies, *Die röm. Vornamen: Studien z. röm. Namensgebung* (Helsinki, 1987), 381–8 (I owe this point to Prof. A.R. Birley).
3 Source: PNH Pr. 20. Memoirs: JV 342. S. Demougin, *Prosopographie des chevaliers rom. julio-claudiens (43 av. J.-C–70 ap. J.-C.). CEFR* 153 (Rome, 1992) 246, denies Sabinus equestrian status, against Stein 1927 (n. 1) 301.

4 Petro Gallic: Graf 7, with n. 25, citing A. Holder, *Alt-celtischer Sprachschatz* (Leipzig, 1896–1913) 2, 976. Gallic connections disgraceful: Cic., *In Pis.* 15, 34.

5 Vespasii: Graf 10; *AE* 89, 201. Senators: *Docs G–N* 369, col. 2, ll. 1–4.

6 Cosa estate: *SV* 2, 1; *TH* 2, 78, 2 (V. inherited it); *DC* 65 (66), 1, 2; size: Nicols 12 n. 2. Cosa: F.E. Brown, *MAAR* 20 (1951) 5–114, esp. 20; *Cosa: the making of a Roman town* (Ann Arbor, 1980). Spoletium house: cf. *CIL* 11, 4778 (*Arch. Epigr. Mitt. Öst.* 15 (1892) 34), dedication to Caligula by a Polla; topography of V.'s paternal and maternal properties: Wellesley 1989, 115. Falacrina: A.M. Reggiani, *Atti* 1981, 286–94. '*Suburbano*': *SV* 5, 2; tr. R. Graves (ed. M. Grant, Harmondsworth, 1979) 281; but cf. *STib.* 11, 1.

7 Accent: *SV* 22. The same vowel shift was affected by patrician Claudii, of Sabine origin: P. Clodius Pulcher (tribune 58 BC). Territory: Strabo 5, 228C; *Homo* 10–13. Reputation: Cic., *In Vat.* 36; cf. E. Dench, *From Barbarians to New Men: Greek, Roman, and modern perceptions of peoples from the central Apennines* (Oxford, 1995) index *s.v.* Rustic contexts on V.'s coins: Levick 1982, 114.

8 Aquae Cutiliae: *SV* 24; *AP* 9, 349; A.M. Reggiani, *Atti* 1981, 278–96. Naturally *PNH* 31, 10, praises the waters.

9 Love of home: *Homo* 9–13. Vitellii: *SVit.* 1. Sabinus' interpretation of the omen of 9 that ('*nepotem . . . Caesarem* (!) *genitum*', *SV* 5, 2) was invented in 69, Tertulla perhaps introduced by V. in a character rôle.

10 Greek: *SV* 23, 1.

11 Uncle's support: Eck 1992–3, 92. Toga at 16: Braithwaite on *SV* 2, 2; Chastagnol 1976, 254 (25 or 26); so Graf 12 with *latus clavus* soon after. Nicols 1 has about 25, Homo 16 26/7; see J. Marquardt, *Das Privatleben der Römer*[2] (Leipzig, 1886) 128f. *Latus clavus*: Chastagnol, *MEFR* 85 (1973) 583–607, argues that *SV* 2, 2, is anachronistic; but cf. Saller 1982, 51 n. 58, and Millar *ERW* 290f., who puts *toga virilis* about 27, *latus clavus* *c*.30 or soon after; see B. Levick, *Ath.* 79 (1991) 239–44. Nicols 2 thinks of a delay of not more than three years. Talbert 77 notes the hesitancy of Seneca and his brother.

12 Vigintivirate and tribunate: D. McAlindon, *JRS* 47 (1957) 191–5 (type (d) 195). Nicols 2, like Graf 12, has the reverse order (vigintivirate *c*.28 or 29). Kienast 1990, 108, has ?26 for the tribunate, like *PIR*[2]*F* 398 and U. Vogel-Weidemann, *Die Statthalter von. Africa und Asia in d. Jahren 14–68 n. Chr. Antiquitas* 1, 31 (Bonn, 1982) 205. Thrace: *TA* 4, 46–51. V Mac.: Nicols 2 n. 9. Braithwaite dates the tribunate to 'the last years of Tiberius', Homo 18 to 29–30, like Graf and Nicols; 30: Chastagnol 1976, 255.

13 *Capitalis*: McAlindon *l.c.*; moneyer: Buttrey 1972, 89; contra, Nicols 2; Levick 1982, 113. No post: Chastagnol 1976, 255. Fall of Sejanus: Levick 1976, 174–9, citing esp. *DC* 58, 11, 5; *EJ* 42. '*Strages*' of 33: *TA* 6, 19, 2f.; *STib.* 51, 4.

14 Required age: G.V. Sumner, *Lat.* 26 (1967) 413–35. Graf 12 argues for 34, from a praetorship of 39, Homo 20 for 34 or probably a little later. Braithwaite on 1, 3, ascribes Sabinus' tenure to 34: he gave thirty-five years' public service, dying 69 (*TH* 3, 75, 1); he assigns V. 35, working back from the aedileship (n. 17 below). So Bengtson 16 and Flaig 356; Kienast 1990, 108, ?35/6. Syme 1975, 64, has Sabinus in 34 or 35, or entering as tribune or aedile. Crete and Cyrene: Talbert 351f. It is unlikely but not impossible that the brothers served in the same year: cf. Vell. Pat. 2, 124, 1. July–June: R. Cagnat, *Cours d'Epigr. lat.*[4] (Paris, 1914) 93; Talbert 497f. rightly denies clockwork precision; T. Mitford, *ANRW* 2, 7, 2 (1980) 1342, has the quaestor under successive governors.

15 Magistracies undesired: *DC* 54, 26, 7; 60, 11, 8, with Talbert 18; Levick 1990, 98. An 'unlucky' career: *EJ* 197.

16 Insufficient time to canvass: Nicols 4; Graf 13, dating the failure to 35, unconvincingly attributes it to Tiberius. Tiberius' health: Levick 1976, 218f.

17 Marius: Plut., *Mar.* 5, 3. Cic., *Pro Planc.* 21, 51, cites consulars failing. V.'s aedileship 38: DC 59, 12, 3, presents it just before Gaius' second consulship; so Weynand 2627f., Vogel-Weidemann (n. 12) 205, and Bersanetti 15 (praetorship 39); Kienast 108. 37: Graf 13. 39: Syme, *Tac.* 652, *RP* 3, 808; J. Morris, *LF* 87 (1964) 319 (due to delayed *latus clavus* and *quaestura*).

18 Popular election: DC 59, 9, 6 (38); repealed: 20, 4, 4–6 (39), adding that there were now 14–16 praetors *p.a.*; accepted by J.P.V.D. Balsdon, *The Emperor Gaius* (Oxford, 1934) 96; cf. Barrett 230f. Date of praetorship: Syme 1975, 64 (39), citing *PIR*² F 398; Nicols 4–7; Bengtson 16 (praetor 39 or, better, 40); Vogel-Weidemann 206 with n. 1410; Kienast 108: 39/40. Interval: Morris (n. 18) 317f. Mud: DC 59, 12, 3 (38); SV 5, 3.

19 Caenis: SV 3, with Graf 16. Property: T. McGinn, *TAPA* 121 (1991) 337 n. 11. Acceptability: 353. V. as praetor: SV 2, 3. 'Conspiracy': Barrett 91–113; Levick 1990, 26f. (bibl.). Campaigns: P. Bicknell, *Hist.* 17 (1968) 496–505. Chronology of 39–40: Nicols 5. V. a candidate of Gaius: Evans 201 n. 2. Dedication to Gaius by V.'s mother? n. 6. New men praetors in 15: Vell. Pat. 2, 124, 4.

20 Financial difficulties: ST 1 ('unpretentious', Jones, *Tit.* 1); the area: Jones 23 n. 2. Praetorian games: Mommsen, *St.* 2, 1, 236–8. ST 1 dates Titus' birth to *'insigni anno Gaiana nece'* (not to his father's praetorship), perhaps a slip (cf. 11, on age at death, 41, in Sept. 81); see *PIR*² F 399; Jones 23 n. 1. Possibly Suetonius is referring not to Gaius' assassination but his slaughter of the 'conspirators'.

21 Domitilla: SV 3, with Homo 184. Ex-slave: [Epit. Aur. Vict.] *Caes.* 10, 1; 11, 1; Jones 3, with n. 10, following Ritter, who sees her as a child exposed, and Evans 201, with n. 2; Braithwaite holds her freeborn. I owe the explanation in the text to Professor J.F. Gardner, who points out that if Liberalis were himself a Roman citizen and freed Domitilla's mother against the *Lex Aelia Sentia*, without good cause shown, he could not marry her: G*I* 1, 67, 71 and 79; J.F. Gardner, *Women in Rom. Law and Society* (London and Sydney, 1986) 223. In *BICS* 33 (1986) 3, she suggested that Domitilla was exposed, reared as a slave, freed as Latin and then claimed as *ingenua* through a *causa liberalis* by her father. She doubts, however, whether Suetonius would have overlooked this romantic tale. (Only some such complication, or her sale, could find room for her being the slave as well as the mistress of Statilius Capella, as Evans *l.c.* supposes.) Prof. Gardner finds two ways in which the situation could have arisen with Domitilla freeborn. The father, a Latin freedman, might have married a Latin freedwoman, but omitted to make a *testatio* when the child was born, with a subsequent *testatio* a year later (*Tab. Heracl.*, Bruns 18, pp. 103, 107; Gardner 1986, 4). He now proved the marital relationship by other means and he (and his daughter) became citizens; alternatively, the father was Roman but mistakenly thought himself Latin and married a Latin. He subsequently proved mistaken, and claimed citizenship (as in G*I* 1, 71), making the daughter a citizen too. *Ingenuitas e libertinitate* : W. Buckland, *Roman Law of Slavery* (Cambridge, 1908) 672f. There is nothing to support Evans' claim *l.c.* that Gaius allowed V. exemption from the rules, the *Lex Iulia de maritandis ordinibus*: the law-suit sufficed. *Scribae quaestorii*: N. Purcell, *PBSR* 51 (1983) 154–61. Liberalis unlikely to have been a freedman: I. Kajanto, *The Latin Cognomina, Soc. Scient. Fenn., Comm. Human. Litt.* 36, 2 (Helsinki, 1965) 220, finds 197 men of that name in *CIL*, only sixteen slave or freed. Ferentium: E.T. Salmon in *PE*.

22 Kinswoman: Jones, *Tit.* 3, regards a connection with V.'s father as 'possible'. A stemma might have a T. Flavius, great-grandfather of V. and grandfather of

Liberalis; he could provide a link with the Arrecini, if he had a grandson who married an aunt of Clemens, Guard Prefect 41. Marriage: remission of one year per child: *Dig.* 4, 4, 2, with Sherwin-White 1966, 74. Domitian: *SD* 1, 1, with the site, '*ad Malum Punicum*', by the Pomegranate (Jones, *Dom.* 1, suggests the Via delle Quatro Fontane). Domitilla: Nicols 8f.; Jones, *Tit.* 24 n. 12, following Suetonius' order; Townend, 'Connections' 62, dates her birth 45.

2 VESPASIAN AND THE ARISTOCRACY: THE COMMAND IN BRITAIN

Nicols 1978, 8f.; 13–22; Jones, *Tit.* 4–17; *Lat.* 43 (1984) 581–3. Britain: G. Webster, *Brit.* 1 (1970) 179–97; G. Webster and D. Dudley, *The Rom. Conquest of Britain*[2] (London, 1973) 69–104; Wiseman 1978; G. Webster, *The Rom. Invasion of Britain*[2] (London, 1993) 84–110; 150; Birley 1981; M. Todd, *Rom. Britain 55 BC–AD 400* (Glasgow, 1981) 60–89; S. Frere, *Britannia*[3](London, 1987) 48–59; W.H. Manning, *Early Rom. campaigns in the S.-W. of Britain. The first annual Caerleon Lecture* (Cardiff, 1988); J.G.F. Hind, *Brit.* 20 (1989) 1–22; A. Barrett, *AJP* 100 (1979) 538–40; N. H. Field, *Dorset and the Second Legion: New light on a Roman campaign* (Tiverton, 1992).

1 Labeo: TA 4, 47, 1; cf. 6, 29, 1; DC 58, 24, 3.
2 Protégés of Nerones: Levick 1976, 95; 160f.
3 Intermarriage: Jones, *Tit.* 4–7 (exaggerating the eclipse 19–37?); Nicols 13–18; Levick 1990, 23 (links with Claudius); Raepsaet-Charlier 1987, 492 no. 606; 496–8 no. 613f.; 502 no. 619; 619f; no. 816f. Plautii: L.R. Taylor, *MAAR* 24 (1956) 7–30; T.P. Wiseman, *New Men in the Roman Senate 139 BC–14 AD* (Oxford, 1971) 252 (cf. Syme 1986, 87); *PIR*[2] P 456–88, with Stemma 20; A. Plautius and Pharsalus: Cic., *Ad Fam.* 13, 29, 4, with Jones 23 n. 4. Plautius' quaestorship, 20: Eck 1996, 50, l.176. Petronii: Wiseman 250; *PIR*[2] P 266–70; 294; 314f; 318–20; 323f; and Stemma 10.
4 Petronia wife of A. Vitellius: TH 2, 64, 1; S*Vit.* 6; *PIR* P[2] 323.
5 Vitellius 'son' of Antonia: TA 11, 3, 1.
6 'Client': TH 3, 66, 3. Narcissus: SV 4, 1. Caenis: Graf 16.
7 Chaucius: S*Claud.* 24, 3; DC 60, 8, 7. Eagles still lost: Florus 2, 30, 38; H. Küthmann, *JNG* 10 (1959–60) 47–50; Levick 1990, 151–3. Josephus' claim: JB 3, 4; Sil. Ital. 3, 599: '*compescet ripis Rhenum*'; cf. Stat., *Silv.* 1, 4, 89 ; Eutrop. 7, 19.
8 Gaius and Britain: TAgr. 13, 2: '*agitasse*'; on the shore: R. Davies, *Hist.* 15 (1966) 124–8; P. Bicknell, *Hist.* 17 (1968) 496–505. Thule: Sil. Ital. 3, 597f.; cf. Val. Flacc. 1, 8f., with E. Birley, *Rom. Britain and the Rom. Army*[2] (Kendal, 1961) 14f., and A. Momigliano, *JRS* 40 (1950) 41f. (not refuted by Birley). V.'s future foreshadowed: TAgr. 13, 3.
9 DC 60, 20, 3 (Sabinus seems subordinated to V.): Birley 1981, 224, accepts the plausible emendation of G. Vrind, *De Cassii Dionis vocabulis quae ad ius publicum pertinent* (The Hague, 1923) 90, making both V. and Sabinus subordinates of Plautius. Prof. A. Barrett comments that the plural *hypostrategountas* is 'weak in the sense of being superfluous': if the singular is kept, *hoi* should still be referred to Plautius. IX Hisp. is a tempting guess for Sabinus' legion. Geta: DC 60, 20, 4.
10 Narcissus: DC 60, 19, 2f. Hind 12 and 16 identifies Dio's 'Bodunni' with the Dobunni round Bagendon, arguing against the Medway and sending a flying column towards Corinium in their support. Harbours: 11–13; Claudius' route: 16f. Monument: Frere 104 n. 21. The pincer movement has won recent support:

N. Hammond and B. Frost, *The Times*, 5 Sept. 1996. Webster 1993, 107, thinks that V.'s offensive began before Claudius arrived, but Plautius would not have split his forces then.

11 Hertfordshire tribes: C. Partridge, *Skeleton Green, a late Iron Age and Romano-British Site, Brit. Mon.* 2 (London, 1981) 353–6 (I owe this reference to Prof. Barrett); Cassivellaunus Trinovantian: E. Black, *Essex Arch. and Hist.* Ser. 3, vol. 21 (1990) 8f. Cogidubnus: T*Agr.* 14, 1; Birley 1981, 208–10; his name as spelt by Tacitus may be Togidumnus and on *Docs G–N* 197 Togidubnus (C.E. Murgia, *CP* 72, 1977, 339, a ref. owed to Prof. A.R. Birley).

12 V. in the West: SV 4, 1; Caledonian Ocean: Val. Flacc. 1, 8; Webster and Dudley 70–88; Frere 58; Hind 3, with the hill forts. Wight: above, n. 8 (Thule). Seafaring: S. McGrail. *Oxf. Jrnl. Arch.* 2 (1983) 299–338, esp. 324; 333; rivers: R. Chevallier, *Rom. Roads* (tr. N. Field, London, 1989) 162. Manning, 9f., argues against Frere that the Dumnonii escaped V.'s attention, and suggests that the second tribe subdued was the Wiltshire and Somerset Belgae (Dobunni under another name?); Webster and Dudley identify a western branch of Atrebates as the second tribe (the 'Belgae') north of the Durotriges, but mention the possibility of two sections of the Durotriges, based on Maiden Castle (later on Dorchester), and Ham Hill (Ilchester): C.E. Stevens, *Proc. Somerset Arch. and Nat. Hist. Soc.* 96 (1951) 188–92. Other strongpoints (50 altogether): Webster 1993, 105, referring (108 n. 51) to R.M. Wheeler, *Maiden Castle, Dorset* (Oxford, 1943) (esp. 61–8; 351–6); (109 n. 57) I.A. Richmond, *Hod Hill 2: Excavations 1951–8* (London, 1968) 103–11, 117–23, dating from samian ware and coins; (for Waddon Hill) G. Webster, *Proc. Dorset Nat. Hist. Arch. Soc.* 101 (1979 [1981]) 51–90 (esp. 54f.); Hamworthy: Webster 1993, 142; Lake Fortress/Farm: *Brit.* 13 (1982) 384–7. Date of S. Cadbury massacre (61): Webster 1993, 108, with n. 51. citing J. Campbell *et al., Antiquity* 53 (1979) 31–8. V. as artilleryman: JB 3, 166, where Thackeray cites Veg. 2, 25, on equipment; so E. Marsden, *Greek and Rom. Artillery: Historical Development* (Oxford, 1969) 180; effects: 96, 181, and Pl. 5. Dr M.G. Simpson believes that there was also an early riverside fort at Wareham. Return with Plautius: D. Eichholz, *Brit.* 3 (1972) 149–63, 46 or 47; so Nicols 8; Graf 18, Webster and Dudley 70, and Bengtson 20, commenting that V.'s speedy success showed that the Britons put up little resistance, are for 44 or soon after. Plautius' stay: DC 60, 21, 5 (stressing Claudius' hasty return); cf. (61) 30, 1f., where the story of Titus saving V.'s life belongs to the Jewish War, probably, as Nicols *l.c.* n. 42, suggests, citing JB 3, 236–9, to the siege of Jotatapa.

13 Corinium: map, Hind 19. Route of XIV: Frere 57. Internal trouble in Britain: Barrett 1979.

14 *Ornamenta*: A.E. Gordon, *Q. Veranius consul* AD 49 (Berkeley-L.A., 1952) 305–30, esp. 318 (43); Kienast 108 has 44. They went to V., Geta, Frugi (who was allowed to ride) and ?M. Vinicius; the knights Rufrius Pollio and P. Graecinius Laco received honorific statues. V. as Emperor conferred *ornamenta* on consular commanders (M.T. Griffin, *CAH²* 11 (forthcoming)). Priesthoods: Nicols 9, citing M. Hoffman-Lewis, *The Official Priests of Rome under the Julio-Claudians* (Rome, 1955) 143, against Homo 24 (pontificate and augurate!); Bengtson 20.

15 Marriage links: TA 12, 7.

16 Vitellius dead before 55: SVit. 3, 1. V.'s consulship: G. Camodeca, *Puteoli* 9/10 (1985/6) 26 n. 71; Nicols 9. Crisis of 47–9: Levick 1990, Ch. 6f. 42 'legal age': Morris, *LF* 87 (1964) 335. Titus, quaestor *c*.64 (66 Bengtson 157), is not known to have held tribunate or plebeian aedileship, suggesting that Claudius advanced V. to the patriciate (Nicols 32); but Birley 1975, 140f., points out that Titus left Rome with Nero and V. in 66 and passed straight to a legateship under V.

17 SV 4, 2: *otium, secessus*.

18 Titus and Britannicus: Ch. 5. End of Claudius: Levick 1990, 75–9.

19 Nero's early years: Griffin 1984, 50–82; B. Levick, *Stud. in Lat. Lit. and Rom. Hist., Coll. Lat.* 180 (Brussels, 1983) 3, 211–25.

20 Vicissitudes: Syme, 'Partisans' 117f. Flaig 358 stresses Vitellius' divorce as a factor. Caesennii: marriage between Paetus (the *cos.* 61?) and a Flavia Sabina (V.'s niece): MW 285, with Townend, 'Connections'; R. Syme, *Hist. Aug. Papers* (Oxford, 1983) 190f.; 'Ministers' 529. Graecina: TA 13, 32, 3–5; A. Plautius: SNero 35, 4. Lateranus: TA 15, 60, 1f. Aelianus: MW 261. Relations with V.: Nicols 33; I owe the point about his deserts to Mrs B.M. Mitchell.

21 Consulship: 44: P. Gallivan, *CQ* 28 (1978) 424; cf. G. Barbieri, *Epigr.* 29 (1967) 7f., and W. Eck, *Hist.* 24 (1975) 34 n. 113; 47: Birley 1975, 225, notes an inscription of Geta and Sabinus using a letter introduced by Claudius: MW 261; M.T. Griffin, *Seneca, a Philosopher in Politics* (Oxford, 1976) 456f. He governed Moesia for seven years (*c.*53–60) and was City Prefect for twelve according to TH 3, 75, 1, necessitating an additional tenure before the governorship (?56–60; 61–8; 69); many suspect text or historian (Griffin, *l.c.*; Syme, 'March' 1009; cf. Nicols 26–30).

3 FROM NERO'S COURT TO THE WALLS OF JERUSALEM

Griffin 1984, 50–118. JB (ed. Niese, 1894), JB, JA, JV (tr. H. Thackeray *et al.*, ed. Loeb, 1927–8; 1930–65; 1926); Laqueur; Weber; H. Drexler, *Klio* 19, NF 1 (1925) 277–312; Graf 19–30; Schürer 1973, 484–513 (bibl.); Smallwood 1976, 256–316; Cohen; E. Gabba, *Atti* 1981, 153–73; Rajak 1983; M. Goodman, *The Ruling Class of Judaea. The origins of the Jewish revolt against Rome* AD 66–70 (Cambridge, 1987); Brunt, *RIT* 282–7; cf. 517–31; S. Applebaum, *JRS* 61 (1971) 155–70; 1977, 373–96, esp. 379–85; Rhoades. Campaigns: A. Barrett, *AJP* 98 (1977) 153–9; Nicols 40–57; M. Gichon, *PEQ* 113 (1981) 39–62; Saddington 1982.

1 Cerialis: TA 14, 32, 6f.; TH 3, 59, 2; Syme, 'Ministers' 529; Birley 1981, 67, like E. Champlin, *ZPE* 32 (1978) 276, A.B. Bosworth, *ZPE* 39 (1980) 275, and Flaig 358, leans towards Townend, 'Connections' 59. Younger Paetus: TA 15, 28, 3 (Stemmata). Marcia: ST 4, 2. Titus' career: Jones 1992, 12–33. Female members of V's family: Raepsaet-Charlier 1987.

2 Africa: SV 4, 3; Sil. Ital. 3, 596–9; cf. TH 2, 97, 2; SVit. 5. V. and Vitellius: Nicolas 1178. Date: Graf 19: 61 or 62; B. Thomasson, *Die Statthalter der röm. Prov. Nordafrikas v. Aug. bis Diocletianus, Skr. utg. av Sv. Inst. i Rom* 8°, 9, 1 (Lund, 1960) 42, 60–2; Bengtson 22 and U. Vogel-Weidemann, *Die Statthalter v. Africa u. Asia . . . 14–68 n. Chr.* (Bonn, 1982) 205, 63–4?; Griffin 1976, 452f., 61–2 or 62–3; repr. 1992, 512f., with 63–4 for a Vitellius; cf. 1984, 265 n. 102; Kienast 1990, 108, *c.*63–4, Flaig 356, 63–4. Fears of 62: TA 15, 18; P. Garnsey, *Famine and Food Supply in the Graeco-Roman World* (Cambridge, 1988) 223f. Moesian grain: MW 261. Pelting: SClaud. 18, 2.

3 Impoverishment: SV 4, 3; cf. Syme, *RP* 1, 396. Mules: Strabo 5, 228 (cf. Wellesley 1989, 116, on 'Marian mules', soldiers); Jones, *Dom.* 18, suggests that he supplied the court. Fee taken in Africa: Weynand 2629. *Arbiter*: *CIL* 6, 1268. Crassus' fate: TH 1, 48, 1; 4, 39, 3.

4 Paetus' reverse: TA 15, 6–17. Gallus: JB 2, 510. Status: Flaig 356.

5 Sura/Soranus brothers: *PIR²* B 55, M 219; importance of marriage: Evans 201. Pigoń 237 n. 11 rejects Nicols 24, connecting Titus' divorce with the Pisonian conspiracy. *Coniuratio Viniciana*: SNero 36, 1; *Docs G–N* 25, ll. 1–7;

B. Warmington, *Nero* (London, 1969) 156. Date: Griffin 1976, 462f.: Nero in Greece early Oct., Corbulo dead late 66 or early 67; Nicolas 251f. Corbulo's connections: Syme, 'Corbulo' 811; 819–23; contra Flaig; threat 359, App. 2. Glitius: TA 15, 56, 4; 71, 6; Orfitus: S*Nero* 37, 1; T*H* 4, 42, 1. Mucianus: Griffin 1976, 465f., hostility to Arrius Varus, who informed on Corbulo.

6 V.'s reputation: T*H* 2, 5, 1. Nerva: TA 15, 72, 2; Sabinus: T*H* 1, 77, 2; *Dig*. 1, 2, 2, 53; Cassius: TA 16, 71–9, 1. V.'s friends: T*H* 4, 7, 2, where 'Sentius' ('*Senecione*', Gudeman) may be Cn. Saturninus, *cos.* 41, but cf. Pigoń 237 n. 13: this man is not known to have played a part comparable with Thrasea's; A. Stein, *RE* 2A (1923) 1509, accepted Ritter's '*Anteio*' (P. Anteius Rufus, TA 16, 14). V.'s complicity is hinted at, T*H* 4, 8, 3: Pigoń. 242. V.'s 'disgrace': TA 16, 5, 5 (Rome, *Quinquennalia* of 65); SV 4, 4, cf. 14, and DC 62, 10, 1a (Greece; so Weynand 2624). Graf 21 has all three derived from Pliny, but the story is not flattering.

7 Origins: JB 2, 117–407; JA 17, 355 – 20, 258 (relation between the two: Cohen 48–66; JB and JV: 67–83, postulating a common sketch); varying accounts: Cohen 152–60; 181–231 insists on participation of aristocrats from the start; he scouts the idea that Florus wanted war (JB 2, 297–300; 305–8; 325–7). T*H* 5, 9f. Smallwood 1976, 256–84 (Caesarea: 285–9); Applebaum 1971 (religious conflict, but noting (168) 'regional particularism crystallizing about strong personalities' and ideological or doctrinal differences' as results as well as causes) and 1977 (the countryside); Rhoades 150–73; Brunt, *RIT* 284–6 (*equites* among the Jews, Josephus' half-heartedness, 'something like class warfare', and notables' opportunism) and 517–31 (less stress on popular animosity to élite); Rajak 65–143; Goodman 1987; Millar 1993, 359–66. Aristocrats in control: Graf 21 with n. 118 (bibl.). Governors' provocation: JB 2, 276; 280–3; 287f.; 292–309.

8 Zealots, *sicarii*: Drexler 283–8; Applebaum 1971, 163f.; Smallwood 299 (bibl. n. 22); C. Hayward in Schürer 1979, 598–606 (bibl.). M. Hengel, *The Zealots: An investigation into the Jewish freedom movement . . . Herod I – 10 AD* (tr. D. Smith, Edinburgh, 1989) 66–145, notes Josephus' use of '*sicarii*' as tendentious, not that of 'Zealots'; see Rhoades 52–9, against continuity between the movement of Judas in 6 and the revolutionaries of 66. (I owe these references to Dr Rajak.) Messianism: n. 12. Judas of Galilee: JB 2, 118; followers 7, 252–74. God: 2, 390. God to be observed: 7, 323; Jews doomed: 327.

9 Opening of war (summary SV 4, 5): JB 2, 284–32 (Florus' scheme also at 283); Cohen 188–91, with Florus' removal an early aim. Berenice's failure: 315. JB uses Macedonian month-names. They might be (1) substitutes for Julian names (e.g. Art. for Maius) or (2) substitutes for Hebrew month-names (e.g. Art. for Airu/ Iyyer), or (3) months of a local (Tyrian) calendar. Nicols 40–7 (tables 46f.) persuasively argues that for campaigning dates (1) is the case: Josephus depended on V.'s *commentarii*, endorsed by Rajak 216 n. 82. Doubt subsists for events not part of a Roman record (a Jewish festival); the end of Vitellius, 3 Apell. (JB 4, 654) is Tyrian. B. Niese, *Herm.* 28 (1893) 203 and *ad loc.*, held that (3) prevailed throughout; Weber 16 n. 3. Gichon 61, like Schürer 1973, 587–601, esp. 596–9, opts for (2) Josephus probably gave dates as he received them; in the Timechart I adopt Nicols' scheme (Table 2 is out of kilter), with alternatives for items probably not from the Roman record.

10 Cestius' emissary: JB 2, 334; 406–10; Florus' refusal of troops: 420f. Agrippa: A.H.M. Jones, *The Herods of Judaea* (Oxford, 1938) 217–61; Schürer 1973, 471–83. His aim: Gichon 41 with n. 11. Pleas: see T. Rajak in L. Alexander, ed., *Images of Empire. Journ. for the Stud. of the O.T., Suppl.* 122 (Sheffield, 1991) 122–34, stressing Agrippa's incompetence. *Sicarii*: JB 2, 425; priestly appointments:

Millar 1993, 63, Antonia siege: 430 (15 Ab). Masada weapons: 433f. (Cohen 193). Departure of local troops: 437f. (Dr Rajak drew my attention to the composition of the survivors.) Withdrawal from part of the palace on 6 Gorp.: 440. Garrison massacred: 450–6. Date: 456 (sabbath!), with Schürer 487 n. 10, and Cohen 3 n. 3 for *Meg. Taan.* 14: withdrawal of Romans from Judah and Jerusalem on 17 Elul (2 Sept.). Caesarea massacre: 457–98; cf. JV 25f.; 46–61. Ti. Alexander: *PIR*[2]J 139.

11 Cyprus and Machaerus: JB 2, 484–6. Expedition, losses: 499–555; JV 24, with Gichon; troops: 500–2, analysed by Gichon 44f; Jerusalem: 45, with n. 29. Size of units: D. Breeze and B. Dobson, *Hadrian's Wall*[2] (Harmondsworth, 1978) 148–56, table 155. Retreat: Smallwood 297; Gichon 56 (topography 58f.), cited Rajak 74 n. 10, with B. Bar-Kochva, *PEQ* 108 (1976) 13–21. Death: JB 2, 540–55; TH 5, 10, 1; XII Fulm.: JB 7, 18; SV 4, 5, with Braithwaite; cf. *RIC* 62n. (69–70); 71 no. 461 (71). Inexperience: Gichon 60.

12 Redeployment: Cohen 197–9. Spreading contagion: JB 3, 3. Magnitude of war: 1, 1 (*topos*); 4f.; 6, 343 (Jews E. of the Euphrates, cf. DC 65 (66), 4, 3; repudiated by Agrippa II: 2, 388f.; cf. Philo, *Leg.* 216f.); note JB 2, 520; war against Parthia (117): DC 68, 32, 1f., with P.R. Davies in L. Alexander, ed., *Images of Empire* (Sheffield, 1991) 175; Egypt involved (41), *Docs G–N* 370, (l. 96–100). Diaspora a target: JB 2, 398f. 'Ruler(s) from Judaea' rumour (JB 6, 312f.; TH 5, 13, 2; SV 4, 5; Eus., *Hist. Eccl.* 3, 8); *ex post facto* justification? (so Dr Rajak). Messianism: Weber 34–48; Graf 21 with n. 118. 'Anti-semitism': Musurillo index *s.v.*; V. Tcherikover and A. Fuks, *Corp. Pap. Iud.* 1 (Cambridge, Mass., 1957) 48–93.

13 Corbulo: n. 5; Scribonii: DC 62 (63), 17, 2–4; Verginius: 63, 24, 1; Capito: TH 4, 13, 1; Aelianus: Ch. 6 n. 37. Pomponius Pius: *Docs G–N* 384. V.'s qualifications and appointment: TH 1, 10, 3; 5, 10, 1; JB 3, 4–7; D. Saddington, *ANRW* 2, 33, 5 (1974) 3492; 3549; Prof. Saddington notes first cavalry pikemen: JB 3, 96; SV 4, 5. Route: JB 3, 8. Legates' status: Nicols 124; son as legate: Birley 1981, 18f. Vettulenus: Syme, 'Ceionii' 330. Marcia: A. Birley, *Hadrian, the Restless Emperor* (London-New York, 1997) 321, n. 17. Titus' connection: E. Champlin, *Ath.* 71 (1983) 259–64, but cf. Raepsaet-Charlier 1987, 439–41, no. 521. (I am indebted to Prof. A. Birley for these refs.)

14 Protégés: Nicols 19, citing JA 18, 143; 19, 276; 360. Alabarch: JA 20, 100 (I owe this reference to Dr Rajak). Son's marriage: JA 19, 277. Advice of Alexander and Agrippa II: Nicols 25f.

15 Title: Chilver on TH 1, 10, 3, suggests '*legatus* in charge of this war'. Corbulo: TA 13, 8, 1 (54); cf. 15, 3, 2. '*Ad componendum statum*': EJ 197 (Cyprus) and *Das SC de Cn. Pisone patre .Vest.* 48 (eds W. Eck *et al.*, 1997) 40, l. 30f, cf; SV 4, 5: '*ad hunc motum comprimendum*'. Cestius succeeded by V. in Syria: TA 15, 25, 5; TH 5, 10, 1; cf. JB 3, 7, criticized by Weber 113: the western legions from Corbulo's war, V Mac., XV Apol., IV Scyth. (replaced by the Syrian X Fret.), are meant, with auxiliaries and 'client' forces: '*exercitus amplior*' (SV 4, 5). *Legatus Aug. pro praetore*: Bengtson 24. Smallwood 306 puts Cestius' death before V.'s appointment. Distribution after Mucianus' arrival: TH 1, 10, 1; 3; 2, 4, 4. October arrival: Nicols 113f.

16 Journeys: JB 3, 8; 29f. (Antioch assembly; V.'s arrival at Ptolemais); 65 implies that Titus found V. there; JV 407–11 (Tyre to Ptolemais); cf. TH 5, 1, 2 (later accretions from Alexandria), with Weber 114f. (bibl.); Graf 27, with n. 149, was for Egypt; so Braithwaite on SV 4, 6; Schürer 1973, 492 n. 31; Bengtson 37; Bersanetti 18 Alexandretta, but against Josephus' usage. Support: JB 3, 29; 68f.; 2, 4. Morale: SV 4, 6, with Weber 119–22.

17 Strategy: Weber 129f.

18 Moderates: Schürer 1973, 489; cf. Cohen 181–8; Dr Rajak notes *JV* 22, where they go with Menahem. Constitution: Smallwood 1976, 298f; mint: 300f.; *Sanhedrin*: *JV* 62. Commands: *JB* 2, 562–8; Eleazar: 564. Josephus in Galilee: 560–84, with Cohen 200–31, estimating 10,000 Galilaeans mobilized, 202; *lestae*, 212; John of Gischala, 222; Josephus intermediary, 214. Misrepresentations: Laqueur 248–55. Agrippa: *JV* 64–9, with Smallwood 303f. Unrest: *JB* 2, 585–646 (Smallwood 304–6). Placidus' attack: 3, 110–14.

19 Forces: *JB* 3, 64–9; *TH* 1, 10, 1; 2, 4, 4; 3; 5, 1. Delay: *JB* 3, 110. Bersanetti 18, Schürer 1973, 492, Smallwood 307, and Nicols 48, accept *JB* 3, 69, 60,000, but cf. Weber 119: he exaggerated unit size (so Chilver on *TH* 2, 6, 2). *SV* 4, 6, has two legions 'added' to V.'s forces, with eight cavalry squadrons and ten cohorts. Braithwaite *ad loc.*, regarding the number of auxiliary units as a slip, suggests that Suetonius thought that there was already a legion in Judaea. Weber's solution was that V. 'added' eight *alae* to six under Titus at Ptolemais, and ten cohorts to Titus' 13. See Saddington 48f., at 102f. estimating 56,000 or 59,000. Significance: Millar 1993, 72. Legates: Nicols 103. Galilees: *JB* 3, 38f.; 127, with Nicols 48–52. Sepphoris: *JB* 3, 30–4; 59; *JV* 373–80; 394–7; *SV* 4, 6; cf. Schürer 1973, 492 n. 32; Cohen 243; 245–8.

20 Organization: *JB* 3, 70–128 ('orders group': J. Peddie, *The Rom. War Machine* (Stroud, 1994) 36). Lowlands Roman: Schürer 1973, 492. Gabara: 132–4; *JV* 123 ('Garaba' J. Benzinger, *RE* 7 (1910) 417). *Virtus*: *TH* 2, 5, 1; Graf 30 compares recent generals, Mrs B. Mitchell earlier: Sall., *Jug.* 100; Livy 21, 4.

21 Jotapata: *JB* 3, 142–339; 258–60: Josephus dates his re-entry 21 Art., with completion of road, the first Roman troops arrive very soon, V. one day later, ?23rd; Jotapata's fall: 1 Pan. makes a forty-two day siege; Josephus writes of 47 (316, 406): 21 Art. is suspect: Thackeray on 142; Schürer 1973, 493 n. 38; Smallwood 308. The details (Dr Rajak observes) are stock stratagems: Cohen 95, n. 35; 235. V. wounded *kata ton tarson tou podos*: 3, 236 (knee, cf. *SV* 4, 6, with Weber 134); fall: 316–39.

22 Josephus' plan: *JB* 3, 193–206; emergence: 340–91. Mourning: 432–42.

23 Japha, Samaritans: *JB* 3, 289–315. Messianic element: Smallwood 311 n. 73.

24 Winter quarters, Joppa: *JB* 3, 409–31.

25 Philippi, Tiberias: 443–57 (site of Sennabis not agreed). Chronology: Weber 132.

26 Tarichaeae: *JB* 3, 462–542, with Thackeray on 462 and Schürer 1973, 494 n. 44: not at Kerak (Beth Yerah) at the S.W. corner of the lake, but N. of Tiberias near Mejdel (Migdal Nunayya); *ST* 4, 3. Triumph: *JB* 7, 147; coins with *VICTORIA NAVALIS*: Schürer 495 n. 45; E. Conrad, *Num. Circ.* (May 1973) 187f.; Smallwood 1976, 309 n. 65, considers the lake battle (*JB* 3, 522–31) minor for it (cf. also Weynand 2632); Weber 282 n. 2, refers it to the victory over Anicetus, Dr Rajak suggests the pirates. The political significance of the issue (G.C. Belloni, *ANRW* 2, 1 (1974) 1060f.) demands the participation of a regular fleet. *CREBM* 2, xlvii, takes it generally: 'Lady Victory of the Fleet'.

27 Captives' fate: 532–42, cf. S*Nero* 19. Labienus: Hirt., *BG* 8, 23, 3–6; Trajan: F.A. Lepper, *Trajan's Parthian War* (London, 1948) 7; Tiberius: *TA* 2, 88, 1.

28 Gamala: *JB* 4, 1–53; Schürer 1973, 495 n. 46. Capture: 62–83, having rebelled 24 Gorp.

29 Tabor: 54–61.

30 Winter quarters, Gischala: 84–120; Schürer 1973, 496, n. 50. Jamnia, Azotus: 4, 130; Lydda, Jamnia: 444.

31 Dissension: 121–365; High Priest chosen by lot: 153–7; Ananus: 151; 158–95; attack on the Temple: 196–207; Idumaeans invoked: 224–304. Slaughter:

305–33; show trials: 334–44. Idumaean departure: 345–55; Niger: 359–63, cf. 2, 520, and 3, 11–28.

32 Immediate attack advised: JB 4, 366f. V.'s plan: 368–76. Slaughter: 377–88. John's rivals: 389–97. Disorder: 406–9; Masada, Engedi: 398–405.

33 Jerusalem, Gadara: JB 4, 410–18 (date 413). Schürer 1973, 498 n. 67 (but cf. 1979, 134f.), argues for Umm Qeis (Gadara of the Decapolis), referred to as a metropolis; cf. Benzinger 1910, 437 followed by Weber 137, n. 1, Thackeray on 413, and Smallwood 310 n. 71; Umm Qeis suits V.'s line of attack less well. Bethennabris: 419–37. Peraea: 438f.; 450.

34 Vindex: JB 4, 440: summary: Nicols 89f. Galba: Flaig 240–92. Date: Levick 1985, 325f.; news in mid-April: Weber 129. V.'s efforts: JB 4, 440–3. Letters: PlG 4, 4; Nicolas 272 believes that V. received one, writtten by the end of 67.

35 Nero recalled: SNero 23, 1; why he fell: Warmington 1969, 155–72; Griffin 1984, 185–207 (expenses).

36 Looting, extravagance: TA 15, 45; 16, 1–3; Griffin 1984, 205–7. Conspirators: n. 5, but esp. TA 15, 48–71. Galba to die: SG 9, 2. Successor: Griffin 189–96.

37 Judaea, Idumaea: JB 4, 443–50. Want of a firm date is suspicious: Weber 141 begins the march only mid-May, Nicols 55 sees JB 4, 443 (the beginning of spring), as c.7 days after the equinox. Antipatris: Schürer 1979, 167. Village casualties (447f.) are particularly implausible. Corea 449.

38 Jerusalem encircled: JB 4, 486–90; capture of 'Gerasa' (Schürer 1973, 499 n. 71): 487f. Smallwood 311, with n. 76, notes Khurbet Qumran (archaeological and numismatic evidence). Surviving fortresses: 555. Simon b. Gioras: 503–44. Hebron: 530–3.

39 Nero's death known: JB 4, 491 (winter, Schürer 1973, 499). End of campaign of 68: JB 4, 497. Weber 139 has the campaign of 68 end 21 June and V., at Caesarea by the 26–27th, hearing of Nero's death by the 30th; Nicols considers 4 weeks too short for a major campaign: two months were required. After arrival in Jericho on 3 June (JB 4, 450), up to three weeks passed before the return to Caesarea: he would arrive about the 16–24th; Alexander knew of the change of government in Egypt by the 21st. Pause for instructions, not wholly cogent: Weber 153. Embassy to Galba: JB 4, 498–502. Events of early 69: TH 1, 1–49; deaths of Galba and Otho, arrival of Vitellius(!): JB 4, 545–9 (Weber 156). Reign of Otho: Flaig 293–355. Jerusalem under John and Simon: JB 4, 556–84; TH 5, 12, 3f.

40 Judaean operations : JB 4, 550–5. Vitellius' victory: 588. Oath: TH 2, 74, 1, with Nicolas 825f.

41 Civil war: JB 4, 491–6; 545–9; but V. neglects Judaea in 502. Simon: 503–44; 556–84. Opening of campaign (close to death of Otho? Some time after Galba's death?) 550. Niese's solution (ad loc.) is followed by Thackeray. (Nicols 47 also dates the move to 68); contra Weber 157. Telescoping: 588–91. Disturbances in Italy begin with the settling of the troops: TH 2, 56; cf. 62; 66; 68; Vitellius enters Rome at 71 (Ch. 4 n. 16).

42 Roads: Isaac and Roll 15–17.

4 THE BID FOR EMPIRE

Garzetti 1974, 622–34 (bibl.). Syme, 'March'; Nicols 40–177; Nicolas; Saddington 1982; 107–36; Wellesley 1989; Flaig 356–416; 451–519. Tacitus: Briessmann 1–83; Syme, Tac. 157–90; Murison 1991, 1693–1706. P. Fabia, REA 5 (1903) 329–82 (Illyricum); Chilver 1957; K. Wellesley, JRS 61 (1971) 28–51 (TH 2, 40). K. Büchner, Die Reise des Titus, Stud. zur röm. Lit. IV (Wiesbaden, 1964) 83–98; Milns 1973; Syme, 'Vestricius'. Townend 1962. O. Montevecchi, Aeg. 61 (1981) 155–70; Rome:

Z. Yavetz, *Hist.* 19 (1969) 557–69, and R. Newbold, *Hist.* 21 (1972) 313–19 (*plebs*). T.P. Wiseman, *AJAH* 3 (1978) 163–75; K. Wellesley, *AJAH* 6 (1981) 166–90 (Capitol); Townend 1987.

1 Declaration: *JB* 4, 592–604; *TH* 2, 79, with Chilver; *SV* 6, 3: 11 July for Judaea (scribal mistake?) for Syria; Kienast 1990, 108; DC 64 (65), 8, 4, with Weber 168 n. 1, Graf 46, Henrichs 52 n. 3. Letter: *JB* 4, 16. Conflicting versions: Graf 33–5. V. and Otho: *JB* 1, 24, with Nicols 73 (Josephus following the official version). According to L. Casson, *Travel in the Ancient World* (London, 1974) 152, ships could not make 10 km an hour; Nicolas 478, has 250 km in favourable circumstances, normal rates 100–150 km a day; the prevailing wind hindered northerly voyages. V.'s motives: Nicolas 1164–7.

2 Prophecy: *JB* 3, 399–408, with Schalit 1975; Rajak 1983, 185–9 (bibl., esp. 189 n. 7). First designs: *TH* 2, 5; *SV* 6. Nero saw the East as a refuge: S*Nero* 47, noted by Nicols 53.

3 T. Vinius, Icelus: *TH* 1, 6, 1; 13, 1f.; 37, 5; 42. Failure to confirm V.: Nicols 61; Flaig 364. Killings: *TH* 1, 6–8; Capito and Macer: 7f.; 37, 3; 58, 2; 3, 62, 2; *SG* 11; Pl*G* 15, 2f. Macer: Murison 1991, 1693–5; A. Kunisz, *L'Insurrection de Clodius Macer . . . en 68 de notre ère. Polska Akad. Nauk* (Wroclaw, etc., 1994); Capito's death: Flaig, 280, Nymphidius' 282–4 (severe on Galba, 196). Reign: Nicolas 431–637. Character: *TH* 1, 12, 2; 18, 1; 49, 2–4. Titus' mission: *JB* 4, 32; 497–501; *TH* 1, 10, 3; 2, 1–4; *ST* 5, 1; Zon. 11, 16, p.49, 1–8D, at DC 64 (65), 8, 3¹; Büchner 97 argues for Tacitus using imperial *commentarii*. Sabinus: Nicols 60f. Nicolas 591–5 associates departure 1 Dec. with news of Galba contemplating adoption.

4 Titus' motives: G. Belloni, *Atti* 1983, 208; Flaig 364 n. 32f. Restoration of Sabinus: *TH* 1, 46, 1, with Chilver (*c.*16 Jan. implied); Pl*O* 5, 4 (March). Discourtesy: *TH* 2, 1, 3; DC 64 (65), 8, 3¹ (cf. Zon. 11, 16, p. 49, 1–8D). Homo 58 sees Galba seduced by Titus' charm – last seen 60. Hostages: *JB* 3, 6.

5 Vitellius' coup: *TH* 1, 12, 1; 51–60; orchestrated: Flaig 326, citing Murison's argument (1979, 191) that Britain was vital (cf. Flaig 336 n. 176); the plot was fomented Sept.–Oct. Tampius a kinsman: 3, 4, 1 (consulship: P.A. Gallivan, *CQ* 28 (1978) 418; W. Eck, *RE* S15 (1978) 97f.; career *AE* 66, 68); advance of 70,000 men (too high): 61–70. Gauls united with legions: Flaig 321. Valens' career: 3, 62. Britain: 1, 60, with Chilver. Nicolas 746f. puts Vitellian forces at 77,000, Otho's at 45,000 (cf. Saddington 109f.). Nicolas 706–11 and Flaig 306 argue that Vitellius' proclamation was concealed until Otho succeeded; concealment, *TH* 1, 50, 1, could not be complete.

6 Ephesus: Wellesley 1989, 43, inferring from *TH* 2, 2, 2. Oracle: *TH* 2, 4, 1f. Josephus' silence: Weber 152 (only *JB* 4, 501, was an indication); see Chilver 1979, 161f.: Tacitus correcting 'cruder propaganda'. Recognition of Otho (*TH* 1, 76, 2; 2, 6, 1) justifying attack on Vitellius: Weber 156. Palm-tree: *RIC* 1², 266 n. 2. Chilver on *TH* 1, 86, 1, suggests that Caesar's statue turning E., Pl*O* 4, 8f., shows Flavian agents active by March.

7 Chilver 1979, 161, notes Josephus exculpating Titus. Eastern and Danubian legions: Flaig 369. Real hesitation: DC 64 (65), 8, 3ᵃ; cf. *JB* 4, 591; *TH* 2, 7, 1; 74–7. Assassination: 75; *SG* 23, with Morgan 1994.

8 Wrangling: *TA* 2, 57f.; 69f.; 13, 9. Shuttling: *JB* 4, 32 and 70 (before 23 Hyp. (Oct.)); apparently in conflict with *TH* 2, 5, 2 (feud ended with Nero's death, followed by Weynand 2634). Traianus' rôle?: Syme *Tac.* 789; Bowersock 1973; Nero's expedition: Nicolas 214 (early autumn; '*hypothèse*' 217 n. 15). Plans of Feb. 69: Nicols 92, cf. Chilver 1957, 34 (Mar.). Mucianus: *TH* 2, 5; 76f., with Graf

34; *JB* 4, 602–5; 3, 8 and 65, suggests that Titus met Alexander at the turn of 66–7: Henrichs 78 n. 93; A. Barzanò, *Atti* 1983, 195–202, postulates a meeting in Cyprus. Agrippa II with Alexander in 66: *JB* 2, 309. Grain: T*H* 1, 73, and Newbold 1972, 316.

9 Ides: T*H* 1, 90, 1, with Chilver; *SO* 8, 3. Otho's generals: 2, 11, 2 (Ap. Annius Gallus *'egregius'*: 4, 68, 1); 23, 4f.; 32f.; 36; undermined by Guard Prefect: 1, 87, 2; 2, 39, 1. Gladiators: 2, 11, 2. Totals: Chilver 269–73, and suggesting, on T*H* 2, 30, 2, that the figures (*c.*54,000; under 30,000) are too high; cf. Garzetti 1974, 210. Balkan reinforcements: Wellesley 1971, 41–5; Chilver on T*H* 2, 46, 1, and 85, 1, and pp. 269–73, rightly doubted a summons as late as 3 Mar. XIV: T*H* 2, 66. Paullinus: T*H* 2, 32; Chilver prefers Pl*O* 8, 2–4. Insubordination: T*H* 1, 80–5; 2, 8–10; 23; 26. Titianus: 2, 23, 5. Peace movement: Powell 838. Chilver on T*H* 2, 41 and 51, hints that Sabinus, who kept his consulship for Apr.–May 69, betrayed Otho. Valens' letter: 55. Bedriacum: Wellesley 1989, 74–89.

10 Sabinus' oath: T*H* 2, 55, 1. Relief: 73. Date of Vitellius' arrival in Rome: Murison 1979, 187. Conduct: T*H* 2, 59f.; Nicols 70. At Bedriacum: T*H* 2, 70, with G.M. Morgan *CP* 87 (1992) 14–29 (ref. due to the kindness of Prof. Nicols). 'Patronage' of Vitellius checking V.: Waters 1963, 214 n. 40. Coinage of Antioch: G. Downey, *A History of Antioch in Syria* (Princeton, 1961) 202f. Disorder: T*H* 2, 7, 1. June conference: 76–8; Ba'al: 78, 3f. Titus with Mucianus: 79. Chronology: Nicols 71f.; Flaig 365 n. 36.

11 Proclamations: T*H* 2, 79f.; MW 41 (so Bengtson 51f.; it may belong to a later episode: Ch. 5).

12 Conference: T*H* 2, 81, 3 (Agrippa's escape). 20–5 July: Nicolas 1170. Kings: *JB* 4, 618–21; T*H* 2, 81, 1 (wealth). Preparations: Saddington 114f. Audiences in Alexandria: Ph*VA* 5, 28. Terms not later used mark the dedication from Perge: *'Imp. T. F. Vespasiano Caesari Aug.'* (*AE* 86, 687).

13 Tiberius: T*A* 1, 47, 4. Blockade: T*H* 3, 48, 3; effectiveness: Wellesley 1989, 125. VI Fer. is claimed by Torelli 1968, 174, for M. Hirrius Fronto Neratius Pansa (n. 58): cf. Hall 1984, 33, and Flaig 575. Collega: Eck, *Sen.* 114 n. 12; 116 n. 24. Invasion from south: T*H* 2, 83, 2, with Syme, *Tac.* 167 and Chilver, also sceptical of the Dyrrachium plan retained once Mucianus knew of Danubian support; the chapter embodies the myth of bloodless victory prevented by Primus' invasion (T*H* 3, 8, 2f.; *JB* 4, 605f.); Flaig 275 rightly stresses that shortage of grain would not win. Danubian movement: below nn. 17, 50. The small task force (T*H* 2, 83, 1) suggests to Nicols 73 and Nicolas, 1092, 1171, that the Flavians always knew that they could rely on Balkan troops. Cavalry: Saddington 115. Speed: 20 km a day: Nicols 74.

14 Money: T*H* 2, 81, 1f.; 82, 1f.; 84 (comments of Flaig 22; 382 n. 94); DC 64 (65), 9, 2. Soldiers' gifts: T*H* 1, 57, 2, with Flaig 335. Mucianus at Rome: DC 65 (66), 2, 5; T*H* 2, 95 (extravagance). Financing: D. Walker, *The Metrology of the Rom. Silver Coinage, BAR Suppl.* 40 (Oxford, 1978) 114–17.

15 Parthians: T*H* 2, 82, 3, cf. 4, 51, 1; S*V* 6, 4. V.'s energy: 82.

16 Vitellius' troops T*H* 2, 56; 88; 93f. (pay: 94, 2; rivalry: 93, 2, cf. 99). Dating: Nicolas 927f.; Coale 49–58, argues for arrival by 4 June.

17 Balkan adherence: 2, 85f.; 96, 1; cf. n. 50, Nicolas 929–31; Wellesley 129. V.'s messengers: T*H* 2, 98. XI Cl.: 3, 50, 1; Nicols 142f.

18 Byzantium and original plan: T*H* 2, 83, 2. Dacians: 3, 46, 2f. Wellesley 1972, 211–15, emends *'gnarus'* to *'ignarus'*: Mucianus, tackling Dacians, was unaware of Cremona. But cf. Syme, 'March': was Mucianus involved? Nicolas suggests (1094, cf. 1120) that Cremona and the Dacians decided Mucianus on the Moesian route in Asia. Rumour of arrival: T*H* 3, 25, 1.

19 Poetovio: T*H* 3, 1–5; date: Nicolas 830 (25–30 Aug.(?)). Primus' control: DC 64 (65), 9, 3f. V.'s orders: T*H* 3, 8, 2. Primus' forces: Nicolas 1019–22. Batavians: T*H* 5, 26, 2f. Flavian fears: Nicolas 945f.

20 Run-up to Cremona: T*H* 3, 6–8. Mistrust of commanders: 10f.

21 Loss of legionaries to Guard: Nicols 159; Flaig 386. Preparations: T*H* 2, 97–100 (troops split up 100, 2f.; 3, 15, 1); Caecina: Nicolas 947–53; Prof. Nicols envisages double-dealing on both sides, forgotten after victory.

22 Caecina's desertion J*B* 4, 634–44; DC 64 (65), 10, 2–4; (and fleet): T*H* 3, 12–14. See Flaig 385; below n. 54.

23 Valens' movements: T*H* 3, 36, 1; 15, 1; 40; Nicolas 897f. Battle and sack of Cremona: J*B* 4, 641–3; T*H* 3, 15–32; DC 64 (65), 11–15; Wellesley 1989, 142–50. Forces: Flaig 386 n. 101: 45,000 Vitellians, and criticizing earlier estimates as too high. Prof. Nicols notes that defeated legions may have been reorganized; junior officers would need watching. Dispersal: T*H* 3, 35.

24 Flight of Valens: T*H* 3, 42f.; 62, 1. Spain and Britain: 44; cf. 53, 3. XI Cl.: 50, 1.

25 Vitellius' reactions: T*H* 3, 36; 54f., with Yavetz 1969, 566f., and Flaig 389–93.

26 Varus: T*H* 3, 36, 2. Origin of II Ad.: Chilver/Townend on 5, 16, 3; contra Flaig 403. Apennines: T*H* 3, 50 3. Nicolas 1094 has Mucianus 1,600 km (Bosporus-Aquileia) behind at the beginning of Oct.; yet he hoped to catch up after Cremona (T*H* 3, 52, 2).

27 Mevania and Misenum: T*H* 3, 55, 3–63. G.M. Morgan, *MH* 49 (1992) 124–30 (ref. due to the kindness of Prof. Nicols), defends Tacitus at 78f., putting Primus in a better light. Effect of displaying head: Nicolas 904f.

28 Negotiations: T*H* 3, 63–5; abdication: 67–9; S*Vit.* 15 (three attempts, see Nicolas 907f.; Murison 1991, 1711); Garzetti 1974, 225, attributes delay to leaders' jealousy of Primus. Sabinus on Capitol T*H* 3, 69–74; awaiting abdication: Nicolas 1010f. On 'Arx', Wiseman 1978; S. height, Wellesley 1981. Grandchildren in refuge: Wellesley 1989, 190. Cerialis: 3, 59, 2; 78, 3–79. Responsibility for fire: P*NH* 34, 38, followed by S*Vit.* 15, 3; J*B* 4, 649; T*H* 3, 71, 4, cf. 75, 3 (Flavians more often blamed); 72, 1 (*'facinus . . . luctuosissimum foedissimum'*); 78, 6 (Cerialis); DC 64 (65), 17, 3. Troop numbers: T*H* 3, 64; 69, 1; Nicols 158; 163. Wellesley 1981, 174. Vitellian praetorians: Nicolas 901f.; others: 1115f.; Othonians: T*H* 2, 67; 3, 24, 3; Urban Cohorts and Watch: 3, 69, 1; H. Freis, *Die Cohortes Urbanae. Epigr. Stud.* 2 (Cologne and Graz, 1967) 13–16. Sabinus' claim: T*H* 3, 70, 2f.; execution: 74, 2. Wallace 350f. is harsh. Tacitus' account: Briessmann 69–83.

29 Delay: T*H* 3, 78; reason: Wellesley 1989, 196; Saturnalia: Nicolas 913; delays in general: 1009–13.

30 March on Rome, embassies, and capture: T*H* 3, 79–84; Nicolas 913–16. Mucianus' arrival: J*B* 4, 654 (one day after Primus! cf. T*H* 4, 11, 1). Callousness: T*H* 2, 55, 1. Vitellius' route: 84, 4–85; Nicolas 1023–5. L. Vitellius: T*H* 4, 2, 2f., with Nicolas 916f. Campania: 4, 3, 1f. Carnage: 4, 1. Dating: Holzapfel 1913, 295–304; 1918, 99–118; Nicolas 919f.

31 V. receives news: J*B* 4, 656 (on arrival); T*H* 3, 48, 3 (Cremona, between Rhinocoloura and Alexandria); 4, 51, 1 (Rome); S*V* 7, 1 (Cremona and Rome). Claudius: Levick 1990, 38. Exactions: above, n. 14.

32 Resources: T*H* 2, 4, 4; 76. Flaig 412f. stresses V.'s need for overall acceptance. Judaea on coinage: Grenzheuser 79. Vettulenus: Ch. 3 n.13. Junior officers: T*H* 2, 5, 2; 81, 3.

33 Calculations: T*H* 2, 74f. Mucianus: 1, 10, 1f. with Chilver; Rogers 1980; Weynand 2634 has Mucianus' reputation making him prefer V. Birth: T*H* 2, 76, 3; Homo 58, 196f., and Wellesley 1989, 117, overestimate; Syme, *Tac.* 791,

suggests Spanish origin. Homosexual: *SV* 13; manner: *TH* 2, 80, 2. Vicissitudes: *PIR*² L 216; with Corbulo: *PNH* 5, 83; Syme, *Tac.* 790, cites geographical knowledge. V. prior in Syria, and a general: Flaig 358–62.

34 Alexander: *TH* 2, 74, 1. Edict: MW 328. For K. Scott, *JRS* 24 (1934) 138–40 Basilides brought V. and Alexander together, for Sullivan 1953, Berenice; nobody is needed.

35 Partisans: *JB* 3, 68; *TH* 2, 81; Agrippa's journey also in *JB* 4, 498–500. Antony's partisans: R. Syme, *The Rom. Revolution* (Oxford, 1939) 273. Resources: above, n. 14. (This paragraph is indebted to the kindness of Prof. J. Nicols.)

36 Anicetus: *TH* 3, 47f. (Aug.–Oct. 69, Nicolas 1173).

37 Military credibility: *TH* 2, 5, 1; 82, 1. Note troops' enthusiasm for the Carmel prophecy, 78, 4: Morgan 1996, 51. Domitian's observation: *TAgr.* 39, 2. Prof. Nicols notes that Verginius became *capax imperii* to his soldiers after defeating Vindex. Contrast with Vitellius: *TH* 2, 73; 76, 4; 77, 3; *JB* 4, 592–5. '*Iudaeorum debellator*': Tert., *Apol.* 5, 7. Galba had jogged: *SG* 6, 3.

38 Respect for Galba: *TH* 1, 10, 3; 2, 6, 1; 76, 2. Piso's significance: Flaig 297 rebutted by Zimmermann 73 n. 87. Verginius: Levick 1985. Birth unimportant: Nicols 167. Emperors' declining status: R. Syme, *Historia Augusta Papers* (Oxford 1983) 189f.

39 Rivals: Sabinus: *TH* 3, 65; 75 (obituary, a stick to beat Vitellians); career: *PIR*² F 352; popularity: *TH* 1, 46, 1 (Urban Cohorts); Wallace 1987. Aelianus: Ch. 2 n. 20. Suetonius: *TH* 2, 37, with Chilver.

40 Merit: Nicols 167, with *TH* 1, 50; cf. 2, 97, 2; Auson., *XII Caes.* 10, 3f. (a persistent view). Vitellius: *TH* 2, 77, 3; 90f.; 3, 86, 1f.

41 Corbulo: Syme, *Tac.* 789f.; 'March' 1013, with Traianus, Nicols 119–24; martinet: *TA* 11, 18, 3–5; 13, 35f. Arrius: *TH* 3, 6, 1; *PIR*² A 1111; betrayal: Verulanus: *TA* 14, 26, 1; 15, 3, 1; cf. *TH* 3, 69, 3. Bolanus: *TA* 15, 3, 1; *TH* 2, 65, 2. Fulvus: *Docs G–N* 51(b); *TH* 1, 79, 5. Alexander: *JB* 2, 309. Networks: I owe this point to Prof. Nicols; contra Flaig 575–85, noting only one officer of Corbulo in the East at the time of V.'s coup (Alexander); that Danubian legates advanced speedily; and that Corbulo's men were not treated as a group by V. Longina: *SD* 1, 3; 3.

42 Prof. Nicols notes that Otho had little time to develop a 'party'. Othonian link: *TH* 2, 75, cf. 77, 3. Otho's letter: *SV* 6, 4. Rubrius: *DC* 63, 27, 1; *TH* 2, 51; 99, 2; *JB* 7, 92. Aquila: *TH* 2, 44, 1; 3, 7, 1. Naso: MW 355 and 421 (Bithynia in 78); cashiered: *TH* 1, 20, 2f., with Chilver; Devijver, *Pros.* 1, 110 no. 139; B. Dobson, *Die Primipilares: Entwicklung u. Bedeutung, Laufbahnen u. Persönlichkeiten eines röm Offizierranges. BJ Beih.* 37 (Cologne-Bonn, 1978) 203f., no. 75 (a ref. I owe to the kindness of Prof. A.R. Birley). Pacensis' career: 1, 87, 2; 2, 12, 1; 3, 73, 2, with Dobson 255 no. 77; cf.; 207f. no. 81 (T. Suedius Clemens); Martialis: *PIR*² C 1404f. Faventius: 3, 57, 1. Epiphanes at Bedriacum: 2, 25, 2. Fuscus: 86, 3, with Syme 1975, 61; Tacitus calls him *dux*; Vienna had militia.

43 Loyalty: *TH* 1, 51, 5 (Lugdunum to Nero); 70, 2; 75, 1 (Procurator and Praetorians to Otho); cf. 2, 46–9; 3, 61, 3; 66; 4, 37, 2 (Vitellianists). Densus: 1, 43, 1 (Piso), with Chilver; *PlG* 26, 8–10. Othonian suicides: *SO* 12, 2. Collective motives: *TH* 2, 37f. 4, 13, 3, does not deny Flaccus patriotism: Wellesley 1989, 174. Seeing who would win: *TH* 2, 86, 4.

44 Executions: *TH* 2, 60, 1; cf. 2, 8, 2 (tokens from Syrian legions to Guard). Flaig 344–8 stresses brutality as Vitellius' worst mistake; the dead of Bedriacum left (like him) unburied. Legionary/auxiliary jealousy: *TH* 2, 88, 1. Favouritism aggravating rivalries: Flaig 351–3. XIV Gem. favoured by Nero: *TH* 2, 11, 1; quarrel with Batavians: 2, 27, 2. Agitation in the E.: 6, 2–72; 79, with

Morgan 1996, 52. Letters to XIV Gem. and I Ad.: T*H* 2, 86, 4; 3, 44. See below, n. 52.

45 Ex-guardsmen: T*H* 2, 82, 3. Significance of change: Flaig 349. Vitellius' new city troops: 93, 2, with Chilver on adherence to Sabinus: they did not get high priority especially as Sabinus was in charge of the change (their pay half that of the Praetorians: Freis 48 (n. 28), based on S*Aug*. 101, 2).

46 Sailors into legionaries: Chilver on T*H* 1, 6, 2; Ravenna: 2, 100, 3; 3, 50, 3. Misenum: 3, 57.

47 Rescue by Valens' troops: T*H* 2, 30; Wellesley 1989, 70. Watch: Nicols 161f; n. 45 above. Verona: T*H* 3, 10, 2f.

48 Contrast between forces: T*H* 2, 76; 3, 2. '*Meliore fato fideque*' on Flavian side: 3, 1, 1. Transfers: 2, 80, 3 (Mucianus); S*V* 6, 4 ('*rumor*', preferred by Graf 47).

49 T*H* 1, 8, 2–9, 3. Verginius a candidate: Levick, 1985. Caecina's ill-treatment: n. 22 above. Caesar's sword: S*Vit*. 8, 4.

50 Moesians: T*H* 2, 85f.; 96; J*B* 4, 619. Danubian legions in E.: Flaig 368. Generals: n. 47 above. XIII: T*H* 2, 67, 2. Fabia 358 draws attention to the initiative ceded to the largest Balkan force. Moesians proclaim V. at Aquileia: S*V* 6, 2f.; S*Vit*. 15, 1, dates the entire revolt to Aug. Supporting Suetonius: Hammond 78, Wellesley 1972, 208f., Barzanò, 1980, and Flaig 373–9, reconstruction 375, with occasion for Aponius' defection before VII Cl. went over (after mid-July). Fabia censures Tacitus' failure to give the outbreak weight; Braithwaite's n. points out that Suetonius' father was tribune in XIII Gem. Graf 43 and Chilver on T*H* 2, 85 (where Flaig 371 n. 52 asks whether it was involved in two episodes or one; the pluperfect '*egerant*' implies two), are sceptical; so Garzetti 1974, 217. Rôle of III Gal. stressed by Nicols 132; cf. Flaig 380: 2, 74, 1; 85, 1; 96, 1; S*V* 6, 3. Fulvus (above n. 41) was not at Cremona, T*H* 3, 10, 1; Syme, *Tac*. 166 n. 7, has him gone to join V.; he might have done more in post.

51 XIV and I: above n. 44; Vitellius; promotions: T*H* 3, 44. Rusticus' action when XX would not swear (T*Agr*. 7, 3): Birley 1981, 269f. and Syme, 'Rusticus' 280f., on MW 464. Reinforcements: T*H* 2, 97f.

52 'Irrational forces': R. Ash in J. Mossman and E. Bowie, eds, *Plutarch and his Intellectual World* (London, 1996) 189–214: events filtered through the glass of 96. Officers' fear: T*H* 3, 26; surrenders: 61. Splits: 1, 7, 2; with Nicols 153f.; Nicolas 1254. *Esprit de corps*: Flaig 378. Nicols postulates an uncommitted officer corps, but each individual made his own calculations.

53 Primus' career: T*H* 2, 86, 1f.; *PIR* ² A 866. *Cognomen* Becco: Syme 1975, 67, on *CIL* 12, 5381.

54 Caecina's career: T*H* 1, 53, 2f.; *PIR* ² C 99. Wallace 350 accepts the unfavourable view; as Prof. Nicols observes, such appointments show contenders desperate for senators (cf. T*H* 3, 4). Caecina and Bassus: 2, 100f.; and the Flavians: 3, 9; 39, 2 (treachery before Vitellius' situation was really precarious); cf. J*B* 4, 635; Briessman 28–45. Valens' career: *PIR*² F 68. As legate of I Valens denounced Verginius to Galba, then assassinated Fonteius Capito: the expected reward, Capito's command, was not forthcoming: T*H* 1, 7, 2; 52, 3; 57, 1. Interpreted by Nicolas 448–51: Valens tried to get Capito to revolt.

55 Festus: T*H* 2, 98, 1; 4, 49, 1, with Nicols 152; consul: *AE* 91, 448. Flavianus: T*H* 3, 4. Flaig 583 distinguishes the Balkan governors: the greatest risk was faced by Flavianus.

56 Silvanus: Wellesley 1989, 156, but calling Bassus (T*H* 3, 50, 2f.) 'a professional servant of the state'. Syme 1975, 66, following W. Eck, *ZPE* 9 (1972) 259f., rates Silvanus higher: designated to a third consulship (83). Tettius' activities: Flaig 375. Aponius: T*H* 2, 85, 2 (murder); 96, 1; 3, 5, 1; 11, 1–3, with Milns 1973.

57 Promises: T*H* 2, 101, 2; Britain: 3, 44. Assured control: I owe this point to the kindness of Prof. Nicols.
58 Varus: T*H* 2, 63, 1; Houston 1972 (possible functions 178); properties: S. Mitchell, *JRS* 64 (1974) 27–39. Marinus: T*H* 2, 71, 2; Wellesley 1989, 109f. Agricola: T*Agr.* 7, 1f., with Ogilvie and Richmond; involved by April: Hanson 37; but drama and Tacitus' concern for his hero to commit himself unhesitatingly are factors. Fuscus and Paulinus: T*H* 2, 86, 3; 3, 43. Pansa (n. 13 and Ch. 9 n. 65): Hall 33, against Torelli 1968.
59 Metz: T*H* 1, 63. Vienna: 66, 1; Spain and Narbonensis joining Vitellius: 76, 1 (*'nusquam fides aut amor: metu ac necessitate huc illuc mutabatur'*); cf. 3, 43.
60 Corsican murders: T*H* 2, 16 (during the Vitellian advance).
61 Mevania: T*H* 3, 59, 1. Apamea: W. Eck, *ZPE* 42 (1981) 242–4; Puteoli and Capua: T*H* 3, 57, 1 (*'municipalem aemulationem'*); 4, 3, 1; Nicolas 989; cf. B. Levick, *G&R* 26 (1979) 121; T*H* 2, 21, 2 (fear of neighbours at Placentia). V.'s 'patriotism': J*B* 4, 589; 616. Cremona: T*H* 3, 30, 1; 32f. Altinum and Opitergium: 3, 6, 2, with Nicols 166. Lugdunum *v.* Vienna: 1, 65, 1. Central Italy: 3, 59, with Nicolas 902. Importance of cities: Flaig 381.
62 V. and the Roman populace: T*H* 3, 69, 1; 74, 2; 80, 1; indifference at end: 83, 1; Flavians known: I owe this point to Prof. Nicols. Galba's memory: T*H* 1, 55, 1. Yavetz 1969, 577; Nicols 164f., citing Newbold 1972. Changing loyalties: Wellesley 1989, 63. Nero's memory: T*H* 1, 4, 2f.; Flaig, sceptical of popularity late in Vitellius' reign, 88 n. 190, notes Flavian difficulties with the *plebs*, 414 .
63 Rewards: T*H* 2, 82, 2; see Ch. 11, with Flaig's reservations 577. M. Ulpius Traianus may have been an intermediary between V. and Mucianus. Traianus, superseded as legate of X Fr. when campaigning was resumed in 70, J*B* 6, 237, may also have accompanied Vespasian to Egypt, but he was road-building in Jezreel in the second half of 69: Isaac and Roll. Expectations of July 69: J*B* 4, 592; 100 *HS* distributed by Mucianus (69), another tip from V. (late summer 70): DC 64 (65), 22, 2; 65 (66), 10, 1ᵃ. Nicols 129f. prefers the 300 *HS* of Augustus' will, totalling *c.*50m Donatives 68–70 and troops paid off by transfer to city units: Flaig 465–9. V.'s policy: Ch. 10 n. 3.

5 IDEOLOGY IN ACTION

Garzetti 1974, 631f. (bibl.). Lattimore; G.W. Bowersock, *Entretiens Hardt* 33 (Geneva, 1987) 291–317. Alexandria: K. Scott, *JRS* 24 (1934) 138–40; P. Jouguet, *Bull. Inst. Egypt.* 24 (1941–2) 21–32; Ph. Derchain, *Chron. d'Egypte* 28 (1953) 261–79; *id.* and J. Hubaux, *Lat.* 12 (1953) 38–52; A. Henrichs, *ZPE* 3 (1968) 51–80; Powell; d'Espèrey 3061–72. Slogans: Wirszubski 97–171; A. Stylow, *Libertas and Liberalitas, Untersuch. zur Innenpolitischen Propaganda der Römer* (Munich, 1972) 48–54; Martin 199–223; Isaac 1984, 143f; A. Watson, *CR* NS 23 (1973) 127f. (*libertas*); Griffin, 1991; Waters. Art, architecture (Ch. 9, bibl.): Hill (coins); Isager; Castagnoli 1981; Bergmann and Zanker; and J. Pollini, *AJA* 88 (1984) 547–55 (reworked portraits); M. McCann, *Röm. Mitt.* 79 (1972) 249–76 (bibl. n. 2). Coins, propaganda, and policies: M. Grant, *Roman Anniversary Issues* (Cambridge, 1950) 88–98; E. Bianco, *RIN* 70 (1968) 145–224; Buttrey 1972; G.C. Belloni, *ANRW* 2, 1 (1974) 1060–6; Kraay; R. Pera, *Atti* 1981, 905–14; J. Babelon, *Hommages Herrmann, Coll. Lat.* 44 (1960) 124–37 (Britannicus). Predecessors: J. Gagé, *REA* 54 (1952) 290–315; Ferrill (bibl.); S. Ramage, *Hist.* 32 (1983) 20 1–14; Griffin 1994; Zimmermann. 'Cult': Scott 1936, 1–39; Fears 1977; J. Deininger, *Die Provinziallandtage der röm. Kaiserzeit. Vest.* 6 (Munich, 1965) 27–32; Fishwick 1987–92; Friesen 1993; R. Herzog, *Urkunden z. Hochschulpolitik der röm. Kaiser, Sitzungsb. d. Preuss. Akad., Phil.-hist. Kl.*

32 (Berlin, 1935) (edicts); Bardon 259–73 and *Atti* 1981, 175–94; Bengtson 146–54; d'Espèrey; M. Durry, in *Hist. et historiens dans l'Antiquité. Entretiens Hardt* 4 (Geneva, [1958]) 215–35 (writings). Patronage: Woodside; Winterbottom; Jones, 1978; Desideri 61–186.

1 Nurturing: T*D* 17, 3; S*V* 15 (injustice only in his absence). *Civilitas*: Graf 138 n. 499. Pliny and Titus: Syme, 'Pliny' 746f.; dedication: P*NH Pr.* 1–12. Pliny's *Hist.*: *Pr.* 20; P*Ep.* 3, 5, 6. The official version is prominent in Weber, esp. 105–8; 136; 183 (V.'s letter to the senate as conclusion); Graf, with stemma, 53. V.'s (war) memoirs: J*V* 342; Titus: 358; 217; d'Espèrey 3079 (Titus helped his father's composition). Bengtson 275 believes that V. wrote 75–9, and is sceptical of memoirs as a source. Josephus' problem: F.W. Walbank in Chr. Schubert *et al.*, eds, *Rom u.d. griechisch. Osten: Festschr. f. H.H. Schmitt* (Stuttgart, 1995) 273–85. J*B* 4–6 written under Titus, 7 Domitianic: Cohen 84–7. J*B* revised: Cohen 17, citing Laqueur 56–96. Authorized by Titus: J*V* 363; dedicated to V.: J*V* 361; J*CA* 1, 50. Titus' clemency: *e.g.* J*B* 1, 27; Yavetz 1975. Josephus a prophet: 77 (cf. 5, 391–3; Jeremiah, cited by Cohen 232); attitude to Titus: M. Stern, *JRS* 76 (1986) 325f.

2 Difficulties: Ch. 13. Ideology/propaganda: Griffin 1991, 23. Simplicity: D*C* 65 (66), 10, 1. Rings: P*NH* 33, 41.

3 Buildings: Ch. 9.1. V.'s sources: Buttrey 1972; Levick 1982; cf. M.T. Griffin, *CAH*² 11, forthcoming: V.'s types 'unoriginal'; so Kraay 1978, esp. 50, 52f. (bronze to 70: few new themes – dynasty, return, liberty, restoration of the Capitol – for development), 55 (*LIBERTAS,* fading: Kraay 1978, 54–6; A. Wallace-Hadrill, *JRS* 76 (1986) 59). *TVTELA*: *RIC* 63 no. 398; 72 no. 480. New buildings on coins: Buttrey 1972, 1 972, 101f. Neronian Concord: Levick 1982, 112f.; other themes: 114f. Vitellius the image of Nero: Ph*VA* 5, 33. Vitellius' Judaean victory type: Ch. 4 n. 6. *AETERNITAS*: *RIC* 28 no. 121(ab); 39 no. 209; 61 no. 384; 65 no. 408 (*P(OPVLI) R(OMANI)*); cf. Tibullus 2, 5, 23; Livy 2, 44, 8; Vell. Pat. 2, 103, 4; *Docs. G–N* 365, 2f. Dr A. Cheung kindly drew my attention to the significance of *SALVS*: Augusta: obv. (21–2; Livia): *RIC* 1, 97 no. 47; revs.: *AVGVSTA, -TI* (Galba): 1, 250 no. 395f.; 256 no. 500. *AVG* (73): *RIC* 21f. nos. 58 and 67; *-TA* (71–8): 70 no. 460, etc.; *–TI* (69–71): 63 no. 392; 74n.

4 Imp. Nero (*Docs. G–N* 25): Griffin 1984, 233, with nn. 69 and 72. Titulatures: Ceausescu 7f.; *RIC* 1, 216; 259f.; L. Vitellius: 262f.; 268 no.7; 272f. nos. 94–8; 'Germanicus': T*H* 1, 62, 2 (an affront to other troops, Flaig 339); S*Vit.* 8, 2. Piso Caesar: MW 2, p. 13. V.'s style in late 69: Isaac 1984; Kienast 1990, 108. 'Augustus': Buttrey 1980, 10f.: papyrus of 16 Sept.: *BGU* 2, 644. *Tabula Siarensis*: J. González, *ZPE* 55 (1984) *e.g.* 58, l. 4; Eck 1996, 38 e.g. l. 4. Vitellius 'compelled' to allow 'Augustus' (with supreme pontificate): T*H* 2, 90, 2; cf. 2, 62, 2; S*Vit.* 8, 2; 11, 2 (18 July); Coale 56 notes him as Augustus in Arval Acts of 5 June (MW 3, l. 14); Caesar: T*H* 2, 62, 2; 3, 58, 3 (with Flaig 338).

5 Milestone: Isaac 1984. Tribunician power: S*V* 12, reading '*ac ne tribuniciam quidem potestatem < . . . > patris patriae appellationem nisi sero recepit*'; scholars supply a copula, < *et* >, <*–que*>, or <*aut* >. Graf 89f., proposed a longer gap: <*nisi invitus* > or <*nisi coactus* >. Possibly there was a reference to the way in which V. used the power. Another explanation, unconvincing, is that the period between the original *SC* and ratification by *comitia* was unusually long (Mommsen, *St* ²⋅ 2, 875 n. 3; Weynand 2635). Successor: T*A* 3, 55, 3. *Dies imperii*: S*V* 6, 3; T*H* 2, 79; Barzanò 1980 interprets it as a concession to Vitellius' legitimacy. Chilver on 1, 47, over-stresses the contrast with predecessors who did not survive to celebrate anniversaries (19 April is referred to as Vitellius' *dies imperii*: MW 2, p. 14). M.T.

Griffin (CAH^2 11, forthcoming) also doubts 1 July as revolutionary: the problem arose only when Galba and Vitellius seized power from outside Rome.

6 New-style ruler: Graf 64. *Arcanum*: TH 1, 4, 2. Marius: E. Rawson, *Phoen.* 28 (1974) 202–6; Sulla: J.P.V.D. Balsdon, *JRS* 41 (1951) 1–10. *Felicitas*: Cic., *De lege Man.* 28.

7 Fortune: Graf 57f., citing A.v. Domaszewski, *Religion des röm. Heeres* (Trier, 1895) 40; JB 4, 622; TA 16, 5, 5 ('*fato*'). Omens: SV 5 (with Graf 36–42 on the sources) has 11; order: Morgan 1996, 42 n. 3, explaining Tacitus' choice. All but two occur elsewhere: oak branch (AD 9); mud (38: in DC 59, 12, 3); dog; ox (both in DC 65 (66) 1, 2); cypress on grandmother's property blown over – to rise again (TH 2, 78, 2: '*iuveni admodum*', where Chilver asks how V. was known to believe prophecies made in his youth; see Morgan; DC 65 (66), 1, 3); Nero's tooth (66–7, in DC); Carmel and Josephus' prophecy (next n.); Nero's dream of Jupiter's chariot leaving the Capitol for V.'s house (in DC); statue (mentioned at Mar. 69 in TH 1, 86, 1; PlO 4, 8f.); eagles fighting (14 April 69); Nile: DC 65 (66), 8, 1, with Scott 1936, 9; Henrichs 1968 suggests an *aretologia* as source; A.D. Nock, *JRS* 47 (1957) 118; De Ste Croix 386. Dio puts the rise after V.'s arrival (November); 28–30 Aug. is the date for Aswan, 5–10 Sept. for Cairo: D. Bonneau, *La crue du Nil. Et. et Comm.* 52 (Paris, 1964) 24 (reference and other help due to the kindness of Dr J. Rea); Weber 255f. defends Dio: the rise was extraordinary. Montou: Bonneau 311 cites E. Drioton, *Fouilles de Médamoud (1926): les inscriptions* 4, 2 (Cairo, 1927) 56 no. 346; statue: PNH 36, 58, with Bonneau 337f.; description: Philostratus, *Imagines* 1, 5 (reference due to Dr K. Forsyth).

8 Ruler from E.: Weber 34–58 (Flavian source); Graf 21–3. Josephus' own prophecy maintains a 'messianic' singular: JB 3, 400–08; cf. 4, 623–6; Morgan 1996, 50 n. 36, accepts his dating. Rajak 185–94 rebuts a messianic element in Josephus and distinguishes the two prophecies, against Zon. 11, 16; his connection with other partisans of V.: Rajak 187, citing Crook 1951, 163 n. 9. Titus' 'miracle': JB 5, 410. V.'s intimations: 3, 404 (after hearing Josephus, 67); 4, 622 (at Berytus, 69); DC 65 (66), 1, 4 (implying the second half of 68). Johanan b. Zakkai: Rajak 188f., with refs n. 7; Smallwood 1976, 314 n. 92. Paphos prophecy: ST 5, 1; TH 2, 2–4, 2; Carmel (convincingly dated to 68 by Morgan 1996, 49): 78 ('*ambages*'); cf. SV 5, 6 (vaguer); both call the god by the name of the mountain. Carmel and Jewish revolt: Oros. 7, 9, 2.

9 V. in Alexandria: TH 4, 81f.; SV 7, with Graf 58–61; DC 65 (66), 8, 1. Primacy of Serapis: DP 32, 12; TH 4, 81, 1; 83f., with Chilver; Paus. 1, 18, 4. 'Basilides' is (1) the priest of Carmel, TH 2, 78, 3; (2) the noble Egyptian (Alexandrian, from his name) acquaintance of V. in the Serapis temple, TH 4, 82, 2; an imperial freedman, SV 7, 1, if the text is correct; (3) an imperial freedman (procurator?) mentioned in a Prefect's edict of 48 (*Docs. G–N* 382, l.35). Scott 1934, 138–40, and 1936 4; 11–13, followed by Henrichs 1968 and Rajak 189, identifies them: Basilides was an emissary to V. from Ti. Alexander, taken by Tacitus for a resident priest of Carmel. (The rheumatism of (2) was advanced in favour: (3), active in 48, was aged); A. Stein, PIR^2 B 60f., distinguished (1) and (2), and hinted at the identity of (2) and (3); Chilver on TH 2, 78, 3, was rightly agnostic. Tacitus' source nodded in giving (1) a name from the later episode: semitic Ba'al was identified with Zeus, but Basilides is Greek. Carmel: O. Eissfeldt, *Der Gott Carmel. Sitzungsb. der deutschen Akad. der Wiss. zu Berlin, Kl. für Sprechen* etc. (Berlin, 1953) esp. 5–14, citing Ps.-Scylax 79M, with 15–24 for his connection with the oracular deity of Heliopolis (*Baal*bek). Second, both authors have (2) ill: so unfit for diplomatic missions. Egyptian participation in the

conference is unattested; the Alexandrians may have been attempting to outdo Carmel.

10 News of Cremona: *TH* 3, 48 3; cf. *JB* 4, 656 (at Alexandria). M.T. Griffin suggests, *CAH* [2] 11 (forthcoming), that the lateness of the miracles in Tacitus is due to dislike of the eastern beginnings of V.'s reign; Flaig 415 sees both authors fitting events to V.'s Romanness, and suspects anti-Oriental propaganda. Early approach: Weber 250–8; Scott 1934; Graf 60; Henrichs 54. Effectiveness and earlier parallels: Derchain 1953, supporting Suetonius' chronology.

11 Nock 118 denies that V. appears as a wonder-worker in his own right. Alexandrian devotion to Antony's family: *Docs G–N* 370, ll.31–4; cf. EJ 320(b).

12 V. as Serapis: Henrichs 71 and comparing V. with Alexander the Great, 55f.; mediator: P.M. Fraser, *Ptolemaic Alexandria* (Oxford, 1972) 2, 803. Alexander's speech: MW 41, esp. ll. 12–16, where Henrichs 71 sees a reference to Serapis (15: *car*; cf. L. Koenen, *Gnom.* 40 (1968), 256); Derchain has the Romans taken in by a lesser ceremony. The foot of the Carmel deity was also particularly venerated: Eissfeldt 15–22.

13 V's difficulties: Flaig 414. Serapis once upper class, and a tutelary deity: Fraser 1972, 1, 246, 248; Serapis and Tyche: Weber 257. Tegea: SV 7, 3.

14 Alexander's responsibility: Bowersock 1987, 301 (with Henrichs 75f.). Alexander in 68: MW 328, with B. Levick, *The Government of the Roman Empire* (London-Sydney, 1985) 179. Henrichs 79 explains Josephus' silence differently: JB 4, 618, revealing that Alexander undertook to win Egypt, is a slip, like JB 7, 123, where V. and Titus spend the night before their triumph in the temple of Isis (not just a token of gratitude: in the Campus Martius Isis was accessible to Titus, who would lose his *imperium* by crossing the Pomerium; but the procession from Isis to Capitol was probably symbolic of their E.–W. progress). The temple, on coins of 71 and 73 (*RIC* 70 no. 453; 78 no. 537, with Hill 212), perhaps refers to this episode, as companion pieces (Mars, Victory, Jupiter Capitolinus) suggest. V.'s loss of favour: DC 65 (66), 8, 4; SV 19, 2, with Ch. 7 n. 22. Titus and Apis: ST 5, 3.

15 Seleucus: *TH* 2, 78, 1; Cramer 130 nn. 447 and 272, identifies him with Otho's Ptolemaeus of *TH* 1, 22, 2, and PlG 23, 4; not named by Juv. 6, 557–9, but Tacitus does not identify them; 'Seleucus', SO 4, 1, is probably a slip; Martin 203f. Divination: Aur. Vict., *Caes.* 9, 4: '*divinis deditus*' (he knew that his sons would succeed him). Barbillus: DC 65 (66), 9, 2, with Cramer 131–46. Bengtson 89 regards V. as sceptical of astrology. Veleda: TG 8, 3; Stat., *Silv.* 1, 4, 90, with Bengtson 68, cf. 136f. (77); oracle: MW 55, after *SEG* 16 (1959) 592, with M. Guarducci, *Rend. Pont. Accad. rom. d'Arch.* Ser. 3, 25–6 (1949–51) 75–87 (V.'s superstition at 80), J. and L. Robert, *REG* 69 (1956) 189f., no. 363; Garzetti 1974, 637; A. Momigliano, *Entretiens Hardt* 33 (Geneva, 1987) 109 (bibl.).

16 Pax: Bersanetti 42 compares Augustus' Ara Pacis. Augustan altars: Hill 220; M. Torelli, *Typology and Structure of Roman Hist. Reliefs* (Ann Arbor, 1982) 38, citing *CREBM* 1, 114 no. 529f.; 123 no. 572, with 261 no. 189. VIRTVS AVGVST. : *RIC* 47 no. 274 (Mars); 56 no., 354f. PACIS EVENT.: 51 no. 308f. (69–70); PACI AVGVSTAE accompanies Victory advancing in 69–71 and 74: *RIC* 52 no. 516; 53 nos. 323, 326; 54 no. 332f.; 55 no. 341f. (Titus); 56 no. 349 (Domitian); 54 no. 337. She ignites a pile of arms in 71: 68 no. 434; 74 no. 493; the legend is found with Nemesis: 31f. nos. 141f., 150 (74–9); and in 73–4 PAX accompanies V. holding a spear and extending his hand to raise a 'towered' woman kneeling before him: 57 no. 356. She is not only 'Augustan', AVGVSTA, but his, AVGVSTI (Stylow 1972, 161 n. 72): *RIC* 50 no. 297 (71); 69 nos. 437–9 (71), etc.; 86 no. 609 (72); 78 no. 534 (73). The ubiquitous VICTORIA occurs in series with PAX: 50 no. 296 (71); 303 (72–3); 93 no. 670 (74); 39 nos. 214–17 (75–9).

ORB(I) TERR(ARUM): 52 no. 317f. (69–70); 53 no. 327; 55 no. 343 (71); 54 no. 338 (74). Tribal dedications: MW 513–16, *CIL* 6, 197. Titus: *CIL* 2, 3732 (Valentia). '*Rabies*': Powell.

17 Peace: PNH 27, 3. Wonders: 36, 101f.; Isager 195f.

18 Triumph: SV 8, 1; JB 7, 119–57 (separate triumphs 121), with Graf 67; DC 65 (66), 12, 1ª; *RIC* 49 no. 294 (?70–1). 'Foreign war': TH 2, 76, 4. Vitellius: *RIC* 1² 268–77 nos. 13–15; 34–8; 46; 61–3; 123f.; 142f.; 151f.; 165; 169; 176; MW 3, cited by Flaig 350. Title: Yavetz 1975, 433 n. 70; *Journ. Jewish Stud.* 44 (1993) 17f. Arches: Ch. 9 n. 14. Spoils carried: JB 7, 148f. MW 53 adorned an arch in the Circus Maximus; the war is not named on the Arch of Titus (Deified: MW 108), but treasures figure; their fate: Schürer 1973, 510. Numismatic commemoration: 509 n. 128; Kraay 52–6, esp. spring and summer 71; *PAX* dominates July–Dec.

19 Salutations: MW 87; dates: Buttrey 1980, 6f.; Kienast 1990, 109.

20 Janus: Oros. 7, 3, 7f.; 9, 8f.; 19, 4, with Syme, *RP* 3, 1192f. Pomerium: Ch. 9.1. Rectifying frontiers: Brunt, 'Tac.' 47; cf. Syme, *l.c.* Claudius: Levick 1990, 107. Campaigns: Ch. 10.

21 V. and Nero: Isager 225–9 (hostility to Vitellius intensified vilification of Nero: Griffin 1994, 311: cf. Ph*VA* 5, 29; *SHA Elag.* 1, 1; 34, 1). Branding a man as a Vitellian was worth doing under Domitian: PNH 1, 5, 2. V.'s troops: JB 4, 592–604; effect of Vitellius' excesses 589–91; slow devastating march: TH 2, 62, 1, Chilver's 'pure Flavian propaganda'; he notes that for Tacitus greed, for S*Vit.* 13f. cruelty as well prevails (but cf. 2, 70, visit to battlefield, and 77, 3); 87 ('*contemptior . . . segniorque*'); Chilver cites Wellesley, *RM* 103 (1960) 287, for a Cologne–Rome march of nearly 14 *m.p.d.*; cf. TH 2, 89; S*Vit.* 11 for military splendour. See also Weber 162 n. 2; Gagé 290f.; Stylow 1972, 48–54; Vitellius' reign: Garzetti 1974, 212–26 (uncritical); Flaig 320–55. V.'s tone: TH 4, 3, 4; cf. DC 65 (66), 10, 1 (70); effect: Ch. 6 n. 3. *LIBERTAS* on coins: *RIC* 46 no. 267 (*PVBLICA* , 69–70); 49 no. 290 (*RESTITVTA*, ?70–1); 68 no. 428 (*AVGVSTI*) – 430 (71); Belloni 1062. Galba's theme: Kraay 52; cf. J.M.C. Toynbee, *The Hadrianic School* (Oxford, 1956) 136. *LIBERT. P. R. VINDEX; ADSERTORI LIBERTATIS PUBLICAE* : *RIC* 65 no. 411; 70 no. 455f. (70 and 71), with K. Kraft, *JNG* 17 (1967) 25; Kraay 55f. '*Adsertor*': Watson. 'Childless': JB 4, 596; Vitellius' legends: *RIC* 1², 264–6f. Portrait: Buttrey 1980, 11.

22 *Dies imperii* : TH 2, 79; SV 6, 3. Erasure: MW 2, pp. 13–15. Otho's avenger: Ferrill 268. Otho rallying Marius Celsus: TH 1, 71. Letter to V.: SV 6, 4. Friendliness towards Otho: Pl*O* 4, 3f., with Nicolas 646f. and Griffin 1994, 311 n. 32. Dr Griffin points out (*CAH* ²11, forthcoming) that feeling might vary between Rome and N. Italy. Otho and Nero: TH 1, 78, 2; S*O* 7, 1 (Golden House). Otho's reign: Flaig 293–320; failings 317f; not rehabilitated: 405 with n. 163.

23 Cf. Waters 208; Stylow 1972, 53 n. 79, citing Gagé 293, and (contra) Timpe 121; Zimmermann 59 (bibl.). Demonstrations: TH 2, 55, 1. Coinage: Kraay 52. Galba's '*honores*': TH 3, 7, 2; 4, 40, 1 (*SC*, Piso's honours abortive); S*G* 23 (statue), with Zimmermann; meaning of the column 62–70, citing H. Jucker, *Chiron* 5 (1975) 362f. V.'s coins: *RIC* 28, no. 119f., with Hill 219, Zimmermann 69 n. 72. Flaig 305 n. 49, 405 n. 166, stresses Galba's exclusion from V's *Lex de imperio* (Domitian rehabilitated him ten days after it was passed) and from later documents: MW 404*B*, l. 8 (94) and Cassiod., *Mon. Germ. Hist., Auct. ant.* 11, *Chron.* 2, 138; but cf. Zimmermann 61 n. 28. Pisones killed: TH 4, 11, 2; 48, 1–50, 3. Irni: González 1986, 153, l. 20, etc.; the Commodan *Tabula Banasitana*, listing even Caligula's citizenship grants, includes Galba, not Otho or Vitellius (explanations A.N. Sherwin-White, *JRS* 63 (1973) 86–98, esp. 90f.). Nero's assassins: S*G* 9, 2. Titus' coinage: *RIC* 148 nos. 245–9; Ferrill 269 (Otho and Vitellius

out). Tacitus on Galba's 'virtues': J. Pigoń, *RM* NF 133 (1990) 370–4; (darker) K. Nawotka, *Phil.* 137 (1993) 258–64.

24 Augustus (stressed by Griffin 1994, 308f.): S*Claud.* 11, 2; Stylow 1972, 53 n. 80. Pliny: see Isager 23f. Actium: Grant 88. Nero's 'innocence': *TA* 13, 4, 1; outstripping Augustus: Sen., *De Clem.* 1, 1, 6. Dynasty: the takeover is shown by sculptural groups: Zimmermann 62 n. 31, cites N. Degrassi, *Rend. Pont. Accad. rom. d'Arch.* Ser. 3, 42 (1969–70) 158–72 (Brescia); K. Hitzl, *Olymp. Forsch.* 19: *Die kaiserzeitliches Statuenaustattung des Metroon* (Berlin-N.Y., 1991) 111–14.

25 Augustan '*Libertas*': Bersanetti 46. Tiberius: S*Tib.* 25, 2; 27–32, 1; *TA* 1, 13, 4; Nero: *TA* 13, 4, 3. Dropped from coins: Stylow 1972, 54. Colosseum: SV 9, 1. Parallels: Graf 81–3, citing *RG* 20, 1, and DC 65 (66), 10, 1ᵃ (building inscriptions). Theatre of Marcellus: SV 19, 1, with Graf 100. Grenzheuser 78 criticizes Timpe 121 for underrating V.'s attention to the previous dynasty; but he notices Claudius.

26 Claudian model: Waters 209; Schmidt 87f. (bibl. n. 18); Flaig 406, but with n. 171; Griffin 1994, 311f., notes ambivalence, the claim of both to '*stabilire*' the state (SV 8, 1; S*Claud.* 11, 1), and in *CAH* ²11 (forthcoming), their industry (Sen., *Cons. ad Pol.* 7, 2). Cult: S*Claud.* 45; SV 9. Titus' education: *ST* 2, 1f.; an issue ascribed to Titus shows Britannicus: *CREBM* 2, 293 no. 306, with H. Mattingly, *NC* 10 (1930) 330–2; Grant 92–4; Darwall-Smith 54, n. 51, reports that Dr I. Carradice considers it Claudian. In Alexandria: Ph*VA* 5, 29. *Pietas*: Graf 82, citing S*Aug.* 31, 5. Potential Nero: *ST* 7, 1, cf. Hitzl, n. 24.

27 Joke: SV 23, 4 (see Ch. 13). Diva Domitilla: Ch. 13, with n. 8. Val. Flaccus' *Proemium* written under Titus: E.M. Smallwood, *Mnem.* Ser. 4, vol. 15 (1962) 170–2, following R. Getty, *CP* 31 (1936) 53–61, against R. Syme, *CQ* 23 (1929) 129–37, and K. Scott, *RFIC* 62 (1934) 474–81; d'Espèrey 3073–5 favours V.; see K. Coleman, *ANRW* 2, 32, 5 (1991) 3091, on the text; Dr P.R. Taylor, University of Birmingham, kindly allowed me to read her persuasive paper before publication. Caledonia: cf. Sil. Ital. 3, 597f., with other echoes of Flaccus.

28 V.'s divinity: *PNH* 2, 18

29 Cult in general: Scott 1936, with 34–7 for spread. Herculaneum: *AE* 51, 217; Formiae: 78, 92 (second half of 70). Pompeii: *Flamen Caesaris Augusti*, *CIL* 4, 1180; H. Mouritsen and I. Gradel, *ZPE* 87 (1991) 149–51, esp. n. 21. Posthumous monuments: Ch. 13 n. 7. Rome: *AE* 10, 197. Tarraco: *CIL* 2, 6095; Philippi: 3, 660.

30 V.'s initiative is accepted *e.g.* by Deininger 1965, 29f. ('*energische Förderung*'), and Hitzl (n. 24) 111 n. 669; the cult of *Divi* with living ruler and Roma grafted on, 114 n. 693, after D. Fishwick *HSCP* 74 (1970) 307. Spain: Fishwick, 1987, 219–39, noting *CIL* 2, 3271, ?first Baetican *Flamen Augustalis*; 3244, with Fishwick, *Hist.* 19 (1970) 96–112; *HSCP* 74 (1970) 299–312. *Flamen divorum*: 1987, 219–39 (Baetica). Narbonensian council: MW 128 (imperial name lost); Fishwick 1964, 349f. (= 1987, 240–56), argues that *IG* 2–3², 4193 shows the first priest Vespasianic. Africa Proconsularis and Nova (Otho's *iura*: TH 1, 78, 1): Fishwick 1987, 257–68; cf. R. Etienne, *Le culte impérial dans la péninsule ibérique d'Aug. à Dioclétien*, BEFAR 91 (Paris, 1958) 447–56; new conventus in N.W. Spain: Etienne 184 (on *CIL* 2, 2637); J. Deininger, *Madrid. Mitt.* 5 (1964) 167–79 (= A. Wlosok, ed., *Röm. Kaiserkult* (Darmstadt, 1978) 441–58). Mauretania and a complete tally: Fishwick 1987, 282–94, denying that activities ascribed to provinces, as in *ILS* 103, imply a *concilium*; caution: Galsterer 1988, 79f., with n. 13 (Stylow 1986 even more cautious). 'Further Spain' refused: *TA* 4, 37f. Lusitania: MW 104 (Mérida), with D. Fishwick, *AJAH* 6 (1981) 89–96. Ipsca: *CIL* 2, 1570, cited by N. Mackie, *Local Administration in Roman Spain* AD 14–212. BAR

Intern. 172 (Oxford, 1983) 126 n. 7; dedication at Olisipo, 73: *CIL* 2, 5217; municipal flamen of (deified) Vespasian and Titus, Tarraco: 6095. *Flamines* for life: Thelepte, Africa: *CIL* 8, 211–16; dated priests: 12028–30; 12039, with 71–3 as the beginning: E. Kornemann, *Klio* 1 (1902) 128f.

31 Houston 1972, 173 n. 26, cites *SEG* 17, 558; *IGR* 4, 1138 and 14, neither dated; MW 89 (to the House and to Nicaea, by Plancius Varus: *kathierosen*); cf. *IGR* 3, 4 (*temenos* and shipowners' 'House', Nicomedia (Izmit)). Houston suggests that Plancius' coins (Halfmann 1979, 104) celebrate V.'s accession, but the two years of his governorship are uncertain. Cestrus: *AE* 72, 644. Prusias: 87, 918. Karanis: *IGR* 1, 1120 (79), cf, 1119 (61); cf. Ch. 12 n. 16.

32 *Maiestas* : R.A. Bauman, *Impietas in Principem. Münch. Beitr. z. Papyrusforsch.*, etc. 67 (Munich, 1974), esp. 157–9; amnesty: DC 65 (66), 9, 1. *Maiestas* under V.: Ch. 6 and 13.

33 Articulate: Aur. Vict., *Caes.* 9. 1; 'Cato': Bengtson 90. V. quotes Greek: SV 23, 1, with J.F. Berthet, *REL* 56 (1978) 321. At Museum: Herzog. Sons' skills: Ch. 12; comet: *PNH* 2, 89, cf. *TA* 14, 22, 1. 100k *HS* for rhetors: SV 18. Quintilian: Juv. 7, 186–9. Teachers etc.: MW 458 (27 Dec. 75; 93–4), with Herzog and (more cautious) W. Hartke, *Gnom.* 14 (1938) 507–12; *TAPA* 86 (1955) 348f.; not philosophers or jurists: Herzog 16f.; immunity from billeting: *Dig.* 50, 4, 18, 30, but cf. Herzog 19f. He suggests that V.'s Alexandrian secretary (libraries, correspondence, and replies to embassies), Dionysius, son of Glaucus (*Suda s.v.*), drafted the Greek version. Vitellius' dish 'the shield of Minerva', S*Vit.* 13, 2, may have been a joke against the Flavians. Control: d'Espèrey 3053.

34 V. patron: *PNH* 2, 117; SV 17; 18f.; Eutrop. 7, 19; Woodside for social purpose. Dionysius' friend Leonidas: C. Cichorius, *Röm. Stud.* (Leipzig-Berlin, 1922) 365–7; Apellaris: Graf 100, with n. 551. Saleius Bassus: TD 9, 5; Juv. 7, 80–7 (possibly Statius). Venus in Temple: *PNH* 36, 27. Privileges of *technitae*: F. Poland, *Gesch. des griech. Vereinwesens* (Leipzig, 1909) 125; Millar, *ERW* 459f.

35 V.'s influence: *TA* 3, 55. *Panegyric*: Durry 1958, 231–5. Hierarchy and luxury: A. Wallace-Hadrill, *G&R* 37 (1990) 85–92.

36 Classicism: E. Cizek, *L'Epoque de Trajan* (Bucharest-Paris, 1983) 496–593. Cicero: Q*IO* 12, 10, 12; TD 26, 7–9; Sil. Ital. 8, 406–11; cf. 12, 218–20, with A.J. Pomeroy in A. Boyle, ed., *The Imperial Muse* (Bendigo, 1990) 132–5. Quintilian: Syme, *Tac.* 103f., on Q*IO* 10, 1, 122, against Tacitus (date and style of TD: 670–3); so Bengtson 149. Pliny his pupil: P*Ep.* 2, 14, 9; 6, 6, 3: see McDermott 1972–3, 347, on Salvius Liberalis. Virgil: Statius, *Theb.* 12, 816f., P. Hardie in Boyle, 3–20, with n. 15. Italicus, Cicero, and Virgil: Mart. 11, 48. Statius: D. Hall in Boyle, 98–118; M. Dewar, ed., *Statius, Theb. IX* (Oxford, 1991) xv-xvii; theme of *Theb.*: W. Dominik in Boyle, 74–97; contrary views n. 9. Italicus' industry: P*Ep.* 3, 7, 5; theme: Pomeroy in Boyle, 122–5. Tributes: Flaccus 1, 1–21 (date: n. 27); Italicus 3, 594–600; Stat., *Silv.* 1, 1; *Theb.* 1; 'fury': D. McGuire, jr., in Boyle, 23, citing F.M. Ahl, *ANRW* 2, 32, 1 (1984) 85–102. Poet's rôle: M. Davis in Boyle, 70, citing Flaccus 4, 558; Bardon 298f., 311–13, has Flavians tolerating literary opposition. 'Court' poets: d'Espèrey 3072.

37 Architectural novelty: G. Lugli, *Atti. 3° Convegno naz. di st. dell'architett., Assisi 1–4 Ott. 1937* (Rome, 1939) 95–102. Portrait painting out: *PNH* 35, 4. Priscus: 35, 120; Isager 133 overplays the point. Sculptural 'illusionism' passing to classicism: McCann 249; 262. Fourth style: Garzetti 1974, 636 (bibl.); J. Liversedge in M. Henig, ed., *Handbook of Roman Art: a survey of the visual arts of the Rom. World* (Oxford, 1983) 86; R. Brilliant, *Visual Narrative: story-telling in Etruscan and Rom. art* (Ithaca-London, 1984) 66–83, links it with the rising taste for the novel. Claudian: V.M. Strocka in V.M. Strocka, ed., *Die Regierungszeit*

des Kaisers Claudius (42–54 n. Chr.): Umbruch oder Episode? (Mainz, 1994) 191–220.

38 Italicus' gods: Pomeroy in Boyle, 123 n. 35, on J.G.W.H. Liebeschuetz, *Continuity and Change in Roman Religion* (Oxford, 1976) 167–81. Egyptian gods: Henrichs 76. Christianity: Ch. 9.

6 A NEW EMPEROR AND HIS OPPONENTS

Hammond; Waters; Griffith. Beginnings: Levi 1938; Briessmann 84–105; Kraay. Advisers: Crook 1955; P.A. Brunt in P. Kneissl and V. Losemann, eds, *Alte Gesch. und Wissenschaftsgesch.: Festschrift f. K. Christ zum 65. Geburtstag* (Darmstadt, 1988) 39–56; P.A. Gallivan, *CQ* NS 24 (1974) 306f. (Vibius); Bradley; Winterbottom. Trials: R.S. Rogers, *TAPA* 80 (1949) 347–50 (*TH* 4, 44); Evans. Opposition: Toynbee 1944; Wirszubski 124–71; Grenzheuser 70–86; A.R. Birley, *CR* NS 12 (1962) 197–9; R. MacMullen, *Enemies of the Roman Order* (Cambridge, Mass.-London, 1967) 46–94; rev. O. Murray, *JRS* 59 (1969) 261–5; Brunt 1975; Melmoux; U. Vogel-Weidemann, *Acta Class.* 22 (1979) 91–107; Malitz; Syme, 'Group'; d'Espèrey 3056–61; Pigoń; M. Griffin in M.-O. Goulet-Cazé and R. Goulet, eds, *Le Cynisme ancien et ses prolongements* (Paris, 1993) 241–58.

1 '*Cuncta . . . solita* ': *TH* 4, 3, 3; cf. DC 65 (66), 1, 1; date: Holzapfel 1918, 103; Kienast 1990, 108; Nicolas 1059 opts for the 22nd. Further motions of Asiaticus: *TH* 4, 4, 3. Consulships: A.E. Gordon, *CP* 50 (1955) 194f. Priesthoods: *RIC* 18, no. 29f.; 32 no. 148. Supreme Pontificate: n. 35. Youth Leaders: MW 85. Delegation: n.10 .

2 Declaration of Galba: DC 63, 29, 1 (with Zon. 11, 13, p. 42, 10–20D) and 6 (senate and people). Otho: on *c.*16 Jan. the Arvals sacrificed '*ob imperium imp. Othonis*', MW 2, p. 13; cf. *TH* 1, 47, 1: '*tribunicia potestas et nomen Augusti et omnes principum honores*'; on the 26th for *comitia* for consulate, p. 13, on 26 Feb. for tribunician power, p. 13, on 5 March for priesthoods, p. 14, and on the 9th for Supreme Pontificate, p. 14. Vitellius: on 30 April they celebrated tribunician *comitia*, p. 14, on 1 May the '*diem imperfii Vitelli German. imp., quod XIII K. Mai. statut. est*', p. 14; cf. *TH* 2, 55, 2: '*cuncta . . . statim decernuntur* '; pontificate: ch. 5 n. 4.

3 Instant taking of powers: DC 59, 3, 2 (Gaius); JB 4, 654f. V.'s letter: *TH* 4, 3, 4 '*tamquam manente bello*': Weber 253. Consistently '*civilis et clemens*': SV 12; DC 65 (66), 10, 1; cf. A. Wallace-Hadrill, *JRS* 72 (1982) 42–8, positing (47) a correlation between civility and respect for the social order itself for V. and Augustus; but only prudence was necessary. Grenzheuser 80 overstresses *TH* 4, 3, 3, '*laetus et spei certus*': civility is second to restoration of peace.

4 Funeral: *TH* 4, 47; MW 97. Mucianus' letter: *TH* 4, 4, 1. Arrival: n. 6. Priscus' suicide: 11, 3.

5 *TH* 4, 39, 1; Nicolas 1086; cf. 1069f. At 1103 he argues implausibly that Domitian got his praetorship only because Mucianus was in Rome (n. 6): Grypus was the first recipient. Chilver on *TH* 2, 85, 2, holds that Tettius kept his office.

6 25 Dec., Syme, 'March' 998. Nicolas 1101–6 implausibly dates Mucianus' arrival (*TH* 4, 11, 1) to about 1 Feb., arguing that DC 65 (66), 2, and modern writers are influenced by the inaccurate *JB* 4, 654 (day after the death of Vitellius) and by *TH* 4, 39, 2; Bengtson 59 seems to favour 21 Dec. '*Socius imperii* ': 2, 83; cf. Vell. Pat. 2, 127f., with A.J. Woodman. Mucianus' supremacy: *TH l.c.*; DC 65 (66), 2, 1–3 (ring); Agrippa: DC 53, 30, 2. '*Trahere in se*' of earlier encroachments: *TA* 1, 2, 1; 11, 5, 1. Executions: *TH* 4, 11, 2 (Galerianus); 80, 1 (Vitellius' son); 4,

39, 3 (Scribonianus). Vitellia: SV 14; [Epit. Aur. Vict.] *Caes*. 9, 2. Clean hands: DC 65 (66), 2, 5. Mucianus and Marcellus: TH 2, 95, 3.

7 Primus–Mucianus feud: TH 3, 52, 2–53, 3. Domitian saluted: 86, 3; friends: 4, 68, 2. Varus and Primus stricken: 11, 1; 39, 3. Varus' transfer: 68, 2. Tarraconensis: MW 261. Primus' reputation: TH 3, 28; 49; 52, 3; 53, 3; 4, 1; 39, 3 (involvement with Scribonianus); 80, 2f.; JB 4, 642.

8 Senate's rôle: TH 1, 84, 3f. Galbian *libertas*: 1, 4, 3. Homo 297 favours Eprius; career: Bradley. New men and attitudes: Grenzheuser 81. Agrippinus and Rusticus: Malitz 245, citing MW 435 and Epict. 1, 1, 28–30; 2, 12f.

9 Helvidius' speech: TH 4, 4, 3 ('*bonus*' against Halm's '*novus*').

10 Embassy: TH 4, 6, 3–8, 5, with Pigoń 237f. (Trajanic evidence for importance of friends) and n. 12 (Nero's victims). He questions (243 n. 39) whether the old practice had been universal. Asiaticus: Townend 1962, 125–9 (why Tacitus suppressed his name); Levick 1990, 61–4. Helvidius–Vitellius quarrel: TH 2, 91, 3; DC 64 (65), 7, 2. Third 'friend': Ch. 3 n. 6.

11 Hostility to 'friends': TA 3, 30; Dr Pigoń compares TH 4, 80 (Primus). V. needing *consilium*: 4, 7, 3; 8, 2. Pigoń writes on *iudicium senatus*, and Griffin, *CAH*² 11 (forthcoming) notes prophecy in Eprius' remarks.

12 V.'s *consilium*: Pigoń 237, citing PPan. 45, 3, for Trajan's choice; Crook 1955, 48–52. Crispus under Domitian: Pigoń 245 n. 47. 'Fish council': Juv. 4, 37–154, with Griffith. Pegasus probably post-dates V. as City Prefect, *pace Dig*. 1, 2, 2, 53: Syme, *RP* 4, 260, on Juv. 4, 77 ('*modo*'). Titus: ST 7, 2.

13 Nerva's and Trajan's friends: DC 68, 2, 3; PPan. *l.c.*; *SHA Sev. Alex*. 65, 5; Crook 1955, 53–5.

14 Capitol; economy commission: TH 4, 9 (Ch. 7 and 9.1); Helvidius' interest: Malitz 236; Darwall-Smith 43f., citing Lana, *Atti* 1981, 1, 89. Vestinus: TH 4, 53, 1. Hod: DC 65 (66), 10, 2, with De Ste Croix 195.

15 Helvidius–Marcellus: TH 4, 6; 43. Wellesley 1989, 211, remarks that the meeting of 1 Jan., hardly summoned by Vitellian consuls, was assembled by Frontinus. Celer: TH 4, 10, with Evans. Date for trial: TH 4, 10; 40, 3; two hearings: Rogers 1949, 348; 9 Jan.: Brunt 1977, 104, followed by Chilver/Townend *ad loc.*; 15th: Malitz 237.

16 Archives: TH 4, 40, 3; 3 Jan.

17 Oath: TH 4, 41, 1, with Chilver for Africanus' fate; Crispus: Juv. 4, 89f., with Griffith 139f.; relations with Vitellius: DC 64 (65), 2, 3; attack on Regulus: TH 4, 42; 3 or 15 Jan.

18 Montanus and Helvidius: TH 4, 42, 2–43, 1. *SC Turpilianum*: Rogers 1949.

19 Confusion: TH 4, 11, 1 (till Mucianus' arrival).

20 TH 4, 44f. (early Jan.: Syme, 'Ministers' 527). Sagitta: TA 13, 44; Sosianus: 16, 14; Dr Pigoń notes that the visit of 66 would not have lasted until 70. Italy and public provinces: TA 13, 4, 3, with Levick 1990, 188.

21 *Lex*: MW 1 (modern title: *CIL* 6, 930); M.H. Crawford, ed., *Roman Statutes* (London, 1996) 1, 549–54 (bibl., tr.). Mommsen, *St*. 2, 876; G. Rotondi, *Leges publicae populi Romani* (Milan, 1922; repr. Hildesheim, 1962) 469f.; F.B.R. Hellems, *Lex de imperio Vespasiani. Journ. Phil*. 28 (Diss. Chicago, 1933); H. Last, *CAH* 11, 404–8; Levi 1938, 8–12; 1975, 187–9; Bersanetti 48f.; Hammond 1956, 9–12; Grenzheuser 70–6; 227–45 (bibl.); M. Hammond, *The Augustan Principate . . . during the Julio-Claudian Period*² (N.Y. , 1968); Garzetti 1974, 629–31 (bibl.); Brunt 1977; Bengtson 63–5; Nicolas 1059; De Ste Croix 1981, 385f.; Wellesley 1989, 207; A. Pabst in W. Dahlheim *et al.*, eds, *Xenia: Festschr. R. Werner, Konst. Althist. Vorträge u. Forsch*. 22 (Constance, 1989), 125–48 (bibl. 141 n. 7).

22 Experts: Pegasus, Nerva, Sabinus? Wrangling: cf. P*Ep.* 3, 20, 1–9; 4, 25. Recess: Talbert 209f.

23 Journey and arrival (hardly as *privatus*, Grenzheuser 180 n. 23, based on DC 65 (66), 10, 1): Aug./Sept.: Halfmann, *Itinera* 178; 180; arrival at end of Sept.: Malitz 238; first half of Oct.: Kienast 1990, 108; cf. Graf 128 n. 329; in Brundisium (Brindisi) 25–30 Sept., after a journey begun 25 Aug.; Rome *c.*10 Oct.: Nicolas 1054 (cf. 1080, end of Oct.). Weber 258–60 notices JB 7, 9, showing that V.'s welcome in the Greek East was known at Caesarea by the beginning of Oct.: he had departed Alexandria in the second half of Aug. The route was Rhodes–Ionia–Greece–Corcyra–Iapygia, thence by land: JB 7, 21f. (leaving before the fall of Jerusalem); DC 65 (66), 9, 2ªf., has only Lycia, by land and sea to Brundisium. Welcome: JB 7, 63–74; upper class: 68. Weber 259–63 notes *RIC* 18 no. 31f.; 19 no. 35. Helvidius: SV 15.

24 Titulature: Ch. 5.

25 DC 65 (66), 12, 1; precision may be apparent only in Xiphilinus' summary (206, 30–208, 1, R. St). Praetors *v.* tribunes: TA 1, 77, 2; 13, 28, 2. Tolerance: S*Tib.* 19; TH 2, 91.

26 Paetus *'exemplar verae gloriae'*: TH 2, 91, 3. Braithwaite's view: on SV 15, based on DC 65 (66), 12. Birley 1975, 142, rightly dismisses the extreme view of M.P. Charlesworth, *CAH* 11 (1936), 9; Wirszubski 149 is too restrictive. See Griffin 1976, esp. 100–3.

27 Thrasea criticized: TA 13, 49, with *'libertate senatoria'* at issue; who his critics were is in dispute, as Dr Pigoń reminds me; perhaps opponents of Nero; but see Wirszubski 139. Helvidius criticized: TH 4, 6, 1f. Fine example, persistent attendance: Epict. 1, 2, 18–24. Melmoux 40 notes *'manque de finesse'*; cf. Toynbee 53 ('disillusioned', 'bitterly disappointed'). Rôle of Dio of Prusa: Moles 86 n. 59; Sidebottom n. 53 also accepts the rôle implied by his work *Against the Philosophers* (Synes., *Dion* 37b) and his link with Nerva, *cos.* 71.

28 Succession crisis: Schmidt 84, citing Grenzheuser 82–6, and Malitz. Graf 108 stressed the predictive character of V.'s asseveration: so Cramer 267 (on astrological grounds); Martin 202f. Tiberius: S*Tib.* 30; TA 3, 56f. (*'petebat'*). Drusus' advancement: TA 2, 44, 1; Titus' implied: DC 65 (66), 12, 1; exile of philosophers at 13, 1f.; Helvidius' death at 12, 3. Sons to succeed, SV 25, cf. Aur. Vict., *Caes.* 9, 4; Eutrop. 7, 20, with Birley 1975, 151, n. 46; *'liberi'*: TH 4, 8, 4.

29 'Adoption' of Piso: TH 1, 15, with Parsi 12–14; Titus 171–3. Adoption: *SEHRE* 586 n. 16; cf. d'Espèrey 3057 n. 52; Grenzheuser 86 on its effect. Murison 1991, 1699, believes that Galba went on to conventional adoption. Waters 205 has Galba's words composed by a Tacitus inspired by the action of Nerva. Vitellius: Waters 206, with TH 2, 59, 3; 89, 2; 3, 66, 2 .

30 Relegation and execution: SV 15; reason: DC 65 (66), 12, 2. In Dio Helvidius plays his part between the return of Titus and the dedication of the Temple of Peace, 75. Exile after the debate on Titus' power: cf. *'altercationibus insolentissimis'*, SV 15; so Brunt 1975, 28–31. Toynbee 56f. widens the causes. Pigoń 240, with n. 25, notes the difficulty of specifying them; dynastic disputes are 'almost impossible to prove' (but he observes, 241, that Marcellus at TH 4, 8, 4, throws V.'s possession of sons in Helvidius' face). Further, SV 25 (cf. Aur. Vict. and Eutrop., n. 28 above) ascribes V.'s determination to a time *'post assiduas . . . coniurationes'*, suggesting a later date than 71. Graf 94, proposing a twofold source, one pro-Flavian and known to Suetonius, the other hostile (Herennius Senecio's biography of Helvidius), rejects the association. Perhaps Dio or his epitomator conflated two unrelated events, Helvidius' quarrel with V. and V.'s

protestation. But what stress can be laid on SV 25, given his bias? (Cf. *'propter assiduos barbarorum. incursus'*, SV 8, 4, discussed Ch. 10). There are later disturbances in ST 6, 1, not to be dated by coins of ?74–9 inscribed *IOVIS CVSTOS* (*RIC* 28 no. 124; 36 no. 176; 39 no. 211), implausibly connected with them by H. Mattingly, *CREBM* 2, xxxix. Syme, *Tac.* 212, held 74 the crucial year ('ruin'; cf. Birley 1975, 152 n. 53, assuming he means death), 671 ('banishment'); 'Ministers' 530f. ('banishment and then execution'), with Eprius (suff. II 74) as chief agent. Birley puts the exile in the censorship: but Helvidius' remark, Epict. 1, 2, 19, that V. could end his rank was true at any time. M.T. Griffin, *CAH*[2] 11 (forthcoming) associates the relegation with Eprius' consulship as well as the censorship. Braithwaite regarded the tribunician arrest of DC 65 (66), 12, 1, as a doublet of the episode of TH 2, 91, 3, but repetition of tried methods is plausible (not so Probus' claim, Sch. Juv. 5, 36, that Helvidius was previously tried and acquitted under V., nor Bersanetti's, 56 (he was inciting popular revolution). *CONCORDIA SENATVI: RIC* 67 no. 418; the preceding *CONCORDIA AVGVSTI* is less acquiescence, more unity imposed. Busyness of the mint in 71: Kraay 51. Ostensible charges and real gravamen: Dr Pigoń notes that in 25 Cremutius Cordus' attack on Sejanus was the real, unpublicized reason (Sen., *ad Marc.* 22, 4; TA 4, 34, 1), and that TH 4, 9, 2, ends: 'There were some who remembered it [his proposal about restoration of the Capitol]', suggesting its use in accusations (he compares TA 16, 21, 3). The execution, Pigoń 240 n. 25, notes, may have been later than Syme believed (74): TD 5, 6 seems to imply that he was alive at the dramatic date of the work (V.'s sixth year: 17, 3; Syme, *Tac.* 670f). Cynics, 75–6: DC 65 (66), 15, 5, with Sherwin-White 1966, 425, and Levi, *Atti* 1983, 167 also for 75, against Braithwaite on SV 15. But, as Mrs B. Mitchell points out, it is tempting to associate the execution with Marcellus' return. Griffin *l. c.* points out the significance of date, *personae*, and subjects (Curiatius Maternus had just offended by reciting his *Cato*); 'condemnation' of Maternus: A. Cameron, *CR* NS 7 (1967) 258–61. End of *LIBERTAS*: Ch. 5 n. 3. Other adherents of Thrasea and Helvidius: Syme 'Ministers'; J. Devreker, *Gnom.* 52 (1980) 351f.

31 Sects distinguished by Homo 294f., with Dio of Prusa as loyalist; Griffin 1993. Helvidius and street philosophers: DC 65 (66), 13, 1, and l[a] ('Stoics'; accepted by Toynbee 53); attacks on Titus and Berenice: 15, 5; cf. DP 32, 9, *c.*71–5 acc. to Jones 1978, 134. Principles: Garzetti 1974, 240. Wirszubski 149. Grooming: PEp. 1, 10, 7. Blossius: Plut., *Ti. Gracch.* 20, 3; Dudley, *JRS* 31 (1941) 94–9. Augustus: G.W. Bowersock, *Augustus and the Greek World* (Oxford, 1965) 30–41. Philosophers' rôle: Malitz is sceptical; Syme, 'Group' 569; 'putting evidence on persons', 573; E. Rawson in M.T. Griffin and J. Barnes, eds, *Philosophia Togata* 1 (Oxford, 1989) 248–50. Thrasea: Wirszubski 138. Grenzheuser 180f. n. 25 holds V. himself influenced by philosophy; Sidebottom 1996 trenchantly criticizes such views.

32 Musonius excepted: Griffin 1993, 248; Desideri 29; 63; 67. Astrologers: DC 65 (66), 9, 2 (before V.'s arrival), with Cramer 244f. Malitz 241 n. 68 cites previous intercourse: PhVA 5, 27–38 (Ch. 5); Sherwin-White on PEp. 3, 11, 5, dates the expulsion *c.*74 or earlier. Mucianus' hatred: DC 65 (66), 13, 1 and l[a]. Misrepresentations: Griffin 246–8. Tutilius: *ILS* 7779 (Rome). Musonius' return: Eus.-Jer., *Chron. s.a.* 79, p. 189 Helm, before dedication of the Colosseum; see H. Sidebottom, *Hist.* 41 (1992) 414.

33 Friends: above, nn. 10f. Homo 197–202; TH 1, 10, 1f.; 2, 84, 2. Mucianus (and Marcellus?) blamed for V.'s 'parsimony': 95, 3; accomplished orator: 80, 2; date of death: Syme, 'March' 1011. *'Ego tamen vir sum'*: SV 13; Marius: Cic., *Tusc. Disp.* 2,

53, with T.P. Wiseman, *New Men in the Roman Senate 146 BC–14 AD* (Oxford, 1971) 113. Marcellus: *PIR*² E 84. Crispus: T*H* 2, 10; Juv. 4, 81–93.

34 Mucianus helps Marcellus: Crook 1951, 163. Marcellus and Crispus as V.'s friends: T*D* 5, 7 (Marcellus' success due to oratory, with Helvidius as his defeated antagonist; Pigoń 244 doubts whether the senate was as hostile as Tacitus makes out); 8, 3; D*C* 65 (66), 16, 3. Crispus' charm: Syme, 'Ministers' 530. Bradley 174f., 178, posits a connection between Sabinus and Marcellus 48–54 when they were respectively governor of Moesia and (?) legate of IV Scyth. (Sabinus' dates: Ch. 2 n. 21). Wealth: T*A* 16, 33, 4 (Marcellus', for prosecuting Thrasea); T*H* 2, 10, 1 (Crispus); T*D* 8, 2. Crispus and the Plinies: Syme, 'Pliny' 764f. Pigoń 229f. points out that T*D* 13, 4, like T*H* 4, 7, 3 (*'reformidet'*), foreshadows Marcellus' fate. 'Conspiracy': Crook 1951; Ch. 12. Catullus: T*Agr.* 45, 1; P*Ep.* 4, 22, 5; Nerva: *PIR* ² C 1227; Sidebottom 1996, 456, suggests that he procured citizenship for Dio of Prusa. D. Novius Priscus: *PIR*² N 187, Lower German legate *c.*79–81; L. Ceionius Commodus: C 603, governed Syria 78–81/2.

35 'Tainted': Evans 102. Cerialis: Birley 1975. Verginius: Levick 1985.

36 Delayed arrivals at Rome: Nicolas 481. Pontificate: Weynand 2636; L. Gasperini in *Scritti stor.-epigr. in mem. di M. Zambelli* (Rome, 1978) 130–2; Buttrey 1980, 13; Isaac 1984, 144 n. 5: late 70. *Redux*: *RIC* 15 no. 4 (Augustus: *RIC* 1², 45 no. 53–6); MW 4 (Arvals); a dedication by a Roman corporation of 13 Oct., year unknown, is suggestive (MW 515); see Kraay 53. *Pater Patriae*: SV 12 ('*sero*', Ch. 5 n. 5); Braithwaite's dating, before 1 July 70, is ill-founded; before Oct.: Buttrey 1980, 13. Cancelleria reliefs: Magi; Ch. 12 n. 12. Double triumph: Val. Max. 2, 8, 2.

37 Changes: Wiegels, 'Hispanier' 198; Aelianus never reached Tarraconensis: MW 261: '*legatum in Hispaniam ad praefectur. urbis remissum*'; 'intrigue or a pestilence at Rome': Syme, 'Ministers' 529, citing Bosworth 1973, 75; cf. W. Eck, *ZPE* 37 (1980,) 60f. (he left after 21 June, when he attended the Capitol ceremony: T*H* 4, 53, 2f); M.T. Griffin, *CAH*² 11 (forthcoming) postulates disagreement on appointments; '*res iniudicata.*', K. Wachtel in *PIR*² P480, p. 198.

38 Plebs: SV 18; Ch. 9 n. 2. Humour, and Pompusianus: SV 14; S*D* 10, 3; D*C* 67, 12, 3; Cramer 267; Jones, *Dom.* 186. Horoscopes: (e.g.) T*A* 2, 30, 1. Accent: SV 22.

39 Waters 214–16; 218. Vitellius: MW 81; S*Vit.* 11, 2 (dating to July 69: see Chilver on T*H* 2, 91, 2; it was Nov.: 3, 55). Flavian consuls: Gallivan 1981, 213–20.

40 Censorship: Buttrey 1980, 15; 23. Jones, *Hist.* 21 (1972) 128, takes mention of censorship on inscriptions after 74 to entail retention of powers. Claudius: Levick 1990, 98–101.

41 *Histories*: P*NH Pr.* 20. In D*C* 65 (66), 13f., Musonius' recall: n. 32. Delators discouraged by Titus: Mart. 4, 5, 4; S*T* 8, 5; D*C* 66, 19, 3; (verbal) *maiestas* 'abolished': 19, 1f., with P. A. Brunt in *Sodalitas. Scritti in onore di A Guarino. Bibl. Labeo* 8 (Naples 1978) 469–80; lenity: Eutrop. 7, 19 (untechnical?). Tiberius: T*A* 2, 34, 1; Levick 1976, 183–200.

7 FINANCIAL SURVIVAL

K. Hopkins, *JRS* 70 (1980), 101–25; R. Duncan-Jones, *Money and Government in the Roman Empire* (Cambridge, 1994). Treasuries: A.H.M. Jones, *JRS* 40 (1950), 22–9 (= *Stud. in Rom. Government and Law* (Oxford, 1960) 99–114); F. Millar, *JRS* 53 (1963) 29–42; 54 (1964) 33–40; Brunt, *RIT* 134–62 ['Fiscus']. Control: Millar *ERW* 133–201; Bosworth 1973; B. Levick, *Entretiens Hardt* 33 (Geneva, 1987) 187–218.

T. Frank, *ESAR* 5, 44–55; L. Homo, *RA* 42 (1940), 453–65; 1949, 163–7; 301–9.
D. Crawford in M.I. Finley, ed., *Stud. in Rom. Property* (Cambridge, 1976) 35–70;
G.M. Parassoglou, *Imperial Estates in Rom. Egypt. Amer. Stud. Papyr.* 18 (Amsterdam,
1978). H. Sutherland, *NAC* 14 (1985) 239–42; Loane 1944.

1 SV 16, 3: '*quadringenties milies opus esse, ut resp. stare posset*', connected with treasury
  shortage. Uniqueness: Frank, *ESAR* 5, 45. It is emended in the Budé edn to
  '*quadragies*'; defended by Bersanetti 61 as a capital fund to provide annual revenue
  (also accepted by Levi 1938, 10, and Bosworth 1973, 58). De Ste Croix 1981,
  468, is sceptical of the MS, Sutherland 1985, 242, non-committal. B. Campbell,
  The Emperor and the Rom. Army (Oxford, 1984) 173, calls the smaller figure a
  'reserve'. The MS figure and the anachronistic idea of building up a capital sum
  are rejected by M.T. Griffin, *CAH*^{2} 11 (forthcoming): revenue at 6 per cent would
  be 2,400m *HS* p.a.; how would interest be obtained? It is almost 50 times
  Hopkins' model-based annual revenue total (at 119, Ms S. Schad has kindly
  pointed out, the total of 824m *HS* needs amending to 773). Earthquakes: TA 2,
  47 3f. (five years' remission in 17) and 4, 13, 1 (three in 23). Lugdunum at 4m
  HS: TA 16, 13, 5. Troops: DC 64 (65), 22, 2; 65 (66), 10, 1^a; virtue: SV 8, 2.
  Nymphidius' promise: PlG 2, 2; Claudius' gifts: Levick 1990, 130f. Vitellius'
  difficulties and tax: TH 2, 94, 2f. Standing grievance: Graf 101. More revenue:
  MW 261; 274. V.'s plan: Flaig 406.
2 Tribute 'attributed': Ulp. *Dig.* 50, 16, 27; 'protection': TH 4, 74, 1.
3 Devastation: S. Mitchell in *Armies and Frontiers in Rom. and Byz. Anatolia, Brit.
  Inst. Arch. Monogr.* 5, *BAR. Intern. Ser.* 156 (Oxford, 1983) 131–50. Restoration:
  SV 8, 5. Loot to be restored: TH 4, 40, 2; SV 10.
4 Nero's expenses: Griffin 1984, 197–207; Sutherland 1985, 241; *RIC* 1^2, 134–7;
  144–6. Rapacity: PNH 18, 35; SN 32; DC 61, 5, 3–6; 62 (63), 17, 1. Building
  famed: Aur. Vict., *Caes.* 5, 2; [Epit. Aur. Vict.] *Caes.* 5, 3. Numbers in pre-
  industrial public building: J. Skydsgaard, *Anal. Rom. Inst. Danici Suppl.* 10. *Città
  e archit. nella Roma imp.* (Rome, 1983) 224. Gifts and recovery: TH 1, 20, 1f.; SG
  15; PlG 16, 3; DC 62 (63), 14, 2; Nicolas 567–9. Statue: PNH 34, 63; cf.
  Libanius 20, 24–33, Galba's parsimony: SG 12; TH 1, 49, 3; 1, 5; PlG 18, 4; DC
  63 (64), 3, 3. Agricola: TAgr. 6, 5, with Ogilvie and Richmond. Gallic tribute
  reduced: TH 1, 8, 1; 51, 4; *portorium* concession revoked: SV 16, 1; Graf 95 n. 529
  cites *CREBM* 1, 345 no. 205; Nicolas 491. Otho and the Domus Aurea: SO 7, 1
  (50m *HS*). Vitellius' largesse: TH 3, 55, 2. Extravagance: PNH 35, 163f.; SVit.
  13, 2 (dish); TH 2, 87, 2; 95 (900m *HS* allegedly spent in a few months), with
  Chilver; Tacitus' figure (from a Flavian source?) recurs in DC 64 (65), 3, 2, for
  dinners.
5 Provinces unequal to demand: MW 466, l. 25. Italian problems: Levick 1990,
  128 and above, Ch. 9. 1.
6 '*Breviarium totius imperii*': SAug. 101, 4. cf. 28, 1; DC 53, 30, 2 (23 BC); 56, 33, 1f.
  (14); publication resumed: DC 59, 9, 4; SCal. 16, 1, with A. Barrett, *Caligula, the
  Corruption of Power* (London, 1989) 224. Aerarium and Fiscus (side by side in SV
  16, 3): Brunt, 'Fiscus'; Parassoglou 27 n. 84 (bibl.); Levick 1990, 127–36. Pallas:
  TA 13, 14, 2. Father of Etruscus: n. 11 below. Funding of Roman building:
  Darwall-Smith 31–2.
7 TH 4, 9 (tr. K. Wellesley (Harmondsworth, 1964) 208), with Darwall-Smith 43f.
  Commission of 62: TA 15, 18, 4.
8 *Bona caduca* etc.: Brunt, 'Fiscus' 141–6; 156. Earliest known confiscations to
  Emperor: Eck 1996, 44, ll. 85–9 (20); TA 4, 20, 1 (24).
9 '*Minuendis publicis sumptibus*': PEp. 2, 1, 9, with Sherwin-White; horse-races, etc.:

DC 68, 2, 3. Water industry: Front., *de Aquis* 116–18: 250,000 *HS* (0.03 per cent of revenue). Revenues' destination: Frank, *ESAR* 5, 47–50.

10 Private loans: TH 4, 47, Chilver suggesting that the loans were of 60m from select individuals, or that the sum was intended for immediate use in paying off praetorians. *Fiscus Alexandrinus*: Frank, *ESAR* 5, 46 n. 31; Bengtson 99. Tiberius: T*A* 3, 53f; a drain of over 50m *HS* p.a. to the E. is deplored in P*NH* 6, 101. The idea that V. participated, apart from selling monopolies (Loane 1944), is implausible. Revenues of *Asiaticus*: Hirschfeld 71f.

11 Ti. Julius' name is inferred: Weaver 1972, 284, with Stat., *Silv.* 3, 3, 85–105. Jewish triumph: 138–42.

12 Praetorians reduced from 16 to 9 cohorts (Ch. 10) would have saved 21m *HS* p.a., 2.7 per cent of revenue: Campbell 1984, 162f. n. 6. 'Doubled tribute': SV 16, 1; DC 65 (66), 8, 3f.; McElderry 1918, 91f., was sceptical of alteration of tribute proper. Roman census, P*NH* 7, 162–4; cf. Phlegon, *FGH* 257, F 37 (centenarians: did age bring remission?). Other censuses: Bosworth 1973, 56, citing P*Oxy.* 2, 311 no. ccclxi (Egypt, 76–7), MW 334 (Tarraconensis; he dates to 71; see Ch. 9.2), and 449, with Stat., *Silv.* 1, 4, 83–8 (Africa, 73–4: see Vita Evrard 1979, 83–7); the census activities of M. Hirrius Fronto may belong to Italy: Torelli 172. See also Brunt, *RIT* 345f. ; *JB* 2, 361–87, noted by M. Corbier in J. Rich and A. Wallace-Hadrill, *City and Country in the Anc. World. Leicester-Nottingham Stud. in Anc. Soc.* 2 (London and N.Y., 1991) 214; C. Nicolet, *Space, Geography, and Politics in the early Rom. Emp. Jerome Lect* 19 (Ann Arbor, 1991) 181f. (derived from Augustus' *Breviarium*). Plundering intensified: TH 2, 84.

13 Remedies: Homo 1940; 1949, 302–9. Restoration: MW 339 (Pompeii); Castagnoli 1948, 280f. (Cannae or Canusium, 76). *Subseciva*: Front., *Contr. agr.* in Grom. Vet. 1, 54L; cf. SD 9, 3; MW 462 (letter of 82 to Falerio. Arausio: A. Piganiol, *Les documents cadastraux de la colonie d'Orange. Gallia Suppl.* 16 (Paris, 1962); MW 447 (77); O. Dilke, *The Rom. Land Surveyors: An introduction to the agrimensores* (Newton Abbot, 1971) 159–77.

14 Claudius: T*A* 14, 18, 2–4; Strabo: *PIR*²A 82. V.'s recovery: Hyg., *Grom. Vet.* 122f.L, with G.I. Luzzato, *Epigr. giurid. greca e rom.* (Milan, 1942) 189, *AE* 19, 91–3 (MW 435) (Paconius in 71, the 'Ptolmeum'); 34, 261 (Tolmetta; a 'garden' in 72). J.M. Reynolds and R.G. Goodchild, *Lib. Ant,* 2 (1965) 103–7; cf. 8 (1971) 47–51, on Apollonia: *AE* 67, 531 (Marsa Susa: the proconsul C. Arinius Modestus (74–5?) oversaw leasing (at 6 per cent of the land's capital value, 1070 *HS* per *iugerum*?); 74, 683f. (Ras el Hilal: Paconius, 74; the leasing); 54, 188 (Ptolemais: Domitian using the proconsul, 88–9); A. Piganiol, *Gallia* 13 (1955), 9f. (Orange, AD 77) for Vespasian elsewhere; Hyg., *Grom. Vet.* 1, 111, with Boulvert 1970, 211f., for land-sales. Corsica: MW 460. Alexandrian palace: DC 65 (66), 8, 4.

15 Provincial boundaries adjusted: Front., *Contr. agr.* 2, 3, 5L, with McElderry 1918, 85. Mirobriga, Sisapo: P*NH* 3, 14; 33, 118. Mines imperial: Frank, *ESAR* 5, 51. *Fossa regia* : G. Di Vita-Evrard, *L'Africa Rom.* 3 (Cagliari, 1986) 31–58 (maps); bibl. D. Mattingly and R.B. Hitchner, *JRS* 85 (1995) 176 n. 135; P*NH* 5, 25; *CIL* 8, 14882 , 23084, 25860, 25967; *ILS* 5955; *AE* 1894, p. 22; 02, 44; 12, 148–51; 36, 28 (= MW 449); 39, 31: '*ex auct.* . . . *Vespasiani* . . . *fines provinciae novae et veter. derecti qua fossa regia fuit*'; course: Leglay 222–8; tax revision: 226 n. 1. Bosworth 1973, 62–70, gives Rutilius 71/2; but see Wiegels, 'Hispanier' 206–8; *AE* 79, 648f., with Vita-Evrard 1979, 83–7: Rutilius took over from the normal proconsul; Syme, 'Rutilius' 515. Sentius is accordingly dated 73–4 by Eck, *Sen.* 119, 70–2 by Bosworth. Status: H.-G. Pflaum, *Hommages A. Grenier, Coll. Lat.* 58, 3 (1962), 1234f. Frank, *ESAR* 5, 46 differentiates property rights E. and W. of the line. Nasamones: DC 67, 4, 6; Jord., *Get.* 13, 76.

16 V.'s interest: McElderry 1918, 97f., citing Stat., *Silv.* 3, 3, 89, for Iberian gold. Reopened lead mines: *PNH* 34, 165. *Lex metallis* etc.: *Docs N–H* 439f. *Lex ferrariarum: CIL* 2, 5181, l. 34; 6, 31863. *Lex Manciana: Docs N–H* 463f.; J. Percival in B. Levick, ed., *The Ancient Historian and his Materials* (Farnborough, 1975) 215, citing C. Courtois *et al., Tablettes Albertini: actes privés de l'Époque vandale* (Paris, 1952) 140–2; T. Curtilius Mancia, suff. 55 (*PIR*² C 1605); Crawford 1976, 47f.: 'possibly a Flavian enactment with widespread application in the province'; so M. Bénabou, *La résistance africaine à la romanisation* (Paris, 1976) 115 (dating to 70–2); Garzetti 1974, 251, 635, is duly sceptical. Further refs: *Lat.* 41 (1982) 70 n. 86.

17 Tax rates: SV 16, 1; DC 65 (66), 8, 3f., with Frank, *ESAR* 5, 46, for Gauls. *Fiscus Judaicus*: Temple tax: *JB* 7, 218; DC 65 (66), 7, 2, with Smallwood 1976, 345 n. 54 (amounts), 371–6 (liability, date and conditions); *Docs N–H* 28 (mitigated). Procurator: MW 203, but cf. Smallwood 375 n. 69. Fire of 80: DC 66, 24, 1f. Population: Philo, *In Flacc.* 43; it would have produced 27m *HS* in 71–2; rejected in *CPJ* 1, 81. Instalments: *CPJ* 2, 132f. nos. 215, 217, etc. Kept separate: 375f. Gentiles: MW 458.

18 Alexandria: DC 65 (66), 8, 3–5, with Bosworth 1973, 59, for priests. (Miracles to induce acceptance: Nicolas 1185–7). Inheritances left in trust by Greeks to Romans or vice versa were confiscated: *Gnomon of the Idios Logos* 18; Rome: *SCal.* 40; urinals: SV 23, 3; DC 65 (66), 14, 5. Titus' dissent: G. Vitucci, *Atti* 1983, 55–67. Customs posts: Homo 1949, 296 (73–4). (I am indebted to Dr J. Rowlandson for advice.)

19 Achaean revenue: Paus. 7, 17, 4. Date: Ch. 9 n. 64; *AE* 82, 877 (alternatively Lemnos). Poll tax: J. Larsen in *ESAR* 4, 455: in Arc.Δelt. 1916, 148, a (Domitianic?) priest pays the province's tax; and *IG* 12, 5, 946, the first or second century endowment of Tenos meeting cost from interest (4,440 at 6 per cent). Poll tax in Spain: McElderry 1918, 89, cites Phlegon, *De Longaevis* (*FGH* 2B, 1185–8). Gallicus in Africa: Bosworth 1973, 62–70, stressing Stat., *Silv.* 1, 4, 83–8. Antiochus of Commagene got 100m *HS* from Gaius on accession: twenty years' revenues: *SCal.* 16, 3; '*tributarios*': MW 372. Note M. Arruntius Maximus, procurator of Asturia and Callaecia, 79: *CIL* 2, 2477

20 Caesarea: *Dig.* 50, 15, 8, 7 (Titus). *Vicesima*: C. Nicolet in *Caesar Augustus: seven aspects*, ed. F. Millar and E. Gruen (Oxford, 1984) 110f.; McElderry 1918, 91f. (Spain), citing *CIL* 2, 1949 etc. Caracalla: DC 78, 9, 5. Trajan: P*Pan.* 37.

21 Levies: DC (65) 66, 2, 5; DP 46, 8, dated *c.*70–80 (Jones 1978, 134). Corruption: SV 4, 3. Procurators: 16, 2. Caenis: DC 65 (66), 14, 3f. Tiberius: Levick 1976, 207f.; Gaius: *SCal.* 39, 1. Hipparchus: SV 13; Domitian: Ph*VA* 7, 23 and 25; DP 7, 12; cf. P*Pan.* 17, 1. Other improper gains: S*T* 7, 1 (Titus abetting). For the problems that Domitian's urgency has caused: M.T. Griffin, *CR* 43 (1993) 114.

22 Avarice: SV 16 with Levick 1982, 60 n. 36. Cybiosactes: Ch. 9 n. 63. Tip: 23, 2; statue base, urine tax: 23, 3; DC 65 (66), 14, 4. V.'s response: Juv. 14, 204f., appositely remarks: 'Gain smells good from any source.' Other smells came from bronze: J. Linderski, *HSCP* 94 (1992), 349–53, esp. n. 6; did Titus collect oiled sculpture?

23 Disbursements: SV 17–19; Eutrop. 7, 19. Nero (2,200m *HS*): *TH* 1, 20, 1; *SG* 15, 1; Pl*G* 16, 2.

24 *Liberalitas*: Amm. Marc. 25, 4, 15. Monarchy: DC 52, 6, 3. *AEQVITAS*: A. Wallace-Hadrill, *NC* 141 (1981) 20–39 (Vespasianic types at 26, with n. 39 (she holds a palm, signifying victory), 29 n. 63. *FIDES PVBLICA*: Levick 1982, 115, citing D.R. Walker, *The Metrology of the Rom. Silver Coinage* 1, *BAR Suppl.* 5 (Oxford, 1976) 83–121, esp. 111; 3, *Suppl.* 40 (1978) 114–17.

25 Sutherland 1985, 242, citing *RIC* 1f.; 15–61; *aes*: Kraay 1978. Centralization: J.P.C. Kent in J. Wacher, ed., *The Rom. World* (London-N.Y., 1987), 568–85.
26 Augustus' wealth: I. Shatzman, *Senatorial Wealth and Rom. Politics. Coll. Lat.* 142 (Brussels, 1975), 371. Jurisdiction: T*A* 4, 25; 12, 60, with Levick 1990, 49–51 (bibl.).
27 *Patrimonium*: Boulvert 1970, 213–24. V. had 'Galbian' slaves: Parassoglou 27. Brick-stamps: R. Matijašić, *MEFR* 95 (1983), 961–95. V.'s will: S*D* 2, 3. Balsam: P*NH* 12, 111–23 (800,000 *HS* p.a. for loppings and shoots); Millar 1963, 30; Brunt, 'Fiscus' 141; Smallwood 1976, 340 n. 39; H. Cotton and W. Eck, *RM* NF 140 (1997) 153–61, which Prof. Eck kindly allowed me to read before publication. Marble: J.C. Fant in N. Herz and M. Waelkens, eds, *Class. Marble: Geochem., technology, and trade* (Dordrecht, 1988) 147–58.
28 M. Rostovtzeff, *Gesch. des röm. Kolonats* (Leipzig, 1910) 291f. n. 2 (local chests). Egyptian estates: *P.Stras.* 267, l. 6f. (Hadrianic); *BGU* 1646, l. 8 (3rd cent.); *SEHRE* 292–5; 670. Boulvert 1970, 224–7, acknowledges (n. 136) doubt over date of *procurator usiacus*; Parassoglou: 25; 27; 52; 74 (list, Hadrianic docs); the new '*ousiaka*' divided between V. and Titus early in 70: Crawford 52f., with nn. 85–92, although she notes that in *Docs G–N* 391, l. 30, the term '*ho Kaisaros logos*' is already found. D. Rathbone, *Cahiers du Centre G. Glotz* 4 (1993) 81–111; radical reorganization 103. Africa: Rostovtzeff 1910, 327; Broughton 1929, 114f. (confiscations: P*NH* 18, 35); Pflaum, *Carrières* 380–5 (headquarters). Asia Minor: Hirschfeld 372 n. 6. H.-G. Pflaum, *Les procurateurs équestres* (Paris, 1950) 46 (but cf. *Carrières* 142) suggested that V. created temporary provinces of Hellespont (MW 336) and Aegean islands (Fest., *Brev.* 10); only financial districts: McElderry 1913, 119; E. Groag, *Die röm. Reichsbeamten von Achaia bis auf Diokletian. Akad. d. Wiss. in Wien, Schrift. der Balkankommission, Ant. Abt.* 9 (Vienna-Leipzig, 1939) 112; Magie 1428. T. Drew-Bear and C. Naour, *ANRW* 2, 18, 3 (1990) 1967 no. 15; *eparcheia* 1974–7; though the post resulted from V.'s reorganization: 1980 n. 266. Syriatica: *AE* 82, 877, citing other regions. Note '*regio*' in *Docs G–N* 368 (46).
29 Homo 1949, 307.
30 Achievement: *SHA XXX Tyrants* 6, 6. Domitian's finances: Levick 1982, 60. Titus' generosity: Jones, *Tit.* 140–6, concluding that V. left a large reserve. The figures of Frank, *ESAR* 5, 51–4, need caution.

8 STABILIZATION: THE WINNING OF PEACE

Graf 60–77; Nicolas 1037–288; Wellesley 1989. Britain: Birley 1981, 62–5. Rhine: G. Walser, *Rom, das Reich, u. die fremden Völker* (Baden-Baden, 1951) 86–128; Briessmann 84–105; Brunt, 'Tac.' 33–52; 481–3; G. Alföldy, *Die Hilfstruppen der röm. Prov. Germ. Inf., Epigr. Stud.* 6 (Düsseldorf, 1968); H. Schönberger, *JRS* 59 (1969) 144–97; Saddington 1982, 120–35; D.J. Knight, *ZPE* 85 (1991) 189–94 (movements); R. Urban, *Der 'Bataverausfstand' und die Erhebung des Iulius Classicus. Trier hist. Forsch.* 8 (Trier, 1985) (timetable 103f.); Murison 1991, 1707–9. Danube: A. Mócsy, *Pannonia and Upper Moesia* (London-Boston, 1974) 41–52; Syme, 'March'; Wilkes 1983. Judaea: Schürer 1973, 501–23; Smallwood 1976, 316–39; I.A. Richmond, *JRS* 52 (1962) 142–55; Y. Yadin, *Masada: Herod's fortress and the Zealots' last stand* (London, 1966; p/b 1985) 204–30; J.H. Feldman, in J. Neusner, ed., *Christianity, Judaism and other Greco-Roman Cults: Studies for Morton Smith at sixty,* 1 (Leiden, 1975) 218–48.

1 No peace: T*H* 4, 1, 1. Low-class revolt: 2, 61. Campanian feuds: 4, 3, with

Chilver/Townend for the cities; Lugdunum and Vienna: 1, 65; Oea and Lepcis: 4, 50. '*Expiato orbe terrarum*': T*H* 4, 3, 3 (Dec. 69).

2 B.R. Hartley and R.L. Fitts, *The Brigantes* (Gloucester, 1988) 1–6; Venutius: T*H* 3, 45; cf. T*A* 12, 40, 2–4 (bibl. Levick 1990, 228 n. 34); S. Mitchell, *LCM* 3 (1978) 215–19, argues for T*H* as giving the correct date, Hanson, *Conquest* 20f., that the accounts refer to the same events. Breastplate: Stat., *Silv.* 5, 1, 149. See Ch. 10 n. 16. Gauls encouraged: T*H* 4, 54, 2; Nicolas 975.

3 Claudius and Germany: Levick 1990, 151–5. Batavian revolt: T*H* 3, 46, 1; 4, 12–37; 54–79; 5, 14–26, using Pliny the Elder; J*B* 7, 75–87; D*C* 65 (66), 3, 1–3; S*D* 2, 1. See Weber 263–7 (origin 264); Wellesley 1989, 168–70. Flavian cover-up: Nicolas 1241, Verginius' story that the Vindex revolt was already nationalist (Levick 1985) part of it. Gauls in revolt only after death of Vitellius: Brunt, 'Vindex' 26. Revolt not separatist: Walser 1951 contra Brunt 'Tac.', Chilver, and Wellesley (commentaries); view revived by Urban 1985, contra Murison 1991; Civilis not punished: Urban 92. Nationalist élan of the Imperium Galliarum is played down by Nicolas 1268–70. T. Wiedemann, *Federazioni e federalismo nell' Europa antica, Bergamo 21–25 sett. 1992* (Milan, 1994) 427–30, stresses sectional interests. Gallo-German assets and Civilis' aims: T*H* 4, 16. Levies: 20. Fissures: 18 (Batavi); 79 (Nervii). Willems 226–31; 241, kindly drawn to my attention by Prof. Saddington, is conclusive for a 'nativistic' Batavian rising. Civilis' appearance: T*H* 4, 13, 2; 61, 1 (noted by Prof. Birley).

4 Swimming: D*C* 60, 20, 2; 6. T*H* 2, 17, 2. Civilis and V. 'friends': 5, 26, 2, with M. Hassall, *Brit.* 1 (1970) 132–4. Batavi among Lingones: T*H* 1, 59, 1. Paulus: 4, 13, 1; 32, 2. Rhine forces: Chilver/Townend p. 15f.; Nicolas 1244. Hordeonius: T*H* 1, 9, 1 ('*debilitate pedum*'); 2, 57, 1.

5 Uprising: T*H* 2, 97, 1; 3, 46, 1; 4, 12–17; Canninefates and Frisii: 15, 2f.; Island lost: 18, 1 (situation: Wellesley 1989, 168; size: Nicolas 1241f.). Attacks on Vetera: 22f.; 34–6; 59f.; on pro-Roman tribes: 28.

6 News of Cremona: T*H* 4, 31, 1. Vocula recovers I, IV, XXII: 37, 2. Choices: 54. Order to stop attacking legions: 32, 1. Leaders: T*H* 4, 55, 1f. Classicus' service: 2, 14, 1. Gauls and Rhine legions: 1, 53, 3; 57; 4, 69, 2. The connection of Cologne conspirators with Vitellius is stressed by Urban 48f., separating them from Civilis. That neglects changes due to the death of Vitellius and opportunities it offered Gauls and Germans. Death of Vocula: 4, 59, 1f. (cf. MW 40). Roman uniform as imperial (in succession to Vitellius): Urban 59f. Civilis and *Imperium*: T*H* 4, 61, 1; fissures, 70. Moguntiacum and Vetera: 59f.; see Chilver/Townend, p. 18. Novaesium and Bonna: 62. Nicolas 1219 estimates 20,000 Romans sworn in.

7 Cologne and Sunuci etc.: T*H* 4, 63–6. Sunuci etc., accede: 66. Defeat of Sabinus: 67, 1f.

8 Mucianus: T*H* 4, 68, 1–4, with Chilver/Townend for a 'Domitianic' account of Cerialis' appointment (J*B* 7, 83; consulship T*Agr.* 8, 2). Annius Gallus: T*H* 1, 87, 2. Tacitus and Upper Germany: Chilver/Townend pp. 17–19. Strategy analysed: Nicolas 1122f. X Gem.: T*H* 5, 19, 1. Origin of II Ad.: *CIL* 16, 10f. (7 Mar. 70); Flaig 403. *Auxilia*: Alföldy 1968, 149; Domitii: 131–5, with MW 299f. Knight 194 notes only five cohorts.

9 Conference: T*H* 4, 67, 2; 69. Trade: J*B* 2, 372. First Roman successes: T*H* 4, 70.

10 Cerialis at Rigodulum: T*H* 4, 71, with Chilver/Townend and Wellesley, Penguin tr., 333, map 8. Treveri at war: E. Wightman, *Rom. Trier and the Treveri* (London, 1970) 43–7. Treatment of Trier and legions: T*H* 4, 72–4; Prof. D.B. Saddington notes the speech as a routine product of historiography. Rebel advance on Trier: 75, 2.

11 Letter to Cerialis: T*H* 4, 75, 1 (early July, Nicolas 1232). Valentinus executed: 85, 1. Strategy and battle of Trier: 76–8, with Chilver/Townend, and Wellesley, Penguin tr., 333, map 9.

12 Surrender of Cologne; XIV Gem. and the fleet: T*H* 4, 79.

13 Battle for Vetera, legionary moves, water diverted: T*H* 5, 14–19, with Chilver/Townend. Ambush: 22.

14 Naval encounter and negotiations: T*H* 5, 23–6, with Chilver/Townend for the Nabalia (Ijssel, Vecht? Heubner *ad loc.* suggests the Lek between Lienden and Maurik). Nicolas' view, 1263f., that Augustus' behest not to expand the Empire (T*A* 1, 11, 7) had to be kept, is implausible. Bructeri: J.G.C. Anderson on T*G* 33, 1. Trier punished: Wightman 1970, 47; J. Krier, *Die Treverer ausserhalb ihrer Civitas*, etc. (Trier, 1981) 174–7. Sabinus: Plut., *Mor.* 770D–771C; DC 65 (66), 3, 1–3; 16, 1f., with *PIR²* J 535. 'Caesar': Nicolas 1252. Gellep battle: C. Rüger in *Rom. Frontier Stud. 1979. BAR Intern.* 71(ii), eds., W. Hanson and L. Keppie (Oxford, 1980) 496f.

15 Destruction: Schönberger 152f.; Vindonissa in stone: *PE s.v. Auxilia*; Bengtson 96.

16 Legions: Chilver/Townend 15f.; older bibl. Graf 131f. nn. 390–401. New forts in northern sector: T. Bechert *et al.*, *Die röm. Reichsgrenze d.v. Mosel bis z. Nordseeküste* (Stuttgart, 1994) 24f. Vetera II: Schönberger 155.

17 Roads and bridges: K. Schumacher, *Siedelungs- u. Kulturgesch. der Rheinlande von der Urzeit bis in das Mittelalter 2. Die röm. Periode* (Mainz, 1923) 227–33. Disbandment: E. Stein, *Die kais. Beamten u. Truppenskörper im röm. Deutschland unter dem Prinzipat* (Vienna, 1932); W. Wagner, *Die Dislokation der röm. Auxiliarformationen in den Prov. Noricum, Pannonien, Moesien, u. Dakien v. Aug. bis Gallienus. Neue Deutsche Forsch., Abt. alte Gesch.* 5 (Berlin, 1938), 224f. Lower Germany: Alföldy 1968, 148f.; H.G. Horn, *Die Römer in Nordrhein-Westfalen* (Stuttgart, 1987) 63–8, with fig. 37 (map), on Burungum and Gelduba. Moves: Knight 195f. cites T*Agr.* 36: six Batavian and Tungrian units in Britain by 83 (cf. A.K. Bowman and J.D. Thomas, *The Vindolanda Writing Tablets* 2 (London, 1994) 22–4); two *alae*, two cohorts (net) from Upper to Lower Germany: 196; I Hisp.: *RIB* 2213. Gaul: G.D. Woolf in J. Rich and G. Shipley, eds, *War and Society in the Rom. World* (London-N.Y., 1993) 188.

18 Tribes: Wilkes 1983. Sido, Italicus, Iazyges: T*H* 3, 5, 1; 21, 2; Mócsy 40f.

19 Julio-Claudian Danube: Mócsy; Syme 'March', 1004–6; *AE* 14, 93, for VIII and 57, 286, for V. VII Cl. moved: H. Parker, *Roman Legions* (Oxford, 1928; repr. Cambridge, 1958) 135.

20 Fleet: J*B* 2, 367. Grain: P*NH* 18, 66. Piracy: B. Isaac, *The Limits of Empire: The Roman Army in the East²* (Oxford, 1992) 45 n. 177, citing T*H* 3, 47. Revenues: *IGR* 1, 860 (Commodus). Claudius: DC 60, 8, 2; T*A* 12, 15–20f.; 63, 3; *Docs G–N* 226. Rhescuporis: *SEG* 19, 504, with Conole and Milns 190 n. 44.

21 MW 261, with L. Mozzewicz and K. Ilski, eds, *Stud. Moesiaca* (Poznań, 1994) 14–17 (bibl.); Conole and Milns 186f.; Bengtson 139f. Criticism: A. Alföldi, *CAH* 11, 85. *Ornamenta* for Tampius Flavianus (suff. II 74): MW 274. Date: Chilver on T*H* 2, 86, 3, against Townend 'Connections' 60 n. 23.

22 Roxolani: T*H* 1, 79, 1–4, with Chilver for 'duty abandoned for ambition'. J*B* 7, 89–95, makes attacks by 'Scyths' coincide with the German uprising crushed by Cerialis. Possible loss of V Alaud.: Flaig 389 n. 109; 402, but Josephus mentions no loss; see also Ch. 10 n. 2. Nicolas 1121 puts Rubrius' mission in May 70; T*H* 3, 46, 2f. (success of VI Fer.; Agrippa's arrival), with Syme, 'March' 1012 and 1975, 62, for Roman control of N. bank; T*H* 4, 4, 2, with Chilver/Townend (Mucianus honoured for success against Sarmatians); 54, 1 (rumours in Gaul of

defeats in Pannonia and Moesia by Sarmatians and Dacians). Blame: Wellesley 1989, 202. Rubrius' legions: H.M. Parker, *The Roman Legions* (Oxford, 1928) 144 n. 2.

23 Danube prime: Luttwak 86f.; Knight 198 (mainly Domitio-Trajanic movement).

24 Anicetus: T*H* 3, 47–8, 2; with Weber 274. Heraclea: *AE* 69–70, 591. Phanagoria: MW 233.

25 Road: *JRS* 66 (1976), 15–19; *ZPE* 55 (1984), 143f. (up to Passover 70: Buttrey 1980, 8f.). Jerusalem: *JB* 5, 2–38. Fatalities: 567–9.

26 Titus appointed: *JB* 4, 658; T*H* 2, 82, 3; S*T* 5, 2; Weber 185–246; in Alexandria: *JB* 6, 341; DC 65 (66), 8, 6, with Smallwood 1976, 317 n. 100. Commission: T*H* 4, 51, 2. Route: *JB* 4, 659–63, with Weber 188–93, calculating 1 Apr. for departure. Troops: *JB* 5, 39–46; Saddington 1982, 131, with legions of 6,000, estimates 55,000 or 69,000. Last allied contributions: Millar 1993, 84; Zeugma legionaries 75. Commanders: *JB* 6, 237f. (Egyptian 'legions'), with Schürer 1973, 502 n. 85; Aeternius, *PIR*[2] L 287; Larcius: 94; Tittius Frugi: *PIR* T 208. Colonus: *POxy.* 2349; R. Syme, *JRS* 44 (1954) 116. Alexander Guard Prefect: MW 329b; 'commanding' Titus' troops in Judaea: *JB* 5, 46; 6, 237, cf. MW 330; for Turner 1954, 61, and Jones 1984, 85, he passed to the Prefecture at Rome; but Syme, *RP* 3, 1277, n. 9 and 1071 n. 7, has him Prefect in Judaea.

27 Siege: Smallwood 1976, 316–27; J. Peddie, *The Rom. War Machine* (Stroud, 1994) 141–7. Arrival and setbacks: *JB* 5, 39–66; 71–97; chronology: Weber 198. Legionary positions: 67–70; 133–5.

28 John's entry: *JB* 5, 98–105. Jewish forces: 248–54. End of feud: 278f. Negotiation: 114, with Smallwood 1976, 318 n. 107. Suburbs razed: 106–8. Move to closer positions: 130–5. Date: 567 (1 May Thackeray *ad loc.*, after Weber 197, cf. his n. on John's entry, 99). Fortifications: 136–247.

29 Titus' plan: *JB* 5, 258–64. Artillery: 267–74; Smallwood 1976, 322 n. 126. Towers and 'Nicon': 291–301.

30 Fall of the first wall (15th day): *JB* 5, 302 (7 Iyyar: see Weber 198); DC 65 (66), 4, 3–5, 2. Unity: 304–6. Attack on N.: *JB* 5, 317. Fall of the second wall: 331–47. Pay-days: *JB* 5, 348–56; G. Webster, *The Roman Imperial Army*[2] (London, 1979) 256; 1 Jan., 1 May, 1 Sept.?

31 1 Panemus crisis in *JB* 5, 567; 6, 22; chronology: Weber 199–207. Double assault: *JB* 5, 356–490, with Smallwood 1976, 320 n. 117. Date: 466. Famine: 371; 424–38; 449; 454; 512; 571; 6, 193–219; 421; other references: Smallwood 321 n. 120. Desertions: *JB* 5, 420–3; 453f.; 548–61 (Roman atrocities); 6, 113–23; 229–32. Captured weaponry: 459. Roman failure: 469–90. Simon's reign of terror: 527–40. Council of war, wall, and new approach: 491–524. Completed: 6, 5. Roman despair: 9–14. Fall of outer and inner walls and Antonia: 15–32; 33–70.

32 Temple attacked, Antonia razed: *JB* 6, 71–94, with Smallwood 1976, 322 n. 128. 17 Tammuz is attested for the end of sacrifices in *mTaan* 4, 6 (Schürer 1973, 505 n. 108). Indecisive engagement: 130–48. Temple siege works: 149–63. Porticoes fired: 164–8; 177–92 with Smallwood 1976, 323. Last phase: 220–8.

33 *Consilium*: *JB* 6, 236–44 (not in DC 65 (66), 5f., and unsatisfactorily placed in the *JB* narrative); Titus exonerated: 241; 254; 262f.; 266. Temple fired: 244–66. Plunder: 271–87, with Smallwood 329 n. 161. Gold: 317. Titus '*imperator*': 316; S*T* 5, 2; Weber 205. New era: Smallwood 331.

34 Titus responsible: Sulp. *Chron.* 2, 30, 6 (for Weber 72 n. 1 this is based on T*H* 5; H. Montefiore, *Hist.* 11 (1962), 156–70, doubts it); Oros. 7, 9, 5f. See also I. Weiler, *Klio* 50 (1968) 139–58 (Jewish verdicts 156–8); Schürer 1973, 506 with n. 115: no evidence of a directive from V., obviating need for deliberation;

Smallwood 326 (Jewish verdicts 324 n. 138); d'Espèrey 3066. Priests executed: *JB* 6, 318–22.

35 Palace: *JB* 6, 358–62. Parley: 323–53. Burning of city: 354f.; 363; 434; 7, 1–4. Underground: 6, 370–3; 402. Assault on Upper City and massacre: 374–407, with Smallwood 1976, 326 n. 150. Towers: 398–400; 409–13; 7, 1. Date of fall: 6, 407; 435: 8 Gorp. Survivals: Schürer 1973, 508 n. 120; Smallwood 1976, 327f.

36 Leaders' fate: 6, 433; 7, 25–36; 118; Simon may have suffered as a 'leveller'. Prisoners: 6, 414–19; 7, 118. Jewish losses: 6, 420 (cf. *TH* 5, 13, 3; Oros. 7, 9, 7), with Smallwood 1976, 327 n. 152; Sulp., *Chron.* 2, 30, 5, gives 100,000.

37 Duration: Weber 207. Tactics: 237–46; Vespasian's advice: 243f. Rewards: *JB* 7, 5–20. Garrison: 5; 17; archaeology: Smallwood 1976, 333 n. 5; *auxilia* 334. Troops depart: 17. Titus' journey: 23–4; 37–40 (birthdays). Agrippa's reward: Millar 1993, 91, on *JB* 7, 97.

38 Cerialis: Smallwood 1976, 332 n. 3. Procurator: L. Laberius Maximus, future Prefect of Egypt and the Guard: *PIR*² L 8. Herodium surrenders: *JB* 7, 163: Machaerus: Schürer 1973, 511 n. 135; *JB* 7, 164–70; 190–209; (plans) A. Strobel, *Zeitschr. d. deutsch. Paläst.-Ver.* 90 (1974) 128; D. Kennedy and D. Riley, *Rome's Desert Frontier from the Air* (London, 1989) 99–101. Bassus' death: *JB* 7, 253. Silva: Smallwood 1976, 335 n. 14.

39 Masada: Schürer 511 n. 137. Siege and fall: *JB* 7, 252f.; 275–84; 304–406, with Smallwood 336–8. Fortifications: Richmond 1962; Roman strength, and circumvallation complete in two weeks, 152f.; cf. Smallwood 338; D.J. Ladouceur, *GRBS* 21 (1980) 245–60; Kennedy and Riley 96–9. 73 is traditional (so Yadin 15), Niese 1893, 211f., having proposed 72 (so Garzetti 1974, 633); 74 was suggested by Eck, *Sen.* 93–103, using Silva's career (so Schürer 1973, 512 and 515); contra, C.P. Jones, *AJP* 95 (1974) 89f., Bengtson 81, and others cited by D. Campbell, *ZPE* 73 (1988) 158 n. 16f.; see also Evans 198 n. 1. H. Cotton, *ZPE* 78 (1989) 157–62, prefers 73 on the basis of dumped papyri, one addressed to Iulius Lupus, perhaps the Prefect of Egypt in office in Feb.–Mar. 73; Eck 1992–3, 95 n. 57. Silva's reward: Eck 1992–3, 95f. Garrison: Smallwood 339, with n. 32.

40 Alexandrian riot in 66: *JB* 2, 489–98. V. and Titus' attitudes: *JA* 12, 121–4; (mention of V. may mean that he too received a petition in 70 or sanctioned Titus' reply).

41 Onias' temple: *JB* 7, 409–36, after Masada's fall, but see Smallwood 1976, 366 n. 39. Paulinus attested by the end of Aug.: *POxy.* 1266, l. 25. Identity: P.J. Sijpestijn, *Hist.* 28 (1979) 117–25. Discontent due to prisoners and tax: 367, cf. 372. Arrears: *CPJ* 1, 80. Smallwood 367f. (phases of closure). *Mishnah*: H. Danby, *The Mishnah* (Oxford, 1933), xiii–xxiii; Schürer 1973, 524f.; Nomenclature: *CPJ* 1, 83–5.

42 Cyrenaica: *JB* 7, 437–53; Smallwood 1976, 369–71, detects a victim of Catullus at *JB* 6, 114. Class: see *EJ*² 311 no. 1. Jewish revolt of 115: DC 68, 32; faction: J. Reynolds, *JRS* 49 (1959) 97. Economic factors: *ead.*, *PCPS*, NS 5 (1958–9), 25f.

43 Africa 68–70: Nicolas 977–88. Macer's legion (see A. Kunisz, *L'Insurrection de Clodius Macer . . . en 68 . . . Polska Akad. Nauk* (Wroclaw, 1994) 56–66) disbanded: Chilver on *TH* 2, 97, 2–98, 1. Piso's death, Garamantian trouble: 4, 48–50, with Chilver/Townend and Leglay 206–9; *PNH* 5, 38. Lepcis fortified: R.G. Goodchild and J.B. Ward Perkins, *PBSR* 21 (1953) 42–73. Festus' honours: MW 266, with Syme, *RP* 4, 281.

44 Legate, *cos. des.*: MW 276f.; *AE* 69–70, 747 ('*utriusque Mauretaniae*'); the equestrian C. Velius Rufus, '*dux exercitus Africi et Mauretanici ad nationes . . .*

244

comprimendas', MW 372, could have been his subordinate, but Bénabou 109–11, implausibly arguing against a rising, was probably right to follow H.-G. Pflaum, *Carrières* 114–16 and 966, in dating intervention to 86. Incursions: Calp. Sic. 4, 37–42; G. Townend, *JRS* 70 (1980), 166–74. 69: T*H* 2, 58, 1. Catalogue: G. Alföldy, *Chiron* 15 (1985) 99–106; interpretation: Bénabou 120–60.

45 Armed subjects: T*H* 1, 68, 1, with Chilver ('an untidy element eliminated by the Flavians'); 2 12, 3; 58, 1. R. MacMullen, *Roman Social Relations 50* BC – AD 284 (New Haven-London, 1974) 35 n. 26, is rebutted by P.A. Brunt, *Phoen.* 29 (1975), 260–70 (= Brunt, *RIT* 255–66). Institutionalization: Saddington 1982, 195f.

9. ENHANCEMENT: THE PHYSICAL AND MORAL RESTORATION OF THE ROMAN WORLD

Plebs: Van Berchem 1939; Yavetz 1987; Griffin 1991; 1994, 307–16. 'Employment': L. Casson, *Bull. Amer. Soc. Pap.* 15 (1978) 43–51; P.A. Brunt, *JRS* 70 (1980) 81–100; J. Skydsgaard in *Città e arch. nella Roma imp.*, *Anal. Rom. Inst. Dan. Suppl.* 10. *Atti del Sem. del 27 ott. 1981 nel 25 ann. dell'Accad. di Danimarca* (Rome, 1983) 223–7. Building: H. Nissen, *RM* NS 49 (1894) 275–98; Blake 87–165; Hill; Castagnoli 1981; Darwall-Smith 35–74. Townend 1987. Colosseum: R. Gall, *RE* 6, 2 (1909) 2516–25; A.v. Gerkan, *Röm. Mitt.* 40 (1925) 11–59 (= E. Boehringer, ed., *Von ant. Architektur u. Topogr.: Gesamm. Aufsätze v. A.v. Gerkan* (Stuttgart, 1959) 29–43); G. Cozzo, *The Colosseum: The Flavian amphitheatre* (Rome, repr. 1971); M.L. Conforto *et al.*, *Anfiteatro flavio: immagine, testimonianze, spettacoli* (Rome, 1988); R. Rea in E.M. Steinby, ed., *Lex. Top. Urbis Romae* 1 (Rome, 1993) 30–5 (bibl.); Kleiner 1990; D.E.E. Kleiner, *Roman Sculpture* (New Haven-London, 1992). W. provinces: Fishwick 1987–91. Spain: McElderry 1918, 1919; Bosworth 1973; H. Braunert in *Corolla memoriae E. Swoboda dedicata. Röm. Forsch. in Niederösterreich* 5 (Graz, etc., 1966) 68–83; H. Galsterer, *Untersuch. z. röm. Städtewesen auf d. iberisch. Halbinsel. Madrid. Forsch.* 8 (Berlin, 1971) 37–50; Galsterer 1988; Wiegels; N. Mackie, *Local Administration in Roman Spain AD 14–212. BAR Intern.* 172 (Oxford, 1983); Stylow 1986; González; A. Fear, *Rome and Baetica: Urbanization in southern Spain c.50* BC – AD 150 (Oxford, 1996) 131–226. Britain: Hanson, *Conquest* 69–83; 'Tac.' 1773–7. Rhine-Danube: D. Planck, *Arae Flaviae: neue Untersuch. zur Gesch. des röm. Rottweil. Forsch. u. Bericht. z. vor- u. Fruhgesch. in Baden-Württemberg* 6, 1, 1 (Stuttgart, 1975); F. Staehelin, *Die Schweiz in Römerzeit*[3] (Basel, 1948); G. Alföldy, *Noricum* (London-Boston, 1974) 106–42; J. Wilkes, *Epigr. Stud.* 4 (1967) 119–21; *Dalmatia* (London, 1969) 78–415; A. Mócsy, *Pannonia and Upper Moesia* (London-Boston, 1974). Africa: McElderry 1913; Broughton 1929, 88–118; Leglay; T. Kotula, *MEFR* 79 (1967) 207–20; J. Gascou, *La politique mun. de l'Empire rom. en Afrique Proconsul. de Trajan à Sept. Sévère, CEFR* 8 (Rome, 1972) 29–66; M. Bénabou, *La résistance africaine à la romanisation* (Paris, 1976); Vita-Evrard 1979; P. MacKendrick, *The North African Stones Speak* (N. Carolina, 1980); D.J. Mattingly and R.B. Hitchner, *JRS* 85 (1995) 165–214. East: A.H.M. Jones, *The Greek City from Alexander to Justinian* (Oxford, 1940) 59–84; 129–46; 170–91; *Cities of the E. Rom. Provinces*[2] (Oxford, 1971); Millar 1993, 80–126; D. Magie, *Roman Rule in Asia Minor* (Princeton 1950) 566–92; Chr. Habicht, *JRS* 65 (1975) 64–91 (assizes); Dąbrowa, *Asie mineure*; S. Mitchell, *HSCP* 91 (1987) 333–65 ['Building']; *Anatolia. Land, men and gods in Asia Minor* (2 vols Oxford, 1993). Syria: G.W. Bowersock, *Akten des VI Intern. Kongr. f. Epigr. Vest.* 17 (Munich, 1973) 123–30; 'Syria'; J.-P. Rey-Coquais, *JRS* 68 (1978) 44–73; M. Rostovtzeff, *Caravan Cities* (tr. D. and T. Talbot Rice, Oxford, 1932); G. Downey, *A History of Antioch in Syria from Seleucus to the Arab Conquest* (Princeton, 1961); D. Van Berchem, *BJ* 185 (1985)

47–86. Judaea: Smallwood 1976, 339–55; Applebaum 1977; B. Isaac, *Journ. Jew. Stud.* 34 (1985) 44–50.

1 Devastation: T*H* 2, 56; S*V* 8, 5. *RESVRGE(N)S*: *RIC* 51 no. 310; 65 no. 407 (70); 69 no. 445 (71); 76 no. 520 (72–3); 101 no. 735 (72–3). Building types: Hill 205. *AETERNITAS*; G.C. Belloni *ANRW* 2, 1 (1974) 1063–5. Kinsmen in conflict: T*H* 3, 25, 2; 51, 1.

2 'Plebs' in politics: T*H* 1, 32, 1 ; 2, 55, 1; 3, 85. Flaig 342 stresses Vitellius' favour with the plebs, Nero's failure. Helplessness: Griffin 1991, 39f., citing T*A* 4, 33, 2. The urban plebs of the thirty-five tribes and the urban plebs in receipt of grain and the thirty-five tribes made dedications to V.: *CIL* 6, 3747; MW 468. Nissen 281 argued for actual refounding of Rome, 13 Feb. 74.

3 Shortage: P. Garnsey, *Famine and Food Supply in the Graeco-Roman World: Responses to risk and crisis* (Cambridge, 1988) 218–27; Tiberius and Claudius: T*A* 2, 87, 1; 4, 6, 6; 12, 43, 1–3; Levick 1990, 109–11; Nero, with *ANNONA AVGVSTI CERES*, *RIC* 1² 139; 159 no. 98f., etc.: Griffin 1984, 106–9; Galba: *RIC* 1², 225f.; 246 no. 291, etc.; Otho: 258f., 260 no. 1; Vitellius: 267, 275 no. 132; *CERES AVGVSTA*, echoing Claudian 127 no. 94, etc.; *ANNONA AVG.* (Flaig 342 notes its absence from dies of Galba and Otho), 266f.; 275 no. 131, etc. V. has both: *RIC* 28 no. 122 (75–9); 29 no. 131–3 (78–9), etc.; 72 no. 469 (71); 82 no. 570 (76); 83 no. 587 (77–8), etc.; Levick 1982, 115 n. 63. V.'s concern: T*H* 4, 52, 2; DC 65 (66), 9, 2ª, coinciding with Titus' departure for Judaea. *Horrea Galbae*: '*instituit*': *Chron. ann.* 334 (inference from the name?); E. Nash, *Pict. Dict. of Anc. Rome* (London, 1961) 1, 481f.; G. Rickman, *Rom. Granaries and Store-buildings* (Cambridge, 1971) 97–104 (plan); 166–8; 170f. (use).

4 S*Claud.* 21, 1, with Levick 1990, 112 n. 25; 131 n. 15: see Van Berchem 142–50: nothing for V. and one distribution for Titus, 149f. (*RIC* 2, 86 no. 606 (72: *CONGIAR. PRIMVM P.R. DAT*); *Chron. ann.* 334 gives 300 *HS* (V.); TD 17, 5; third distribution: *RIC* 2, 127 n.*. Cash on return: DC 65 (66), 10, 1ª.

5 Aqueducts restored, 71: MW 408(a) ('*Curtia et Caerulea*', i.e. Claudia: Front., *De aquis* 1, 13f.). Tiber: MW 443; *CIL* 6, 1238; *Bull. Com.* 1887, p. 15 (73; the latter records restoration of the *ripa Veientana*: the r. bank below the Farnesina); *Eph. Epigr.* 4, 807 : '*Ex auctoritate . . . Vespasiani*'; cf. *Docs. G-N* 307(b) (Claudius); M.T. Griffin, *CAH²* 11 forthcoming, contrasting the Augustan '*ex SC*': e.g. EJ 295; so O.F. Robinson, *Ancient Rome: City planning and administration* (London-N.Y., 1992) 88: the five-man board had become one ex-consul. Pliny on Claudius and Agrippa: Isager 202f.; 210.

6 Ruins: S*V* 8, 5. Flood: T*H* 1, 86, 2; S*O* 8, 3. Builder: P*NH* 36, 102; S*V* 9, 1, with Braithwaite; cf. Darwall-Smith 74. V. preserver: MW 151. '*Correcta disciplina*': Graf 78.

7 Ceremony: T*H* 4, 53, with Townend 1987, esp. 245 ('*Lapis*'); A. Keaveney, *Giorn. Ital. di Fil.* 39 (1987) 213–16; Darwall-Smith 44f. Dedication of cult-statue: MW 163. Hod: S*V* 8, 5; DC 65 (66), 10, 2. Imperialism symbolized: P*NH* 36, 101, with Griffin 1991, 20.

8 Capitol: *e.g. RIC* 70 no. 452; 74 no. 496 (both 71), apparently continuing until 108 no. 793 (77–8), with Hill 210f.; diversity makes Hill 205 and Darwall-Smith 46f. cautious on coins as evidence for the Temple; two stages may be shown. Honos et Virtus: P*NH* 35, 120; Marius: *CIL* 1, p. 195. Vesta (undamaged in 69) attracted attention on coins: Hill 208, citing *asses* of 72 and 73: *CREBM* 2, 144 no. 648 etc. Marcellus theatre: S*V* 19, 1; Plut., *Mor.* 974A. Builders' names: DC 65 (66), 10, 1ª; cf. S*Aug.* 29, 4; *RGDA* 19, 1; 20, 1; Elder Pliny as source: Graf 81.

9 Claudius' temple: SV 9, 1; A.M. Colini, *Atti della Pont. Accad. rom. d'Arch.* Ser. 3, *Mem.* 7 (1944) 137–61 (illustr.); Darwall-Smith 48–52, (history; and stressing the massive 180 by 200 m platform (Mart. *Sp.* 2, 9f.)). See also Charlesworth 1937, 57–66, noting Front., *De Aquis* 1, 20; 2, 76 (Nero using the site as a distribution centre for Aqua Claudia); R.B. Lloyd, *AJA* 86 (1982) 93–5; L. Richardson, Jr., *New Topogr. Dict. of Anc. Rome* (Baltimore-London, 1992) 87f.; G. Buzzetti in Steinby 1993, 277f. Date of remains: A. Boethius and J. Ward Perkins, *Etruscan and Rom. Architecture* (Harmondsworth, 1970) 219. Golden House: Mart., *Sp.* 11f.; *TA* 15, 42; S*Nero* 31, 1f., with A. Boethius, *The Golden House of Nero* (Ann Arbor, 1960); Griffin 1984, 132–42 (bibl.); Darwall-Smith 36–8, both the latter stress its public shrines.

10 Temple (*temenos*): JB 7, 158; DC 65 (66), 15, 1. A.M. Colini, *Bull. Com.*. 65 (1937), 7–40; J.C. Anderson, Jr., *AJA* 86 (1982) 101–10 (plans); Richardson 1992, 286f. Garden: Lloyd 1982, 91–3. Kleiner 1992, 181; Darwall-Smith 55–67. Library: A. Gell. 5, 21, 9; 16, 8, 2. Beauties: *PNH* 36, 102; JB 7, 159–61; *PNH* 34, 84; 35, 74; Nile: 36, 58; Darwall-Smith 61 doubts the heifer (Procopius, *BG* 4, 21, cf. *PNH* 34, 57). Ara Pacis: *RGDA* 12, 2. Another temple inscription: *CIL* 6, 939. V.'s Plan: E. Rodriguez-Almeida, *Forma urbis marm.: aggiornamento gen. 1980* (Rome, 1981); Castagnoli 1948, 395 n. 1, dating to 77 on basis of *CIL* 6, 935; G. Canettoni *et al.*, eds, *La Pianta marm. di Roma ant.: forma urbis Romae* (2 vols, Rome, 1960) 1, 218; census: Robinson 1992 (n. 4) 20.

11 Collecting: A. Rouveret in J. Pigeald and J. Oroz, eds, *Pline l'Ancien: témoin de son temps. Conventus Plin. intern. Namneti 22–26 Oct. 1985 hab.* (Salamanca-Nantes, 1987) 431–49 (I am indebted to Mlle V. Naas for knowledge of this paper), bibl. 432 n. 4, on *PNH* 36, 101, JB 7, 158–62, and *PNH* 34, 62, for Tiberius (cf. S*Tib.* 44, 2). Balsam: Ch. 7 n. 27. Spending: Cic., *Pro Mur.* 36, 76; nationalization: *PNH* 35, 26; Nero's *sellariae*: 34, 84; Golden House a 'prison': 35, 120; see Isager 83f.; 120; 133. Exclusive: S*Nero* 39, 2, cited by Skydsgaard 223; Mart., *Sp.* 2, with Griffin 1994, 312. Helius: SV 18; *PNH* 34, 45f.; Graf 83 (symbolizing unification of E. and W.), Emperor as patron: Griffin 1991, 33f., distinguishing (35–7) supply from dole. 'Brokers': R. Saller, *Personal Patronage Under the Early Empire* (Cambridge, 1982) 68; 73–5. Claudius: Levick 1990, 105–14.

12 Bibl. above; Darwall-Smith 76–90, Bede: Migne, *Patr. Lat.* 94, 543, with H.V. Canter, *TAPA* 61 (1930), 150–64, cited by Darwall-Smith 75 n. 2; '*amphitheatrum*': MW 11 (p. 19), reserving places for Arvals; '*Caesareum amphitheatrum*': Mart., *Sp.* 1, 7. Upper-class enjoyment: Griffin 1991, 36; 43–5; philosophers: Sen., *NQ* 7, 32, 3. Not Tiberius: B. Levick, *Tib. the Politician* (London, 1976) 122. Model: Darwall-Smith 90; J.-C. Golvin, *L'Amphithéâtre romain* (Paris, 1988) 273; dated lists: M. Wilson-Jones, *Röm. Mitt.* 100 (1993) 391–442. Puteoli: A. Maiuri, *Studi e ricerche sull'anfiteatro flavio puteolano* (Naples, 1955); Carthage: *CIL* 8, 12567c; Urbs Salvia: Eck 1992–3, 97f. 'Hunting theatre' struck: DC 79, 25, 2. Inscription: G. Alföldy, *ZPE* 109 (1995) 195–226 (*ILS* 5633): '*Imp.<T.>Caes. Vespasianus Aug./Amphitheatrum Novum (?)/ex manubis fieri iussit*'. (I am indebted to the kindness of Prof. F.G.B. Millar for the original information); so already M.A. Levi, *Atti* 1983, 169. V.'s rôle: SV 9, 1 ('*fecit*'); K.M. Coleman, *JRS* 80 (1990) 73 n. 242, supports Gerkan's chronology, but kindly drew my attention to Wilson-Jones 1993: lower storeys stressed to take the load of upper; Titus' rôle: *Chron. Ann.* 354, p. 146f. ('*dedicavit*'), used of Titus by S*T* 7, 3); Mart., *Sp.* 2; Eutrop. 7, 21: '*aedificavit {Titus}*'; cf. Jones, *Tit.* 173 n. 169; Darwall-Smith 78f.; Design: Homo 375f. ('*froid, monotone*'); 387; Boethius and Ward Perkins 1970, 221–4. Size: Nissen 297f. (numerological significance); Conforto 10 (arena). Construction: Skydsgaard 223f. Titus' games: DC 66, 25, with

K.M. Coleman, *JRS* 83 (1993) 58–74, on aquatic displays; Darwall-Smith 82–9.

13 Colossus: *SV* 18, 1; *SN* 31, 1 (120 *pedes*); *PNH* 34, 45 (?106.5; Nissen 297 n. 1); DC 65 (66), 15, 1 (100). C. Lega, *Bull. Com.* 93 (1989–90) 339–78, and in Steinby 1993, 295–8; fig. 17. Site: 296, cf. Griffin 1984, 131; Darwall-Smith 68f.

14 Arches: DC 65 (66), 7, 2; 'Via Labicana' (Musei Vaticani, Museo Gregorio Profano, Inv. 9997): Kleiner 1990 131–4; bibl. 131 n. 19; cf. Darwall-Smith 69f. and 276f., who follows F. Castagnoli, *Bull. Com.* 69 (1941) 59–69.

15 Genius: *CREBM* 2, 124 no. 576, cf. *RIC* 71 no. 463 ('temple'); Kleiner 1990, 134–6; *SNR* 68 (1989) 85–91. Darwall-Smith 70 envisages this as one of Dio's arches (temporary).

16 '*Plebeculam meam*': *SV* 18, 2, with De Ste Croix 1981, 194f.; Skydsgaard 226f., scrutinizing employment as an end in public building; but cf. Brunt 1980 and Darwall-Smith 28f. Pompeii: J.D. Dobbins, *AJA* 38 (1994) 629–94, esp. 632, 689–94 (ref. owed to the kindness of Dr R. Laurence). Butchers: *SV* 19, 1. Members of a *collegium* of excavators made a dedication for Titus (*CIL* 6, 940), and V.'s slave, clerk in the marble works, to Hercules Augustus (301). Building inscriptions: Newton 46–50 nos. 89–98; *AE* 54, 61 (corner of Via Veneto and Via Aemilia).

17 Squatters: *SV* 8, 5, with n. 1 above. V.'s edict and *SC*: *Cod. Iust.* 8, 10, 2 ('*negotiandi causa*'); *SC Hosidianum*, modified by *Volusianum* of 56: *Docs G-N* 365, ll. 41–4, cited by Graf 79, with Levick 1990, 113f., 126; Griffin 1994, 313; Bengtson 171. Augustan building: Strabo 5, p. 235. Streets: MW 412. Graf 135 n. 446, notes who should have done the work: S*Aug.* 30, 1. Claudius on predecessors: *Docs G-N* 308(b); 368, l. 11; *JA* 19, 284. Crowds etc.: Juv. 3, 243–8; Mart. 7, 61, cited in Robinson 1992 (n. 4) 59–82 (streets). V.'s humiliation: above, Ch. 1. '*Plostra*': *SV* 22, with *FIRA* 1², 146 , 65–8, and Robinson 1992, 73–5; 81.

18 Cookshops: DC 65 (66), 10, 3; *SN* 16, 2; DC 60, 6, 7; Robinson 136.

19 Scope of census: Bosworth 1973, 50f., citing *PNH* 7, 162–4. Longevity: Phlegon, *FGH* 257, F 37.

20 Population: P.A. Brunt, *Italian Manpower* (Oxford, 1971) 120–9; under V.: Bengtson 101. Recruitment: Ch. 10. Decline perceived: *TH* 2, 56, 2. *Alimenta*: R. Duncan-Jones, *The Econ. of the Rom, Emp.*² (Cambridge, 1982) 288–319; *Docs G-N* 223 (first known private scheme); cf. G. Woolf, *PBSR* 58 (1990) 197–228 (sceptical). Pomerium extension (minor, Nissen 295): *PNH* 3, 66; *ILS* 248 (St Paul's Gate); *CIL* 6, 31538a (Pincian); c (Sta. Cecilia, Trastevere); *Not. dei Scavi* 1933, 241 (Campus); MW 1, 14–16; cf. M. Labrousse, *MEFR* 54 (1937) 165–99 (plan 169), with fiscal motives; Homo 296; M.T. Griffin, *CAH*² 11 (forthcoming), stresses the wording ('*auctis p.R. finibus . . .*'), suggesting the conquest of Judaea as possible justification and noting the antiquarianism of V. and Claudius (V.'s: Buttrey 1972). Claudius: Levick 1990, 107; dating: 120f.; 149. Hadrian: *CIL* 6, 31539a-c; *Not. dei Scavi l.c.*

21 C. Gracchus: E. Badian, *Roman Imperialism*² (Oxford, 1968) 44f.; Claudius: Levick 1990, 114. Via Flavia: MW 415; *CIL* 5, 7988f. (78–9). Vineyards: MW 430. Tifatina: MW 444; *ILS* 3240; *AE* 71, 80, with K. Rigsby, *TAPA* 106 (1976), 321f. Cannae: *AE* 45, 85; cf. Castagnoli 1948, 286, noting *Lib. Col.* 261L.

22 Capua, Puteoli: M. Frederiksen, ed. N. Purcell, *Campania* (Rome, 1984) 331, with nn. 127f.: *ILS* 6331 and 8351 belong to Puteoli; rivalry: *TH* 3, 57, 1. Capua 'Flavia' by 84: *AE* 69/70, 635. Puteoli: MW 140 (86). Reate: MW 378; *CIL* 9, 4682f.; 4685, 4689; cf. *TA* 14, 27, 3. Nola: *Lib. Col.* 1, *Grom. Vet.* 1, 236L; Sinuessa: *CIL* 10, 4735; Paestum: p. 52f.; *Eph. Epig.* 2, p. 457; Bovianum: MW 354; N. Italy: G.E.F. Chilver, *Cisalpine Gaul* (Oxford, 1939) 227, citing *TH* 2,

17, 1 and 21, 1. Brixia: N. Degrassi, *Rend. Pont. Accad. rom. d'Arch.* Ser. 3, vol. 42 (1969–70) 135–7; Patavium: W.V. Harris, *ZPE* 27 (1977) 288–90; Dr E. Bispham, kindly providing this reference, suggested that the Patavine era began soon after 173 BC: the '*IIIIvir . . . e lege Iulia municipali*', *CIL* 5, 2864, belongs early in V.'s reign.

23 Appia, Flavia: MW 413, 415 (78); *CIL* 10, 6817 (76); Latina: 6894; 6896; 6901 (Jan.–June 77); Flaminia: Aur. Vict., *De Caes.* 9, 8; [Epit.] 9, 9f.; R. Chevallier, *Rom. Roads in Italy and France* (London, 1972) 104–6; Viterbo: 414 (77); W. Eck, *Die staatl. Organisation Italiens in der hohen Kaiserzeit. Vest.* 28 (Munich, 1979) 30f.

24 Victoria: MW 432; cf. Hor., *Ep.* 1, 10, 49 (Newton 50, no. 99); Herculaneum: *CIL* 10, 1406 (76), with Newton 51 no. 100. Salernum building restored, 74–8: *AE* 66, 72.; Forum Livii in Aemilia: *CIL* 11, 598. Firmum: *AE* 75, 353. *Aeternitas*: *Docs G–N* 365, l. 4.

25 Judicial functions: Millar, *ERW* 507–37. Galba: *SG* 14, 3. Restoring loot: *TH* 4, 40, 2; *SV* 10; sittings: *SV* 13, with T. Honoré, *Emperors and Lawyers* (London, 1981) 8. Claudius: Levick 1990, 116–23 (bibl. 120). Busyness: refs in Crook 1955, 26–8.

26 Eprius and Crispus: *TD* 8, 4: Aper: 7, 1; Trachalus: *PIR²* G 30; Liberalis: *SV* 13; MW 311. Jurists: Honoré 1981, 10. B.W. Frier, *CAH²* 10, 978 (unfavourable, but drawing attention to Plautius (?D. Plotius Grypus, *cos.* 88)). Taints: Juv. 4, 75–81; *DC* 67, 13, 3f.; F. Sturm, *Atti* 1981, 105–36 (favourable). Priscus: Syme, 'Neratius'.

27 Legislation: Bersanetti 69. Tiberius: *TA* 3, 54, 3; Nero: Talbert 442f. (*SCC*); G. Rotondi, *Leges publicae populi Romani* (Milan, 1922) 468 (*leges*). Claudius: Levick 1990, 123–6. *Claudianum*: 123, with 222 n. 265; the requirement of a complaint by the master is ascribed to V. by M.T. Griffin, *CAH²* 11 (forthcoming). Children of women not known to be slaves: *GI* 1, 85, E. Seckel and B. Kuebler *ad loc.* suggesting peregrines of an unspecified area, and Griffin *l.c.*, like J. Crook, *CR* 17 (1967) 8, and P.R.C. Weaver in B. Rawson, ed., *The Family in Ancient Rome* (London-Sydney, 1986) 148f., more convincingly Junian Latins (mentioned 1, 81, *Leges Aelia Sentia* and *Junia* in 80). *Macedonianum*: *SV* 11; D. Daube, *ZSS* 65 (1947) 261–311; Levick 124; 222f. n. 29 (bibl.); *PIR²* M 9 (refs); loan non-actionable: Griffin, 1994, 313, and *CAH²* 11 (forthcoming); Talbert 443f. no. 70. *Pegasianum*: Talbert no. 68, with refs: *GI* 2, 254–9 (the quarter); 286a (*fideicommissa*); cf. Muirhead *ad loc.*; Ulp., *Reg.* 25, 14–16; Paul, *Sent.* 4, 3; 4, 5, *5; Just., *Inst.* 2, 23, 5–7; *Cod.* 1, 17, 2, 6; W. Buckland, *Textbook of Rom. Law from Aug. to Justinian³*, ed. P. Stein (Cambridge, 1966) 355f.; Sturm, *Atti* 1981, 117–20. *Iunia*: A.N. Sherwin-White, *The Rom. Citizenship²* (Oxford, 1973) 332–4; modified by Pegasus and Pusio: *GI* 1, 31; Ulp., *Reg.* 3, 4. Talbert no. 69 cites *GI* 1, 31, and Ulp., *Reg.* 3, 4.

28 Provincials employed: Ch. 10f. Boldness: Homo 298; quotation: Fishwick 1987, 300. Italy provincialized: *Verona List* of 312–14 (A.H.M. Jones, *Later Roman Empire* 3 (Oxford, 1964) 384); cf. N. Méthy, *Lat.* 55 (1996) 101–11; *DC* 52, 22, 1, with F. Millar, *Phoen.* 40 (1986) 295–315, on taxation. Change from Augustan policy: Graf 84f.; Bersanetti 60. Italy eulogized: *PNH* 3, 39–42; 37, 201–3; Tiberius' misgivings: *TA* 3, 54, 6–8; Italian senators: *TA* 11, 23, 5f. Vine edict: *SD* 7, 2. Tiberius benefactor: A.S. Hunt and C.C. Edgar, *Sel. Papyri* (Cambridge, Mass.-London) 2, 211, l. 39; Titus darling: *ST* 1; cf. Aur. Vict., *Caes.* 10, 6, with mention of provinces; [Epit. Aur. Vict.,] *Caes.* 10, 6; Eutrop., 7, 21. *Patria*: *PNH* 3, 39.

29 Peace: *PNH* 27, 1–3; Empire established: *JB* 7, 158. Early success: *SV* 8, 1; cf. Aur. Vict., *Caes.* 9, 8; cf. [Epit. Aur. Vict.] *Caes.* 9, 9. Asia Minor: Magie 566–92:

Ch. title; N. Africa: Leglay 201–3; governors: 209–13; Romanization: 234f. Trade: H.J. Loane, *CP* 39 (1944) 10–21; Bengtson 105f. 'Epigraphic habit': S. Mrozek, *Epigr.* 35 (1973) 113–18, esp. 14; C. Eilers, *Roman Patronage of Greek Cities* (Oxford, forthcoming), should be read. 'Administration': F.G.B. Millar, *JRS* 56 (1966) 166.

30 Neglect: *Docs G–N* 368, l. 11. Asseria: MW 451 ('*in re praesenti*'). Lepcis/Oea: *AE* 79, 648f. (first half of 74); line: Vita-Evrard 1979, 87–91. At Thagaste (Souk-Ahras) Suppenses and Vofricenses were segregated: *AE* 42, 35 (Domitian); J. Lancel, *Libyca* 3 (1955) 292 (V.). Lac(in)imurgenses: *AE* 86, 323 (Mar.–Dec. 73), with Stylow 308. Corsica: MW 460 (?77); V. confirms privileges which the Vanacini had kept until Galba's reign (i.e. Galba's successors were ignored). Dalmatia: *AE* 67, 355 (Iader). Vienna: 66, 243 (Col du Jaillet); MW 446 (Col de la Forclaz); without mention of censorship. Ceutrones Latin: *PNH* 3, 135, perhaps since Claudius: *CIL* 12, 104; so B. Galsterer-Kröll, *Chiron* 3 (1973) 289; Thasos: MW 457; Sparta: *AE* 05, 188; Mopsuhestia: *AE* 66, 486 (under P. Nonius Asprenas Caesianus or Caesius Cassianus: *PIR*^{2} N 123f.); later disputes: DP 34.

31 Pius: Ael. Arist., *On Rome* 33; J.H. Oliver, *The Ruling Power, Trans. Amer. Phil. Soc.* 43, 4 (1953) 919.

32 Promotions: Magie *l.c.,* Flamma: TH 4, 45, 2; J. Reynolds, *JRS* 49 (1959), 97. Bassus: *PEp.* 4, 9,1, cited by Bengtson 102; not necessarily *repetundae*, despite Sherwin-White's n.; not in Brunt, *RIT* 93; the procedure seems anomalous. Interpretation: B. Levick, *Lat.* 41 (1982) 63f. Eprius in Asia: *PIR* ^{2} E 84. Modestus: Eck, *Sen.* 119 (Catullus: Ch. 8). Domitian: *SD* 8, 2; Magie 578–80. Praise: TH 2, 82, 2.

33 'Specialists': Torelli 174. Agricola in Gaul: T*Agr.* 9, 1; hopes: 42, 1. Pliny's career: A.N. Sherwin-White, *The Letters of Pliny* (Oxford, 1966) 72–82.

34 *Iuridici*: McElderry 1919, 86–9, citing *PNH* 19, 37. Proconsul's legates as model: Eck, *Sen.* 38 n. 5; cf. *Dig.* 1, 16, 4, 6. Development: G. Alföldy *Fasti Hispanienses* (Wiesbaden, 1969) 236–52; Birley 1981, 404–7. Licinus: *PEp.* 3, 5, 17 (advocate: 2, 14, 9–11); cf. *PNH* 19, 35 ('*iura reddenti*'); 31, 24: Syme *RP* 7, 503f.: *iuridicus* (Alföldy, 1969, 70f.), not acting-governor (Sherwin White 1966, 223, rebutted by Eck, *Sen.* 225 n. 476). Liberalis (*PEp.* 2, 11, 17; SV 13) and Javolenus (*Dig.* 36, 1, 48 (46)): Syme 1980, 25f.; Birley 1981, 211–14, dates them 78– or 79–81 or 81–4 and between 83 and 86 respectively, suggesting (210 n. 16) that Fishbourne was constructed for the *iuridicus*. Cogidubnus' death (T*Agr.* 14, 1): Birley 1981, 207f.; cf. A. Barrett, *Brit.* 10 (1979), 241f. (mid-60s). Galatia-Cappadocia: R. Sherk, *The Legates of Galatia from Augustus to Diocletian* (Baltimore, 1951) 41f.; Eck, *Sen.* 3, with n. 9; Rutilius: Syme, *RP* 5, 518f. Polemaeanus: MW 316. Legates as administrators in Augustan Celtiberia: Strabo 3, p. 166f. Alföldy 1969, 67, starts the series with L. Piso in 25 and suggests, 74f., that Q. Pomponius Rufus functioned in Spain 75– or 74–8, succeeding Licinus.

35 *Mandata*: J.M. Reynolds and R.G. Goodchild, *Lib. Ant.* 2 (1965) 106. Augustan injunctions: EJ^{2}311; B. Levick, *The Government of the Rom. Empire* (London and Sydney, 1985), 10 no. 6, on J.H. Oliver, *AJP* 100 (1979) 551–4. See Brunt, *RIT* 179, on procurators (T*Agr.* 9, 4), V. fattening them (SV 16, 2), and jurisdiction exercised, under Domitian, by those of the Fiscus Judaicus (*SD* 12).

36 Urbanization: Graf 76f., with n. 415 (list and bibl., including Weynand 2681–4; J. Assmann, *De coloniis et oppidis Rom., quibus imperatoria nomina . . . imposita sunt* (Langensalza, 1905); E. Kornemann, *RE* 4 (1901) 511f.); Homo 298 ('*romanisation du monde*'); Garzetti 1974, 249f.; H.-G. Pflaum, *ZPE* 17 (1975) 262. Africa: Leglay 220f. Madaurus: *ILA* 2070; 2064 *bis*; 2152, but Leglay 221 n. 2 dates after V.; Broughton 104; Leglay 221 adds Icosium, with population transferred to

Ilici to make way for the Augustan colony Rusguniae: *PNH* 5, 20; *CIL* 8, 20853 (July 74–6). Aventicum: Staehelin 1948, 205–11 (cf. 223 n. 4); R. Frei-Stolba, *ANRW* 2, 5, 1 (1976) 391–3. D. Van Berchem, *Chiron* 11 (1981) 221–8: Latin colony keeping local leaders in power. 'Foederata': J. Nollé, in C. Schubert and K. Brodersen, eds, *Rom u. der griech. Osten: Festschrift f. H. Schmitt z. 65 Geburtstag* (Stuttgart, 1995) 356f. Brigantium etc.: H.-J. Kellner, *Die Römer in Bayern* (Munich, 1971) 41–6. Forum Segusiavorum: Assmann 101, citing *CIL* 13, p. 221. Flaviobriga: *PNH* 4, 110 (= Portus Amanum); Ptol. 2, 6, 7. Conquest: Syme, *RP* 2, 825–54; victory: DC 54, 11, 2–6; Neronian revolt: *Docs G–N* 183; gold: *PNH* 33, 78. A N.W. Spain under separate administration was rebutted by McElderry 1918, 85.

37 Sirmium: *CIL* 3, 10220. Siscia: *PNH* 3, 148. Scupi: Mócsy 116; *IMS* 6, p. 25f.; 57 no. 15. E. Birley, *ZPE* 64 (1986) 209–16. Ex-sailors in Balkans: *CIL* 3, p. 850f. (71).

38 Thrace: Jones 1971, 17f., with nn. 24 and 26.

39 Caesarea: *PNH* 5, 69; *HN* [2] 802; centre: *TH* 2, 78, 4; rights: *Dig.* 50, 15, 1, 6; 8; 7; '*Prima*' refers to primacy, not to V.'s proclamation. No settlers: B. Isaac *Talanta* 12–13 (1980–1) 38–43. Ptolemais: Levick 1990, 183. Camulodunum: *TA* 12, 32, 5; 14, 31, 4f. Ammaedara: *CIL* 8, 308. Initiative: J.C. Mann, *Legionary Recruitment and Veteran Settlement. Inst. Arch. Occas. Publ.* 7 (London, 1983) 56–63.

40 Egyptian dyke (75): *POxy.* 1112, l. 2. *Vehiculatio*: MW 457. Africa: Hippo-Carthage: *CIL* 8, 10116 (first half of 76). Asia Minor: D. French, *ANRW* 2, 7, 2 (1980) 698–729; *Roman Roads and Milestones in Asia Minor* 2, 1. *BAR Intern.* 192 (i) (Oxford, 1988) 430. Asia: nos. 479f., 688; *CIL* 3, 470; 7203f.; *IGR* 4, 267 nos. 479f.; *483 (Ephesus-Pergamum); 688 (nr. Thyatira). N.W.: 304, 308 = MW 421, of 77–8. Cilicia: 461; Seleuceia: R. Heberdey and A. Wilhelm, *Reisen in Kilikien ausgeführt in 1891 u.1892. Denkschr. Wien* 44 (Vienna, 1896) 101 ('*ek demosion*').

41 Via Augusta: MW 418 (first half of 79), at the Baetis. Bracara-Asturica road: *CIL* 2, 4814 (77); Calpetanus Rantius: MW 417; *ILS* 5833; Eck, *Sen.* 127f. n. 73. Newton 64 nos. 131–4, 136f., collects others (Titus, or uncertain date); bridge in Gallaecia: MW 87 (first half of 79).

42 Vicissitudes: Garzetti 1974, 641. Deportation: *TA* 2, 85, 5 ('*latrociniis*'). Boundaries: MW 455. '*Procurator et praefectus*' in 74: MW 337; *CIL* 10, 8024 (milestone); 8005 (first half of 70). Corsica: *TH* 2, 16; MW 460 (?77): '*beneficia . . . quae in tempora Galbae retinuistis, confirmo*'.

43 Transpadana: Sherwin-White 1973 (n. 27 above) 157–9; Maritime Alps: *TA* 15, 31, 1, with Sherwin-White 367–73. Claudius: Levick 1990, 165–7. Spain: *PNH* 3, 30: '*iactatum procellis reipublicae*'; Bosworth 1973, 51–5, adopts '*iactatus*', V.'s plight in 69–71. Fear 145f., rightly stressing V.'s self-interest, 143, agrees. But Hirschfeld's doubt, *Kl. Schrift.* (Berlin, 1913) 303 n. 4, whether Pliny would have admitted that, remains. Mackie 1983, 215f., saw that '*iactatum*' referred to generosity on the part of V.'s predecessors, notably Vitellius when Spain had gone over: *TH* 1, 78, 1; 3, 55, 2; the grant was precarious until confirmed. 73–4: McElderry 1918, 79, arguing that inscriptions (*CIL* 2, 1049) mention the censorship, that Titus is V.'s colleague as benefactor, and that references to the grant are all 75 or later (*e.g. CIL* 2, 2096; 1610 (Cisimbrium, dated by Stylow 290–5 to 84; Igabrum)). Bosworth's date, 70–1, was questioned by Wiegels 197–208 (prosopographical grounds); Bengtson 129, González 201, and M.T. Griffin, *CAH*[2] 11 (forthcoming) accept 73–4. Civilis (*TH* 4, 68, 4): Fear 146. Charters not granted immediately: Millar *ERW* 405. Date and purpose of Law: 147–51, citing *Tab. Irn.* Ch. 20 for modifications.

44 Whole peninsula: Mackie 1983, 216f.; MacElderry 1918, 68–79. Fear 138–40, 148, noting need for 129 charters for Baetica, 172 for the rest; contra. Galsterer 1971, 46–60. Charters: MW 453f.; González 1986; fragments: A. D'Ors, *Emérita* 73 (1985), 31–41 (local emulation 40); A.M. Canto, *ZPE* 63 (1986), 217–20; J. González, *ZPE* 70 (1987), 217–21 (modern Cortegana or Italica) (I owe these references to Dr Fear's kindness; see also Fear 132 n. 6). Content, effects: Braunert (private rights, rebutted by Galsterer 1971); Galsterer-Kröll 1973, 280–4; H. Wolff, *BJ* 176 (1976) 56–62; Wiegels 211; Millar, *ERW* 485; 630–5; Galsterer 1988, 82–8; Fear 133–8; survival of *Latini coloniarii* 136.

45 Ipsca: *CIL* 2, 1570, 1572, 1597, with Mackie 25. Stylow, 301–3, stresses the intermediate phase as one in which communities adopted Roman ways. Variants and eligibility for magistrates: Galsterer 1988, 83 and 86, citing *Lex Irnitana* 21. Ch. 31 refers to provisions operative '*ante hanc legem rogatam*', reflecting 'the incorporation . . . without proper rephrasing, of a chapter of a general law . . ., passed in the comitia at Rome' (González 1986, 208). Stability: Fear 155; 167: no Latin-Roman *conubium*.

46 Saborenses: MW 461. [Caes.] *Bell. Hisp.* 8, 3–5, is cited by Mackie 1983, 15 n. 20. Vibius (MW 334) is dated 71–4 by Bosworth 1973, 70–7; but cf. Wiegels 196–205; Eck 1982, 288 n. 24; Stylow 299 n. 26, for appointment after the second consulship; Syme, 'Ministers' 530 is for 73. Munigua rebuked: *AE* 62, 288.

47 Latinity and public works: Mackie 126 n. 7; no contribution: 146 n. 10. Fear 167; 221–4. Munigua: W. Grünhagen in *Segovia, Symposium de arqueol. rom.* (Barcelona, 1977) 201–8. Conimbriga: *PE s.v.*, on *AE* 69/70, 247. Cartima: *CIL* 2, 1956f. Ipsca temple: 1570. Lepcis: Vita-Evrard 1979, 91–8 (date: 74–7); *Bull. Arch. du Com. de Trav. hist. et scient.* NS 17b (1981) 198–209, esp. 204; arch to V. and Titus: *IRT* 342 (78); 348 (Domitianic temple).

48 Dated inscriptions: R. Duncan-Jones, *Structure and Scale in the Anc. Economy* (Cambridge, 1990) 60f.

49 Criteria: Galsterer-Kröll 1973, 303. Scardona: Wilkes 1969, 218, on *CIL* 3, 2809f.; Doclea: Wilkes 259–61 (ascribing grant to Titus); 425. Others: 290. Solva: *PNH* 3, 146 ('*oppidum*'), with Alföldy 1974, 81f.; 94f. (plans); 309 n. 20 (Quirina); *CIL* 3, 13707, apparently mentions '*municipium Flavia Solva*'; Scarbantia (*CIL* 3, 4243; 14355) belonged to Quirina; cf. *PNH* 3, 146; *PE s.v.*; others: Mócsy 115 ('policy'). Volubilis: *Docs G–N* 407(b). Africa: Leglay 221f. Hippo, Bulla: Gascou 33–5; Sufetula: *CIL* 8, 23216; Flavii at Cillium: 211–16; Kotula 207; Thysdrus: *AE* 91, 1635. Inscriptions: Bengtson 128. Thugga: *AE* 86, 1023; Sabratha: *AE* 71, 485; cf. *IRT* 342 (Leptis). Dedications: Leglay 233 n. 2. Arches: Mattingly and Hitchner 185.

50 Cirta tribes: MW 448. Cirta/Tigisis: *AE* 57, 175; 1969/70, 696; sedentary: A. Berthier, *Bull. d'arch. Alg.* 3, (1968) 293–300. Sofeggin: Mattingly and Hitchner 194f; 'Romanization': 206. Mancian tenure: Ch.7 n. 16.

51 Arae Flaviae: Planck 1975, 220–4; Aquae Flavianae: *CIL* 8, 17727; Vindonissa: *CIL* 13, 5195. Danube: Mócsy 139; Corinth: *HN*[2] 404 (Domitian onwards); restored (and Perinthus refounded as Heraclea!): Malalas 261f.D. Claudia Paphos Flavia after the earthquake: *ANRW* 2, 7, 2 (1980) 1310f. n. 86. Traianus benefactor: *BCH* 12 (1886) 281.

52 Flaviopolis: Jones 1971, 204; Dąbrowa 14; 71, Assizes: Habicht 1975, Flaviopolitae 66, 73f. Cities: *JB* 2, 366; *PhVS* 548; coinage etc: *ESAR* 4, 715, 746; Bengtson 132.

53 *TAgr.* 21; *PNH* 3, 39, with Fear 22f.

54 M. Millett, *The Romanization of Britain, an Essay in Archaeological Interpretation*

(Cambridge, 1990); East: G. Woolf, *PCPS* 40 (1990) 116–43 (bibl.). Seasons: Mattingly and Hitchner 205f., on cultural perspectives; see also Bénabou, esp. 331–80.

55 African change: Leglay 246 (based on Baal-Hammon: M. Leglay, *Saturne africain: monuments* (2 vols, 1961, 1966)); different emphasis: Gascou 11: little urbanization Augustus–V., slow recovery under Flavians, vigorous policy only with Trajan; initiative with rulers, 36; cf. Bénabou 417f. (cautious); P. Leveau, *Annales* 33 (1978) 89–92 (parameters of discussion); Mattingly and Hitchner 177; 185; 205. Lepcis a '*Sufet-municipium*': Gascou 35. 'Our army': Lucian, *Alex.* 48.

56 Houses: Fear 26; Loans: DC 62, 2, 1. Verulamium inscription: Birley 1981, 73. Trebellius: T*Agr.* 16, 3, with Ogilvie and Richmond. Demetrius: *ibid.* p. 32f., on Pl., *Mor.* 410A, 419E–20A; *RIB* 662f. Camulodunum: TA 12, 32, 5, cited by Hanson, *Conquest* 73; Flavian building: 75–8; 'Tac.' 1775f. Economic change: B.W. Cunliffe in B.C. Burnham and H.B. Johnson, eds, *Invasion and Response: The case of Roman Britain. BAR Brit. Ser.* 73 (Oxford, 1979) 363f. Urbanization in London, Exeter, and Leicester: P. Salway, *Roman Britain* (Oxford-N.Y., 1981) 156f.; S.S. Frere, *Britannia*³ (London-N.Y., 1987) 193.

57 Gallic advance: J. Drinkwater, *Roman Gaul: the three provinces, 58* BC – AD 260 (London and Canberra, 1983) 35–92; 'Julii': *Lat.* 37 (1978) 817–50. Claudius: Levick 1990, 167–72. North: E. Wightman, *Gallica Belgica* (London, 1984) 53–74; 80–100; 158–190; Mann 1983 (n. 39). Routes: Strabo, 4, p. 199, with W.B. Cunliffe in S. Macready and F.H. Thompson, eds, *Cross-Channel Trade between Gaul and Britain in the Pre-Roman Iron Age. Soc. Ant. Occ. Papers* (London, 1984) 6f.; 242; cf. C. Partridge, *Skeleton Green, a late Iron Age and Romano-British Site, Brit. Mon.* 2 (London, 1981) 351f.

58 Prosperity: Bengtson 128f. Cillium: Gascou 31f.; MacKendrick 50; Thysdrus oil: Leglay 229f; ceramics: 231; *tria nomina*: 234 (Antonines reaped what Flavians had sown); *ex voto* development: 237f.

59 African dedications: Leglay 233 n. 2. Comment on grants: JCA 2, 40; Sen., *Apoc.* 3, 3, with Levick 1990, 172f.

60 Eastern affairs: TH 1, 2, 1. Progress: JB 7, 21f.; DC 65 (66), 9, 2ª. Houston 1972, 177 n. 45, has M. Plancius Varus on Perge's embassy, noting others: JB 7, 22, and *IGR* 4, 120 (Mysian Apollonia, before 26 September 70).

61. MW 458, cf. SV 17f.: see P.A. Brunt, *BICS* 39 (1994) 25 n. 1 (teachers of rhetoric benefit). Not philosophers (also mentioned in *Dig.* 50, 4, 18, 30): G.W. Bowersock, *Greek Sophists in the Rom. Emp.* (Oxford, 1969) 32f.; M.T. Griffin, *CR* NS 43 (1993) 116.

62 Nero's philhellenism: *Docs G–N* 64, ll. 40–2. Favoured: JA 20, 154. False Neros: TH 1, 2, 1; 2, 8f. (69); John of Ant., Fr. 104M (80–1); S*Nero* 57, 2 (88). Malcontents: G. Bowersock, *Entretiens Hardt* 33 (Geneva, 1987) 308–11; Parthians preferred: DC 48, 24, 8; 49, 20, 4 (40–38 BC). *Or. Sib.* 4 (Jerusalem 125–36, Nero's return 138f., enrichment of Asia 145–77); Eus.-Jer., *Chron. s.a.* 77, p. 188 Helm, has three Cypriot cities destroyed. Origin of oracles: J. Geffcken, *Komposition und Entstehungszeit der Or. Sib.* (Leipzig, 1902) 18–21; *Revelation*: R. Bauckham in L. Alexander, ed., *Images of Empire* (Sheffield, 1991) 47–90, noting *Or. Sib.* 3, 350–80, and 4, 145–8. R. Moberly, *Bibl.* 73 (1992) 376–93, puts *Revelation's* genesis in 69. Interested benefactions: *Babylon. Talmud* 33b, in Yavetz 1975, 411.

63 Cybiosactes: SV 19, 2 (with Strabo 17, p. 796; DC 39, 57, 1). Caesar: DC 65 (66), 8, 6. Freedom: SV 8, 4, lists Achaea, Rhodes, Byzantium, Samos, Lycia, with dependent monarchies Cilicia, Thrace (for Trachea, describing Cilicia; cf. Malalas 262D), and Commagene; so Eutrop. 7, 19, 4; Oros. 7, 9, 10; Eus.-Jer., *Chron., s.a.*

74, p. 188 Helm; PhVA 5, 41 (Achaea only, mentioning disorder; cf. Paus. 7, 17, 4), with M.T. Griffin, *CAH*² 11 (forthcoming). Cos: Magie 1428f. n. 10 (inconclusive); see S. Sherwin-White, *Ancient Cos. Hypomn.* 51 (Göttingen, 1978) 148 (Cos unfree *c*.27 BC – 78, made immune from tribute 53). Lycia: n. 65. Corinth's coinage: C.J. Howgego, *NC* 149 (1989) 199.

64 Byzantium, Samos: *PNH* 4, 46; 5, 135. Achaea: Paus. 7, 17, 3; E. Groag, *Die röm. Reichsbeamten v. Achaia bis auf Diokletian. Schr. d. Balkankomm.* 9 (Vienna-Leipzig, 1939) 41. Date: 70: PhVA *l.c.*; Syncell. 646D, accepted by C.P. Jones, *Plutarch and Rome* (Oxford, 1971) 18 n. 30, and Bosworth 1973, 60f.; 73–4: Eus.-Jer. *l.c.*, accepted by R.J.A. Wilson, *CAH*² 10, 445. Houston 1972 suggests Plancius Varus as first governor; the chronology of his career is uncertain. Rhodes: Jones 1978, 168 n. 17; H. Sidebottom, *Hist.* 41 (1992) 409 n. 27.

65 Asprenas: *TH* 2, 9, 1. Bengtson 111 follows Eus.-Jer.; Kreiler 101 suggests that it returned to provincial status in 69: *'libertas'* implies freedom from governors (105 n. 5). Lycia never freed: Eck, 'Leg.' (older views 71 n. 24); *Sen.* 4; Eck cites *TAM* 2, 396, from Patara: Marcius serves an emperor whose name is erased (Nero) and V.'s substituted. At Lydae (MW 287) he is 'legate of Vespasian and of all emperors since Tiberius' (which may refer generally to long service). C.P. Jones, *Gnomon* 1973, 690f., holds Lycia unviable as a province, but cf. S. Şahin, *Lykia* 1 (1994) 130–7; Eck 1982, 285 n. 16, rebutted doubts; A. Balland, *Fouilles de Xanthos* (Paris, 1981) 4 n. 23 (hesitatingly), Strobel 1985, and Mitchell 1993, 2, 153f., rallied; contra, R. Syme, *Anatolica: Studies in Strabo* (Oxford, 1995) 274–80. Hall 1984 argued for M. Hirrius Fronto as first governor of the reunited province 71/2; so Halfmann, 1991, Mitchell 1993, I 154, with n. 57; critique by Strobel who, like Eck, 'Leg.', has Pansa in Lycia alone, 70–2; for M.T. Griffin, *CAH*² 11 (forthcoming), the number of V.'s legates suggests early reannexation.

66 *Lex*: M. Wörrle, *Stadt u. Fest im kaiserzeitl. Kleinasien. Vest.* 39 (Munich, 1988) 97–100. *Vespasianeia*: *IGR* 3, 487; N.P. Milner and S. Mitchell, *Anat. Stud.* 55 (1995) 96f. Myra: *AE* 91, 1534 (73); Xanthus: *TAM* 2, 270, 275; Balbura: *IGR* 3, 466; *AE* 78, 834 (?74–6); Patara: *TAM* 2, 396 ('synterethenton'); Cadyanda: *TAM* 2, 651 (MW 437); 652 ('anasothenton'):, with S. Mitchell in S. Macready and F.H. Thompson, eds, *Rom. Architecture in the Greek World, Soc. Ant. Occ. Papers* 10 (London, 1987) 21; J.J. Coulton, *ibid.* 73f.; J.R. Patterson in J. Rich and A. Wallace-Hadrill, eds, *City and Country in the Ancient World. Leicester-Nottingham Stud. in Anc. Soc.* 2 (London and N.Y., 1991) 157–65. C. Roueché in M.M. Mackenzie and C. Roueché, eds, *Images of Authority. Papers presented to J. Reynolds on . . . her 70th birthday. PCPS Suppl.* 16 (1989) 211, cite A.M. Mansel in D. Ahrens, ed., *Festschrift M. Wegner* (Münster, 1962) 38–41, and *Bell.* 28 (1964) 185–208 for a monument at Side (first half of 74), and *SEG* 34 (1984) 1306 for Perge's neocorate. Attaleia: *AE* 72, 601 (early in reign?). Dedication also at Cestrus: 643 (first part of 76, to V. and Titus). Ephesus, with Traianus *'diataxantos'*: *BCH* 10 (1886) 95 (80). Caution on payment: Mitchell, 'Building'; the list in Garzetti 1974, 640, is undifferentiated. A gift to Sparta seems implied by *CIG* 1305 (78)); note the ?architrave from a ?bathhouse at Lappa, kindly drawn to my attention by the late W.G. Forrest, *Horos* 6 (1988) 61f.

67 Eprius: n. 32. Galatia-Cappadocia and roads: Ch. 10. *'Nova iura'*: *TH* 1, 78, 1. Melitene: Kreiler 74. Troops in transit S. Mitchell, *Armies and Frontiers in Asia Minor. Proc. of a Colloquium . . . 1981. BAR Internat.* 156 (Oxford, 1983) 139–45. Bithynia: P*Ep*. 10, with Sherwin-White; B. Levick, *G&R* NS 26 (1979) 119–31. Creteia: Jones 1971, 159; *HN*² 514. (Flaviopoleis in Asia: n. 52.)

68 Fronto: Halfmann 1979, 109 no. 32; priesthood: MW 132.

69 Claudian famine: Levick 1990, 179. Domitianic: *Revelation* 6, 6; edict: *SD* 7, 2;

14, 2, with B. Levick, *Lat.* 41 (1982) 66–73. Riot: DP 46, 8. Cibyra: *IGR* 4, 914f., with L. Homo, *RA* 42 (1940), 462 (promoting cereals).

70 Syrian roads: Ch. 10. Antioch: *JB* 2, 479; Smallwood 1976, 361 (Roman troops present). Damascus: *JB* 2, 561; (and all Syrian cities) 7, 368, with divergent figures; see Millar 1993, 78. First accusation: *JB* 7, 41–53; fire: 54–62, Petitions: *JB* 7, 96–111; *JA* 12, 121–4. See Downey 204f.; 586f.; Smallwood, 358–64, suggesting (362) that Christianizing Jews were attacked; date of second petition: 363 n. 29.

71 Spoils and theatre: Malalas 260f.D, with Downey 206f. (V. is credited with a temple of the Winds, 262.) Purpose: Millar 1993, 79. Canal: D. Feissel, *Syria* 62 (1985) 77–103; cf. Ch. 10 n. 46. Berytus: *CIL* 3, 170. Bostra, Gerasa: Bengtson 122f. Palmyra: J.F. Matthews, *JRS* 74 (1984) 158–73; sites: Rostovtzeff 1932.

72 PhVA 5, 27–40; (V.); 6, 29–33 (Titus). Euphrates: *PEp.* 1, 10. Epictetus: F. Millar, *JRS* 55 (1965) 140–8. Dio of Prusa: Jones 1978 (esp. 14–16). In Alexandria: Syn., *Dion* 316, 21f. (Sidebottom 1996, 448 n. 11 sceptical). Eastern senators: Ch. 11.

73 Post-war Judaea: Millar 1993, 366–74. Legate: Eck, *Sen.* 5 (garrison commander only). X Fret.: *JB* 7, 17. Emmaus: 217 (not the toparchy capital Nicopolis: Schürer 1973, 512 n. 142; Smallwood 1976, 341 n. 42). House of David: Eus., *Hist. Eccl.* 3, 12 (Hegesippus), with Smallwood 351f. Agrippa II received gifts: Phot., *Cod.* 33 (Justus of Tiberias); *JB* 7, 97, names Arcea in Lebanon; Smallwood 339f. with n. 35.

74 'Iron ring': Rostovtzeff 1932, 67, discussed by B. Isaac, *The Limits of Empire: the Roman army in the East*[2] (Oxford, 1992) 346–9. Cities not founded: *JB* 7, 217, accepted by Cohen 139 against M. Avi-Yonah, *The Holy Land . . . a hist. geogr.* (Grand Rapids, 1966) 110f. Toparchies: *JB* 3, 54f. Landed rulers: Brunt, *RIT* 526f. Reconstruction: *JB* 4, 442. Caesarea: n. 39; V. in office: *CIL* 3, 170; Weber 271 n. 2; cf. E. Kornemann, *RE* 4 (1901) 552 no. 273. 'Greek' city: Dr Rajak notes *JB* 2, 266: it had a sizeable Jewish clement. Odeion: Malalas 261D. Joppa: *JB* 2, 507–9; 3, 424–7; *PNH* 5, 69; *HN*[2] 803 (with Neapolis); Emmaus-Nicopolis: Smallwood 343 n. 48. Neapolis: Jones 1971, 228 and 278; Schürer 1973, 520 n. 36; Millar 1993, 368; the new name took time to root: *JA* 4, 449.

75 'Private possession': Schürer 1973, 512. Julianus: *JB* 6, 238, with Smallwood 1976, 317 n. 104. Taxes: Schürer 513 n. 143 (bibl.); Smallwood 344. Temple tax: Ch. 7 n. 17. Disposal: *JB* 7, 216, with Smallwood 340f. n. 40; 342. Agrarian conditions: Applebaum 1977, 385–95 ('leasing' 388–91); he cites *Midrash de-Bei Rav* 317, and compares TA 14, 31, 5. Settlers: *JB* 4, 438; 444.

76 Jamnia: Smallwood 1976, 347–51; Schürer 1973, 513; 521–8; Cohen 138–41; Pharisaic: 237f. Morality: P.R. Davies in L. Alexander, ed., *Images of Empire* (Sheffield, 1991) 175; later Diaspora: F. Millar in J. Lieu *et al.* eds, *The Jews among Pagans and Christians in the Roman Empire* (London-N.Y., 1992) esp. 120. Christianity: S. Brandon, *The Fall of Jerusalem and the Christian Church, a Study of the Effects of the Jewish Overthrow of AD 70 on Christianity*[2] (London, 1957). Flight of community: Schürer 498, citing (n. 65) Eus., *Hist. Eccl.* 3, 5, 2f.; Epiph., *Haer.* 29, 7; *De Mens.* 15. Circumcision: *Acts* 15, 5–29.

77 Edict: *Docs G–N* 391. Tax: DC 65 (66), 8, 3f. Sedition: *JB* 2, 487–98; Eus.-Jer., *Chron.*, *s.a.* 74, p. 188 Helm. *Fideicommissa: Gnom. of Idios Logos* (A. Hunt and C. Edgar, eds, *Sel. Pap.* 2 (Cambridge, Mass., 1934) 206) 18. Vitellius: C. Préaux, *Mél. G. Smets* (Brussels, 1952) 576 (Thebes). Prefect's decline: Brunt, *RIT* 215; experience: 222f.

78 Batavi: Willems 242.

10. IMPERIALISM: VESPASIAN'S ARMY AND THE EXTENSION OF THE EMPIRE

Bibl.: Ch. 8f., E.N. Luttwak, 51–126; Alföldy 1968 (Ch. 8) 148–59; P. Holder, *Stud. in the Auxilia of the Rom. army from Aug. to Trajan. BAR Intern.* 70 (1980); Saddington 1982, 107–92; D.J. Knight, *ZPE* 85 (1991) 189–208 (movements); V.A. Maxfield, *The Military Decorations of the Rom. Army* (London, 1981). Britain: Garzetti 1974, 641f. (bibl.). E. Birley, *Rom. Britain and the Rom. Army*[2] (Kendal, 1961) 10–19; Birley 1973; M.W.C. Hassall, *Brit.* 1 (1970) 131–6; W.H. Manning, *Early Rom. Campaigns in the S.W. of Britain. The first ann. Caerleon Lecture* (Cardiff, 1988); N. Reed, *Brit.* 2 (1971) 143–8; Hanson, *Conquest* 46–142 (maps); 'Tac.' 1757–84. Germany: R. Syme, *CAH* 11, 131–87; H. Schönberger, *JRS* 59 (1969) 144–97 (bibl.); B. Zimmermann, *Jahresb. aus Augst u. Kaiseraugst* 13 (1992) 289–303 (Clemens); P. Filtzinger, *Arae Flaviae, das röm. Rottweil* (Rottweil 1995). Danube: Mócsy 1974 (Ch. 9) 80–9; Wilkes 1983; L. Pitts, *JRS* 79 (1989) 45–58 (kings). Euphrates: N. Debevoise, *A Political Hist. of Parthia* (N.Y., 1938) 196–202; Magie 566–92; K.-H. Ziegler, *Die Beziehungen zwischen Rom und dem Partherreich. Ein Beitrag zur Gesch. des Volkerrechts* (Wiesbaden, 1964) 78–81; Kreiler 1975; Bowersock, 'Syria'; A.B. Bosworth, *Antichthon* 10 (1976) 63–78; *HSCP* 81 (1977) 217–55; H. Hellenkemper in *Stud. zu den Militärgrenzen Roms* 2. *Vorträge des 10 intern. Limeskongr.* (Cologne, 1977) 461–71; T.M. Mitford, *ANRW* 2, 7, 2 (1980) 1169–228; Dąbrowa, *Asie Mineure*; *Klio* 62 (1980) 379–88 ('Limes'); *Syria* 58 (1981) 187–204; *Lat.* 41 (1982) 614–19; in *The Rom. and Byzant. Army in the E. Proc. of Coll. of Sept. 1992* (Krákow, 1994) 19–27; B.W. Jones, *RM* 128 (1985) 346–52 (Titus, 70–1); Halfmann, 'Alanen'; M. Heil, *Chiron* 19 (1989) 165–84; B. Isaac, *The Limits of Empire: The Roman Army in the East*[2] (Oxford, 1992); E.L. Wheeler in V.A. Maxfield and M.J. Dobson, eds, *Rom. Frontier Stud. 1989: Proc. of the XVth intern. congr. of Rom. front. stud.* (Exeter, 1991) 505–11; Millar 1993, 80–90; S. Mitchell 1993 (Ch. 9) I, 117–42.

1 Nightmare: W. Eck *et al.*, eds, *Das SC de Cn. Pisone patre. Vest.* 48 (Munich, 1996) 42, l. 52f. Fear: TH 4, 46, 2: SV 8, 2.

2 Recalcitrance: TH 4, 2, 2. Mucianus' measures: 4, 46, 2–4. Fleets honoured: C.G. Starr, *The Rom. Imperial Navy 31 BC–AD 324* (Westwood 1941) 185f. Cashierings: SV 8, 2; Graf 71 and n. 356 singles out XV; not so Chilver/Townend p. 14; see also C. Ritterling, *RE* 12 (1925) 1760; Nicolas 1278–82; L. Keppie, *The Making of the Rom. Army: From Republic to Empire* (London, 1984) 213–15; Flaig 403 n. 158. V Alaud.: TH 1, 61, 2; Syme, 'March' 1007 and DP 105, favours survival; Wilkes 1983, 279 n. 42, and K. Strobel, *Hist.* 37 (1988) 504–8, are against. Origin of Alaud.: SCaes. 24, 2; earlier bibl. Garzetti 1974, 638. Destruction in Moesia: Ch. 8 n. 22. Cremona legions to Illyricum: TH 3, 35, 1. Scupi: E. Birley, *ZPE* 64 (1986) 211. Vitellian praetorians: MW 375, 381f. (capitulations: TH 3, 63, 1): transfers: Chilver/Townend on TH 4, 46; Flaig 401f. on difficulties. Skill: E. Marsden, *Greek and Rom. Artillery: Hist. development* (Oxford, 1969) 185, on MW 375.

3 Late payments: SV 8, 2. Gift exchange: Flaig 454. Sternness: SV *l.c.*; Graf 70 compares SCaes. 65; SAug. 24, 1; STib. 19; SG 12, 2f. Losses of VII Gem.: TH 3, 22, 4, with Wellesley 1972, 222. *Flaviales* (Veget. 2, 7, with N. Milner) belong, as Prof. Saddington kindly notes, to the second Flavian dynasty.

4 Proletarians: Homo 138–40, 320f., like Graf 71 following *SEHRE* 573 n. 8; see E. Birley, *Britain and the Roman Army*[2] (Kendal, 1961) 124. Ignorance of politics: H. Last, *CAH* 11, 396.

5 Legionaries' origins: G. Forni, *Il reclutamento delle legioni da Augusto a Diocleziano*

(Milan-Rome, 1953) 177–86; *ANRW* 2, 1 (1974) 339–91, esp. 380–5; G. Webster, *The Roman Imperial Army*[3] (London, 1985) 108. *Alimenta*: P*Pan*. 28. Tiberius' complaint: T*A* 4, 4, 4; 5, 5. Germany: J. Mann, *Legionary Recruitment and Veteran Settlement During the Principate. Inst. Arch. Occ. Publ.* 7 (London, 1983) 25–9, with Table 11f.

6 Recruitment: W. Wagner, *Die Dislokation der röm. Auxiliarformationen in den Prov. Noricum, Pannonien, Moesien, u. Dakien v. Aug. bis Gallienus. Neue Deutsche Forsch., Abt. Alte Gesch.* 5 (Berlin, 1938) 96f.; Holder 1980, 16–18 ('Flavia' as a battle honour); 142; Leglay 220 n. 3; arrangements for *auxilia* Saddington 1982, 127–35. New areas: 161. I am indebted to Professor Saddington for help on these topics.

7 Older views: Homo 322. Double units: Holder 1980, 5f.; 142, cf. J*B* 3, 67; Corbulo's device: D. Kennedy, *ZPE* 61 (1985) 181–5; D.B. Saddington in Y. Le Bohec, ed., *La hiérarchie (Rangordung) de l'armée rom. sous le Haut-Empire. Actes du Congrès de Lyon* (Paris, 1995) 54 on *Acts* 21, 31. Citizens: *AE* 66, 187: Ala Sulpicia c.R. German problem: Ch. 8 n. 16. Neronian institutionalization: Saddington 1982, 195–7; cf. H. Callies, *BRGK* 45 (1965) 146–8 (Tacitean 'cohorts' as native units). Native commanders: T*H* 4, 12, 3 (in imperfect tense) with Chilver/ Townend following Brunt, 'Tac.' 38 (they lost the privilege in 70); see A.R. Birley, *ZPE* 88 (1991) 97f. nn. 48f.; A.K. Bowman, *Life and Letters on the Roman Frontier* (London, 1994) 25–7, citing (n. 18) the loyal Labeo of T*H* 4, 18, 4 (note his feud with Civilis); Sulpicia: A.K. Bowman and J.D. Thomas, *The Vindolanda Writing Tablets* 2 (London, 1994) 218 no. 247; H. Elton, *Frontiers of the Roman Empire* (London, 1996) 50, notes the Gallic-sounding prefect of *ILS* 2734. Service abroad: T*Agr*. 31, 1.

8 Nine cohorts: MW 400; ten: *CIL* 16, 81, with Chilver/Townend on T*H* 4, 46, 4, cf. 2, 93, 2; criticism of Th. Mommsen and M. Durry's view (*Ges. Schr.* 6 (Berlin, 1910) 8; *Les cohortes prétoriennes. BEFAR* 47 (Paris, 1938) 80) on reduction: A. Passerini, *Le coorti pretorie* (Rome, 1939) 55–7. One thousand in each: Flaig 354. Analogy between Titus and Drusus Caesar: M.T. Griffin, *CAH*[2] 11 (forthcoming). Alexander Prefect: Ch. 8 n. 26.

9 Four *urbanae*: MW 400; H. Freis, *Die Cohortes urbanae. Epigr. Stud.* 2 (Cologne-Graz, 1967) 13–16. Commanders: Syme, 'Prefects'. Carthage: MW 376, cf. Z. Visy, *AH* 30 (1978) 49–54; F. Bérard, *MEFR* 100 (1988) 173–9 (I am indebted to Prof. Saddington for these references). Lugdunum: *ILS* 2119.

10 Domitian *v.* predecessors: M.T. Griffin, *CR* 43 (1993) 115; Tiberius' withdrawal: Levick 1976, 126f. Decorations: A.E. Gordon, *Q. Veranius Consul* AD *49* (Berkeley-Los Angeles, 1952) 320f.; Newton 10–14 (Silvanus: L. Mrozewicz, *Eos* 82 (1994) 167–71; Clemens: Zimmermann 1992, 296); Maxfield 1981, 153–7; 189f.; 122. Patriciate: MW 299f.; Ch. 11.

11 Power: Luttwak 1–50, distinguishing Julio-Claudian and Flavio-Trajanic systems; so Flaig 406; Augustus: Garzetti 1974, 253. Gauls: T*H* 4, 54, 1. Fates: T*Ger*. 33, 2. Deflection of revolt: J*B* 3, 108; Aramaic *Bellum*: Rajak 1983, 179–84, citing (179 n. 16) Laqueur 126f.; Thackeray 20–50; F.W. Walbank, in Chr. Schubert *et al.*, *Rom. U. d. gr. Osten: Festschr. f. H.H. Schmitt* (Stuttgart, 1995) 280 (ref. owed to Prof. D. Saddington). Rubrius' action: J*B* 7, 94f. Tarraconensis' loss: T*A* 4, 5, 2; S*G* 10, 2.

12 Extreme formulation: Boulvert 1970, 209. Injunction: T*A* 1, 11, 7.

13 N. African survey: A. Piganiol, *Atlas des centuriations rom. en Tunisie* (Paris, 1954); O. Dilke, *The Roman Land Surveyors* (Newton Abbot, 1971) 151–8; 246f. (bibl.); *Fossa Regia*: Ch. 7 n. 15. Roads: EJ 290f. (Tiberian, from winter quarters at Tacape). Separate command: T*H* 4, 48, 2; DC 59, 20, 7. Varying legate's title:

B.E. Thomasson, *Die Stattshalter d. röm. Prov. Nordafrikas v. Aug. bis Diokletianus. Skr. utg. av svenska Inst. i Rom.* 8, 9, 1 (Lund, 1960) 66f. 'Numidia': *ILS* 1177f. (227–30). Tullus: MW 300.

14 Disturbances: T*H* 4, 48–50; Bénabou 69–100; Leglay 203–5 (the proconsul helpless). Tacfarinas: T*A* 2, 52; 3, 20f.; 32; 73f.; 4, 23–6; Galba: S*G* 7. Maternus: Ptol. 1, 8, 4: F. Desanges. *Lat.* 23 (1964) 713–25 (*c*.86); Bénabou 106–8.

15 Decisive phase: Leglay 220; later Mauretanian trouble: MW 372: see Ch. 8 n. 44. T. Kotula, *MEFR* 79 (1967) 219 ('*stabilisation et consolidation*'); Bénabou 111f. similarly. Ammaedara: Ch. 9 n. 39; *CIL* 8, 308; centuriation: P. MacKendrick, *The North African Stones Speak* (N. Carolina, 1980) 33. Whether III was already at Theveste in 69 is disputed: Leglay 217, following V. de Pachtère, *CRAI* 1916, 273–84 dates the move 75; bibl. Flaig 258 n. 82. Cillium, Madaurus: J. Gascou, *La politique mun. de l' Empire rom. en Afrique Proconsul. de Trajan à Sept. Sévère, CEFR* 8 (Rome, 1972) 31–3, with *Inscr. Lat. d'Alg.* 1, 2152. Sufetula: Broughton 102; Kotula 215f, Aquae Flavianae: *CIL* 8, 17727, mentioned by Bénabou 114 along with Mascula and Vazaïvi (*CIL* 8, 17725; 17633; 17637); Lambaesis: L. Leschi, *Libyca* (*Arch. Epigr.*) 1 (1953) 189–97 (81). Milestones: Hippo-Cirta: *AE* 55, 145: '*ab Alpibus*'; repaired *CIL* 8, 22210; –Theveste: MW 419 (bridge, 76); Flavian *limes*: Bengtson 125f., citing J. Baradez, *Fossatum: Recherches aériennes sur l'organisation des confins sahariens . . .* (Paris, 1949); flexibility of *limes*: Baradez 360; cf. MacKendrick 240f.; fig. 9.4: they 'established a line' fortified by Trajan etc.; B.H. Warmington, *The North African Provinces from Diocletian to the Vandal Conquest* (Cambridge, 1954; repr. Westport, Conn., 1970) 20–6: 'towards the end of the first century'; D. Mattingly and R.B. Hitchner *JRS* 85 (1995) 174–6. Town development: Ch. 9; military: Gascou. Chalcideni: *ILS* 2927n.

16 'Job': E. Badian, *Rom. Imperialism in the Late Republic*[2] (Oxford, 1968) 22f. (contra, J.-M. Bertrand, *JS* 1989, 191–215), A.W. Lintott, *Imperium Romanum: Politics and Administration* (London-N.Y., 1993) 198 n. 4. Bengtson 134 has Rome seeking a natural frontier, the Humber–Mersey line unsatisfactory. Agricola's predecessors, esp. Bolanus: T*Agr.* 13–17; Birley 1961; Birley 1981, 57–65; Hanson, *Conquest* 174–88, avowedly minimalist. Cogidubnus hardly surviving V.: Birley 1981, 210.

17 Manning 26.

18 Cerialis, Frontinus: Birley 1981, 66–81; Hanson, *Conquest* 6 (Carlisle established 72–3); 39.

19 Birley 1981, 70 n. 8, suggests service in Africa and Spain for Frontinus; Armenia (based on Front., *Strat.* 2, 9, 5): Syme, 'Partisans' 128. Policing: Hanson, *Conquest* 50–4.

20 Career: T*Agr.* 6f; campaigns: 18–39; Homo 200f. (aiming at a 'scientific and inviolable frontier'); 'scientific' is also Luttwak's word (51). Agricola appointed 77: Birley 1981, 77–9; Hanson, *Conquest* 40–5, 'Tac.' 1751–4, following D.B. Campbell, *ZPE* 63 (1986) 97–200, in dating consulship late 76; so M.T. Raepsaet-Charlier, *ANRW* 2, 33, 3 (1991) 1842–4. Ordovices: Hanson, *Conquest* 46–8; Mona 49f., on T*Agr.* 14, 3; 18, 3–6. Second season: 20, 2f. Brigantes: Hanson, *Conquest* 54f.; extent 57. In 56–64 on '*novas gentes*', T*Agr.* 22, 1, he gives credit to predecessors. Peacetime activities: T*Agr.* 21; see Ch. 9. 2.

21 79: T*Agr.* 22; Hanson, *Conquest* 84–9.

22 Titus Imp. XV: DC 66, 20, 3 (date: Buttrey 1980, 25). Halt: T*Agr.* 23, 81–2: 24–7 (Ireland 24; rescue of IX Hispana 26), with Hanson, *Conquest* 115–26.

23 83: T*Agr.* 24: '*ignotas ad id tempus gentes*'. Forts: Hanson, *Conquest* 108–13 (first frontier demarcated by military installations). The reconnaissance of Demetrius of Tarsus (Pl., *Mor.* 419E, on imperial instructions) probably belongs to 82; but

C.P. Jones, *Plutarch and Rome* (Oxford, 1971) 136 n. 1, suggests a dramatic date before 83. Mons Graupius: T*Agr.* 29–39; Hanson, *Conquest* 128–42, cuts the battle down and discusses sites; K. Strobel, *Hist.* 36 (1987) 198–212, dates to 84 but cf. Raepsaet-Charlier *l.c.* (n. 20 above; ref. owed to the kindness of Prof. A. Birley). Withdrawal: Hanson, *Conquest* 6; 143–73. Troops removed: MW 322 (IX Hisp., cf. T*Agr.* 26, 1); one unit sent in replacement was a Cohors Usiporum (28, 1).

24 Augustus: C. Wells, *The German Policy of Augustus* (Oxford, 1972) esp. 3–13; 246–50, following Brunt, *RIT* 96–109, 433–480. Claudius: TA 11, 18–20. Bengtson 95 has '*Befestigungspolitik*' after Civilis' attack: it went further: Luttwak 50–126.

25 Bructeri: Stat., *Silv.* 1, 4, 89f.; *CIL* 16, 23, Lower Rhine diploma of 15 April 78, in Eck, *Sen.* 123; *AE* 66, 187 (decorations). Veleda: Ch. 5 n. 15; successor: DC 67, 12, 5, 3. Spurinna: Syme, 'Vestricius' 543–5 (ref. owed to the kindness of Prof. A. Birley).

26 Forts E. of upper Rhine: Schönberger 153, with n. 64; cf. 40f. (Heidelberg, Neuenheim, Ladenburg Claudian); Wiesbaden, Hofheim, and N.E. route: 155; M. Klee, *Der Limes zwischen Rhein u. Main* (Stuttgart, 1989). '*Decumates*': TG 29, 4, with A.A. Lund, *ANRW* 2, 33, 3 (1991) 2109–24. Vesontio: Levick 1985, 326–8.

27 Clemens: *Chron. Fred.* 2, 36, in *Mon. Germ. Scr. Rer. Merov.* 2, 60; F. Hertlein, *Die Gesch. der Besetzung des röm. Württemberg* (Stuttgart, 1929) 28–31. Aventicum: Ch. 9 n. 36; Augusta Raurica, Vindonissa: Graf 132 n. 401; gains to Helvetii and Raurici: 36f.; Praefectus Equitum at Günzberg 77–8: 24. '*Vicani Vindonissenses*': Newton 93 no. 202. Technique: TG 29, 4. Forces: MW 399 (21 May 74: six cavalry, twelve infantry units); *AE* 69/70, 420. Milestone: MW 416 (Offenburg): '*iter de{rectum ab Arge}ntorate in R{aetiam}*', or '*r{ipam Danuvii}*': *CAH* 11, 160 n. 4; Zimmermann 1992, 293f. *Ornamenta* etc.: MW 50; 298f.; '*Felix*': *CIL* 2, 2477. Homo 201; 333 (defensive changes). Schönberger 156 and Zimmermann discount any campaign by Clemens; cf. n. 10; Hertlein too referred *Chron. Fred.* to the revolt of 70. Rhine and *castella* : Graf 132 n. 401, from K. Schumacher, *Siedelungs– u. Kulturgesch. Der Rheinlande von der Urzeit bis in das Mittelalter 2. Die röm. Periode* (Mainz, 1923) 41f., Hertlein 28–35; Filtzinger Taf. 6; list 66; J. Heiligmann, *Der 'Alb-Limes', ein Beitrag z. röm. Besetzungsgesch. Südwestdeutschlands. Forsch. u. Ber. z. Vor- u. Frühgesch. in Baden-Württemberg* (Stuttgart, 1990) 187–99 (maps). A coin of 72–3 from the E. fort at Rottweil suggests date and route; pre-Flavian occupation has been proposed: Schönberger 157. Arae Flaviae: Ptol. 2, 11, 15 (cult: Scott 1936, 34f., opting for Domitian, D. Fishwick, *ANRW* 2, 16, 2 (1978) 1224, for V.); W. Schleiermacher, *Germania rom., Gymn. Beih. 1* (1962) 59–63 (sceptical on status); D. Planck *Arae Flaviae: neue Untersuch. Zur Gesch. Des röm Rottweil. Forsch. u. Bericht. z. vor–u. Fruhgesch. In Baden-Württenburg* 6, 1, 1 (Stuttgart, 1975): *castella* map 218; Filtzinger 21f. overinterprets his no. 4, having temple and forum by 75. Augst 'Victory monument': F. Staehelin, *Anz. f. Schweiz. Altertumskunde* (1930) 1–14. Roads: Schumacher 237–9; Hertlein 32–7; F. Hertlein and P. Goessler, *Die Strassen u. Wehranlagen des röm. Württemburg* (Stuttgart, 1930).

28 Raetia: Hertlein 20–5, noting Mengen-Ennetach, 9 km from Laiz, as new. N. bank: 24. See also H.-J. Kellner, *Die Römer in Bayern* (Munich, 1971) 46f. (map).

29 Domitian's advance: Schönberger 155–7 (map 176); Heiligmann 1990 (n. 27), map.

30 Syme, *CAH* 11, 161, raised the question.

31 Suebians: Pitts 1989, 48, citing T*H* 3, 5, 1; 21, 2. 'Third zone' and Marcomanni: 55. The problem: Wilkes 1983, 261. Defeats: Jones 1992, 138f; 141–3. Gallus: *JB* 7, 94f., and Ch. 8.

32 Redeployment: Mócsy 1974, 81; Germany-Balkans: Knight 196; in general 198–204; 5 transfers Germany–Moesia, 12 Pannonia–Moesia, 199f.; Dacia: 201f. Imerix: *AE* 71, 299. Carnuntum (73): *CIL* 3, 11194–7; *PNH* 4, 80. Brigetio: *CIL* 16, 26; Vindobona: *ILS* 9140; *CIL* 16, 31, 47, 57; Aquincum: *CIL* 16, 30, cf. 84; *AE* 86, 590. Ala I Aur . . .: 69/70, 477. Pannonian *auxilia* of 80 (four *alae*, thirteen cohorts): *CIL* 16, 26, cited by Wilkes 1983, 279 n. 43. IV Fl. from Dalmatia to ?Viminacium: Jones 1992, 228 n. 110, following Wilkes 282f. nn. 67, 74. (I am indebted to Professor Saddington for references and other help.)

33 V Alaud.: n. 2 above; Syme, 'March' 1007, is against Durostorum (C. Patsch, *Sitzungsb. d. Österr. Akad. d. Wiss.*, phil.-hist. Kl. 217, 1 n. 3); VII road-building: *AE* 1896, 17. Jones, *Dom.* 137, stresses V.'s work as presaging Domitian's; Wilkes 1983, 266, details construction. Taliata: *Starinar* Ser. 4, vol. 18 (1967) 21f.; Appiaria attested 76: *AE* 57, 307.

34 Infantry: Mócsy 81. Naval bases: Wilkes 1983, 267; 280 n. 51. No defence in depth: Bengtson 96. Colonies: Ch. 9.2.

35 Nero's war: W. Schur, *Die Orientpolitik des Kaisers Nero. Klio Beih.* 15, NF 2 (repr. Aalen, 1963); Debevoise 179–202; Magie 550–65; Ziegler 67–77. Geography: Isaac 1992, 9–14.

36 Settlement: Griffin 1976, 464f.; 1984, 226f. Favourable to Parthia: John. Ant., Fr. 104M. Reaction against hellenism: Debevoise 196. Vologaeses peaceful: T*A* 15, 5, 3. Diplomacy: T*H* 2, 82, 3. Discourtesy: DC 65 (66), 11, 3. Reinforcements: T*H* 4, 51; S*V* 6, 4 (40,000 archers). Crown: *JB* 7, 105.

37 Paetus and Collega: *JB* 7, 59. Celsus: *PIR²* M 296; Syria: MW 93 (July 72 – April 73: Buttrey 1980, 7 and 23); with Corbulo: T*A* 15, 25, 3; fidelity to Galba: T*H* 1, 45; PlO 1, 1f.; with Otho: T*H* 1, 71; Germany: *AE* 79, 413, ending March– June 73. Origin: Syme, *Tac.* 682f., with John Lyd, *De Mag.* 3, 33 for tactics. Traianus: Bowersock, 'Syria' 133–5; with Corbulo: Syme, *Tac.* 790. Suff. 70: R. Syme, *JRS* 68 (1978) 12; L. Vidman, *LF* 98 (1975) 66f. (72); contra Eck, 'Prokonsuln' 146–8. Titus in E.: Jones, *Tit.* 56–9.

38 V.'s arrangements: S*V* 8, 4: ' . . . *item Trachiam Ciliciam et Commagenen . . . in provinciarum formam redegit. Cappadociae propter adsiduous barbarorum incursus legiones addidit consularemque rectorem imposuit pro equite Romano*'; '*thraciam*' MS and Eutrop. 7, 19, 4; [Epit. Vict.] *De Caes.* 9, 13 ('*Ciliciaque ac Trachia*'); Oros. 7, 9, 10.

39 Aristobulus: Bosworth 1976, 66 nn. 22, 24, for survival until 70–1; the local era began 72/3 (n. 24). Armenian boundaries: Wheeler 1991, 507–9. V.'s motive: Mitchell 1993, I 124, citing T*A* 13, 39, 1f. Antiochus: *JB* 7, 219–43, with Isaac 1992; at 22 he cites *JB* 2, 379 and 389, for Parthian anxiety not to rouse Rome. Rajak 182 dates both annexations to 72, citing R. Sullivan, *ANRW* 2, 8 (1977) 790–4; see also Kennedy 1983, 186–8. Paetus' rôle: Bengtson 111. Samosata base: Ptol. 5, 14, 8. Recruitment: Millar 1993, 88, citing *CIL* 16, 36 etc. Velius: MW 372; *AE* 63, 368. III Gal. and *cochlea*: MW 93; importance in V.'s motivation: Magie 574. Other units, *e.g.* at Tille: Millar 1993, 83. Speculation about Commagene: Dąbrowa 1994.

40 Cilicia: Magie 576, with n. 27. Emesa: R.D. Sullivan, *ANRW* 2, 8 (1977) 218; Millar 1993, 84, cautious. Beroea and Apamea: Isaac 1992, 39.

41 XII Fulm.: *JB* 7, 18, with T.M. Mitford, *JRS* 64 (1974) 166 and 1980, 1186 (arriving May 71 at earliest); E. Dąbrowa, 1982, 619 n. 30 (speedy departure from Jerusalem). Raphaneae a base: *JB* 7, 219–43, with Weber 270 n. 3; Isaac 1992, 39 n. 132. Militarization: Festus, *Brev.* 20, cited by Wheeler 1991, 509.

Praetorian legate: Bosworth 1976, 65; first consular 76: B.E. Thomasson, *Laterculi Praesidum* 1 (Gothenburg, 1984) 264.

42 Traianus legate of Galatia-Cappadocia: Syme, *Tac.* 31 n. 1, based on MW 263; Bowersock, 'Syria' 134f.; doubted by Kreiler 37; approved by Eck, 'Jahresfasten' 287 n. 20, citing *JRS* 43 (1953) 153; rebutted by Dąbrowa 1988, 162 n. 657 (I owe this ref. to the kindness of Prof. A. Birley): 'Why did V. . . . entrust A. Marius Celsus, legate of Germania Inferior, with Syria . . . rather than Traianus . . . in the neighbouring province?' XVI Fl. *stationed* at Satala: *AE* 75, 817, with T. Mitford, *ZPE* 71 (1988) 168 n. 7, against D. Van Berchem's scepticism, *MH* 40 (1983) 185–96 (canal: *AE* 83, 927; *BJ* 185 (1985) 86); Isaac 1992, 36, sees the garrisoning of Satala as a second stage in the militarization of Cappadocia. Creation of XVI: Dąbrowa 1982.

43 Threat: P*Ep.* 9, 13, 11, with Syme, *Tac.* 631f.; quarrelling governors: Ch. 4.1.

44 Chabinas: L. Jalabert and R. Mouterde, *Inscr. gr. et lat. de la Syrie* 1, 38–43. Milestones w. of Satala: T.B. Mitford, *JRS* 64 (1974) 166; *ANRW* 2, 7, 2 (1980) 1186–92 (Cappadocian auxiliaries 1188–92); overall strength: Isaac 1992, 37. Black Sea strength (Apsarus): M. Speidel in S. Mitchell, ed., *Armies and Frontiers in Rom. and Byz. Anatolia. Proceedings of Coll. at . . . Swansea, 1981. Brit. Inst. Arch. Ankara Mon.* 5, *BAR Intern.* 156 (Oxford, 1983) 16f. Routes: Isaac 1992, 10f. Trapezus: Mitford 1974, 163; *AE* 75, 783. Anicetus: *TH* 3, 47f.

45 Milestones (W): D. French, *ANRW* 2, 7, 2 (1980) 430; (N.E.): Cn. Pompeius Collega, 75/6 from Melik, Serif/Yurtbaşı on the Nicopolis–Satala road or the frontier road (MW 86 = French 365 (Erzıncan); French 910 (Erikli, 78); 983 (Aşahı Ihsaniye nr Amastris (Amasra)). Macedo and Gallus: Mitchell 1993, I 122 and 124. Cilicia: milestone of 75/6, Olba-Diocaesareia, 2 km from Uras towards Uzunburç: *AE* 73, 543; bridge at Seleucia on Calycadnus: *IGR* 3, 840 (77–8). Domitian and Mylasa-Passala road: *AE* 88, 1028. Road grading: D. French, *AS* 24 (1974) 143–9; Isaac 1992, 34 n. 94. Appraisal by Mitchell *l.c.*

46 Antioch–Ptolemais: *AE* 07, 193 (234th stone); Apamea–Raphaneae: 74, 652. Palmyra–?Sura: 33, 205, with Bowersock 1973, 133; 136; Isaac 1992, 34f.: Millar 1993, 83. Crossroads: *AE* 74, 653 (Qorsi). Seleucia: D. Van Berchem, *MH* 40 (1983) 185–96; *BJ* 185 (1985) 47–87, esp. 53–61, on *IGLS* 3, 1131–40; Millar 87f., citing Paus. 8, 29, 3; Downey 1961 (Ch. 9, bibl.) 207, citing L. Robert, *CRAI* 1951, 255f. Canals: above, n. 42; Ch. 9 n. 71. Fleet: Millar 90.

47 Defensive strategy: J.G.C. Anderson, *CAH* 10, 780; Homo 341; Luttwak 1976, 57, cited by Isaac 1992, 50 n. 206; Dąbrowa, 'Limes'; Mitchell 1993 1, 118: 'frontier defences'; H. Halfmann, *Stuttgart. Koll. z. hist. Geogr. d. Altertums* 4, 1990 (Amsterdam, 1994) 577–88. Parthian weakness: R. Syme, *CAH* 11, 141–3. Offensive: Weber 275f.; Bosworth 1976; 1992, 33; 40f.; 50–3, citing (n. 205) F. Cumont, *Acad. roy. de Belg. Bull. de la classe des lettres* (1905) 197–117. Euphrates: E.W. Gray, *JRS* 55 (1965) 270, on Osrhoene and Sophene (still Roman in 54: T*A* 13, 7, 2); Wheeler 1991. S. sector: Millar 1993, 4: desert frontier or police posts lining roads, illustrated in D. Kennedy and D. Riley, *Rome's Desert Frontier from the Air* (London, 1989). Nero's plans: *TH* 1, 6, 2; S*Nero* 19, 2; *DC* 62 (63), 8, 1; P*NH* 6, 40, with Griffin 1976, 462–6; 1984, 228f.; J. Kolendo in J.-M. Croisille and P.-M. Fauchère, eds, *Neronia 1977 Actes du 2ᵉ Coll. de la Soc. intern. d'Et. Néron* (Clermont, 1982) 21–30 (propaganda aim). Geography: n. 49. Trajan's aims: F.A. Lepper, *Trajan's Parthian War* (Oxford, 1948) 158–213.

48 Alani, with Halfmann, 'Alanen': T*A* 6, 33, 3; *JA* 18, 97 (35); *SV* 8, 4?; *SD* 2, 2; *JB* 7, 244–51, between the fall of Antiochus IV and the arrival of Silva in Judaea (Ch. 8 n. 38). Route: Halfmann, 'Alanen' 44. Request: *SD* 2, 2; *DC* 65 (66), 15, 3, which Halfmann assigns to 76/7: certitude is impossible; 72/3 seems to be the

terminus a quo. Peaceful relations: Ziegler 78f. Traianus' *ornamenta*: MW 263; P*Pan.* 14, 1 ('*Parthica lauro*', but '*ferociam superbiamque Parthorum ex proximo auditus magno terrore cohiberes*'); 16, 1. Threat: T*H* 1, 2, 1, with Chilver: '*mota prope etiam Parthorum arma falsi Neronis ludibrio*', which Syme, *CAH* 11, 143 n. 5, invoked against hostilities; false Neros: Ch. 9 n. 62. [Epit. Aur. Vict.] *Caes.* 9, 12: '*metu solo in pacem coactus est*'; cf. Aur. Vict., *Caes.* 9, 10: '*ac bello . . . in pacem coactus*', with Cohn's '*sine*' before '*bello*' or Gutschmidt's replacement of '*ac bello*' with '*ab illo* '. See Rajak 1983, 182f. Relationship of Victor and the 'Epitome': F.A. Lepper, *JRS* 47 (1957) 97–100. Pansa: Torelli 1968, 173, rebutted by Heil (he is legate of '*exercitus qui est in Africa*'); supported by Halfmann 1991. Halfmann like Syme believes in an immediate Parthian riposte, citing *aurei* of Domitian (77–8) celebrating a success against Parthia: *CREBM* 2, 42 nos. 231–3 (Domitian cos. V); cf. 37f., nos. 201, 204; 40 no. 223f. ('Victory', the first time since 72). Strain: Ziegler 80. Commagene: Bowersock 1973, 135.

49 Caucasus: Debevoise 201–2; Bosworth 1976, 75; 1977, 226–8. Apsarus and Dioscurias: P*NH* 6, 12; 15. Harmozica: *SEG* 20, 112; Bosworth 1977, 226 n. 37. Centurion: MW 369; Bosworth n. 38; location: R. Heidenreich, *ZPE* 52 (1983) 213f. Caucasus in literature: Stat. *Silv.* 4, 4, 63f.: '*metuenda . . . limina*'; Val. Flacc., *Arg.* is cited by Debevoise 202 n. 62; A. Hollis, *G&R* 41 (1994) 209f. connection with the Alani: Syme, *CAH* 11, 143; Ziegler 80; Mitchell 1993, 1, 118f. Their history: Bosworth 1977, 220–4. Isaac 1992, 42–5, is cautious on Roman ambitions in the Caucasus and the Alan factor is denied by Weber 275, Bosworth 1976, 67–70, arguing that they were friendly and useful in their attack on Parthia; Heil 1989 (geographical factors; reinterpretation of *AE* 68, 145); Isaac 47; Wheeler 1991, 509; for Debevoise *l.c.* the Roman presence was 'ostensibly' aimed against the Alani. The '*barbari*' of S*V* 8, 4, Pontic: Cumont 1905, 207; Kreiler 1972, 76 n. 7; Bosworth 1976 71f. They are not Parthians: S*Tib.* 9, 1.

11 ELITES

M. Hammond, *JRS* 47 (1957) 74–81; Syme, *Tac.* 585–97; Houston 1971; Bengtson 113–20. Eck, *Sen.*; Eck 1974; Houston, 'Adlection'; Halfmann 1979; Dąbrowa, *Asie Mineure* 54–70. Devreker, 'Adlectio'; 'Composition'; Talbert. Syme, 'Ceionii'. McDermott 1972–3; Eck 1992–3. Houston, 'Nonius'.

1 Homo 290–3. Claudius: *JA* 19, 265. Praise: Bengtson 92; 120.

2 Losses: Griffin 1991, 33f.; S*V* 9, 2: both orders suffering '*caede .. neglegentia*'; cf. Aur. Vict., *Caes.* 9, 9; [Epit.] 9, 11 (savage emperors). Flaig 412 minimizes effects. Augustus: C. Nicolet, in E. Segal and F. Millar, eds, *Caesar Augustus: Seven aspects* (Oxford, 1984) 89–128; *Equites*: S. Demougin, *L'Ordre équestre sous les Julio-Claudiens, CEFR* 108 (Rome, 1988) 184–8. Claudius censor: Levick 1990, 98–101.

3 Polemaeanus: MW 316; Halfmann 1979, 111f.; Grypus (*PIR* [2] P 506); T*H* 3, 52, 3; 4, 39, 1; Syme *RP* 5, 612f.: to command a legion, then to hold a praetorship; Bassus, still commanding fleet(s), 9 Feb. 71 (MW 398), T*H* 2, 100, 3, cf. 3, 12, with *PIR*[2] L 379; J*B* 7, 163–216; L. Antistius Rusticus' wait (MW 464): Eck, *Sen.* 66; cf. C. Caristanius Fronto (MW 315). Tenure of censorship: T*Agr.* 9, 1 (Agricola patrician 73 or 74); Bosworth 1973, 49 n. 2, cites MW 93f. and *CIL* 5, 4312, for opening, Censorinus, *De die nat.* 18, 14, and P*NH* 7, 162, for closing; Houston, 'Adlection'; Kienast 1990, 108 ('*vor 1. Juli 73–Ende 74*'). Domitian: DC 67, 13, 1; obsolete: 53, 17, 3; cf. 7.

4 Conduct: *SV* 8, 1; 9, 2; Aur. Vict., *Caes.* 9, 9, and [Epit.] 9, 11. Claudian standards: *Docs G–N* 369, col. 2, ll. 3f.: contributing funds: *TA* 11, 24, 10; Italian investment: *PEp.* 6, 19, 4, with Sherwin-White.

5 M. Palfurius Sura: *PIR*² P 68; Juv. 4, 53, with Schol. Syme, *RP* 4, 88. Subsidies: *SV* 17 ('*liberalissimus*'); Augustus and Tiberius: *TA* 1, 75, 5f.; 2, 37f. (the earlier gift); 48; Vell. Pat. 2, 129, 3; Talbert 47–53.

6 Reservations: *TH* 2, 82, 2. Massa: 4, 50, 2; cf. Bengtson 91. Bassus: n. 3 above.

7 Galba: Syme 1975, 63, on *TH* 2, 53, 1. Numbers of *novi*: Flaig 408, stresses effect, with n. 143, estimating up to 15 per cent and citing Hammond 1957, 77, for 69 *novi*. '1,000': Aur. Vict., *Caes.* 9, 9; [Epit.] 9, 11. Membership of 600: Talbert 134. Houston, 'Adlection', revises Eck, *Sen.* 103–5; Nicols 109f.; Talbert 134 counts three adlections for Claudius, about twenty for V., thirty-five in the second century. First known *adlectus inter consulares*, praetorian prefect in 182: P. Leunissen, *Konsulen und Konsulare in der Zeit v. Commodus bis Severus Alexander (180–235 n. Chr.)* (Amsterdam, 1989) 3 n. 8. Claudius: *Docs G–N* 370, l. 45; Levick 1990, 100f. Italians: Grenzheuser 82.

8 Neratii: *AE* 76, 195; Syme, 'Neratius'; *PIR*² N 60. Sempronius Fuscus: *AE* 84, 435. Maturus Arrianus: *PEp.* 3, 2; Syme, 'Ministers' 530. Minicius Macrinus: *PEp.* 1, 14, 5. Catilius Longus, adlected *inter praetorios*, may have distinguished relatives and may belong, as Prof. A. Birley points out, to the same city and the same tribe, Clustumina, as Catilius Severus; he had been tribune of IV Scyth. and commander of Cohors III Sagittariorum: Halfmann 1979, 133–5 ; W. Eck, *ZPE* 42 (1981) 243; Syme, *RP* 4, 23n.; 5 473; 555; Dąbrowa 1998, 90–2. According to E. Tóth, *Acta Arch. Acad. Scient. Hung.* 35 (1983) 3–61 = *AE* 83, 773, the Savaria victory monument bore the name of C. Helvidius Priscus, son of V.'s opponent, also the honorand of *AE* 72, 394, who was thus adlected *inter praetorios*: implausible so close to the execution of Priscus' father; and the 'obliteration' of the honorand on the monument looks like accidental damage.

9 Maternus: *AE* 73, 293 from Liria (his native place?), with G. Alföldy and H. Halfmann, *Chiron* 3 (1973) 331–73; rivalry with Trajan: *PEp.* 9, 13, 11, Syme, *RP* 3, 1388f.; 4, 277, was reserved; less so, as Prof. Birley points out, in 5, 602, cf. 6, 464f.

10 Pactumeius Fronto: *MW* 298, with A.R. Birley, *Septimius Severus: The African Emperor* (London, 1971) 42; T.D. Barnes, *CR* 21 (1971) 332, held that Clemens was consul; rebutted by W. Eck, *ANRW* 2, 1 (1974) 196 n. 174; G. Alföldy, *Konsulat und Senatorenstand unter den Antoninen. Antiquitas* Ser. 1, 27 (Bonn, 1977) 81 n. 34; M. Le Glay, *Epigr. e ord. sen. Atti del coll. intern. AIEGL, Roma 14–20 mag. 1981* II, *Tituli* 5 (Rome, 1982) 766f.

11 Break: Flaig 382. Dedication: I. Kaygusuz, *Epigr. Anat.* 4 (1984) 3. Few easterners: Houston, 'Adlection'; Halfmann 1979, 78, lists nine under V., three of Flavian origin. Tertullus (117 no. 22) was connected with M. Plancius Varus (104, no. 8; Ch. 4 n. 58). Quadratus, an Arval in 72 (*MW* 5, p. 16), may have been adlected in 69 (so Braithwaite on *SV* 9, 2). Kin to Claudius and Julius Severus: *Docs N–H* 215; *PIR*² I 507 (stemma); Devreker, 'Composition'. Caristanius: Halfmann 109 no. 13; son-in-law of L. Sergius Paullus (cf. for his services S. Mitchell, *Anatolia: Land, men, and gods in Asia Minor* 2 (Oxford, 1993) 6). Marinus: Halfmann, 110, suggests descent from a Tiberian intellectual (*TA* 4, 58, 1; 6, 10, 2); he was son-in-law of Cn. Caecilius Simplex. Syme distinguishes Trajanic magnates from Hadrian's municipal intellectuals: *RP* 6, 107f. Philopappus: Halfmann 132 no. 36; stemma 121.

12 Claudian *latus clavus*: Levick 1990, 101; Flavian adlection: Eck, *Sen.* 103–5: *AE* 73, 293, Curiatius Maternus; *MW* 289, C. Fulvius Lupus, equestrian officer,

inter praetorios (V.); 291, L. Baebius Avitus, procurator of Lusitania, *inter pr.*; 298, Pactumeius Fronto, *inter pr.* (V. and Titus); 311, C. Salvius Liberalis Nonius Bassus, *inter tribunicios, inter pr.* (V. and Titus); 315, with Birley 1981, 211–13, and Eck 1992–3, 100–3, Caristanius Fronto, equestrian officer, *inter trib.*, then *inter pr.*; 316, Polemaeanus, tribune of III Cyr., *inter aedilicios* (V.); 321, Cornutus Tertullus, ex-quaestor and aedile *inter pr.* (V. and Titus censors); 464, Antistius Rusticus, tribune of II Aug., *inter pr.* (V. and Titus).

13 V. making a new aristocracy, abandoning the policy of Augustus, etc.: Bersanetti 74f. Provincials are played down by Flaig 410. Caesar: S*Iul.* 76, 3; known admissions: T.P. Wiseman, *New Men in the Roman Senate 139 BC–14 AD* (Oxford, 1971) 190. Claudian civil war: *id.*, *JRS* 72 (1982) 57–67.

14 Transpadana: Syme, *RP* 7, 635–46. Change of tone: T*A* 3, 55, 2–6; restored: P*NH* 36, 8; 117. Syme, *RP* 6, 45; Brixia and Patavium, P*Ep* 1, 14, 5f. Verona connections: Syme, *JRS* 58 (1968) 149. Senate: Sil. Ital. 1, 608–29, in Homo 360f. Bourgeois takeover: Bersanetti 91 ('*patriziato/borghesia*'). Glory: T*H* 1, 84, 3. Marriage: P. Veyne, *Annales: écon., soc., civilisations* 33 (1978) 37f.; M. Corbier in B. Rawson, ed., *Marriage, Divorce and Children in Ancient Rome* (Canberra-Oxford, 1991) 59; health: P*Ep.* 10, 17a; Sherwin-White 1966, index, *s.v.* illness; Fronto and M. Aurelius: E. Whitehorne, *Lat.* 36 (1977) 413–21; Tiberius: T*A* 6, 46, 9; S*Tib.* 68, 4; Plut., *Mor.* 136D; 794C.

15 Succession: Syme, *Tac.* 11; 35; 130. Hadrian: A. v. Premerstein, *Das Attentat der Konsulare auf Hadrian im Jahre 118 n. Chr., Klio Beih.* 8 (1908, repr. Aalen 1963); T. Barnes, *JRS* 57 (1967) 65–79; A.R. Birley, *Hadrian, the Restless Emperor* (London-New York, 1997) 87–9. *Lex'*: Ch. 6 n. 21; elections: P*Ep.* 3, 20; 4, 25.

16 Antonine forebears (Stemma II): Syme, *RP* 1, 325–38; Nicols 1978, 173. Traianus: P*Pan.* 9, 2 (Eck, *Sen.* 109; Syme, *RP* 4, 402, has Trajan adlected); consulship: *AE* 85, 130; his daughter was Ulpia Marciana, his wife perhaps kin to Titus' Marcia Furnilla. M. Annius Verus: *SHA M. Aur.* 1, 2; *Pius* 1, 6. Curvii: next n. Ceionius: *PIR*² C 603. List: Eck, *Sen.* 108f., including ?T. Aurelius Fulvus; *PIR*² A 1510, grandfather of Antoninus Pius. Flaig 409, 577, is sceptical of rewards for civil war activity by Traianus and others, esp. as late as 73–4: V. needed men of merit. But loyalty and merit combined were a standard criterion: T*A* 3, 48, 2. Nicols 1978, 171, is judicious.

17 Patricians: Graf, 69; Claudius: *Docs G–N* 369, l. 45; Levick 1990, 101. Non-military: J. Morris, *LF* 87 (1964) 336. Military men: Eck, *Sen.* 109–11; Flaig 409. Agricola: T*Agr.* 9, 1. Note Sex. Frontinus' nephew: Syme, *RP* 4, 401. Curvii: G. Alföldy, *Die Hilfstruppen der röm. Prov. Germ. Inf., Epigr. Stud.* 6 (Düsseldorf, 1968) 131–5; G. Di Vita-Evrard, in A. Mastino, ed., *L'Africa rom. Atti del IV convegno di stud. Sassari, 12–14 dic. 1986* (Sassari, n.d.) 509–29. Sex. Vettulenus Cerialis: Eck, *Sen.* 33; 92f.; 109, 115–17; 121–5; legateship: *JB* 3, 310–15; *ILS* 988. Silva: Eck 1992–3, 87–99. Aurelius Fulvus' (n. 16) consular ornaments as legate: T*H* 1, 79, 5. The claim of L. Luscius Ocrea of Lanuvium (*AE* 29, 27; 1981, 829; R. Syme, *Hist.* 13 (1964) 119; Eck, 'Leg.' 73–5), ex-praetor adlected patrician or attaining both ranks by adlection, is unknown. L. Pedanius Secundus Pompeius Festus, of Italian or Spanish (Barcino) descent, quaestor of V., was too young for the civil wars: Eck, *Sen.* 107 n. 84. Crystallization, rules for patricians: Eck 1974, 218; V. A. Maxfield, *The Military Decorations of the Rom. Army* (London 1981) 23.

18 Eprius: Eck, *Sen.* 115–18.

19 Vitellius' consulship: S*Vit.* 11, 2, with MW 81 ('*cos. perp.*' which Kienast 1990, 29 and 106 thinks made from '*P(ater) P(atriae)*'; Prof. T. Wiedemann interprets '*perpetuus*' as implying uninterrupted tenure without re-election. Pre-election:

Flaig 352. Favourable aspect: Appian, *Civ. Wars* 1, 103. Flavian consulships: Gallivan 1981, 187–9; 195f.

20 Nerva: Ch. 6. Ap. Messalinus: P*Ep*. 4, 22, 5f., with Sherwin-White. Novius Priscus: *PIR*² N 187. Ceionius: n. 16.

21 Dates of second consulships: Gallivan 1981, 201; 213–15. Flavianus: MW 274; *AE* 66, 68. Cerialis: Ch. 3 n. 1.

22 Vettuleni: Bengtson 116f.; Syme *RP* 1, 324–32. Sex. Cerialis: n. 17; Reate: *CIL* 9, 4742; 4694 (Pituanii); 10, 7245 (marriage). Civica: Eck, *Sen.* 130–3; 138; 86; death: T*Agr.* 42, 1. Firmus: A.B. Bosworth, *ZPE* 39 (1980) 267–72. 'Marshals': Syme, *Tac.* 44–58. L. Flavius Silva, *cos.* 81, legate of Judaea, would be attractive as a relative; 'L.' is against it: Eck, *Sen.* 111 n. 14; cf. Bengtson 118. Flaig 408, with analysis of groups and noting dangers of adlection at will, holds that groups of supporters and office-holders did not coincide.

23 '*Viri militares*': Syme, *Tac.* 50; contra, J. Morris, *LF* 87 (1964) 336 n. 39; B. Campbell, *JRS* 65 (1975) 11–31 (refs n. 1); Flaig 569–73 rebuts modified versions because Campbell's argument was that the '*viri*' were functionally distinct; but cf. D. Saddington, *ANRW* 2, 33, 5 (1991) 3493 (Tacitus' conception) and A.R. Birley, *Locus Virtutibus Patefactus? Zum Beförderungssystem in der hohen Kaiserzeit* (Opladen, 1992). Quirinius: TA 3, 48; *Luke* 2, 2. Tiberius: TA 4, 6, 2.

24 Final development: P*Pan.* 66, 4. *Consilium*: Cic., *Pro Rab. perd. reo* 3. Early civility: TH 4, 3, 4; 51, 3; frugality: DC 65 (66), 10, 3f; council and attendance: 5. Coins: *CREBM* 2, xlvii; 124 no. 576, with Kleiner 1990, 134–6; Pl. 33, 2.

25 Augustus: DC 55, 24, 9–25, 6; Claudius: TA 11, 23–5, 2. Nero: TH 4, 8, 3, with Pigoń 1992; Domitian: T*Agr.* 45, 1f.

26 Claudian *SCC*: Talbert 440–2; Levick 1990, 97f. Vespasian: Talbert 443f. Content: Ch. 9 n. 27. Education: Woodside. Aelianus' *elogium*: MW 261.

27 Openness: SV 12; DC 65 (66), 10, 4–6. Claudius: 60, 3, 3; S*Claud.* 35, 1, with Levick 1990, 51f., with n. 29. Grading: P*NH* 33, 41, with Mommsen, *St.* 2, 2, 834. V.'s humiliation: SV 14, cf. 4, 4; DC 65 (66), 11, 2.

28 Republican conflict: TA 12, 60. Survival: T*Agr.* 9, 4, with Ogilvie and Richmond. Quarrel: SV 9, 2. Parity: Garzetti 1974, 240.

29 Claudius' measures: Levick, 1990, 47–51. Sardinia: Ch. 9 n. 42. Fleet: C.G. Starr, *The Rom. Imperial Navy, 30 BC–AD 324. Cornell Stud. in Class. Phil.* 26 (Ithaca, N.Y., 1941; repr. Westport, Conn., 1975) 33. Friend: MW 460.

30 C. Velius Rufus' '*ius gladii*': MW 372. Fuscus: TH 2, 86, 3f., with Chilver. Flaccus: Houston, 'Nonius'. Liberalis: above, n. 12.

31 Claudian knights: Sen., *Apoc.* 14, 1. *Ornamenta*, Etruscus' father: P.R.C. Weaver, *Familia Caesaris* (Cambridge, 1972) 282–94, on Stat., *Silv.*. 3, 3. Vitellius' freedmen: TH 2, 57, 2 ; 65; 95. Hormus: TH 4, 39, 1, see Flaig 341. Larcius: P*Ep*. 3, 14, with Sherwin-White; probably son of the rich and successful freedman A. Larcius Lydus, DC 62 (63), 21, 1 (62–8): W. Eck, *EOS* 1 (1982 [1984]) 301f.; *Die Verwaltung d. röm. Reiches in d. hohen Kaiserzeit: ausgewählte u. erweiterte Beiträge* (Basel, 1995) 177f. (I am much indebted to Prof. A. Birley for help with this note.)

32 Warning: Ph*VA* 5, 36. Paradigm: Sen., *Ep.* 47, 9. German superiority: TG 25, 2. Claudius' failing: P*NH* 33, 134; 35, 201. Vitellius: S*Vit.* 12. Hormus: TH 3, 12, 3; 28 (Cremona); cf. Mart. 2, 15. V. and Narcissus: SV 4, 1. Vipstanus: Syme *Gnom.* 1957, 520; *Hist.* 1962, 149f.; 1975, 67. Caenis: DC 65 (66), 14, 3–5 (V. profiting); cf. SV 23, 2 (a minister). Rights over freedmen: TH 2, 92, 3, with Chilver, citing G*I* 3, 56; *Dig.* 25, 3, 5. 19–26 (25f. allowing escape on grounds of insufficient means; 37, 14, 4); *Cod.* 6, 3.

33 Knights' takeover: Chilver on T*H* 1, 58, 1, noting MW 338 and 347 (ex-military tribunes heading three or two departments); Jones 1992, 178 is over-cautious.
34 Levelling: Sen., *Ep.* 47, 10. Similarly, M.T. Griffin in V.M. Strocka, ed., *Die Regierungszeit des Kaisers Claudius (41–54 n. Chr.): Umbruch oder Episode?* (Mainz, 1994) 314. Vitellii: S*Vit.* 1, 1; 2, 1; Gabinii: Cic. *De Leg.* 3, 35; Livy, O*xy.* 54. Cf the *Salvii* of Urbs *Salvia*: McDermott 1972–3, 338f. Pallas' posterity: *PIR*² A 858f.

12 VESPASIAN AND HIS SONS

Weber 55–8; 210–84; Buttrey 1980; Pick; Hammond; Parsi; Sullivan 1953; Bengt-son 155–78; Girard 1989. M.P. Morford, *Phoen.* 22 (1968) 57–72 (training); Jones 1975; *Tit.* 1–113; *Dom.* 1–21, D. Fishwick, *AJAH* 6 (1981) 89–96. Crook 1951; Rogers 1980. B.W. Jones and R. Develin, *Antichthon* 10 (1976) 79–83; G. Menella, *Ath.* NS 59 (1981) 205–8. Literature: Luck; d'Espèrey; L. Herrmann, *REG* 92 (1979) 113–19.

1 Succession: Homo 167–9; Griffin 1984, 189–93. Flaig 204 denies 'legitimacy'; attention given it is surprising. Augustan scheme: Levick 1976, 19–81. Recom-mendation to Galba: M. Corbier in B. Rawson, ed. *Marriage, Divorce and Children in Ancient Rome* (Canberra-Oxford, 1991) 70; too late for renewed oath of Jan. 69: Flaig 297; nobility a disadvantage to Piso, 298; problems of narrative: 461–5. Otho's status late 68: 301f., citing Pl*G* 20, 3; T*H* 1, 24, 1; S*O* 4, 2. Sons: J*B* 4, 596; T*H* 2, 77, 1 (Titus '*capax iam imperii*'), with Chilver; Martin 1982, 213f. Sons may be the point of V.'s response to Mucianus' complaints, S*V* 13 (cf. [Epit. Aur. Vict.] *Caes.* 9, 3): 'Still, I am a man'. Grandsons: J*B* 7, 73 (71); A*P* 9, 349 (a child for Domitian implied). See Ch. 5 n. 24.
2 Health: S*V* 20. *Principes Iuventutis*: *RIC* 2, 17f. nos. 23–7 (69–71); 30 no. 139 (Domitian only, ?75–9); 31 no. 145 (72–); 49 no. 292 (?70–1); 62 no. 390f. (69–70). Titus' training: Morford. Labour divided: T*H* 4, 52, 2. V.'s nomenclature: Buttrey 1980, 8–11; 'Caesar': Kienast 23, citing Parsi 53–5; 'imp.' and 'Caes.' movable: Fishwick 1987, 234–7. Claudius: Levick 1990, 42 n. 4; already in 20 (Eck 1996, 48, l. 148). Achievements: Rajak 1983, 204–13; complementary: J*B* 4, 597; Titus' speech: 6, 341.
3 Dissidents: Ch. 6. Office of State: Levick 1990, 41–52. Galba's adoption: T*H* 1, 15f. Titus' qualities: S*T* 3; poet: *PNH Pr.* 5; 11; Aur. Vict., *Caes.* 10, 1; [Epit. Aur. Vict.] *Caes.* 10, 2; Eutrop. 7, 14; 21 (Latin orator, Greek poet); Eus.-Jer., *Chron., s.a.* 79, p. 189 Helm; T*H* 5, 1, 1; Desideri 137–9; remiss in Forum: S*T* 4, 2; Bardon 274–80; A. Grilli, *Atti* 1983, 133–45; L. Alfonsi, *ibid.* 183–7; d'Espèrey 3078f. Distinction not won as early as DC 60 (61), 30, 1, claims: Ch. 2. Divine protection: Weber 222f.; new Nero: S*T* 1, 1; 6f.; DC 66, 18, 4f. Independence, debauchery: T*H* 2, 2, 1. '*Amor et deliciae generis humani*': S*T* 1, 1. Cosmopolitan: Weber 58; cf. S. Gély, *Atti* 1983, 313–23. Anti-semitism: P*Lond.* 2785 (Musurillo 25); P*Oxy.* 1242 (Musurillo 48). Berenice: below, n. 20f. R. Syme, composing *RP* 7 (1991) 647–63 under Edward VIII, will have thought that she aimed at marriage and a title. T*H* 2, 2, 1, suggests a liaison notorious before Titus left Judaea in 68. Defection: n. 6.
4 Promotion: Ch. 6. Homecoming: S*T* 5, 3; J*B* 7, 119; DC 65 (66), 12, 1ᵃ. Arrival: Chambalu 517; Jones, *Tit.* 78; end of June: Weber 270; Graf 66f. has July, Halfmann, *Itinera* 180f. May/July for journey. Success everywhere celebrated: Weber 279–84; Graf 67. Agrippa: DC 54, 28, 1; Nero: T*A* 12, 41, 2 (51);

salutation on accession 69, 2; Tiberius: S*Tib.* 21, 1 (13). '*Summi fastigii vocabulum*': T*A* 3, 56, 3. Titus' salutations: Buttrey 1980, 18f. Arvals: MW 6–8, cf. *AE* 91, 1635.

5 Prophecies: Ch. 5. Bravery: *ST* 4, 3; generalship: Ch. 8; compared with Caesar: Weber 226–37. *Imperium proconsulare*, 71: Homo 185; Crook 1951, 164. Bengtson 156f. is cautious. Tiberian parallel: Graf 67. O. Montevecchi, *Atti* 1983, 353, notes Titus' praetorian troops and Prefect as conferring *quasi*-parity; bibl. Jones *Tit.*, 81, with nn. 15–21 (late 70 or early 71). Birley 1975, 152 n. 51, suggests 70 on the basis of the salutation known at Tarsus by February 71 as confirmed at Rome (Ph*VA* 6, 30). *TH* 4, 3, 4 (cf. DC 65 (66), 1, 1), has no grant at the end of 69, only the absentee consulship of 70, attested 24 May, MW 191, but ending before Jerusalem fell: either Titus became V.'s legate again until his salutation, recognized by the senate, occasioned the grant of proconsular *imperium*, or he was awarded it on leaving the consulship. Sharing power: Ph*VA* 7, 8: *Praenomen*: *RIC* 2, 55 no. 339–46 (71 and 74), 56 no. 351 (69), 58 no. 369 (?69) (eastern mints); *ILS* 260, MW 260 (Italian cities); MW 103 (Valentia); *ILS* 988 (Carthage); MW 86; 421 (milestones); Sabratha: *AE* 68, 551 (77–8); Jones, *Tit.* 102 n. 20. V. and Titus '*imperatores*' in V.'s lifetime: *PNH* 3, 66; 7, 162. Coins apparently making Titus '*imperator designatus*' 70–2: Buttrey 1980, 40–3, following Pick 192–7. 'Pontifex Maximus' on Syrian milestones: *AE* 74, 653; 1983, 927 (75–6), Naples 1988, 323 (74). Augustus-Tiberius: T. Barnes, *JRS* 64 (1974) 23. Mistakes about Domitian: n. 9.

6 Ambitions: *ST* 5, 3; crown(s): *JB* 7, 105; Ph*VA* 6, 29 (*ethne*). *JB* 6, 34: Titus addresses 'fellow-soldiers'; cf. S*Caes.* 67, 2; S*Aug.* 25, 1; correctly interpreted by B. Campbell, *The Emperor and the Roman Army 31 BC–AD 235* (Oxford, 1984) 32–9, 44, citing *TH* 2, 5, 2. As Dr Pigoń notes, 69–70 made the address common: *TH* 1, 35, 2; *SG* 20, 1. See Montevecchi 1983, 349; Bengtson 103. Caenis: *SV* 3; unmarriageable, Ch. 2. Titus' travels: *JB* 7, 19; 23; 37; 39; 96; 100; 105f.; *POxy.* 2725, with n.; Downey 205 n. 21; chronology: Weber 270f.; Halfmann, *Itinera* 180f.

7 Consulships: Buttrey 1980, 18f.; 77: O. Salomies, *Ktèma* 18 (1993) 104. Arches: Ch. 9 n. 14; Titus' arch, which Richmond 1969, 218–21 dates to Trajan's reign: S. Reinach, *REJ* 20 (1890) lxv–xci, cited by Rajak 1983, 203–7; F. Magi, *Röm. Mitt.* 82 (1975) 99–116; Darwall-Smith 166–72 (Domitian). First to capture Jerusalem: MW 53. Census with consular power: *RGDA* 8, 3f.

8 Prefecture: *ST* 6, 1 (with Flaig 74); J. Crook, *CQ* NS 6 (1956) 289. Co-regent: *ST* 6; Ph*VA* 6, 30; Garzetti 1974, 237. Personality cult: Ch. 5. Statue of Titus, Emerita, 77: MW 104 ('from 5 lb of gold'); Valentia calls him '*conservator pacis Aug.*': 103.

9 Priesthoods: *ILS* 258 (71); '*Sodalis Augustalis*' by *SC* before 5 Apr. 71, requiring a twenty-eighth decury: *ILS* 5025. Domitian: MW 115 (73–6); *CIL* 3, 12218; 9, 4955; Arval: 6, 2054 = 32361 (75). Nero: *PIR*[2] D 129 (p. 36). Domitian included: *e.g.* MW 131 (vexillation in Belgica); MW 475 (Pompeii), for safety of V. and offspring ('*liberi*', cf. 513 and *PNH* 2, 18); cf. gymnasium at Prusias ad Hypium 'consecrated' *c.*75/6 to 'the Augustan house of the *Imperatores*': *AE* 87, 918; 1951, 217: oath by Genius of V. and his *liberi* (Pompeii). Mistakes: testamentary dedication of MW 84; censor: *AE* 78, 804 (Balbura): cf. *IGR* 3, 366; the Side monument (Ch. 9 n. 66) probably contained Domitian's statue as well as V. and Titus'.

10 Domitian's relegation: Homo 186f.; Bengtson 102f. (underrating *ST* 6); '*parità*': M.A. Levi, *Atti* (1983) 165f. Magistracies: *TH* 4, 39, 1; *SD* 1, 3; Buttrey 1980, 28f.; above n. 7 for 77. Obverses: *RIC* 33f. nos. 155–60 (Titus, 71–2); 41 nos.

230–2 (Domitian, 73): the point is made by M.T. Griffin, *CAH*² 11 (forthcoming), comparing the position of Tiberius 4–14. *Princeps Iuventutis*: MW 117, of 80; *RIC* 121f. nos. 39–51; *spes*: 30 no. 139 (?75–9); 41 no. 233 (74–5); 60 no. 380 (74–5); Levick 1982, 113 n. 43. Tiberius' will: n. 12. Julia: *SD* 22. Griffin, *CAH*²11, notes stress on harmony in the family, citing *JB* 4, 597, and 7, 119, and *PNH Pr.* 5. Vows: MW 11, p. 19.

11 Clemens; journey: T*H* 4, 68, 2; 85f.; *SD* 2, 1; *JB* 7, 82–8; n. 16. *PIR*² F 259 (p. 148); Nicolas 1051–3. Malitz 1985, 238 n. 44 (Helvidius' rôle on the Capitol, 21 June, due to Domitian's absence?). Played up later: Front., *Strat.* 4, 3, 14; n. 16 below; riding in triumph: *SD* 2, 1; *JB* 7, 152; cf. S*Tib.* 6, 4; arch: n. 7. Head laureate/bare: *RIC* 95–7 nos. 687–707 (72–3). Parthians: *SD* 2, 2. Consolation: Halfmann, 'Alanen' 41, on *CREBM* 42 nos. 231–3.

12 Cerialis approached: T*H* 4, 86, 1. Escape: 3, 74, 1; DC 64 (65), 17, 4; *SD* 1, 2; *PIR*² F 259 (p. 148). Obelisk (Darwall-Smith 145–50): Isis: side III sec. 4; royalty: side III, sec. 1, elucidated by Grenier 1987, 949 (Domitian V.'s heir); cf. side I, sec. 1: 'whom his father has crowned'; tr. Darwall-Smith 146f. Domitian Caesar: T*H* 3, 86, 3; 4, 2, 1. Achievement in 69: Stat., *Theb.* 1, 21f.; *Silv.* 1, 1, 79–81; cf. Q*IO* 10, 1, 91; *SD* 13, 1; poem: Mart. 5, 5, 7; Tonans' son: 9, 65, 3–6. Forgery: 2, 3, with M.A. Levi, *Atti* 1983, 166; Tiberius' will: Levick 1976, 220; Claudius': Levick 1990, 78. Cancelleria reliefs: Magi 1945; Toynbee 1957; A.M. McCann, *Röm. Mitt.* 79 (1972) 249–76 (Hadrianic); Darwall-Smith 172–7 (from arch in Porticus Divorum). Heirs: *SD* 15, 1.

13 Warning: T*H* 4, 52, 1 (embroidered). Journey (Ch. 6 n. 23) advanced: Bersanetti 39, from DC 65 (66), 9, 2ᵃ. Misbehaviour: 2, 3; 3, 4; Beneventum: 9, 3; '*moria*' of Claudius (Levick 1990, 14f.); discredited by Graf 65f.

14 Literature: *PNH Pr.* 5; Q*IO* 10, 1, 91; Val. Flacc. 1, 12; *SD* 2, 2; Ph*VA* 7, 4 (Nero); the works: Bardon 281–8; K.M. Coleman, *ANRW* 2, 32, 5 (1991) 3088–95. Principate: Levick 1982.

15 Titus' daughters: Ph*VA* 7, 7; Julia Arrecina's: Castritius 1969, 492–4, against Townend 1961; cf. *PIR*² M 265. Homo 187 exploits hindsight over Titus' lack of sons.

16 *JB* 7, 82–8 (Gaul) with Weber 186 ('*durchweg panegyrische*'); cf. 266f., date: Ch. 5 n. 1. Domitian's friends would hold office 82–5: Eck, *Sen.* 60f. '*Liberi*' on dedications, etc.: n. 9 above. Arrecinus: MW 302, with Jones and Develin; contra, Menella 1981; S. Demougin, *MEFRA* 90 (1978) 325f.; death and its date: *SD* 11, 4; MW 14 (p. 27), with Jones and Develin 79–83: 22 Sept. 87; Rutilius was Praefectus in 89: Stat., *Silv.* 1, 4, 90–4, with Syme, 'Rutilius' 515. Domitia and Aelianus: *SD* 3, 1; 10, 2; DC 65 (66), 3, 4; Juv. 4, 154. Son: Vinson 447, citing J.-L. Desnier, *REA* 81 (1979) 54–65. Officials and Domitian: *AE* 69/70, 634 (Karanis), commemorates the temple founded in 73 by the Prefect of Egypt on behalf of V., Titus, Domitian, and the whole house (cf. Ch. 5 n. 31); 63, 11, set up at Adana, 77/8, by the governor; Domitian is jointly credited with restoring Bithynian roads by the procurator: MW 421 (78). Coins with '*AVG.*' for '*AVG. F.*': *RIC* 2, 56 n. (71).

17 Bengtson 172, like S*T* 1, stresses contrast between heir and Emperor. Journey: Helvidius: *SV* 15 and Ch. 6. Exculpation of V.: Syme, *Tac.* 212. Birley 1975, 152 n. 53, citing the boast (S*T* 3, 2) and *SV* 6, 4 (a letter from Otho); S*T* 6, 2 (death of Marcellus, below); *SD* 2, 3 (Domitian's accusation); see Malitz 1985, 243. Drafting documents (S*T* 6, 1) as M.T. Griffin observes, *CAH*² 11 (forthcoming), shows where power lay. Advancements under Domitian: Ch. 13.

18 'Conspiracy': DC 65 (66), 16, 3f.; S*T* 6, 2; [Epit. Aur. Vict.] *Caes.* 10, 4 (Berenice the motive; she 'returned' to Rome after V.'s death, below, n. 21; so also Bengtson

157f.); Crook 1951, 168f., justifiably suspicious, but dismissing Caecina as secondary. Josephus on Caecina: *JB* 4, 644, with Rajak 1983, 195 n. 23, arguing for freeing the 'conspiracy' from 79; see n. 16; Dr Pigoń notes Townend 1964, 340, dating to 79: Josephus was always free to state his truth about Caecina. Pigoń 238 acutely notes an intimation of Marcellus' 'conspiracy' in *TH* 4, 7, 3. Accepted: Grenzheuser 254f.; Rogers 1980, 93, with n. 39. Bengtson 144 suspects forgery of the speech. For Pigoń (240) Marcellus' end is a 'mystery'. Scapegoats: M.A. Levi, *Atti* 1983, 168.

19 Scripts: Sen., *Contr.* 3, *Pr.* 6. Nymphidius: PlG 14, 3. Consulars: Ch. 11, n. 15. Misgivings about Titus: above, n. 3.

20 Ascendancy, rivalry: Crook 1951, 162; 'Queen': 163. Quintilian's case: *QIO* 4, 1, 19. Berenice's stay: DC 65 (66), 15, 3f.; the justification for 75 is the context: dedication of Temple of Pax and erection of Colossus, 75; Parthians ask for help (*SD* 2, 2); possible support: MW 237. Her dismissal may have come in 79: Dio connects it with the punishment of philosophers and the capture of Sabinus, after nine years (*TH* 4, 67). Warning: above n. 13, with Crook 1951, 163–5. Crook invokes 'Concord' on coins of 71–3, but other references are possible.

21 Berenice's return: DC 66, 18, 1; [Epit. Aur. Vict.] *Caes.* 10, 7; *ST* 7, 2, with Schürer 1973, 479 n. 41. Rogers 1980 argues that Mucianus lacked ambition. Date of death: *TD* 37, 2; *PNH* 32, 62.

22 Caecina, Antonius, and V.: *JB* 4, 644; *TH* 3, 31, 4; 4, 80. Pigoń 239 acutely stresses anxious imperial friendships (*TH* 4, 8, 3).

13. CONCLUSION: IDEOLOGY IN THE AFTERMATH

Josephus: Ch. 3, bibl.; Tacitus: Ph. Fabia, *Les sources de Tacite dans les* Hist. *et les* Ann. *St. Hist.* 49 (Paris, 1893) ix–xvi; 1–306; E. Groag, *Jahrb. f. Class. Phil., Supplbd.* 23 (1897) 709–98; Briessmann 1955; Syme, *Tac.* 130–216; V. Pöschl, *Atti* 1981, 515–22; Murison 1991, 1711–13; Syme, 'Vestricius'. Suetonius: Graf; A. Wallace-Hadrill, *Suetonius: The scholar and his Caesars* (London, 1983). Aftermath: Jones, *Tit.* 114–80; *Dom.* 22–125; 160–98. Divinity: Buttrey 1976; H. Gesche, *Chiron* 8 (1978) 377–90; Schmidt; Lattimore 1934; Scott 1936, 61–82; 189–92; Friesen; Darwall-Smith 97f.; 153–78. Domitillae: D. Kienast, *ZPE* 76 (1989) 141–7. Portraiture: Ch. 5, bibl.; Bergmann and Zanker 332–5; K. Fittschen and P. Zanker, *Katalog d. röm. Portraits in d. Capitol. Museen u. d. anderen kommunalen Sammlungen d. Stadt Rom* (Mainz, 1983–5) 1, 33–8; Daltrop *et al.* 2, 1, 9–17.

1 Lifestyle: SV 21; [Epit. Aur. Vict.] *Caes.* 9, 15; cf. P*Ep.* 3, 5, 9; Ph*VA* 5, 31; DC 65 (66), 10, 5; cf. Garzetti 1974, 228. Theatre: Plut., *Mor.* 974A. Caenis' tombstone: MW 210. Propositioned: SV 22, with A. Hudson-Williams, *CR* NS 2 (1952) 72f. Propaganda: Graf 103; credited *TA* 3, 55, 5.

2 Death: SV 23f. (omens 23, 4; the comet that inspired Titus' poem (in his fifth consulship: *PNH* 2, 89) must have appeared by 76); DC 66, 17, 1–4 (omens 2f.); 17, 2f.; 18, 1ᵃ; [Epit. Aur. Vict.] *Caes.* 9, 17f.; Eutrop. 7, 20, 2; Oros. 7, 9, 12 (pestilence at 11; Eus.-Jer., *Chron.* p. 189 Helm dates to 77). Graf 106f. (successor of Julio-Claudians); Jones, Tit. 114f. Mausoleum: SN 46, 2. Parthian dissension, 78–81: A. Hollis, *G&R* 41 (1994) 205–12. Resort (unlike Augustus and Tiberius): M. Frederiksen, *Campania*. ed. N. Purcell (Rome, 1984) 335, citing Millar, *ERW* 24–8. Cutiliae waters; Strabo 5, 228C; *PNH* 31, 10.

3 Date: 24 June: Weynand 2673f.; Holzapfel 1918, 74–81: the night of 23–4 accounts best for discrepancies; Braithwaite on *SV* 24; Kienast 1990, 108. Dying on his feet: SV 24; [Epit.] DC 66, 17, 2; cf. S*Tib.* 73, 2. 'Becoming a god': SV 23,

4; DC 66, 17, 3, with Fishwick 1987, 295–300; Schmidt on Sen., *Apoc.* 4, 3, cf. 8, 3.

4 Claudius' symptoms: V. Grimm-Samuel, *CQ* 41 (1991), 178–82. Suspicions of Titus: DC 66, 17, 1; rebutted by Jones, *Tit.* 114. Schmidt 88 n. 23, recalls Nero's 'mushroom' joke (SN 33, 1; DC 60 (61), 35, 4). Titus *Imp.* XV: DC 66, 20, 3, in Buttrey 1980, 25 (other titles: 20).

5 Consecration: Buttrey 1976. V. is not *DIVVS* on the Domitilla reverse *RIC* 134 no. 154 (she predeceased him); see 121n., where Domitian in 80 is *COS.VII* and *AVG.F.*; Titus with *DIVVS VESPASIAN.* rev.: 120 no. 32; *DIVI F.* obv. of Titus, with rev. of the deified: 133 nos. 143–6; the deity on obv. 134 nos. 147–52; Domitian liked *AVG.* on his coins, retaining it with *DIVVS*: 136–9 nos. 162A-175. Aqueduct: *ILS* 98; so MW 11 of ?29 May 80 (both sons); Syme, *RP* 4, 399f., notes that V. is not always '*Divus*' on later inscriptions: neither V. nor Titus is in MW 299f. Gesche's interpretation, 384, that Titus like Pius and M. Aurelius was co-regent, is criticized by Schmidt 88 n. 20; Darwall-Smith 98f. accepts delay in ratification, rejecting Blake's attempt, 97, to determine how much of V.'s temple was built by Titus; cf. J.B. Ward-Perkins, *Rom. Imperial Architecture* (Harmondsworth, 1981) 72f. Motive: PP*an.* 11, 1f. Titus' saying: DC 66, 19, 1f.; Tiberius in TA 1, 73, 5. A.R. Birley's argument, *CR* 12 (1962) 197–9, that the oath of DC 75, 2, 1, goes back to V., is not strong: TH 4, 41, 1. Domitian's refusal: DC 67, 2, 4. Titus vindicator: PP*an.* 35, 4; Mart., *Sp.* 4. P. Herz, *ANRW* 2, 16, 2 (1978) 1167, n. 215, stresses continuity. Minerva: PhV*A* 7, 24 and 26; she appeared on V.'s coins: *RIC* 65 no. 407 (70); 69 no. 445 (71); 101 no. 735 (72–3). *PROVI-DENTIA*: Fears 1977, 221 Arvals: MW 11 (p. 19) ll. 38–40.

6 Julia: SD 17, 3. V's temple: Eus.-Jer., *Chron.* p. 191 Helm; Flavian Temple: SD 1, 1; Mart. 9, 20 and 34; Val. Flac. 1, 15f. *CIL* 6, 938; Hill 206f., on *CREBM* 343 no. 229 (95–6); Jones, *Dom.* 87f.; Darwall-Smith 159–65, arguing (266f.) for Titus as constructor of Flaccus' '*delubra genti*' (date of passage: Ch. 5 n. 27). *Sodales*: Newton 95–7; Scott 1936, 79–81 (Domitian founder); Momigliano 1975, 2, 657–76 (linked with Jupiter). Obelisk, Cancelleria reliefs: Ch. 12 n. 12. Cumae: *CIL* 10, 3698.

7 *Flamines*: H. Mouritsen and I. Gradel, *ZPE* 87 (1991) 149–51, and personal communication: flamen of deified V. and Titus at Tarraco: *CIL* 2, 6099; 4212 (= MW 344). The flamen at Portus, Ostia: *AE* 87, 204, is from *c.*100–50; Ostia: *CIL* 14, 292, 298; 4641, 4664; *AE* 86, 113; 10, 197; 13, 190; flamens of Augustus, V., and Trajan at Eporedia and of V., Nerva, and Trajan at Vardagate: *CIL* 5, 6797, 7458; of V. at Augusta Taurinorum: 7021; Terventum: 9, 2600; Histonium: 2855 (= *ILS* 5501); Volcei: 10, 413; Pisae: 11, 1447a; Aquileia: *AE* 34, 232. At Aquinum 'Juvenal' is flamen, MW 156 (not the satirist, b.62–70: Syme, *RP* 3, 1121f.). Other honours: Olisipo altar (Domitianic?): *AE* 87, 478d; Newton 94 nos. 211f.; Munigua, posthumous: *AE* 72, 256. Miletus: nymphaeum architrave ?dedicated to the deified V.: 04, 226. Freedmen commemorating Tiberius, Drusus Caesar, and V. (35, 47, Philippi) show personal devotion; so the dedication to the deified V., 39, 55 (= MW 134, Baalbek), 56. V. and Titus at Ephesus: *IvE* 3, 710b and c; cf. 7, 1, 3038 (temple warden), with Friesen 37; date of cult: 41f.; 48.

8 Graf 2 unconvincingly cites SV 1, 1 for uncertainty. *CREBM* 343, no, 229 (95–6); *EG* 2, 697. Domitian's mistress: SD 17, 3; DC 67, 3, 2; cf. PhV*A* 7, 7; Schol. Juv. 2, 29; critique of stories: M.P. Vinson, *Hist.* 38 (1978) 431–49. '*Diva*': *PIR*[2] F 426 cites *RIC* 204, no. 400 (90–1); Mart. 9, 1, 7; Italian and provincial *flaminicae*: Novaria: *CIL* 5, 6514; Aeclanum: MW 147. *DIVA DOMITILLA AVGVSTA*: *RIC* 124 no. 69 (rev.); 70–3 (obv.) of uncertain dates; cf. MW 146

(Patavium). V.'s wife, *PIR*[2] F 416, where A. Stein denies that she is '*Diva Dom-itilla*'; daughter, 417, claiming deification for her; granddaughter 418. Kienast 1989 argues that the deified sister ('*soror*') alluded to in Stat., *Silv.* 1, 1, 98, is Julia, Domitian's niece. V.'s wife Augusta: *CIL* 6, 31287; '*MEMORIAE*' and/or *carpentum*: *RIC* 134 no. 153f. seven children of Domitilla and Clemens: MW 221. Cerialis: Ch. 3 n. 1.

9 Titus' reputation Ch. 12; rebutted: Luck 66–9; illness: Bengtson 163–5; Garzetti 1974, 258f., is judicious. Achievements: *ST* 1, 1; 11; *DC* 66, 18, 1–19, 3ª; Oros. 7, 13; 15; Aur. Vict., *Caes.* 10; [Epit. Aur. Vict.] *Caes.* 3; 6–11; 16; Eutrop. *Brev.* 7, 21, 2; Aug., *Civ. Dei* 5, 21; Jones, *Tit.* 121f. Disasters: *ST* 8, 3; *PEp.* 6, 16; *DC* 66, 21, 1–24, 4; [Epit.] 10, 12f.; Oros. 7, 9, 11. Natural disasters under V.: Oros. 9, 11; *Orac. Sib.* 4, 128f., cf. 143f.; 5, 450–4; 7, 5.

10 Domitian 'heir': *ST* 9, 3; no joint ruler: Bengtson 160; no military training: M.P. Morford, *Phoen.* 22 (1968) 69–71. Sabinus: *SD* 10, 4; *PhVA* 7, 7; *PIR*[2] F 355. Contradictions on Domitian's treatment of V.'s and Titus' friends: *ST* 7, 2; *DC* 67, 2, 1f.; 3, 3. Note temporary Campanian relegation of Claudius Etruscus' father, V.'s *a rationibus* and Titus' protégé: Stat., *Silv.* 3, 3, 138–42, with Weaver 1972, 289. Jones, *Dom.* 65, attempts reconciliation but cf. M.T. Griffin, *CR* 43 (1993) 115: the authors have different perspectives; slow careers of men advanced by V.: Eck, *Sen.* 66. Cerialis: Birley 1981, 69; cf. Syme, *RP* 7, 645 n. 63. Censor: *DC* 67, 4, 3; *RIC* 161–5 nos. 60–98; 166–77 nos. 100–203. Purges: *SV* 10. 2–4; MW 14 (p. 27).

11 Revisionists: K.H. Waters, *Phoenix* 18 (1964) 49–77; Vinson (n. 8); Jones, *Dom.* 196–8: see Bengtson 281. *Libertas*: *RIC* 223 no. 7; 227 no. 64 (96); 224 no. 19; 225 nos. 31 and 36 (97). MW 66 (= *Docs N–H* 27a); *PEp.* 9, 13, 4; *TAgr.* 3, 1. '*ROMA RENASCENS*' (stronger than '*RESVRGENS*'): *RIC* 227 no. 67 (96); 229 no. 91 (97). The dynasty: *SV* 1. 1. Ephesus: MW 139, with Friesen 32–7. Calculation: *SV* 25, with Graf 108. Sabinus: Plut., *Mor.* 771C, with C.P. Jones, *Plutarch and Rome* (Oxford, 1971) 25.

12 V.'s friends: n. 10. Syme, 'Saturninus'; probably governor of Judaea *c.*78–81 and involved in the erection of a loyal inscription to V. and Titus: *AE* 78, 825; Syme, 'Ceionii'.

13 God: above, n. 3. Favor the mime: *SV* 19, 2; merit: *TH* 2, 77, 3. Unifying rumour: P.A. Lienhardt in J. Beattie and R.G. Lienhardt, eds, *Studies in Social Anthropology: essays in memory of E.E. Evans-Pritchard* (Oxford, 1975) 105–31. V. and *veritas*: *TD* 8, 3; *SV* 13. Gladiators: *DC* 65 (66), 15, 2; Tiberius: *STib.* 47 (another reason for absence). Mud: *DC* 59, 12, 3; Ch. 1; source: Townend, 'Cluvius' 233f.; freedman: 65 (66), 11, 2, cf. 62 (63), 10, 1a; vowels: *SV* 22; urinals: 23, 3; *DC* 65 (66), 14, 5; cf. Juv. 14, 204f.: a cliché: 208f.

14 Fate: Graf 18. Pliny: '*A fine Aufidii Bassi*' and on German wars (*PNH Pr.* 20. Syme, *Tac.* 288f.). Criticism: *TH* 2, 101, 1 (Caecina and Bassus). Rajak 1983, 195–8, rebuts the idea that Josephus' works – JB belongs to the late 70s, JA and JV to 93–4 – were official history. Later writers: *TAgr.* 13, 3; Graf also cites *DC* 60, 20, 3f.; 60 (61) 30, 1. Primus and Hormus: JB 4, 642; *TH* 3, 28 (Messalla *v.* Pliny). Messalla covering the Moesian outbreak until the Flavians entered Rome: Milne 1973, 293 n. 70. Verginius and Vindex: Levick 1985. Caecina: Ch. 12.

15 Tacitus first: Rajak 1983, 199, citing *PEp.* 5, 8, 12. Sources: *TH* 2, 37, 1; Fabia; Groag (principles of selection 765); Syme, *Tac.* 675–6; Chilver 1979, p. 25f.; d'Espèrey 3063; M.M. Sage, *ANRW* 2, 33, 2 (1990) 893–7; Murison 1991, 1711–13. *PNH* 3, 28, unpublished in his lifetime. Cluvius: Townend, 'Cluvius'; 1964; cf. Griffin 1976, 429 n. 2; defended: T.P. Wiseman, *Death of an Emperor:*

Exeter Stud. Hist. 30 (Exeter, 1991) 111–18; D. Wardle, *Herm.* 120 (1992) 466–82.; bibl. n. 1; *fides*: P*Ep* 9. 19. 5; source of the accent on irrational soldiers as a factor in 69–70: R. Ash in J.M. Mossman, ed., *Plutarch and his Intellectual World* (London, 1997) 205 n. 9, citing Powell. Mud: n. 13. Extent of Cluvius' *Histories*: Chilver on T*H* 1, 78, 2, questioning whether he dealt with 69; Wardle 477 n. 64, noting Townend's views (destruction of Capitol at latest). Fabius Rusticus (Sage 1015): T*A* 13, 20, 3; T*Agr.* 10, 3; if alive in 108 (*CIL* 6, 10229, l. 24), a young and impressionable disciple of Seneca (I owe caution on this to Prof. A. Birley); Townend 1964, 343, is sceptical and argues for Pliny; Sage 897 concurs. Date of Pl*G* and Pl*O* : Ash 213 n. 57.

16 Rufus: P*Ep.* 9, 19; oration: 2, 1, 6; Tacitus on him: Levick 1985, 344–6. Spurinna: T*H* 2, 11, 2, with Chilver; Syme 'Vestricius' 543 and 547 (consular date). Agricola: Birley 1981, 75f.

17 '*Praecipuus adstricti moris auctor Vespasianus fuit, antiquo ipse cultu victuque*': T*A* 3, 55, 5. Improvement: T*H* 1, 50, 4 (so Aus., *De XII Caes. per Suet. Tran. script.* 12); Ceausescu 1989 reinterprets. Meanness and '*egregium principatus temperamentum, si demptis utriusque vitiis solae virtutes miscerentur*': 2, 5, 1; Mucianus also 1, 10, 1f. '*Saevum*': 1, 2, 1. Friends: T*H* 2, 95, 3; Vinius, 1, 6, 1, with Chilver; 37, 5 (and Icelus, *PIR*² J 16); 48, 2–4; Valens: 3, 62, 2; Asiaticus, 2, 57, 2. Caecina and Bassus: 2, 100. Messala: 3, 28 (d'Espèrey 3062f.). Capitol: Ch. 4 n. 28.

18 Suetonius' sources: Graf 109 and *passim*; standing: Bengtson 177; attitude: Wallace-Hadrill 1983, 186–9. Commission: S*V* 10; T*H* 4, 40, 2 (same source); see Graf 86; generally Fabia and Groag.

19 Dio: Bengtson 279; Malitz 1985, 246. Pliny and Mucianus: *PIR*² L 216 (p. 51); *Acta* and letters: T*D* 37, 2.

20 See Aur. Vict., *Caes.* 9, and [Epit. Aur. Vict.] *Caes.* 9; *SHA Elagab.* 1, 2; Aug., *Civ. Dei* 5, 21; Aus., *l.c.* (n. 17), cited by Bengtson 280: both V. and Titus are '*iusti*'.

21 Cult: n. 7; *Flaviales*: n. 6; *CIL* 8, 7062. Temple renamed: Homo 387. Municipal *seviri Flaviales* from Italy, Narbonensis, and Dalmatia: Newton 87f.

22 Colosseum: Ch. 9.1 with n. 12. Amm. Marc. 16, 10, 14; Bede, *Coll.* 1, 3, but the words on the '*Colisaeus*' were originally applied to the Helius statue: C. Lega in E.M. Steinby, ed., *Lex. Top. Urtis Romae* 1 (Rome, 1993) 296, cf. G. Lugli, *Rom. antiqua: il centro monumentale* (Rome, 1946) 321f. Last shows: Cassiodorus, *Var.* 5, 42 (beasts); Theodoret *Hist. Eccl.* 5, 26 (gladiators).

23 Oros. 7, 3, 8; 9, 8f., has Flavians vindicating Christ; Dante, *Parad.* 21, 82, with M.P. Stocchi, *Encicl. Dante* 6, 91–3; tradition, incl. Turin poem: V. Canotta, *Atti* 1983, 217–42. Romance: Hook and Newman, Intr., with bibl. and citing (xx n. 5) F. del Paso y Troncoso, *Déstrucción de Jerusalén, auto en lengua mexicana (anónimo)*, etc., *Bibl. Nahuatl* I, 4 (Florence, 1907).

24 Bersanetti 89–92; Britain 86 (from T*Agr.* 21?). Homo, title page; 170–83; 190–5, with Bengtson 180 (Napoleon).

25 Emperors from provinces: T*H* 1, 4, 2. Fairs: *e.g.* Cremona, 3, 30, 26. Gaius: DC 59, 20, 4; Claudius: 60, 14, 1; Nero: e.g. T*A* 13, 50, 1f. Irony: [Epit. Aur. Vict.] *Caes.* 9, 17; cf. Tiberius: B. Levick, *Hist.* 27 (1978) 95–101.

26 'Epigraphic habit': S. Mrozek, *Epigr.* 35 (1973), 114. Functional Principate: Garzetti 1974, 228. Antonine aristocracy: Homo 386. '*Civilis Princeps*': A. Wallace-Hadrill, *JRS* 72 (1982), 32–48; S*V* 12. Military monarchy: Bengtson 31; reservations: Flaig 207. Tiberius on functions: e.g. T*A* 3, 53, 3.

27 Jokes: S*V* 22f. Braithwaite on S*V* 20, 'straining' cites J.J. Bernoulli, *Röm. Ikonographie* 2, 2 (Stuttgart etc., 1891), 27.

28 Physique, deportment: Levick 1990, 15. Two types of portrait: Graf 102, n. 560,

citing Bernoulli 21–8. Taf. 7 (Thermae; ?a little after 79); A. Hekler, *Greek and Rom. Portraits* (London, 1912): idealizing type 218a; Thermae 218b; R. Delbrück, *Ant. Porträt* (Bonn, 1912) Taf. 39a (Naples); F. Poulsen, *Röm. Mitt.* 20 (1914) 44–9. (Ny Carlsberg 45); Daltrop *et al.* 9–17 (age as criterion). Bergmann and Zanker 332–40, in the context of reused monuments; their two coin types are J.P.C. Kent, B. Overbeck, A. Stylow, *Die röm. Münze* (Munich, 1973) 228 and 225. Uffizi: Bergmann and Zanker Taf. 3, 12a; Ny Carlsberg: Daltrop Taf. 3; London 1890: Taf. 2; Vatican: Taf. 3; Cancelleria: Taf. 5; Ch. 12 n. 12 above; Capitoline: Fittschen and Zanker 1, 33, no. 27 ('*Hauptypus*'). Realism: J. Liversedge in M. Henig, ed., *Handbook of Roman Art: A survey of the visual arts of the Roman World* (Oxford, 1983) 102f.

29 Descriptions: *SV* 20; baldness: 23, 4; *DC* 66, 17, 1 (gout, *podagra*).

30 Hekler (n. 28) xxxiv. Pallor, but '*in corpore*', the face often suffused: P*Pan.* 48, 4, with M. Durry. Titus: *ST* 3, 1.

CONCORDANCE

To M. McCrum and A.G. Woodhead, *Select
Documents of the Principates of the Flavian Emperors* (MW)
(Concordance to *Docs G–N* : Levick 1990, 239f.)

1	*ILS* 244; *FIRA* 1, 15; Bruns 56
2–10	G. Henzen, ed., *Acta Fratrum Arvalium* (Berlin, 1874) XC–CIV; A. Pasoli, ed., *Acta Fratrum Arvalium quae post annum MDCCCLXXIV reperta sunt* (Bologna, 1950) 22–8; cf. *Album* 1, 125, 127, 129, 131, 141, 144
23	*ILS* 982
24	*CREBM* 1, 287 no. 5
25	*CREBM* 1, 292 no. 12
26	*CREBM* 1, 293
27	*CREBM* 1, 297 no. 31
28	*CREBM* 1, 318 no. 63
29	*CREBM* 1, 345 no. 205
30	*ILS* 238
31	*IRT* 537; *Afr. ital.* 7 (1940) 99f.
32	*CREBM* 1, 364 no. 1
33	*BMC Phoen.* 209 no. 42
36	*CREBM* 1, 388 no. 99
37	*CREBM* 1, 375 no. 47
38	*CREBM* 1, 306 no. 65
39	*CREBM* 1, 308(d)
40	*ILS* 983
41	*PFuad* 1, 8; P. Jouguet, *Mélanges Ernout* (Paris, 1940) 201–10
42	*CREBM* 2, 87 no. 425
43	*CREBM* 2, 120 no. 559
44	*CREBM* 2, 131 no. 604
45	*CREBM* 2, 81 no. 397
46	*CREBM* 2, 118 no. 549
47	*CREBM* 2, 129 no. 597
48	*CREBM* 2, 139 no. 629
49	*ILS* 9198

50	*ILS* 997
51	*Not. d. Scavi* (1933) 241; cf. *MEFR* 54 (1937) 165–99; *Album* 1, 135
52	*CREBM* 2, 169 n.
53	*ILS* 264
55	*SEG* 16, 592; cf. 14, 611
73	*ILS* 237
74	*IGR* 1, 1174
75	*CREBM* 1, 344 no. 201
76	*ILS* 240; *Album* 1, 126
77	*BMC Syria* 177 no. 214
78	*CIL* 11, 7417
79	*BMC Alexandria* 27 no. 218
80	*CREBM* 1, 372 no. 27
81	*ILS* 242
82	*CREBM* 1, 369 no. 10
83	*CREBM* 2 180, no. 748B
84	*ILS* 246
85	*CREBM* 2, 7, ‖
86	*ILS* 8904
87	*ILS* 254
88	*IGR* 3, 223
89	*IGR* 3, 37
90	*CREBM* 2, 194, ¶
91	*CREBM* 2, 129 no. 596
92	*CREBM* 2, 75 *
93	*ILS* 8903
94	*IG* 7, 3418
95	*TAM* 2, 275; *IGR* 3, 609
96	*TAM* 2, 1188
97	*ILS* 984
98	*ILS* 257
99	*CREBM* 2, 246 no. 138
100	*ILS* 8306
101	*CIL* 6, 948a; Newton 230
102	*ILS* 258
103	*ILS* 259
104	*ILS* 261
105	*ILS* 263
106	*CREBM* 2, 242 no. 147
107	*IGR* 4, 715
108	*ILS* 265
109	*CIL* 6, 12355; Newton 234
110	*CREBM* 2, 247 no. 141
111	*TAM* 2, 506; *IGR* 3, 573

112	*ILS* 8906
113	*ILS* 271
114	*CREBM* 2, 311 no. 62
115	*ILS* 267
116	*EE* 8, 15 no. 73; Newton 211
117	*CIL* 3, 12218
118	*CREBM* 2, 301 no. 12
119	*CREBM* 2, 358 no. 284
122	*ILS* 269
128	*ILS* 6964; *FIRA* 1, 22; Bruns 29
129	*Hesp.* 10 (1941) 72–7 no. 32; 11 (1942) 80
130	*CREBM* 2, 94 no. 449
131	*ILS* 3453
132	*JRS* 2 (1912) 102
133	*MAMA* 6, 177
134	*Bull. du Musée de Beyrouth* 1 (1937) 78
135	*CREBM* 2, 241 no. 106
136	*IGR* 4, 211; Newton 215
137	*Ann. du Serv. des Ant. de l'Egypte* 39 (1939) 605
138	*Inscr. Bulg.* 1, 58; cf. *IGR* 1, 594
139	*Forsch. in Ephesos* 2, 166 no. 48
140	*Bull. com.* 67 (1939), App. 45f.
150	*ILS* 7357
151	*ILS* 252
152	*ILS* 5025
153	*Rev. de Phil.* Sér. 3, vol. 25 (1951) 195–201
154	*ILS* 3001; *Bull. com.* 63 (1935) 171
155	*ILS* 1010
156	*ILS* 2926
157	*IRT* 347
163	*ILS* 2995
168	*ILS* 5172; cf. *AC* 22 (1953) 79–88; *Rev. Arch.* 1954 (1) 80–2
173	*ILS* 1012
174	*ILS* 3534
179	*ILS* 3663; *Album* 1, 138
181	*ILS* 3673; *IGR* 1, 704
188	*IGR* 1. 1120; *OGIS* 671
190	*CREBM* 2, 189 no. 780
191	*Not. dei Scavi* 1914, 363
192	*CIL* 10, 7
198	*CIL* 6, 8833
199	*Jahresh. Öst. Arch. Inst.* 26 (1930) Beibl. 59f.
200	*ILS* 1517
201	*ILS* 1489f.

202	*ILS* 1518
203	*ILS* 1519
204	*ILS* 1523
205	*ILS* 1567; *PBSR* 15 (1939) 24
206	*ILS* 1943
208	*ILS* 1679
210	*CIL* 6, 12037
211	*Bull. de la Soc. des Antiq. de France* 1929, 173–9
218	*ILS* 7733a
221	*ILS* 1839
225	*Röm. Mitt.* 27 (1912) 309f.
233	*IGR* 1, 903
234	*IGR* 1, 881
235	*Vestnik Drevnei Ist* . 1955, 207f. no. 3; cf. *Bibl. Class. Orient.* 1 (1956) 199
237	*ILS* 8795; *IGR* 3, 133; *OGIS* 1, 379; *JRS* 33 (1943) 85f.
238	*SEG* 15, 836
239	*ILS* 8958
240	*BMC Syria* 110 no. 1
241	*IGR* 3, 1244; *OGIS* 1, 419
242	*IGR* 3, 1144; *OGIS* 1, 425
243	*IG* 2 3449; *OGIS* 1, 428
244	*Mél. de l'Univ. St. Jos. Beyrouth* 15 (1942–3) 32; *Beyrouth ville rom. hist. et mon.* 8f.
245	*BMC Parthia* 210 no. 5
246	*BMC Parthia* 203 no. 1
247	*BMC Parthia* 195 no. 14
253	*BMC Troas* 63 no. 44
254	*CREBM* 2, 113 ß
255	*CIL* 5, 5812
256	J. Serra Vilaró, *Excavaciones en Tarragona* (1932) 110f.; cf. *PIR*² G 64
257	*CIL* 6, 1528
258	*ILS* 8816; *IGR* 3, 486; *OGIS* 558
259	*CIL* 14, 2173
260	*ILS* 999; 3, 2, p. clxxiii
261	*ILS* 986; *AC* 3 (1934) 121–61
262	*BMC Bithynia* 145 no. 44
263	*ILS* 8970; *Milet* 1, 5, 53f.
264	*BCH* 12 (1888) 281; Newton 258
265	*Antioch-on-the-Orontes* I, *Excavations of 1932* (1934) 53
266	*Inscr. Ital.* 10, 4, 30; *ILS* 989
267	*ILS* 987; *Phil.* 91 (1936–7) 238–45
268	*Inscr. Cret.* 4, 292; *Phil.* 91 (1936–7) 238–45
269	*Sitzungsb. Akad. Berlin* 1931, 831

270   *IGR* 4, 644l; *OGIS* 482; *MAMA* 6, 262
271   *ILS* 992
272   *IGR* 4, 524; *OGIS* 476
273   *BMC Aeolis* 114 no. 99
274   *ILS* 985; *Arch. Ertes.* 52 (1939) 103–7
275   *CIL* 4, 2560
276   *ILS* 8969
277   *CRAI* 1940, 131–7
278   *ILS* 3596
279   *ILS* 980
280   *IGR* 1, 863; *Inscr. ant. orae sept. Ponti Euxini* 12, 421
281   *IGR* 3, 125
282   *BMC Cappadocia* 47 no. 8
283   *ILS* 8704a; R.P. Wright, *Cat. of . . . Stones in the Grosvenor Mus., Chester* ([Chester,] 1955) 199
284   *BMC Bithynia* 104 no. 4
285   *ILS* 995
286   *JRS* 3 (1913) 301–9; cf. *Jahresh. Öst. Arch. Inst.* 29 (1935) Beibl. 179f.
287   *TAM* 2, 131; *IGR* 3, 522
288   *CIL* 3, 335
289   *CIL* 12, 3166
290   *ILS* 1000; 3, 2, p. clxxiii
291   *ILS* 1378
292   *ILS* 1003; *Album* 1, 140
294   *CIL* 10, 1258
295   *ILS* 1002
296   *CIL* 6, 1495; Newton 163
298   *ILA* 2, 644; cf. 643
299   *ILS* 990
300   *ILS* 991
302   *Ath.* NS 18 (1940) 145–63
304   *ILS* 1007
305   *ILS* 9499
306   *ILS* 1008
307   *ILS* 1005
308   *CIL* 8, 21365
309   *ILS* 1015; 3, 2, p. clxxiii
311   *ILS* 1011
315   *JRS* 3 (1913) 260; *ILS* 9485
316   *ILS* 8971; *Forsch. in Ephesos* 5, 1, 62–6 no. 3; cf. *IGR* 4, 1509
319   *CIL* 3, 250
320   *IGR* 4, 384; *OGIS* 486; *IGR* 4, 373–83, 385–97; *TAM* 2, 566
321   *ILS* 1024

328   H.G. Evelyn-White and J.H. Oliver, *The Temple of Hibis in El-Khargeh Oasis* 2 (N.Y., 1938) 23–45 (Text B); *SEG* 15, 873

329   *Papyrus Hibeh* 215; cf. *JRS* 44 (1954) 61

330   *IGR* 3, 1015; *OGIS* 586

331   *AJA* 39 (1935) 588f.

332   *SEG* 14. 853; *SB* 8958; L. Robert, *La Collection Froehner* 1 (Paris, 1936) 75

333   *CIL* 11, 5382

334   *Bull. du Mus. de Beyrouth* 1 (1937) 80–2

337   *CIL* 10, 8024

338   *ILS* 1447; cf. *PBSR* 15 (1939) 23

339   *FIRA* 3, 76(c); *ILS* 5942

340   *ILS* 2729

341   *ILS* 6905

342   *ILS* 2711

345   *SEG* 2, 850

346   *ILS* 1910

353   *CIL* 9, 1132

354   *CIL* 9, 2564

355   *ILS* 9199

356   *CIL* 11, 390

357   *ILS* 2641; *Album* 1, 142

358   *ILS* 2647

359   *Syria* 5 (1924) 324–30

360   *CIL* 3, 6603

361   *ILS* 2118

363   *ILS* 9089

369   *Vestnik Drevnei Ist.* 1950, 1, p. 177f.; *Epigr.* 16 (1954) 118–20

370   *Raccolta di scritti in onore di A. Giussani* (Milan, 1944) 147–55; *CIL* 3, 14349^2 (rev.)

372   *ILS* 9200

373   *CIL* 9, 4688

374   *Not. d. Scavi* 1951, 1–6

375   *ILS* 2034; 3, 2, p. clxxvi

377   *JRS* 38 (1948) 103f.; *Ant. Journ.* 29 (1949) 84

378   *ILS* 2460

379   *CIL* 5, 889

381   *ILS* 2035

382   *ILS* 2036

385   R.P. Wright, *Cat. Grosvenor Mus., Chester* 29

386   *ILS* 2284

390   *Röm.- Germ. Korr.* 4 (1911) 25f.

391   *ILS* 2497

392   *ILS* 2507; 3, 2, p. clxxviii

393   *ILS* 2544
394   *ILS* 2566
396   *CIL* 16, 7; *ILS* 1988
397   *CIL* 16, 10
398   *CIL* 16, 13
399   *CIL* 16, 20; *ILS* 1992
400   *CIL* 16, 21; *ILS* 1993
401   *CIL* 16, 24; *JRS* 16 (1926) 95–101
408   *ILS* 218
409   *CIL* 6, 1246
412   *ILS* 245
413   *ILS* 5819
414   *CIL* 11, 2999
415   *Inscr. Ital.* 10, 1, 705; *ILS* 5832
416   *ILS* 5832
418   *ILS* 5867
419   *CIL* 8, 10119; *ILA* 1, 3885
421   *ILS* 253
424   *Syria* 13 (1932) 276f.
425   *CREBM* 2, 133 no. 614
426   *CREBM* 2, 17 no. 90
429   *CIL* 6, 814
430   *ILS* 249; *Album* 1, 136
432   *ILS* 3813
433   *ILS* 250
434   *Ant. Journ.* 36 (1956) 8–10; *JRS* 46 (1956) 146f.
435   *SEG* 9, 166
437   *TAM* 2, 651; *IGR* 3, 507
438   *IGR* 3, 840
439   *ILS* 8710
440   *Proc. Soc. Ant. London* 31 (1918–19) 37
443   *ILS* 5927; cf. J. Le Gall, *Rech. sur le culte du Tibre* (Paris, 1953) 138f.
444   *ILS* 251
445   *ILS* 5982
446   *ILS* 5957
447   *CRAI* 1951, 366–73; *Gallia* 13 (1955) 9
448   *Libyca* 3 (1955) 289–92
449   *Bull. Arch.* 1934–5, 391f.; cf. *ILS* 5955
450   *IRT* 854
451   *ILS* 5951
453   A. D'Ors, *Epigr. jurid. de la España rom.* (Madrid, 1953) 281–309;
       FIRA 1, 23; *ILS* 6088; Bruns 30a
454   A. D'Ors, *ibid.* 311–41; *FIRA* 1, 24; *ILS* 6089; Bruns 30b
455   *FIRA* 1, 59; *ILS* 5947; Bruns 71a

456	Bruns 57
457	C. Dunant and J. Pouilloux, *Rech. sur l'hist. et les cultes de Thasos* 2 (Paris, 1958) 82–7, no. 186
458	*Sitzungsb. Akad. Berlin* 1935, 967–72; *FIRA* 1, 77; cf. *TAPA* 86 (1955) 348f.
460	*FIRA* 1, 72; Bruns 80
461	*FIRA* 1, 74; *ILS* 6092; Bruns 81
462	*FIRA* 1, 75; Bruns 82
468	*ILS* 6045
470	*Mem. dell'Accad. di Arch., Lett. e Belle Arti di Napoli* NS 3 (1955) 88f.
471	*IG* 14, 760; *IGR* 1, 453
475	*AJP* 68 (1947) 389
477	*ILS* 5350
478	*CIL* 2, 3250
479	*ILS* 256
481	*ILS* 1981
482	*CIL* 8, 20853
483	*Bull. Arch* 1934–5, 94f.
484	*IRT* 300
485	*IRT* 42(a); cf. *Libyca* 2 (1954) 383f.
486	*ILS* 6105; *Ann. du Mus. Nat. arch., Plovdiv* 1 (1948) 59
487	*Fouilles de Delphes* 3, 4 no. 34; *Syll. Inscr. Gr.*[3] 3, 817
488	*IG* 22, 3283b
495	*BCH* 6 (1882) 286f.; Newton 195
501	*BMC Phrygia* 95 no. 150
502	*BMC Lydia* 51 no. 69
513	*ILS* 6049
514	*ILS* 6050
515	*ILS* 6051
516	*ILS* 6052
532	*CREBM* 2, 86 no. 423

BIBLIOGRAPHY

Items from this bibliography are cited in abbreviated form (author, date). When only one work of an author is cited the date is omitted; several works of an author published in the same year, and a few others, are distinguished by abbreviated titles.

Applebaum, S., 'Judaea as a Roman province: the countryside as a political and economic factor', *ANRW* 2, 8 (1977) 355–96.

Bardon, H., *Les Empereurs et les lettres latines d'Auguste à Hadrien*² (Paris, 1968).

Barrett, A., *Caligula: The Corruption of Power* (London, 1989).

Barzanò, A., 'Il "dies imperii" di Vespasiano', *Iura* 31 (1980) 148–50.

Bénabou, M., *La résistance africaine à la romanisation* (Paris, 1976)

Bengtson, H., *Die Flavier. Vespasian, Titus, Domitian. Geschichte eines römischen Kaiserhauses* (Munich, 1979).

Bergener, A., *Die führende Senatorenschicht im frühen Prinzipat* (Diss. Bonn, 1965).

Bergmann, M., and Zanker, P., ' "Damnatio Memoriae": umgearbeitete Nero- und Domitiansportraits. zur Ikonographie der Flavischen Kaiser u. des Nerva', *Jahres. Deutsch. Arch. Inst.* 96 (1981) 317–412.

Bersanetti, G.M., *Vespasiano* (Rome, 1941).

Birley, A.R., 'Petillius Cerialis and the conquest of Brigantia', *Brit.* 4 (1973) 179–90.

—— 'Agricola, the Flavian dynasty, and Tacitus', in B. Levick, ed., *The Ancient Historian and his Materials* (Farnborough, 1975) 139–54.

—— *The Fasti of Roman Britain* (Oxford, 1981).

Blake, M.E.R., *Roman Construction in Italy from Tiberius through the Flavians. Carnegie Inst. Publ.* 616 (Washington, D.C., 1959).

Bosworth, A.B., 'Vespasian and the provinces: some problems of the early 70's AD', *Ath.* NS 51 (1973) 49–78.

Boulvert, G., *Esclaves et affranchis impériaux sous le Haut-Empire romain: rôle politique et administratif. Bibl. di Labeo* 4 (Naples, 1970).

—— *Domestique et fonctionnaire sous le Haut-Empire romain: la condition de l'affranchi et de l'esclave du prince* (Paris, 1974).

Bourne, F.C., *The Public Works of the Julio-Claudians and Flavians* (Diss. Princeton, NJ, 1946).

Bowersock, G.W., 'Syria under Vespasian', *JRS* 63 (1973) 133–40 ['Syria'].

Bradley, K.R., 'The career of T. Clodius Eprius Marcellus Cos. II AD 74: some possibilities', *Symb. Oslo.* 53 (1978) 171–81.

Braithwaite, A.W., ed., *C. Suetoni Tranquilli Divus Vespasianus, with an Introduction and Commentary* (Oxford, 1927).

Briessmann, A., *Tacitus und das flavische Geschichtsbild. Herm. Einzelschr.* 10 (Wiesbaden, 1955).

Broughton, T.R.S., *The Romanization of Africa Proconsularis* (Baltimore, Md., 1929; repr. Westport, Conn., 1968).

Brunt, P.A., 'The revolt of Vindex and the fall of Nero', *Lat.* 18 (1959) 531–59 (= *RIT* 9–32) ['Vindex'].

—— 'Tacitus on the Batavian revolt', *Lat.* 19 (1960) 494–517 (= *RIT* 33–52) ['Tac.'].

—— 'Stoicism and the Principate', *PBSR* 43 (1975) 7–35.

—— 'The *Lex de imperio Vespasiani* ', *JRS* 67 (1977) 95–116.

Buttrey, T.V., 'Vespasian as moneyer', *NC* Ser. 7, vol. 12 (1972) 89–109.

—— 'Vespasian's Consecratio and the numismatic evidence', *Hist.* 25 (1976) 449–52.

—— *Documentary Evidence of the Chronology of the Flavian Titulature. Beiträge zur kl. Phil.* 112 (Meisenhanheim am Glan, 1980).

Castagnoli, F., 'Cippo di "restitutio agrorum" presso Canne', *RFIC* 26 (1948) 280–6.

—— 'Politica urbanistica di Vespasiano in Roma', *Atti* 1981 261–75.

Castritius, H., 'Zu den Frauen der Flavier', *Hist.* 18 (1969) 492–504.

Ceauscescu, G., 'Vespasian: Princeps in melius mutatus', *Tyche* 4 (1989) 3–16.

Chambalu, A., 'Flaviana', *Phil.* 44 (1885) 106–31; 502–17.

Charlesworth, M.P., 'Flaviana', *JRS* 27 (1937) 55–62.

Chastagnol, A., 'Le laticlave de Vespasien', *Hist.* 25 (1976) 253–6.

Chilver, G.E.F., 'The army in politics, AD 68–70', *JRS* 47 (1957) 29–35.

Clarke, G.W., 'The date of the consecratio of Vespasian', *Hist.* 16 (1966) 318–27.

Coale, A.J., 'Dies Alliensis', *TAPA* 102 (1971) 49–58.

Cohen, S.J.D., *Josephus in Galilee and Rome. His vita and development as a historian. Columbia Stud. in the Class. Trad.* 8 (Leiden, 1979).

Conole, P., and Milns, R.D., 'Neronian frontier policy in the Balkans: the career of Ti. Plautius Silvanus', *Hist.* 32 (1983) 183–200.

Cook, S.A., *et al.*, eds, *CAH* 11: *The Imperial Peace* AD 70–192 (Cambridge, 1936, repr. 1954).

Cramer, F.H., *Astrology in Roman Law and Politics. Mem. Amer. Phil. Soc.* 37 (Philadelphia, 1954).

Crook, J., 'Titus and Berenice', *AJP* 72 (1951) 162–75.

—— *Consilium Principis: Imperial councils and counsellors from Augustus to Diocletian* (Cambridge, 1955).

Dąbrowa, E., *L'Asie mineure sous les Flaviens: recherches sur la politique provinciale* (tr. E. Willmann, Wroclaw, 1980) [*Asie mineure*].

Daltrop, G., Hausmann, U., and Wegner, M., eds, *Die Flavier: Vespasian . . . Domitian. Das römische Herrscherbild* 2, 1. *Deutsches Arch. Inst.* (Berlin, 1966).

Darwall-Smith, R.H., *Emperors and Architecture: A study of Flavian Rome. Coll. Lat.* 231 (Brussels, 1996).

Desideri, P., *Dione di Prusa, Un intellettuale greco nell'Impero Romano. Bibl. di Cultura contemporanea* 135 (Florence, 1978).

Devreker, J., 'L'adlectio in senatum de Vespasien', *Lat.* 39 (1980) 70–87 ['Adlectio'].

—— 'La composition du Sénat romain sous les Flaviens', in W. Eck, H. Galsterer,

H. Wolff eds, *Stud. zur ant. Sozialgeschichte: Festschrift F. Vittinghoff* (Cologne etc., 1980) 257–268 ['Composition'].

Downey, G., *A History of Antioch in Syria from Seleucus to the Arab Conquest* (Princeton, NJ, 1961).

Eck, W., 'Die Legaten von Lykien und Pamphylien unter Vespasian', *ZPE* 6 (1970) 65–75 ['Leg.'].

—— *Senatoren von Vespasian bis Hadrian. Prosopographische Untersuchungen mit Einschluss der Jahres- und Provinzialfasten der Statthalter, Vest.* 13 (Munich, 1970) [*Sen.*].

—— 'M. Pompeius Silvanus, consul designatus tertium – ein Vertrauter Vespasians und Domitians', *ZPE* 9 (1972) 259–75.

—— 'Beförderungskriterien innerhalb des senatorischen Laufbahn, dargestellt an der Zeit von 69 bis 138 n. Chr.', *ANRW* 2, 1 (1974) 158–228.

—— 'Jahres- und Provinzialfasten der senatorische Statthalter von 69/70 bis 138/9', *Chiron* 12 (1982) 281–362 ['Jahresfasten'].

—— 'Prokonsuln von Asia in der Flavisch-Traianischen Zeit'. *ZPE* 45 (1982) 139– 53 ['Prokonsuln'].

—— 'Zur Familie der Neratii aus Saepinum', *ZPE* 50 (1983) 193–201.

—— 'Statius *Silvae* 1. 4 und C. Rutilius Gallicus also Proconsul Asiae II', *AJP* 106 (1985) 475–84.

—— 'Urbs Salvia und seine führenden Familien' in *Picus: studi e ricerche sulle Marche nell' Antichità* 12–13 (1992–3) 79–108.

—— et al., eds, *Das SC de Cn. Pisone patre. Vest.* 48 (Mainz, 1996).

d'Espèrey, S. Franchet, 'Vespasien, Titus et la littérature', *ANRW* 2, 32, 5 (1986) 3048–96.

Evans, J.K., 'The trial of P. Egnatius Celer', *CQ* NS 29 (1979) 198–202.

Fears, J.R., Princeps a diis electus: *the divine election of the emperor as a political concept at Rome. Papers and Monogr. of the Amer. Acad. at Rome* 26 (Rome, 1977).

Ferrill, A., 'Otho, Vitellius, and the propaganda of Vespasian', *Class. Journ.* 60 (1965) 167–9.

Fishwick, D., *The Imperial Cult in the Latin West: Studies in the Ruler Cult of the Western Provinces of the Rom. Empire. Et. prélim. aux religions orient. dans l'emp. rom.* 108 (2 vols in 4, Leiden 1987, 1991–2).

Flaig, E., *Den Kaiser herausfordern: die Usurpation im röm. Reich. Hist. Stud.* 7 (Frankfurt a.M.–N.Y., 1992).

Friesen, S.J., *Twice Neokoros: Ephesus, Asia Minor and the Cult of the Flavian Imperial Family. Religions in the Graeco-Rom. world*, 116 (Leiden etc., 1993).

Gallivan, P.A., 'Some comments on the Fasti for the reign of Nero', *CQ* NS 24 (1974) 290–311.

—— 'The Fasti for AD 70–96', *CQ* NS 31 (1981) 181–220.

Galsterer, H., 'Municipium Flavium Irnitanum: a Latin town in Spain', *JRS* 78 (1988) 78–90.

Garzetti, A., 'L. Cesennio Peto e la rivalutazione flaviana di personaggi neroniani', in R. Chevallier, ed., *Mélanges . . . offerts à A. Piganiol* (Paris, 1966) 777–90.

—— From Tiberius to the Antonines. A history of the Rom. Empire AD 14–192 (tr. J.R. Foster, London, 1974).

Girard, J., 'L'Idée dynastique sous les Flaviens', *Ktèma* 12 (1989) 169–73.

González, J., 'The *Lex Irnitana*: a new Flavian municipal law', *JRS* 76 (1986) 147–243.

Graf, H.R., *Kaiser Vespasian, Untersuchungen zu Suetons Vita Divi Vespasiani* (Stuttgart, 1937).

Grassi, H., *Untersuchungen zum Vierkaiserjahr 68/69 n. Chr. Ein Beitrag zur Ideologie und Sozialstrukture des frühen Principats. Graz Diss.* 23 (Vienna, 1973).

Greenhalgh, P.A.L., *The Year of the Four Emperors* (London-N.Y., 1975).

Grenier, J.-C., 'Les inscriptions hiéroglyphiques de l'Obélisque Pamfili', *MEFR* 99, 2 (1987) 937–61.

Grenzheuser, B., *Kaiser und Senat in der Zeit von Nero bis Nerva* (Inaug. Diss. Münster, 1964).

Griffin, M.T., *Seneca, a Philosopher in Politics* (Oxford, 1976; p/b with additions, 1992).

—— *Nero, the End of a Dynasty* (London, 1984).

—— 'Urbs Roma, Plebs and Princeps', in L. Alexander, ed., *Images of Empire Journ. for the Stud. of the N.T., Suppl.* 122 (Sheffield, 1991) 19–46.

—— 'Claudius in the judgement of the next half-century', in V.M. Strocka, ed., *Die Regierungszeit des Kaisers Claudius (41–54 n. Chr.): Umbruch oder Episode?* (Mainz, 1994) 307–16.

Griffith, J.G., 'Juvenal, Statius, and the Flavian establishment', *G&R* NS 16 (1969) 134–50.

Halfmann, H., *Die Senatoren aus dem östlichen Teil des Imperium Romanum bis zum Ende des 2. Jh n. Chr. Hypomnemata* 58 (Göttingen, 1979).

—— *Itinera Principum, Gesch. u. Typologie der Kaiserreisen im röm. Reich. Heidelb. Althist. Beitr., Epigr. Stud.* 2 (Stuttgart, 1986) [*Itinera*].

—— 'Die Alanen und die röm. Ostpolitik unter Vespasian', *Epigr. Anat.* 8 (1986) 39–51 ['Alanen'].

—— '"Nachbehandlung": M. Hirrius Fronto Neratius Pansa', *Asia Min. Stud.* 3 (1991) 41–3.

Hall, A.S., 'An unidentified governor of Lycia-Pamphylia under Vespasian', *Epigr. Anat.* 4 (1984) 27–36.

Hammond, M., 'The transmission of the powers of the Roman Emperor from . . . AD 68 to 235', *MAAR* 24 (1956) 61–133.

Hanson, W., *Agricola and the Conquest of the North*[2](London, 1991) [*Conquest*].

—— 'Tacitus' "Agricola"', *ANRW* 2, 33, 3 (1991) 1741–84 ['Tac.'].

Henrichs, A., 'Vespasian's visit to Alexandria', *ZPE* 3 (1968) 51–80.

Hill, P.V., 'Buildings and monuments on Flavian coins', *NAC* 8 (1979) 205–24.

Hirschfeld, O., *Die kaiserlichen Verwaltungsbeamten bis auf Diocletian*[2] (Berlin, 1905).

Holzapfel, L., 'Römische Kaiserdaten', *Klio* 12 (1912) 483–933; 13 (1913) 289–304; 15 (1918) 99–121.

Homo, L., *Vespasien, l'empereur du bon sens (69–79 ap. J.-C.)* (Paris, 1949).

Hook, D, and Newman, P., eds, *Estoria do muy nobre Vespesiano emperador de Roma* (Exeter, 1983).

Houston, G.W., *Roman Imperial Administrative Personnel during the Principates of Vespasian and Titus (AD 69–81)* (Diss. North Carolina, 1971; Univ. Microfilms, Ann Arbor, MI, 1979).

—— 'M. Plancius Varus and the events of AD 69–70', *TAPA* 103 (1972) 167–80.

—— 'Vespasian's adlection of men in senatum', *AJP* 97 (1977) 35–63 ['Adlection'].

—— 'Nonius Flaccus: a new equestrian career from Firmum Picenum', *CP* 72 (1977) 232–8 ['Nonius'].

Isaac, B., 'Vespasian's titulature in AD 69', *ZPE* 55 (1984) 143f.

Isaac, B., and Roll, L., 'A milestone of AD 69 from Judaea', *JRS* 66 (1976) 9–14.

Isager, J., *Pliny on Art and Society: The Elder Pliny's Chapters on the History of Art* (London and N.Y., 1991).

Jones, B.W., 'Titus and some Flavian *amici* ', *Hist.* 24 (1975) 454–62.

—— *The Emperor Titus* (London, Sydney, and N.Y., 1984) [*Tit.*].

—— *The Emperor Domitian* (London-N.Y., 1992) [*Dom.*].

Jones, C.P., *The Roman World of Dio Chrysostom* (Cambridge, Mass.-London, 1978).

Kennedy, D., 'C. Velius Rufus', *Brit.* 14 (1983) 183–96.

Kienast, D., *Römische Kaiserttabelle: Grundzüge einer röm. Kaiserchronologie* (Darmstadt, 1990).

Kleiner, F.S., 'The arches of Vespasian in Rome', *Röm. Mitt.* 97 (1990) 127–36.

Kraay, C.M., 'The bronze coinage of Vespasian: classification and attribution', in R.A.G. Carson, and C.M. Kraay, eds, *Scripta mummaria Romana: Essays presented to Humphrey Sutherland* (London, 1978) 47–57.

Kreiler, B., *Die Statthalter Kleinasiens unter den Flaviern. Inaug. Diss. zur Erlang. des Doktorgrades der Phil. Fak. der Maximilians-Univ. zu München* (Munich, 1975).

Lana, I., 'La politica culturale dei Flavi', *Atti* 1981, 85–103.

Laqueur, R., *Der jüdische Historiker Flavius Josephus: eine biographischer Versuch auf neuer quellenkritischer Grundlage* (Giessen, 1920; repr. Darmstadt, 1967).

Lattimore, R., 'Portents and prophecies in connection with the Emperor Vespasian', *CJ* 29 (1934) 447f.

Leglay, M., 'Les Flaviens et l'Afrique', *MEFR* 80 (1968) 201–46.

Levi, M.A., 'I principii dell' impero di Vespasiano', *RFIC* NS 16 (1938) 1–12.

—— 'Flavi', *ANRW* 2, 2 (1975) 177–207.

Levick, B.M., *Tiberius the Politician* (London, 1976).

—— 'Propaganda and the imperial coinage', *Antichthon* 16 (1982) 104–16.

—— 'L. Verginius Rufus and the Four Emperors', *RM* NS 128 (1985) 318–46.

—— *Claudius* (London, 1990).

Loane, H.J., 'Vespasian's pepper warehouses', *CP* 39 (1944) 10–21.

Luck, G., 'Über Suetons "Divus Titus"', *RM* NS 107 (1964) 63–75.

Lucrezi, F., *Leges super principem: la 'monarchia costituzionale' di Vespasiano* (Naples, 1982).

Luttwak, E.N., *The Grand Strategy of the Rom. Emp. From the First Century* AD *to the Third* (Baltimore, Md-London, 1976).

McDermott, W.C., 'Flavius Silva and Salvius Liberalis', *CW* 66 (1972–3) 335–51.

McElderry, R.K., 'Some conjectures on the reign of Vespasian', *JRS* 3 (1913) 116– 26.

—— 'Vespasian's reconstruction of Spain', *JRS* 8 (1918) 53–102; ('Addenda') 9 (1919) 86–94.

Maehring, H.R., 'Joseph ben Mathia and Flavius Josephus: the Jewish prophet and Roman historian', *ANRW* 2, 21, 2 (1984) 864–944.

Magi, F., *I relievi Flavi del Palazzo della Cancelleria* (Rome, 1945).

Magie, D.M., *Roman Rule in Asia Minor* (2 vols, Princeton, NJ, 1950).

Malitz, J., 'Helvidius Priscus und Vespasian. Zur Geschichte der "stoischen" Senatsopposition', *Herm.* 113 (1985) 231–46.

Martin, J.-P., *Providentia Deorum: recherches sur certains aspects religieux du pouvoir impériale. CEFR* 61 (Rome, 1982).

Melmoux, J., 'C. Helvidius Priscus, disciple et héritier de Thrasea', *PP* 30 (1975) 237–40.

Millar, F.G.B. *The Roman Near East 31 BC–AD 337* (Cambridge, Mass.-London, 1993).

Milns, R.D., 'The career of M. Aponius Saturninus', *Hist.* 22 (1973) 284–94.

Moles, J.L., 'The career and conversion of Dio Chrysostom', *JHS* 98 (1978) 79–100.

Momigliano, A., *Quinto Contr. alla stor. degli stud. class. e del mondo ant.* (2 vols, Rome, 1975).

Morgan, M.G., 'Vespasian's fears of assassination', *Phil.* 138 (1994) 118–28.

—— 'Vespasian and the omens in Tacitus *Histories* 2, 78', *Phoen.* 50 (1996) 41–55.

Murison, C.L., 'Some Vitellian dates: an exercise in methodology', *TAPA* 109 (1979) 187–97.

—— 'The historical value of Tacitus' "Histories"', *ANRW* 2, 33, 3 (1991) 1686–1713.

Musurillo, H.A., ed., *The Acts of the Pagan Martyrs (Acta Alexandrinorum)* (Oxford, 1954).

Newton, H.C., ed., *The Epigraphical Evidence for the Reigns of Vespasian and Titus* (N.Y.-London, 1901).

Nicolas, E.P., *De Néron à Vespasien. Etudes et perspectives historiques, suivies de l'analyse, du catalogue, et de la réproduction des monnaies 'oppositionelles' connues des années 67 à 70* (2 vols, Paris, 1979).

Nicols, J., *Vespasian and the Partes Flavianae. Hist. Einzelschr.* 28 (Wiesbaden 1978).

Niese, B., 'Zur Chronologie des Josephus', *Herm.* 28 (1893) 194–229.

—— 'Der jüdische Historiker Josephus', *Hist. Zeitschr.* 76 (1896) 193–237 (tr. in J. Hastings, ed., *Encycl. of Religion and Ethics* 7 (Edinburgh, 1914) 569–79).

—— and Destinon, I., eds, *Flavii Iosephi opera. VI, De Bello Iudaico libros VII* (Berlin, 1894).

Ogilvie, R.M., and Richmond, I.A., eds, *Cornelii Taciti De Vita Agricolae* (Oxford, 1967).

Parsi, B., *Désignation et investiture de l'Empereur rom. (I*^er *et II*^e *siècles après J.C.)* (Paris, 1963).

Pflaum, H.-G., *Les Procurateurs équestres sous le Haut-Empire romain* (Paris, 1950).

Pick, B., 'Zur Titulatur der Flavier: I. Der Imperatortitel des Titus. II. Die Consulaten Domitiens als Caesar', *ZfN* 13 (1885) 190–238; 355–83.

Pigoń, J., 'Helvidius Priscus, Eprius Marcellus, and *iudicium senatus*: observations on Tacitus, *Histories* 4.7–8', *CQ* NS 42 (1992) 235–46.

Powell, A., *'Deum ira, hominum rabies'*, *Lat.* 31 (1972) 833–48.

Rajak, T., *Josephus: the historian and his society* (London, 1983).

Rhoades, D.M., *Israel in Revolution 66–74 CE: A Political Hist. Based on the Writings of Josephus* (Philadelphia, 1976).

Richmond, I.A., 'Two Flavian monuments', in P. Salway, ed., *Roman Archaeology and Art. Essays and Studies* (London, 1969) 218–28.

Riposati, B., ed., *Atti del congresso internaz di studi vespasianei, Sett. 1979, Rieti* (2 vols, Rieti, 1981) [= *Atti* 1981].

—— *Atti del congresso internaz. di studi Flaviani* (2 vols, Rieti, 1983) [= *Atti* 1983].

Ritter, H.W., 'Zur Lebensgeschichte der Flavia Domitilla, der Frau Vespasians', *Hist.* 21 (1972) 759–61.

Rogers, P.M., 'Titus, Berenice and Mucianus', *Hist.* 29 (1980) 86–95.

Saddington, D.B., *The Development of the Roman Auxiliary Forces from Caesar to Vespasian (49 BC–AD 79)* (Harare, 1982).

Ste Croix, G.E.M. De, *The Class Struggle in the Ancient Greek World* (London, 1981).

Saller, R.P., *Personal Patronage in the Early Empire* (Cambridge, 1982).

Schalit, A., ed., *Zur Josephus-Forschung. Wege der Forschung.* 84 (Darmstadt, 1973).

—— 'Die Erhebung Vespasians nach Flavius Josephus, Talmud u. Midrasch. Zur Geschichte ein messianischen Prophetie', *ANRW* 2, 2 (1975) 208–327.

Schmidt, M.G., 'Claudius und Vespasian: eine Interpretation des Wortes "vae, puto, deus fio" (Suet. Vesp. 23, 4)', *Chiron* 18 (1988) 83–9.

Schürer, E., *A History of the Jewish People in the time of Christ*[2] eds F. Millar, G. Vermes, *et al.*, (4 vols, Edinburgh, 1973, 1979, 1986, 1987).

Scott, K., *The Imperial Cult under the Flavians* (Stuttgart-Berlin, 1936; repr. N.Y., 1975).

Sherwin-White, A.N., *The Roman Citizenship*[2] (Oxford, 1973).

—— *The Letters of Pliny: A Historical and Social Commentary* (Oxford, 1966).

Sidebottom, H., 'Dio of Prusa and the Flavian dynasty', *CQ* 46 (1996) 447–56.

Simon, E., 'Zu den flavischen Reliefs von der Cancelleria', *Jahr. Deutsch. Arch. Inst.* 75 (1960) 134–56.

Smallwood, E.M., *The Jews under Roman Rule from Pompey to Diocletian. Stud. in Judaism in Late Ant.*, ed. J. Neusner, 20 (Leiden, 1976).

Strobel, K., 'Ein neues Zeugnis für die Statthalterschaft des M. Hirrius Fronto Neratius Pansa in Lycia-Pamphylia aus Oinoanda', *ZPE* 61 (1985) 173–80.

Stylow, A.U., 'Apuntes sobre epigrafia de épocaflavia en Hispania', *Gerión* 4 (1986) 285–311.

Sullivan, P.B., 'A note on the Flavian accession', *CJ* 49 (1953) 454–62.

Syme, R., 'Some Antonine relatives: Ceionii and Vettuleni', *Ath.* 35 (1957) 306–15 (= *RP* 1, 324–32) ['Ceionii'].

—— 'The jurist Neratius Priscus', *Herm.* 85 (1957) 480–93 (= *RP* 1, 339–52) ['Neratius'].

—— *Tacitus* (2 vols, Oxford, 1958) [*Tac.*].

—— 'Pliny the procurator', *HSCP* 73 (1969) 201–36 (= *RP* 2, 742–73) ['Pliny'].

—— 'Domitius Corbulo', *JRS* 60 (1970) 27–39 (= *RP* 2, 805–24) ['Corbulo'].

—— 'Notes on Tacitus, *Histories* iii', *Antichthon* 9 (1975) 61–7.

—— 'The enigmatic Sospes', *JRS* 67 (1977) 38–49 (= *RP* 3, 1043–61) ['Sospes'].

—— 'The march of Mucianus', *Antichthon* 11 (1977) 78–92 (= *RP* 3, 998–1013) ['March'].

—— 'Antonius Saturninus', *JRS* 68 (1978), 12–21 (*RP* 5, 514–20) ['Saturninus'].

—— *Some Arval Brethren* (Oxford, 1980).

—— 'Partisans of Galba', *Hist.* 31 (1982) 460–83 (= *RP* 4, 115–139) ['Partisans'].

—— 'Antistius Rusticus, a consular from Corduba', *Hist.* 32 (1983) 359–74 (= *RP* 4, 278–94.

—— 'Statius on Rutilius Gallicus' *Acta Phil. Fennica* 15 (1984) 149–56 (= *RP* 5, 514–20) ['Rutilius'].

—— *The Augustan Aristocracy* (Oxford, 1986).

—— 'Prefects of the City, Vespasian to Trajan', in *Estudios de derecho romano en honor de A. D'Ors* (Pamplona, 1987) 1057–74 (= *RP* 5, 608–21) ['Prefects'].

—— 'Ministers of the Caesars', *RP* 7 (1991) 521–40 ['Ministers'].

—— 'A political group', *RP* 7 (1991) 568–87 ['Group'].

—— 'Vestricius Spurinna', *RP* 7 (1991) 541–50 ['Vestricius'].

Talbert, R.A., *The Senate of Imperial Rome* (Princeton, NJ, 1984).

Thackeray, H. St. J., *Josephus, the Man and the Historian* (NY, 1929).

Timpe, D., 'Römische Geschichte bei Flavius Josephus', *Hist.* 9 (1960) 474–502.

—— *Untersuchungen zur Kontinuität des frühen Prinzipats. Hist. Einzelschr.* 5 (Wiesbaden, 1962).

Torelli, M., 'The cursus honorum of M. Hirrius Fronto Neratius Pansa', *JRS* 58 (1968) 170–5.

Townend, G.B., 'Some Flavian connections', *JRS* 51 (1961) 54–61 ['Connections'].

—— 'Traces in Dio Cassius of Cluvius, Aufidius and Pliny', *Herm.* 89 (1961) 227–48 ['Cluvius'].

—— 'The consuls of AD 69/70', *AJP* 83 (1962) 113–29.

—— 'Cluvius Rufus in the Histories of Tacitus', *AJP* 65 (1964) 337–77.

—— 'The restoration of the Capitol in AD 70', *Hist.* 36 (1987) 243–8.

Toynbee, J.M.C., 'Dictators and philosophers in the first century AD', *G&R* 13 (1944) 43–58.

—— *The Flavian Reliefs from the Palazzo della Cancelleria in Rome* (Oxford, 1957).

Turner, E.G., 'Tiberius Iulius Alexander', *JRS* 44 (1954) 54–64.

Van Berchem, D., *Les distributions de blé et d'argent à la plèbe rom. sous l'Empire* (Geneva, 1939; repr. N.Y., 1975).

—— 'Un banquier chez les Helvètes', *Ktèma* 3 (1978) 267–74.

Vidman, L., 'Die Familie des L. Neratius Marcellus', *ZPE* 43 (1981) 377–84.

Vinson, M.P., 'Domitia Longina, Iulia Titi, and the literary tradition', *Hist.* 38 (1989) 431–50.

Vita-Evrard, G. Di, 'Quatre inscriptions du Djebel Tarhuna: le territorie de "Lepcis Magna"', *Quad. di Arch. della Libia* 10 (1979) 67–98.

Wallace, K.G., 'The Flavii Sabini in Tacitus', *Hist.* 36 (1987) 343–58.

Waters, K., 'The second dynasty of Rome', *Phoen.* 17 (1963) 198–218.

Weaver, P.R.C., *Familia Caesaris, a Social Study of the Emperor's Freedmen and Slaves* (Cambridge, 1972).

—— 'Social mobility in the early Roman Empire: the evidence of the imperial freedmen and slaves', *Past and Present* 37 (1967) 3–20 (= M.I. Finley, ed., *Studies in Ancient Society* (London, 1974) 121–40).

Weber, W., *Josephus und Vespasian. Untersuchungen zu dem jüdischen Krieg des Flavius Josephus* (Berlin etc., 1921).

Wellesley, K., ed., *Cornelius Tacitus, The Histories Book iii . . . with Text, Introduction and Commentary* (Sydney, 1972).

—— *The Long Year* AD 69² (Bristol, 1989).

Weynand, P., 'T. Flavius Vespasianus', *RE* 6, 2 (1909) 2623–95.

Wiegels, R., 'Das Datum der Verleihung des ius Latii an die Hispanier: zur Personal- u. municipal Politik in den ersten Regierungsjahren Vespasiens', *Herm.* 106 (1978) 196–213 ['Hispanier'].

Wilkes, J.J., 'Romans, Dacians, and Sarmatians in the first and early second centuries', in B. Hartley, and J. Wacher, eds, *Rome and her Northern Provinces: Papers Presented to S. Frere* (Gloucester, 1983) 255–89.

Willems, J.H.W., 'Romans and Batavians: a regional study in the Dutch eastern river area. II', *Bericht. v. d. Rijksdienst. voor het Oudheidkundig Bodemonderzoek* 34 (1984) 39–332.

Winterbottom, M., 'Quintilian and the vir bonus', *JRS* 54 (1964) 90–7.

Wirszubski, Ch., *Libertas as a Political Idea at Rome during the Late Republic and Early Empire* (Cambridge, etc., 1950).

Wiseman, T.P., *Titus Flavius and the Indivisible Subject* (Exeter, 1978).

Woodside, M. St. A., 'Vespasian's patronage of education and the arts', *TAPA* 73 (1942) 123–9.

Yavetz, Z., 'Reflections on Titus and Josephus', *GRBS* 16 (1975) 411–32.

—— 'The urban plebs in the days of the Flavians, Nerva and Trajan', in A. Giovannini, ed., *Opposition et résistances à l'Empire d'Auguste à Trajan, Entretiens Hardt* 33 (Geneva, 1987) 135–86.

Zimmermann, M., 'Die *restitutio honorum* Galbas', *Hist.* 44 (1995) 56–82.

INDEX OF PERSONS

Emperors and well-known members of their families, and celebrated writers, are listed under the name most familiar to English readers, other Roman citizens by *nomen*.

INDEX OF PEOPLES AND PLACES

City names are given in Graeco-Roman form followed by modern equivalents; rivers and some other geographical features vice versa.

INDEX OF SUBJECTS AND TERMS